INTERNATIONAL AVIATION LAW

This is the third edition of a now-renowned guide that provides an extensive account of the state of the aviation industry and the law that regulates it. This new edition, revised and updated throughout, focuses on environmental and sustainability considerations, and includes a new chapter on innovations aimed towards meeting the 2050 Net Zero Emission targets endorsed by the International Civil Aviation Organisation (ICAO) and the International Air Transport Association (IATA).

International Aviation Law: A Practical Guide explains the international context and application of the law as it applies to commercial and recreational aviation, and to the broader aviation environment. It provides a comprehensive introduction to all aspects of aviation law, from criminal law to contract law, to the legal duties and responsibility of aircrew and other aviation personnel including airport operators, air traffic controllers and aircraft engineers. Each area of the law is clearly explained in accessible language and supported with practical case studies to illustrate the application of the law within an operational aviation context. It also provides advice on how to avoid or minimize legal liability for those working in the aviation industry.

The book is written for a very broad readership of those working within the aviation industry, those aspiring to work within it and those within the legal profession dealing with air transportation, as well as students within the same industries. The third edition will additionally find favour with new readers seeking information on environmental issues and answers to the question of how the aviation sector will meet the 2050 emission targets.

Professor Ronald I. C. Bartsch AM is a world-renowned aviation lawyer, academic, airline executive and international consultant. The author has been a pilot for 50 years and holds a current Air Transport Pilot Licence. Ronald was appointed a Member of the Order of Australia for his 'significant contribution to aviation law, and safety and compliance' in the Australia Day Honours in 2021.

International Aviation Law

A Practical Guide

Third Edition

PROFESSOR RONALD I. C. BARTSCH AM

BA (Syd), BSc (Syd), LLB (NSW), LLM (UTS), MPhil (Syd), Dip ED (Syd)

informa law
from Routledge

Designed cover image: Ivcandy/Getty Images

First published 2025
by Informa Law from Routledge
4 Park Square, Milton Park, Abingdon, Oxon OX14 4RN

and by Informa Law from Routledge
605 Third Avenue, New York, NY 10158

Informa Law from Routledge is an imprint of the Taylor & Francis Group, an informa business

First edition published by Ashgate 2012
Second edition published by Routledge 2018

British Library Cataloguing-in-Publication Data
A catalogue record for this book is available from the British Library

Library of Congress Cataloging-in-Publication Data
Names: Bartsch, Ronald I. C., 1954– author.
Title: International aviation law : a practical guide / Professor Ron Bartsch AM.
Description: Third edition. | Abingdon, Oxon [UK] ; New York, NY : Routledge, 2025. | Includes bibliographical references and index.
Identifiers: LCCN 2024027559 (print) | LCCN 2024027560 (ebook) | ISBN 9781032652061 (hardback) | ISBN 9781032652108 (paperback) | ISBN 9781032652146 (ebook)
Subjects: LCSH: Aeronautics—Law and legislation.
Classification: LCC K4095 .B37 2025 (print) | LCC K4095 (ebook) | DDC 343.09/7—dc23
LC record available at https://lccn.loc.gov/2024027559
LC ebook record available at https://lccn.loc.gov/2024027560

ISBN: 978-1-032-65206-1 (hbk)
ISBN: 978-1-032-65210-8 (pbk)
ISBN: 978-1-032-65214-6 (ebk)

DOI: 10.4324/9781032652146

Typeset in Palatino
by Apex CoVantage, LLC

This book is dedicated to the Hon Michael Kirby AC CMG, former justice of the High Court of Australia. A compassionate human being of absolute integrity and infinite wisdom.

Contents

About the Author

Professor Ronald I. C. Bartsch AM has over 45 years' experience in the aviation industry in a variety of senior operational, safety and regulatory roles. As former head of safety and regulatory compliance at Qantas Airways Limited and a senior manager with the Australian Civil Aviation Safety Authority, he has both industry and government experience across all sectors of the aviation industry.

Ronald is a director of Regional Express Holdings Limited – Australia's largest independent regional airline – and Chair of the airline's Board Safety, Environment and Risk Management Committee. Ronald is a director of Dovetail Electric Aviation in which Rex Airlines has a shareholding. He is also Director of the international aviation consultancy firm Avlaw Aviation Consulting and President of the Asia-Pacific RPAS Consortium. For the past three decades Ronald has conducted assignments in over 30 countries across six continents.

As an experienced pilot, Ronald has been flying for 50 years and has in excess of 7,500 flying hours, a current Air Transport Pilot Licence and ratings on over 30 aircraft types, including command endorsements on the Beechjet and Boeing 717. He also has formal qualifications in law, education, science and the arts. Admitted as a Barrister to the High Court of Australia in 1993, Ronald has also served as an aviation specialist and Presiding Member of the Commonwealth Administrative Appeals Tribunal until 2017. Ronald was appointed a Member of the Order of Australia for his 'significant contribution to aviation law, and safety and compliance' in the Australia Day Honours in 2021.

A former high school mathematics and science teacher, Ronald is also a Senior Visiting Fellow at the University of New South Wales for the past two decades and at the Australian National University. In 2016 Ronald was appointed as the inaugural Professor of International Law at AeroX's School of Aviation in New Delhi, India and has been a visiting Professor at the University of the South Pacific since 2019. He is the author of numerous publications, including the best-selling *Aviation Law in Australia* (6th edn) and co-author of *Drones in Society* and a contributing author for the aviation title of *Laws of Australia* and *Halsbury's Laws of Australia*. Ronald's most recent international publication on creative thinking is *The Corona Dilemma: 20–20 Thinking for the Next Normal* which was released globally in 2021.

Preface

A comment I often hear from readers of this book is that they welcome the way in which I explain the law within the practical context to which it applies. This feedback may seem rather unremarkable, but I feel many publications about the law tend to be rather dry, particularly for a lay audience. But for those who work in the aviation industry – the aviation practitioners – they know only too well, that the law encroaches upon virtually every aspect of their industry. The challenge they face, on a daily basis, is interpreting the law and applying it to their workplace duties. To me, this is why explaining the law in context is of utmost importance.

By 'aviation practitioners', I am referring to those who work in the aviation industry and those who likewise aspire. They are the pilots, the aircraft engineers, those who work for operators of airports, airline personnel, aviation insurers and underwriters, air traffic controllers, regulators and so many other aviation professionals. And in saying 'those who likewise aspire', I am thinking of students undertaking aviation-related studies and those within the general population who are drawn by the aura and excitement of this wonderful technology we call aviation.

International Aviation Law: A Practical Guide is precisely as the name suggests. It is a 'guide' in that it provides direction and assistance to the reader so that he or she is better positioned to understand the law as it impinges upon his or her day-to-day duties. But perhaps the question that first needs to be asked is: why do I, the reader, an aviation practitioner, need to know about aviation law – and, moreover, why *international* aviation law? To me there are three important components of the answer to this question.

The first part of the answer relates to the reason why lay practitioners even need to study aviation law. Surely that is why we have lawyers. There is no doubt whatsoever of the need for aviation lawyers. Aviation is a highly capital-intensive and specialized industry. Risks, if not effectively managed, may be extreme and the resolution of operational issues quite often legally complex. As with many aspects of society, specialist branches of the law have developed – aviation law is no exception.

I am certain that those readers who work in the aviation industry know only too well the extent to which laws and regulations abound. In fact it is generally acknowledged that aviation is the most strictly and extensively regulated of all industries. One simply cannot perform a professional day's work without confronting some aspect of the law. Simply stated, an aviation practitioner must be able to understand the law as it applies to his or her area of professional responsibility.

The second reason why an understanding of the law is important is because of the scope and degree of exposure of aviation practitioners to legal liability. This liability, in some instances, may be incurred personally. In other words, an individual employee or contractor may, for example, be personally liable for fines, an award of damages and in some instances subject to criminal prosecution. This is not meant to 'shock' the reader but more to act as a reminder of the fact so eloquently expressed in the adage 'ignorance of the law is no defence in a court of law'. Never have truer words been spoken.

An important aspect of this exposure to liability relates to the underlying purpose of most aviation regulation, namely the promotion of safety. In general, society expects, and quite often demands, continually improving levels of operational and workplace safety. In an increasingly litigious society, both aspects of this part of the answer are compelling reasons why acquiring a more comprehensive understanding of the law makes a lot of sense.

The final part of the question posed relates to why there is a need to study *international* aviation law. The answer to this really goes to the very essence of what this publication is all about and indeed what makes this book unique. To attain a truly meaningful understanding of the law – to the extent that you have a high degree of confidence in what you do and the decisions you make – you must have acquired that level of knowledge to *know* that you are in fact legally correct. It is my genuine belief that one needs to study aviation law in its international context to attain this level of understanding of the law. Let me elaborate.

There is *no* industry that is more affected, and indeed controlled, by international standards than is the case with the aviation industry. These standards, most of which derive from the Chicago Convention of 1944, are more than just standards – they are in fact *the law*. No less than 193 sovereign states of the world have agreed to be bound by the Standards and Recommended Practices of the 19 Annexes administered by the International Civil Aviation Organization (ICAO). These standards or SARPs, as they are more commonly referred to, find their way, through the 193 varying legal systems, to each and every one of the readers' respective workplaces. This is *that* part of the domestic aviation law of each individual state with which most readers would have a fair degree of familiarity, but, quite often and unfortunately, the *only* part.

It is my contention that aviation law as a professional academic discipline is, with the utmost respect, in the main taught – to use a British colloquialism – 'arse about tit'. Translated for a multicultural audience, this expression, in this context, simply means taught in the reverse order to the way in which it *ought* to be taught. Studying international aviation law provides not only the contextualization of the 'bigger picture' but, more importantly, provides both awareness and understanding of the legal basis upon which *all* civil aviation law – both domestic and international – is founded.

Finally, it is worth mentioning that the trend of international harmonization – towards universal conformity of aviation standards – is not only increasing but is doing so at an ever-increasing rate. The catalyst for this was the First World War and the trend has continued to be fuelled by subsequent major worldwide events including: the Second World War; international terrorism; government economic rationalization; airline strategic alliances; pandemics and epidemics; customer loyalty (frequent flyer) programmes; code-sharing; global reservation systems; highly dynamic oil prices; the proliferation of low-cost carriers; Internet bookings; the Global Financial Crisis; and increased government liberalization towards more and more 'open skies' policies.

For the preceding reasons I believe that explaining the law within the practical context of the aviation industry is of utmost importance. For me, the law without context is like grammar without words – a vast collection of principles and rules devoid of any meaningful application.

Quite unlike any other mode of transportation, aviation activities are not restricted by political and geographical boundaries. The 'internationalization' of aviation activities, and the legal processes that support and assist this development, commenced with the invention, has continued ever since and will persist until international harmonization is absolute. I believe that such a future is not beyond rational contemplation and is conceivably quite likely to occur within most of our respective lifetimes.

Professor Ronald I. C. Bartsch AM, Sydney, Australia

1
Introduction to International Aviation Law

INTRODUCTION

It has now been more than a decade since the first edition of this publication, at a time when the aviation industry was booming. Year on year more and more people were flying than ever before, and the sky-high passenger numbers showed little sign of abating. Then in 2020 the uncontemplatable event happened with the outbreak of COVID-19. The pandemic wreaked financial devastation across the entire aviation value chain, most notably for airlines. Apart from freight forwarders and cargo airlines, all subsectors of the industry suffered massive losses. Even previously reliable value creators, such as airports and manufacturers, were not spared the pandemic's economic impact. There's no sugar-coating the diagnosis: the coronavirus was without doubt the most devastating event to have ever impacted the aviation industry.

Back in 2021 in *The Corona Dilemma* (2021: 51) I made the following observation:

> The effects of COVID-19-related border closures and stay-at-home orders around the world have had devastating effect on international and domestic travel. On the other side of the pandemic and in the years to come, airlines and travel will emerge as an entirely new industry as those who do survive attempt to recover their massive losses.

Fast forward five years and the aviation industry worldwide has made a near full recovery from the coronavirus. According to a 2024 air travel outlook, released by the International Air Transport Association (IATA) and the Airports Council International (ACI), global passenger traffic in 2024 will surpass the pre-pandemic levels with over 9.4 billion passengers and push operating profits to over USD 60 billion. Government, international agencies such as the International Civil Aviation Organizations (ICAO) and industry associations like IATA and the ACI, have all played a significant role in this recovery and reformation, but above all, because of the globally harmonized regulation of the aviation industry, this recovery has been swift and complete.

Ever since its invention, aviation has been inextricably linked with the law. This relationship, while essential, is synergetic in nature for both the development of aviation and of aviation law. As is stated later in this text: 'The aviation industry is what it is today not in spite of, but rather because of, the law that regulates it'. To truly appreciate the nature and workings of the aviation industry, anyone working, or intending to work, in the industry should be conversant with both the international and domestic aviation legal and regulatory framework.

DOI: 10.4324/9781032652146-1

Working in the Aviation Industry

The sales of this publication have confirmed there is a significant demand by people working in, or associated with, the aviation industry for a text that provides an easily digestible overview of the structure and workings of the entire legal and regulatory framework for international aviation. Likewise, there is a similar demand from aviation training institutions and universities for a text that provides students with the requisite background and understanding of international aviation law, so they are better prepared to enter the aviation industry and readily apply this knowledge to their workplace. This third edition was necessary as it has incorporated changes to the post-pandemic operating environment and other developments in the global aviation sector and looks to the future challenges – in particular the 2050 Net Zero Emission targets – and how these will be integrated into the international regulatory framework.

Irrespective of the particular discipline being studied, it is always desirable to understand the background and development of how and why the subject matter evolved. In respect to the study of international aviation law this understanding is essential. There is no other field of human endeavour or branch of law that is so harmonized as is the international aviation regulatory regime, and that has only occurred because of the close cooperation of sovereign states collaborating for national and international objectives. The following sections describe the development of the very first aviation laws and explain the motivations and objectives of governments in respect to how aviation was to be regulated. It will be further highlighted that certain aspects of this branch of law that has developed essentially remain unchanged from their humble beginnings because of the unique features and requirements of the international aviation industry.

The Very Beginning

Ever since humankind's earliest attempts to unleash its earthly chains, people have been feverishly developing rules and regulations that would attempt to curtail such foolhardy endeavours. Long before even the Wright brothers' historic flight at Kitty Hawk in 1903, regulations relating to flights in balloons and airships had been developed and promulgated as early as the eighteenth century.

So what is it about the activities of aviation that attract the attention of such misfeasance and malice? Surely the burden of having to submit to the laws of gravity ought to have been sufficient laws with which our aeronautical ancestors had to contend without the imposition of additional 'man-made' laws? But apparently not so.

It all began in France in the early 1780s with Joseph-Michel and Jacques-Etienne Montgolfier, sons of a wealthy papermaker of Annonay. The brothers noticed that bags, when held above an open fire, grew lighter and lifted into the air. They discovered that hot air did not leak through paper. They experimented with balloons of paper and manufactured larger balloons capable of lifting considerable weight. Monsieur Montgolfier had forbidden his sons to ever fly in their invention, but Jacques-Etienne had already disobeyed his father and made a tethered flight to almost 400 feet. Around the same point in time, but on the other side of the Atlantic Ocean and in a hot air balloon constructed by a lawyer, Peter Carnes became the first American to venture aloft in a tethered balloon.

At the time it was widely believed that altitude sickness would restrict manned assents to within close proximity of the earth's surface. To test this hypothesis, the Montgolfier brothers, on 19 September 1783 in Versailles, put a sheep called Montauciel – French for 'climb to the sky' – a duck and a rooster in a basket attached to a hot air balloon. They named the aircraft the Aerostat Réveillon. The flight, in front of Louis XVI and Marie Antoinette, lasted just eight minutes, covered two miles and reached an altitude of approximately 1,500 feet before crashing to the ground. Nevertheless, the flight proved that life was sustainable in the atmosphere well above the surface of the earth with the three recruited farmyard 'passengers' having survived the ordeal.

Unfortunately, this inaugural untethered balloonist ascension also resulted in the first injury on board an aircraft. During the flight, most probably during the approach and landing phase, the sheep had apparently stepped on the rooster and broke its leg. Had there been aviation lawyers at the time, it is quite conceivable that counsel for the cockerel might still be pursuing compensation. It has been suggested that this precursor ought to have warned of the dangers of single-class carriage by air well before the advent of low-cost carriers.

The first manned flight in an aircraft took place two months later from the Château de la Muette in Paris on 21 November 1783 (Figure 1.1). Before a crowd of 100,000 spectators, in a paper-lined silk balloon designed by the Montgolfier brothers, scientist Jean-François Pilâtre de Rozier took off with fellow aviator Marquis d'Arlandes. The balloon soared over Paris, once tilting, belching out black smoke, and on descent nearly catching fire.

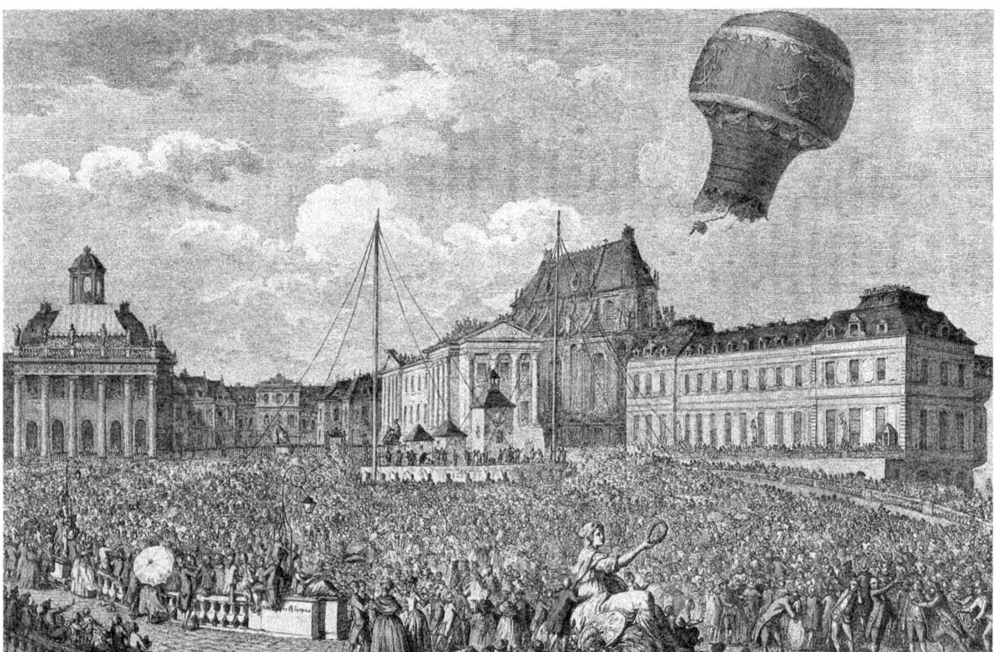

Figure 1.1 The first manned balloon flight, 21 November 1783

Source: Wellcome Collection 36351i

A few days later on 1 December, Professor Jacques Alexandre Charles – the French scientist of Charles' Law fame – stayed aloft for almost two hours in his hydrogen-filled balloon. Professor Charles, accompanied by Nicolas-Louis Robert as co-pilot of the 380-cubic-metre balloon, took off from the Jardin des Tuileries in Paris and travelled 27 miles (36 kilometres) before landing in the small town of Nesles-la-Vallée. This time a crowd of over 400,000 Parisians and others assembled to witness the spectacle. Among them was Benjamin Franklin, then the US Ambassador to France. Someone in the crowd asked of the Ambassador 'What's the use of a balloon?', to which Franklin immediately replied: 'What's the use of a new-born baby?' And this was certainly the birth of aviation. Even today in France, hot air balloons are still called Montgolfières and hydrogen balloons are referred to as Charlières.

Less than four months after this historic feat, the first aerial regulation was promulgated on 23 April 1784. The Paris police, in their apparent wisdom, introduced a law forbidding balloons to fly without a special licence. The inextricable link between aviation activities and regulatory standards had been established. This symbiotic relationship would continue and become the basis for all future aviation legislation.

Aviation law as we know it today has developed to the extent it has not due to any absence of reason but rather because of particular, yet peculiar, characteristics of travel by air. Unlike any other mode of transportation and, indeed, unlike any facet of human endeavour, travel by air challenges and defies all boundaries and frontiers – be it political, geographic or celestial. As expressed so eloquently by Banner (2008: 28–9), 'by its immensity and its fluidity the atmospheric layer resists all possession'.

To fully understand aviation law as an autonomous discipline, we must consider it within its broader international context. In short, we must study an international aviation law. Aviation is something very different, something very exciting and indeed something very much worthy of regulation.

How can this be? Why the *need* for regulation? Is it that I the author – the pilot turned lawyer and safety regulator – have now betrayed the reader? Have I been brainwashed and indoctrinated by the evil forces of aviation regulation to the extent that it has clouded my vision of the noble and majestic art of flight? Or is there perhaps – just perhaps – some element of truth in what I suggest? Is it conceivable that the regulation of aviation is both *necessary* and *desirable*? So here beginneth the lesson – International Aviation Law 101.

Why Study International Aviation Law?

Many publications on the subject of aviation law often approach the topic of international aviation law almost as an afterthought – if it is addressed at all. Such works typically begin by explaining the application of aviation law at the national level and within the legal system and jurisdiction of the country to which the publication is targeted. This book takes a somewhat different approach. It is strongly asserted that because of the unique characteristics of aviation activities, any meaningful appreciation of the regulatory regime that 'controls' the aviation industry can *only* be achieved by first considering aviation law within its broader, international context – that is, by studying *international aviation law*.

The adoption and proliferation of international aviation treaties such as the Chicago Convention is quite unique to the aviation industry. This particular treaty not only *influences* all aviation activities – that is, international, domestic and, to an increasing degree, military – but also, to a large and increasing extent, *dictates* all operational, technical, safety and security standards within the industry. We should study international aviation law not just to gain an insight into aviation in its international environment, but rather to provide a clearer and more comprehensive understanding of the legal basis upon which *all* aviation law is founded.

As an industry, what makes aviation somewhat unique can be explained in terms of its development and how it is regulated. These two aspects of aviation, although quite distinct, are in fact highly interrelated and to a significant extent account for why there is a greater degree of international harmonization of aviation legislation than there is with any other industry.

At its most fundamental level, the proliferation of aviation regulation has evolved from developments of the law directed towards the protection of proprietary rights of both the individual and the state. At the personal level, the law seeks to protect the property rights of the individual landowner. At the national level the sovereignty of the airspace above a state and its territorial waters is of utmost importance to the independence and security of that state. By way of illustration the current proliferation of drones in society, and the fact that both domestic and international regulations have not been able to adequately address the protection of proprietary rights, highlights the importance of this issue. But let us first begin in considering the proprietary rights of the individual.

Individual Proprietary Rights

The concept that an aircraft in flight may operate over a person's land without infringing that person's property rights is a unique feature of aviation law that has also developed with the expansion of aerial operations. Traditionally, property law defined a person's land or real property as extending from a line drawn around the boundary of the land to the centre of the earth and to the extremities of the heavens. This was derived from customary law and based on an old Roman maxim *cujus est solum ejus est usque ad coelum*, meaning 'whose is the soil, his is also that which is up to the sky'. If one infringed these proprietary rights, an action for trespass or nuisance could be brought.

There are early recorded instances involving ballooning accidents in which damage to personal property occurred. One particular accident occurred in France on 12 May 1903, while attempting to land in a suburban Parisian street. Upon impact with the ground, the balloon suddenly burst into flames. The ignited gas entered a window of a nearby building, with the resulting fire seriously injuring eight occupants. So, from the very beginning of manned flight, it was manifestly obvious that the law needed to develop – and to develop quickly – to protect the rights of innocent victims of aviation-related accidents.

***Guille v Swan*, 19 Johns 381 (NY Sup Ct, 1822), Supreme Court of New York**

Mr Guille, the defendant balloonist, landed his balloon in the vicinity of the plaintiff Mr Swan's garden. When Guille descended, he was in a dangerous situation and asked for assistance from a person who was working in Swan's field. The spectacle attracted the attention of hundreds of local residents who, in all the excitement, broke through Swan's fences and spoiled his vegetables and flowers. The damage caused to the balloon was minimal, totalling approximately $15, whereas the damage resulting from the stampede of people was in the order of $90. In this appeal the Supreme Court found Guille liable for all the damages that occurred on the premise and, in terms of establishing causation, he should have anticipated that his descent and landing would most likely have attracted such a crowd.

Another more contemporary example in which the adverse causal effects of aircraft operations have played a decisive role was with an American balloon called the Double Eagle. This balloon, the first to cross the Atlantic Ocean non-stop, arrived in France on 15 August 1978. When it landed, thousands of enthusiastic fans ran towards it, damaging a wheat field. The French farmer lodged a claim for $1,000 with his insurance company, but the company refused to pay. However, the farmer eventually did receive his $1,000 from the American Consul-General in France, which avoided legal proceedings.

The question that needs to be asked is to what extent does the law protect the proprietary rights of individuals with respect to aircraft operations? The English courts, and for that matter most common law countries, follow the general principle enunciated in the following case.

***Baron Bernstein of Leigh v Skyviews and General Ltd* [1978] 1 QB 479, Court of Queen's Bench**

The defendant company took a single aerial photograph from a plane while overflying the plaintiff's country residence. In bringing an action for trespass, the plaintiff claimed, as owner of the land and airspace above, that he had a right to exclude any entry into that airspace. The court dismissed the case and held that the landowner's rights did not extend to an unlimited height. Griffith J stated that it was necessary to balance the rights of an owner to enjoy land against the rights of the general public to take advantage of all that 'science now offers in the use of airspace'. The rights of an owner in the airspace above his land are restricted to such height as is necessary for the 'ordinary use and enjoyment of his land and the structures upon it'. The landowner has no greater rights than any other member of the public.

Territorial Sovereignty of States

At the national or domestic level, the proprietary rights that are protected under international aviation law are those relating to issues of territorial sovereignty of the state. In international aviation the concept of sovereignty is the keystone upon which virtually all aviation law is founded. Long even before the Wright brothers' historic flight in 1903, tensions between nations regarding issues of sovereignty had emerged because of transnational sorties of balloons.

Somewhat ironically, it was the First World War that brought about a realization of the potential importance of aviation in terms of its economic and social benefits. But also, with the War came a sombre awakening of the dangers to states and their citizens of its use in hostile hands. This was not the first aviation-related event to raise the issue of sovereignty in respect to aircraft operations. Later in this chapter we review sovereignty issues relating to ballooning operations that date back to the late nineteenth century between France and Germany.

The law that has developed in relation to each of these two concepts of ownership – that is, personal property and state sovereignty – is all part and parcel of what has been termed international aviation law. In Chapter 2 we will consider the way in which international aviation law is defined and how it may be classified. We shall see how international aviation law has both a public and private component, as well as drawing from the domestic aviation law of individual states.

Those readers who are aviation practitioners will be well aware and familiar with the aviation rules and regulations that relate to their day-to-day duties and responsibilities. What will become apparent in reading this book is the extent to which the local or domestic aviation law of individual nations has derived from treaties and other instruments of international law. Moreover, since aviation, by its very nature, is to a large extent international, its optimal benefits cannot be realized if it is confined to national boundaries. Therefore, it is advantageous for aviation practitioners first to consider the law relating to aviation in its broader international context to better understand its application under the domestic aviation legal regime.

International Aviation Law Today

In more recent times, with the vast improvements in aircraft technology, and in particular since the introduction into service of the jet engine, aircraft have greater range and performance capabilities. Modern transport airliners are able to traverse multiple international boundaries in a single flight. Moreover, improved levels of safety and operating efficiencies and increased competition have all helped reduce the cost of air travel and thereby greatly increased its demand. On the political side of aviation there has been a more liberalized approach by governments around the world with a trend towards more 'open skies' policies. All of these factors have increased the demand and appetite for international air travel.

Together with the commercial, economic and social benefits of air travel, certain adverse effects of aviation operations have been fuelled by a rapidly expanding demand for air travel. While the advantages derived from international cooperation between nations of aviation activities are obvious, with this also comes a downside. With the increased 'sharing' of the benefits derived from international air transport, its risks are also *shared* globally. Issues relating to aviation safety, security and the environmental impacts of aircraft operations all need to be addressed through international dialogue leading to agreed standards which then must be consistently translated into domestic law. The global environmental 2050 target of net zero carbon emissions has been endorsed by both ICAO and IATA as they work together to assist the aviation industry to meet this challenge.

Every state is sovereign in its territory, but it is unable to regulate these aspects of international civil aviation effectively without the cooperation of other states and international agencies. For instance, in respect to the regulation of drones and with the development of sustainable aviation fuels (SAF) and electric and hydrogen powered aircraft, it can be seen how the societal benefits are yet to be fully realized mainly because an international regulatory framework is yet to be developed to permit their usage.

The role of developing consistent international aviation standards and ensuring they are consistently applied and enforced is the role of the International Civil Aviation Organization (ICAO). But the international aviation system is indeed only as strong – and as safe – as its weakest link. The 11 September terrorist attacks on the World Trade Center in 2001 proved this in a most devastating way. Following these attacks the ICAO was swift to promulgate international security standards to address the deficiencies apparent with the international aviation system.

Moreover, unless the 193 contracting states to the Chicago Convention, through their respective National Aviation Authority (NAA), promulgate and oversee the relevant ICAO Standards and Recommended Practices (SARPs) in a consistent manner, the international aviation system will falter. The perceived necessity since 2005 of the European Union (EU) to maintain an 'Air Safety List' of airlines prohibited from entering European airspace to maintain safety standards is evidence of the vital importance of the consistent worldwide application of international aviation standards. As we shall see later, the ICAO through its audit oversight programme has increased its vigilance of the level of compliance with the SARPs by its member states.

The following extract from Shawcross, Beaumont and Martin (1977: 2), stated almost half a century ago, provides a good summary of the unique characteristics of international aviation law:

> The use of aircraft has destroyed all effective frontier barriers, even the barrier of the ocean. So the sovereign states of the world have been forced to try to replace their differing systems of national laws by one international system for the flow of international traffic and trade. So far the system is still very far off. But no other system of law has been so rapidly developed by sovereign states collaborating for national and international objectives.

Before we go into detail of how international aviation standards are applied today, it is important to understand how international aviation law evolved. What we will discover is that the reasons why this area of the law developed in the first place are precisely the same reasons why it is absolutely necessary today. The law relating to aviation needs to be developed, standardized and enforced on an international basis to provide for sustainable growth.

THE DEVELOPMENT OF INTERNATIONAL AVIATION LAW

Hot Air Balloons and Police

As previously stated, from its very beginnings, aviation activities have been subject to strict regulatory control. Soon after the first manned hot air balloon assents in 1783, the

Paris police required flight permits to protect the safety of persons and property on the ground. One prominent commentator suggested:

> It seems as if regulators feared a sinister element in the navigation of the air, born of ancient superstition and sought to safeguard the people from some diabolical power attacking the human race from the heavens.
>
> (Colegrove 1930: 2)

Perhaps this emotive view is a little overstated, but nevertheless it certainly makes the point.

Sometime later, again with the Parisian gendarmes, the Chief of Police of the Seine introduced regulations in 1819 requiring all balloon operations be equipped with a parachute. While earlier legislation focused more on addressing issues relating to aircraft impacting the ground, this rule appears to have been the first to promote safety on board the aircraft.

In stark contrast to other modes of transportation, such as road, rail or maritime, rules requiring licences or other measures of control came long after the implementation of the invention. But aviation regulation went even further. Unlike, for example, the development of road and rail transport, aviation acquired its own specialized area of the law. As Banner (2008: 354) suggests: 'we may infer that technological change, in itself, does not cause lawyers to create new categories of law. New technologies are assimilated into the old categories'.

Transport law was sufficient to accommodate, for example, road, rail and maritime operations – even at the international level. But as Diederiks-Verschoor (2006: 2) points out in respect of international aviation law, 'this was one of the rare instances where legal process went ahead of technology'. The law relating to aviation was literally growing at a faster rate than the technology it was meant to regulate. In hindsight this was really quite an extraordinary situation.

A significant contributory factor as to why aviation law developed autonomously occurred in Europe towards the end of the nineteenth century. Political tensions between neighbouring states had heightened as a consequence of a rapid increase in ballooning operations. Certain nations – in particular France and Germany – became increasingly concerned of the discharge of projectiles and explosives from balloons and of their use for covert operations. This led to the convening of the first international aeronautical congress in Paris in 1889. High on the agenda were issues of national sovereignty and the seeking of resolutions proclaiming a state's right to prohibit war and spying from balloons. However, it took some time. In fact, a decade later at The Hague Peace Conference of 1899, the first international declaration relating to the prohibition of aerial warfare in balloons was signed.

Freedom of the Air

At the turn of the twentieth century, a French academic lawyer by the name of Paul Fauchille wrote a treatise titled *Le Domaine Aérien et le Régime Juridique des Aérostats* (1901). In his publication Fauchille argued that there should be a 'freedom of the air', that is, unrestricted freedom of travel for airships in the airspace over the territory of any other country, although a year later he did concede that naturally 'the state must have the right to prohibit war and spying from balloons over its territory'.

In 1902 the Institute of International Law (*Institut de Droit International*) met in Brussels and considered a proposed convention on the regulation of aerial navigation. Drafted by Fauchille, the regulations were later endorsed at its 1906 meeting in an amended form. So effective was Fauchille's argument that, in its 'pure' form – and during times of peace – the theory of 'freedom of the air' never became very widespread as there was no real opposition to the concept. During the first decade of the twentieth century, most people supported this liberalized approach. As it then was, aviation was embraced by all and heralded as the coming of a new era. Fauchille and his approach to travel by air continued to gain support and earned him the title of 'the father of aviation law'.

The endorsement by the Institute of International Law of Fauchille's draft regulations appears to have been the first diplomatic effort to actually formulate the principles of international law relating to air navigation. And so, by the turn of the previous century, books had been written, institutions formed and legal processes established, all in the name of international aviation law and – what makes this even more extraordinary – all before the first powered flight in an aircraft – now that's keen!

Powered Flight in Aircraft

The first aircraft to attempt a controlled powered flight was in a non-rigid airship or dirigible – nowadays also referred to as a 'blimp'. The German Count Ferdinand Von Zeppelin was responsible for what became known as the first 'Zeppelin' flight on 2 July 1900. Unfortunately, the flight lasted only 18 minutes due to a failure of the winding mechanism to balance the distribution of weight on board the aircraft. Because of the balancing problem, this design did not win the confidence and support of potential investors.

The next advancement in airship manoeuvrability was attributed to a pilot by the name of Alberto Santos-Dumont. Santos-Dumont was able to effectively attach an internal combustion engine to his balloon. In an aerial competition in 1901, he flew his airship named Number 6 over Paris from the Parc de Saint Cloud, around the Eiffel Tower and then finally returned to his departure point. The flight lasted just under 30 minutes and was deemed to be the fastest, and for his efforts and ingenuity he won the prestigious Deutsch de la Meurthe Prize.

The next significant development in the design of the dirigible occurred in 1902, as a result of the efforts of an engineer named Leonardo Torres Quevedo. Torres Quevedo developed his own 'Zeppelin' designed in such a way to overcome the previous balance problems, but issues relating to aircraft controllability were yet to be resolved.

Then in 1903 the Wright brothers, Orville and Wilbur, were the first to successfully carry out a powered flight in a heavier-than-air aircraft. It should be noted that all previous flights were conducted in aircraft that were lighter than air. The historic flight, at Kitty Hawk, North Carolina, lasted just 12 seconds and spanned a mere 120 yards. Although short in time and distance, its significance was profound as it established the foundation for future aircraft design and technology.

The main difference between the Wright brothers' flight and other flights in balloons and airships during the previous 120 years – beginning way back in 1783 – was the degree of control that the brothers managed to achieve over their aircraft. Their invention of the three-axis control enabled them to steer the aircraft effectively and maintain its equilibrium. The problems associated with travelling in the third dimension of space had been resolved. This unique feature became – and remains today – the standard for all fixed-wing aircraft.

NATIONAL SOVEREIGNTY

Introduction

By 1910, with a changing political landscape across Europe, issues of national sovereignty had begun gaining public attention. An increasing number of politicians and academics were becoming increasingly critical of Paul Fauchille's concept of 'freedom of the air'. The Dutch-born Johanna Nijeholt in his publication *Air Sovereignty* (1910) and England's Professor Harold Hazeltine in *The Law of the Air* (1911) strongly opposed the concept, so much so that Fauchille's opponents came down heavily in favour of complete national sovereignty of airspace. Franz von Liszt, a highly esteemed expert on international aviation law, proclaimed: 'In peacetime there can be no talk about absolute "freedom of the air" in view of the danger to the state from airships dropping objects, observing military installations and so on' (Kislov and Krylov 1956: 35).

With developing international political tensions, and the real prospects of war in Europe, the very first supporters of complete sovereignty of airspace based their views above all on national interests and notions of national security.

Although Europe was the first continent where the 'containment' of aviation activities attracted the attention of governments, the USA was not far behind. In 1909 the Chief Justice of the Supreme Court of Connecticut, Professor Simeon Baldwin, wrote a treatise titled *Will Airships Change Our Laws?* The publication highlighted the impact of airships on the legal framework of aviation. Professor Baldwin raised the issue of whether airships should have the right to fly over people's property. His view was that government regulation of airships was necessary because there was no line of authority in customary or common law to settle such a dispute.

In an article published in the *New York Times* on 20 November 1909, Baldwin further argued his position in contrasting the ramifications of an accident in the air compared with one at sea. When there is a shipwreck, he explained, the only people affected are those on board or the owners of the vessel or its cargo. If, however, such a situation was to occur in aviation, the accident may impact upon many parties and may involve property damage and possible injury to persons on the ground. On reflection and considering the extent and complexity of litigation in this area today, Baldwin's prophesies displayed a remarkable degree of wisdom and insight.

Following the attention created by Baldwin's publications, Holland Forbes of the Aero Club of Connecticut drafted the first aeronautical regulations in the USA. Forbes' proposal was passed by the Connecticut legislature and was signed into law by the now Governor Baldwin on 8 June 1911. Baldwin was then appointed Connecticut's first Commissioner of Aeronautics and was responsible for the first regulation of public transportation by air in America.

In the same year that Baldwin was arguing the need for legislation to protect the property rights of individuals in the USA, issues of proprietary rights of nations were raised throughout Europe. Concepts of state sovereignty reached new levels when in

1909 a French pilot, Captain Louis Blériot, crossed the English Channel and landed at the port of Dover – but without any permission.

International Conventions

The first attempt at creating a set of rules and regulations for aviation on an international scale was initiated by the French government in 1910. This was in response to German balloons making frequent flights above French territory – just as they had towards the dawn of the previous century. According to Sand *et al.*, it was reported that 'at least ten German balloons crossed the frontier and landed in France carrying over twenty-five aviators at least half of whom were German officers' (1960: 30). As the French government wanted to prevent international confrontations, it proposed summoning an international conference to discuss the operations of flights into and out of foreign countries.

The resulting international conference – the Paris International Air Navigation Conference (1910) – can be viewed as the first political effort to compose principles of international aviation law. Although the conference did not succeed in drafting an international convention, it did identify and address key issues for the future with regard to international air navigation.

As a result of the previous Blériot 1909 incident and the Paris Convention in 1910, the British Parliament passed the *Aerial Navigation Act 1911*. This statute conferred upon Parliament the power to close British airspace – including the English Channel – from all foreign aircraft when considered necessary. At the time, Britain was anticipating war with Europe and so the fundamental purpose of the statute was to protect the nation from attack from the air rather than to enhance the safety of air navigation.

So, by 1911, two of the most powerful nations, Britain and the USA, had both passed domestic aviation laws to regulate aviation activities. Significantly, both legislative instruments were motivated by a perceived need by the legislature to protect their citizens from the adverse effects of aircraft operations. In the case of Britain, the greatest threat was the use of aircraft by hostile, foreign protagonists; in the case of the USA, it was designed to protect the public from those who attempted these aerial activities.

The Two World Wars

After the Paris Convention of 1910, discussions and international dialogue on the subject of aviation law would most likely have continued had it not been for developing hostilities between certain European nations – all of which were major aviation players. After the outbreak of The Great War in 1914, international cooperation in respect to aviation activities immediately ceased – even between allied nations. The aircraft was about to become one of the primary weapons of war.

Indeed, it was the First World War that also brought about a realization of both the importance of aviation and its potential danger to states and their citizens in threatening their sovereignty. However, it was not until 1919, immediately following the War, that the issue of sovereignty was finally resolved on an international basis. Once again, the nations of the world convened in Paris for the first major international conference on aviation.

The conference resulted in the drafting of the *Convention Relating to the Regulation of Aerial Navigation*, which is more commonly known as the Paris Convention. This Convention defined the status of international airspace and gave authority to each individual operating an aircraft to act in accordance with the law of the state of registration.

The first article of the Convention strictly specifies that states have complete and exclusive sovereignty over their own airspace in stating:

> The High Contracting Parties recognize that every Power has complete and exclusive sovereignty over the air space above its territory.

This proclamation finally put to rest the debate, which had begun in the previous century, of whether the airspace was 'free' – as it is with the high seas – or whether it was 'part' of the subjacent state or territory. It is important to realize that the Paris Convention did not *create* the principle of exclusive air sovereignty, but rather *recognized* it. Article 1 was drafted in such a way that it was declaratory of pre-existing customary international law.

Furthermore, the principle of air sovereignty extends to all nations – that is, 'every Power' – irrespective of whether a particular state has signed or ratified the Convention. It is a role of the executive of the state to represent that state at international conventions and then to 'sign' or otherwise agree to an international convention (or treaty). It is then for the legislature to adopt the obligations imposed by the convention into the domestic law of the particular state. This process is known as ratification. The Paris Convention 1919, as we will consider in more detail in Chapter 2, was the first true instrument of international aviation law.

So let us now summarize the importance of the concept of national sovereignty to aviation. In international aviation, the concept of sovereignty is the basis and essence upon which virtually all aviation law is founded. The concept, ever since the Paris Convention 1919, has been the backbone of all international aviation law around the world. Governments throughout the world – including the 38 nations that were represented at the Convention – were almost unanimous in their desire to harness, through strict regulatory control, this thing called aviation.

Somewhat ironically, the intervention by governments in terms of their seemingly insatiable appetite to control aviation was motivated more by the demonstrated capacity of the technology to destroy rather than provide any beneficial attributes. The driving force behind the state's need to control aviation through regulation was, of course, an awareness of the dangers that hostile enemy aircraft pose to a nation's security. This 'awareness' turned to fear following the demonstrated destructive capabilities of aircraft during the First World War.

Governments' fear of aircraft as a potentially destructive technology continued to develop and was further heightened as a consequence of rapid advances in aircraft design and performance during the Second World War. There was widespread destruction across Europe resulting from enemy aircraft assaults, culminating at the War's end in the Pacific with the devastating aftermath of the atomic bomb attacks on Nagasaki and Hiroshima in Japan in 1945.

Aviation law had up to this time become, as its primary purpose, an instrument of regulatory control by governments rather than specifically focusing on promoting and enhancing the safety of aerial activities. It is only relatively recently – that is, since the

Second World War and with the convening of the Chicago Convention in 1944 – that safety outcomes became the predominant driving force for aviation regulation.

Quite ironically, three of the most influential events that have shaped and directed the course of international aviation law have been directly associated with aviation's destructive capabilities. The First and Second World Wars and, most recent, the 9/11 terrorist attacks on the World Trade Center in 2001 have significantly and permanently influenced the direction and structure of international aviation law.

In conclusion, it is important to emphasize the impact these world events have had upon the development and style of international aviation law. Indeed, the traditional highly prescriptive style of the actual aviation rules and regulations was a consequence of the unique combination and interrelationship between issues of state sovereignty, military influences and aircraft technological development. This aspect of aviation operations, and the development of this entirely new branch of law to control such activities, cannot be overstated.

2
Sources of Aviation Law

'Necessity' as they say in the classics, is the 'mother of invention'. Aviation law was born out of necessity. Almost from the time of the invention the rate of advancement in aircraft design and performance necessarily required the intervention of governments from around the world to effectively control this rampaging technology.

The purpose and need for aviation law has been fuelled by the increasing globalization and expanding nature of aviation activities. Due to the unique attributes of travel by air, in certain instances, aviation law is, by application, considered to be *international* aviation law. This view has been eloquently expressed by Justice Peters in the case of *Scandinavian Airlines System, Inc. v County of Los Angeles*, 56 Cal. 2d 11 (1961):

> As the vessel which sails the seas is subject to admiralty law, airplanes flying international skies are subject to all manner of international aviation law.

DEFINITIONS AND TERMINOLOGY

In this chapter the various sources from which international aviation law has derived will be explored. In addition, the way in which the different branches of aviation law are defined and classified will be examined. To begin with, and consistent with the central theme of this publication, a consideration of the law within an international aviation context will be provided.

International Law

International law has been described as a body of legal rules which apply between 'sovereign' states and such entities that have been granted international legal personality, such as international organizations. The concept of international legal personality extends to organizations such as the United Nations (UN) and the International Civil Aviation Organization (ICAO), both of which are key players in international aviation law. International conventions – for example, the Chicago Convention 1944 with regard to the ICAO – detail and confer international personality upon these respective organizations.

There has been significant debate amongst jurists and scholars as to the true nature of international law. The 'law of nations' – as it was once called – developed in the sixteenth century amongst a few Western European civilizations, predominantly those of Ancient Greece and Rome. Their shared heritage of Christianity gave these civilizations some sense of commonality, before the development of the modern Westphalian state

DOI: 10.4324/9781032652146-2

system that saw the collapse of these empires. Nevertheless, with the interconnectedness of the world and the inevitability of globalization, a shared set of rules is becoming more important to the international community of sovereign states.

There is no doubt that states, in many respects, refuse to surrender their sovereignty. The Belgian scholar Charles de Visscher (1957: 92) argued that it was a

> pure illusion to expect from the mere arrangement of inter-State relations the establishment of a community order; this can find a solid foundation only in the development of the true international spirit of men. . . . There will be no international community so long as the political ends of the State overshadow the human ends of power.

This provides some insight into the notion that international law has a fundamental political element.

As there is no sovereign international authority with the power to enforce decisions or even to compel individual states to follow rules, international law has sometimes been referred to as a 'toothless tiger' in not being a *true* law. In aviation, however, because of the extensive and important role of international institutions like the ICAO and the International Air Transport Association (IATA), and the proliferation of honoured bilateral air services agreements between nations, including the almost universal ratification of international conventions concerning international civil aviation, the existence of an international aviation law is beyond dispute.

What is a Treaty?

International treaties formulate the backbone of international law. However, it is often the case that treaties are long, complex, difficult to follow and in many cases too general to understand. Sometimes they are just plainly unclear. Practitioners in the aviation industry may have worked all their life in aviation but have little to no understanding of the principles of treaty law, and how critical principles of the Chicago Convention and the Montreal Convention apply to the practicalities of the industry.

International treaties are, in many ways, like contracts. They are a document entered into by two or more sovereign states containing legally binding rules that each contracting state must follow. The typical procedure is:

- The treaty is drafted.
- The treaty is then *signed*.
- Sometimes, a state's signature is subject to ratification, where a state indicates its consent to be bound if the parties intended to show their consent. This simply means that a state can sign a treaty but refuse to ratify it and refuse to show their consent to be bound. The signature thus becomes a mere gesture.
- Usually, for a treaty to have legal effect, a certain number of states need to ratify it.
- If a state did not become party to a treaty at the time it was given legal effect, they may *accede* to the treaty later and show their intent to be bound.
- In many states, the passage of legislation will be required in order to make that treaty binding as part of domestic law.

In some states – which are referred to as *monist* states – international and domestic law are seen to be part of the same order. In this case, domestic legislation is not required in order to give legal effect to a treaty. France and Germany are two examples of states where international treaties are automatically binding in their territories. In *dualist* states, by contrast, that passage of legislation is required in order to make treaties legally binding. International and domestic law are seen in these states to be part of two separate orders, as it is the consent of states to be bound which gives international law its legitimacy.

In order to interpret treaties, states are often required to apply the principles of treaty interpretation contained in another treaty – the *Vienna Convention on the Law of Treaties* 1969 ('the VCLT'). An extensive discussion on the VCLT will not be provided here, but an overview of its most important principles should be outlined.

Article 31 of the VCLT reads that a treaty is to be interpreted 'in good faith and in accordance with the ordinary meaning to be given to the terms of treaty in their context and in light of its object and purpose'. This means that one should avoid interpreting the text to the detriment of a state unless that detriment is explicitly stated. It also means that interpreting a treaty's provisions will require looking at contextual factors including:

- its preamble and Annexes (interpreting the Chicago Convention will therefore require an appreciation of ICAO Annexes);
- any agreement relating to the treaty made between all parties in connection with the treaty's conclusion;
- any instrument that was made by the parties in connection with the conclusion of the treaty and accepted by the other parties as an instrument related to the treaties; and
- if the treaty's provision is unclear, or if its application leads to an unreasonable result, looking at the *travaux préparatoires* (preparatory work) is permitted. This may involve looking at emails sent about creating the treaty, handwritten notes, memos, etc.

Article 19 allows states to make *reservations* to parts of a treaty. This is where a state aims to exclude or modify the legal effect of a treaty, a part of which it does not accept. They are still bound by the treaty itself, but some provisions may be modified or excluded as a condition for their acceptance to be bound. They are, however, prohibited from making a reservation if:

- the reservation is prohibited by the treaty;
- the treaty provides that only specified reservations, which do not include the reservation in question, may be made; or
- the reservation is incompatible with the object and purpose of the treaty.

This last point means that states are forbidden to exclude themselves from a provision that is so fundamental to the purpose of the treaty, as not giving it legal effect may practically go against the entire reason the treaty was made. For instance, it would make no sense if a state was to make a reservation to provisions in the UN Torture Convention that prohibit torture. Otherwise, you may as well not have the treaty at all.

International Aviation Law

International aviation law is essentially a combination of both public and private international aviation law. It has been suggested that its principal purpose is to provide a system of harmonized regulation for international aviation operations and to eliminate conflicts or inconsistencies between the domestic aviation laws of states. The following definition (Bartsch 1996: 9) provides a pragmatic, workable and generally accepted account of the term: 'International aviation law is that branch of law that comprises rules and practices which have been created, modified or developed that apply to all aviation activities'.

In a later section of this chapter, we will see that this definition has been derived from a generally accepted definition of *aviation law*. International aviation law is usually associated with civil aviation operations, although many defence operations are conducted in accordance with civil aviation procedures. Military or 'state' aircraft are often specifically excluded from instruments and treaties of international law; however, in the interests of the safety of air navigation – military aircraft after all *do* operate in the same airspace – military aircraft by and large operate in accordance with the same operational and procedural rules of the air.

International aviation law derives from a number of sources, the most important of which are:

- international treaties and conventions;
- bilateral and multilateral air services and safety agreements;
- domestic aviation law;
- judicial decisions with respect to the interpretation of international treaties and other areas of the law that specifically relate to aviation activities;
- contracts between states and airlines;
- commercial alliances and other agreements between airlines;
- in certain instances, regional safety programmes and other initiatives.

Figure 2.1 provides an overview of the structure of international aviation law and the various components and institutions from which it derives.

In the next section of this chapter, we will see that international aviation law has both a public and private component, as well as drawing upon the domestic aviation law of

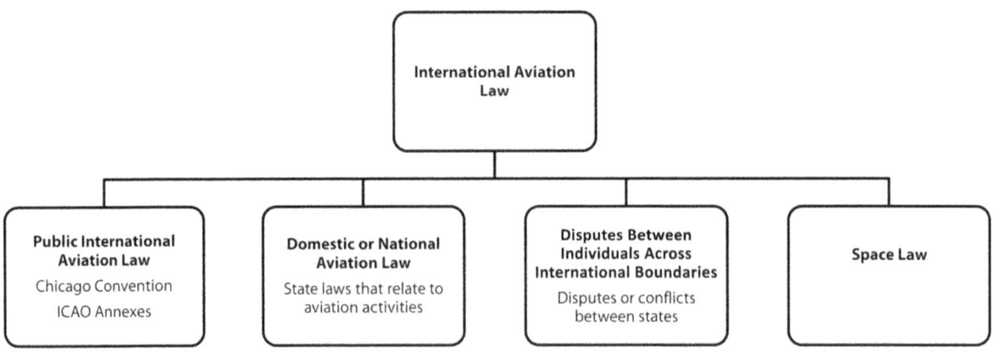

Figure 2.1 Structure of international aviation law

individual states. In brief, *public international aviation law* essentially refers to agreements between nations and is often in the form of international conventions or treaties. *Private international aviation law*, on the other hand, relates to legal *jurisdictional* issues – that is, the scope of the legal authority of a state or body – when conflicts or ambiguities arise between the laws of different states with respect to aviation activities.

Public international aviation law more specifically is that branch of international aviation law that determines the rules between contracting states and other international personalities. The Paris Convention 1919 and the Chicago Convention 1944 are true charters of public international aviation law. This term contrasts with the law relating to private disputes in which one of the parties may be from another state. This is the realm of private international aviation law, which is sometimes referred to as *conflict of laws*.

Towards the end of this chapter, in the section titled 'Domestic Aviation Law', definitions of the terms *air law* and *aviation law* will be provided. In Chapter 3, the various types of systems of law that exist around the world will be examined, together with definitions and characteristics of these varying systems of law. Additionally, the fundamental nature, attributes and defining qualities of what constitutes a 'law' in general will be explained.

At this stage it is important for the reader to appreciate the reason why it is of utmost importance to clearly define terms, concepts and indeed the branches or divisions of law when studying and applying 'the law'. The basis upon which aviation rules and regulations will be developed is intrinsically related to the doctrinal basis, classification and definition of these terms. In the aviation industry – because of the almost universal application of technical, safety and operational terms – this becomes even more critical. It may appear to the reader that an inordinate amount of time seems to have been spent on this particular topic, but that is not so – it is all for good reason. Let me explain.

To highlight the importance of maintaining a consistent approach and understanding when applying aviation terminology, take the following illustration. Consider, for example, the term 'accident'. If this term does not have *precisely* the same meaning and interpretation whenever and wherever this term is used, its application will not and indeed *cannot* be consistently applied. So, in continuing with this example, when collecting and comparing worldwide accident data, or when considering the operational requirements in the case of an aircraft accident, or the legal liability of airlines or aircrew resulting from an aircraft accident, or passenger rights in the event of an accident during an international flight, all require and rely upon a consistent understanding and application of this term.

Moreover, continuing with this example, the term 'accident' may have a different meaning (and therefore definition) which will depend upon the context to which it refers. So, what constitutes an 'accident' for the purposes of the Montreal Convention 1999 in respect of carrier liability for airlines and passengers may and does differ from the meaning of 'accident' in respect of Annex 13 of the ICAO relating to aircraft accident investigation. In an aviation context, the term 'accident' has many different meanings depending upon the circumstances and context to which it refers. The reason why the term *is* consistently applied throughout the aviation world is that all countries – at least the 193 states that have adopted the Chicago Convention and other international aviation treaties – have taken on (through ratification into domestic legislation) the same precise meaning (that is, the definition) that has been provided under international conventions and treaties. This is what international aviation law is all about – the consistency of application of technical standards and terms.

PUBLIC INTERNATIONAL AVIATION LAW

Introduction

The first fixed wing scheduled passenger air service commenced operations on New Year's Day 1914 from St Petersburg, Florida, to Tampa, Florida, a distance of 17 miles. The service was operated by the St Petersburg–Tampa Airboat Line. The first regular international passenger air service was a weekly flight between Paris and Brussels which commenced on 22 March 1919. For a fare of 365 francs, *Lignes Aériennes Farman* operated Farman F60 Goliath biplanes between the two cities with a flying time of 2 hours 50 minutes. Only six months after the commencement of the inaugural service, 38 nations attended the *Convention Relating to the Regulation of Aerial Navigation* in Paris in October 1919. The Paris Convention 1919, as discussed in Chapter 1, heralded the true beginning of international aviation law in confirming, virtually at the dawn of airline operations, the desire of governments throughout the world systematically to control aviation.

As a consequence of the First World War, aircraft design and technology progressed at an astonishing rate. By the end of the War, and in only four years, the plane had developed from a flimsy single engine biplane to a large, multi-engine, alloy construction transporter. Aircraft were now capable of flying significantly increased payloads higher and farther than ever before and at previously unimaginable speeds. The number of aircraft also increased dramatically. At the beginning of the War in 1914, Great Britain possessed only 12 military airplanes. By the War's end in November 1918, there were 22,000 airplanes. Civil airliners were waiting in the wings to play an important role in the advancement of world trade and commerce.

Apart from astonishing military aviation developments during the War years, there had also been significant developments in civil aviation. In April 1919, customs examinations of passengers in Brussels commenced, as did international mail and cargo air services operations from Paris. The first 322 Junkers F13 aircraft was manufactured and performed its maiden flight on 25 June to become the world's first all-metal commercial aircraft. KLM (*Koninklijke Luchvaart Maatschappij voor Nederland an Kolojien*) Royal Dutch Airliners was formed and began operations later that year.

The first private organization of air carriers was formed on 28 August 1919 with six European airlines establishing the International Air Traffic Association in The Hague. This was the precursor to the International Air *Transport* Association (which also uses the acronym 'IATA') that was created in October 1945 with similar aims of collaboration between members to promote the safe and efficient development of international air commerce. The IATA's headquarters are now located in Montreal, Canada.

The Paris Convention 1919

During the War, the Inter-Allied Aeronautical Commission was established in 1917 with the aim of considering the limits of commercial aviation with a particular focus on the developments in Germany. In the aftermath of the War, Germany was forbidden to develop military or naval air forces. More specifically, the Commission was encouraged to prepare a convention on international aerial navigation in the period when peace was evidently present. Albert Roper had been retained as an aviation expert to the French Cabinet of the Under-Secretary of the State for Aeronautics.

During discussions at the Paris Peace Conference in Versailles earlier in 1919, a committee led by Monsieur Albert Roper was officially formed on 6 March and was instrumental in convening the Paris Convention of 1919. Although the commercial potential of this now vastly improved means of transportation was universally accepted, it was more specifically the demonstrated capacity of aviation as a weapon that catalyzed governments to act so swiftly and harmoniously to control this potentially destructive new technology.

The preamble to the Paris Convention included the words 'to encourage the peaceful intercourse of nations by means of aerial communications' and 'to prevent controversy'. These words reflected the determination of the allied nations to agree upon consistent international legal regulation. It is of little surprise that most of the drafters formulating the principles of international air law were in fact military officers.

As we discovered in Chapter 1, the Paris Convention defined the status of international airspace and gave authority to each individual operating an aircraft to act in accordance with the law of the state of registration. There were not many laws governing aviation before 1919, so this development, as we learnt in the previous chapter, was particularly significant in regard to issues of *sovereignty*.

With the signing of the Convention by 27 of the 38 states on 13 October 1919, the first multilateral instrument of international aviation law relating to air navigation was enacted. The nations that signed the instrument included: Belgium, Bolivia, Brazil, the British Empire, China, Cuba, Czechoslovakia, Ecuador, France, Greece, Guatemala, Haiti, the Hedjaz (Saudi Arabia), Honduras, Italy, Japan, Liberia, Nicaragua, Panama, Peru, Poland, Portugal, Romania, the Serbo-Croat-Slovene state, Siam, Uruguay and the USA.

Although the Paris Convention is no longer in force and even though it was not accepted by every nation – significantly, it was never ratified by the USA or Spain – it nevertheless provided the framework for post-First World War developments and cooperation in international aviation. The Convention did resolve the issue of air sovereignty and also became the basis for the adoption by many nations of their first regulations relating to civil aviation.

The Paris Convention also created the first official organization responsible for the international oversight of aviation activities with the establishment of the *Commission Internationale de Navigation Aerienne*. This commission provided the all-important foundation of today's technical and safety standards for aviation which is now the role and function of the ICAO.

The Chicago Convention 1944

The *Convention on International Civil Aviation* of 1944, or the Chicago Convention as it is commonly referred to, essentially updated and replaced the Paris Convention. Today the Chicago Convention is by far the most prolifically adopted international treaty. Some 193 sovereign states have ratified (made into domestic law) this convention and in so doing have agreed, under international aviation law, to be bound by the technical and operational standards developed by the ICAO as detailed in the 19 Annexes to the Convention.

Without doubt, this Convention is by far the most important instrument of public international aviation law and *is* the reason why we need to study international aviation law. The Conference in total lasted 37 days – 12 days longer than anticipated – and was eventually signed on 7 December 1944. It remains by far the world's most ratified international treaty with all of the UN 193 member states having ratified it. It is therefore important for us to understand how this Convention has gained universal support and why it is the basis of practically *all* aviation law, both domestic and international.

With the onset of the Second World War, passenger flights virtually ceased, but this did not prevent international aviation from continuing to grow – in fact, it flourished – just as it had during the previous World War. Although the War resulted in widespread destruction and the loss of millions of lives, the increased demand for, and utilization of, aircraft during this period led to significant advancements in technical and operational aspects of aircraft. By the War's end, advancements in aircraft design and technology had culminated in the development of the first jet engine. The potential of this technology, in times of peace, had finally been realized.

This astonishing development clearly showed that there was a need for an international organization to regulate international aviation and to assist with its growth and development. Following preliminary discussions initiated by the British government earlier in 1944, the USA called for an international conference to be held in Chicago in November of that year. It was the intention of the USA and its allied nations to establish post-war civil aviation arrangements and institutions and, in particular, the USA sought to promote the freedom of international exchange by removing the restrictions to international air travel imposed by absolute air sovereignty.

The principal parties at the conference were, of course, Britain and the USA. With the war in Europe still six months from being over, none of the 'opposing' states were invited or present. Of the 54 invited states, the USSR was the only notable absentee. The USSR had originally planned to attend, but at the last moment decided to withdraw its delegates from Montreal while en route to Chicago. Some commentators believe that the reason why it refused to participate may have stemmed from the fact that Portugal, Spain and Switzerland were all invited and the USSR had no real diplomatic relations with any of these countries. From a practical viewpoint, the absence of the USSR had the effect of prohibiting the use of Soviet airspace to international aviation for almost the next half-century.

The conference began on 1 November 1944 and was held at the Stevens Hotel, Chicago, which is now the Chicago Hilton. At the time the Stevens Hotel was considered one of Chicago's grand but nevertheless 'ageing' hotels. The less than salubrious accommodation did not meet the expectations of all the delegates, with some having described the venue as a mammoth second-rate hotel whose reception was likened to New York's Grand Central Station.

In total, 955 people attended the conference, including delegates, advisors, aviation experts, consultants, secretaries, clerks and stenographers and press representatives. The conference at that time was the largest international conference ever held in the USA and possibly the world. As a consequence of the number of attendees, a few 'inconveniences' were experienced, including up to an hour's wait for the use of the hotel's lifts and for external telephone connections.

Included in the conference agenda was to 'make arrangements for the immediate establishment of provisional world air routes and services' and to establish 'an interim council to collect, record and study data concerning international aviation and to make recommendations for its improvement'. The conference also aimed to 'discuss the principles and methods to be followed in the adoption of a new aviation convention'. It is important to note that, under Article 3(a), the Convention applies only to 'civil' aircraft and specifically excludes 'state' aircraft. Aircraft used for military, customs or police services are deemed to be state aircraft for the purposes of the Convention.

The overarching concern of the majority of the conference delegates was maintaining state sovereignty, just as it had been at the Paris Convention almost exactly a quarter of a century earlier. This issue was even more controversial, particularly with the USA's liberal position and push towards 'freedom of the air' being well known to all states.

The general objectives of the conference in terms of promoting international air transportation were twofold – of both an economic and a technical nature.

The economic objectives sought to:

- promote the freedom of airspace to nations and airlines;
- develop procedures for determining air fares, frequencies, schedules and capacities; and
- make arrangements for simplifying customs procedures and standardizing visas and other documentation.

The technical objectives were concerned with establishing international standards with respect to:

- technical standards, including the licensing of pilots and mechanics, registering and certifying the airworthiness of aircraft;
- the planning and development of navigational services and facilities; and
- the establishment of standard systems of communication procedures.

These two quite contrasting objectives were the central theme of the conference and extensive debate ensued as to whether universal navigational standards for both technical issues and consistent international rules concerning the economics of air transport could be agreed. In terms of the technical objectives, there was almost unanimous agreement. In fact, as it turns out, by far the most important contribution of the Chicago Convention overall was the almost unanimous agreement over technical matters and the groundwork which led to the establishment of the ICAO. The functions, structure and role of the ICAO are discussed in more detail in Chapter 4.

The two opposing positions and philosophies in respect of the economic and commercial aspects were essentially between countries led by the USA on the one hand and by Britain and its former colonial territories on the other. Although both nations, along with nearly all 52 nations represented, shared the same view regarding the conference's technical objectives and support for the establishment of the ICAO, in terms of economic outcomes, their idiosyncratic views differed vastly.

In contrast to Britain, the USA had well-established airlines and route structures, and wanted unrestricted operating rights for all nations on all international sectors. With an almost complete monopoly on the production of large four-engine transport aircraft, the USA was bargaining from a position of strength. According to one contemporary industry source (*The Aeroplane*, 22 December 1944) from 1939 to 1944, the USA produced some 17,000 multi-engine transport aircraft.

Britain's strength, in terms of negotiations, lay in its influence over the member nations of the then British Empire, many of which were located on major strategic air routes, so vital for international flights at the time because of the limited aircraft range. The British government in October 1944 had even issued a White Paper which proposed a multilateral surrender of sovereignty to an international airline regulatory authority. Australia, along with New Zealand in consideration of their geographic isolation from the rest of the world, proposed an even more radical plan in calling for the complete ownership and operation of airlines with the establishment of an international authority. It was, however, the proposal submitted by the Canadian delegation that became known as the 'five freedoms' which won the greatest support.

Freedoms of the Air The USA advocated for a complete 'freedom of the air' for commercial air transportation, while Britain, supported by all nations of the British Empire, proposed varying degrees of international regulation. The 'Five Freedoms Agreement' was documented as the International Air Transport Agreement, with only 20 states signing at Chicago, including the USA, and not all subsequently ratifying it. Only a handful of South American countries and countries with minimal aviation infrastructure signed, as they had more to gain by air alliance with the USA than any loss of fifth freedom rights.

The five freedoms can be summarized as follows:

1 the freedom of Country A's aircraft to overfly other countries;
2 the freedom of Country A's aircraft to land in other countries for non-traffic purposes, for example, for fuel or repairs;
3 the freedom of Country A to deliver traffic from Country A to other countries;
4 the freedom of Country A to pick up from other countries traffic destined for Country A;
5 the freedom of Country A's aircraft to pick up and discharge traffic between other countries (Countries B and C) on multi-sector journeys which originate/terminate in Country A.

Because only the first five 'freedoms' have been officially recognized by international treaties, the ICAO refers to the remaining 'freedoms' as being 'so-called' freedoms. These freedoms are discussed in more detail in Chapter 4.

Without the addition of the fifth freedom, the USA would not have been able to achieve its objective of dominating the major trunk routes. Obviously, in the absence of any regulatory control, if the five freedoms were adopted, the USA would be strategically placed to use its overwhelming air operating superiority to monopolize whichever major trunk routes it cared to operate in. Such a proposal was therefore unacceptable to Britain and its Empire and most other nations represented at the conference.

Although nearly all the delegates agreed that some degree of regulatory control was desirable, and indeed necessary for a cooperative development of international civil aviation, there was no consensus apart from agreement on the first two freedoms. It was hoped that the other freedoms might be settled on a multilateral basis, but this was not practicable as the more powerful nations stood more to gain through negotiating bilateral arrangements. As the free market approach was not acceptable and multilateral approaches were not practicable, the only other way to secure international air travel consensus appeared to be by way of individual bilateral air services agreements.

As with the Paris Convention 1919, the Chicago Convention restated and thereby reinforced the principle of absolute air sovereignty in Article 1, which states:

> The contracting states recognize that every state has complete and exclusive sovereignty over the airspace above its territory.

As was the status quo under the Paris Convention, air transit and traffic rights between contracting states required specific agreement.

'Two Freedoms' Agreement Under the Convention, all scheduled international air services must acquire prior permission before flying into or over foreign territories. To fill the gap with regard to scheduled international air services, most states, including Britain and the USA, signed the International Air Services Transit (Two Freedoms) Agreement. The Two Freedoms Agreement is also known as the Transit Agreement. This agreement was signed by 32 states at the Chicago Convention and has subsequently been ratified or accepted by over 135 states.

It is at the contracting state's unfettered discretion whether to adhere to the Transit Agreement. Bilateral agreements can, and usually do, include terms exchanging these two freedoms. This is an alternate arrangement for overflight rights where one or both states are not party to the multilateral agreement. The Transit Agreement does not specifically require contracting states to obtain a permit prior to exercising transit or non-traffic stopovers. In practice, irrespective of how overflight rights have been established, the filing of flight plans for operational purposes is usually all that is required to provide the requisite safety, technical and security information.

Also during the Chicago Conference, the 'Five Freedoms Agreement' was documented as the International Air Transport Agreement with only 20 states signing the agreement at Chicago, including the United States, but not all subsequently ratifying it. It was only a handful of South American countries and countries on 'the road to nowhere' that signed, as they had more to gain by air alliance with the United States than any loss of fifth freedom rights.

Bilateral Air Service Agreements Today, due to the unconformable nature of international dialogue, bilateral air service agreements ('bilaterals') are negotiated in respect of the other 'freedoms' just as they were prior to the Convention. So as not to deny certain rights of the parties, the wording of these agreements is often intentionally self-contradictory and general. Not surprisingly, bilateral agreements are often the source of a significant proportion of international air disputes.

The first bilateral air services agreement negotiated was between the USA and Britain in 1946. The so-called Bermuda 1 agreement permitted reciprocal rights of designated airlines of each nation to operate services to specified 'gateway' airports. The agreement did not restrict the number of flights and the format of this agreement became the basis for many other such bilateral agreements throughout the world.

It is estimated that as many as 3,500 bilateral agreements currently exist throughout the world, but the trend of governments is towards a more liberalized approach to international aviation policy. This has resulted in more 'open skies' agreements, particularly bilateral 'open skies' agreements. Such agreements have been established between the USA and Canada and between Australia and New Zealand with their single aviation market in the 1990s. Apart from the 2001 Multilateral Agreement on the Liberalization of International Air Transportation (MALIAT) between Brunei Darussalam, Chile, New Zealand, Singapore and the USA, there have been relatively few regional agreements – the major exception being of course in Europe.

Open Skies The primary rationale for open skies arrangements is obviously economic. Open skies promote greater airline productivity, better targeting of markets and improved operational flexibility for the airlines. Opening up routes to competition and allowing more scope for airlines to serve particular routes drive improvements in productivity. Competition places greater pressure on airlines to lower costs which are ultimately passed on as cost savings to passengers. Moreover, additional flexibility in operations and route development enables airlines to further reduce costs. The European experience has shown that low-cost carriers (LCCs) gain most from a more liberalized environment.

The EU's open skies market is by far the most comprehensive in any region. It has essentially created a single aviation market in the EU since January 1993. This allows, for example, an Irish-owned airline operating out of the UK to offer services between Spain and Italy. The EU–US open skies agreement is another very significant open skies agreement covering civil aviation traffic between two of the world's three biggest markets.

In Asia, the world's fastest growing aviation market, the Association of Southeast Asian Nations (ASEAN)'s open skies arrangement, the Single Aviation Market (SAM), was announced in 2015.

PRIVATE INTERNATIONAL AVIATION LAW

Introduction

Private international aviation law is the area of international aviation law that deals with private disputes in which one of the parties may be from another state. As previously stated, this branch of law is also referred to as conflict of laws. The first real attempt to address the problems associated with conflict of laws in aviation was an initiative of the French government in 1925 in convening the first international conference on private air law in Paris.

In the six years following the signing of the Paris Convention in 1919, there had been a proliferation of new airlines and the creation of a far more extensive network of international scheduled air services. With this expansion, and the inevitable increase in aircraft incidents and accidents, many disputes arose in respect of the associated damages and losses. *Conflict of laws* issues, particularly those relating to claims by passengers and owners of aircraft and cargo, were dramatically increasing and, in the absence of any international normative legal framework, disputes were not able to be effectively considered or resolved.

Under the direction of Albert Roper, the Secretary General of this International Conference on Air Law, the final protocol resulting from this conference proposed the creation of a special committee of experts. The *Comité International Technique d'Experts Juridiques Aériens* (CITEJA) was established to further examine the issues relating to the responsibility of international airlines and to set about the enormous task of *codifying* this rapidly expanding area of private air law. The work of the CITEJA was subsequently taken over by the ICAO with the creation of the Legal Committee in May 1947. This issue and the work of the ICAO generally are discussed in greater detail in Chapter 4.

Although there is no single equivalent forum or institution in private international aviation law as with the ICAO with respect to public international aviation law, since the creation of the CITEJA in 1925 there has been a proliferation of internationally accepted conventions. These include the Warsaw Convention 1929 and more recently the Montreal Convention 1999 and the Cape Town Convention of 2001. All three of these conventions are discussed in detail in Chapter 9.

Collectively, these conventions, and to a lesser extent organizations, of private international aviation law more than satisfy the essential elements in recognition of a true law. However, by far the most significant and one of the earliest conventions on private international aviation law was the Warsaw Convention of 1929.

The Warsaw Convention 1929

In the 1920s, the Legal Commission of the IATA produced standard conditions of carriage by air. The effectiveness of these conditions of carriage was, however, limited. They were not comprehensively adopted and were subject to differing interpretations between jurisdictions. This all changed with the Warsaw Convention of 1929.

Prior to the adoption of this convention, there were no uniform rules of law concerning international carriage by air. The rights of passengers and owners of cargo, most of which had been previously stated in the contract of carriage, would vary from country to country and in accordance with each country's own laws – that is, its domestic or national laws. The Warsaw Convention or, more formally, the *Convention for the Unification of Certain Rules Relating to International Carriage by Air* was agreed for signature at Warsaw on 12 October 1929. This convention represented the first uniform international effort to implement laws relating to international air carriage, especially with respect to a carrier's liability.

The Warsaw Convention imposes on the carrier – that is, the aircraft operator, which is usually an airline – a liability that is strict. The concept of *strict liability* means that the carrier will be held accountable without the need to prove negligence or fault. For this reason, strict liability is also referred to as *no-fault liability*. In practical terms this means that just as long as the passenger or owner of the cargo can show that the injury or damage suffered (by the *plaintiff*) resulted from the carriage by air, then the carrier will be held responsible (or liable) for the resulting damages.

In the case of the Warsaw Convention, apart from being strict (that is, no-fault), the carrier's liability is also *limited* to an amount specified by the Convention. As such, the carrier's liability under the Warsaw regime is considered to be 'strict and limited' liability. The form of liability arose more to protect the development of the fledging airline industry – most of which was owned by the state – rather than to benefit the passengers.

The trade-off in the application of the doctrine of strict liability (to the benefit of the passengers or owners of cargo) on the one hand was to limit the liability to the carrier on the other, a sort of quid pro quo arrangement whereby both parties accrued some benefit from the arrangement. Nowadays under the Montreal Convention 1999 – which has practically replaced the Warsaw Convention – liability is no longer limited in most instances. Today travel by air is far safer – airliner accidents are extremely rare – and the need to 'protect' the development of the airline industry is no longer a relevant factor in the equation.

Under the Warsaw system, there are some instances in which the carrier will be liable to damages in excess of this limitation. This only applies if the individual suing someone else (the *plaintiff*) can show that the carrier (the *defendant*) was guilty of *wilful misconduct*. Wilful misconduct can be described as the perpetrator being aware of their misbehaviour and the potential for damage ensuing, without necessarily intending a specific injury. An interesting fact is that the delegates to the Warsaw Convention agreed to limiting passenger compensation for loss of property or harm to a passenger by an airline to $8,300, where the amount was given in gold francs.

Where the Convention continues to apply, it covers transportation of persons, baggage and goods by air for hire. It imposes strict liability on carriers in respect of 'accidents' causing death or bodily injury to passengers, destruction of or damage to cargo and baggage, and damage caused by delay in the carriage of passengers, cargo and baggage.

In summary, the underlying objectives of the Warsaw Convention were to:

- protect the infant airline industry by imposing a limitation of liability;
- benefit passengers on the grounds of liability against the carrier; and
- achieve the maximum degree of uniformity for the international carriage by air.

The stated objectives of the Warsaw Convention were achieved for approximately two decades after it came into effect before its usefulness and support were gradually eroded to an extent that the Montreal Convention of 1999 was adopted to overcome the deficiencies of the previous regime and thereby replace it as the primary international convention governing international air carriage.

The Montreal Convention 1999 has fundamentally altered this area of private international air law. The new liability rules were developed during an International Conference on Air Law called by the ICAO to modernize the Warsaw Convention system. Dr Assad Kotaite, then President of the Council of the ICAO, stated in respect of the new agreement:

> We have succeeded in modernizing and consolidating a seventy-year old system of international instruments of private international aviation law into one legal instrument that will provide, for years to come, an adequate level of compensation for those involved in international air accidents.

However, back in 1929, the importance of the Warsaw Convention cannot be overstated.

The Montreal Convention 1999

The Montreal Convention is the most recent international convention governing international air carriage and was intended to consolidate and update the 'patchwork' nature of the various Warsaw system amending protocols. As a consequence of many nations, including Canada, Chile, Cuba, Malaysia, the Philippines and the USA, having not ratified the subsequent amendments to the Warsaw Convention, a non-uniform international system of liability of carriers governed international air carriage for some time. With this development, one of the fundamental objectives of the Warsaw Convention – namely to achieve the maximum degree of uniformity for the international carriage by air – had been fundamentally frustrated.

The lack of uniformity has largely been resolved following the Montreal Convention's entry into force and progressive adoption by most nations of the world. The

USA's ratification of the Convention represented another important step in the unification of international air carriage governance. However, some states who are parties to the Warsaw Convention have yet to ratify the Montreal Convention 1999 and for these states the Warsaw system – as it applies in terms of the adoption of subsequent 'Warsaw' protocols to that particular nation – continues to apply.

Prior to the introduction of the Montreal Convention, compensation limits remained generally low, in line with the early philosophies aimed at supporting a fledgling industry. The industry, despite present-day challenges, has developed significantly in respect of its commercial stability and relative safety standards. Commercial arrangements such as inter-carrier, code-shares and airline alliance agreements, and the complex nature of international trade have led to practices never envisaged by the drafters of earlier conventions, such as electronic documentation in place of traditional paper tickets and air waybills.

The Montreal Convention came into force on 4 November 2003 and although it updated many aspects of the Warsaw system, it is in fact an entirely new treaty that unifies and replaces the system of strict and limited liability established under the Warsaw Convention and its subsequent amendments and protocols. The Montreal Convention has a number of important differences, distinguishes between international and domestic carriage and, like its predecessor, only relates to international carriage by air.

The Convention establishes a new two-tier scheme to govern passenger compensation. The first tier, which operates up to 128,821 (since 2019 but originally 100,000) *Special Drawing Rights* (SDRs), imposes strict liability upon the carrier. The carrier's liability under the first tier can only be reduced by the demonstrated contributory negligence of the passenger. Liability under the second tier is unlimited if damages are proven in excess of 128,821 SDRs but can be avoided by the carrier proving that the damage was not caused by its negligence or was caused solely by the negligence or other wrongful act or omission of a third party. The rationale for a system of strict liability is essentially to get over the difficulty for passengers to prove fault.

Other notable changes include the promotion of the English text to a position of authority equal to the French text that controlled the Warsaw Convention. This means that courts will no longer be forced to resolve ambiguities and other interpretation-based issues by reference to French dictionaries. Further, reliance upon gold francs is replaced by a new generic currency system based upon SDRs, the value of which is determined by the International Monetary Fund.

Under the previous Warsaw system, there were four locations – in legal terms referred to as forums – where a plaintiff could bring an action against a carrier. These forums were:

- the domicile of the carrier;
- the principal place of business of the carrier;
- the country where the contract of carriage was made – provided it carried out business there;
- the destination country.

A 'fifth forum' of jurisdiction that has been created under the Montreal Convention enables a passenger to bring an action in the state party to the Convention in which, as at the time of the accident, the passengers have their principal place of residence, so long as the carrier operates, directly or indirectly, to that state.

It was this additional forum and the increased compensation available to the plaintiff under the Montreal Convention that was the main reason why it is preferred over the Warsaw System and has, as of the beginning of 2024, been ratified by more than 137 states.

The Cape Town Convention 2001

Another relatively recent 'addition' to the branch of private international aviation law is the Cape Town Convention of 2001, which resulted from 20 years of work to develop an international security interest convention for mobile equipment including aircraft. The Convention provides incentives to finance certain types of transactions including aircraft and aircraft engines in the international marketplace.

The Convention came into effect 1 April 2004 and initially covered only large commercial transport aircraft, but in 2006 an accompanying Aircraft Protocol extended its application to include regional jets, helicopters and corporate jets. The main advantages provided under the Convention and Protocol are:

- the right of repossession by creditors of aircraft and/or engines in case of default;
- the establishment of an International Registry in Ireland giving first-in-time priority to creditors having registered an 'International Interest'; and
- various other 'rights' to persons with registered interests with respect to aircraft.

It is hoped that over time the Convention will result in lower financial charges and will reduce the complexity of aircraft leasing or funding arrangements with respect to aircraft and/or aircraft engines.

Now that we have reviewed the various components and branches of international aviation law, Figure 2.2 may be useful in showing the relationships between each of these divisions and classifications.

CUSTOMARY INTERNATIONAL LAW

The root of all international law stemmed from custom – rules which grew up over a significant period of time by the common, tacit consent of states. The world community is much larger than when custom first developed, so whether or not something is actually custom can sometimes be the topic of debate. The core notion of custom is that states engage in acts because they see it as the right thing to do and expect other states to engage in those sorts of acts as well. Generally accepted forms of custom today include the duty not to intervene in the internal affairs of other states (sovereignty), immunity for heads of state from foreign jurisdiction, the prohibition on torture and the prohibition on the use of chemical weapons in war.

The wonderful, yet perhaps strange, element of international law is that customary rules are 'discovered' throughout the course of time. Custom exists as we know it, but we don't know if it exists for sure until it is mentioned in a treaty, or recognized by the

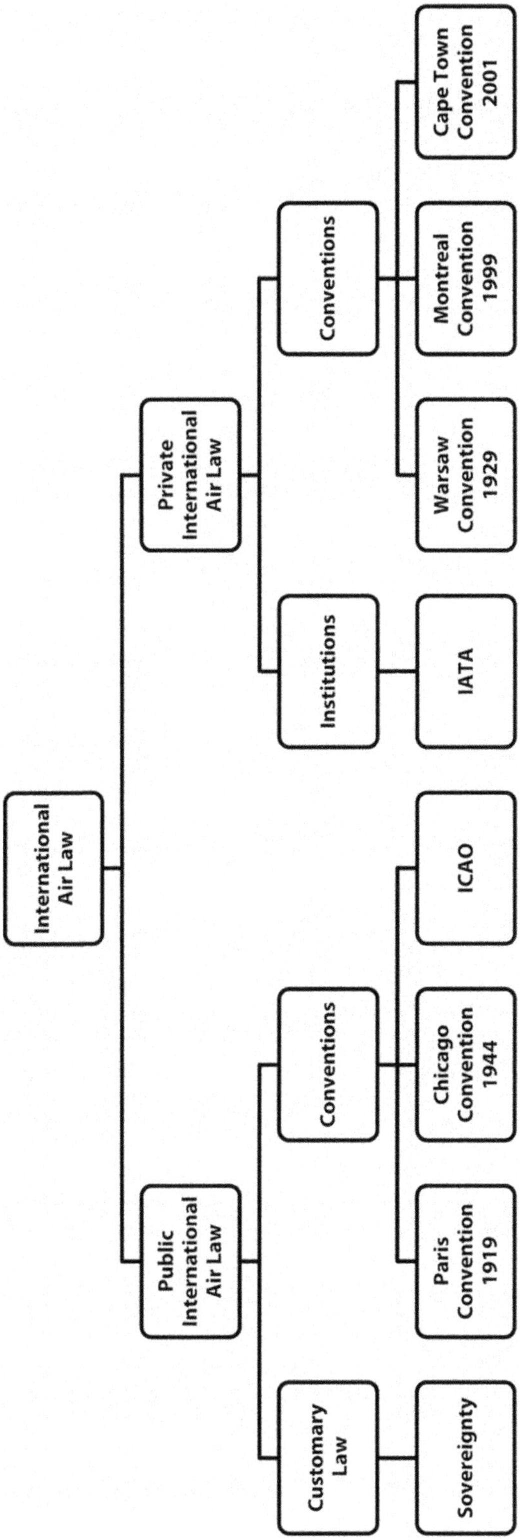

Figure 2.2 Structure of international air law

International Court of Justice, or by a scholar from the International Law Commission, etc. For a customary rule to exist there needs to be:

- general, consistent and uniform state practice, i.e. there needs to be fairly widespread participation of an act with the absence of substantial dissent;
- *opinio juris*, i.e. the subjective belief of states that they have a legal obligation to perform that particular act.

The impact of recognized customary law is that, even though a state has not ratified a particular provision of a treaty, it may still be bound by it as a matter of customary law. An example is the existence of *jus cogens* peremptory norms, which are norms of international law that all states have to follow no matter what. This includes the prohibitions on genocide, war crimes, crimes against humanity, torture and so on. As such, whilst a state may have refused to ratify the UN Torture Convention, it is still bound by *jus cogens* customary norms not to engage in acts of state-sanctioned torture.

The customary rule of sovereignty is recognized in Article 1 of the Chicago Convention, though it is debatable whether or not other provisions formulate custom. Because of the largely uniform state practice that has developed with the commitment of states to undertake aviation legal harmonization – such as airworthiness standards, safety requirements, the requirement for states to conduct investigations in the event of an aircraft accident, etc. – there is probably a lot of scope to make an argument that customary international aviation law exists.

DOMESTIC AVIATION LAW

Introduction

We have now arrived at that section of the book which is typically the starting point for many other publications on the subject of aviation law. Having provided the background to how aviation law developed – that is, within international aviation forums and conventions – we can now understand precisely what domestic aviation law is all about and what it is designed to achieve.

Contracting states to the Chicago Convention 1944 – all 193 of them – in having *ratified* or made into domestic law its obligation to comply with the Convention, must now, through their respective National Aviation Authorities (NAA), enact laws so as to create an aviation regulatory regime. This regime must include legislation that will ensure all the SARPs contained in the 19 Annexes of the Chicago Convention are complied with. In consideration of the fact that there are far in excess of 10,000 SARPs, this is by no means an easy task.

Structure of Domestic Law

We will discover in Chapter 3 that there is no universally accepted definition of what constitutes 'a law' or 'the law'. The terms are quite broad and vary in their application in the various types of legal systems throughout the world. At this stage it is sufficient to consider *the law* in terms of requiring the following three essential elements:

- an institution to make a law (sovereignty);
- sufficient scope to which the law applies (adequate jurisdiction); and
- the authority necessary to ensure that laws are applied and followed (usually by way of the imposition of sanctions or penalties).

In Chapter 3 we will overview the various types of legal systems that exist throughout the world. To remain effective and therefore relevant, any legal system must be responsive to changes in social behaviour, technological advancements, societal attitudes and mores within its jurisdiction. This is particularly true in rapidly changing technocentric industries such as aviation where business efficiencies can be impeded if the law cannot readily accommodate the uptake of new technological enhancements within its regulatory regime. To cater for the needs of society as a whole, various branches or divisions of law have developed over time.

Domestic Aviation Law

Any classification, division or branch of law exists, or is created, so that the subject matter can be better considered or understood within a contextual framework. For example, it is convenient to consider insurance law as a separate division of law when studying the subject. Even though a contract of insurance derives from the law of contract, it has sufficient peculiarities to justify its consideration as a separate branch of law.

For some time, indeed since its advent, aviation has been considered as a separate and unique science. It has been suggested that aviation is 'no less a science in itself, whose autonomy requires that it be presented separately from other closely related sciences' (Matte 1981). The insurance industry has long since established its own body of rules and so too has the aviation industry. Just as insurance law has evolved from contract law, aviation law has evolved with the development of an aviation industry.

As aviation activities have expanded and evolved, so too has that area of the law which supports and applies to these activities. The law has responded to the needs of aviation because society has so demanded.

Even though aviation law has existed since the birth of the invention – one could argue from the time the Paris police required special balloon permits in 1784 – the need for a pragmatic, working definition of aviation law was long overdue. Moreover, and consistent with a fundamental principle of international aviation law, it is imperative that such a definition is universally accepted. The acceptance, use and application of such a definition are of far greater benefit to aviation generally than its possible contribution to debate or intellectual rigour.

By way of comparison, consider the way in which *industrial law* has evolved, developed and expanded from employment law. In a similar manner, aviation law has evolved, developed and expanded from air law. Its relation to, and distinction from, air law is of far more importance than a purely academic pursuit. Proper terminology and doctrinal categorization allow the subject matter to be better understood within its contextual framework, that is, the aviation industry.

Throughout the world there has been considerable debate in relation to any universally agreed definition for the terms 'air law', 'aeronautical law' and 'aviation law'. Sometimes the terms are even used interchangeably. With respect to the terms 'air law' and the 'law of the air', if they were to apply to the literal or common meaning of the word 'air' as the 'medium' or the 'atmosphere', then this would logically include all the law associated with the use of the air, including radio and satellite transmissions. In the main, air law, as it applies to aviation, has a far narrower interpretation and is generally considered to apply to the body of rules governing the use of airspace.

According to Diederiks-Verschoor (1993), *air law* can be broadly defined as that body of rules governing the use of airspace and its benefit for aviation, the general public and the nations of the world.

Aviation Law Defined

The following definition of *aviation law* (Bartsch 1996) is sufficiently broad, and has gained widespread acceptance, to not only encompass the diversity of the subject matter as it exists today but also accommodate its expansion as it increasingly impinges upon other areas of contemporary society and indeed other established branches of law.

> Aviation law is that branch of law that comprises rules and practices which have been created, modified or developed that apply to aviation activities.

By way of analogy, aviation law is to air law as maritime law is to the law of the sea. To assist with the clarity of expression and to reduce the potential for problems to arise in the application (or misapplication) of these terms in this publication, the preceding definitions will respectively apply to the terms 'air law' and 'aviation law'.

According to Milde (2008: 43):

> A law is new – as is the case with air law – not only because it is an isolated legal discipline, but also on account of the new object to which it refers, the new legislation, and the way in which former principles are understood and adapted to new situations.

The same can be said in relation to aviation law – not that aviation law is a new law per se, but rather a newly *defined* law.

Air law (or *aeronautical law*) is therefore a subset of aviation law just as the 'aeronautical uses of the airspace' is a subset of 'aviation activities', but, nonetheless, both are part of the aviation industry. Aviation by definition relates to 'flight by mechanical means' and so by adapting the earlier definition, aviation law would include *space law* – the law that encompasses national and international law applicable to and governing activities in outer space (Figure 2.3). Air law by definition would necessarily exclude space law as it is beyond the navigable airspace.

Aviation law therefore encompasses the business aspects of airlines and general aviation activities and their regulation. Likewise, those aspects of insurance law, commercial law, competition law and so on that peculiarly relate to aviation activities will all form part of aviation law. Security and environmental regulations applicable to aviation activities are also within the scope of aviation law. Also included within the domain of aviation law is the regulatory oversight of aviation activities by regulators, government agencies and others.

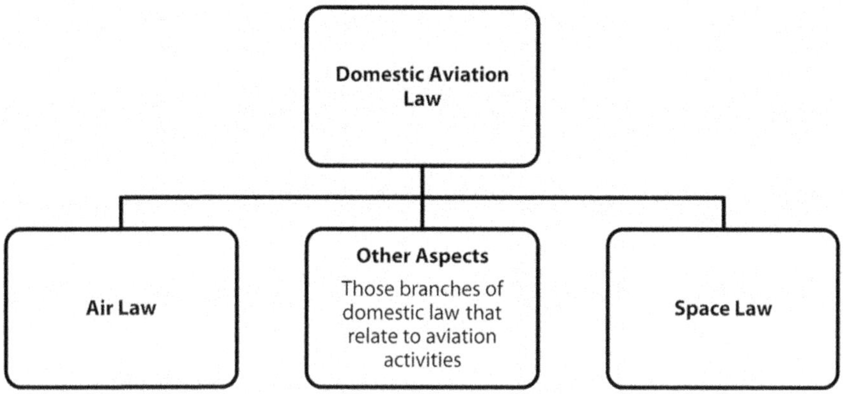

Figure 2.3 Structure of domestic aviation law

Aviation law is not separate from other divisions of law in the way that, say, the law of contract and the law of negligence are. Also, in certain less litigious jurisdictions – as compared with, for example, the USA – there are relatively few reported cases on aviation, with many cases being resolved as insurance cases, the bulk of which are settled on financial terms. This practice has tended to obscure and inhibit the development of a specialist branch of law in such countries.

CONCLUSION

In studying aviation law, it is necessary to review aspects of contract law, tort law, criminal law and so on, but to do so from an aviation perspective. When dealing with, for example, defences to a claim of negligence, stress of weather would be considered as one such defence, whereas normally, when studying the law of negligence, it would not.

What *is* important when studying aviation law is to consider its application and interaction with other areas of the law within the legal system. Aviation, whilst undisputedly unique, nevertheless operates within the wider legal normative framework. In Chapter 3 we will examine aviation law in the context of varying legal systems that exist throughout the world.

As aviation law is now a recognizable area of law it would be a retrograde step to try to categorize it within any other established branch of law. After all, its uniqueness is the reason for its particular development and its enduring presence.

3
The Law and Legal Systems

INTRODUCTION

Understanding the Law

Legal systems or systems of law vary considerably throughout the world. Moreover, even within the major recognized 'families' of legal systems, such as the *common law system* and the *civil law system*, the domestic legal system varies considerably between individual nations or sovereign states. Irrespective of the source or basis of any legal systems, no two countries 'share' an identical system of law.

For instance, the USA as a former British colony has its system of law founded on the common law of England. However, in certain areas of the law, it is considerably different from the law in England, and indeed, to the law of any other former British colony. Following America's independence in 1776 and with the establishment of its own Constitution (in 1789), the USA's legal system developed significantly and in a different direction from other former British colonies such as Australia, Canada, India and the Republic of South Africa.

Similarly, the German legal code differs from the French legal code, although both are described as civil law nations. To add further complexity to the issue, there are situations where the same legal term has different meanings in various legal systems or where different legal terms have the same legal effect.

This begs the following question: how can a single legal text possibly hope to cover *any* area of law on an international basis? The answer to this question was partially explained in Chapter 1. There it was elucidated how the aviation industry is unique with respect to the degree to which it is regulated and the internationally harmonized manner in which it is regulated. Moreover, because of the proliferation of international aviation treaties – most significantly the Chicago Convention of 1944 – the law relating to aviation has in some areas almost universal application.

Another reason why this seemingly arduous task of presenting and explaining a particular branch of law in a single publication encompassing all jurisdictions is even possible is because this book is *not* written for lawyers or for students of law. It is important to remember that this book is targeted at aviation professionals and to explain to them in simple lay terms the relevant law as it applies to their workplace. Aviation practitioners need not be concerned with a detailed account of general legal principles and legal processes as they apply within a particular (legal) jurisdiction. That is why we have – and dare I say *need* – aviation lawyers.

DOI: 10.4324/9781032652146-3

Aviation Practitioners and the Law

Aviation practitioners are mostly concerned with the application of aviation law in terms of how it will apply to the workplace. As there is almost universal conformity of technical, safety, operational and security standards, the *outcomes* of the application of these standards should be universal. For example, consider the situation where an aircraft system or component of a commercial transport aircraft operated by an international airline needs to be replaced in a foreign country by a foreign maintenance organization. The maintenance and engineering standards required under international aviation law are practically the same irrespective of the legal system of either the country in which the airline is based or where the repairs are undertaken. In both instances the output – that is, the maintenance undertaken – must be in accordance with international standards, as prescribed in the ICAO SARPs.

In the preceding example, the application of local laws of the foreign country were not really relevant as the standards applied (to the maintenance activity) would have been the same had the maintenance been carried out in the country of domicile of the airline. Nevertheless, there are situations in which the aforementioned will not be the case and when it is desirable for an aviation practitioner to have at least a basic understanding and awareness of the local foreign legal systems.

Sometimes knowledge of the system of law or legal system of a foreign country in which, say, an international airline operates *is* important. Indeed, the operations manuals of many airlines require that flight crew and other company employees *must* comply with not only the relevant aviation law of their own country but also *any applicable laws of the country in which they operate*. If you are working for an international airline, why don't you have a look now at your operational documentation – I would be most surprised if this is not the case.

The following provides a few examples of instances in which an understanding of some basic fundamentals of the legal system of a particular foreign country in which an airline (or any other aviation-related organization) operates may be useful:

- a crew member (or other employee) while operating in a foreign country may be subject to a legal process, e.g. a civil action or possibly a criminal charge;
- local laws relating to immigration, customs and security requirements;
- contractual negotiations or disputes between aviation companies located in different countries, for example, agreements for ground handling services in foreign countries;
- legal issues associated with conditions of employment and other industrial matters relating to airline staff employed or based in foreign countries.

And the list goes on. Needless to say, in most instances there may – and most probably *will* – be the need for specialized and local legal expertise to advise on matters such as those listed. But in each instance, at the very least, a basic understanding of the laws and the legal systems of the foreign country may be sufficient to avoid exposure to, or at least mitigate, the risk of legal liability associated with such events that may arise in the course of their employment as an aviation practitioner.

Accordingly, this chapter provides an overview of the varying types of legal systems that operate throughout the world and seeks to explain the process by which over 190 sovereign nations have adopted an almost universal system of international aviation law. Yet, despite the diversity of the legal systems of individual states, there is a common basis from which all systems of law are derived. This is known as the *rule of law*.

The Rule of Law Fundamental to any legal system is what is known as the rule of law. Traditionally, the rule of law had been regarded as the means of maintaining the balance between personal freedom and the power of the state. Ultimately, the rule of law aims to promote and instil fairness amongst members of society, and it could be said that it is what makes civil society civil. In a system operating under the rule of law, any sovereign power or government must ascribe to a minimum standard of fairness in content and procedure. State or governmental actions must not be arbitrary; that is, a use of power or force should not be without reason, necessity or principle.

It follows that no person can be punished unless there is a breach of the law warranting punishment and that persons within society must make reparation for their own breaches of the law, either to the state or to other individuals wronged through their breach of the rules of society. Further, every person, regardless of their status, is subject to the same rules and laws, meaning that *everyone*, including kings and presidents, is subject to the law. The rule of law forms the very basis of the proper functioning of any modern legal system and its relationship with sovereign power and individuals.

AVIATION PRACTITIONERS AND LEGAL SYSTEMS

Introduction

The international aviation industry extends across more than 190 sovereign nations – each of which has its own unique, and often quite complex, legal system. How then can a single publication on aviation law even hope to provide any meaningful guidance or assistance to such a seemingly insurmountable challenge?

Let me explain. This publication aims to assist the aviation practitioner by attempting to provide an international context to the law as it applies to any particular aviation scenario or workplace issue. As the full title implies, it seeks to provide the reader, as a professional within the aviation industry, with an understanding of the application and influence of the broader, and fundamental, international aviation legal framework and the underlying 'purpose' for a particular rule or standard. Then, and only then, is the reader in a position to apply his or her specific knowledge of the local regulatory provisions – with which he or she is most likely to be intimately familiar – to the facts at hand to predict a legal outcome. Sometimes the scenario or issue at hand may not directly relate to a particular piece of legislation of even a specific procedure, but nevertheless a legal consequence may result.

This begs the following question: why is there a need to understand the law in an *international* context? How is the attainment of this additional 'international' legal context going to assist me to do what I do on a regular basis *locally*? No doubt as an aviation professional you are most probably already able to apply your understanding of the law and how it applies to your day-to-day tasks and then set about getting on with your work. Also, no doubt you will be familiar with any applicable corporate policy, procedures or guidance material that will need to be considered when deciding how a particular law, rule or procedure is to be applied. For those who work in the aviation industry, this is an everyday occurrence.

Deviation from 'The Law'

All the preceding discussion regarding the importance of knowing and following the applicable law and regulations is good advice and mostly common sense. But where this approach comes unstuck is when you are confronted with a situation or predicament that is something out of the ordinary – something, perhaps, that your workplace practices or standard operating procedures (SOPs) do not specifically address. Because the aviation industry is such an open and dynamic system, it is not uncommon for unforeseeable situations to arise. The following is an account of some notable aviation occurrences to illustrate such a point.

British Airways Volcanic Ash Incident In 1982, whilst on a scheduled night service from Kuala Lumpur to Perth, a British Airways Boeing 747–200 inadvertently and unknowingly entered a dense cloud of volcanic ash. The ash had resulted from a recent volcanic eruption from Mount Galunggung in Indonesia, which was directly below the flight path. The crew detected a pungent acrid smell and fine dust (which the crew initially believed to be smoke) that had entered the cabin through the aircraft's air conditioning system. In addition, extensive 'sparks' appeared on the flight deck windshield, which the crew believed to be 'St Elmo's fire' effect. Then one-by-one all four engines of the aircraft failed. The jumbo now was essentially a 400-ton glider. Once the aircraft was out of the ash cloud, the crew eventually managed to restart the engines in succession. However, the continued malfunction of the number 2 engine led the crew to conduct an in-flight shutdown of that engine. As a result, an en route diversion was made to Jakarta on the remaining three engines. The crew, under the command of its captain, somehow managed to land the stricken airliner safely. The actions and procedures adopted by the crew were *not* in accordance with the company's mandated standard operating procedures as there were no SOPs that covered this extraordinary situation.

In 2010, in another spectacular aviation event, a Qantas Airways Airbus A380 suffered a catastrophic engine failure during the climb and was forced to make an emergency return landing at Singapore's Changi International Airport. On inspection, it was found that the aircraft's number 2 engine, a Rolls-Royce Trent 900, had a missing turbine disc. The warnings displayed on the aircraft's onboard computers (over 70 of them!) could not all be addressed with due dispatch, which therefore made the application of mandated SOPs crucial in such a situation. The captain made the decision – again, not in accordance with mandatory SOPs – to determine what systems remained operative rather than attempt the impossible task of actioning the displayed alerts and failures. Captain Dave Evans, a highly experienced Senior Check Captain who was on board the flight, commented after the event: 'We may have well thrown the checklist out the window as we had to get back to the fundamental priority of every pilot – fly the aircraft'. The crew were highly commended for their performance and the decisions they made during the in-flight emergency.

But what of the crew's actions in these scenarios? In both instances the captain decided *not* to follow standard company operating procedures. Fortunately, on both occasions there were no injuries. But what if the actions of the crew had *not* resulted in a positive outcome? What then would be the position at law in terms of legal liability with respect to the crew's failure to follow operating procedures that had been mandated by the airline and therefore covered under civil aviation law? We will consider the answer to these questions later in this chapter.

It is not only the spectacular scenarios that call for novel solutions to be created. It is also the more mundane and routine processes that are likewise subject to the influence of variables to create novel situations. The variables at play in our industry include the weather, complex mechanical systems, highly specialized procedures, cutting-edge computer systems and many others. Things don't always go to plan. However, given the dynamic and time-critical nature of our industry, the show must go on – solutions need to be found and time-critical decisions need to be made.

This is when things get a little complicated. Given that aviation is a highly capital-intensive industry, together with the fact that the inherent risks of travel by air are enormous – even the seemingly most minuscule, unimportant or trivial issue or event may have significant and sometimes dire ramifications. The potential for disaster is very real, as the following events highlight.

The Challenger Disaster On 28 January 1986, the Space Shuttle *Challenger* broke apart 73 seconds into its flight, leading to the death of seven crew members including a civilian, a school teacher. This was the first space flight that allowed a civilian to be involved and consequently was a highly publicized launch. The shuttle was actually scheduled to be launched for the tenth time on 22 January, but due to problems such as bad weather and faulty ground equipment it was further delayed. When the launch was finally approved on the morning of 28 January, the temperature was very low – forecasted to be as low as −7.7 degrees Celsius. At such a temperature, the o-ring (a flat ring made of rubber or plastic, used as a gasket) was not able to stop gases from passing through the joint. It was found on investigation that the accident was caused by a faulty o-ring seal on the joint between the two lower segments of the right-hand side solid rocket booster (SRB). The compromised seal allowed flames and hot gas to pass through the joint which subsequently caused the rocket booster to strike the external fuel tank. This in turn caused a rupture in the external fuel tank, which was exacerbated by the aerodynamic forces on the vehicle, which eventually led to the in-flight breakup of the shuttle.

Although the cause of the *Challenger* disaster can be pinpointed to a specific technical problem, the main contributing error, and last line of defence, was NASA's decision to launch. Members within the team who were responsible for the launch decision knew that the o-ring could not withstand the pressure inside the SRB at the current temperatures, but they proceeded with the launch anyway (Rogers Commission 1987).

The *Challenger* disaster is also an example of what has been termed *normalization of deviance*. Under tremendous schedule pressures, the NASA team accepted a lower standard of performance on the solid rocket booster o-rings, i.e. they repeatedly accepted heat damage that was never expected. The team slowly fell into the trap of believing their repeated success in accepting that the deviance implied future success.

Admittedly, the *Challenger* accident involved space travel, but closer to earth the following accident case study involving an American Airlines DC-10 highlights the importance of following standard operating procedures. This example shows how aviation practitioners – in this case aircraft maintenance personnel – had succumbed to the practice of deviating from standard operating practices in an attempt to do what was considered at the time the 'right' thing.

The American Airlines DC-10 Accident On 25 May 1979, American Airlines Flight 191 in a McDonnell-Douglas DC-10 aircraft crashed moments after take-off from Chicago's O'Hare International Airport. During the take-off rotation, the left engine and pylon assembly and about 3 feet of the leading edge of the left wing separated from the aircraft and fell to the runway. The aircraft continued to climb and began to roll to the left. It continued to roll to the left until the wings were past the vertical position and, whilst rolling, the aircraft's nose pitched down below the horizon. This resulted in the aircraft crashing into the open field and the wreckage being scattered into an adjacent trailer park. All 258 passengers and 13 crew on board were killed, along with two people on the ground. The accident remains the deadliest airliner accident to occur on US soil.

The National Transportation Safety Board (NTSB) determined that the primary cause of the accident was the use of a new maintenance procedure to change engines. The procedure recommended by McDonnell Douglas called for the removal of the engine prior to the removal of the engine pylon, but American Airlines, along with Continental and United Airlines, had begun to use a procedure that saved approximately 200 maintenance hours per aircraft. The new procedure involved aircraft mechanics removing the engine with the pylon as one unit, rather than the engine, and then the pylon. A large forklift was used to support the engine while it was being detached from the wing – a procedure that was found to be extremely difficult to execute successfully, due to difficulties with holding the engine assembly straight while it was being removed.

What the preceding scenarios have attempted to illustrate is the extent of the disastrous ramifications that may result from the actions of those working in the aviation industry – including actions which at the time may not have been considered to be overly significant in terms of their potential outcomes. Both the *Challenger* and American Airlines accidents were not a result of a 'deliberate' violation of the rules or procedures but were what has been termed to have been the result of a *normalization of deviance* – a situation where a past and 'successful' deviation from standard procedures has become the 'norm'.

In terms of the legal ramifications that may arise in respect of such actions by aviation practitioners, the following extract from Esler (2009) provides some valuable information:

> It is important here to pause and consider the difference between intentional actions that knowingly violate law, regulations or accepted practices and unintentional errors or mistakes, either of which could lead to death, injury or property damage. In the first instance – which can also include intentional fraud or felonious actions, e.g., terrorism or deliberate attempts to threaten the safety of an aircraft – there is universal agreement within the international aviation community that perpetrators should be charged and prosecuted to the fullest extent of the law.

These case studies are not meant to 'frighten' professionals who are working in the aviation industry, but rather to provide the reader with an awareness of the types of situations in which gaining a better understanding of 'the law' – and the legal system in which it operates – may reduce one's exposure to the liability that may result from one's actions.

We will now review the major types of legal systems that exist throughout the world and highlight the similarities and differences of these various systems. Therefore, if you are operating or working in a foreign country which has a legal system which is different from your own, you will be more aware – and thus better prepared – to adequately and professionally respond to situations that may require other than standard operating procedures.

LEGAL SYSTEMS

The Law Defined

The meaning of the word 'law' has long been the subject of debate and philosophical discussion. This fact is not surprising when one considers the diverse cultures in which legal systems have inevitably created difficulties in finding an exact definition of the law. Any definition of law must be sufficiently broad to include all these systems.

The *law* can be defined in many ways, but the underlying notion of this term is that law encourages and ensures certain standards of conduct are upheld in human behaviour. These standards or rules are formed to specifically govern individuals and groups by establishing guidelines to encourage or prohibit certain types of behaviour. Therefore, the law accomplishes its purpose by providing for orderly dispute resolution, protecting the rights of property and preserving the structure and integrity of government. A good definition is provided in the following extract:

> *Law* as it exists in the modern community may be conveniently, although perhaps not comprehensively, defined as the sum total of all those rules of conduct for which there is a state sanction.
>
> (Stone 1915: 3)

The law is administered and enforced by a system commonly referred to as the 'legal system'. This system, in every nation of the world, encompasses:

- lawmakers (e.g. Parliament/Congress);
- interpreters of the law (e.g. the courts);
- law enforcers (e.g. the police and government regulatory authorities);
- administrators of the law (e.g. government officials and civil aviation regulators);
- legal advisors (e.g. solicitors, barristers and attorneys).

It is the responsibility of those who administer and enforce the law, such as the courts, to determine an appropriate balance between society's conflicting interests. The decisions taken by the custodians of power are meant to maintain a balance, one which may be described as being for the overall good of society. In every sovereign nation, this involves a balancing act – sometimes requiring the agility and finesse of a tightrope walker – for someone or some institution to decide how the balance is determined and where the lines are to be drawn. In democratic societies we elect governments who are responsible for the 'line drawing'.

The law or legal systems can then be seen as a means of providing a system of social order, whereby individuals are accorded a greater degree of personal freedom than would otherwise exist. Quite obviously, a legal system is concerned with far more than just providing an infrastructure that allows for personal freedoms. Laws relating to the environment, for example, protect natural resources for the benefit of present and future generations.

We have already discovered the diversity of legal systems that subsist throughout the world. These systems, all of which are unique, have developed in response to a variety of reasons including local influences, customs and cultural norms. Although we identified certain general classifications of the law – such as the common law and civil law systems – there is no single formula that can be applied to provide legal solutions or even to determine how the courts will decide a particular matter.

Accordingly, no legal principle or rule of statutory interpretation can be applied to the extent of determining 'legal' outcomes to specific scenarios or individual cases involving the law. The legal ramifications or legal outcomes to specific issues or disputes can only be addressed at the domestic law level and even then quite often at the state, county, municipality or provincial level – most 'law' is local. The complexity and diversity of the law is one of the main reasons why lawyers usually confine themselves to particular legal jurisdictions and even then, perhaps, to specific areas or branches of the law. Such is the case in particular in respect of specialist aviation lawyers.

Legal Systems

In Chapter 1 we learnt how and why international aviation law developed. In Chapter 2 we identified the various sources from which international aviation law may derive and defined and classified the various branches of aviation law. In this chapter we now turn our attention to examining the various types of legal systems throughout the world. What becomes immediately apparent are the diversities and contrast between such legal systems. But the important point to remember is that, irrespective of the various types of legal systems – or how they operate – in respect of the technical, operational and safety standards of aviation, they all must – or at least are obliged to – comply with the SARPs set down by the ICAO as Annexes to the Chicago Convention.

As we shall see in this section, even though there are unique differences between the various legal systems (for example, between common law systems and civil law systems), there are also unique differences between jurisdictions within each 'family' of legal systems (for example, differences between French law and German law, although both are civil law systems). It should be noted that in this book it is assumed that all common law systems are alike in essential respects and likewise all civil law systems are alike in essential respects.

THE COMMON LAW SYSTEM

The evolution of the common law system can be traced back to England at the time of the Norman Conquest, which was in 1066. It began with sending people (that is, judges) out to country areas to resolve disputes. In the time before the Conquest, disputes were decided by local lords, barons and petty kings according to local customs. By sending his judges in a 'circuit' around the English countryside, King William I had the goal of merging all these disparate local laws into a single 'common' law throughout England.

The circuit judges, as they became known, were instructed to decide cases on a consistent basis, such that similar cases would yield similar decisions. As such, William's 'common law' developed on a case-by-case basis, such that legal principles were developed through a succession of cases based on consistent reasoning towards principled conclusions. This common law legal system was later adopted in the USA, Canada, Australia, New Zealand and the countries of the British Commonwealth (Figure 3.1). Even the term 'circuit judges' is still used in many common law countries.

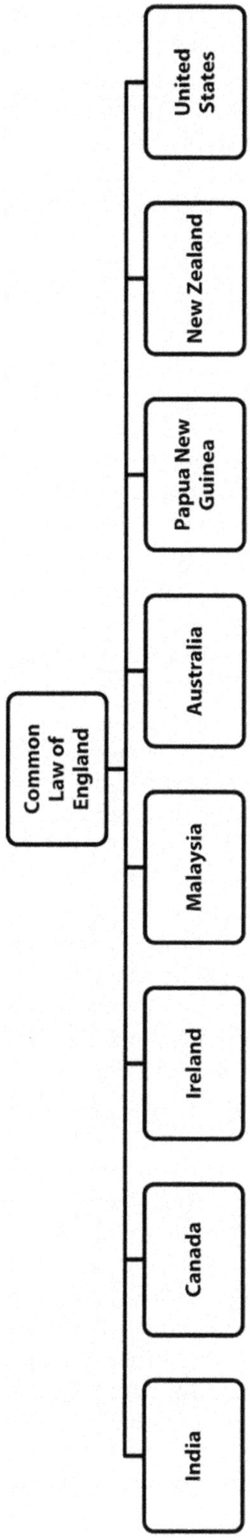

Figure 3.1 Major common law countries

In the archetypal common law system, the system is *uncodified*. This means that there is no set compilation of legal rules and statutes, but the law is dominantly created by judicial decisions. This difference is the result of the different role of legislators in civil law and common law. In very general terms, in civil law systems, the law is predominantly based on the doctrine of the *separation of powers*, whereby the role of legislators is to *create* the law, while the courts are to *apply* the law. On the other hand, again in general terms, in common law systems, the courts' main task is in *creating* the law. However, in both systems the courts also *interpret* the law.

Common law procedure is usually *adversarial* – a legal approach where advocates represent the respective parties' positions before an impartial person or group of people – usually a jury or judge, or both. This means that the judge acts as an impartial arbiter between the parties in the dispute as they each present their case. The judge is the *trier of fact* as well as the *trier of law*. When a *jury* is present, the jury acts as trier of fact and the judge retains the role of trier of law. The parties in the case lead the proceedings, whereas the position of the judge is rather passive, not undertaking any independent investigation into the subject matter of the dispute. The basic role of the judge is to oversee the proceedings and maintain that all aspects of legal procedure are followed.

The judge's role is not to interrogate the witnesses but to ensure that the parties' questions are legally and procedurally acceptable. In this way, the role of a judge in a courtroom during the presentation of argument in a trial may be compared to that of a referee or umpire in a game of sport – to ensure that the game is played according to the rules.

One of the most distinctive features of the common law system is that judges decide cases according to the doctrine of precedent. The doctrine of precedent is also known as *stare decisis*, which roughly translates as 'standing by settled points'.

This doctrine is essentially based on William I's instructions to his judges following the Norman Conquest as discussed earlier: cases involving the same or similar essential or material facts must be decided in the same way. Precedents are maintained in court records, and important cases are historically documented more fully and publicly in collections of case law. Until the fourteenth century, these were known as yearbooks, but they are now known as law reports. The modern technological era has allowed many of these reports to be published online, making the law more readily accessible to anyone who wants to read it than ever before in history.

In contrast to common law, the doctrine of precedent does *not* apply to civil law courts. In those countries, court decisions are not binding on lower courts in subsequent cases, nor are they binding on the same courts, and it is not uncommon for courts to reach opposite conclusions in similar cases. However, courts and judges make some effort to be consistent between cases and thus will give some consideration to the decisions made in other cases, although it must be stressed that they are not *bound* to follow previous decisions as common law judges are.

The claim that common law is created solely by case law is only partly true, as the common law is based in a large and increasing part on statutes which the judges are supposed to apply and interpret in much the same way as the judges in civil law courts. This is the result of legislatures creating more law. Generally speaking, laws enacted by a legislature override the precedents made before them. The difference is, however, that the interpretation applied by one court *becomes* a precedent to be applied by other courts in the system.

The term *codification* is used to describe the process whereby common law (that is, judge-made law) is 'converted' into legislation through the legal process. Many common law countries are undergoing a process of codification – the process of writing into legislation those rules that were developed by cases. Codification and the pull of legislation is especially felt in aviation as aviation law is almost exclusively legislative. Therefore, the role of the courts in both common law and civil law systems – with respect to aviation cases – is to interpret and enforce the aviation regulations.

THE CIVIL LAW SYSTEM

The term 'civil law' is derived from the Latin expression *ius civile*, which is the law applicable to all Roman *cives* (citizens). Civil law systems are *codified*, which means that the main rules in civil law systems are contained in comprehensive documents which they call 'civil codes'. One commentator has described the civil code as:

> a systematic, authoritative, and guiding statute of broad coverage, breathing the spirit of reform and marking a new start in the legal life of an entire nation.
>
> (Schlesinger *et al.* 2009: 271)

The codes set the general rules of the law and the courts then make their own interpretations of those general principles afresh in each case to arrive at conclusions about how those general principles can provide solutions on a case-by-case basis. Essentially, the assumption is that all cases can be resolved by applying these codes, but where certain cases are not regulated by the code, the courts should apply general principles to fill legislative gaps.

Table 3.1 provides a summary of the major types of legal systems that exist throughout the world, including legal systems in addition to the common law and civil law systems, which are compared in Table 3.2.

Countries with civil law systems have comprehensive and updated legal codes that are based on Roman law. In the sixth century, the Emperor Justinian took the initiative to bring together all Roman laws in what came to be known as the *Corpus Iuris Civilis* or *Corpus Iuris Justinianis*. The *Corpus Iuris* formed the legal basis of the Byzantine Empire for many centuries.

Around the turn of the nineteenth century, two distinct systems of civil law emerged which were Napoleon's law, known as the Napoleonic Code, and the Germanic Code. The Napoleonic Code spread throughout Central and South America, and had an impact on the laws of the Asian Peninsula (Laos, Cambodia, Vietnam and Thailand), while the Germanic Code was introduced into Japan and recently China. The codes of civil law detail all issues that are capable of being brought before a court and the appropriate punishment for such an offence.

The role of judges in civil law systems is to determine the facts of the case and to apply the relevant codes. This system is known as an *inquisitorial system* – a legal system where the court or a part of the court is actively involved in investigating the facts of the case. The reason this legal system is called an 'inquisitorial' system is because the judge examines the witnesses and the parties to the case have little to no authority in leading the proceedings. The judge in civil law thus plays an active role in the proceedings. Judges in civil law systems have the main role in establishing the relevant issues of the case based on the available evidence provided by all parties to the case.

Table 3.1 Legal systems in various jurisdictions

Common Law	Australia, Canada, Great Britain (except Scotland), India, Israel, Jamaica, New Zealand, Trinidad and Tobago and the USA
Civil Law	China, France, Germany, Indonesia, Italy, Japan, Korea, Switzerland and Turkey
Canon Law	Personal and church law within countries – Christian Church
Islamic Law	SUNNI school of thought: Hanafi (Afghanistan, the Balkans, Egypt, Jordan, Lebanon, Libya, Pakistan, Sudan, Syria and Turkey) Maliki (Algeria, Libya, Morocco, Nigeria and Somalia, Sudan and Tunisia) Sh'afii (Indonesia, Malaysia, the Philippines and Sri Lanka) Hanbali (Saudi Arabia) SHI'A School of Thought (Iran and Yemen)
Talmudic Law	Personal law in many countries for Jewish people, e.g. in Israel, Lebanon and Morocco
Hindu Law	India and Bali (Indonesian island)
Customary Law	Adat law in Indonesia and Malaysia, Aboriginal customary law in Australia, Indigenous customary law in the Americas
Scandinavian Law	Denmark, Finland, Norway and Sweden
Socialist/Marxist	China, Cuba and the USSR pre-1989

Table 3.2 Comparison between common law and civil law

Common Law	Civil Law
Derived from legal system of England and the British Empire	Derived from Roman and French Empires
Consists of both case law or judge-made law (based on precedents) and statutes	Almost exclusively codified where rules and principles are set out in codes
Nature of legal system is adversarial	Nature of legal system is inquisitorial
Judge acts as an impartial umpire, applying their understanding of the law to the facts and directing the jury on matters of law	Judge acts as an investigator, extracting information from witnesses

With respect to the resolution of legal issues, the civil law system is based on the principle *jura novit curia*, which translates to mean 'the court is supposed to know the law' and therefore does not require the parties to plead. In contrast, in common law systems, 'pleading' relates to outlining the facts to which legal principles are to be applied to a particular case.

Although the judges enforce the formal charges, investigate and decide on the case, judges in this system work within the framework established by the comprehensive, codified set of laws. It could be said that the decisions made by the judges have a less crucial role in shaping the civil law as opposed to judges in the common law system.

In an inquisitorial system, the role of the judge is more interventionist, whereby the trial, including the questioning of witnesses, is controlled by the judge. The judge in civil law courts is more an 'investigator' than an 'umpire' as in the common law courts. This more active role affects the way in which court records are established and proceedings are conducted, and the approach to appeals, and it derives from the core civil law notion that a trial is a search for the truth.

CLASSIFICATION AND BRANCHES OF LAW

In Chapter 2 we briefly considered the various branches and divisions that have developed in the specific area of aviation law generally and international aviation law in particular. In this section we now examine the broader classifications that exist and essentially apply across all systems of law throughout the world. It is important that, as an aviation professional, you are aware of the reason for the creation of these different categories of the law and the names they have been given. Upon reviewing the relevant section of Chapter 2, you will see that each of the following categorizations also applies to each of the various branches and divisions of aviation law.

Private and Public Law

Public law regulates legislatures, governments, courts and civil institutions in their dealings with citizens and is aimed at protecting the freedom of individuals, whereas private law deals with the relationships and transactions between individuals. Public law is categorized into constitutional, administrative and criminal law. Constitutional law deals with the interpretation and enforcement of the constitution and its regulation of the organs of government. Administrative law regulates the way in which governments make decisions and enforce these decisions in the community. Criminal law deals with offences committed by individuals against the state. *Private law* is the law of actions which allows individuals to take action against another person. It involves the law of contract, property law and the law of torts.

A fundamental division in all civil law systems is between private and public law. The distinction has its roots in Roman law, but there is no uniformity among countries as to its precise scope and effects. Private law is often used interchangeably with civil law. Strictly speaking, however, private law comprises two grand divisions of its own of which civil law is one and commercial law the other. Both the French *Code Civil* and the German *BGB* are codifications of private law to the exclusion of commercial law. They comprise the legal rules that govern the relationship between private parties. The commercial activities of businesspeople are governed by a separate commercial code. Interestingly, civil codes adopted during the twentieth century tend to be less reluctant in incorporating commercial law. Examples are the Swiss Civil Code of 1907, the Italian Civil Code and the Dutch *NBW*.

It is not possible to place the law applying to aviation neatly into any of these categories. Certain aspects of aviation law relate to private law (for example, contracts and the law of torts), whereas other areas are part of the public law (for example, criminal offences and government regulation of the industry).

Substantive and Procedural Law

Another basis of classification is whether the law relates to rules or statutes (*substantive law*) or to that part of the law concerned with the procedural aspects of the law (*procedural law*, Figure 3.3). Substantive law is sometimes called 'black letter law', whereas procedural law refers to the rules relating to court procedures and the rules of evidence. It may be considered that procedural law dictates how the substantive law is to be applied and enforced. Since aviation law would be exclusively contained within the area of

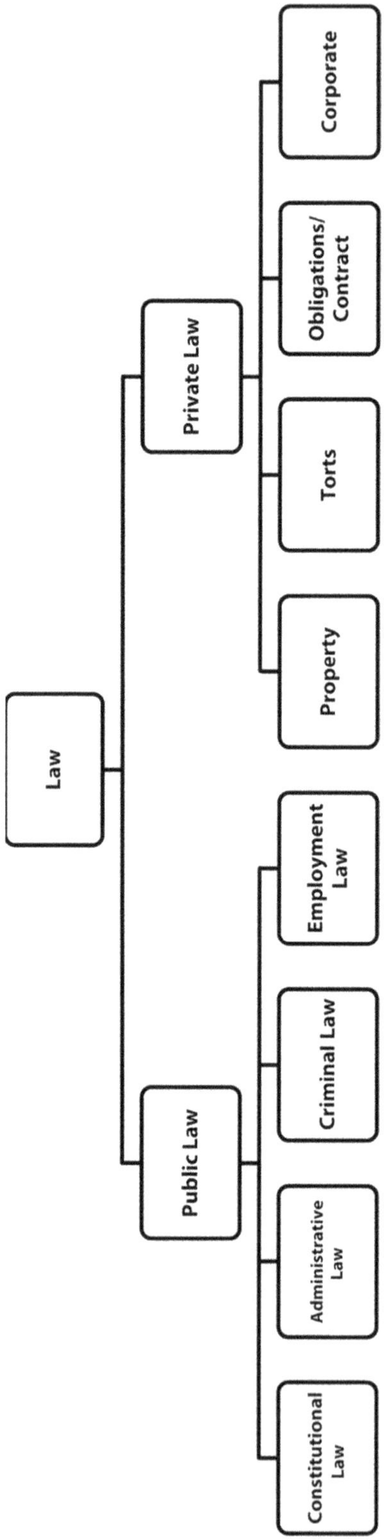

Figure 3.2 Public and private law

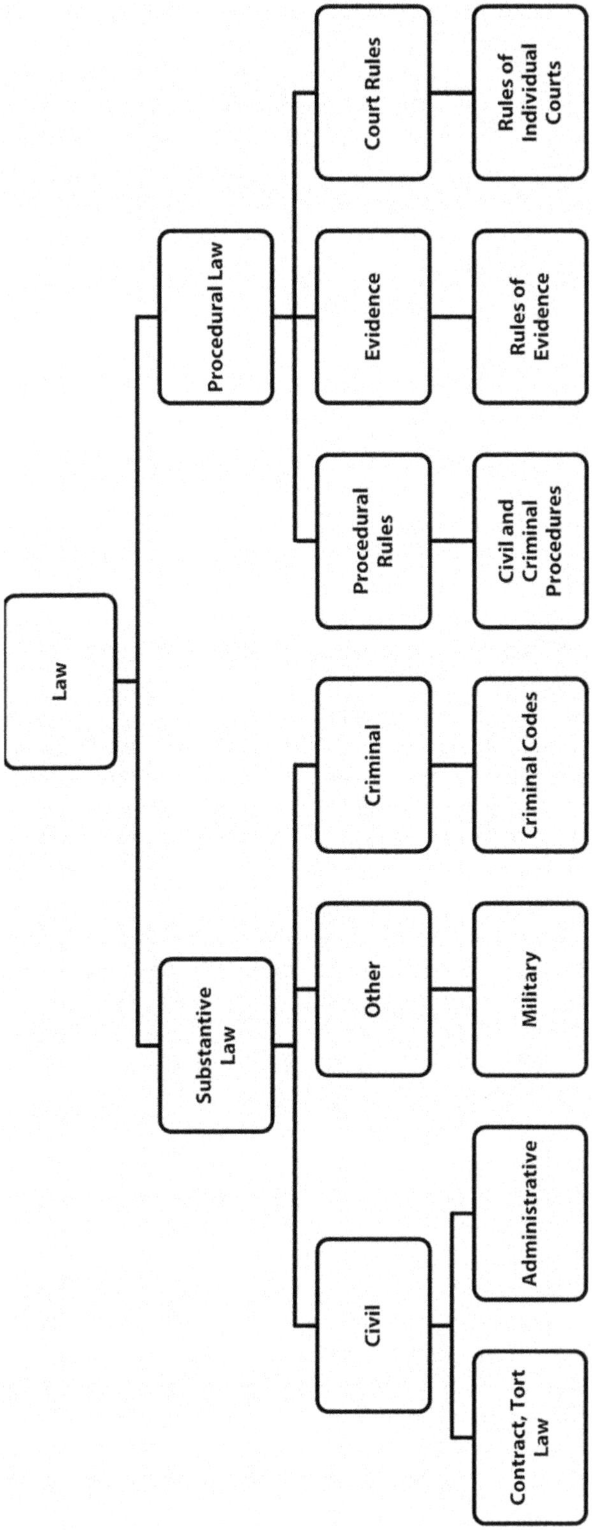

Figure 3.3 Substantive and procedural law

substantive law, this classification provides little assistance in gaining a better understanding of the subject, but provides some insight into how legal systems work.

As previously mentioned, aviation law is wholly contained within the substantive law. The difficulty arises as to which of the subclassifications it belongs. Aviation law is predominantly civil law in the sense that it relates to the law between individuals, as does contract law and the law of negligence. However, certain aspects of aviation law concern criminal provisions, being actions enforceable by the state. Aviation is also an important part of military law and space law; however, these areas of aviation activities are beyond the scope of this book.

AVIATION AND THE LAW

The Fundamental Objective of Aviation Law

As was previously stated, under the Chicago Convention 1944, contracting states – all 193 of them – are obliged to comply with all applicable ICAO standards, except (as we will discover in Chapter 4) to the extent that they have notified 'differences' from the ICAO. While the legal systems of each particular state vary enormously, the technical standards, by definition, must remain just that – *standards* – and therefore must be consistently applied. Moreover, each of these standards is designed to achieve a particular, usually safety-related, outcome.

Each of the 193 varying state legal systems must then determine how it will establish and enforce the ICAO standards as law within its own system. The legislature of each state will pass an Act or statute that *ratifies* the Chicago Convention – and any other international treaties it has agreed to. It is usually the responsibility of the local regulator, sometimes referred to as the National Aviation Authority (NAA), to draft the appropriate civil aviation regulation or rule that will give (legal) effect to that state's obligations under the treaty. In the case of the Chicago Convention, this entails establishing a regulator regime that will give effect to all the SARPs as contained in the 19 ICAO Annexes. What the governments (through their respective NAAs) of the 193 state members of the ICAO then attempt to do is, through their 193 varying systems of law, achieve the same technical aviation standards specified in each and every SARP. This happens every single day across 193 nations – with varying levels of success.

With the benefit of hindsight, had the architects and designers of the ICAO known the degree to which future aviation was to become harmonized – not only with respect to technical standards but also various commercial aspects of the industry, such as global alliances, code-sharing and liberalized international aviation policy – their approach to the issue may have been very different. Just imagine if the ICAO had in its wisdom, from its very beginning, drafted the primary civil aviation legislation for all the member states of the Chicago Convention. This 'common' *enabling* legislation would then provide a common regulatory framework or regime to give effect to all the technical aviation standards as and when they are developed.

With such a universal regulatory framework – essentially a common civil aviation statute for every nation – when developing and drafting the multitude of SARPs, the ICAO's lawyers could also have drafted, as and when required, common regulations or rules to give effect to these technical standards – in all 193 states simultaneously, consistently and unambiguously. Never say never – we can live in hope.

CONCLUSION

Considering the fact that there are far in excess of 10,000 SARPs, one can only hope at best to master the application of those aviation regulations that apply to their particular area of speciality within their specific legal system. The extent to which laypersons (that is, non-lawyers) need to know the law is only so that they are able to understand their legal obligations and to be aware of the legal ramifications of their actions - and to know when they need to seek legal advice. In practical terms, this translates into having confidence in what you do as being acceptable behaviour within your particular legal system.

This book does not attempt to make you - as an aviation professional and practitioner - into what is sometimes described as a *bush lawyer* - that is, a layperson who pretends or acts as if he or she *is* in fact a 'lawyer'. Day-to-day situations arise in the aviation industry in which a legal determination, by an experienced aviation lawyer, is required. What is hoped is that this book will provide you with sufficient information and practical guidance to allow you to better and therefore more professionally perform your duties, but also to make a determination as to when legal assistance may be required.

The ability to make such an informed judgment is most important in terms of an organization's overall risk management strategies. *Legal liability* is just another component of the overall risk profile of an organization. As previously stated, there is no other industry that is so extensively regulated as the aviation industry. Being able effectively to manage this aspect of risk is an important daily challenge.

4
The Regulation of Aviation

INTRODUCTION

Aviation is widely regarded to be the most regulated industry in the world. To develop a thorough understanding of the foundations of the current aviation regulatory framework, one must go back to the days when manned flight was in its infancy. In what is now recognized to be one of the most rapidly developed industries, with the efficiency and capabilities of modern aircraft, it is quite astonishing that it has been just over a century since the advent of powered flight.

The event that was the catalyst for this phenomenal growth of aviation was the First World War. This war, as tragic as it was, will forever be acknowledged as the event which facilitated a paradigm shift in military strategy, whereby those involved in warfare could no longer focus only on the threat posed by the enemy from the ground, but where the threat from the air was now fully appreciated. This was the basis for governments throughout the world to insist and demand unfettered sovereignty over their own airspace:

> The war was a tremendous lever for aviation. In a feverishly accelerated rhythm, at the command of the state, every door was open to discovery. Success was achieved, the aim reached, astounding progress made. . . . War was the hellish laboratory in which aviation became adult and was shaped to flawless perfection.
>
> (Allaz 2004: 32)

The origin of the freedom to fly over other countries is founded on Hugo Grotius' 1609 principle *Mare Librium* (freedom of the seas). The source of this ideology centred on the belief that any country should have the freedom to sail on the seas without restrictions being imposed on it by other nations. The role played by pioneers such as Grotius and the rationale for this evolution of thought help illustrate the social and cultural framework upon which concepts of contemporary regulation are based.

Just as the acceptance of the notion of freedom of the high seas enabled maritime activities to change the world, so too has an adoption of this principle to international airspace for aviation activities changed the world in which we live. It is almost impossible to imagine a world today without commercial international air transportation and it is equally impossible to imagine the world of aviation without regulation. This view is encapsulated in the following quote:

> The aviation industry is what it is today not in spite of, but rather because of, the law that regulates it.
>
> (Bartsch 2012b)

DOI: 10.4324/9781032652146-4

In this chapter we begin with a brief account of the basis for the regulation of aviation activities and then provide an overview of the structure and institutions responsible for the current regulatory regime for both domestic and international aviation.

FUNDAMENTALS OF REGULATION

To create a truly effective aviation regulatory environment, it is suggested that three essential elements must exist, namely:

- *effective legislation*: the regulatory framework, that is, the supporting legislation, must be clearly stated and structured so that it can achieve the statutory objectives intended by the *state*;
- *competent regulatory agencies*: there is a need for an effective and competent regulatory authority, and it is essential that properly trained, resourced and committed professionals are given the administrative tools by which they can effect the statutory objectives with which they have been entrusted; and
- *a culture of compliance within the aviation industry*: those who are regulated should be understanding and supportive of the regulatory process. This commitment requires more than just a preparedness to comply, but also a willingness to embrace common goals that a regulatory regime is designed to achieve.

The last two elements are considerably intertwined and require a paradigm shift in attitude on the part of the regulator as well as those on which requirements are imposed to ensure that both are working towards a 'shared' set of goals. It is a symbiotic relationship between operator and regulator, who are jointly responsible for the determination of the parameters of regulations and their intent. While the regulator's role is to give a clear set of instructions to the operator reflecting the expectations of the regulator, the operator must ensure their compliance as well as maintain close coordination with the regulator.

The long-term benefits associated with this are paramount, and none more so than the importance of educating aviation professionals and the travelling public. It is just as important to develop a collective culture of compliance where society will benefit from the advantages that the regulatory regime was designed to achieve, as well as ensuring that the rules being enforced address the risks inherent in aviation activities.

There are, however, quite divergent views on the concept of aviation regulation. Some take the view that those who conduct commercial air operations should be self-regulating and that the responsibility for deciding and enforcing safety standards should be left to the individual operators or the operators collectively. This line of reasoning is founded on the underlying assumption that if operators are not obligated to meet standards and enforce certain practices, then this exposes the industry to the risk of having to police those opportunistic operators looking to take advantage of any leeway in the regulatory framework. Such operators will likely seek to gain an advantage over their competitors, knowing that those who prioritize commercial objectives over operational safety will eventually encounter catastrophic events that will damage reputation, lose customers and therefore not pose an ongoing threat to the profitability of other carriers.

This all sounds quite straightforward. So why wouldn't this approach work in practice? The reason is that we live in a commercially driven world of aviation, a world where the dynamics of the international and highly competitive marketplace mean that lax approaches to regulatory oversight will be exploited – especially considering the continual pressure on the corporate workforce to maintain profits.

Regulatory Structure

The basis for the establishment of regulatory systems that define and oversee the aviation industry derives from a variety of sources. The aviation regulatory system is unique by global standards, and the international aviation law that has developed is inextricably linked and founded upon the underlying regulatory structure. The various sources and institutions from which the international aviation regulatory system has been founded are:

- international conventions and treaties;
- customs and customary law;
- court decisions, legal instruments and treatises; and
- general and domestic laws of the states.

The *Vienna Convention on the Law of Treaties* (Vienna Convention) defines a treaty as an international agreement concluded between states in written form and governed by international law, whether embodied in a single instrument or in two or more related instruments and whatever its particular designation. The Vienna Convention provides that it is a general rule that when state parties enter into a treaty through ratification they must intend to create legally binding rights and obligation. This obligation is explained in Article 26 of the Convention with the principle that every treaty in force is binding upon the parties to it and must be performed by them in good faith.

For the aviation industry, conventions (or treaties) are by far the most important source of standards from which derives the basis for regulatory systems. The Vienna Convention in Article 31 (1) and (2) states that a treaty must be interpreted in good faith in accordance with the ordinary meaning to be given to the terms of the treaty in their context and in the light of its object and purpose.

Essentially, conventions are agreements between sovereign nations that have been formally ratified into the domestic legislation of each nation involved. They can take one of two forms: (i) bilateral – between two nations; or (ii) multilateral – involving three or more nations. Both forms of agreement will be discussed (with specific examples) in more detail later in this chapter under the heading 'Commercial and Economic Regulation'.

Another way of describing conventions, in very general terms, is by way of analogy. They can be seen as a 'facilitator' and as a medium for collaboration, whereby many nations are invited by a sponsoring international organization, for example, the ICAO, to discuss matters of global significance. The ICAO's activities and area of responsibility as it relates to aviation will be discussed in more detail later in this chapter under the heading 'Safety and Technical Regulation'.

The Evolution of Aviation Regulation

The regulatory framework within which air operations are conducted today is the product of a continuous process of development which initially came to the forefront of policy-makers' attention during the early twentieth century. Tracing back and identifying the root causes of the need to introduce regulatory reform about air transportation provides the context of its origin and assists in providing a better understanding and interpretation of the rules. Basic principles and arrangements for the development of international civil aviation were established by the Chicago Convention 1944.

The Chicago Convention 1944

Towards the end of the Second World War, a greater appreciation and acknowledgement by those involved in the War was beginning to take place with regard to the development of civil air transportation. The three major powers at the time – the USA, Russia and Great Britain – had conflicting ideologies as to the future direction of civil aviation, which was indicative of the position each held upon the conclusion of the War.

The USA, which had financially prospered because of the War, was of the view that airlines and the entire civil aviation industry should essentially be an open and free system and that competitive market forces should be allowed to prevail. The Russians were almost diametrically opposed in that they proposed a 'closed skies' regulatory and economic environment with agreements permitting the entry of passengers and freight. In essence, this meant that if Russia's policy was adopted, only Russian planes could operate into and out of Russia. Great Britain stood somewhere in between the nationalist approach of Russia and the liberalized stance of the Americans, suggesting that the civil aviation industry should be regulated on an international basis.

Freedoms of the Air

The varying approaches and proposals of the state representatives at the Chicago Conference were discussed in Chapter 2. Although Russia was not represented at the Convention, the 52 states present eventually established a system for categorizing 'rights', which became known as the 'freedoms of the air'. Although there was not universal agreement as to which rights would be agreed in a multilateral treaty, there was consensus as to how such rights should be defined. The freedoms of the air can be explained as follows:

- *First Freedom of the Air*: the right or privilege, in respect of scheduled international air services, granted by one state to another state or states to fly across its territory without landing.
- *Second Freedom of the Air*: the right or privilege, in respect of scheduled international air services, granted by one state to another state or states to land in their territory for non-traffic purposes.
- *Third Freedom of the Air*: the right or privilege, in respect of scheduled international air services, granted by one state to another state to put down, in the territory of the first state, traffic coming from the home state of the carrier.

- *Fourth Freedom of the Air*: the right or privilege, in respect of scheduled international air services, granted by one state to another state to take on, in the territory of the first state, traffic destined for the home state of the carrier.
- *Fifth Freedom of the Air*: the right or privilege, in respect of scheduled international air services, granted by one state to another state to put down and take on, in the territory of the first state, traffic coming from or destined to a third state.

It should be noted that the ICAO refers to all freedoms beyond the Fifth Freedom as 'so-called' freedoms. The reason for this is that only the first five freedoms have been officially recognized as such by way of international treaties resulting from the Convention. The remaining 'so-called' freedoms can be described as follows:

- *Sixth Freedom of the Air*: the right or privilege, in respect of scheduled international air services, to transport, via the home state of the carrier, traffic moving between two other states. This freedom, unlike the first five, is not incorporated as such into any widely recognized air service agreements such as the 'Five Freedoms Agreement'.
- *Seventh Freedom of the Air*: the right or privilege, in respect of scheduled international air services, granted by one state to another state; that is, the service need not connect to or be an extension of any service to or from the home state of the carrier.
- *Eighth Freedom of the Air*: the right or privilege, in respect of scheduled international air services, of transporting *cabotage* traffic between two points in the territory of the granting state on a service which originates or terminates in the home country of the foreign carrier or (in connection with the Seventh Freedom of the Air) outside the territory of the granting state.
- *Ninth Freedom of the Air*: the right or privilege of transporting cabotage traffic of the granting state on a service performed entirely within the territory of the granting state (also known as the 'stand-alone' cabotage).

The Chicago Convention is the basis for international aviation regulation and therefore represents the primary source of *public* international aviation law (see Chapter 2). The invitation for states to attend was made with the general objective for the Convention to establish the basic principles and direction upon which all future civil aviation would proceed internationally. Essentially this meant that the foundations were set for the development of international civil aviation to occur in a 'safe and orderly manner' and to establish international air services on a basis of 'equality and opportunity' and sound economic operation (Heilbronn 2008).

The Convention can essentially be broken down into two components. The first (Articles 1–42) addresses how all previous sources of international law, such as the Paris Convention 1919 and the Havana Convention 1928, were to be unified under this new standard of international aviation law. The second part (Articles 43–96) contains details of the charter under which the ICAO was to be created and thus obliged to comply with.

SAFETY AND TECHNICAL REGULATION

A key stepping stone for the aviation industry during the early development of regulation was to develop a tailor-made set of tools by which aviation technical issues and standards could be addressed. Discussions and groundwork with regard to this issue at the Chicago Conference in 1944 led to the establishment of the Provisional International Civil Aviation Organization (PICAO). In 1947, the Organization was no longer provisional upon the ratification of the Chicago Convention by 50 per cent, being 26 of 52, of the signatory states. As such, it was renamed the International Civil Aviation Organization. The ICAO is the medium by which international cooperation and coordination in civil aviation can occur. Through a series of mechanisms, the ICAO works to uphold the principles underlying the Chicago Convention.

The ICAO

The ICAO was set up to implement the fundamental principles of safety, regularity and efficiency of air navigation. The ICAO became a Specialized Agency of the United Nations on 13 May 1947 and is for that reason invested with special powers, pursuant to Article 64 of the Chicago Convention.

The ICAO develops and adopts internationally agreed standards and practices for the regulation of civil aviation, coordinates the provision of air navigation facilities on a regional and worldwide basis, collates and publishes information on international civil aviation, and acts as the medium by which aviation law develops on an international scale. Apart from technical matters, the ICAO has been instrumental in providing the organizational structure for the determination of less contentious economic arrangements. The ICAO, with beneficial outcomes, has addressed matters such as customs procedures and visa requirements. The ICAO has also assumed responsibility for collecting statistical data for international civil aviation, including information on safety-related issues like accident and incident statistics.

The ICAO's objectives under Article 44 are:

- to ensure the safe and orderly growth of international civil aviation throughout the world;
- to encourage the arts of aircraft design and operation for peaceful purposes;
- to encourage the development of airways, airports and air navigation facilities for international civil aviation;
- to meet the needs of people from around the world for safe, regular, efficient and economical air transport;
- to prevent economic waste caused by unreasonable competition;
- to ensure that the contracting state has the right to a fair opportunity to operate international airlines;
- to avoid discrimination between contracting states;
- to promote safety of flight in international air navigation; and
- to promote on a general basis the development of all aspects of international civil aeronautics.

In 2012, ICAO, realizing that it should do more than just 'foster the development of air transport' as prescribed in the Chicago Convention, took the bold step of identifying three aspects of the rubric 'sustainability of air transport' to be: social, economic and environmental. It went further afield by adding on a brand-new Strategic Objective of the Organization to be termed 'economic development of air transport'. This is an all-encompassing objective and should mean a defragmented approach to air transport which considers an in-depth study of world economics, present and future, and where air transport would fit into a market driven industry.

Air transport liberalization would be key to this ICAO objective, and it would be up to ICAO to suggest a viable economic system that would ensure connectivity; the best deal for the passenger and the removal of barriers such as restrictions on ownership and control.

The mechanisms by which the ICAO implements change and achieves its set objectives will now be discussed.

The ICAO Safety Standards Safety is paramount to all aviation activities and is the ICAO's most fundamental objective. The ICAO consistently emphasizes the importance of air safety: 'Safety is and always must be of paramount importance in the operation and development of air transport and there is a need to continuously update and implement safety standards and practices' (Kotaite 2000).

The dynamics and unique characteristics of the aviation industry mean that the regulatory framework within which operations are conducted is constantly under development to ensure that the standards and criteria that are considered the benchmark are not outdated, and takes into consideration the current aspects affecting the industry. The various ICAO Annexes are continually being amended and developed to ensure that the regulatory requirements with respect to air safety remain effective. As part of this development, since early 2000, the ICAO has mandated that various aviation operators have approved Safety Management Systems (SMS).

Operators of airports in 2003 became the first aviation industry sector required to establish and maintain their own 'approved SMS'. Since that time, the ICAO has mandated SMS requirements for air operators and maintenance organizations. Annex 6 in this regard prescribes: 'From 1 January 2009, states shall require, as part of their safety programme, that an operator and maintenance organization implement a safety management system acceptable to the state of the operator'.

The adoption of this standard has highlighted the ICAO's belief that there is a close correlation between a robust safety framework and profitability. The more aviation has evolved, the less significant is the trade-off between commercial goals and safety objectives. In the twenty-first century, aviation stakeholders operate in an environment where the customer demands high levels of safety.

With increased competition in the aviation industry – especially since the introduction and proliferation of LCCs – air safety to customers *must* be assured, even by those carriers who are competing predominantly or exclusively on price. Developing and implementing a business model, system or process that provides for both increased levels of safety and improved business efficiencies can be referred to as a *safety quinella*. This principle is consistent with the ICAO's most fundamental (dual) objectives to 'ensure the *safe* and orderly *growth* of international civil aviation' (emphasis added). In aviation these two terms are far from being mutually exclusive and, indeed, it is suggested that they are in fact complementary in application. Airlines and aviation enterprises will only grow if they are perceived to be safe.

Technical Standards International specifications for civil aviation appear in 19 Annexes to the Chicago Convention, each Annex dealing with a particular subject matter. It is the Council of ICAO which adopts such amendments, which are then sent to member states of ICAO for comment. Standards and Recommended Practices (SARPs) of Annexes and Procedures for Air Navigation Services (PANS) are the foundation leading to harmonization of global aviation safety and efficiency in the air and on the ground and are the backbone of ICAO's meaning and purpose which is to advance the principles and techniques of air navigation and foster the development of air transport.

The technical specifications are divided into two categories, namely, *standards* and *recommended practices*, although they are collectively, and most commonly, referred to as SARPs. There are 12,000 such SARPs contained in the 19 Annexes. When it comes to amendments to the SARPs and PANS ICAO follows a structured, transparent and multi-staged process – often known as the ICAO '*amendment process*' or '*standards-making process*' – involving a number of technical and non-technical bodies which are either within the Organization or closely associated with ICAO. Typically, it takes approximately two years for an initial proposal for a new or improved Standard, Recommended Practice or procedure to be formally adopted or approved for inclusion in an Annex or a PANS. Occasionally, this timescale can be expanded or compressed depending on the nature and priority of the proposal under consideration.

The 19 Annexes to the Chicago Convention 1944 are as follows:

Annex 1	Personnel Licensing
Annex 2	Rules of the Air
Annex 3	Meteorological Service for International Air Navigation
Annex 4	Aeronautical Charts
Annex 5	Units for Measurement for Air/Ground Operations
Annex 6	Operation of Aircraft
Part I	Commercial Air Transport – Aeroplanes
Part II	General Aviation – Aeroplanes
Part III	Helicopters
Annex 7	Aircraft Nationality and Registration Marks
Annex 8	Airworthiness of Aircraft
Annex 9	Facilitation
Annex 10	Aeronautical Telecommunications
Annex 11	Air Traffic Services
Annex 12	Search and Rescue
Annex 13	Aircraft Accident and Incident Investigation
Annex 14	Aerodromes
Vol I	Aerodrome Design and Operation
Vol II	Heliports
Annex 15	Aeronautical Information Services
Annex 16	Environmental Protection
Vol I	Aircraft Noise
Vol II	Aircraft Engine Emissions
Annex 17	Security – Safeguarding International Civil Aviation Against Acts of Unlawful Interference
Annex 18	Safe Transport of Dangerous Goods by Air
Annex 19	Safety Management

The following provides a brief summary of the various ICAO Annexes (King 2012).

Annex 1: Personnel Licensing

In the Chicago Convention 1944 it is stated that members of the operating crew of aircraft engaged in international navigation shall be provided with licences issued or rendered valid by the state in which the aircraft is registered. Annex 1 is established for the licensing of flight crew, air traffic controllers, flight operations officers, aeronautical station operators and aircraft maintenance personnel.

A state having issued a licence shall ensure that the privileges granted by that licence are not exercised unless the holder maintains competency and meets the requirements for recent experience established by that state. Recent provisions have been introduced to allow for the use of electronic pilot licences, which are increasingly being used by ICAO member states. It introduces a new common format to provide for simplified licence verification by other states. This amendment should assist ICAO member states in the wider adoption of e-licences, whilst also reducing the number of printed licences in circulation and realize cost reduction and environmental benefits.

The Annex also details the medical and other provisions required for licences and ratings held by these categories of personnel.

Annex 2: Rules of the Air

In the Convention, each state undertakes to keep its regulations uniform, to the greatest possible extent, with those established under the Convention – thus ensuring safety of operations. States undertake to ensure the prosecution of all persons violating the regulations regarding the Rules of the Air. Annex 2 specifies the general, visual and flight rules which the pilot in command is responsible for complying with, unless those rules conflict with the regulations of the state being overflown.

Annex 3: Meteorological Service for International Navigation

The Convention provides for states to undertake and provide meteorological services to facilitate international navigation in accordance with the Annex. The regulatory material in the Annex is identical to the technical and other regulations issued and authorized by the World Meteorological Organization.

States are obliged under the Convention to provide or designate a Meteorological Authority, regional forecast centres, meteorological offices and aeronautical meteorological centres and arrange for observations to be made by aircraft.

Annex 4: Aeronautical Charts

The Convention requires that contracting states shall maintain and provide aeronautical charts and that they are kept up to date through a standard revision service. The Annex establishes detailed operational requirements for all charts concerned and specifies which charts shall be available, specifying aerodrome obstacle charts, precision approach terrain charts, en route charts, area charts, standard departure and arrival charts, instrument and visual approach charts and world aeronautical charts.

Annex 5: Units of Measurement for Air/Ground Operations

The standardized system of units in the Annex is based upon the International System of Units (SI) and other non-standard units necessary to support the safe operation of international aviation.

Annex 6: Operation of Aircraft

Annex 6 contains minimum standards required to ensure that civil aviation operations are carried out in a safe and consistent manner. It contains mandatory material on the responsibility of the operator to maintain operations manuals, promulgation of performance limitations, maintenance procedures, crew training and the overall supervision and management of flight operations.

The Council of ICAO has recently introduced another amendment to Annex 6 which contains comprehensive provisions aligned with the ICAO *Technical Instructions for the Safe Transport of Dangerous Goods by Air* (Doc 9284). These provisions assist in the safe and efficient carriage of dangerous goods by helicopters which should be receiving the same oversight as other aircraft. Alternate safe landing considerations for offshore helicopter operations is another significant area addressed in these provisions.

Annex 7: Aircraft Nationality and Registration Marks

The Annex specifies the use and application of aircraft registration marks, how they shall be selected, where they shall be positioned on the aircraft and the requirement for states to maintain a register listing certificates of registration. Recent amendments to Annex 7 include the introduction of a standardized certificate of de-registration to aid states in clearly communicating the transfer of an aircraft from one state to another (Annex 7), and assuring that mandatory continuing airworthiness information relating to aircraft modification or repair should be distributed (Annex 8).

Annex 8: Airworthiness of Aircraft

The Convention states that every aircraft shall be provided with a Certificate of Airworthiness issued or rendered valid by the state in which the aircraft is registered. The standards in Annex 8 are broad specifications that state the objectives rather than provide a methodology or system of how the objectives shall be realized by individual states. New provisions in Annex 8 concerned the now required availability of cargo compartment fire suppression system details to help improve cargo safety risk mitigation efforts.

Annex 9: Facilitation

The Annex requires that contracting states shall provide certain specified minimum levels of facilitation for passengers and aircrew. Additionally, it seeks to reduce the amount of paperwork required to handle and clear filters through ports of entry and focuses upon entry permits, customs procedures, etc. It is important to note that Article 9 bestows on the state a 'right' and not a responsibility, giving the state the power to decide. This brings to bear the inevitable question as to whether a right in this context is linked to responsibility.

A case in point which brings Article 9 into focus is Flight MH 17 which was shot down by Russian backed rebels over Ukrainian airspace in July 2014. The discretion given to the state in Article 9 is transformed into an obligation in Article 28 that the state is obligated to provide 'other air navigation facilities' (i.e. air traffic control advice) which in the case of flight MH 17 the Ukrainian authorities ought to have known they were not able to provide over the rebel held area over which the aircraft was shot down.

Annex 10: Aeronautical Telecommunications

The Convention requires that states comply with standards for the operation and maintenance of radio equipment, navigational facilities and radio frequencies. The standards are applicable to both manufacturers and users of technical facilities designed for aeronautical telecommunications, and the Annex also details how Aeronautical Information Services shall be provided and operated.

Annex 11: Air Traffic Services

This Annex covers the establishment of airspace, units and services so that air traffic services are provided to aircraft in a uniform and consistent way. States are required under the Annex to determine how the airspace is organized, where and how the air traffic services shall be provided within that airspace, the communications requirements and the procedures to be adopted.

Annex 12: Search and Rescue

The basic provision of this Annex is that all states shall provide Search and Rescue (SAR) services on a 24-hour basis. This required the establishment of a Rescue Coordination Centre (RCC), rescue units, and the responsibilities and functions of those units and the procedures to be adopted, whether provided by private or public organizations.

Annex 13: Aircraft Accident and Incident Investigation

The Convention requires states to investigate any aircraft accident within such laws that may be permitted under procedures recommended by the ICAO. The Annex requires the state to take all reasonable measures to protect the evidence and maintain the safe custody of the aircraft for the purposes of the investigation.

Annex 14: Aerodromes

Annex 14 provides states with guidance and instructions on the physical characteristics of airports and the technical services to be provided. The Annex prescribes in considerable detail the dimensions of runways, taxiways, strips, runway end safety areas and terminal areas, etc. In addition, it requires the provision of aerodrome rescue and fire services and provides the operational and technical characteristics of such services with regard to manning levels, response times, equipment levels, etc.

Annex 15: Aeronautical Information Services

All states are required under the Convention to provide and maintain an Aeronautical Information Service (AIS), the purpose of which is to collate, collect, edit and publish information concerning aviation operations in that state. The AIS may be provided by a private or public agency, provided that the requirements of the Annex are properly met. Attention of states is also drawn to the provision of Annex 15 related to the publication of differences between their national regulations and practices and the related ICAO Standards and Recommended Practices through the Aeronautical Information Service, in addition to the obligation of states under Article 38 of the Convention.

Annex 16: Environmental Protection

Annex 16 deals with aircraft noise and engine emissions. It provides an international noise exposure unit for land use planning and establishes noise abatement procedures. The Annex also requires that aircraft shall be noise certificated to predetermined levels as promulgated by the ICAO and that the noise certification granted by one state shall be recognized by another state. States shall recognize, as valid, certifications granted by another state provided that the requirements are no less stringent than the provision of the Annex.

ICAO does not officially link efficiency in aircraft engine emissions and safety. At the 40th Session of the Assembly of ICAO in September 2019 the Assembly also adopted Resolution A40–19: *Consolidated statement of continuing ICAO policies and practices related to environmental protection – Carbon Offsetting and Reduction Scheme for International Aviation (CORSIA)* which *inter alia* requests the Council to update the Annex 16, Volume IV and Environmental Technical Manual, Volume IV, with the technical contribution of the Committee on Aviation Environmental Protection (CAEP), as appropriate. CAEP is a technical committee of the ICAO Council established in 1983. CAEP assists the Council in formulating new policies and adopting new Standards and Recommended Practices (SARPs) related to aircraft noise and emissions, and more generally to aviation environmental impact. CORSIA is to be implemented through an Annex – Annex 16 Volume IV, Part II – to the Chicago Convention which prescribes a monitoring, review and verification (MRV) model, the applicable scope of which is stipulated in Chapter 2, to the effect that the Standards and Recommended Practices (SARPs) of the Annex are applicable to an aircraft operator that produces annual CO_2 emissions greater than 10,000 tonnes from the use of an aircraft(s) with a maximum certificated take-off mass greater than 5,700 kg conducting international flights, on or after 1 January 2019, with the exception of humanitarian, medical and firefighting flights.

Annex 17: Security – Safeguarding International Civil Aviation Against Acts of Unlawful Interference

The Annex requires that all states shall: establish an organization, develop plans and implement procedures to meet security threats; establish a national security programme; designate an authority to be responsible for the security programme; and establish means of coordinating activities between the departments, agencies and other organizations concerned with aspects of the national security programme. The Annex also details requirements for training programmes, airport security committees, contingency plans, facilities to be provided for security services, etc.

Annex 18: Safe Transport of Dangerous Goods by Air

Annex 18 details the requirements for ensuring that dangerous goods can be safely carried by air. They are derived to a large extent from the UN Committee of Experts on the Transport of Dangerous Goods and establish inspection, surveillance and enforcement procedures.

Annex 19: Safety Management

Annex 19 is ICAO's newest Annex. It became applicable on 14 November 2013 after having been proposed at the Organization's High-level Safety Conference in 2010. The purpose of creating this Annex was to address safety risks associated with aviation in a proactive manner. It was found that, with air traffic projected to double in less than 20 years, safety risks must be addressed proactively to ensure that capacity expansion is carefully managed and supported through strategic developments in both regulations and infrastructure.

Most of the Annex consists of provisions which were duplicated or transferred from other Annexes. It requires each state to establish a state safety programme (SSP) for the management of safety in their territory, in order to achieve an 'acceptable level of safety performance in civil aviation'. The SSP should include:

- state safety policy and objectives;
- state safety risk management;
- state safety assurance;
- state safety promotion.

Importantly, these components of the SSP had previously been recommended practices, but Annex 19 raised them to standard status and as such, contracting states are required now to have these. Annex 19 on Safety Management in Standard 3.1.1 requires each state to establish a State Safety Program (SSP) for the management of safety in the state, in order to achieve an acceptable level of safety performance in civil aviation. The SSP must include state safety policy and objectives; state safety risk management; state safety assurance; and state safety promotion.

As can be seen from the preceding summary by King (2012) of the various Annexes the ICAO develops and promotes technical standards across virtually every sector of the aviation industry. The development of these technical standards, as we will examine later in this chapter, requires the input of highly experienced technical specialists within the ICAO. Once the standards have been developed there is then the task of implementing and overseeing these standards. In particular, the ICAO's main areas for promulgating technical requirements are:

- safety initiatives;
- standardization;
- international specifications;
- recommended practices;
- the development of SARPs;
- the implementation of SARPs;
- the Universal Safety Oversight Audit Programme (USOAP);
- regional planning; and
- facilitation.

Safety standards were discussed in the previous section. Each of the main areas of the ICAO's functions will now be reviewed.

Standardization One of the ICAO's most important functions is the development of internationally agreed standards for international aviation. Article 37 of the Chicago Convention encourages contracting states to 'collaborate in securing the highest practicable degree of uniformity in regulations, standards, procedures, and organization in relation to aircraft, personnel, airways and auxiliary services'.

The ICAO develops and amends international standards in relation to communication and air navigation systems, airports, rules of the air, personnel licensing, aircraft design and airworthiness, registration and identification of aircraft, meteorology, facilitation, accident investigation, search and rescue, aviation security, environmental protection and a variety of other matters that fall within the scope of activities deemed to be the responsibility of the ICAO.

Members of the ICAO are not obliged to adopt international standards for solely domestic applications; however, apart from the threat to safety this poses, it makes little sense for a country to have one set of rules applied to international aviation and another to domestic aviation. Thus, the international standards developed by the ICAO apply de facto to domestic aviation. More specifically, Annex 13 implies that states are expected to apply its provisions domestically, and Annex 17 was amended in the wake of the terrorist attacks of 11 September 2001 to 'require' states to implement certain security standards domestically, except where it is impractical to do so.

International Specifications Article 37 of the Chicago Convention provides for the Council of the ICAO to make SARPs dealing with a wide range of matters concerned with the 'safety, regularity and efficiency of air navigation', and that it may, 'for convenience', annex them to the Convention. Once a rule or procedure is adopted by the ICAO Council as a standard, states are obliged to implement that rule or procedure. Standards use words like 'shall' and 'shall not', and they appear as normal text in the bodies of the Annexes.

Under Article 38 of the Convention, if a state cannot comply with a standard, it is obliged to notify the ICAO of that non-compliance, and the ICAO holds a repository of all such *differences*.

Unfortunately, until recently, the obligation to notify differences under Article 38 was more honoured in the breach than in the observance, and states were often unable formally to determine the compliance status of other states. It is for this reason that the USOAP was developed and implemented.

Recommended Practices According to the ICAO, recommended practices are specifications, the adoption of which is desirable in the interests of the safety, regularity or efficiency of international civil aviation. Recommended practices are formally adopted as such by the ICAO Council, and compliance by states with recommended practices is not mandatory. Standards use words like 'should' and 'may', and appear as bold, italicized text in the bodies of the Annexes.

So how does the ICAO Council make the distinction between something that it deems important enough to be enforced as a requirement as opposed to something that is merely recommended? One explanation is that some states may lack the technical expertise or the financial backing to be able to implement a recommended practice, or a particular practice may be politically unacceptable to a state at a particular time. As countries gain access to technology, allocate resources, implement reform and/or change government, recommended practices may be adopted on such a widespread basis that they are eventually adopted by the Council as standards.

Development of SARPs The process for development and adoption of SARPs is, on paper, a simple exercise. Under the direction of the Council and the Secretary General, the Air Navigation Bureau of the ICAO Secretariat undertakes research and technical studies, with the assistance of specialist panels and study groups. On the basis of these studies, recommendations are made to the Air Navigation Committee of the Council on the content and effect of rules and procedures for the regulation of international civil aviation.

The Air Navigation Committee then resolves the contents of the SARP and, except in those cases where immediate action is required in the interests of safety or security, invites all the ICAO member states to comment on their proposals, before placing them before the Council for adoption by vote. A two-thirds majority vote is required for the Council to adopt the new or amended Annex.

Implementation of SARPs Once a SARP has been proposed, it is up to each member state to implement it through its own domestic arrangements. Implementation of a standard is mandatory, at least in the absence of a notification of the Council of a member state's inability to comply, while implementation of a recommended practice is voluntary. The ICAO defines a standard as:

> Any specification for physical characteristics, configuration, material, performance, personnel or procedure, the uniform application of which is recognized as necessary for the safety or regularity of international air navigation and to which contracting states will conform in accordance with the convention; in the event of impossibility of compliance, notification to the Council is compulsory under Article 38 of the convention.

Recommended practices are viewed only as desirable, meaning that a state is not in breach of its arrangements with the ICAO if the practice is not implemented and notification is not given. The ICAO defines a recommended practice as:

> [A]ny specification for physical characteristics, configuration, material, performance, personnel or procedure, the uniform application of which is recognized as desirable in the interest of safety, regularity or efficiency of international air navigation, and to which contracting states will endeavor to conform in accordance with the convention. States are invited to inform [the] Council of non-compliance.

Under Article 12 of the Chicago Convention, it is the responsibility of every member state to keep its own regulations uniform 'to the greatest possible extent' with the SARPs promulgated by the ICAO. Under Article 37, states are obliged to 'collaborate in securing the highest practicable degree of uniformity' in their domestic law, regulations and procedures with the SARPs.

In the event that the SARP is deemed to be 'impractical to comply' with, under the conditions detailed in Article 38, the relevant authorities from the state in question are to notify the ICAO and provide details of the differences between its own practices and those established by the SARPs.

The Universal Safety Oversight Audit Programme The ICAO has traditionally relied upon member states to inform it of non-compliance with SARPs in accordance with their obligations under Article 38. However, states have often been less than forthcoming in notifying the ICAO of differences, even when those differences were informally known to exist. It was clear to some member states of the ICAO that there were other states that were simply not complying with large portions of the Annexes.

The ICAO Universal Safety Oversight Audit Programme (USOAP) was initiated by a worldwide ICAO conference of Directors General of Civil Aviation (DGCA) in 1997. This audit commenced, on a voluntary basis, in 1996, and a few years later in 1998 became a universal audit programme with all member states of the ICAO being audited on a progressive basis.

By the end of 2001, all of the then 185 states had received at least one audit of legislation, procedures and practices in relation to personnel licensing and the operation and airworthiness of aircraft. The USOAP has progressively expanded to include aerodromes, air traffic services and aircraft accident investigation, and will eventually cover the standards in all safety-related Annexes to the Chicago Convention.

Under the USOAP, each contracting state to the Chicago Convention is audited at least once every five years. The audit is conducted from a systems approach to safety perspectives and is broken down into three phases. Phase 1 aims to identify the extent to which the ICAO Annexes have been implemented, and the differences from the ICAO SARPs are identified through a series of State Aviation Activity Questionnaires and Compliance Checklists. Phase 2 is when the ICAO sends its own audit team to conduct an on-site audit to note any discrepancies between the information provided during Phase 1 and the actual state of affairs.

The post-audit formalities make up the third and final phase of the audit process, which ends with the audit team preparing a confidential audit report. The state is first given the opportunity to respond to this report, and once an agreement is reached between the ICAO and the state on what differences are to be notified, the state prepares a plan to address the differences. Follow-up audits are scheduled to assess the degree to which the deficiencies identified by the audit team have been rectified. The USOAP is closely linked to the ICAO's Global Aviation Safety Plan (GASP) which, in collaboration with states and industry, focuses on achieving a significant decrease in accident rates.

The UK Department for Transport (DfT) is the primary government body responsible for civil aviation in the UK and played a central role in the ICAO USOAP audit that took place in February 2009. The Department is responsible for establishing the aviation policy for all the territories over which it has jurisdiction, including the overseas territories that make up the remainder of the UK.

Elsewhere in Europe, on 15 July 2002, a milestone moment took place for the aviation industry with the adoption of *Regulation (EC) No 1592/2002 of the European Parliament and of the Council*. This regulation provided the authority for the establishment of the European Aviation Safety Agency (EASA). This was then repealed upon the creation of *Regulation (EC) No 216/2008*. We will discuss this further later in this chapter.

Fast forward two decades at the ICAO's 41st General Assembly on 7 October 2022, the ICAO team responsible for the ICAO Universal Safety Oversight Audit Programme (USOAP) Continuous Monitoring Approach (CMA) came to a consensus on ICAO's budget and work programme for the next three years to 2025, to continue to support the ICAO Universal Safety Oversight Audit Programme.

Regional Planning Not all aviation problems can be dealt with on a worldwide scale, and many subjects are considered at a regional level. The ICAO therefore recognizes nine geographical regions that must be treated individually for planning the provision of air navigation facilities and services required on the ground by aircraft flying in these regions.

Planning is done at the ICAO regional air navigation meetings, which are held from time to time for each of the regions, where the need for facilities and services is carefully considered and decided upon. The plan which emerges from a regional meeting is designed so that when the states concerned implement it, it will lead to an integrated, efficient system for the entire region and will contribute to the global system.

In December 2006, an Industry Safety Strategy Group, in cooperation with the ICAO, handed down the second part of its Global Aviation Safety Roadmap. This initiative outlines strategies for improving safety in 12 focus areas to help rectify global air safety oversight and regulation issues. The Roadmap, as with the USOAP, has been incorporated into the ICAO's Global Aviation Safety Plan.

In the Asia-Pacific region, the Pacific Aviation Safety Office (PASO), headquartered in Port Vila, Vanuatu, has utilized the Roadmap in establishing a regional aviation safety and security oversight programme for its 12 member nation states. PASO is enabled through the Pacific Islands Civil Aviation Safety and Security Treaty (PICASST). The author was fortunate in being able to assist with the development of the regulatory oversight programme and surveillance procedures for PASO, having been seconded from the Australian Civil Aviation Safety Authority (CASA) to assist and promote the development of safety oversight in the Pacific region.

Most recently in September 2022 in Montreal, Canada, the International Civil Aviation Organization held its 41st Assembly. One of the items on the agenda was the launch of the Pacific Regional Aviation Strategic Plan for 2022–2032, a document developed with input from the Pacific Island States, ICAO and the Pacific Aviation Safety Office (PASO).

The Plan has a ten-year strategic focus across seven strategic goals that reinforce and reflects PASO's contribution to achieving the 2050 Strategy for the Blue Pacific Continent. PASO stands ready to deliver a broader scope of services, and play the multi-functional role now desired by members. Once again, the author was fortunate in being able to assist with the development of the Plan as the legal and regulatory advisor in the project team.

Aviation Ministers of PASO member states endorsed the Pacific Regional Aviation Strategy which commits to review the PICASST and the transition of PASO to an enhanced multi-functional regional aviation organization. This strategy details a suite of priorities that complement and operationalize overarching regional commitments made by states through their participation in the 2050 Blue Pacific Strategy. This strategy takes the goals and priorities determined at the regional level and operationalizes them with specific actions and performance measures to enable PASO to track its progress and success.

The next few years will see considerable change for PASO as it transitions to become a Regional Aviation Organisation as envisaged with an amended PICASST and the Pacific Regional Aviation Strategy. This next phase will need to be carefully planned and managed to ensure continuity of service and seamless transition.

The growth and change in PASO's focus and form occur at a time with significant external challenges, including an environment still considerably impacted by the COVID-19 pandemic, increasing labour shortages and constrained state budgets needed to fund PASO's activities as well as a broader suite of Pacific Regional Aviation Strategy commitments.

The Strategy places PASO and the future Regional Aviation Organisation in an ideal position to take Pacific aviation forward and deliver tangible outcomes for the Pacific region. It lays out a ten-year plan which is intended to guide PASO's governing Council, management and officers on what to strive for, what to focus on, why, how and when.

Facilitation States have imposed border controls on persons and goods for centuries. The Chicago Convention recognizes these controls as legitimate and necessary, but with the advent of fast and cheap air transport, the need to streamline the controls and minimize their impact on trade has come into sharp relief. Article 22 is particularly instructive, providing that:

> Each contracting state undertakes . . . to facilitate and expedite navigation by aircraft between the territories of contracting states, and to prevent unnecessary delays to aircraft, crews, passengers and cargo, especially in the administration of the laws relating to immigration, quarantine, customs and clearance.

Annex 9 of the Convention, titled 'Facilitation', sets out the SARPs with respect to border control for persons and goods transported by air, setting minimum standards. Its underlying policy is set out in Article 22 – that is, it serves the purpose of curtailing the demands that states can make in securing their borders.

The International Air Transport Association

The IATA is the air transport industry's global trade organization. At its foundation in 1945, the Association consisted of 57 members from 31 different countries, a figure which today has grown to represent the interests of 320 members from over 120 countries, equivalent to 83 per cent of the total scheduled international air traffic globally.

The IATA acted as successor to the International Air *Traffic* Association, which was formed in the same year (1919) as the first scheduled international air service.

The IATA has always promoted the interests of its members, but the evolution of aviation and the growth of its members across a greater geographical landscape has meant that the organization's prior ability to start small and grow gradually is no longer an effective means of implementing change in today's aviation environment. Instead, the IATA now operates as an organization with an international influence using systematic procedures and larger infrastructure to meet each of its goals and responsibilities to its members. The 1945 Articles of Association identified the IATA's aims upon which it would base its methodology. Over time, the IATA has been able to sustain growth without altering the objectives upon which the organization was established. In order to maintain relevance, these objectives were redefined to take into account the contextual changes that have occurred in the environment in which airlines now operate.

The IATA's mission and goals are stated as follows:

- *safety and security*: to promote safe, reliable and secure air services;
- *industry recognition*: to achieve recognition of the importance of air transport to worldwide social and economic development;
- *financial viability*: to assist the industry to achieve adequate levels of profitability by optimizing revenues while minimizing costs;
- *products and services*: to provide high quality, value for money, industry-required products and services that assist the airlines in meeting the needs of the consumer;
- *standards and procedures*: to develop cost-effective, environmentally friendly standards to facilitate the operations of international air transport; and
- *industry support*: to identify and articulate common industry positions and support the resolutions of key industry issues.

These areas of specialization are not exhaustive but do represent the core of the IATA's activities today.

COMMERCIAL AND ECONOMIC REGULATION

The rules by which air transport is governed are different from those relating to most goods and services. Businesses operating in other industries generally trade freely unless they are specifically restricted, whereas trade in scheduled international air services is prohibited unless specifically allowed by either multilateral or bilateral air service agreements.

International trade in most services is regulated by the *General Agreement on Trade in Services* (GATS) and agreements between members of the World Trade Organization (WTO). In contrast, international air transport services are unique in that they are permitted if and only if 'permission' or 'authorization' has been granted, as prescribed in Article 6 of the Chicago Convention, which states: 'No scheduled international air service may be operated over or into the territory of a contracting state, except with the special permission or other authorization of that state, and in accordance with the terms of such permission or authorization'.

Article 6 has the result that an international agreement is required between nations seeking to have international airline services between them *before* the airline service commences. A mere contract between private individuals or companies in each country is not sufficient; there must be an agreement at government level. It is important to point out that trade in ancillary aviation services is not covered under this provision, so that services in aircraft maintenance or computer reservation systems can be negotiated between operators without the need for government involvement.

Multilateral Regulation

The *International Air Services Transit Agreement* or 'Two Freedoms Agreement' is the most important agreement by which freedoms are granted multilaterally and has been ratified by more than 135 of the 193 member states to the Chicago Convention. Globally there is a growing recognition of the inefficiencies inherent in the bilateral system which for so long was the primary tool used to facilitate liberalization. A shift towards 'open skies' policies in key aviation markets was brought about by the emergence of globalization, and more specifically the expansion of the EU and a review of the USA's international aviation policy.

The EU aviation liberalization process was completed in 1997 with the establishment of a single European common aviation market. On 1 May 2001, the *Multilateral Agreement on Liberalization of International Air Services* (MALIAT), which promotes the establishment of multilateral open skies agreements, was signed by the USA, New Zealand, Singapore, Brunei and Chile. Australian and Japanese delegates were present and participated in the negotiations; however, these two nations did not sign the finalized agreement.

For countries like the USA and New Zealand that were official parties to the MALIAT, the pre-existing bilateral agreement that was in place upon the commencement of negotiations was to be suspended for as long as the multilateral agreement was the framework upon which both were bound. The MALIAT provides a model to facilitate agreements that can exchange up to seven and eight freedom rights and eliminates airline 'substantial ownership' requirements and other restrictions relating to frequency, capacity and routes.

European Regulations

As previously mentioned, *Regulation (EC) No 216/2008 of 20/02/2008* establishes the common rules in the field of civil aviation in Europe and creates a European Aviation Safety Agency (EASA), repealing the former 2002 and 2004 regulations that originally covered the matter. The new Regulation expanded EASA's responsibilities and extended their role to air operations, pilots' licences and the safety of non-EU Member State aircraft. The primary purpose of the law is to ensure a high protection of European citizens in civil aviation through the adoption of 'common safety rules' and measures ensuring products, persons and organizations in the community comply with such rules. The economic purpose is also intertwined, as the Regulation prescribes that safety for European citizens should contribute to facilitating 'the free movement of goods, persons and organizations in the internal market'.

The Regulation is detailed and comprehensive, and applies to the 'design, production, maintenance and operation of aeronautical products, parts and appliances, as well as personnel and organizations involved in the design, production and maintenance of such products, parts and appliances' and also the personnel and organizations involved in operating the aircraft. However, the Regulation does not apply when these products and personnel are engaged in military, customs, police or similar services – it is solely *civil* aviation.

EASA has become critical to the EU's aviation safety strategy, and works with both the European Commission and Member States to achieve uniform application of laws across the board. It is truly 'pan-European', with the involvement of other non-EU countries in Europe like Iceland, Norway, Switzerland and Liechtenstein (and soon to be UK). EASA prepares draft rules for consideration in the EU legislative processes and consults with a range of organizations across the industry.

The European Regulations are vast, and are essentially separated into three components:

- Regulations and Implementing Regulations (hard law);
- Acceptable Means of Compliance (AMC) and Guidance Material (GM) (soft law);
- Certification Specifications (soft law).

The 'hard law' is the law that must be complied with, and includes everything listed in Figure 4.1. The other soft laws offer guidance for industry players; they do not have to be complied with exactly, but they are of good use for the industry because following them – or something similar to them – will help comply with the Regulations and Implementing Regulations.

For example, in the context of initial airworthiness, *Commission Regulation (EU) No 748/2012* is the Regulation – the hard law – with which airlines must comply. In Annex 1 of the Regulation, section 21.A.35(a) prescribes:

> Flight testing for the purpose of obtaining a type-certificate shall be conducted in accordance with conditions for such flight testing specified by the Agency.

This does not provide much guidance. However, AMC/GM to Part-21 – Issue 2, Amendment 4 provides guidance material, including very specific guidance in creating the Flight Test Operations Manual (FTOM). Then there is a significant amount of certification specification under this Regulation, including 'CS-25', which provides certain specifications for large airplanes, proceeding to regulate a variety of features such as stall speed and take-off speeds, including providing complex formulas like:

CS 25.103 Stall speed
(See AMC 25.103)

(a) The reference stall speed V_{SR} is a calibrated airspeed defined by the applicant. V_{SR} may not be less than a 1-g stall speed. V_{SR} is expressed as:

$$V_{SR} \geq \frac{V_{CLMAX}}{\sqrt{n_{zw}}}$$

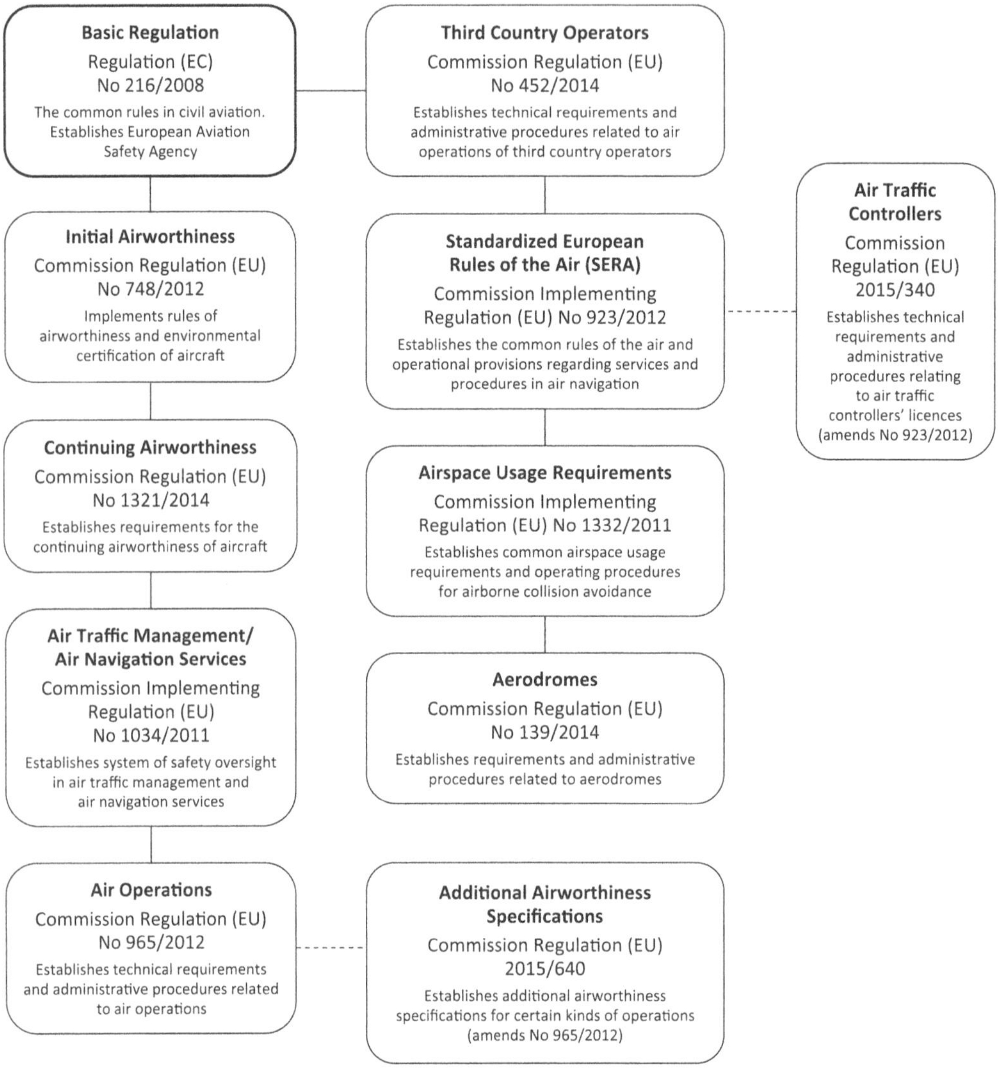

Figure 4.1 A broad framework of European aviation regulations

Source: EASA

The EASA has not restricted its operations to Europe. In March 2017, EASA and ICAO jointly hosted the Global Forum on Regional Safety Oversight Organizations (RSOOs) in Switzerland where progress was made on initiatives to improve the recognition, efficiency and cooperation worldwide of such organizations. EASA therefore also takes an advisory role in strengthening regional initiatives for the benefit of aviation safety on an international basis. RSOOs are essentially regional collaboration mechanisms that are created to fulfil states obligations under Article 37 of the Chicago Convention, which provides that each state undertakes 'to collaborate in securing the highest practicable degree of uniformity in regulations, standards, procedures and organization in relation to aircraft, personnel, airports, airways, and auxiliary services in all matters in which such uniformity will facilitate and improve air navigation'. ICAO believes that when such regional aviation safety organizations are implemented effectively, 'regional arrangements can help States overcome specific challenges, such as a lack of resources and qualified technical personnel, while helping to harmonize regulatory systems, reduce duplicative functions, create economies of scale, and ensure long-term sustainability and self-sufficiency'. EASA is often cited as an RSOO that works extremely well.

United States Regulations

United States aviation regulations find their basis in the *Federal Aviation Act 1958*, which delegates authority to the Federal Aviation Administration (FAA) to oversee and regulate safety in the airline industry and the use of US airspace, including in both civil and military aviation. It is unlike EU regulation in this way, as EU regulations do not apply to military aircraft. The Federal Aviation Regulations (FARs) are regulations created by the FAA to govern all US aviation activities, and are part of Title 14 of the Code of Federal Regulations (CFR), 'Aeronautics and Space'. Chapter 1 of the FARs consists of three volumes which the FAA regulates. Chapter 2 is specifically overseen by the Office of the Secretary of the Department of Transportation, and Chapter 3 by the Office of Commercial Space Transportation of the FAA. Chapter 5 created the National Aeronautics and Space Administration (NASA), and Chapter 6 created the Air Transportation Stabilization Board (ATSB), which is an office of the Treasury formed to help American airlines after 9/11.

The FAA, like the EASA, lays out airworthiness standards and the requirements for aircraft registration. It also provides rules for airspace and air traffic and a whole range of other matters. More about US regulations as they apply to different branches of aviation will be explored extensively in this book.

EU–US 'Open Skies'

To identify the source that triggered the process by which an EU–US open skies agreement was reached in 2007, we must go back over a decade to when the Transatlantic Common Aviation Area (TCAA) was introduced by the Association of European Airlines (AEA) in 1995. The principle upon which this suggestion was made, and what formed the core of the AEA philosophy, was that the liberalization and harmonization of competitive conditions should be intertwined. This stance would eventually have a significant influence on the mandate which represented a key stepping stone for an EU–US open skies agreement being reached.

In 2002, the European Court of Justice ruled that individual EU Member States entering bilateral air service agreements with the USA were considered to be in breach of single market rules. Given the size of the American and European markets relative to the rest of the world, it was important at that stage to establish the effective processes through which aviation regulation could be developed. The identification of this breach meant that the process by which air service agreements were negotiated between EU nations and the USA had to be reconsidered fundamentally. Indeed, it meant that a process for negotiations between the EU itself and the USA needed to be established. Based upon a mandate from EU Member States, the Commission began negotiations with the USA in June 2003. The main order of business was to develop and implement an agreement that would facilitate the liberalization and harmonization of aviation activities between the EU and the USA, a milestone that would eventually bring an end to individual bilateral air service agreements between any EU Member State and the USA.

From 2003 to 2007, a total of 11 rounds of negotiations took place to reach the final agreement that was signed at the EU–US summit on 30 April 2007. The impediments that stalled the agreement being signed any earlier could be found on both sides of the Atlantic. On one side, EU transport ministers deemed certain results of negotiations to be insufficient based on the minimum requirements of the mandate, whereas the US Congress was not satisfied with the action that was taken during particular phases of negotiations to rectify what it considered to be fundamental constitutional issues.

Consensus was reached in April 2007 and the air services agreement came into effect on 30 March 2008. The outcomes of the changes in the regulatory framework resulting from the first of the two phases of implementation are explained as follows:

- All EU and US airlines can fly transatlantic routes to and from the airports of their choice without restrictions on capacity, frequencies and types of aircraft. Airlines are free to propose transatlantic services that originated and or terminated outside the open aviation area as long as they include a stopover in the home region (the EU or the USA). Unlimited code-sharing is now permitted between the EU, the USA and third party countries.
- Restrictions on fares on transatlantic routes have been removed. Up until the open skies agreement was signed, airlines were required to register fares and governments were given the authority to block any they considered to be anti-competitive. A prohibition remains, however, on US airlines undercutting prices on intra-EU flights.
- The agreement provides a formal commitment from both sides towards compatible practices and improved cooperation in the areas of safety, security, government subsidies and the environment.
- The agreement also creates new cooperation arrangements between the EU and US competition authorities, facilitating the joint assessment of alliances between EU and US carriers.
- Opportunities are created for foreign carriers to wet lease aircraft to US airlines for use on international routes between the USA and any other third party country.
- Global Distribution Systems (GDSs) service providers operating in Europe have expanded to include services in the USA and vice versa. Equality is of paramount importance, and under no circumstances can European regulators impose tougher requirements on US systems, and vice versa.
- Global airline alliances will benefit from streamlined US regulatory processes, which for European airlines means that they pre-qualify for immunity from US antitrust laws when planning commercial cooperation with other EU and US carriers.

It should be noted that immunity from US antitrust laws enables airlines party to this agreement to discuss joint pricing and to coordinate flight schedules and other related matters without the threat of legal ramifications.

Impact of Brexit

The referendum held in the United Kingdom on 23 June 2016 resulted in a vote for the UK to leave the European Union, a vote that would require the nation to trigger Article 50 of the Lisbon Treaty in order for them to officially withdraw. The following November, the UK's High Court ruled that the government had to consult Parliament in order to do this, and the government's Brexit bill passed through the Commons easily.

As a member of the EU, the UK has benefited from EU's single air market for air transport and from rights negotiated at the EU supranational level with other nations, including the creation of agreements such as the EU–US open skies agreement. It is unclear at the moment exactly what is going to occur, with a lot of the impact being speculated. By leaving, it is believed that UK airlines will no longer enjoy automatic access to the single market. This will mean that their rights to operate to, from and within the EU would need to be provided through fresh agreements with the EU. They could also save their access by acceding to the European Common Aviation Area (ECAA) agreement (to which also Norway and Iceland – both non-EU nations – are parties). The UK could have some leverage in negotiating bilateral agreements, given that their aviation market is one of Europe's most important. As the UK may no longer be a party to the EU–US open skies agreement, they may have to draft a bilateral agreement to ensure they retain access to the US market.

On the technical front, the UK plays a crucial role in the European Aviation Safety Agency (EASA) and UK aircraft must comply with the EU's safety regulations. Countries that are not EU Member States, like Norway and Lichtenstein, may participate in the EASA processes when they have entered into agreements with the EU. So participation, importantly, is not a right, but a possibility that is subject to negotiation. After Brexit, the UK will surely lose influence over the development of the EASA framework. Countries that are not full EU members lose power to influence the final form of regulations. If the UK attained membership in the European Economic Area (EEA), it could obtain some influence on future EU laws but not as much as they had as an EU Member State.

Today the UK aviation post-COVID industry skills shortage continues to be exacerbated by a failure to reach agreement on the movement of labour across borders following the country's departure from the European Union (EU). The UK government remains at loggerheads with the EU over UK demands to amend aspects of the terms under which the country left the community in January 2020. These mainly hinge on disagreements over how cross-border trade is regulated between the British mainland and Northern Ireland.

In February 2021, with the support of the UK DfT, an industry partnership created the Aviation Skills Retention Platform as a free service to help companies fill vacancies. But other issues for the aviation industry remain as a legacy of Brexit. From 1 January 2023, holders of EASA pilot and maintenance engineer licences will no longer be permitted to work for UK companies or operate UK-registered aircraft. The UK Civil Aviation Authority advised aviation companies and their employees that they should start the process of securing UK licences well ahead of this deadline.

Liberalization of the ASEAN Market

The economic prosperity of China coupled with a downturn in the American market has contributed in part to the Asia-Pacific region being recognized as the largest aviation market in terms of passenger movements in 2009. The global airline industry has taken notice and many of the long-term strategic initiatives being implemented today are underpinned by the continued growth in this region, which only shows signs of growing in the years to come.

The continual rise of LCCs has proven to be the leading cause of a gradual phasing out of what were traditionally known as 'national carriers', leading to a paradigm shift in the development of route structures, fleet selections and management principles. Although there are still many true 'national carriers' throughout the world today, the trend of economic rationalization which began with governments of Western economies in the 1980s has, in general, led to governments divesting themselves of the responsibility – and hence the associated economic burden – of owning and running their own national airlines.

The combination of all these factors which now make up the global aviation marketplace has in turn contributed to the ASEAN countries embarking on a path towards liberalization. The current regulatory framework that these ten Member States (Brunei, Cambodia, Indonesia, Laos, Malaysia, Myanmar, Philippines, Singapore, Thailand and Vietnam) comply with does not facilitate growth and, more importantly, does not enable these carriers to negotiate with the largest airlines in the world from a position of strength due to the constraints imposed on them in relation to ownership and control, market access and external relations.

ASEAN's open skies policy – the ASEAN Single Aviation Market (ASEAN-SAM), finally came into effect on 1 January 2015. It removes restrictions on third, fourth and fifth airspace freedoms for airlines based in ASEAN Member States. Unfortunately, it still places restrictions on the seventh freedom on the air – removing these restrictions would permit airlines to transport passengers and cargo between two foreign countries, which is critical to allow for the development of regional carriers. Each ASEAN state will have to completely open up their international airports to other ASEAN members and remove restrictions on the frequency and maximum capacity of flights. The general aim of ASEAN-SAM is really to encourage airline competition, lower the cost of tickets and elevate the status of domestic airlines to become regional players.

A few nations were reluctant to ratify the full agreement, being the ASEAN Multilateral Agreement on the Full Liberalization of Air Freight Services. But, in May 2016, Indonesia and Laos finally ratified it and the Agreement has achieved full ratification by all ten ASEAN Member States (Brunei, Cambodia, Indonesia, Laos, Malaysia, Myanmar, Philippines, Singapore, Thailand and Vietnam). This open skies policy will allow the foreign carrier of one ASEAN state to land at any airport of another ASEAN state on any number of occasions with unlimited seat capacity.

But it is not all going smoothly. The Agreement requires the parties to completely open up their international airports to other ASEAN Member States, but this is not being carried out to its fullest extent. Indonesia's *Presidential Regulation No. 12/2016* only allows *five* Indonesian airports to be part of the policy. Laos has also not yet freed Vientiane and Luang Prabang for Thai carriers. The Philippines is also limiting access to Manila due to capacity and overcrowding.

The rationale behind this reluctance is primarily protectionist. Several members are reluctant to liberalize as they fear domestic airlines could not compete on an open market. Many also have significant government-owned airlines. Laos fears its airlines – the largest of which is government-owned – would be run out of business by competitors from larger markets such as Indonesia. Furthermore, subsidies for government-owned carriers and foreign ownership restrictions are common in the region. Another source of reluctance is that there are practicalities making it difficult for ASEAN airlines to expand – that is, inadequacies with infrastructure. Manila's Ninoy Aquino International Airport (NAIA) is a case in point. It was named the worst airport in the world in 2013 by the Guide to Sleeping in Airports' annual survey. It was found to have incredibly poor infrastructure and overcapacity, which contribute to lengthy delays and traveller frustrations. Newer Clark Airport tries to ease some burdens – it is about 100 kilometres from Manila but lacks effective rail and highway support.

Despite these obstacles, it should be interesting to see how the ASEAN-SAM develops in the next few years.

Bilateral Air Service Agreements

The topic of bilateral air service agreements was briefly discussed earlier in this chapter. However, within this section on commercial and economic regulation, a more detailed account of such agreements is warranted. Bilateral air service agreements – commonly referred to as 'BASAs' or even more generally as 'ASAs' – are binding international treaties between sovereign states, which represent the deregulation of air services between each country.

The primary function of an ASA is to outline the mutual agreement upon the exchange of rights granted to airlines to overfly, stop in and transport passengers and cargo to, from and within their territories. An ASA will usually define route and airline capacity, frequency of flights, destinations and city pairs, stopover rights and conditions on code-sharing. The various combinations of origin, destination and transit points are categorized into the nine 'freedoms of the air' and rights are allocated as between the two countries. The traffic rights granted in these types of ASAs usually have frequency or capacity limits, controlled in terms of aircraft type, the number and frequency of services and/or the number of seats.

Such arrangements are coming under increasing pressure from the forces of globalization to become multilateral (more liberalized and with a more flexible framework), and both the ICAO and the IATA are supportive of these initiatives, but they differ on the best path to increased liberalization. On the one hand, the ICAO believes that the most promising channel for further liberalization remains the ASA, both through bilateral agreements and through regional multilateral agreements. However, the IATA highlights the apparent deficiencies in this framework, saying that the bilateral system must change because it prevents airlines from acting like normal businesses. It says the ability for airlines to serve markets based on supply and demand serves as the most appropriate alternative to governments negotiating access on their behalf.

Remotely Piloted Aircraft Systems (RPAS)

The emergence of unmanned aerial vehicles (UAVs) or remotely piloted aircraft systems (RPAS) – otherwise known as drones – came as a shock to the international legal framework, and as of 2018 international and domestic laws are struggling to keep up with regulating the legal and constitutional issues associated with drones.

Whilst the dominant regulations are domestic, the international community has made efforts and, indeed, should make more. Article 8 of the Chicago Convention reads 'no aircraft capable of being flown without a pilot shall be flown without a pilot over the territory of a contracting State without special authorization by that State and in accordance with the terms of such authorization'. ICAO held informal meetings in 2006 and 2007 where it was decided that the development of SARPs for unmanned aircraft systems (UAS) was a necessary task and that ICAO should serve as a focal point for global harmonization of drone laws.

The regulatory framework ICAO is currently developing is being shaped within the context of a statement in the Global Air Traffic Management Operational Concept (GATMOC) – a concept to be discussed in more detail later in Chapter 14. The following definition was presented and endorsed at the Eleventh Air Navigation Conference held in Montréal from 22 September to 3 October 2003.

> An unmanned aerial vehicle is a pilotless aircraft, in the sense of Article 8 of the *Convention on International Civil Aviation*, which is flown without a pilot-in-command on-board and is either remotely and fully controlled from another place (ground, another aircraft, space) or programmed and fully autonomous.

ICAO's new RPAS Panel aims to deliver standards for unmanned aircraft to the governing council in 2018. Once these are approved, the standards will guide ICAO's 19 member states in setting their own domestic regulations regarding UAS.

The main purpose of this framework is to maintain the highest possible uniform level of safety. Part 2.9 of ICAO Cir 328 – Unmanned Aircraft Systems (UAS), published in 2011, reads:

> Identifying the commonalities and differences between manned and unmanned aircraft is the first step toward developing a regulatory framework that will provide, at a minimum, an equivalent level of safety for the integration of UAS into non-segregated airspace and at aerodromes. Technical specifications to support airworthiness, command and control (C2), detect and avoid, and other functionalities are being addressed by various industry standards development organizations around the world. ICAO's focus will remain on the higher-level performance-based standards, e.g. specifying minimum performance requirements for communications links, rather than how to achieve said requirements, along with harmonizing terms and definitions needed to support this activity.

The Circular therefore makes it clear that technical specifications are being developed by 'various industry . . . organizations around the world' and that ICAO's job is merely to specify the minimum requirements that states can then develop further once the SARPs have been developed.

ICAO published its Manual on Remotely Piloted Aircraft Systems in 2015 and then in 2020 released its Model Regulations for unmanned aircraft systems applicable to certification and safe operations of UAS (RPAS). The Manual introduces several governing principles, some of which are:

- The remotely piloted aircraft (RPA) is to hold a Certificate of Airworthiness issued by the state of registry.
- Individual remotely piloted systems (RPS) should not have piloting control of more than one RPA at a given time.
- The remote Pilot-in-Command (PIC) is expected to have continuous control over the RPA under normal operating conditions. An interruption of the C2 link is

considered an abnormal operation condition. RPAS design should consequently take into account potential interruption of the command and control link.
- An RPA is considered airworthy when an RPAS has been demonstrated to conform to an approved type design and is compliant with instructions for continuing airworthiness (ICA) through maintenance actions or inspections.

The ICAO Model Regulations for Unmanned Aircraft Systems, Parts 101 and 102 are accompanied by Advisory Circulars (AC) and guidance material to assist NAA personnel in the implementation and oversight of UAS or Remotely Piloted Aircraft Systems (RPAS) operations. The ACs and guidance material serve as an example for ICAO member states to create, add or amend, existing or future national UAS guidance material by the respective state aviation regulators.

The Model Regulations are not intended to be prescriptive, mandatory or construed in any way as to pre-empt individual states' legal structures. They are meant to offer model language for states to facilitate the establishment of UAS regulations. In developing the document, it was recognized that the specific national legislative requirements might not be the same for all states, and therefore the states are free to adapt the Model Regulations, as appropriate, to meet their specific needs.

One of the principles in the Model Regulations is that a person must not operate an unmanned aircraft (UA) within segregated airspace unless the person has approval to do so from the administering authority responsible for the segregated airspace area. Neither can a person operate a UA in controlled airspace without authorization from the ATC unit responsible for that airspace, and without a relevant qualification for the use of an aeronautical radio.

It is rather unusual that a manual was developed before SARPs were developed but in the case of drones, it was considered necessary due to the rapid advancement of the technology. Essentially, UAS is going to operate in accordance with ICAO standards already existing for manned aircraft. The term remotely piloted aircraft (RPA) is being introduced to mean an aircraft piloted by a licensed 'remote pilot' situated at a 'remote pilot station' located external to the aircraft, like on the ground or in another aircraft, who monitors the aircraft at all times and can respond to instructions issued by air traffic control. RPA will be made a subset of unmanned aircraft – 'unmanned aircraft' or 'unmanned aircraft system' are all-encompassing whereas RPA will refer to just the piloted subset.

The development of UAS SARPs has given rise to significant legal matters concerning the Chicago Convention. Article 3 recognizes that every state is entitled to require the landing at some designated airport of a civil aircraft flying above its territory without authority, and that every aircraft shall comply with an order of this nature. As such, an RPA pilot will require the ability to comply with these instructions provided by the state, visually or electronically, and have the ability to divert the RPA to the specified airport at the state's request. A remote pilot is critical if a UAS is to operate closely to other civil aircraft, as Article 8 places emphasis on the requirement that pilotless aircraft '*shall be so controlled* as to obviate danger to civil aircraft' (emphasis added).

Article 12 of the Convention stipulates that aircraft shall comply with the rules and regulations relating to the flight and manoeuvre of aircraft of the territory in which they are flying. With RPA, the possibility may arise whereby RPA operations, including the responsibilities of the pilot, are to be transferred over to another operator as the aircraft is in flight. ICAO's Circular on UAS elaborates on this issue:

> The remote pilots may be co-located or situated thousands of kilometres apart, e.g. for an oceanic flight of a long range RPA, handover of piloting responsibilities to a remote pilot situated in Asia from a remote pilot situated in North America or between an en-route remote pilot and a local (terminal) remote pilot. Handover may also occur as a result of routine shift work of the remote pilots.

Consequently, changes in the legal framework will be necessary to address the handover of these responsibilities.

ENVIRONMENTAL REGULATION

Over the past 50 years, the environmental impact of aviation, in particular relating to noise, air quality and climate change, has become a contentious issue. This period has seen a sharp rise in awareness for the environment as a whole and the contribution of the transport sector to its deterioration has led to the creation of new industries, as well as a new set of requirements for aviation stakeholders to comply with. Given that the projected growth figures for commercial aviation activity is about 5 per cent per year over the next 20–25 years, the environmental impacts of aviation are expected to gain more significance against a background of declining impacts from many other sources.

The International Civil Aviation Organization (ICAO) adopted the Carbon Offsetting and Reduction Scheme for International Aviation (CORSIA) back in 2016, which was heralded as the first global market-based environmental initiative for any industry sector. At the 77th International Air Transport Association (IATA) Annual General Meeting in Boston, USA, on 4 October 2021, a resolution was passed by IATA member airlines committing them to achieving net zero carbon emissions from their operations by 2050.

Then in 2022 at the 41st ICAO Assembly in Montreal, 184 member states adopted the Long Term global Aspirational Goal (LTAG) of net zero carbon emissions from international aviation by 2050 in support of the UNFCCC Paris Agreement's temperature goal to limit global warming to well below 2 degrees Celsius. This was a most important development by ICAO in aligning governments with the IATA Net Zero by 2050 resolution at the 77th IATA AGM a year earlier.

IATA's pledge, consistent with ICAO's goals, brings the entire air transport sector in line with the objectives of the Paris Agreement. ICAO's Fly Net Zero commitment is for airlines to achieve net zero carbon emissions by 2050 through a combination of maximum elimination of emissions at the source, offsetting and carbon capture technologies. IATA says the aviation industry won't be able to completely eliminate emissions at the source, and will need to mitigate the rest using a variety of offsetting mechanisms. This is the process where emissions are compensated for by the financing of a reduction in emissions elsewhere.

IATA has subsequently published a series of roadmaps to net zero by 2050. These roadmaps are the first detailed assessment of the key steps necessary to make net zero by 2050 an aviation success in covering technology, infrastructure, operations, finance and policy. The roadmaps are not just for airlines but also for governments, suppliers and financiers. All stakeholders must deliver the products, policies or investments needed to decarbonize.

At the IATA Annual General Meeting (AGM) and World Air Transport Summit on 4–6 June 2023 in Istanbul, Türkiye, IATA's Director General Willie Walsh stated:

> The sustainability challenge is, bar none, the biggest that we will face as leaders of the aviation industry. This will be difficult and take time. As pioneers building the net zero emissions age for aviation, scrutiny of our efforts will be extreme. We must welcome it as a means of telling the impressive story of aviation's decarbonization and its contributions to society.
>
> (ICAO Pressroom 2023)

Due to the ever-increasing importance of this topic to the aviation industry and indeed for the entire international community, it is quite apt that a chapter of this publication be dedicated to the rapidly evolving areas of the aviation industry, and of aviation law, that will be instrumental toward achieving the internationally agreed Net Zero Emission target by 2050. Chapter 17 has been dedicated to the subject. At this stage it is sufficient to give an overview of the topic from an international aviation regulatory perspective.

Now more than ever, it is important to ensure that there is a balance between the various tools which can be used to influence positive environmental outcomes for the aviation industry, be it engine technologies, air traffic management (ATM) strategies or the focus of this section, regulation. Such an assessment requires understanding the trade-offs among technologies, operations, policies, market conditions, manufacturers and airline economics, and the environmental impacts of aviation activities.

The costs and benefits of mitigating these impacts are often difficult to discern because of the complex interdependencies among environmental impacts, aircraft design, operating procedures and industry responses to policies. The nature of policy development and the bureaucracies that come with it make it difficult for regulations to be implemented in a timely manner. This issue is only magnified when considered in the context of aviation, which is widely regarded as being extremely sensitive to external factors and is constantly going through a period of transition with regard to some aspects of the industry's activities.

Development of ICAO Aviation Environmental Standards

The need for a holistic approach with regard to regulating aviation's impact on the environment became evident during the 1960s. The very nature of aviation and the freedoms given to airlines to fly over one another's sovereign boundaries required a global perspective to be adopted in respect of the environmental footprint of the industry.

Aircraft noise, the most readily perceived community impact, was the first area to be regulated by the ICAO. The ICAO first published Annex 16 on noise standards in 1971 with subsequent increases in stringency since then, brought about by a combination of community initiatives, improvements in technology and a clearer understanding of the environmental challenges facing twenty-first-century citizens.

Emissions standards were next to follow with the implementation of the ICAO SARPs for aircraft emissions in the 1980s to improve air quality in the vicinity of airports. The ICAO emissions standards are prescribed in an amended Annex 16, which now addresses general environmental standards.

The need to reconsider the international aviation community's approach to managing the effects of the industry's impact on the environment was brought about by a number of factors, which, when combined, pose the biggest threat to the sustainability of an industry providing key logistical support to the travelling public and industries operating on a global scale. When one looks at the context within which the Chicago Convention was signed, it is clear that many of the environmental issues which face the airline industry today would not have been considered, and for this reason it is important for an arm of the ICAO to be solely dedicated to this area.

It was back in 1968 that the first significant move was made on the part of the ICAO in acknowledging the importance of remaining proactive on the issues regarding the environment. This resulted in an instruction handed to the ICAO Council to establish international specifications and associated guidance material to control aircraft noise after it was demonstrated that the noise in the vicinity of airports was not sustainable. Only a few years later, in 1971, it was clear that environmental management was becoming a higher priority than had previously been considered. The scope of the ICAO's activities was broadening during this period and now included the responsibility to guide the development of international civil aviation in such a manner as to benefit the travelling public and to achieve maximum compatibility between those reliant on the services supplied by the aviation industry and those who are not.

Annex 16 was adopted in 1971 on the basis of recommendations of the 1969 Special Meeting on Aircraft Noise in the Vicinity of Aerodromes. Matters considered at the Special Meeting included procedures for describing and measuring aircraft noise, human tolerance to aircraft noise, aircraft noise certification, criteria for the establishment of aircraft noise abatement procedures, land use control and ground run-up noise abatement procedures. What was to result from this meeting was the establishment of a new committee that would assist the ICAO on issues surrounding the development of noise certification requirements for different classes of aircraft. This committee would be referred to as the Committee on Aircraft Noise (CAN), and it wasted little time, its first contribution to the regulatory framework being the first amendment to Annex 16.

In 1973, the CAN adopted an amendment to Annex 16 that addressed noise certification of future production and derived versions of subsonic jet airplanes. During subsequent meetings, the CAN developed certification standards for future subsonic jet airplanes and propeller-driven airplanes, and for the future production of existing supersonic transport airplane types and helicopters. It also developed guidelines for noise certification of future supersonic and propeller-driven short take-off and landing (STOL) airplanes as well as installed APUs (auxiliary power-units) and associated aircraft systems when operating on the ground.

The issue of engine emissions was yet to be addressed under any of the ICAO's formal requirements. However, a resolution was agreed upon in 1971 during an ICAO Assembly focused on reviewing proposals for the ICAO standards for the control of engine emissions from certain types of aircraft engines. The result of this meeting was the formation of the Committee on Aircraft Engine Emissions (CAEE), with a view to developing specific standards for aircraft engine emissions. These standards were later adopted in 1981 and essentially set limits for the emission of smoke and certain gaseous pollutants for large turbojet and turbofan engines to be produced in the future.

As a result, the scope of the existing Annex 16 was widened to include engine emissions provisions and hence led to this particular Annex being split into Volumes I and

II: Volume I contains provisions relating to engine noise, whilst the provisions relating to aircraft engine emissions were contained within Volume II.

Recent Developments in Environmental Regulation

To keep pace with the environmental challenges facing the aviation industry, a number of bodies and initiatives have come to the fore over recent years. Given that the Chicago Convention makes no reference to the regulation of the environment, the ICAO has reacted in due course by adopting and continually updating SARPs on aircraft noise and subsequently on aircraft engine emissions and designated them as Annex 16 Volumes I and II, respectively.

Today the internationally agreed 2050 Net Zero Emission aviation targets have been agreed to and supported by the International Civil Aviation Organization and the International Air Transport Association. To meet these targets, technological innovation is needed across the entire aviation sector including the production of low-emission and sustainable aviation fuels, design improvements in aircraft and engines, and operational fleet optimization. With the escalating increase in aviation traffic in the post-pandemic era, demand restraint scenarios also need to be considered to curb growth in emissions and ultimately reduce them this decade. But to achieve these objectives there needs to be a more collaborative approach, not only between aircraft and engine manufacturers and the airlines and airport operators, but between governments, internationally and domestically, to develop policies and regulations that support and promote these objectives.

In conclusion, the entire aviation industry agree that environmental issues are a global challenge that needs a global solution. This topic will be discussed at length in Chapter 17.

5
Contract Law

INTRODUCTION

The day-to-day operations of any business – aviation-related or otherwise – would simply not be possible without the law of contract. Contracts are fundamental to any commercial enterprise and their application is so widespread that people may enter into contractual arrangements without even knowing it. There are many different forms in which contracts can be established, and they do not always have to be in writing. For example, you become a *party* to a contract when you purchase a cup of coffee, a newspaper, a bus ticket or even groceries.

One of the main reasons why it is important to acquire a working understanding of the law of contract – not only because of its widespread application – is that in entering contractual relations, the law imposes certain obligations and responsibilities on the parties to a contract. Without having some knowledge of how contract law applies and of the obligations and responsibilities that the law imposes, an individual may be exposed to unacceptable levels of risk within their private or professional capacity.

Understanding the law of contract is of paramount importance to the international aviation community, and its application comes at a time when the global aviation industry is recovering from the devastating and unprecedented impact of the COVID-19 pandemic. The chaos it has unleashed upon every carrier and air traveller in the world is unprecedented, and this impact relates directly to the contract of carriage by air. The increased awareness by consumers of their rights, or lack thereof, resulting from this 'extraordinary event' is yet to be fully explored, but there is no doubt that it will be far greater than the trend of improved passenger rights identified immediately prior to the onset of the coronavirus.

This global event has shown the effectiveness of existing legal rights and regulatory and contractual consumer protection provisions but also, and most relevantly, has highlighted their deficiencies. This is a classic example of an area of the law – and particularly the law of contract – where the law has been modified because of the inadequacy of traditional legal recourses and of the uniqueness of the aviation operating environment.

Practitioners in the aviation industry such as pilots, maintenance engineers, flight attendants and air traffic controllers all need to be familiar with the various aspects of the law of contract so that they can conduct their business and personal relationships with a degree of certainty. Likewise, even the users of aviation services, passengers and owners of freight or cargo all need to be familiar with the terms and conditions of carriage. Until relatively recently, technical professionals working in the aviation industry had little, if any, training in contract law or for that matter in any aspects of the law.

DOI: 10.4324/9781032652146-5

Consistent with the underlying purpose of this book, it is hoped that this chapter will provide some useful and helpful guidance to the reader in this area of the law.

As stated, passengers on board an aircraft need to be familiar with the circumstances in which they may or may not be contractually bound. What are the conditions governing a passenger airline ticket? What are the legal rights of a passenger when there is damage to his or her baggage resulting from a flight? Who is held responsible if a passenger is injured on board an aircraft? Most of these questions will be discussed in this chapter, with the remaining issues addressed in Chapter 10.

One very important initial observation on this topic is that the general principles of contract law apply universally around the world. The international commercial economy – of which multinational corporations are such an important part – effectively dictates this to be the case. There are certain standards that are used globally in aviation that have also developed from international conventions relevant to international air carriage.

One of the most important areas of contract law that relates to international aviation law is contract for air carriage. The Warsaw Convention 1929 was the first convention to establish uniform rules of law concerning international carriage by air. However, the subsequent amendments made to the Warsaw Convention, by way of protocols, were not ratified by the USA and some other states as they considered that the compensation provided under the Convention had become inadequate.

The limitations of liability for death or injury of passengers as contained in the Warsaw system were increasingly questioned by countries all over the world. This is one of the reasons why the effectiveness of and support for the Warsaw Convention gradually diminished – it was eventually replaced by the Montreal Convention in 1999.

The Montreal Convention 1999 is the most recent international convention to govern international air carriage and has updated and replaced the Warsaw Convention. Up until its introduction, there was no uniform international system in place to govern international air carriage as the Warsaw system (the term given to the original Convention and the subsequent protocols), due to lack of universal adoption, degenerated into a non-universal system and thereby frustrated one of its primary objectives.

Although the Montreal Convention is now probably the most important area of *private* international aviation law (see Chapter 2 for a definition of this area of law) relating to contracts, it is certainly not the only area. Contracts of employment for aviation practitioners, sale and leasing of aircraft and other equipment, global alliances, third party contractors for ground services and aircraft maintenance services contracts are all instances in which the law of contract applies. Moreover, as this book is directed at the international world of aviation, it is important that those airlines or other businesses that contract with foreign parties are familiar with how the relevant state law applies to each particular contract.

A final point that is most important in this area of the law relates to the increasing importance and usage of e-commerce and in respect of contracts being created online. Although most countries have introduced legislation to cover contracts entered into through the Internet, the purchaser of such items and services may be unaware of the *jurisdiction* (that is, the legal area or scope of authority) or *forum* (that is, the court or other institution where contractual disputes may be heard) in which the contract has been formed and to which any remedies for breach of contract may apply. For all the aforementioned reasons, it is therefore necessary for aviation personnel – especially those involved with international travel – not only to understand how the law of contract developed and how it applies but also to have a broad understanding of the *differences* that may apply in its application throughout the various legal systems of the world.

The Development of Contract Law

For those not familiar with the basic differences between common law systems and civil law systems of mainland Europe and elsewhere, it may be worthwhile briefly to revise the relevant section in Chapter 3. As stated from the outset, contract law necessarily has a high degree of similarity across *all* jurisdictions throughout the world and therefore only those areas of significant difference, in respect of contract law, will be considered in the following section.

The development of the civil law system and the common law system both stem from the Middle Ages. In the civil law system, the doctrine of *causa* provided the basis of all contracts in the medieval era and such a concept is still frequently used today. This doctrine was a useful way of solving cases in which there were no technically valid formal contracts. If the parties to the agreement had a legitimate reason or cause for making such promises, this would be sufficient for the courts to enforce the promise as a legally binding contract. In the late Middle Ages, the French adopted this concept in which one article in their civil code (Article 1131 of the *Code Civil*) provides that promissory contracts are valid only if they have a cause. As the French adopted such a doctrine in their customary laws, it consequently became a part of the modern codes of the many civil law countries.

The common law system on the other hand took a different approach to contracts. Throughout the Middle Ages, this system kept with the traditional contract referred to as either a deed or a contract under seal. To guarantee that an executory promise was binding between parties, these formal documents were used. This was to make sure that the promises created were binding in the future. What is meant by an *executory* promise is that some item or service is given or accepted in return for a promise, with the intention of that promise being performed in the near future. The traditional method of making a deed in the Middle Ages was to attach a seal to a document, which is often referred to as a 'promise', and then hand it over. It is from this procedure that the expression 'signed, sealed and delivered' originated. One characteristic of these contracts was that it was not necessary to formulate any general theory of contractual obligation. This was due to the notion that enforcement was established automatically once the individual put his or her seal to his or her promise. It should be noted that many of the civil law systems, particularly those drawn from Roman law, were well established before the advent of the common law system. This is why in common law there can be seen traces of civil law relating to contracts.

According to Marsh (1994: 22), the contractual principles that apply to *all* legal systems that derived from the civil law are:

- a contract is formed by offer and acceptance, also called 'agreement';
- intention to create legal relations;
- the theory of *consensus ad idem* (meeting of the minds of all parties);
- the 'will' theory that the contract is a product of the intentions of the parties and it is the function of the court simply to determine what the parties have agreed upon;

- the rules relating to the recovery of damages in contract as applicable to common law systems in which the principle formulated in the English case of *Hadley v Baxendale* applies.

One of the most significant treatises of common law, *De Legibus et Consuetudinibus Angliae* (*On the Laws and Customs of England*), has categories drawn from Roman law. The medieval English jurist Bracton wrote this treatise with parts of it largely influenced by the division of the law in Justinian's Institutes found in civil law.

Development of Common Law Contracts The first contract in the common law of England was referred to as the real contract or commonly now referred to as 'bailment'. This form of contract included the legal duty of the delivery of a *chattel*. The transaction involved the duty of the *bailee* returning the chattel (*personal property*) or its value to the original owner. Such a duty was referred to as a debt and the action of 'debt' was used for its enforcement.

In the eighteenth century, the earliest form of human transaction was a form of trade known as *bartering*. The basic idea of bartering was exchanging goods or services directly with another individual without needing a medium of exchange (today, the most common medium of exchange is money). This meant that there was no need for any obligations to be made as the agreement was instantly fulfilled when exchange took place. This explains why executory contracts were very rare during the eighteenth century and why the courts did not recognize expectation damages in that period. *Expectation damages*, in the context of contract law, are the monetary equivalent of what was promised under the contract, or, in other words, the value of the benefit that the party not in breach would have received if the other party had performed the contract as agreed.

In situations where goods or services were not exchanged straightaway, executory contracts were used and became quite important for 'future' agreements. *Executory consideration* is a thing given or accepted in return for a promise where that promise is due to be performed in the future. These promises were not enforceable by law, but nevertheless were a feature that made up a loan.

This initial action led to the development of a loan, where a chattel was to be delivered to one party by another to be used by them and then returned to the lender when specified. In such a transaction, a high level of trust exists in the lender giving its property to the borrower. There is also the duty of the borrower by law to return to the lender what is rightfully its property. This is commonly referred to as an obligation. As the borrower had benefited from a loan, the obligation stemmed from the requirement to repay the debt. For example, if a mechanic fixed a car, the obligation would be to pay the mechanic for the services rendered. The history of early contract law in the common law system transitioned from the conception of contractual duty imposed by law to that of contractual obligation resulting from a promise.

The modern law of contract was developed in the *laissez-faire* society of England in the late-nineteenth century. *Laissez-faire* is the notion of individuals and society being free from the intervention of governments in economic affairs and workings of the markets. With regard to contracts, it meant that a person or business could enter into any contract without government restrictions. However, there were exceptions to this in cases where contracts were either offensive to policy or were established to commit crimes.

During the nineteenth century, there was great popularity in the notion of *laissez-faire*, particularly with regard to economics. The theory was that a person could achieve the best results given the freedom to do so and that the state's function was to maintain order without interfering in these activities. This changed, however, due to the Industrial Revolution, as there was significant growth in production methods in agriculture and manufacturing. The impact of commercialization meant that the notion of *laissez-faire* was no longer adequate for society. This was because there was a greater degree of commercial transactions taking place with an expansion in economic activities, which created the need for establishing commercial agreements as opposed to mere social arrangements. This gave rise to the importance of legally binding agreements.

Development of Civil Law Contracts The development of contract law in the civil law system can be traced back to the fourth and fifth centuries BC, in the period when the Greeks and Romans came to rely on laws designed to deal with international transactions. Athens was said to be importing grain from Russia, Sicily and Egypt, and these activities are now commonly known as the grain trade (Hasebroek 1965). The upper class of Greek society enjoyed quality foods, textiles and other luxuries from all over the Mediterranean (Casson 1984).

Although it seemed as though the trade system was very sophisticated and prosperous, this was far from the case. In those times the trading activities were very primitive, limited and a slow process. Due to these features, only necessities were largely traded, including products such as corn and grain. The law at that time was general in nature, simple and quite scarce. It may seem surprising, but these laws were suitable for that period of time. Ancient trade in Athens was seen as one of the early forms of customs in ancient society.

In ancient Athens there were laws known as 'emporial laws' which were designed to deal with imports and exports, the supply of food and necessities and bottomry activities. The term 'bottomry' was used between the seventeenth and early nineteenth centuries to describe the legal relationship based on mortgage or pledge. A shipowner, for example, might borrow money from a lender in order to undertake a voyage. The lender would provide the money but only exchange for the ship temporarily until the loan was repaid (this including the interest or premium stipulated); this was known as a 'pledge' or a sign of a solemn promise (executory consideration).

'Bottomry' also referred to a form of loan contract based on the mortgage of a ship. It was a contract entered into by the owner to obtain funds from a lender. The funds, including the stipulated interest, needed to be repaid upon the successful completion of a voyage; however, if the ship was lost, there was no obligation to repay the loan amount. If the voyage was successful but the loan was not repaid in accordance with the terms specified in the bottomry contract, the lender took possession of the vessel. Such a contract today is known as a conditional loan.

A fundamental distinguishing feature of the contemporary civil law system, as compared to the common law system, is that it originated to a very large extent in Roman law. Roman law was the most highly developed system of law in the ancient world, and reached its zenith in what is known as the 'classical period', between 117 AD and 235 AD. In 528 AD, Justinian, the Emperor of Byzantium, organized a compilation of Roman law sources. This compilation was completed in 534 AD and became known as the *Corpus Juris Civilis*. It was comprised of four parts, namely, the Digest, the Institutes, the Code and the Novels. The Digest and the Institutes were the most important parts in the development of the Civil Law. The Digest contained excerpts from the writings of the most prominent Roman jurists of the classical period, and the Institutes was a textbook which contained a succinct summary of Roman law. The Corpus Juris was almost entirely private law. Roman law was a formulary system, by which a litigant had to bring his case under a particular form of action. Roman law never developed general rules or abstract legal concepts. The writings of the jurists contained in the Digest focused mainly on the solving of problems arising in individual cases.

DEFINITION OF A CONTRACT

Simply stated, a contract is an agreement between two or more persons that is enforceable at law. The words 'two or more persons' in this context refer to a legal person or legal entity, which includes a corporation.

CLASSIFICATION OF CONTRACTS

Written and Verbal Contracts

A contract can be created in a number of ways. Some contracts can be formed by being expressed in words, either written (referred to as *acte sous seing privé* in French law) or spoken. These types of contracts are no less binding than written documents, provided all the essential elements are included.

A written contract could be a person signing a contract to buy a house, whereas a verbal contract could be for the sale of a cup of coffee. There are, however, problems associated with verbal agreements with regard to evidentiary proof. In other words, if a contract is verbally constructed, how will third parties know the circumstances under which the contract was agreed upon? Issues will arise when trying to enforce a verbal contract, as it is very difficult to distinguish which party is telling the truth. In the courts, the true intentions of the parties at the time of contracting need to be recognized, and if the contract is verbal, it is much more difficult to prove what each party's intention was at the time.

A contract can also be created impliedly by the actions and conduct of the parties. These contracts need not be created by words, either written or spoken, but are created by the very actions of the parties in the context in which those actions occurred. If, for example, in the normal course of business a company has been supplied with particular goods on the same day of each week for a year and would pay the invoice which is delivered with the goods, the courts are likely to imply that a contract exists from the time of delivery even though there has been no expressed agreement prior to each delivery.

There are some contracts that are of a standard form type that are commonly referred to as adhesion contracts. These contracts are between two parties where the terms and conditions are set by one of the parties, and the other party is placed in a 'take it or leave it' position with very little room to negotiate the terms. Some common examples include carriage by air, bus and train tickets, lottery entries and credit card accounts. An interesting fact is that most standard form contracts are not usually read as the terms are commonly found in the fine print and are written in complicated legal language, which most customers find difficult to follow. Other written contracts may be specifically prepared on each occasion, as occurs in everyday business.

Form of a Contract

There are two forms of a contract in common law: either a *simple* contract or a *formal* contract. The difference between them is essentially whether or not the contract requires *consideration*. Although a simple contract can come in many forms and is not just found in writing, it will always have the notion of consideration as an essential element. This type of contract is by far the most common form of contract. On the issue of consideration, contract law has a much wider ambit in civil law than it does in the common law, in the sense that agreements which create only duties on one party and only rights in the other party are recognized under the civil law system.

On the other hand, a formal contract requires that the agreement be written in a particular form. As previously stated, these contracts were traditionally 'signed, sealed and delivered' and are commonly referred to as contracts under seal or 'deeds'. If this form of contract is used, the element of consideration is not needed but nevertheless is still enforceable by law.

It may be of assistance to think of the difference between simple and formal contracts as being one of how the parties indicate they are serious about forming a legally enforceable agreement. In the case of a simple contract, the parties indicate their seriousness by exchanging things of legal value, whereas for a formal contract, each party must be serious – that is, the only implication that can be drawn from the solemn act of affixing one's seal to a document. The solemn act of sealing justifies to the law that the agreement is legally enforceable, and so no consideration is required for a formal contract.

In common law countries, it is not unusual for the legislature to have created laws altering the common law position to require certain contracts to be in writing. The sale of land and a contract of marriage are two important examples. In civil law countries, there are also certain types of contracts that must be in writing. In France, for example, certain types of contracts must be written and require public office holders, commonly referred to as either a *maire* or a *notaire,* to compose the contract. Such a document is known as an *acte authentique* and would include contracts that involve parties donating property, marriage contracts or contracts altering matrimonial property rights after the marriage is dissolved.

Contracts may also be classified by their mode of acceptance. In a *bilateral contract,* the parties come to an agreement and are then under obligations to perform their various undertakings in accordance with the contractual terms. It may be stated that, after the contract is formed, both parties are obliged to perform. On the other hand, a *unilateral contract* involves an 'offer to the world', open for anybody to accept. Acceptance occurs when the accepting party gives a full and complete performance of the terms of the contract. Only then is the offering party obliged to perform its promises to the party that accepts. Since the contract is formed only *after* the accepting party has fully performed all its promises, it may be said that only one party is left to perform after the contract is formed, thus justifying the name 'unilateral' contract. The difference may become clearer with some examples.

For example, if Samantha agrees to buy a car from Amin, the contract is formed as soon as agreement is reached as to the terms of the sale. Once the contract is formed, Amin has the obligation to deliver the car into Samantha's possession, and Samantha has the obligation to pay Amin the sale price. This example would be known as a *bilateral* contract, because at the moment the contract is formed, both parties have obligations remaining for performance.

An example of a *unilateral* contract could be a reward for finding a pet. For example, Diane's dog, Murphy, is missing and she places an advertisement in a newspaper offering a reward to anyone who can find and return Murphy to her. Beau finds her beloved dog and accepts the offer of the reward by reuniting Murphy with Diane. Beau has, in effect, both accepted the offer and performed the contract in the one motion. This is a unilateral contract because only one party – Diane, the party making the offer – remains to perform her obligations after the moment the contract is formed.

Validity of a Contract

Another way of classifying a contract is in terms of its validity. In this connection, contracts may be valid, void, voidable or illegal. A *valid* binding contract possesses all elements, and the law will enforce the contract.

A *void* contract is one having no legal effect and that cannot therefore be enforced by a party or by anyone else. A void contract is said to be *void ab initio* ('no effect from the beginning') in circumstances where the contract is void from the outset, as if the contract were never formed. An example could be a murder or drug dealing, which would be voided from the beginning as the terms of the contract are illegal. In civil law, a void contract applies when there is complete nullity due to the parties either not really consenting or the agreement lacking an objective or there was no lawful cause or *causa* (Marsh 1994: 83 and 95). A contract may also become void at some point after formation, in which case any rights that had accrued as between the parties are still enforceable, even after the contract is no longer valid. In this case, consider a contract for the international sale of goods. For example, a company in Utopia contracts to buy 1,000 steel chairs from a company in Ruritania, to be delivered in five shipments of 200 chairs each. After the first two shipments, war breaks out between Utopia and Ruritania, and both the Utopian Parliament and the Ruritanian Congress pass laws prohibiting contracts with persons of 'enemy states'. The contract between the two companies was quite legal upon its formation, but is now illegal due to the new laws. As such, the contract is void from the time the laws were passed, but the Utopian company is still obliged to pay the Ruritanian company for its 400 chairs, since they have already been delivered.

A *voidable* contract is one which has some deficiency that allows the innocent (affected) party the choice of either declaring the contract void or allowing it to continue. The party is not bound by the contract and this right is usually given to the injured party. Examples include misrepresentation (false information), duress (threats) or undue influence (involuntary acts). An *illegal* contract is one where the purpose or object of the contract is unlawful. An *unenforceable* contract is a valid contract that has some defect in how it is constructed or mannered that will make it unenforceable by law. If the defect is corrected, it is possible for the courts to enforce the agreement.

Validity Under Civil Law Systems

In civil law systems, contracts can be made void if they are found to lack a lawful 'cause'. This will be discussed at length in this chapter, but it is worth mentioning it here briefly. In French law, for example, Article 1131 of the *Code Civil* states that 'an obligation without "cause" or with a false "cause" or a "*cause illicite*" is without any legal effect or deemed a void contract' (Marsh 1994: 95). *Cause illicite* basically translates from French to mean an unlawful cause. Article 1133 of the *Code Civil* states that a cause is unlawful when it is prohibited by legislation, for example, if a contract is formed for the lease of a shop for the purposes of operating a black market. The *objet* of the obligations is for the lessor to give shop possession and the lessee to pay rent. Both of these obligations are legal activities; however, the motivating reason for gaining this lease is illicit. In this case, the external cause would provide the basis for making this contract void. Civil law systems also require that the price of the sale of an item in a contract must either be determined or objectively determinable at the time the contract is concluded. The *Code Civil* in French law states 'that the price must be fixed and settled by the parties' (Article 1591 of the *Code Civil*) and the price can be left to the evaluation of the third party, although 'if they are unable or do not want to make an evaluation there is no sale' (Article 1592 of the *Code Civil*).

With regard to the price being objectively determinable under the contract, it needs to be established in the absence of factors that are dependent on the will of either of the parties. Basically the sale will be considered void when the price is based on the will of only one of the parties, as they could fix the price and by doing so disadvantage the other party. There are exceptions to this general rule, though. For example, a contract for works can be valid in the absence of a price either determined or objectively determinable. Article 1787 of the *Code Civil* provides that 'the prior agreement on the cost of the works is not an essential element for a contract for works'. An underlying element that remains the same in both sales contracts and contracts for works is that the contract will be deemed void if the price is fixed by either party, rather than by both parties acting jointly.

Other civil law systems such as Germany's are more flexible with what the term 'determinable' means in the context of contract price. If the price is determined on the basis of good morals and is conducted in good faith, then the contract will be treated as valid. The price also does not need to be objectively determined at the time of contract, but can be established at the date of delivery.

In the case of aleatory contracts, validity will be determined on whether or not the *alea* (Latin for chance) can be said to be genuine. In Article 1964 of the *Code Civil*, aleatory contracts are defined as contracts where the extent of one party's performance depends on some occurrence of a particular event. Some aleatory contracts include *rente viagére* and the variation of *baux à nourriture*. *Rente viagére* is where one party hands over its property rights in exchange for periodic payments for income support over its lifetime, by way of annuity. *Baux à nourriture* is a variation of this which involves a promise to provide board, lodging and care instead of a life annuity (Vranken 1997: 98).

Consider the following example to illustrate this principle. If Francesca agrees to give her house to Thomas in exchange for personal care over the period of her life, this is deemed to be *baux à nourriture* provided Thomas cares for her until she dies. The *Code Civil* does not require the object of the obligations to be substantial (Vranken 1997: 98).

Performance of a Contract

How a contract is performed is another way of classifying contracts. A contract that has had both parties carry out their side of the agreement is known as an *executed contract* or *discharged contract*. A contract that requires the performance of some task by one or more of the parties at some time in the future is called an *executory contract*.

In civil law systems, there can be obligations relating to the actual conduct of negotiations and also to the continued process of the negotiations when they become more advanced. Delictual liability, which is known as tort liability in common law countries, can arise under Article 1382 of the *Code Civil* when conducting negotiations. Such liability can arise due to the fault caused by bad faith or lack of good faith of one party in the conduct of negotiations. In this situation there does not need to be any proof that the party intended to injure the other party.

ESSENTIAL ELEMENTS OF A CONTRACT

For an agreement to be a legally enforceable contract under common law systems, the agreement must fulfil six basic requirements:

- *An intention to create legal relations*: the parties must have intended for their agreement to be legally enforceable.
- *An agreement*: there must be a meeting of minds, which is often evinced by one party making an offer and the other party accepting it unconditionally. However, agreement may be reached without there ever being an offer that is accepted, as long as it is clear that both parties fully understand that they are to be bound by the terms of the contract and can at least be imputed to know what those terms are.
- *Consideration*: each party must support the agreement by 'giving something in exchange for something else', also known as a quid pro quo. It should be noted that a formal contract under seal (a 'deed') does not require consideration. As outlined previously, it is all about how the parties demonstrate their legal seriousness in relation to the deal.
- *Legal capacity of the parties*: the law restricts certain individuals from entering into some contracts, such as those of unsound mind and infants.
- *Genuine consent*: the courts have identified various 'vitiating factors' where agreement to enter a contract is not real or given freely, for example, duress or undue influence.
- *Lawfulness of the activity*: the object or purpose of the contract must be legal. Both the common law and statute may prohibit certain contracts.

An Intention to Create Legal Relations

An underlying feature of any contract is intention regardless of the legal system. Parties to a contract must have genuinely intended to enter into a legal relationship for any promises they had made to be legally enforceable. Normally an intention to create legal relations will be assumed from the circumstances governing the negotiation. For example, agreements classified as either social (between friends) or domestic (within families) are presumed not to intend legal relations in the common law system. The presumption is rebuttable, however, as are most presumptions in the common law.

Generally, a person will not be sued for breach of contract if he or she accepts an invitation to a dinner or social function and fails to attend. However, if the person was paid to attend the dinner – which might occur, for example, if the person is to deliver an after-dinner speech or presentation of some kind – then the circumstances have changed and by obligation (being paid) the person would need to attend. This would thus form a legal relationship. This presumption seems sensible and reasonable: just imagine if such a presumption did not exist – there would be thousands upon thousands of social and domestic cases entering into the courts based on legally enforceable obligations. Therefore, to determine whether there was an intention to create legal relations, the nature of the agreement needs to be examined.

However, in the nature of commercial relations, there is a strong presumption by the courts that the parties to an agreement had intended to enter into a legal relationship. Even if an agreement is made in the absence of words and is between friends or family members, if it is undertaken in the course of business dealings, then a legal relationship is formed. Again, the presumption is rebuttable in court if the party defending can prove to the satisfaction of the court that there was clearly no such intention.

The following common law case illustrates the extent to which the courts will 'presume' an intention of the parties to be legally bound in commercial negotiations.

***Edwards v Skyways Ltd* [1964] 1 WLR 349**

A pilot, Mr Edwards, who was employed by the company Skyways Ltd, was made redundant and so, as instructed, left the company. The company had informed Edwards that 'pilots declared redundant and leaving the company would be given an *ex gratia* payment equivalent to the company's contribution to the pension fund'. On 19 April 1962, the pilot informed the company he had decided to take the refund and the *ex gratia* payment. On 1 May, he accepted redundancy and the following day the company paid the pilot only the amount of his own contributions, the board rescinding its previous decision to make *ex gratia* payments to redundant aircrew. The counsel for the company argued that the agreement had no legal effect because there was no intention to enter into legal relations in respect of the promised payment. The company relied on the use of the phrase '*ex gratia*' to rebut the presumption that legal relations had been intended. The court rejected the respondent airline's argument and held that the airline was legally bound by the agreement.

In civil law systems, when a promise is made and the cause is a charitable intention, if sued by the other party, the courts will look at the personal relations of the parties involved (Mason 1941). There will be no significance in this area with regard to fraud, mistake or duress. Alternatively, if the promise is found to have the cause in an intention of commercial exchange, the court will look at whether fraud, mistake or duress occurred.

AGREEMENTS UNDER COMMON LAW SYSTEMS

Agreement

In order to create a legally binding agreement, there usually needs to be an offer and an acceptance of that offer. Once the offer is accepted unconditionally and there is *consensus ad idem* (a meeting of the minds), a contract is created. *Consensus ad idem* is an expression that means when two parties to an agreement have the same understanding as one another on the terms of that agreement. If there is not a *consensus ad idem*, the courts will state that a contract does not exist as there was not a sufficient agreement between all the parties involved.

To illustrate this principle by way of an example, in a situation where the parties are mistaken as to the subject matter of the contract, the courts will usually consider the contract void or invalid or even *void ab initio*. The contract may have never existed because of the deficiency of one of the elements, in this case confusion in the subject of the contract. The courts will therefore need to examine the documents and circumstances surrounding any agreement to determine the true intentions of the parties.

It should be kept in mind that in the common law, a donation is not recognized as a contract. The reason is that it is not classified as an exchange of items, but rather is considered a 'gift'. The very notion of it being a gift means the *donee* (the person who receives the gift) has no contractual right to demand anything from the *donor* (the person who gives the gift) as he or she has not themself given anything to the donor – there is no consideration.

Offer and Acceptance

As previously stated, an agreement is most often constituted by the valid acceptance of a valid offer. Agreement is the very essence of what a contract is all about. Basically, an offer in the legal context is defined as a statement of intent addressed by one party to another, stating certain terms and conditions to another party in which that other party will be bound if it accepts such terms. An agreement arises when an offer made by one party (the offeror) is accepted by the other (the offeree).

Common law systems on the other hand express an offer as one which incorporates a promise and a request for an act. However, common to both systems is the intention of the person making the offer to be contractually bound and that the offer is sufficiently complete to allow acceptance.

The law of contract has developed certain rules outlining whether or not a genuine offer exists. The following scenario illustrates the point.

> Offer: 'I will sell you my Cessna 172 for $25,000'.
> Acceptance: 'I will accept the offer of buying your Cessna 172 for $25,000'.

However, to form a contract, the acceptance must be unconditional. If the offeree puts conditions on acceptance, then what has actually occurred is that the offeree has made a *counter-offer*. A counter-offer is just that, an offer. It is *not* an acceptance. As such, if an offer is answered by a counter-offer, there is no concluded contract. A counter-offer is a new offer by the offeree to the original offeror. It has the effect of rejecting the original offer in common law systems. Only when both parties agree on the offer will a valid agreement be reached:

> Counter-offer: 'How about I buy your Cessna 172 for $20,000?'
> Acceptance of the counter-offer: 'OK, I will accept $20,000 for the aircraft. You drive a hard bargain!'

The rules of an offer can be stated as follows (Bartsch 2024: 158):

- An offer must be distinguished from an invitation to treat.
- An offer must be communicated to the party to whom it was intended, which could be composed of an individual, a group of individuals or the world at large.
- All the terms of the offer need to be known to the person accepting the offer.
- An offer will terminate if it is either rejected by the offeree, revoked (withdrawn) by the offeror, at any time specified for the offer to lapse or if any one of the parties dies (either the offeror or the offeree).

Invitation to Treat

The term 'invitation to treat' can be described as an invitation or willingness of one party to negotiate a contract. The person responding to the invitation can make an offer and the person who made the invitation can then decide to accept or reject the offer. When making the offer, a person must have clearly intended that, if accepted, the offer would be legally binding.

In common law, the case of *Pharmaceutical Society of Great Britain v Boots Cash Chemists (Southern) Ltd* was a landmark decision in recognition of changed retailing practices.

This case remains the leading authority in common law countries for the proposition that the mere display of goods on the shelves of a supermarket is an invitation to treat. The offer made is by the customer when the selected goods are presented to the cashier at the checkout counter. Interestingly, it developed because of changes in the retailing of goods in the UK at the time with the increase in 'self-service' shopping. It is a good example of where the law responded to the changing needs of society. In contract law, which is entrenched within the commercial sector of society, it is a most important and fundamental characteristic of the law that it responds to such societal changes and needs, otherwise the law, as Charles Dickens suggested, may become an 'ass'.

***Pharmaceutical Society of Great Britain v Boots Cash Chemists Ltd* [1953] 1 QB 401, Court of Appeal**

Boots Cash Chemists implemented a new method for customers to buy pharmaceuticals. The method included customers taking medication off the shelves of the chemist and then paying for these at the checkout point ('self-service') rather than purchasing them from behind the counter. The Pharmaceutical Society of Great Britain argued that the display of goods (pharmaceuticals) was considered an 'offer' and when a customer selected and put an item into his or her shopping basket/trolley, this implied 'acceptance'. The Pharmaceutical Society argued that according to the Pharmacy and Poisons Act 1933, it was an unlawful practice to sell certain drugs unless there was supervision by a registered pharmacist at the point where 'the sale is affected'. Due to there being insufficient supervision, it was argued by the Pharmaceutical Society that Boots Cash Chemist was in breach of the Act. However, Boots argued that the display of goods was not an offer but merely an 'invitation to treat'. It followed that placing items into a trolley or basket was an offer made by the customer to buy the goods and could either be rejected or accepted by the cashier. The sale is therefore 'affected' at the checkout point, which had a supervising pharmacist, and thus there was no breach of the Act. The court held that the sale takes place at the checkout point and therefore Boots had not committed an offence.

Consider a further example on the topic. A shirt in a store window would be classified as an invitation to treat in common law systems. The reason for it being classified as an 'invitation' is that anyone can make an offer to the shopkeeper and negotiate the price; the offer is not necessarily the amount on the price tag (although someone offering a price less than that displayed on the price tag is likely to get very short shrift from a salesperson). If a person takes the shirt to the counter to purchase, he or she is making an offer to purchase that piece of clothing. The seller (shopkeeper) is entitled to accept or reject the price offered by the buyer (customer), as acceptance has not taken place and therefore no contract has formed. However, when payment is made, this action implies that acceptance of the offer has been made and it is too late for the seller to alter the price.

Advertisements

Advertisements, price lists, circulars and catalogues that promote the availability of goods and services are also viewed as invitations to treat rather than offers in the common law system. They are usually seen as statements indicating the availability for sale or supply of certain things. By definition, supplying information in response to an inquiry is not an offer. Similarly, an advertisement for a vacant position is also an example of an invitation to treat. This is because the person who responds to the advertisement makes the offer. The person advertising for an employee is then free to either accept or reject that offer.

Not all advertisements, however, are considered to be invitations to treat. In order to distinguish between an offer and an invitation to treat, the courts will need to look at the facts of each particular case to determine the intentions of the parties. The case of *Carlill v Carbolic Smoke Ball Co*, an old English case, illustrates this point.

Carlill v Carbolic Smoke Ball Co **[1893] 1 QB 256, Queen's Bench Division**

The defendant was a manufacturer of smoke balls who placed an advertisement promoting its product in certain newspapers. It claimed that inhalation of 'medicated' powder in the smoke would prevent the user from catching influenza and other respiratory illnesses. To back its rather extravagant claims, the defendant offered £100 to anyone who caught influenza after using the smoke balls in the manner directed. Further, the advertisement went on to say that £1,000 had been deposited in a London bank, 'shewing our sincerity in the matter'. Relying on the advertisement, Mrs Carlill bought the smoke balls and used them in accordance with the instructions. Several weeks later she contracted influenza and subsequently claimed the £100. The defendant refused to pay, so Mrs Carlill sued the company for breach of contract and succeeded.

The type of offer made by the smoke ball company is referred to as a unilateral offer and results in a unilateral contract. You will recall that a unilateral contract is one involving the exchange of a promise for an act, whereby the contract is formed upon the first party's performance of the terms of the contract, leaving only one party to perform after the contract is formed.

In the result, this case is perhaps the exception that proves the rule. It is a case that shows how to rebut the presumption that an advertisement is an invitation to treat – in this case, the advertisement was held to be an *offer*. What impressed the Court of Appeal about this particular advertisement was that its terms seemed to evince an intention on the part of the company that this was no ordinary advertisement. The claim to have deposited £1,000 in the bank, and thus 'shewing our sincerity in the matter', was taken to raise the advertisement beyond the level of the 'mere puff' in which most advertisers engage and into the level of the 'offer to the world'. Mrs Carlill, by obtaining (she purchased it from the company, but it could be argued that she could have obtained it in any other way, even by theft) the so-called Carbolic Smoke Ball and using it as directed, fulfilled the terms of the contract and presented her claim to the company for payment of the £100. The court held this act to be the acceptance of the contractual terms, and so the contract was validly formed – and the company breached it when it refused to pay.

Advertisements in the electronic media, such as television and the Internet, are treated similarly in the common law system. The following is a case of just such a 'mere puff' that is typical of modern advertising and was rightly held to be such.

***Leonard v Pepsico Inc*, 210 F 3d 88 (2nd Cir 2000), United States Court of Appeals, Second Circuit**

Pepsi advertised on television a new promotion whereby 'Pepsi Points' could be collected by purchasing Pepsi products or bought for 10 cents each. The advertisement showed a range of redeemable products including sunglasses, T-shirts and caps. It showed a school student wearing these products and then arriving at school in a Harrier Jump Jet under which appeared the banner 'Harrier Fighter 7,000,000 Pepsi Points'. The plaintiff acquired the 7 million points and claimed the jet. Pepsico refused to deliver a jet (probably because it didn't have one) and the plaintiff sued. The court found that the jet was clearly intended to inject humour into the advertisement and that no reasonable person would believe that such an exaggerated and far-fetched statement would be considered binding on the party.

It should, of course, be noted that in the foregoing case, the advertisement was held not even to be an invitation to treat – it was a humorous statement that was intended only to be funny and to attract attention in the manner that good advertising should. Indeed, it was a fantastic commercial because it engendered the attention of the audience. This case has also been the subject of a 2022 Netflix docuseries detailing the story of John Leonard and how he set about trying to 'claim' his Harrier jet. However, this advertisement is not an invitation to treat because, it is submitted, an invitation to treat must involve at least an intention to entertain or consider offers, even if not automatically to accept them. The reasoning of the Second Circuit seems to bear this out, calling the advertisement exaggerated and far-fetched, implying that Pepsico really did not mean to indicate that it would even accept offers to 'purchase' a Harrier Fighter for 7 million 'Pepsi Points'.

Auctions

An auctioneer's call for bids is also classified as an invitation to treat under common law. Basically, an offer is made when any of the bidders make a bid. An agreement is formed if, and only if, the auctioneer accepts a particular bid, usually confirmed with the falling of the hammer, which concludes the auction of that item.

***Peter Smythe v Vincent Thomas* [2007] NSWSC 844, Supreme Court of New South Wales, Australia**

The defendant was an Australian aviation enthusiast and a registered user of the online auction site eBay. He listed his vintage Wirraway aircraft VH-WIR on eBay with a 'minimum bid' of $150,000 for a period of ten days. Prior acknowledgement and acceptance by all participants of the auction house's terms and conditions was required. One of the conditions stated that the seller must sell the goods for the minimum specified amount if a bid of that amount or greater was received. The plaintiff made a bid of $150,000 within the prescribed period and in accordance with eBay rules. He was deemed the successful bidder and received an email from eBay to that effect. The defendant refused to sell the aircraft to the plaintiff, claiming that he had a telephone conversation with him stating that he would not accept any offer less than $220,000 and that an inspection must be carried out prior to making the offer. The court found that the telephone conversation between the parties did not constitute a contract of sale and therefore held that there was a binding contract between the parties that should be specifically enforced.

Tenders

Similar to an auction, the tendering process is also normally an invitation to treat in common law systems. Tenders are most commonly used in government and commercial contracts. A call for a tender is generally not considered an offer. Basically, a call for tender is a structured invitation to suppliers for the supply of goods and services. The tenderer in calling for tenders seeks expressions of interest from parties to buy or sell an item, or to provide a service for a nominated price. The person calling the tender then has the authority to reject any tender and is not obliged to accept the separate offers provided in response to the tender.

Communication of the Offer

An essential component of acceptance is that it is given in response to an offer. The offer must be communicated to the offeree, that is, the person or class of persons to whom the offer was made. The offering of a reward is a further example of an offer made to an unspecified class of persons. Without communication, there can be no 'meeting of the minds', because the offeree cannot know the terms of the offer and therefore agreement cannot follow.

Notification of the Terms of the Offer

For there to be agreement between the parties, it is necessary for both parties to be aware of any term upon which the offer is conditional. This rule has been relied upon in a number of so-called ticket cases. This will be explained in detail in Chapter 9.

Termination of an Offer

An offer can be terminated in a number of ways. These include (Terry and Giugni 2009):

- the time specified lapsing or if not specified after a reasonable time;
- failure of a condition in the offer;
- rejection by the offeree (the person who has been offered) or the making of a counter-offer;
- revocation by the offeror either verbally or in writing (the person who makes the offer); and
- the death of the offeree or offeror.

In common law, an offer can always be revoked or varied at any time prior to acceptance. This will even apply to those businesses specifically stating that a contract is irrevocable (permanent). This is because before acceptance no consideration is given, signifying that nothing has been promised between the parties, and as acceptance has not taken place, it is not yet a legally enforceable contract.

Acceptance

Acceptance of an offer completes the agreement and, provided that all essential elements of a contract are satisfied, it will also complete the contract. An essential element of acceptance is that it provides consent of the offer and a promise to perform the acts required by the offer. Acceptance of an offer will either be expressed or implied. Express acceptance occurs when the offeree directly agrees to the offeror's terms. Implied acceptance, on the other hand, is inferred from an examination of the conduct of the parties.

In common law systems, performing the requested act (consideration) is the only element that can transform an offer into a contract.

As with an offer, there are a number of rules that the courts have developed for determining if an acceptance establishes an agreement.

Acceptance must be:

- made in reliance of an offer;
- communicated to the offeror by the offeree unless this rule is not required under the specified contract;
- unconditional; and
- affected in the manner stipulated in the offer.

Acceptance Made in Reliance of the Offer A person needs to be aware of an offer in order to accept it. Acceptance usually occurs when someone acts on something; however, the doing of an act does not always correspond with acceptance. For example, if Wayne finds Tracey's dog Fifi and returns her to Tracey without having any knowledge of a reward, this means there was no knowledge of the offer. Therefore, the act of returning the dog does not amount to acceptance (and thus Wayne is not entitled to the reward) as the act was not a result of the offer, even if there was an 'offer to the world' in the form of signage specifying a reward for Fifi's safe return.

Communication of Acceptance The offeree must communicate acceptance of the offer to the offeror. The confirmation to anybody other than the offeror is classified as insufficient acceptance. The action of silence also does not amount to acceptance; however, this will depend on the circumstances surrounding the offer. As a general rule, though, silence does not constitute acceptance. Consider a case of the sale of a car. Even if the seller says to the prospective buyer 'the price is $40,000, and if I don't hear from you by Friday, I'll assume you don't want the car', the buyer cannot complain if he remained silent and the seller then sold the car to someone else on Sunday – he had not accepted the seller's offer.

Acceptance Must be Unconditional As agreement requires a meeting of minds, acceptance must be absolute and unconditional. Conditional acceptance is not considered an effective form of acceptance as it can easily be altered and is not 'set in cement'. This is considered universal in both common law and civil law systems.

A conditional acceptance constitutes a counter-offer in common law systems, which the law considers to be a new offer altogether. Once a counter-offer is made, the original offer is deemed to have been rejected and can therefore not be revived by any subsequent acceptance. French law, however, differs in the idea of a counter-offer (Dickson 1994). There must be an agreement in the essential terms of the contract in order to form a contract on the basis of the 'wills' of the parties.

It is important, however, to appreciate that 'agreement' is the essence of all contracts and as such the courts in the common law systems will always look at the subjective intention of the parties at that time. The following common law case relating to an international airline illustrates this point.

***Baulderstone Hornibrook Pty Ltd v Qantas Airways Ltd* [2003] FCA 174, Federal Court of Australia**

Qantas Airways (the respondent) planned to extend Domestic Terminal 3 at Melbourne International Airport. Tenders were called to undertake the work. Baulderstone Hornibrook (the applicant) was subsequently notified by a 'Letter of Acceptance' that it had been selected as the successful tenderer. Ten days later, the written contracts were signed and exchanged. The work on the terminal was commenced but, due to a variety of factors, was excessively delayed beyond the dates listed in the contract documents. A dispute arose and the applicant sued for breach of contract for delay and disruption. The date that the parties were bound in contract was critical because information about an issue that caused significant delays came to the attention of the applicant after receiving the 'Letter of Acceptance' but before the contract was signed. The applicant argued that the contract came into existence upon receipt of the 'Letter of Acceptance' and both parties were bound by the terms as they existed at that time. The respondent argued that negotiations over 'crucial matters', including the issue that caused delays in construction, were taking place during the ten-day period and the terms were not agreed to, and the parties were not bound until the contract was signed. The court held that the contract came into existence at the earlier date, that is, at the date the 'Letter of Acceptance' was received by the applicant. It analysed the intentions of the parties and found that despite ongoing negotiations over some terms, when examined in the context of the contract as a whole, the parties clearly intended to be bound from the time the 'Letter of Acceptance' was received prior to the signing of the contract.

Withdrawal From Negotiations and Letters of Intent

Acceptance Must be Affected in the Manner Stipulated in the Offer If there is no specified method of acceptance, the general rule is that acceptance is not complete until received by the offeror in both common law and civil law systems. Communication of acceptance can be in writing or in the form of a face-to-face conversation or on the telephone between the two parties.

An exception to this rule is an acceptance of an offer by post. In common law systems, the *postal acceptance rule* states that acceptance becomes effective at the time of posting a letter accepting the offer. This rule is also extended to telegram submissions at a post office, but does not apply to 'instantaneous' modes of communication (for example, telephone, facsimile or telex). In these instant message cases, the general rule is that acceptance occurs at the time the offeror receives the communication. The common law position with respect to email is still unclear, but it is submitted that the rule of 'instantaneous' communications would apply to email as well as the other forms of electronic transmission. Withdrawal of an offer by post will not be complete until it reaches the offeree.

Silence Does Not Constitute Acceptance Common law systems both regard the action of silence as non-acceptance. This is not a definitive rule, however, and it will often depend on the individual case. The leading English case is *Felthouse v Bindley* (1862) 142 ER 1037. In that case, a man decided to purchase a horse from his nephew. After a series of letters were written, the nephew stopped responding. His uncle wrote, 'If I hear no more, I consider the horse mine at 30 pounds'. The nephew did not reply, and the Court ruled that it was unfair to impose this sale on the nephew. His silence did not amount to acceptance. On the other hand, silence will be enough to constitute acceptance. In some circumstances, the subsequent conduct of another party will be indicative of their willingness to be bound.

AGREEMENTS UNDER CIVIL LAW SYSTEMS

Agreements under civil law systems have similar elements to agreements under common law systems, but there are important differences. Practitioners must be aware that international contracts between civil and common law countries will not all the time have the same legal principles applying to them.

For a start, there are differences in what constitutes a contract under the civil law system. For example, a donation under French law is deemed a contract as there has been a 'meeting of the minds' between parties on what is to be exchanged been the parties (Marsh 1994: 41). In English law, as explained previously, a donation is not recognized as a contract. In civil law, there is a legal *causa* that a court will recognize from the intention to be generous to the other party. The notion of *causa* will be explained in detail later in this chapter.

Offer and Acceptance

An offer in civil law systems is conveyed as the willingness to contract according to a set of terms. It is not an offer as one which incorporates a promise and a request for an act. The offer and acceptance process is practically performed in the usual way of purchasing and selling, and counter-offers can be made to reject the original offer. For counter-offers, however, it will depend on the facts of the case and the intention of the offeree. Unlike common law, counter-offers in civil law do not automatically terminate the original offer. Rather, this is decided upon after examining the expressed intentions of the parties concerned in each particular case.

Invitation to Treat

'Invitations to treat' as established in the *Pharmaceutical Society* case does not apply in civil law systems. For instance, in French law, the mere display of priced goods in a shop window, on supermarket shelves or in catalogues can be treated as an offer rather than an invitation to treat provided the item and price are clearly stated (Weill and Terré 1986). However, this may depend on the intentions of the parties and the circumstances surrounding that agreement. The French courts have not established any firm legal rules governing these situations. Therefore, when purchasing goods from a French online catalogue, one should review the terms and conditions carefully that relate to what constitutes a sale.

When items in a shop window are considered or are displayed in a catalogue, this is considered a sign of a continuing intention of the seller to sell the items concerned and the intention to purchase (buyer's acceptance) is when the buyer places an order or action that implies intention to purchase. As with all contracts, the courts will look at the facts of the case and determine the intentions of each party.

In the case of a person buying items from a supermarket, a contract is made when the customer places the item marked with a fixed price in his or her basket (implying acceptance) before he or she reaches the checkout. This indicates that the contract is formed from the moment the buyer indicates (placement of item in basket) that he or she would like to purchase the item. Therefore, when injuries occur to a shopper from the items in his or her basket, the store would be held liable to the shopper in damages for breach of contract under Article 1147 of the *Code Civil*. The following case illustrates such a point.

***Soc. des Eaux de Vittel v Dehen Soc. Supermag Rennes GP* [1962] I 135**

Lady Dehen was shopping at a 'self-service' store of the company Rennes Supermag and purchased, among other things, a bottle of beer and a bottle of 'Vittel – delight'. The bottle of 'Vittel – delight' was felt to be abnormally warm by Dehen; however, she purchased the bottle anyway. She took her purchases to the checkout to pay for them and, as she was waiting for the bill to be printed, packed her shopping bags. As she packed the 'Vittel – delight', it coincidently knocked against other groceries, which made the bottle explode, injuring her right eye. She sued Supermag and the manufacturer on the basis of Articles 1382, 1383, 1384 (the tort provisions) and 1147 (breach of contract) of the *Code Civil*. The court found that due to improper storage of the bottle (being close to a source of heat) and causing the bottle to be 'abnormally warm', the store was held to be liable to Dehen in damages for breach of contract under Article 1147 of the *Code Civil*. Although the claim was made under Articles 1382, 1383 and 1384 of the *Code*, which cover delictual responsibility (torts), it was rejected because the store was held liable for breach of contract.

Advertisements

In civil law systems, activities such as advertisements, price lists, circulars and catalogues would be considered offers capable of acceptance provided that the item and price were clearly stated (Weill and Terré 1986). However, such a general rule will not always apply in countries that are governed by a civil law system. Germany's law, for example, is closer to English law (a common law system) with regard to the distinction between an offer and an invitation to treat. The activities mentioned in the common law section on advertisements are considered to be invitations to treat rather than offers in themselves (Marsh 1994: 41–3). An offer that is qualified as *freibleibend* or 'without engagement' is an offer which is not binding and is more the equivalent of an invitation to treat.

Termination of an Offer

Offers can be terminated in numerous ways, but there are important differences in civil law systems. In civil law, an offer has binding character and cannot be revoked (cancelled) after being given (Pejovic 2001). The offeree is bound by the terms of the offer for the period specified or, if not specified, for a reasonable period established by the courts. Being bound by the terms of the offer will also depend on the content of the offer. If the offer is not accepted, it will be considered revoked, or if it was not accepted in the specified period, it will also be revoked. However, it needs to be noted that a legally enforced contract be revoked or amended if there is a mutual consent between all parties involved.

There is an exception to the binding of offers under German law. When the offeror has qualified his or her offer as *freibleibend,* it is much the same as an invitation to treat and basically means 'without engagement' (Marsh 1994: 41–3). An offer classified as *freibleibend* is an offer that is not binding by law.

***Chastan v Isler*, Cass. civ., 17 December 1958**

In this case, a period during which the offer would not be revoked was implied. The seller of a chalet was aware that the proposed purchaser was intending to visit him on 15 or 16 of August and could not therefore revoke his offer to sell before this time.

The legal principle in this case is that an offer is revocable as long as it is not accepted, but it must be kept open for any period stated in it or, if no period is stated, for a reasonable period.

If an offer is not accepted within a reasonable time, it will lapse. What is considered reasonable will depend upon the nature and circumstances surrounding a particular offer. It should be noted that stating the time period in an offer is quite beneficial in circumstances when an offer lapses rather than waiting for what the courts hold to be 'a reasonable time'.

Acceptance

Acceptance in civil law systems is the element that provides evidence that the other party has agreed to the terms proposed and thus leads to the formation of a contract. As with common law, a person needs to be aware of an offer in order to accept it and the offeree must communicate acceptance of the offer.

There can, however, be certain requirements that need to be met for acceptance to be effective. For example, in German law, acceptance will only be in effect when it is communicated to the offeror and acceptance comes within the 'zone of control' of the recipient, which could, for example, be during working hours at their business address. In French law, only agreement as to the essential terms is needed for acceptance to be made. With regard to other terms, which are referred to as *accessoires* (accessories), there will be an obligation on all parties to seek to reach agreement on these. If they are not able to reach an agreement on these terms, they will be governed by *les dispositions legislatives supplétives* or by general trade customs under Article 1135 of the *Code Civil* (Marsh 1994: 43). If, however, the term is essential to either party, the contract will not be formed and it will be at the discretion of the judge as to whether the essential term is normally regarded as an *accessoire.*

Agreements must also be unconditional, i.e. acceptance must be absolute and with no strings attached. If there is a conditional acceptance, it will be considered a counter-offer. French law, however, requires that there is an agreement in the essential terms of a contract in order to form a contract on the basis of the 'wills' of the parties.

Withdrawals from Negotiations and Letters of Intent

Pre-contractual agreements made in negotiations and letters of intent have a degree of legal value in civil law systems. Legal value in this context means the usefulness of a document as legal proof of a business transaction.

As countries around the world have differing legal systems, there are as a result differing legal consequences when undertaking negotiations. When establishing international contracts, it is important to realize that a letter of intent will not necessarily have the same legality in the country the party is undertaking negotiations with. Each party needs to be aware of the risks associated with pre-contractual agreements and legal documentation when undertaking international business dealings.

Under French law, there can be obligations relating to both the conduct of negotiations and the progression of the negotiation (for example, in the advanced stages of negotiation). The conduct of negotiations can be classified under delictual liability (Article 1382 of the *Code Civil*) when fault arises from one party. Article 1382 states that anyone who causes damage to another person is obliged to compensate that person. This liability arises from the fault (bad faith or lack of good faith) of one of the parties without the need for any evidence that there was intention to cause harm or injury to the other party.

The fault may consist of the following:

- Abruptly breaking off negotiations when in an advanced stage without any sufficient reason to explain why. This becomes quite significant when a large expense is incurred from the negotiation and there is the expectation of concluding such an agreement.
- Conducting negotiations with separate parties (two or more companies) but concealing from each party that other negotiations were taking place at the same time. The fault does not lie in conducting negotiations with more than one party but in the concealment of it, as parties are led to believe that there is a greater degree of certainty that they could obtain such a contract.

The damages recoverable from these 'faults' would include the loss of time and the expenses incurred from the negotiation, including those that were incurred in preparing to execute the contract. The damage costs recovered are arguable and will usually be decided upon by the *juge de fond* (judge).

The preceding 'faults' would not be considered under common law to have any legal effects. Although these faults would be viewed as unethical under common law, this does not provide sufficient grounds to commence legal action against another party. In addition, broken promises under the common law system will not be actionable under tort law, but could be under contract law provided the contract has all the essential elements.

Letters of intent are used widely in both the common law and civil law systems; however, there is a major difference in the legal implications of these documents in each system. In common law systems such as England, contracts can only be established in the terms agreed upon by the parties. On the other hand, when a letter of intent is issued following a significant progression in negotiations, French law may treat such a document as an *accord de principle* (agreement in principle). In such a situation there is an obligation to conclude the negotiations in good faith and this will be considered to be contractual.

The effect of an *accord de principle* is that parties cannot go back on their word with what has already been agreed upon and they must maintain good faith in all matters when negotiating. The intention of the letter of intent is to be contractually binding by forming an obligation to undertake the negotiation in good faith and having the other party accept such a contract. If the intention is not for the letter to be legally binding, some form of an expression stating clearly that it is not binding needs to be provided on the letter. An expression such as *bon pour lettre d'intention seulement sans être contractuel* (translating to 'subject to contract' in English) will suffice.

There is a slight difference between common and civil law as to when an offer is accepted by telephone. In the civil law system, the contract will be formed at the time when the acceptor notifies acceptance, whereas in common law, the contract will be formed at the time when the acceptee hears the acceptance. In international telephony, this can be two slightly different times.

There have been two differing views based on when contracts are formed by post in civil law. The two views are referred to as '*réception*' and '*expédition*' (Marsh 1994: 70). The theory of *réception* states that a contract is formed when the acceptance letter is received, whereas the theory of *expédition* states that a contract is formed when the acceptance letter is sent. Although both these theories were applied in French law, it seems that the *Cour de cassation* has decided in favour of the theory of *expédition*, although the final word will always rest with the *juges de fond* or judges. This rule also extends to contracts formed by fax – the contract would be formed upon the sending of the fax and the place where the contract was formed would be from where the fax originated. This is different from the common law position, which suggests that contracts would be considered to form at the time the acceptance was received and at the place where acceptance is received.

As with common law, generally, silence does not constitute acceptance. It is not a definite rule, but an exception can be found to this in German law in respect of commercial letters of confirmation (*kaufmannische Bestätigungsschreiben*) in contracts between businesspeople (Marsh 1994: 73). Such a letter states the expressed and implied content of the negotiations that preceded the conclusion of the contract. It makes sense that the letter would be issued after the negotiations are completed due to its content. The principle of 'consent by silence' when faced with the letter will apply even on the first time the other party has seen it, with the exception of the letter containing new or altered clauses.

Offers Made Solely in the Interests of the Offeree One exception to the general rule of silence is when offers made are only in the interest of the other party. This exception was established by a case in which a motorcyclist had an accident on his motorcycle that caught fire and left him injured and unable to move. A garage mechanic saw this scene, immediately provided assistance and was consequently burnt in doing so. The French *Cour d'appel* held that there was a contract of assistance (known as 'contract of help' or *convention d'assistance*) and that the motorcyclist was subsequently liable to the mechanic in damages for providing assistance.

CONSIDERATION

The Element of Consideration

Consideration can be defined as something done or promised by one party in exchange for something done or promised by the other party. The essence of consideration is said to be the benefit to the promisor or detriment to the promisee. In common law systems, a contract has no binding effect unless supported by consideration or made under seal. Since the sixteenth century, the law of contract in common law countries has required the element of consideration. Normally consideration takes the form of a mutual exchange of promises between the parties to a contract.

A gratuitous promise is unenforceable by the common law system as there is a complete absence of consideration on the part of the other party. A gratuitous promise is one in which there is a promise to do something without seeking any return. The promise has acquired no contractual rights. If, however, the same promise is made under a seal, it is binding because the formality of the deed implies the seriousness of the transaction and arguably is no longer gratuitous.

The common law system has developed certain rules that apply to the doctrine of consideration. They are:

- past consideration is no consideration;
- consideration need not be adequate;
- consideration must be sufficient;
- consideration must move from the promise but need not move to the promisor; and
- application of the doctrine of promissory estoppel.

Past Consideration is no Consideration

Consideration may be executed or executory, but cannot be past. Executed consideration is where an act has been performed in return for a promise. A person responding to a reward gives (executed) consideration. Executory consideration is the norm and refers to the situation in which a promise is given in response to another's promise. Consideration must be bargained for and form part of the contract. Promises made after the event or made independently of the contract in question cannot be consideration. The rule that 'past consideration is no consideration' was the principle developed in the following old English case.

Roscorla v Thomas **(1842) 3 QB 234; (1842) 114 ER 496, Court of Queen's Bench**

Roscorla bought a horse from Thomas and after the sale Thomas promised that the horse was sound and free of vice. The horse was in fact extremely vicious. Roscorla sued Thomas for breach of warranty (promise). The action failed because Thomas' promise was made after the sale and did not form part of the contract. Roscorla had given no consideration except the past consideration of the sale.

Consideration Need Not be Adequate

The common law system is not concerned with what each of the parties to an agreement has given or promised. The very nature of a contract is that it allows the contracting parties the freedom to make any agreement they choose, provided it is not illegal. Traditionally, the role of the courts was simply to interpret the contract and not to rewrite it according to their own standards or notions of fairness. This common law rule allows consideration to be nominal or trivial, just so long as it represents something of value. The term 'peppercorn rental' refers to the lease of premises for the amount of one peppercorn per year (in modern times, often actually a nominal amount of money, such as $1 per year) – a totally insignificant amount but still sufficient to constitute good consideration at law.

Consideration Must be Sufficient

Sufficiency of consideration refers to the giving of something of legal value. For example, consideration that is illegal (such as a criminal act) or contrary to public policy would not be sufficient consideration. The question of whether consideration is sufficient often arises when that which is given appears to be of value but is quite often illusory. Examples of insufficient consideration include the performance of a pre-existing duty, whether a public duty imposed by law or the performance of a duty already imposed by contract. For instance, in respect of the performance of a public duty, a safety inspector with a NAA may be under a duty to provide for the safety of air navigation, but this duty is normally limited to times when that officer is 'on duty'. When the safety inspector is 'on duty', the safety inspector cannot use the duty to provide for the safety of air navigation as consideration in any contract (other than the contract of employment the safety inspector must have with the NAA, of course).

Consideration Must Move from the Promisee but Need Not Move to the Promisor

The promise of the promisor will remain unenforceable if not supported by an exchanged promise (consideration) on the part of the promisee. The promisee must provide the consideration agreed to with the promisor. However, consideration may move to a third party rather than to the promisor. A situation in which this rule has been applied is where there are more than two parties involved.

Consider, for example, Maria promises Frances to pay Delphine $50. This contract is legally enforceable as between Maria and Frances, despite the fact that the benefit of the payment goes to Delphine. As an aside, however, it should be noted that Delphine has no rights to enforce this contract because she is not a party. The doctrine of *privity* of contract effectively prevents stipulations in favour of third parties being enforced by those third parties (but note that such stipulations can still be enforced by the parties to the contract). According to this doctrine, a contract cannot impose obligations on, or give rights to, anyone other than the contracting parties: only a person who is a party to a contract can sue on it. Present legislation in some jurisdictions has modified the strictness of this common law rule to allow, in certain instances, a third party beneficiary to enforce a contract even though that person is not a party to the contract.

Privity works slightly differently in civil law. Parties to a contract may agree that contractual rights can be transferred to a third party. For example, in the German Civil Code, 'a contract may stipulate performance for the benefit of a third party, so that the third party acquires the right directly to demand performance'. This right, however, cannot be imposed upon the third party.

The Doctrine of Promissory Estoppel

In common law systems, the doctrine of promissory estoppel allows a party to enforce a promise even though the element of consideration is not present. It is basically a principle that prevents a party from reneging on its original promise. For example, if a landlord states that his tenant does not need to pay rent for a certain period, the landlord would be 'estopped' from denying that he made such a statement if he sues the tenant claiming rents for that period. The doctrine of promissory estoppel essentially evolved to overcome the problems related to the element of consideration.

Common law estoppel works as a rule of evidence. It prevents a party to a legal case (Party A) from admitting evidence denying the truth of a representation that party made in certain circumstances. To succeed, the other party (Party B) must satisfy the following elements:

- Party A made a statement of past or present fact;
- Party B relied on that statement;
- as a result of that reliance, Party B suffered detriment (that is, Party B has suffered from 'detrimental reliance'); and
- Party A's act of making the original statement was unconscionable.

Normally, estoppel may only be used as a defence – in normal circumstances, it cannot be used to commence an action. It is thus said that estoppel is a 'shield', not a 'sword'. However, in cases involving severe unconscionability, estoppel may be used as a 'sword' and may even relate to statements to the future. This latter form is known as *promissory estoppel.*

CAUSE OR *CAUSA*

The Notion of 'Causa'

In civil law systems, a contract cannot exist without a lawful cause or *causa,* a term that originated from Roman law. Basically *causa* can be defined as a comprehensive term for any proceeding in a court of law whereby an individual seeks a legal remedy.

In civil systems, cause is the reason why a party enters a contract and performs contractual obligations. The main difference between lawful cause and consideration is the circumstances at which the party is bound. Parties can be bound without needing to obtain something in return; exchange does not need to take place for a contract to be established (Pejovic 2001: 42). For example, gratuitous contracts will be enforced under civil law systems, whereas this is not the case in common law systems.

It should be noted that there is a double meaning of the term 'cause': a cause can be internal or external. The principle of internal cause seeks to answer why one party legally commits itself to a contract with another party. On the other hand, the principle of external cause looks at the overriding motive that triggers the legal commitment of either party.

Absence of Causa–Les Contrats à Titre Onéreux *and* Synallagmatiques Commutatifs

The notion of cause needs to be found as the immediate objective (*le but immédiat*) so that it is present in the action of the other party to execute the obligation required to be performed under the contract. For example, in a contract of sale, the cause for the buyer is the duty performed by the seller to deliver the goods and transfer the item in exchange for payment. However, when there is an absence of cause, the contract needs to be examined as to whether or not there exists any genuine and serious counterpart obligation, which is looked at objectively by the courts. To put it another way, the court is not interested in the parties' personal motives or whether the obligations are even; it is concerned as to whether there is a sufficient *objet* (object) and consequently a sufficient cause (Marsh 1994: 73).

Absence of Cause Post-Contract

In civil law systems, if there is a valid cause when a contract has formed, it follows that there are no grounds to seek declaration that the contract is void for lack of cause even if one of the parties fails to perform its obligation. This notion is stated in Article 1131 of the *Code Civil*.

Contracts for Payment in Respect of an Existing Obligation

If a promise is made in the belief that a certain obligation would be fulfilled and no such obligation existed, it is considered void for *fausse cause*. *Fausse* in this context is defined as a cause that is non-existent and the contract was agreed upon in the mistaken belief that a certain obligation would be undertaken. This is referred to as the doctrine of *erreur sur la cause*.

Illicit Cause

As mentioned in the preceding discussion on the validity of contracts, when a contract is established and the cause is of an illegal or immoral motive, the contract will be deemed void and consequently unenforceable by law. In some civil law courts such as the French *Cour de cassation*, it has also been decided that a contract can only be void if the illicit or immoral purpose was agreed upon by both parties. This makes sense because if one of the parties involved did not know that the motive of the other party was illicit or immoral, it would appear unjust if the innocent were not protected under law.

Unjust Enrichment

Under the German Civil Code (*Burgliches Gesetzbuch*) in paragraph 818, there is a provision that states that the obligation to return or to provide a benefit is excluded where the recipient is no longer enriched. This principle has been used by the courts to protect the recipient in circumstances where it has incurred losses financially from the transaction, at least up to the time that it has knowledge of the defect.

***Bundesgerichtshof 1971*, NJW 1971, 609, Seventh Civil Senate, Germany**

On 27 August 1968, the defendant, who was born on 5 September 1950, took a scheduled flight operated by the plaintiff from Munich to Hamburg, after having purchased a ticket for this flight. At Hamburg, he managed to join the transit passengers and to re-enter the plane for a flight to New York, without being in possession of a valid ticket for this part of the journey. He was refused entry to the USA because he did not have a visa. The plaintiff thereupon made the defendant sign a document according to which the defendant owed the plaintiff the sum of $256, issued the defendant with a ticket for the return journey and, on the same day, took the defendant back to Munich on a scheduled flight operated by the plaintiff. The defendant's mother as his statutory agent (the plaintiff was still a minor at the time) refused to grant consent to legal transactions concluded between the defendant and the plaintiff. The court held that the defendant had to pay the fixed flight rates for the journeys from Hamburg to New York as this was considered unjustified enrichment against the plaintiff.

Although this principle has not been adopted by English law, this law does recognize what is known as a defence of change of position where the plaintiff acted in good faith and it seems unjust that it has to provide a remedy for injuries suffered from the wrongful act (which is known as restitution). There are exceptions as some common law systems have adopted this doctrine. For example, the doctrine of unjust enrichment has been accepted in Canadian law. The case *Air Canada v Attorney General of British Columbia* (1989) 59 DLR 161 is authority in support of this principle.

Action De in Rem Verso

The *action de in rem verso* (unjust enrichment) in the French *Code Civil* is based on preventing a person instigating self-enrichment at the expense of another, in the same fashion as in the German Civil Code. This enrichment would occur when one person is enriched to the detriment of the other without having a legitimate 'cause' and the other party obtains no benefit.

LEGAL CAPACITY OF THE PARTIES

The validity of a contract may be affected by the legal capacity of one or both of the parties. There are several classes of persons who are restricted in their capacity to enter into a contract. A party that contracts with a person who does not have full legal capacity or is declared 'incapable' by law may render that contract either void or voidable, depending on the circumstances. The following classes of people are subject to varying degrees of incapacity with respect to entering into a contract in both the civil law and common law systems:

- minors;
- persons of unsound mind.

Civil law systems generally only have specifications regarding age and mental capabilities in the capacity to contract with another person. However, there are other classes of people subject to varying degrees of incapacity, which include:

- intoxicated persons;
- corporations;
- other grounds for legal incapacity.

Minors

Under the common law and civil law systems, minors are considered not to have the capacity of entering into any legal obligations. The main purpose for introducing legislation on this subject has been to protect the interests of minors. In both the common law and civil law systems, a contract can be voidable on the grounds of incapacity if a minor is involved. There are exceptions to this when the contract is made for the purpose of providing the minor with 'necessities', such as for his or her support or education, or a purpose related to his or her business activities. Other, non-necessary contracts with minors are *voidable* at the option of the minor – note that the other party to the contract, if over the age of majority, is bound by the contract unless and until the minor 'voids' it.

The age at which a person is considered an adult (sufficient legal capacity) is known as the *age of majority* and depends on local laws. The most common age is 18 years in many of the civil law systems including Germany (Section 2 of the German Civil Code (BGB)), France (Article 388 of the *Code Civil*), Italy (Article 2 of the *Codice Civile*) and the Netherlands (Article 1:234 of the Civil Code of the Netherlands (BW)). In common law jurisdictions, the age varies between 18 and 21 years, depending on the jurisdiction – once again, practitioners should check the local laws.

Persons of Unsound Mind

As agreement in both common law and civil law requires a 'meeting of the minds', it follows that a person suffering from a mental disorder is unable to provide this essential element. In Australian common law, the case of *Gibbons v Wright* (1954) 91 CLR 423 ruled that there was no 'fixed standard of sanity', but simply a requirement that each party be of 'such soundness of mind as to be capable of understanding the general nature of what he [or she] is doing by his [or her] participation'. This is generally the case in most common law countries.

Each civil law country has its own laws to that respect. In French law, adults protected within the meaning of Article 488 of the *Code Civil* are incapable of entering into a contract. These are adults that have 'impaired personal faculties' as stated in the *Code Civil*: see Article 488. Similarly, in German law, a person is incapable of contracting if 'in a state of pathological mental disturbance, which prevents the free exercise of will, unless the state by its nature is a temporary one': see Section 104 of the BGB.

For a person to plead insanity successfully in the common law system, the person must show that:

- the person did not understand the person's own actions as a result of the mental condition; and
- the other party was aware, or ought reasonably to have been aware, of that person's mental incapacity.

Intoxicated Persons

In common law, the law of contract treats people under the influence of alcohol and other drugs in much the same way as it does regarding people suffering from a mental disorder. It is for the person claiming intoxication at the time of agreement to satisfy the two points listed earlier. Arguably, however, the standard to which those elements must be shown is higher due to the self-inflicted nature of most intoxication – leaving 'drink spiking' to one side. In many situations, refusing to enforce a contract on the mere basis that a person was inebriated at the time that it was made would not be reasonable or convenient.

Corporations

A corporation is defined as a legal person and therefore has the ability to sue and be sued in its own name. Under common law, a corporation is one class that is subject to incapacity with respect to entering into contracts. Corporations have the capacity to enter contractual relations, but these arrangements are only binding on the company if those acting on behalf do so accordingly to the discretion of the company. A more full discussion of a corporation's ability to enter into contracts appears in Chapter 9.

Other Grounds for Legal Incapacity

If an adult under the *Code Civil* in French law compromises the fulfilment of his or her family obligations due to 'prodigality, insobriety or idleness', then he or she is categorized as a protected adult. This means that such an adult is incapable and thus protected from entering into a contract by law: see Article 488.

GENUINE CONSENT

There is no valid consent to the making of a contract if the consent was only given because of a mistake or misapprehension (*erreur*) or if the consent was exercised as a result of duress (*violence*) or if the contract was brought about by misrepresentation (*dol*) in both the civil and common law systems.

Misrepresentation

Misrepresentation occurs where the parties have agreed to be bound by the terms of an agreement but where one of them has relied upon a representation or undertaking that is false. For example, Fernando gives information to Krystyna whilst negotiating (a pre-contractual situation) with the intention of persuading her decision in favour of his own interests. If the situation is that Fernando is an expert in the field and Krystyna relies upon the information provided, Fernando owes a duty of care to Krystyna and consequently will be liable in damages for economic loss if it is found that the information is false and consequently had influenced Krystyna's decision.

In common law systems, if the representation made is knowingly false, or made without belief in its truth, or if the maker was reckless as to whether it was true or not, then it is *fraudulent misrepresentation*. If, however, the person making the representation believed it to be true, then it is *innocent misrepresentation*. A subset of innocent representation is where the representation made is false and was made without reasonable care or concern as to its accuracy. This is known as *negligent misrepresentation* and has developed from the tort of negligence with respect to negligent misstatement.

A similar principle applies in civil law systems. For example, in France, the term is '*dol*' and may consist of false representation or fraudulent misstatement. In the *Code Civil*, the term *dol* is a cause of nullity when the *manoeuvres* (tricks) of one party persuade the other party to enter into a contract that it would not have otherwise entered into. *Manoeuvres* can include the action of issuing false documents or giving false information with the intention of deceiving the other party (Marsh 1994: 96). This lack of consent does not include innocent misrepresentation.

Mistake

In common law systems, the courts are, in general, very reluctant to provide relief on the basis of a mistake. This may seem a harsh approach, but the reasoning is consistent with a principle of law applicable to contractual relations, *caveat emptor*, which means 'let the buyer beware'. However, if consumers dealing with corporations can prove that any representation has led to such misunderstanding, then such conduct will usually provide legal grounds in the associated legislation of that country.

The law of contract recognizes the following types of mistake:

- *common mistake*, where each party makes the same mistake;
- *mutual mistake*, where the parties are at cross-purposes; and
- *unilateral mistake*, where only one of the parties is mistaken.

In relation to the types of mistakes, the law of contract will only recognize mistakes of fact that relate to matters of vital importance. The mistake must relate to a *condition precedent* to the formation of the contract – that is, a term that, had it been known to exist at the time of contracting, the parties would not have agreed. This notion is also encompassed in civil law systems around the world, with Germany and France being two such examples explained in the following.

In German law, a party is allowed to retract its 'expression of will' (*Willenserklärung*) if a mistake has been made and this mistake was an essential element as to why it had contracted to start off with. The mistake needs to relate either to the expression or content of the *Willenserklärung* itself or the characteristics of a thing or person that are important in the business transaction.

Similarly, in French law, a contract can be void on the basis of a mistake, commonly referred to as *erreur* (French for 'mistake' or 'error'). Error or mistake is a cause of nullity of an agreement only when it touches the very substance of the thing that is its object. The mistake could be in the identity (for example, the nationality, age, marital status or even reputation) of the person if this element was one of the main causes of the agreement. Whether the party's mistake was essential for the contract will be left to the discretion of the judges (Marsh 1994: 96–101).

With regard to a work of art, the authenticity of the artwork by an artist will be seen as an essential element that could lead to a possible *erreur*. The following case illustrates this point.

***Epoux Saint-Arroman v Réunion des musées nationaux et autres*, Civ. Ler, 13 December 1983, Bull. Cil. No. 293 (the Poussin case), Cour de cassation**

A couple named Saint-Arroman owned a painting that family tradition attributed to the French seventeenth-century artist Nicolas Poussin. In 1968, they decided to sell the painting at an auction, and they contacted a famous Parisian auctioneer who had it evaluated by an expert. The expert concluded that the painting was, in fact, not by Poussin, but was rather a minor work of the Italian School of Carracci for which he gave an estimated price of 1,500 francs. The painting was therefore sold at auction as a Carracci for a price of 2,200 francs. With a view to acquiring the painting, the Louvre Museum exercised its right of per-emption afforded by the law to national museums in these circumstances. In the weeks following the sale, various articles were presented stating that the painting was in fact by Poussin and consequently in 1969 it was exhibited in the Louvre stating that it was by Poussin. The Saint-Arromans found out about this and were very upset with this situation. They decided to sue the Louvre Museum to revoke the contract of sale. The courts held that the Saint-Arromans could obtain annulment of the sale by auction on the grounds of the art being mistaken that it was definitely not a Poussin.

The *Cour de cassation* stated that the issue of importance was that the seller (the Saint-Arromans) sold their painting on the advice of the expert at the auction, who said that it was not a Poussin when in fact it might have been. Therefore, an *erreur* in French law can happen if the plaintiff's belief is questionable.

Duress

Duress is defined as a situation where a person enters into a contract because of actual or threatened violence or some other form of illegitimate pressure. This definition applies to both the common law and civil law systems; however, there is a slight variation in how it operates.

In common law, the English case of *Barton v Armstrong* [1976] AC 104 held that a contract may be ruled invalid on the grounds of duress if the use of illegitimate pressure was one of the causes for a party to enter into the agreement. If that pressure is established, the burden will then be on the person who applied the pressure to demonstrate that the pressure did not operate to cause the party to enter into the agreement.

In French law, by contrast, duress, which is known as *violence* in French law, is a cause for nullity of a contract both when it is 'exercised against the contracting party, but also applies when this action is performed against the spouse, descendants or ascendants of the contracting party' (Article 1113 of the *Code Civil*). To determine whether a person acted under *violence*, the judges look at whether a reasonable person in the same situation would have acted in the same manner: see Chapter 6.

Undue Influence

Undue influence occurs where one party (the dominant party) influences the will of the other party (the subservient party) to consent to the contract. In common law systems, undue influence does not require an act of violence but only the exertion of some power or influence by the other party such that the person's free will has been compromised. On the other hand, in civil law systems, violence is encompassed in 'undue pressure' (in contrast to 'undue influence' in common law systems) rather than 'duress', given the very wide scope that this principle has in the codes of civil law countries.

For the contract to fall into the category of undue pressure in civil law, there needs to first be a threat which causes the other party to fear a 'considerable and present harm' to a person or fortune (Article 1112 of the *Code Civil*). A threat could be bodily violence or a person's mental well-being (for example, threat of defamation) or even a threat to economic well-being.

Unconscionable Conduct

In common law systems, unconscionable conduct occurs when the dominant (stronger) party takes advantage of a 'special disability' of the subservient (weaker) party. The most commonly held 'disabilities' are drunkenness, poor literacy skills and low levels of education, and age-related deterioration in mental faculties.

Contracts may be declared void if it can be established, on the part of the person claiming the defence, that:

- the terms of the contract provide for harsh consequences; and
- there existed at the time of contracting an inequality of bargaining power.

The most likely remedy for unconscionability is that the contract is voidable and the contract will likely be set aside.

DISCHARGE OF A CONTRACT

A contract is said to have been *discharged* when the rights, obligations and responsibilities created by it come to an end.

Performance

The most common way in which a contract comes to an end is by performance by each of the parties of their respective obligations arising out of the contract. However, difficulties sometimes arise as to what constitutes actual performance.

Agreement

In the same way that parties are free to enter a contract, so too can the parties to a contract agree to terminate it. As long as both parties mutually agree to discharge the contract, no legal ramifications will apply.

Frustration

In common law systems, the *doctrine of frustration* operates so as to relieve the parties of their duty to perform when performance has either become impossible or totally impracticable without fault on either side. The effect of frustration is that the contract is considered terminated at the time of the frustrating event and no party is liable for damages.

In civil law systems, and of growing significance in the common law, is the principle of *force majeure*. *Force majeure* is approximately the equivalent of frustration in the Common Law. This principle translates to mean unforeseen and unexpected events outside the control of the parties, which make performance of the contract impossible. *Force majeure* in effect excludes liability of a party for non-performance of the contract. This principle in civil law operates independently of the party agreement. In other words, the party will not be liable in case of *force majeure* because, as highlighted previously, liability is based on fault.

However, in common law systems the principle of *force majeure* is not clearly defined, which means that parties to the contract need to specify those events in which *force majeure* will apply to exclude liability for non-performance. Civil law systems only apply the principle of *force majeure* when the unforeseen circumstances make the performance of the contract impossible.

Breach of a Condition

A breach occurs when one or more of the parties fail to comply with a contractual obligation, whether expressed or implied, in which case the innocent party is entitled to some form of relief. If it is a breach of a condition or a serious breach of a less important term (either a 'warranty' or an 'intermediate term'), the innocent party usually has the right to end the contract and/or seek damages or other remedies that may apply.

In the common law, when there has been a breach of contract, the plaintiff is entitled to damages as of right. This is the primary remedy in the common law for breach. However, in two specific situations, the plaintiff will also be entitled, if he so desires, to terminate the contract. If he does so elect, the termination will be in addition to the plaintiff's right to seek damages. The two situations in which a plaintiff may elect to terminate arise when there has been either a fundamental breach or when there has been repudiation. When either of these two situations occurs, the plaintiff may treat the contract as having been terminated. It is at the discretion of the plaintiff whether to do so, and he need not seek the permission of the court.

By way of contrast, in civil law, when a contract is terminated or 'resolved' as it is properly known, there are specific rules or codes that apply. For example, in French law the wording of Article 1184 indicates that it is possible, in principle, for a creditor to seek resolution in any circumstances where there has been a breach. Article 1184 reads as follows:

- A resolutive condition is always implied in *synallagmatic* contracts to provide for the case where one of the parties does not fulfil his undertaking.
- In this case the contract is not resolved by operation of law. The party in whose favour the undertaking has not been performed has the choice either of forcing the other to perform the agreement, where that is possible, or of claiming resolution with damages.
- Resolution must be claimed by action at law and further time for performance may be granted to the defendant depending on the circumstances.

Note in civil law systems, a 'synallagmatic' contract is simply a contract in which each party to the contract is bound to provide something to the other party.

It is worth briefly discussing the differences between a condition, intermediate term and warranty for the purposes of common law. The division of these three types of contractual provisions has been dubbed the 'tripartite classification system'.

Contractual terms in the common law are classified as conditions and warranties. Conditions are the most important terms, and their breach entitled the plaintiff to terminate the contract. Warranties were the less important terms, and their breach only entitled the plaintiff to sue for damages, while the contract itself remained ongoing. Conditions are those terms which are essential to the substance of a contract, or in other words they were 'essential' to the contract. Put more frankly, a person would not have entered into a contract without the expectation of performance of these conditions. The breach of a condition will give rise to a right to terminate a contract. Intermediate terms are broad terms that would create injustice if it was ruled either a condition or a warranty.

The test of essentiality is whether it appears from the general nature of the contract considered as a whole, or from some particular term or terms, that the promise is of such importance to the promisee that he would not have entered into the contract unless he had been assured of a strict or substantial performance of the promise, as the case may be, and that this ought to have been apparent to the promisor.' Diplock LJ explained the historical development of the distinction between conditions and warranties in the following case.

> ***Hong Kong Fir Shipping Co Ltd v Kawasaki Kisen Kaisha Ltd* [1962] 2 QB 26**
>
> Hong Kong Fir Shipping hired out one of its skips to Kawasaki Kisen Kaisha. The terms of the contract required Kawasaki to keep the ship in a 'seaworthy condition'. Kawasaki did not do this, keeping the ship in the dry dock for seven months, which led it to deteriorate to the point of needing repairs. The Queen's Bench found that the term 'seaworthy condition' was a broad one and that, if it was ruled to be a condition, a 'loose nail' could lead to a breach of a term and, if ruled to be a warranty, would mean huge faults would be considered acceptable.

The test to discover an *immediate term* assessed if the term could be breached in a variety of ways, and if the breach was serious enough of the other party to be deprived of substantially or entirely the benefit of the contract. In this case, 'seaworthy condition' could be breached in a variety of ways, but the breach in question did not deprive Hong Kong Fir Shipping of a substantial benefit of the contract because the route could still have been performed.

Warranties, the third classification, are the terms that remain. A breach of a warranty will not give rise to a right to terminate, but it could give a right to damages. Basically, if a party fails to comply with an obligation under common law systems, it is in breach of its contract whether it is at fault or not. Damages can be awarded even if there is no fault associated with the breach.

However, in civil law systems, a party will only be in breach of its contract if it was found to be at fault in failing to uphold its obligations. The element of fault, therefore, is required for awarding damages to be involved (Pejovic 2001: 42). In addition, recovery of these damages can only be awarded if the breach of contract is caused at least by negligence.

REMEDIES

In both the common law and civil law systems, remedies are approached in much the same way. The essential goal of remedies is to put the party that has suffered in the position it would have enjoyed had the other party performed its obligations, or to restore it to its original position before the breach took place.

In both the common law and civil law there are three basic remedies available for breach of contract, namely:

- damages;
- specific performance; and
- termination.

In civil law there is the additional temporary remedy of *withholding performance.* Although the contractual remedies in the two systems are essentially the same, the ways in which these remedies are applied in the two systems vary considerably.

In the common law there is a definite hierarchy with regard to the remedies. The remedy of damages is undoubtedly the most important. In the great majority of cases of breach of contract a plaintiff will be awarded damages, which will be the only remedy available to him. Specific performance is an equitable remedy and will only be awarded, at the judge's discretion, when damages are inadequate. Termination for breach is a remedy which can be exercised only in certain circumstances.

In civil law, on the other hand, the remedies for breach are ranked in a different order of importance from those in the Common Law. For example, Article 1184 of the French Civil Code, which sets out the remedies in French law, appears to place specific performance and termination on a higher footing than damages, in that it permits a creditor to claim either specific performance, where this is still possible, or termination, in all circumstances. The article puts damages in a secondary role by stating that if the creditor seeks termination he may also claim damages.

Damages

The general measure of damages in common law and civil law systems is the calculation on the basis of compensating (as far as money can) for the loss suffered by the innocent party as a result of the other party's breach. Damages would include the loss that the aggrieved party had suffered and the gain of which it had been deprived. In this context the term 'aggrieved party' means a party that has had its monetary, personal or property rights denied or infringed by another party's actions. Generally, the damages recoverable are those that naturally arise from the breach.

For both systems, an award of money for the damage suffered is usually sufficient as a remedy for mere delay. However, it should be noted that when the effects of a delay are sufficiently serious, monetary remedies are not sufficient in themselves and termination of a contract (rescission) should be available. This is also the case in situations when there are slight deviations in contract conditions. These minor faults in performance that contribute to delay are not severe enough to lead to contract termination. On the other hand, in cases where one party does not perform at all, this would be sufficient for the innocent party to terminate the contract and may also entitle the innocent party to suitable remedies. The normal remedy taken will depend on whether the obligations can be performed or not. In French and German law, the normal remedy to non-performance is that the aggrieved parties are entitled to performance by the other party with monetary compensation for delay.

In civil law systems, damages are awarded only if the aggrieved party has suffered a loss as a result of the non-performance of the contract by another party. This is slightly different in common law systems, as the aggrieved parties that suffer no loss are still granted damages, which are known as *nominal damages*.

In common law systems, instances when the courts will award nominal damages include:

- the loss suffered was either nil or negligible;
- there was no evidence of loss or not of the type recognized at law; or
- there were instances when the plaintiff's behaviour was disapproved of by the courts.

However, both legal systems agree that damages are not awarded if this results in a gain for the defaulting party but no loss to the aggrieved party.

As a concluding comment, the difference in approach between the two legal systems in respect to remedies can best be explained by the very different historical development of the two systems. The legal rules of a particular legal system are never simply rules, but rather 'encode experiences' and are 'the outward manifestation of an implicit structure of attitude and reference'. The 'structure of attitude and reference' which underpins the rules relating to breach of contract in civil law has developed largely based on moral considerations, whereas the 'structure of attitude and reference' which underpins the rules in the common law has developed largely based on economic considerations.

6
Tort Law

INTRODUCTION

In everyday life, every aspect of human endeavour involves a certain degree of risk to life, person and property. The contemporary concept and application of the law of tort seeks to protect legal persons – that is, individuals or corporations – from the wrongful tortious acts or omissions of others. Tort law does not have defined limits on the application of this area of the law and the scope as to what acts or inactions will be held to be 'wrong'. These will be determined in accordance with notions of what 'the law' considers to be 'reasonable' in the circumstances of each particular case.

For the aforementioned reason, tort law has developed in accordance with changing societal values. As commerce and industries develop – and the aviation industry is a good case in point – tort law will respond by seeking to protect society from those within such an industry who cause 'damage' or harm to others by not having behaved reasonably. The way in which the law responds to protect contemporary society ensures that tort law will continue to remain relevant even when there is rapidly developing technology and new operating procedures – once again, such is the case with the aviation industry.

The range of situations that may lead to a cause of action arising under tort law is therefore quite diverse. Consider, for instance, the workplace. Tort law seeks to protect employees (and others) from the intentional or negligent acts (or omissions) brought about by fellow co-workers or others. Tort law has also developed in that it may protect the environment by providing remedies against individuals and businesses with regard to air, land and water pollution in instances where it is found to constitute the tort of nuisance. This could include an aircraft's noise, vibrations, smell and fumes when flying over another person's land or that has otherwise interfered with the occupier's enjoyment of the land. With the increased restrictions imposed upon aircraft operations in respect to their adverse impact upon the environment, together with a reduced tolerance by the community, an extension of tort law as the industry strives toward the 2050 Net Zero Emissions target may well eventuate.

The extent to which the law should compensate individuals who, as a consequence of another's wrongful actions or inactions, suffer loss, injury or other damage is a difficult notion to resolve. The law of torts, which is also referred to as the *law of delict* in some civil law systems, attempts to resolve such issues should they arise between individuals, corporations, governments, public authorities and other such bodies. Although there are differences in how each legal system applies this area of law, there is, in general, a common approach by the courts with respect to the main aspects of tortious behaviour. Courts in any legal system that view behaviour to be socially unacceptable usually provide some form of compensation to the innocent party.

DOI: 10.4324/9781032652146-6

In some instances the court may provide an order prohibiting the other party from undertaking certain actions or even compelling it to do other things (this is known as an *injunction*). The law of torts seeks to assist or compensate the innocent injured party as a consequence of the wrongdoer's actions or inactions. This area of the law seeks to 'regulate' human behaviour by threatening to impose economic loss, through the award of damages, and thereby encourage individuals and corporations to act in a careful, safe, responsible and prudent manner.

The Law of Tort

The term 'tort' is derived from the Latin word *tortum*, which means 'something twisted, wrung or crooked' and from the Norman-French word *tort* meaning simply a 'wrong' (Markesinis 2011). It is a term used by lawyers to refer to certain types of action which give rise to a civil cause of action. Specifically, a tort refers to a breach of a duty, other than one arising under a contract, which gives rise to a civil remedy. In other legal systems, different terminology is used, such as unlawful acts (German-inspired legal systems) and *délits* (French-inspired legal systems). The main functions of tort law are to provide compensation to the victim, loss shifting and spreading, deterrence and avoidance of behaviour that is not considered acceptable by law.

The law of tort is a concept that originated from criminal law. The difference between a crime and tort is that criminal offences are focused on protecting society and punishing those who have committed a wrong against society as a whole (and thereby compensating society as a whole), whereas torts are focused on compensating those who have innocently suffered. Basically, the main goal of a tort is to 'right a wrong', in other words, to restore the party to its original position before the 'wrong' took place.

Development of Tort Law

The development of tort law is linked to the evolution of laws aimed at resolving conflicting social claims and interests, and at encouraging peace and order in the community. In the early development of tort, it was for a long time classified under the same branch of law as criminal law. Historically, offences committed against the community or the king's interests fell under the branch of criminal law. For example, the certain wrongs of an anti-social kind, such as treason, murder, theft and arson, were offences against the king or the state and were viewed as criminal acts within that framework of law (Markesinis 2011).

On the other hand, when wrongs were committed against an individual, this fell within the law of torts. These types of wrongs were generally handled by the person claiming to be injured or wronged, who would decide on their own (without the help from the courts) whether action should be taken or not. In early tort law, the law was predominantly concerned with the most serious kinds of wrongs, such as bodily injury, damage to goods and trespass to land. It was only in the nineteenth century that the law of torts then extended to include intentional infliction of economic loss. The separation of tort law from criminal law occurred as a result of developments in 'law and order' during the Middle Ages.

The modern function of tort law is to compensate those parties that have been injured by a wrong committed by another party. An example of this could be where one person has been injured by another due to negligence.

PROTECTION OF LIFE, LIMB AND FREEDOM OF MOVEMENT

Intentional Interference

In all legal systems, there is a common goal of protection to life, health and physical integrity in which these elements are considered important. This can be viewed in offences that are related to personal injury (e.g. battery and assault), which are causes of action in trespass under common law.

Battery is a term that refers to the intentional action of force and may include harmful or offensive contact with another individual. This harmful or offensive action does not need to be known by the victim for it to be classified as battery. For example, an airline passenger who intentionally and offensively touches another passenger who is sleeping could be found guilty of battery.

Assault is where the plaintiff had a reasonable belief of being in danger of the direct application of force. An individual has been assaulted if he or she has been subject to the threat of immediate harm or offensive contact or any threat or action that causes him or her to be reasonably fearful or apprehensive of imminent harm. An example of this could be a passenger checking in for a flight at the ticketing desk and an argument erupting with regard to weight of the bag. Assault would occur if a threat was made that was likely to be carried out by that person, or at least if the person threatened had a reasonable belief that it would be carried out. In other words, if the person making a threat is an elderly man, this is less likely to be classified as assault as the threat or imminent harm posed is very low. However, in the same situation, if the person carrying out the threat is a bodybuilder, this threat is likely to be classified as assault. These offences (both battery and assault) can fall under both branches of law concerning torts and also crimes capable of attracting serious criminal sanctions.

This is also the case in situations where there is a complete restriction of the plaintiff's freedom of movement without lawful excuse. This is known in common law systems as *false imprisonment*, which is a cause of action for trespass to a person, as there is total restraint upon the liberty of the person. There are two main elements of false imprisonment: detention of a person which is unlawful and the confinement of that person in such a way that it takes away his or her freedom of movement. Such a restriction is actionable under both tort law and criminal law. There are, however, exceptions to freedom of movement where there are criminal statutes that allow lawful arrest to occur, for example, by a police officer, but this will depend on the motives of the legal enforcement. The following case highlights this point.

***Fuerschbach v Southwest Airlines*, 439 F.3d 1197 (2006), United States Court of Appeals, Tenth Circuit**

The plaintiff (Fuerschbach) worked as a customer service representative for Southwest Airlines at the Albuquerque airport. A common activity that was enacted on new employees when they successfully completed a probationary period was to conduct a prank by pretending to arrest them. The plaintiff's supervisor conducted a prank by asking two police officers to come and pretend to arrest her at work. They handcuffed her and commanded her to walk to a room in which all the employees surprised her with a party. The plaintiff was so devastated by these events that she began to cry and could not stop for the duration of the party. She saw a psychologist who said she suffered from post-traumatic stress disorder. She sued everyone connected with the event, including the City of Albuquerque on numerous grounds, including assault, battery, false imprisonment and intentional infliction of emotional distress. The court held that the officers' actions of placing a person's hands in a position to be handcuffed and then leading the individual to walk 15 feet offended a reasonable sense of personal dignity. As the officers intended to touch the plaintiff's arms to handcuff her, this would be viewed by the court as offensive contact which constitutes battery.

Other examples of unlawful restriction of freedom of movement could include border security confining a passenger to a room and contacting the police on the suspicion that he or she is a terrorist. In this case, border security could be held liable for damages due to false imprisonment if it turns out that security had no grounds to justify that the passenger was a terrorist. However, if there were clearly an exit door to leave, it is less likely that the plaintiff (the passenger) would be able to claim false imprisonment unless there was a threat made that limited his or her choices of action.

Other exceptions can be where there is a condition of contract. For example, an action of false imprisonment was brought against American Airlines by a passenger who demanded to be allowed off an aircraft delayed on the ground prior to departure for 11 hours. The action failed, the court holding that by purchasing a ticket, the passenger had consented to such reasonable constraint.

NEGLIGENCE

Definition of Negligence

In certain situations, the law will require an individual to ensure that a requisite level of care is taken with regard to the welfare of other people. If, as a result of the actions or omissions of that person who owes a duty of care to the other person, that other person suffers injury or damage, then the person who has breached his or her duty is guilty of negligence. For example, if a captain on board an aircraft intentionally ignores warning signals in the cockpit and as a result overruns a runway, this may be considered negligence. Any aviation professional who is found to be careless, based on the circumstances of each case, can be liable for damages to those individuals who have suffered as a result of his or her carelessness. The following case illustrates this.

***Nichols v Simmonds, Royal Aero Club of Western Australia and Commonwealth* [1975] WAR 1, Supreme Court of Western Australia**

The plaintiff (Nichols), the pilot of a Comanche aircraft, sued the defendant (Simmonds), the pilot of a Musketeer aircraft. The aircraft had collided as they were landing at Jandakot aerodrome, about nine miles southwest of Perth. The plaintiff also sued the Royal Aero Club of Western Australia, the employer of the defendant, claiming that the club was vicariously liable for the alleged negligence of the air traffic controller on duty at the airport at the time it took place. On appeal to the Full Court of the Supreme Court of Western Australia, the Court agreed with the trial judge that all parties were guilty of negligence or contributory negligence to varying degrees. The two pilots were negligent in failing to keep a good lookout and maintaining a safe separation from other aircraft as was required when operating in a secondary control zone. The duties imposed on the pilots did not absolve the controller from also keeping 'a proper lookout . . . and to give a warning if two aircraft are abnormally close'. The appeal was dismissed.

Although the common and civil law systems take a different approach to the concept of negligence, they do have similarities. In circumstances where personal injury is involved, in all systems there must be conduct that is intentional or careless, that cannot be justifiable and that causes harm to the party.

Negligence in All Legal Systems

In English tort law, the essential element for negligent conduct is the breach of duty and not solely the duty of care provided. Basically, the breach of duty test aims to find out whether there was sufficient care exercised by the defendant towards the plaintiff. The method of establishing whether sufficient care existed is by making a comparison between the conduct of the defendant and what a *reasonable person* would do in the same situation. This is known as an *objective test*. This is explained in more detail later.

Similarly, in Germany, another civil law system, the courts also apply an objective standard in deciding whether negligence took place. When viewing each case, the judge will make a comparison between the conduct of the party and that of a typical party. For example, the judge will compare the conduct of a pilot with that of a typical pilot and the conduct of an air traffic controller with that of a typical air traffic controller. Where there are differences in this comparison, the subject party has acted with *Verschulden*, regardless of whether he or she cannot be individually blamed for his or her conduct. The term *Verschulden* is described as meaning either intention or negligence, suggesting that the generic term could be used for both. Those individuals who have a lack of knowledge or ability provide no defence against liability. The following case illustrates this point.

***Reichsgericht*, First Civil State, Germany, 14 January 1928**

On 23 October 1921, whilst undertaking a journey through the English Channel to Gothenburg, the German three-masted schooner *Lisbeth* ran aground on the sandbank off the Dutch island of Texel. The schooner could not be recovered, which led to the plaintiff owner of the vessel suing the defendant captain of the ship, claiming damages on the ground that he negligently caused the loss of the vessel. The court found that because the plaintiff had knowledge of the defendant's inexperience and lack of skills and still gave him the schooner to operate, he (the shipowner) was found to be grossly negligent in failing to perceive the danger to the ship as a result of the defendant's lack of ability.

The Elements of Negligence

Objective Tests The objective test is the basic rule that applies in all legal systems. This test aims to establish what the defendant should have known about the risk and what he or she ought to have done to avoid it. Modern legal systems resort to objective criteria to determine the requisite standard of care. The question of whether negligence existed is decided upon by a general negligence test. This involves a comparison of the actions of an individual against those of what a *reasonable person* would make, which is referred to as an objective test, as discussed previously.

In civil law systems, a similar standard is used. In French tort law, for example, the *bonus pater familias* ('good family father') is a concept that applies in much the same way as the objective test in common law systems in considering what a reasonable person would be capable of doing. In other words, the actions of an individual are compared to the actions of an average careful person in the same situation. When there are differences in the conduct of the individual compared to that of a reasonable person, it can usually follow that the standard of care was not met and thus the element of breach of duty of care is established.

The negligence test of the reasonable person focuses both on his or her conduct and personal capacities. This test has an outer aspect that is apparent when looking at the circumstances and an inner one that is not self-evident. Basically, the test answers whether the defendant behaved as a reasonable person would have done in the same circumstances (outer care) and whether the defendant possessed the reasonable person's knowledge and skills (inner care). This standard enables the courts to establish the magnitude of injury, the cost of avoiding it and the likelihood of the circumstances being realized or foreseen.

If the defendant belongs to a particular group or has professional experience, this individual will be judged against the standard expected to be achieved by other individuals of that same profession. Skilled professionals such as airline pilots, lawyers and doctors are expected to perform their duties to the standards of their profession.

Nobody expects the passenger on the Clapham omnibus – a colloquial term coined by the distinguished English judge Lord Denning – to have any skill as a surgeon, a lawyer, a doctor or a chimney-sweep unless he is one, but if he professes to be one, then the law requires him to show such skill as any ordinary member of the profession or calling to which he belongs, or claims to belong, would display.

In an aviation context, pilots, aircraft maintenance engineers and air traffic controllers are held to very high standards of conduct. As aviation is a highly regulated industry, upholding these standards is necessary for compliance with regulations and to prevent civil liability. For example, a pilot will be compared to the standard of a reasonable pilot in the same situation, regardless of the skills that the pilot actually possessed. If the pilot does not have the required skills to fly a certain type of aircraft, then the pilot will be deemed negligent in attempting to fly that aircraft.

Existence of a Duty of Care

In the common law, the law of tort assumes that every individual in society owes a duty of care to protect other individuals. The landmark case in this area was *Donoghue v Stevenson* in 1932, in which Lord Atkin delivered the leading speech. The case is illustrated as follows.

> ***Donoghue v Stevenson* [1932] AC 562, House of Lords**
>
> In this case, the plaintiff (Mrs Donoghue) had drunk from a bottle of ginger beer purchased by a friend from a retailer. After she had consumed half the bottle, she found a badly decomposed snail in it. As a result of having consumed the drink, she became ill and sued the defendant (the manufacturer Stevenson) for negligence. The court held that the defendant owed the plaintiff a duty of care to ensure that the bottle contained no harmful contaminants and awarded the damages to the plaintiff.

Prior to this case, the plaintiff could only take action against a manufacturer of defective goods under contract law. However, with the increasing specialization of industries, distribution chains of goods have become increasingly complex. The doctrine of privity of contract often prevented injured parties from being able to bring a claim for breach of contract. Such would have been the case for Mrs Donoghue, as the ginger beer she drank was bought by a friend and so she had not contracted with either the shopkeeper or the drink manufacturer.

Donoghue v Stevenson introduced the *neighbour principle* to the common law of tort. This principle remains the touchstone in determining whether a particular circumstance or relationship will attract negligent liability in common law systems. In his judgment, Lord Atkin put it in this way:

> The rule that you are to love your neighbour becomes in law, you must not injure your neighbour; and the lawyer's question, Who is my neighbour? receives a restricted reply. You must take reasonable care to avoid acts or omissions which you can reasonably foresee would be likely to injure your neighbour. Who, then, in law is my neighbour? The answer seems to be – persons who are so closely and directly affected by my act that I ought reasonably to have them in contemplation as being so affected when I am directing my mind to the acts or omissions which are called in question.

In all systems, there can be no liability for negligent omissions unless there is a duty to act.

Similarly, in civil law systems, the notion of the duty to care remains. If there is a breach of a rule of conduct imposed by legislation or regulation, or a failure to conform to a general standard of due care and diligence, liability can be established. This is a very similar notion to the duty of care principle as defined in *Donoghue* insofar as there seems to be an underlying moral obligation not to harm your neighbour.

One case that illustrates the issue of a duty of care involves the tragic collision of two Boeing 747 aircraft in the Canary Islands.

***Burke v Pan World Airways, Inc.*, 484 F. Supp. 850 (S.D.N.Y. 1980)**

Following the well-known air accident involving two Boeing 747 jets at Tenerife in 1977, the plaintiff (Burke) sued Pan World Airways for negligently causing her mental distress. She was the twin sister of one of the passengers on board the ill-fated Pan American jet and claimed that at the moment of the accident, she felt as if she had been 'split in two'. She claimed that a kind of 'extrasensory empathy' exists between some sets of identical twins, and because of this psychic connection with her sister, she felt incredible mental distress when her sister was killed in the accident. The court dismissed her claim, however, reasoning that the theory of 'extrasensory empathy' is too unusual for any reasonable person to foresee the damage that occurred and thus take care to guard against.

Factors Determining Whether There is a Breach of Duty

In both legal systems, the courts consider a number of factors in determining whether there has been a breach of a duty of care. These factors are comparable between these two legal systems. Such factors include (Dam 2006):

- the seriousness of the expected damage (common law system) is similar to the nature and value of the protected interest (civil law system);
- the probability that an accident will happen (common law system) is similar to the dangerousness of the activity (civil law system);
- the character and the benefit of the conduct (common law system) is similar to the aspects of the relationship of proximity or special reliance between those involved (civil law system); and
- the burden of precautionary measures (common law system) is similar to the availability and the costs of precautionary or alternative methods (civil law system).

Although common law systems rely more heavily on these factors, civil law systems nevertheless encompass these factors in their legal literature.

The four-factor approach can be illustrated by the English case of *Bolton v Stone*, which is explained as follows.

***Bolton v Stone* [1951] AC 850, House of Lords**

As a result of a well-hit six during a cricket match, a ball passed over a seven-foot-high boundary fence and struck Miss Stone. At the time she was standing outside her house across the road from the grounds. As a result of the injuries she sustained, she commenced proceedings against the cricket club for negligence. Although the court held that the accident was foreseeable, the probability of such injuries resulting were so unlikely that a reasonable person would not have been expected to have taken any additional precautions than did the appellants. The cricket club had not breached its duty of care and was therefore not negligent.

In a postscript to the case, the club paid Miss Stone damages and costs after the decision of the Court of Appeal. However, after having the decision overturned in its favour by the House of Lords, it did not recover the money from Miss Stone and indeed made efforts so that she 'did not suffer financially'.

The preceding case can be approached using the four factors. The seriousness of the expected damage was personal injury to the plaintiff, the probability that an accident would happen was very low (highly unlikely), the burden of precautionary measures entailed the cost of constructing a high fence, and the character and benefit of the conduct can be grounds for justification in special circumstances.

Seriousness of Injury

If there is no risk, there is generally no care required. This, in English tort law, is where the victim did not owe a duty of care, and in German tort law it means that there has not been an infringement of a protected right. Negligence can be established even if the risk of it happening is low. For example, in the English case *Paris v Stepney Borough Council* [1951] AC 367 at 385, an employee sustained a splinter in his sole healthy eye. As the probability of an accident was low, the employees did not take any safety precautions, such as using protective glasses. The employer was held liable, however, because it should have taken into consideration the employee who was an exception to the rule, as he only had one functional eye. This draws on the notion that damage to his only functional eye would have caused him greater damage than other employees in the same situation as he had impaired faculties.

Probability of Injury

The probability of the harm needs to be established from the point of view before the harmful event has occurred, and not with the benefit of hindsight. Since the degree of probability is usually underestimated in day-to-day life, the use of available empirical data can be useful. The case *Haley v London Electricity Board* had such data available. This case was about a blind man who fell down a manhole and as a result of the fall lost his hearing. The workmen only marked the hole with a handle of a hammer, which was clearly not a sufficient precaution for someone who was blind. The House of Lords decided that any accident to a blind person could have been expected with a reasonable degree of probability, referring to the statistics in which there was evidence that a number of unaccompanied blind people used this same pavement.

It is interesting to note that in German law, if it is found that more than one party could be held responsible for injury to another, those parties are held jointly liable for the total damages: see Section 840 of the German Civil Code. The landmark case was that of two hunters who shot and killed someone they mistook for a deer. As it was unclear which direction the bullet had come from, the parties involved were therefore all jointly liable.

Precautionary Measures

Negligence is established by balancing risk and care. When there is a bigger risk involved, more precautionary measures are required. In the case of *Bolton v Stone*, the probability of someone being struck by the ball would be very rare, so a high degree of precautionary measures would not be worth taking. In many cases precautionary measures need to be undertaken on an ongoing basis. For example, an airline should maintain its aircraft in accordance with approved maintenance programmes so that the risk to passengers is at an acceptable and reasonable level. Likewise, licensed aircraft maintenance engineers should conduct regular inspections of aircraft, again in accordance with applicable maintenance schedules, and should do whatever in the circumstances would be considered reasonable. What is reasonable in the aforementioned circumstances is usually judged against that which is generally considered reasonable by one's peers.

Obviously, the costs associated with increased levels of maintenance, oversight and inspections need to be balanced against the risks in order to find an appropriate level of responsibility. Take, for example, the case in the Court of Brussels where a plaintiff sued a shop owner for damage to his car caused by shopping trolleys in the shop's car park. The shop owner had taken several measures to prevent this damage from occurring. This included signs displaying the rules of the car park, the frequent collection of trolleys and an indicated place where trolleys should be left. These measures seemed sufficient, and more precautionary measures seemed too expensive and were not needed.

Precautionary measures can also be related to the care of the party and not necessarily a high level of risk. In *Qantas Airways Ltd v Cameron* (1996) 66 FCR 246, the full bench of the Federal Court of Australia found Qantas had breached its duty of care in subjecting the respondent passenger to 'environmental tobacco smoke' during an international flight, thereby causing discomfort and ill health. In awarding damages of $3,000, the Court held that it was 'Qantas' breach of a duty to warn that caused the loss' after the passenger had specifically requested a 'non-smoking' seat prior to contracting with the carrier and was entitled to expect those 'healthy conditions' during the flight.

Public Utility of the Defendant's Conduct

In certain situations, the potential danger created by a defendant's conduct may be justified in terms of the overall benefit conferred on society by such actions. For example, consider the situation of a crewmember who, when following company procedures, caused injury to a passenger during a hijacking. Such conduct may be held not to be in breach of any duty owed on the grounds of public policy.

Foreseeability and Adequate Cause

The law of negligence requires that for a duty of care to exist, the negligent act (or omission) must have been *reasonably foreseeable* (common law system) or have an *adequate cause* (civil law system). In common law systems, this means that a *reasonable person*, put in the position of the defendant, would have foreseen that damage might result from the negligent conduct. It is not necessary for the defendant actually to foresee the specific nature of damage but that actual damage would have been reasonably foreseeable to a reasonable person.

In civil law systems, the test of causation is determined by the 'adequate cause' theory. The adequacy theory can set realistic limits of liability by relying on common-sense notions of causal connection (Markesinis and Unberath 2002: 113). The adequate cause is applied to all forms of tort liability and is not limited merely to cases of liability based on fault. Both of these concepts, although different, keep liability within reasonable bounds.

Good Samaritan Principle For a long time, common law systems contrasted significantly with civil law systems in terms of potential liability associated with failure to come to the rescue of another human being. With regard to liability, common law systems (for example, the USA) in recent years have increasingly focused on the area of failure to render assistance to victims of traffic accidents. The laws generally consisted of imposing a duty to come to the aid of another person. This is known as the Good Samaritan Principle, which has been incorporated into most common law systems. It is an act that sets out to protect those individuals who choose to serve and tend to others who are injured or ill. The act is intended to reduce the hesitation of bystanders to assist as there is a fear that they may be sued or prosecuted for unintentional injury or wrongful death.

On the other hand, in civil law systems, it is a criminal offence not to render assistance to those in need. In this legal system, individuals have a general duty to aid a person when he or she is subjected to physical danger, taking into consideration of course that such a rescue would not be risky to the rescuer. This principle is referred to as the 'duty to rescue'.

By way of example of the application of this principle, in 1953 the German Criminal Code 330c was amended to read:

> Whoever does not render help in cases of accident, common danger or necessity although help is required, and under the circumstances is exactable, and in particular is possible without danger of serious injury to himself, and without violation of the important duties, will be punished by imprisonment up to one year or by fine.

With regard to liability, the rescuer will only be held liable if the victim's position has deteriorated due to the rescuer's intervention. On the other hand, to claim for compensation for the rescuer's expenses and the possible damage he or she has suffered can be a tort law claim if the rescued individual had been responsible for the dangerous situation.

PROTECTION OF PROPERTY

Land

Civil law systems provide protection for property under provisions in both the property and tort sections in their corresponding civil code. In civil law systems, intentional interference with the substance of a thing, whether it is movable or immovable, would be actionable under the corresponding legal systems. The term 'movable property' basically means personal property and immovable property means real estate or real property. As a general observation, it can be said that in all legal systems, the courts have always treated the protection of real property in a 'special' way in consideration of its particular importance to individuals and society in general.

In common law systems, property owners are afforded such protection under the law of torts only. This means that physical intrusion to property or individuals falls within the tort of *trespass*. The term 'trespass' basically means the unlawful intrusion that interferes with an individual's self or property. Civil law systems have not made such a clear delineation that common law systems have in general made with regard to lawful visitors and trespassers. It should be noted, however, that in some common law countries, the courts have not required such a determination to be made as to the 'status' of the intruder.

A trespass to land is committed when there is any direct interference with another person's lawful possession of land. It has been said that the ownership and possession of the column of space above the surface is *ad infinitum* (meaning 'to infinity'), but current legislation seems to limit this claim to the height below which a spacecraft cannot orbit. Therefore, the infringement of the airspace directly over another person's land is deemed to be trespass.

***Bernstein of Leigh (Baron) v Skyviews & General Ltd* [1978] 1 QB 479, Queen's Bench Division**

A landowner claimed damages for trespass against a firm that had taken an aerial photograph of his home from a height of about 630 feet, crossing his land to do so. The court held that an owner of land at common law had rights over his land to such a height as was necessary for the ordinary use and enjoyment of the land and the structures upon it. It was found that the plane was not interfering with the landowner's right and therefore was not trespassing. Bernstein claimed that the maxim of *cujus est solum ejus usque ad coelum* (the owner of the land owns the land up to the heavens) should be applied, but the court did not agree on this, so the claim was dismissed.

Section 76 of the *Civil Aviation Act 1982* (UK) (a common law act) holds that if an aircraft flies at a reasonable height, this does not create a trespass into the airspace. However, if anything falls upon the land from an aircraft, it is a trespass even if the aircraft was flying at a reasonable height. In such a case, damage is compensable without proof of fault (Markesinis and Deakin 2003: 445).

An aircraft that does not fly at a reasonable height can have action brought against it in the form of nuisance. Nuisance is a legal action to redress harm arising from the use of a person's property. In order to be actionable as a nuisance, the conduct involved must be an interference which is unreasonable as judged by the courts. The following case illustrates this.

***United States v Causby*, 328 U.S. 256 (1946), United States Supreme Court**

The plaintiff (Causby) owned a dwelling and a chicken farm near a municipal airport. One of the runways of the airport passed directly over the plaintiff's property at 83 feet, which was 67 feet above the house, 63 feet above the barn and 18 feet above the highest tree. The government leased the use of the airport for a term of one month commencing on 1 June 1942, with a provision for renewals until 30 June 1967. Various military aircraft of the USA used this airport. They frequently came so close to the plaintiff's property that they barely missed the tops of trees, the noise was startling and the glare from their landing lights lit the place brightly at night. This destroyed the use of the property as a chicken farm and caused loss of sleep, nervousness and fright on the part of the plaintiff. The plaintiff sued in the Court of Claims to recover for an alleged taking of his property and for damages to his poultry business. The Court of Claims found that the government had taken an easement over the plaintiff's property and that the value of the property was destroyed and the easement taken was $2,000, but it made no finding as to the precise nature or duration of the easement.

Nuisance does not need to be tangible (damage to poultry business) but also can be intangible (decreased value in property), as illustrated in the following case.

***Cie. Air France v Sté ERVE et al.*, 8 May 1968; [1968] RFDA 327, Cour de cassation (2e Ch. Civ.)**

A high-rise apartment building in Nice, France had been constructed on the outskirts of the city, but the apartments were difficult to sell because of the noise produced by jet aircraft using Nice Airport. An action was filed against the operator of the airport, the Chamber of Commerce. The court held that it had no jurisdiction to hear the case because the Chamber of Commerce was a public corporation set up by the French government. The case should therefore have been brought before the *Conseil d'Etat*. The builder of the apartment building subsequently filed a claim against Air France, although that company was only one of the many users of the airport, and the residents also sued for compensation. Air France was required to assume the burden of proof and to demonstrate that the noise caused by its aircraft did not in fact exceed legal limits. The court eventually decided that the operator of the aircraft was liable for damage caused by manoeuvrings of the aircraft.

Pure Economic Loss

The term 'pure economic loss' is the financial loss someone suffers that is not the result of death, personal injury or damage to movable or immovable objects. Most legal systems are reluctant to award compensation for pure economic loss when there is no physical harm or injury sustained. This reluctance stems from the fact that if individuals are compensated for pure economic loss, such an action will open up the means for various other claims to be made. For example, if a car accident occurs, other car drivers could be affected and thus would be able to lodge claims for the delays caused. Generally, in all legal systems, there needs to be a sufficient reason for awarding compensation for pure economic loss. In order to keep this liability within limits, certain control mechanisms are therefore used.

PROTECTION OF HONOUR, REPUTATION AND PRIVACY

Personality Rights of the Individual

Civil law systems have encompassed in their civil code both general and specific personality rights. For example, the landmark case that established the general personality right in Germany is known as the *Schacht* case. Up until that point, there was no protected right of personality under the German Civil Code. The *Budesgerichtshof* (BGH – the German court) therefore not only settled this case but also created the general personality right as a protected right within the framework of the Code. Consequently, this led to creating specific rights, such as the right to privacy and to honour and reputation. The case is as follows.

***Budesgerichtshof* (First Civil State), 25 May 1954, BGHZ 13, 334 = NJW 1954, 1404 = JZ 1954, 698**

In its weekly journal, the defendant (a publishing company) published on 29 June 1952 an article that criticized the establishment of a new bank by the plaintiff (Dr Schacht). Dr Schacht instructed his attorney to approach the journal and to ask for the publication of certain corrections in the contents of the article. The journal's editor decided to publish an extract of the lawyer's letter in the column 'Letters from Readers'. In viewing the published letter, it appeared that the attorney had expressed his own views rather than his client's. The plaintiff viewed this type of publication to be an injury to his right of personality, in that publishing the letter under the heading 'Letters from Readers' deliberately misled the public. The result of this was an incorrect impression to the public that the letter was merely an expression of opinion by one of the readers. The court held that it was irrelevant whether or not the defendant had been guilty of a crime; rather, the plaintiff's general right of personality had been infringed. This general right of personality was held to deserve recognition as a basic constitutional right, considering that there were already articles in the German Civil Code on general personality rights.

On the other hand, common law systems do not recognize a general liability for invasion of privacy and infringement of other personality rights. Protection of personality rights falls under several torts, such as deceit, malicious falsehood, libel (defamation in a permanent form such as a written text), slander (defamation by spoken words or gestures), nuisance, breach of confidence, assault, battery and passing off. The right to general privacy in common law is covered under the *Human Rights Act 1998* (UK). Only recently has this legal system slowly recognized the tort of invasion of privacy. The following case highlights the leading case in Australia for the tort of invasion of privacy.

***Grosse v Purvis* [2003] QDC 151, District Court of Queensland, Australia**

The female plaintiff, a shire councillor, became romantically involved with the defendant whilst working on various community-related ventures. From 1992 the relationship soured and in April 2002 the plaintiff commenced action in the District Court of Queensland, seeking damages pursuant to various causes of action including harassment, nuisance, negligence, trespass to person and the intentional infliction of physical harm to the plaintiff. The plaintiff's claim was based on the defendant's conduct, which was described as the act of 'stalking'. This claim fell within an actionable civil claim for invasion of privacy. The court held as such because it reasoned that the acts of the defendant were 'willed' and intruded on the plaintiff's privacy in a manner highly offensive to a reasonable person of ordinary sensibilities, and that those willed acts caused detriment to the plaintiff.

A general right of personality specifically in a name is protected under paragraph 823 I of the BGB. In a court in Frankfurt, the German airline Lufthansa, which has a crane as its emblem, in 1982 brought a claim against a defendant who had produced a sticker depicting two copulating cranes, accompanied by the word 'Lusthansa', but in this instance failed as the court considered that it had not breached the relevant code.

THE SCOPE AND BASES OF LIABILITY

Liability Based on Fault

Fault in this context refers to a person failing to uphold a certain standard of care. In most circumstances, fault liability refers mainly to negligence liability. There are differing requirements for liability based on conduct in each legal system. For example, there is one in France (*faute*), two in England (*duty of care* and *breach of duty*) and three in Germany (*Tatbestand, Rechtswidrigkeit* and *Verschulden*). It would appear that a French individual would have it far easier than a German individual because the latter has to prove two more requirements than the French individual. However, on closer inspection, each legal system has comparable formal requirements, with the only difference lying in limiting the scope of liability.

The traditional approach to tort liability in the civil law system was that fault constituted the legal basis for liability. This approach focused on punishing only those individuals who were 'bad' (at fault) by getting them to pay for the harm or damage they caused. It was on the notion that 'innocent' parties (who are not at fault) should be protected and those who had wronged should be punished. Traditionally, the compensation required was basically greater the greater the degree of blameworthiness. Previously, the concept of fault liability did not apply to guardians or keepers of animals, as this type of liability was without fault. The following case highlights this.

***Case of Montagnier*, Cass civ, 27 October 1885**

A mule that was owned and guarded by the defendant knocked stones from the top of a wall onto the plaintiff (Montagnier), who was seated at the base of the wall, causing him significant injury. The plaintiff sued for damages; however, the court rejected a claim of liability on the basis of Article 1385. It held that the defendant had taken care at all material times and that the mule's actions (unexpectedly bucking) were beyond the control of the defendant.

In the preceding case, the damage was caused by the mule and not by its handler; therefore, as the handler did not alone cause the fault, he was not found liable. However, this decision is flawed, as a legal regime ought to exist to guardians of animals. This case led to the *Cour de cassation* announcing a change in policy by ruling that Article 1385 establishes a presumption of fault that can only be rebutted by proof of an unforeseeable event (*cas fortuit*) or of a fault committed by the injured party. Previously, a claim of liability on the basis of Article 1385 was not given. The significance of *Montagnier* lies in the fact that it cut the link between Article 1385 and Articles 1382–3 of the *Code Civil*.

The fault principle is not sufficient for damage caused by aircraft in special air damages (damages to property on the ground or to a person). The reason for this is in many cases it would be impossible to know the exact cause of an aircraft incident. It could be that those on the ground involved in the incident would not be able to tell how the injury was caused, as the person on the ground could not possibly know what caused the injury from up in the sky, and the pilot (if still alive) might genuinely not know or refuse to give information due to fear of legal ramifications.

In the aforementioned instance, even had the injured party known the cause, how would he or she have been able to provide proof when in court? This problem is resolved by applying a basic rule for the rule of liability for special air damages where these damages can only be derived from the principle of absolute liability. This type of liability has been adopted in Article 1 of the Rome Convention of 1952.

The term 'absolute liability' in this context means that a pilot will be held liable for air damages even if it can be proven that the pilot committed no fault, was unable to prevent the accident or that a duty of care was upheld. When there are damages that occur from unknown causes or from external events, the liability is placed on the aviation company rather than the sole individual. The owner of the aircraft can easily be identified through the registration markings on the aircraft.

Strict Liability

Strict liability can be defined as liability without fault and in this context fault is generally considered to mean intentional or negligent conduct. Basically, strict liability can be considered as liability without negligence. It is sufficient for the plaintiff to prove that the defendant was responsible for the act that caused the damage.

The doctrine of strict liability is very important to the aviation industry, particularly in relation to commercial air carriage. Strict liability often applies to damage caused by movable objects that present a higher level of risk, for example, motor vehicles, animals or defective products such as drugs. Aerial navigation, however, falls into a grey area as aerial navigation is a high-level risk activity and has great dangers associated with all parties. Therefore, it cannot be said that whoever is responsible for this dangerous undertaking should be regarded as being solely at fault as other factors may play a part.

***Reichsgericht* (Sixth Civil Senate), 11 January 1912, RGZ 78, 171**

On the morning of 5 August 1908, the defendant landed his airship on a field near Echterdingen due to an engine failure. Thousands of people gathered around this spot to view the airship. This led to the landing area being blocked off by the military, while the fire brigade and the various army units were placed at the defendant's disposal. At around 3 p.m., a storm began which caused the airship to break loose from its moorings and be dragged about 1,200 metres, where it burnt. The plaintiff, who was one of the spectators, was standing near the place of anchorage. The plaintiff became caught in the mooring cables and was injured. The plaintiff sued the defendant for damages, alleging that the accident was caused by the defendant's negligence. Both lower courts rejected the plaintiff's claim.

The application for review for the aforementioned case was denied for the following reasons. The Court of Appeal judged the claim only on the basis of two articles (Articles 823 and 831) of the Civil Code and disregarded any other legal provisions that impose 'liability for danger'. This was due to the plaintiff's injuries being sustained outside any contractual relations, so only the provisions of the Civil Code dealing with torts could apply. The defendant followed all corrective measures in ensuring the airship was anchored safely and had no doubt that it would also be adequate for other weather conditions. The emergency landing was only expected to last a few hours so the airship was quite properly anchored. As there were no signs of the weather conditions changing when landing, no further measures needed to be undertaken for anchoring. Therefore, the Court of Appeal stated that the defendant did not breach his duty of care in these circumstances and that the airship being torn away by the unexpected gust of wind must be seen as the consequence of an act of God.

Similarly, in Germany, the *Luftverkehssgesetz* (Air Traffic Act) establishes strict liability for the operator of a plane. This rule also applies to damage caused by the noise of an airplane, for instance, when the driver of a motor vehicle, distracted by the noise of a low-flying jet plane, collides with a tree (BGH, 1 December 1981, VersR 1982, 243).

The area of strict liability also raises interesting questions in relation to aerial agricultural *spray drift* claims where an agricultural operator sprays crops on one property but wind carries the spray to an adjoining property and the spray causes damage to produce. The following case illustrates the effects of spray drift on an adjacent property.

***Lenk v Spezia*, California Court, 22 December 1949**

This case involved a beekeeper who lost 14 tonnes of honey due to the death of his bees. The bees were killed when they flew onto nearby farm fields that had been sprayed with toxic insecticides to protect farm crops. As there was no evidence that the insecticides were sprayed onto the plaintiff's land, the case did not involve trespass. Instead, the beekeeper brought the case as a negligence action on the grounds that the farmer failed to use due care in his operations.

In this case, it was found that the insecticide sprayer regularly notified the beekeeper in advance of the spraying and asked him to move the hives or to keep the bees temporarily confined. The beekeeper refused to do so, even though he was fully aware of the risks to the bees. Had the farmer been negligent in his spraying, the court agreed, he would be liable for damage caused.

***Ecuador v Colombia* (Aerial Herbicide Spraying Case), International Court of Justice**

In March 2008, Ecuador seized the International Court of Justice of a dispute between itself and Colombia concerning the alleged 'aerial spraying by Colombia of toxic herbicides at locations near, at and across its border with Ecuador'. In its application, Ecuador stated that 'the spraying has already caused serious damage to people, to crops, to animals, and to the natural environment on the Ecuadorian side of the frontier, and poses a grave risk of further damage over time'. It further contended that it had made 'repeated and sustained efforts to negotiate an end to the fumigations' but that 'these negotiations have proved unsuccessful'. This case highlights the serious ramifications of spray drift occurring across two states.

Liability for Others

Damage caused by an employee is not always easily recoverable from the employee, since employees generally are not insured, nor do they have financial means to pay compensation. Thus, all legal systems contain special regimes for the liability of the employer for damage caused by their employees. *Vicarious liability* is liability imposed on the employer when an employee commits a tort in the course of his or her employment. This is a form of strict liability, since the 'innocent' party (the employer) is made liable for the fault of its employee. In all legal systems, a business will be found liable for damages unlawfully caused by conduct that can be reasonably attributed to, or identified with, the business. Readers should refer to Chapter 7 for further details on this.

Damage

In general, the purpose of tortious damages is to put the plaintiff in the position, as far as money can, that he or she would have been in had there been no breach by the defendant. In other words, it is the defendant's obligation to pay the plaintiff a certain amount of money in order to repair the harm done. This payment to the victim (reparation) can be through restoring the individual to the position he or she had been in before the tort was committed or through monetary compensation. For example, if a passenger is injured at the airport by a worker handling the baggage trolleys, the *tortfeasor* (the baggage worker) has to pay the victim's (the passenger) costs of medical treatment and his or her loss of income and/or loss of earning capacity.

The Montreal Convention 1999 (see Chapter 2) contains details that a carrier is liable for damage sustained in the event of the death or bodily injury of a person and/or the destruction or damage to baggage. What does the Convention mean by 'bodily injury'? Does it also include mental injury? The answer is that it will vary on a case-by-case basis. For example, in the common law case of *Rosman v Trans World Airlines*, only mental injury that was the direct result of bodily injury could be compensated. On the other hand, in *Husserl v Swissair*, the common law court was willing to award compensation for mental injury regardless of whether this had resulted from bodily injury or not.

Punitive Damages

Punitive damages are considered to be related to misconduct that is intentional, malicious or consists of action or inaction that is grossly wilful or is in intentional disregard for others that could be of a criminal nature. These damages are also referred to as *exemplary* damages as they are intended to make an 'example' of the defendant's wrongful conduct by punishing them rather than simply compensating the plaintiff. In the USA, these damages are more often awarded than in many jurisdictions and in some cases they can be quite significant. This has led to manufacturers being required to pay enormous sums of money in recent years. It should be noted, however, that strict liability is applied in nearly all states of the USA and in some civil law systems such as France. English, German, Dutch and Canadian laws are also developing in their application towards the standard of strict liability.

Causation

If someone has acted negligently or has violated a statutory rule, the question arises as to whether there is a causal connection with the resulting damage. All legal systems apply various tests for the element of causation, but in practice the courts' approaches are also driven by policy considerations. This explains why the application of the same test can lead to various outcomes, whereas the application of different tests can lead to similar outcomes.

The basic requirement for causation in any legal system is that the *conditio sine qua non* (the 'condition without which there is nothing') test or *but for* test is met. *Conditio sine qua non* literally means condition without which the damage would not have occurred. The court asks whether, but for the conduct of the defendant, the plaintiff would have suffered the damage alleged, and compares what actually happened to what might theoretically have happened. Causation requires that the negligent act complained of, even if shown to have been in breach of duty, *necessarily* caused the damage in question. In other words, if the defendant can show the damage would have resulted irrespective of his or her wrongdoing, then the defendant may escape liability. The damage must be proven to have been *caused* by the defendant's negligence. The following case illustrates such a point.

***Public Trustee v Commonwealth* [1996] NSWSC 110, Supreme Court of New South Wales (Australia), Court of Appeal**

In 1980 at Sydney's Kingsford-Smith Airport, a fully laden (slightly overloaded) Advance Airlines' Beechcraft Super King Air lost power shortly after take-off. Unable to maintain altitude, the captain attempted an emergency landing, but struck the embankment of Runway 34. All 13 people aboard the aircraft were killed. The claim brought by the dependents of the deceased passengers was not finally settled until 1995. At trial in the Supreme Court of New South Wales, Abadee J agreed that the air traffic controllers who had allowed an Ansett Airlines' jet to land ahead of the crippled Advance Airlines' Beechcraft Super King Air had breached their duty of care in not giving appropriate instructions to the King Air captain. The claim against the then Civil Aviation Authority (being vicariously liable for the actions of their employee controllers) was rejected because the judge was of the opinion that the plane would have crashed anyway, and so the air traffic controllers' breach of duty of care did not cause the crash. On appeal, the majority (Mahoney and Clarke JJA, and Kirby P dissenting) upheld the judgment of Abadee J.

PRODUCT LIABILITY IN AVIATION

Product liability is a broad concept relating to the liability imposed on the manufacturer of a product for defects that cause injury to its users. Liability is not confined to the original manufacturer, but includes manufacturers of component parts, maintenance organizations, distributors and second-hand dealers.

The three elements that are required to potentially succeed in a product liability claim are:

1 defective design;
2 defective construction;
3 inadequate instructions for handling a product put on the market.

As product liability developed in America, most cases related to the growth are American cases, as stated by Diederiks-Verschoor (2006). Court cases relating to product liability grew immensely in number in the 1930s and aviation was not unique in this respect. American judges established that aircraft manufacturers were legally responsible for product safety and reliability standards similar – or at least comparable – to those imposed by law on manufacturers of ordinary consumer goods. An early case of product liability relating to aviation is given next.

***Maynard v Stinson Aircraft Corp* [1940] US AvR 71, State of Michigan, Circuit Court for Wayne County, 22 October 1937**

A passenger was awarded damages when she suffered injuries caused by an aircraft catching fire. The manufacturer was held by the court to have been negligent in the design of the airplane on two counts. First, the 'exhaust stacks' were too short to discharge the hot exhaust gases free and clear of the body of the plane; second, the carburettor drain design was such that gasoline escaping from it was likely to accumulate on the underbody of the airplane where it was ignited by the exhaust gases.

Another aviation case that is a perfect example of a situation that involves product liability is *Moyer v Martin Marietta Corp*, 481 F. 2d 585 (5th Circ [Fla], 1973). In this case, action was brought against a manufacturer of an aircraft and a manufacturer of an ejection seat for death to a test pilot caused by premature activation of the ejection seat mechanism.

The scope of product liability has continued to grow and now extends to liability imposed on those other than the manufacture of defective parts. This led to the introduction of strict liability to manufacturers. The following common law case provides such an example.

***Berkebile v Brantly Helicopter Corporation*, 281 A.2d 707 (Pa. Super 1971)**

On 9 July 1962, Berkebile flew alone from his home to an airport at Franklin in his Brantly B-2 helicopter. There he asked for a certain type of gasoline (100-octane) which was not available. The airport manager offered to get the gasoline from an airport in Oil City ten miles away. However, Berkebile said he had sufficient gasoline to fly to Oil City and took off anyway. When he had flown only two miles, his helicopter fell into a wooded area and he was killed. While the helicopter was still in the air, and before it disappeared into the trees, a seven-foot section of one of the three rotor blades broke off. This led to him crashing near Franklin, being killed as a result. The plaintiff (Berkebile's executrix) sued Brantly Helicopter Corporation, which manufactured the helicopter, under the wrongful death and survival statutes. The court found that Brantly Helicopter Corporation was liable in this case as it was one of strict liability. This means that the seller is subject to liability to the consumer regardless of whether all possible care was taken in producing and selling such a product. In other words, the court decided 'that no current societal interest is served by permitting the manufacturer to place a defective article in the stream of commerce and then avoid responsibility for the damages caused by the defect'.

There are also some instances where it was not possible to take legal action against a manufacturer on the basis of a defective product. The following case illustrates this point.

***Bruce v Martin-Marietta Corp and Ozark Airlines*, 14 Avi 472 (1976), United States Court of Appeals (10th circuit), 24 September 1976**

An aircraft of a Martin 404 type, built in 1952 by Martin-Marietta, had been chartered to carry a Wichita State University team and supporters to a football match in Logan, Utah. On its way to Logan, the aircraft crashed into a mountain west of Silver Plume, Colorado. As a result of the horrific impact, the passengers' seats broke loose from their attachments and were thrown against the bulkhead of the airplane, blocking the exit. Shortly after the crash, the aircraft caught fire, and the accident resulted in 32 out of the 40 passengers being killed. The manufacturers were sued for damages on three counts: 'negligence', 'implied warranty' and 'strict liability'. The court stated that an aircraft manufacturer was not liable for damage arising from the crash on the grounds just mentioned for alleged defects in the adequacy of the seat fastenings and the lack of fire protection in an aircraft built as long ago as 1952. There was nothing to indicate that the ordinary consumer would expect a 1952 vintage aircraft to have the safety features of one manufactured in 1970.

As a concluding comment on tort law, as was the situation with the previous chapter regarding contract law, each country's legal system has a differing application of this area of law. What is important, from the perspective of an aviation practitioner, is that you are aware of the fact that there *will* be different approaches taken by the courts in applying the various areas of law. Therefore, as an aviation professional, or an aspirant to become one, if you are in a situation in which the laws of other countries may be applicable, in acquiring such knowledge and awareness, you are at least better positioned to be mindful of any potential legal ramifications of your actions or inactions.

7
Employment and Industrial Law

INTRODUCTION

As individuals, and as a nation, work plays a central part in our lives and economic success. Business enterprises require a skilled, competitive and committed workforce to succeed. Most adults spend the majority of their waking hours at work – or post COVID-19 – working from home. The often-asked question 'What do you do?' reflects the considered importance in contemporary society of employment and work. This is because our vocation or occupation – be it as an air traffic controller or an airline reservations supervisor – largely defines our place in society and the respective responsibilities and obligations associated with that position. Therefore, there is a need for both employees and employers to understand their rights and obligations in order to prevent breaches of constantly changing employment laws, which may have direct effects on them as professionals and on their business.

In recent years the nature of the workplace has significantly changed for many workers as expressed by the following extract (Bartsch 2021: 02):

> The COVID-19 pandemic absolutely blindsided us all, and its impact on our personal lives and on businesses around the world is undeniable. Life as we knew it before 2020 will likely never be the same. The world has changed, likely irrevocably so.

And nowhere in our everyday life have these changes been more evident than in our workplace environment. By way of example, in Australia alone, an estimated 25,000 people left the commercial aviation industry during the COVID-19 pandemic after airlines made drastic staffing cuts and accreditations lapsed. In the years following the pandemic, many workers retrained in other industries and didn't return to aviation. Now with the increased demand for international travel, airlines are trying to claw staff back, but industry commentators say the industry has a 'reputation' problem.

Today work from home and hybrid-working arrangements have redefined the way in which we engage with our employers. As individuals and as business leaders, we're sitting at the crossroads of something extraordinary. From pilots to baggage handlers, maintenance engineers and technicians – the aviation sector is contending with a worker shortage. But to better understand the nature of the contemporary industrial environment, we need to go back to first principles and consider the nature and legal basis of workplace arrangements.

One of the main goals of employment or labour law is to ensure that no employer can be allowed to impose – and no worker can be obliged to accept – conditions of work which fall below what is understood to be a decent threshold in a given society at a given time. In other words, labour law is not just about regulating employment contracts but is adopted to provide both the employer and the employee with 'decent

DOI: 10.4324/9781032652146-7

work'. Initially, this body of law was intended for the protection of manual workers in industrial enterprises, but it has gradually changed to fulfil two functions: the protection of the worker and the regulation of the relations between organized interest groups (industrial relations).

A distinguishing feature of industrial relations – also referred to as labour relations – in aviation is its industrial nature. Every day, thousands of airliners travel to foreign countries with varying legal systems and jurisdictions. Most international airlines establish bases and sales offices abroad and recruit foreign employees or contract with foreign aviation service providers. These common, everyday occurrences reinforce the importance of gaining an awareness of this area of law and its application within an international context.

Employment law is frequently based upon the requirement that for the courts or authorities to provide protection or some remedy to the parties, a *contract of employment* needs to be established. The employment contract provides the legal foundation for the employment relationship. Workers who performed work or provided services under an employment relationship are protected by labour law, while those who are not under contract do not acquire such protection at law.

The underlying basis of the legal relationship between any aviation worker and his or her employer is contractual. Just like any other contract, when there is acceptance, the contract usually becomes binding and the terms of the agreement – whether expressly or implied – form part of the contract at the time of accepting an offer.

As was discussed in Chapter 5, there are certain essential elements required for the formation of a contract. One of these elements – that of offer and acceptance – also plays a fundamental role in the context of a contract of employment. Likewise, the application of the doctrine of *privity of contract* is equally applicable to the workplace, whereby only those who are party to an employment contract acquire the protection (and the obligations imposed) provided under the terms of the contract.

Every nation has its own unique laws and, as such, differing laws define employment and labour conditions and entitlements. Therefore, this chapter cannot provide a detailed examination of the law of employment applicable to each legal jurisdiction; rather, it seeks to explain and highlight some of the more important employment issues within the context of the international aviation environment.

THE EMPLOYMENT RELATIONSHIP

Types of Workplace Relationships

The nature of the workplace relationship may vary; however, throughout the world there are certain common legal classifications within employment law. The most fundamental classification of a worker is as either an *employee* or an *independent contractor*. The two distinct types of employment contracts are that of the employer and employee and that of the principal and independent contractor. The majority of legal systems around the world have more obligations to an employee than to an independent contractor. The benefits and entitlements that are afforded to employees, as opposed to independent contractors, come at a cost to the employer.

To illustrate the obligations that may be imposed upon an employer, consider the following. Companies who employ workers can be held liable to provide benefits (for example, wages and leave entitlements) not only to the employee but also to the government for unpaid employment taxes if employees are 'misclassified' as contractors. By way of an aviation example, consider a pilot working for a small general aviation company. In order to determine the respective rights and obligations of that pilot and the company, it is first necessary to consider whether the pilot is in fact an employee of that organization or simply provides services under some other type of arrangement. The correct classification of a worker is a most important issue in any business, including the aviation industry. The courts have developed certain tests and standards to determine the distinction between the employment relationship and the independent contractor.

The two main types of workplace relationships recognized under employment law are:

- *contract of service*, which creates the employer–employee relationship; and
- *contract for services*, which gives rise to the relationship between a principal and an independent contractor.

While different jurisdictions use different standards and tests for determining the nature of the relationship, in most countries, the determination essentially relates to one factor – the degree of *control* that the employer asserts. For example, the French legal system states that an employment contract is one that contracts for:

1 the performance of an activity;
2 remuneration provided for work conducted;
3 an existence of a superior–subordinate relationship between the parties.

The notion of 'superior–subordinate relationship' under the civil law system has close parallels to the English common law 'master–servant' relationship. This term originates from the Victorian era when it was considered that the servant/employee was essentially an *agent* of the master – working to perform the master's chores.

The tests used by the courts to determine the true workplace relationship vary from country to country. Sweden, for instance, utilizes a ten-part test, whereas Canada uses a four-part test. In most common law systems, however, the basic legal principle applied to identify a workplace relationship is known as the *control test*. What is considered by 'control' is the nature and degree of power that a person can exercise over the tasks performed of another person. If the 'employer' can control not only *what* work is done but also *how* it is performed, then the relationship is usually deemed to be that of an employer–employee.

Employees

The relationship between an employer and an employee is recognized at law as being the result of a contract. This is referred to as a 'contract of employment'. A contract of employment can only exist if the law recognizes that the parties to the contract are an employer and an employee. The *employment relationship* is a contract whereby one party (the employee) agrees to perform certain services for the other party (the employer) in return for remuneration – usually in the form of wages and conditions.

According to Vranken (1997), the labour courts of many nations in mainland Europe have, to a large extent, derived from the Probiviral Court or *Conseil de prud'hommes* (literally, 'court of wise men'). This court was set up at Lyon, France pursuant to a Napoleonic law of 1806. In many European codes or treaties, there is no definition of 'employee'. The word 'workers' is usually used to describe employees. However, the term 'worker' does not have a universal definition.

The definition that is used in EU *directives* is that 'workers' are those who are economically dependent or self-employed, engaged on temporary contracts and those who are engaged through labour agencies. A *directive* is basically a legislative act that requires Member States to achieve a particular result. The European Court of Justice on the other hand defines a 'worker' as covering all persons engaged in economic activity even without a contract of employment and including even those without a contract at all, but who are seeking work.

Independent Contractors

Independent contractors are required to do the job they have been contracted to perform. Unlike the employee, the independent contractor controls the methods and the means to do the job. In the world of aviation, aviation medical examiners, owners of small charter operations and certain flight instructors who undertake freelance work may be considered to be independent contractors.

Principals and Agents

The agency relationship differs slightly between the common law and civil law systems. Under the common law, an undisclosed *principal* is bound to contracts with third parties if the agent forming the contract has actual authority to enter into those contracts. The principal will then be able to hold the third party to the contract. In civil law systems, the 'principle of lack of communication among parties that have no knowledge of each other's existence' prevails, making the principal not bound. In other words, the principal is not able to hold the third party to the contract unless they had knowledge of the principal's existence.

If there is a situation where a principal and an agency establish an agency relationship by writing a written contract, the agent has actual authority to act on behalf of the principal. Under common law systems, the agent can enter into a contract with a third party and the principal would not be liable to the third party unless it had some authority over the agent. However, in civil law systems, the agent's power to perform is independent of the validity of the agency contract – in other words, the principal is liable to the third party (Meiners, Ringleb and Edwards 2009).

***Hallock v Trans World Airlines Inc*, 364 SW 2d 636 (1963), Missouri Court of Appeals, Kansas City District**

Proceedings commenced by Maria Hallock in respect to her deceased husband, Thomas Hallock. The main issue for the court to resolve was who, at the time of Thomas' death, was his employer? Maria claimed her husband was an employee of Trans World Airlines (TWA), whereas TWA rejected this assertion and claimed he was an employee of Ethiopian Air Lines (EAL) and had never been a TWA employee. The court found that TWA was acting only as an agent of the employer, hiring the now-deceased pilot on behalf of EAL, rather than as an employer. Hallock's contract of employment had precisely identified EAL as the master of the relationship which undertook all related obligations, including the payment of regular salary, notwithstanding that in fact TWA had also provided the pilot with certain benefits. The referee and the Industrial Commission ruled that he was not a TWA employee and denied compensation. On appeal, the Circuit Court affirmed this decision.

A common and important component of labour law in both the civil and common law systems is that of the equality – or, in most instances, inequality – of the employment relationship. The relationship is fundamentally unequal because one party (the employee) is economically dependent upon the other party (the employer) to provide a livelihood. The inequality is further entrenched in that the relationship is ongoing, as opposed to other contracts, where there is often only a one-off relationship. Airline pilots, air traffic controllers, flight attendants and essentially anyone else who works on a more or less ongoing basis fall into this relationship category.

Although the approaches to labour law of the civil law and common law systems are different in many ways, the same approach to addressing this inequality remains. In both systems there is always direct legislative intervention in the employment relationship. *Work councils* are commonplace in most civil law countries; however, they differ widely in their composition between nations. Basically, work councils have been established at the place of work so that employers and employees can meet and confer on an equal footing.

In common law countries, this is an area of the law that has been subject to a high degree of *codification*. As previously mentioned (see Chapter 3), civil law systems have comprehensive 'codes' that encompass a wide range of statutory rights for the protection of individual employees, in that they dictate the nature of their relationship with their employer. These statutory rights go far beyond the protection of employees in the course of their employment. For instance, they not only cover situations where unfair termination actions have been initiated by the employer but also address the conditions under which temporary work arrangements may be entered into, part-time work, privacy, working time and even the impact of strike action on the individual contract of employment.

Labour relations are power relations and this impacts on the outcome of collective bargaining in the civil law as well as in the common law. Due to the extensive individual employment laws in the civil law, the collective bargaining stakes are less high. Civil law systems promote a cooperative approach to the employee–employer relationship through two main forms of worker participation, these being work councils and employee representation on the supervisory boards of companies.

Vicarious Liability

One of the consequences of the inequality of the employment relationship is that employers are very often financially better placed to absorb risk. The concept of *vicarious liability* addresses this very issue by allowing an aggrieved party, especially in tort law, to hold the employer responsible for the acts of its employee. Whilst the employee is still legally responsible for his or her own actions, plaintiffs will more often commence action against the employer, who is more likely to have 'deep pockets' – that is, the employer has a greater capacity to pay a claim for damages.

For an employer to be held vicariously liable for the acts of an employee, a number of criteria must be satisfied:

- The employee must be an employee and not a contractor. In other words, there must be an employer–employee relationship rather than a principal–contractor relationship.
- The employee must be acting within the actual or apparent authority of an employee in the circumstances.
- The employee's acts must be performed in the course of the employee's employment and not on a 'frolic of his own'.

If the preceding criteria are not met, then the employer cannot be held liable for the employee's actions.

THE CONTRACT OF EMPLOYMENT

The basic feature of labour law in any legal system around the world is that the rights and obligations of the employee and the employer to one another are mediated through the contract of employment. In writing up a contract of employment, there is a general duty to provide the essential terms to the employee. The aim of stating the specific terms is to confirm that the employee understands what is to be expected of him or her and what to expect, the terms of his or her wages and holiday rights, what happens in the event of termination and the overall role of his or her job.

In the contract of employment there are usually terms that are stated by the parties which have been specifically agreed upon as applying to their relationship. In common law systems, these terms are known as *express terms* and are conditions of employment that are expressly agreed upon by all parties. Basic matters include hours of work and pay commonly.

Express Terms

Commonly, the employer must provide the employee with a written statement of terms and conditions of employment, setting out minimum information as required by certain legislation. *Express terms* may also extend to 'work rules' or the terms of an employer's policy. These will be incorporated into a contract of employment in circumstances where the terms are clear and unequivocal and the document is brought to the attention of the employee before the commencement of the contract or freely adopted later in time.

Implied Terms

With most employment contracts, not all the terms and conditions are expressly agreed upon – either verbally or in writing – at the time when the contract is formed.

For this reason, the courts may imply various 'unspoken' terms into the contract. At common law, there is an implied duty in a contract of service that each party will treat the other with such a degree of consideration and courtesy as will enable the contract to be carried out. The implied basic duties of an employer include a duty to provide work, a duty to provide remuneration and a duty to ensure the safety of employers. This duty was evident during, and in the aftermath of, the COVID-19 pandemic in that the employer had to ensure the safety of all workers from the virus, which included the wearing of face masks and in some instances required mandatory vaccinations.

On the other hand, the implied duties of employees include the duty to conduct themselves in a professional and respectful manner, to obey the employer's lawful commands, to perform work in a skilful and competent manner and to provide a faithful service. It is plain to see how these implied duties of an employee have derived from the concept of the master–servant relationship.

Hours of Work

In common law countries, the hours of work are usually set out in the individual employee's employment contract. These conditions must be less than or equal to any applicable working hours prescribed by legislation of applicable industrial awards. In mainland Europe, however, minimum standards for hours of work or 'working time' for those employed in the civil aviation sector are well established and date back over two decades when they were specifically stated in an EU Directive, *Council Directive 2000/79/EC of 27 November 2000*. This Directive concerns the European Agreement on the Organization of Working Time of Mobile Workers in Civil Aviation. This agreement was concluded by the Association of European Airlines (AEA), the European Transport Workers' Federation (ETF), the European Cockpit Association (ECA), the European Regions Airline Association (ERA) and the International Air Carrier Association (IACA).

The 2000 EU Directive prescribes the following requirements:

- a maximum annual working time of 2,000 hours, with the total flight time limited to 900 hours (block flying time), spread as evenly as practicable throughout the year;
- a certain number of days free of all service (seven days per month and at least 96 days per year);
- at least four weeks' paid annual leave and specific health and safety measurements appropriate to the nature of work;
- a free health assessment before employees are assigned, and then at regular intervals, subject to medical confidentiality requirements;
- an obligation on the employer to adapt the pace of the work to the worker;
- health and safety protection appropriate to the nature of work.

In respect to the last point, and in the aftermath of the COVID-19 outbreak, states, including government regulators, airports, airlines and aircraft manufacturers among other stakeholders of the aviation ecosystem, developed – in coordination with public health authorities – a set of measures aimed at reducing health risks to air travellers, aviation workers and the general public.

In terms of working conditions those employees who are working in the aviation field excluding pilots and flight crew are treated similarly to employees in other fields of work. According to the *ILO Hours of Work (Industry) Convention 1919*, the working hours of people employed in any public or private industry shall not exceed eight hours in a day and 48 hours in the week, with exceptions to those holding positions of supervision or management, different specifications agreed upon and those undertaking shift work.

Annex 6 of the Chicago Convention sets out the rules and regulations regarding work and rest periods for aviation personnel. Limitations, set by states in their national aviation regulations, are prescribed by daily, monthly, quarterly or annual flight time limitations. These limitations will vary depending on factors including the number of aircrew (for example, single-pilot or multi-pilot operations), facilities for rest during the flight and adequate rest facilities at operational ports.

Specifying and limiting flight and duty times for aircrew and other aviation operational personnel (air traffic controllers) are a most important factor in ensuring the safety of aviation activities. More recently, state NAAs have promulgated regulations that permit airlines and other aviation organizations to develop their own *fatigue risk management systems* (FRMS).

Due to the increasing diversity of airline services and networks – particularly fuelled by the increased level of competition resulting from the proliferation of LCCs – custom-designed organizational FRMS provide for greater flexibility for rostering of aircrew and scheduling of services. FRMS can provide both increased business efficiencies – more efficient allocation and use of aircrew – together with improved levels of safety resulting from less fatigue. This 'win-win' outcome is another example of achieving a *safety quinella* and is consistent with the ICAO's approach of creating a less prescriptive regulatory regime.

Workplace Safety The aviation industry is always striving to provide a safe, secure and healthy working environment for all employees – both above the wing (flight crew) and below the wing (ground and ramp personnel) – and of course for passengers. There are steps that employers can take to prevent serious injuries among workers, from looking for structural issues in the workplace to providing employees with training on human factors and error. By being proactive, aviation companies can build a healthy safety culture that will improve productivity and, most importantly, reduce injuries across the entire workplace.

Apart from compliance with statutory work health and safety (WHS) requirements for air operators and employers the aviation industry, and indeed all other workplace environment, there are always emerging challenges that employers face and this was demonstratively evident during the SARS and COVID-19 pandemics. During these times the industry requires the support and assistance of government agencies at both the local and international level.

In October 2021 the International Civil Aviation Organization's (ICAO) Council Aviation Recovery Task Force (CART) released the fourth edition of its Guidance for Air Travel through the COVID-19. These measures, applicable to states, airport operators, airlines and others in the air transport industry, were designed to enable a consistent and predictable travel experience. They also contributed to the efficient, safe, secure and sustainable transport by air of an increasing number of passengers and cargo, and minimize the risk of COVID-19 transmission between and among these groups and the general public. The implementation of these measures significantly facilitated and strengthened the global recovery from the COVID-19 pandemic.

Termination of Employment

An employment contract may come to an end for a number of reasons. It may be due to the contract ending due to time (fixed-term contract), an employee reaching a certain age (see later in this chapter for information on the age limit on pilots) or as a consequence of a breach of a condition stated in the contract. Where the contract is for an indefinite period and no provision is made for its termination, the majority of legal systems provide that it may be ended upon giving reasonable notice. Notice provisions are normally stipulated in the employment contract.

In some jurisdictions, such as France, there does not need to be a legally valid reason for discharging employees. The following article by Debost (2007) illustrates this point.

> *The New Hiring Contract*
>
> The *Contrat Nouvelles Embauches* (CNE) or 'New Hiring Contract' represents a revolution in the world of French employment contracts. Indeed, the US law rule of 'at will-employment', which allows employee discharge for no reason, was not a familiar notion in French law until an ordinance of 2 August 2005 (hereinafter 'the Ordinance') created the CNE, which is a type of indefinite-term employment contract under which the employee is more or less 'employed at will' for the first two years.
>
> The general rule under French employment law remains that anyone is entitled to be hired under an indefinite-term employment contract, which, after a fairly short trial period (no more than six months), cannot be terminated by the employer without 'real and serious' cause and due process.
>
> Fixed-term employment contracts that terminate automatically upon the expiry of their term are only authorized in specific cases. If they fail to comply with strict requirements, they are then deemed to be entered into for an indefinite term.
>
> As an exception to these general rules, the Ordinance now provides that any company employing up to 20 employees in France can hire anyone under a CNE, which allows the employer to terminate the contract without cause, provided it:
>
> i sends a termination letter to the employee by registered mail with return receipt requested;
> ii complies with a short notice period – except in certain circumstances;
> iii pays the employee an indemnity equal to 8 per cent of all remuneration due to him or her up to the termination date; and
> iv pays an indemnity equal to 2 per cent of the same to the unemployment fund.

Basically a termination-at-will system, as is common in the US and other common law countries, operates whereby if a worker refuses to accept changes imposed by the employer to the terms or conditions of their contracts of employment, they can easily be dismissed. This differs from a legal system where workers are protected against unfair dismissal.

Unfair Dismissal

Protection against unfair dismissal is the most commonly found form of statutory protection in both the civil law and common law systems. In a number of instances, action of the member states was triggered by the adoption of a recommendation on this issue by the International Labour Organization in 1963 (*ILO Convention No 119, 1963 concerning Termination of Employment at the Initiative of the Employer*) (Vranken 1997). The principle was also strengthened in 1982 by the *Termination of Employment Convention*. The following case provides an example of a pilot being unfairly dismissed, and although it is an early case it nevertheless demonstrates the paramount importance placed by the judiciary (and tribunals) upon safety with carriage by air.

***Alidair Ltd v Taylor* [1978] ICR 445, Court of Appeal, England**

The applicant was a pilot employed by the respondent company. On landing at Guernsey Airport, as pilot-in-command of a Vickers Viscount, Captain Taylor 'bounced' the aircraft, causing structural damage to the undercarriage. Following an investigation by the company, the pilot was summarily dismissed on the ground of incompetence. On appeal from the Employment Appeal Tribunal, the applicant alleged that he had been unfairly dismissed as a consequence of a single and isolated instance or error of judgment. The Court of Appeal held that the findings of the Tribunal were correct and that the appeal should be dismissed.

In the judgment of the Employment Appeal Tribunal, Bristow J stated:

> Where the degree of professional skill required of an employee was high and the consequences of the smallest departure from that high standard were serious and could bring about a major disaster, *one* failure to perform in accordance with that high standard was sufficient to justify dismissal.
>
> (*Alidair Ltd v Taylor* [1977] ICR 445 at 447 per Bristow J, emphasis added)

The main reason for citing the preceding reference is to emphasize the extent to which the courts throughout the world will err on the side of the travelling public when deciding upon matters pertaining to aviation safety.

CONTEMPORARY EMPLOYMENT ISSUES IN AVIATION

As employment law is one of the most complicated and complex areas of the law, it is simply not possible in a book such as this – or for that matter any single publication – to provide a detailed insight into labour law in every jurisdiction throughout the world. Moreover, cases that appear before the court are usually decided on the basis of particular issues relating to the individual and the conditions under which they are employed rather than the application of a general principle of law.

This section will examine a variety of contemporary and important issues of employment law that relate specifically to the aviation industry. Most of these issues have an international context and therefore will provide the reader with an appreciation of how they may relate to their particular workplace and, indeed, perhaps to their own individual contract of employment.

Retirement Age of Pilots

In respect of the retirement age of pilots, Annex 1 of the ICAO provides that if the licence holder is aged 60, he or she is not allowed to act as the pilot-in-command or commander of an aircraft engaged in international commercial air transport operations. However, on 10 March 2006, the ICAO Council adopted an amendment to Annex 1 stating that if there is more than one pilot and that if the other pilot on board is *younger* than 60 years of age, the age of the pilot can be *above 60* but can be no more than 64. This amendment has increased the age limit by five years for commercial pilots operating an aircraft carrying at least two appropriately qualified and licensed pilots.

In 1959, the US Federal Aviation Administration (FAA) introduced the *Age 60 Rule* (the previous age limit) as it concluded that the rule would promote air safety. According to Speciale, this determination was based on the finding that:

> available medical studies show that sudden incapacitation due to heart attacks or strokes becomes more frequent as men approach age sixty and present medical knowledge is such that it is impossible to predict with certainty those individuals who are most likely to suffer attacks.
>
> (2006: 273)

Internationally, the age limit in the ICAO standards was again increased in November 2006 from 60 to 65, although some countries are yet to adopt this standard. For example, the German airline Lufthansa has set an age limit of 60 in its collective agreement (BBC News 2011b).

***Prigge and others v Deutsche Lufthansa AG* [2011] ECJ C-447/09 (13 September 2011)**

In this case, Mr Prigge, Mr Fromm and Mr Lambach were employed for many years by Deutsche Lufthansa as pilot captains. Their employment contracts terminated in 2006 and 2007 respectively when they reached 60 years of age, pursuant to Article 19(1) of Collective Agreement No 5a. The Lufthansa pilots alleged that they were victims of discrimination on the grounds of age, contrary to a directive on equal treatment in employment and occupation as per Council Directive 2000/78/EC of 27 November 2000. These pilots brought an action before the *Arbeitsgericht Frankfurt am Main* (Frankfurt am Main Labour Court) for a declaration that their employment relationship with Deutsche Lufthansa had not terminated at the end of the month during which they reached 60 years of age and an order that Deutsche Lufthansa should continue their employment contracts. The *Arbeitsgericht Frankfurt am Main* dismissed their action and the *Landesarbeitsgericht Hessen* (Higher Labour Court) dismissed their appeal. The applicants therefore lodged an appeal on a point of law before the *Bundesarbeitsgericht* (Federal Labour Court, Germany). The *Bundesarbeitsgericht* looked at whether, after the entry into force of the Directive, an interpretation of Article 14(1) of the Collective Agreement has the effect of rendering the age limit of 60 for Deutsche Lufthansa pilots invalid. Deutsche Lufthansa's Collective Agreement states that the age of their pilots is to be limited to 60 to guarantee air traffic safety, whereas national and international legislation fixes that age at 65 and this limitation is not a measure that is necessary for public security and protection of health, within the meaning of the aforementioned Article 2(5). National and international legislation considered that it was not necessary to prohibit pilots from acting as pilots after the age of 60, but merely to restrain those activities. Therefore, the prohibition on piloting after that age, contained in the measure at issue in the main proceedings, was not necessary for the achievement of the pursued objective. The court therefore held that fixing a retirement age at 60 could not fall within the exception in this case, as the German national law had set the age at 65. The collective agreement was therefore contrary to national law and, as such, was unlawful.

In summary European Union's highest court – the European Court of Justice – held that governments may impose safety restrictions on pilots above the age of 60, but that they cannot ban them from flying completely. In a court statement issued at the time of the handing down of this landmark decision it was stated:

> Prohibiting airline pilots from working after the age of 60 constitutes discrimination on grounds of age, While the right to act as a pilot may be limited from that age, total prohibition goes beyond that which is necessary to ensure air traffic safety.

Sometimes the requirement relating to a 'maximum' age at which a pilot can fly may be determined by factors other than those specifically prescribed in either international standards (for example, by the ICAO) or by individual NAAs (for example, the FAA 'over 65 rule') and may be determined by individual employment contracts. The following case from the High Court of Australia found that there were certain 'inherent' conditions of employment that may be relevant in determining a maximum age.

Qantas Airways Ltd v Christie [1998] HCA 18

In this case, Qantas allegedly dismissed Mr Christie, a 60-year-old international airline pilot, on the basis of his age. In deciding whether the pilot could fulfil the inherent requirements of his position, the High Court considered it relevant to look at the surrounding context of his employment, as well as his physical ability to perform the task. Mr Christie's inability to fly on any flights except those to Indonesia, New Zealand and Fiji, all of which were short flights, could not be accommodated by the airline's bidding system, which determined the rostering of pilots. Because the short flights were used by all pilots to round their flying hours up to the required number, if all such flights were allocated to Mr Christie, the remaining pilots would be under-utilized. Therefore, the Court held that the surrounding context meant that he was not able to fulfil the inherent requirements of the job even though he might be physically capable of flying.

The following article illustrates the change in the pilot retirement age by the then Bush government in the USA in 2007 (Unnikrishnan 2007).

Pilot Retirement Age in the United States

In December 2007, US legislation governing commercial pilots was amended by [Congress] to allow commercial pilots to fly until the age of 65. The legislation, which is known as the Fair Treatment for Experienced Pilots Act, allows both pilots on a domestic flight to be up to the age of 65. For international flights, one pilot may be up to the age of 65 provided the other pilot is under the age of 60, which is consistent with the November 2006 ICAO standard. While the law is not retroactive, airlines do have the option to rehire pilots who are under the age of 65. The rehiring of pilots is not mandatory and is the decision of each airline.

Licensing Requirements

Fundamental to any aviation licensing regime is the necessity of the state NAA to check the competency of personnel who perform aviation activities which, unless carried out properly, could jeopardize aviation safety. This competency standard is achieved through the issuing of licences to aviation professionals who perform operationally critical tasks. Those aviation professionals who require licences include flight crew members (pilots and flight engineers), aircraft maintenance technicians, aeronautical station operators, flight dispatchers and air traffic controllers. As required by the ICAO, all aviation professionals who wish to attain a licence must undertake approved training courses, demonstrate competency for the licence they are applying for, be compliant with any relevant medical fitness standards and have sufficient experience for the corresponding licence.

The basic principles of personnel licensing for aviation personnel are:

- the licence is the authorization which allows the holder to perform specific activities;
- issuing of a licence will go to those who have demonstrated an acceptable degree of competency;
- there are different types of licences where each one grants specific privileges.

Industrial Action and Disputes

Industrial disputes are typically disagreements between an employer and employee, usually represented by a trade union, over some aspect of the terms or conditions of employment. In other words, employees engage in industrial action when they want something done about a certain issue. Aviation is no exception to this, with airlines worldwide engaging in industrial action. The effects of industrial action can be varied, ranging from tarnished reputations of companies to loss of productivity for the company.

Resulting from the impact of increased competition within the worldwide aviation market and the increased financial pressure imposed upon airlines as a result of the Global Financial Crisis, there have been a number of high-profile industrial disputes. More recently, with the EU debt crisis, there has been an escalation in industrial action by unions within the aviation industry, as the following articles demonstrate. Such employment-related tensions will most likely continue for the foreseeable future. The following cases highlight the rise in industrial action.

British Airways Cabin Crew Dispute (2009–11 and 2016–17)

On 21 January 2011, cabin crew employed by British Airways (BA) voted in favour of strike action and walking off their job. It was part of an ongoing dispute between the crew and BA since 2009, when the airline announced plans to cut 1,700 cabin crew jobs and freeze their pay. The airline had been running at a loss, and unilaterally decided – after failed union negotiations – to reduce crew complements on long flights, change cabin crew allowances and introduce a significant voluntary redundancy programme. Over a three-year period, the union engaged in 22 days of strikes and resulted in an agreement to restore travel concessions and a two-year pay deal. About 96 per cent of cabin crew are represented by the labour union Unite. The dispute provides some interesting insight into the industrial legal framework utilized by British Airways to seek injunctions against strike action.

The framework regulating the conduct of industrial action in the United Kingdom is Part V of the *Trade Union and Labour Relations (Consolidation) Act 1992* ('TULRCA'). In 2010, Unite held a ballot voting for strikes and BA applied to the UK High Court for an injunction – after succeeding in obtaining one in 2009 – claiming that the union had not complied with the obligation to inform all persons entitled to vote in the ballot as soon as reasonably practicable. The key provision was section 231 of TULRCA, which required the union to provide its members with, *inter alia*, information about the number of votes cast and the full results of the ballot. Unite received the report of the ballot scrutineer and sent SMS messages and emails to its members announcing the outcome of the ballot, but not in the exact way required by TULRCA. All of the necessary information was available on public and internal websites, notice boards and news sheets, and complaints of breaches of section 231 by employees was not in evidence. Nevertheless, the High Court found that the text messages to members containing a link to Unite's website containing the relevant information was not taking 'active steps' to provide the information as required by the broad interpretation of section 231 in *Network Rail Infrastructure Ltd v NURMTW* [2010] EWHC 1084 and granted the injunction.

On appeal to the Court of Appeal, a majority lifted the injunction. The judges found that the 'active steps' requirement was not a proper interpretation of section 231. The legislation did not contain a test requiring that every single eligible member needed to be sent the full results. The cabin crew were required to take some action online, but that was not a problem according to the court since the crew were computer literate. Personal notification of the outcome was also not a requirement. Their Lordships found that taking such steps as were 'reasonably necessary' was a lesser burden than BA pressed for and did not require that *every* possible means had been attempted.

Another industrial dispute arose again in 2016, where cabin crew voted to strike over 'poverty pay and broken promises'. There were cases of cabin crew sleeping in their cars between shifts as they could not afford to purchase the gas needed to travel home. After a long chain of disruptions, strikes and protests, discussion in September 2017 concluded with seeing salaries rise by between £1,404 and £2,908 by March 2018.

The issue stemmed from the creation of a 'mixed fleet' category of cabin crew, which comprised about 15 per cent of BA's total cabin crew. In order to compete with low cost carriers such as Ryanair and easyJet, BA created these 'mixed fleet' crews with inferior terms and conditions compared to the other crews on Eurofleet and Worldwide. In 2015, the mixed fleet starting salary was about £12,000, compared to an average of £37,200 (Harvey and Turnbull 2017). Surveys indicated that less than 10 per cent of staff reported their pay was adequate to support their lifestyle. None reported their pay was enough to support their future life goals. Uncertainty with rosters also worsened the conditions. They would change at very short notice, and mixed fleet members were told to continuously check their rosters on holidays and their days off in order to see when they were next working. An unofficial motto of the cabin crew was *'To fly, to starve'* – a modification of BA's tagline *To fly, to serve*.

2014 Air France Strike

For two weeks in September 2014, Air France pilots stopped flying to protest the airline's plan to have Transavia, a lower-cost KLM unit, to undergo most of the short routes in Europe, cutting down labour costs and increasing their profits. It was similar to what Lufthansa had done, which saw most of its shorter continental routes being shifted to Germanwings. Pilots were worried about the plan as it involved up to 1 billion euro in investment for new planes and hiring many pilots, eventually leading to longer hours and lower wages.

After a long 14 days, Air France pilots called an end to the action in 'the interest of passengers and the company'. Costing over 250 million euro, it was said to have been an enormous threat to France's fragile economic situation. Negotiations between Air France, KLM and the National Union of Airline Pilots were unfortunately not making any progress and only ended after huge pressure to bring an end to the longest halt in Air France's history.

Air France expressed relief at having arrived at the end of a 'costly and damaging' strike, which began Sept. 15 and has cost its struggling French-Dutch parent, Air France-KLM, as much as 20 million euros, or [US]$25.4 million, a day. But the airline said it 'deplored' the union's refusal to endorse management's revised strategic plan and sign an accord bringing a formal end to the dispute.

Nonetheless, management reiterated its intention to accelerate the expansion of the group's Transavia budget carrier in France in order to compete head-to-head with larger regional rivals like Ryanair and easyJet.

'This expansion will take place, as planned, under competitive economic and social conditions', Air France said in a statement.

'The emergence from the conflict only reinforces the company's determination to advance its business model', it said. 'The strategic interest of the company must remain the goal of all' employees.

Prime Minister Manuel Valls welcomed the end of the strike and said that the French government, which owns a 16 percent stake in Air France-KLM, would 'stand by the company and its employees, who were plunged into uncertainty by this episode'.

(Clark 2014)

Conclusion

Almost the entire global aviation workforce was exposed to the risks of job instability and virus infection since the global outbreak of COVID-19 in 2020. It is irrefutable that airport and airline workers are more seriously exposed to physical safety and job insecurity issues than other business sectors in a pandemic world. Since that time many aviation professionals have been active in searching for more safe and stable job opportunities in other sectors and this has fuelled the current global shortage of aviation professionals – especially aircraft engineers and aircrew.

Airport operators and airlines are addressing the staffing challenges by offering higher pay and wage supplements, working with government to fast-track work permits, visas and background checks, and even sending office personnel to the front lines. Some airports even capped the number of passengers at times because of labour shortages, forcing airlines to cancel flights.

Increased collaboration between airports, airlines and key third-party suppliers has also assisted to lessen the impact of the labour struggles. Enhanced data sharing and planning for travel peaks have also reduced disruptions. In addition, identifying best workplace practices and sharing them across the entire aviation sector can improve efficiency and ease the transition. The rebuilding of confidence and commitment to employment security by all aviation businesses is fundamental for a return to workplace stability and industrial harmony in the post COVID-19 era.

8
Criminal Law

INTRODUCTION

Aviation and crime is not a relationship that engenders assurance to those who fly. Nor is it a combination traditionally associated with the 'noble art of flying'. The uncomfortable reality is that the commercialization of aviation has brought with it a corresponding increase in the level of aviation-related criminal activity. Governments and regulators throughout the world have responded to acts of terrorism and sabotage and other antisocial behaviour committed within the aviation industry by creating a broad range of offences and by imposing severe sanctions to dissuade the perpetrators of such crimes.

Due to this increasing commercialization of aviation, there have been significant changes in both the nature and scope of aviation-related criminal activity. This has particularly been the case since the terrorist attacks on the World Trade Center in New York on 11 September 2001 – a topic which is considered at some length in Chapter 13. However, acts of sabotage and unlawful interference with aircraft are but two examples of aviation-related criminal behaviour. Acts or omissions that are considered by the state to be sufficiently serious and worthy of the imposition of criminal sanctions are prescribed in legislation. After all, at the end of the day, a crime is what the state says is a crime.

Although crime is widespread, there is no definitive definition across all legal jurisdictions. Essentially, a crime constitutes an act or omission which is prohibited under state or federal statutes or criminal codes. More formally, criminal law regulates the conduct of individuals in a society concerned with protecting the rights of the community as a whole (Michaelides-Mateou and Mateou 2010). This chapter will seek to highlight the common features of criminal activity throughout the world and in particular offences related to aviation activities.

Criminal law is punishable by the state, which differs from civil or private law, which primarily concerns actions between individuals (Bartsch 2024). There are, however, certain activities that are actionable either as a crime or as a civil wrong (tort). Assault and negligence, as we have seen in Chapter 6, are two examples.

In this chapter, an overview of the criminal law is provided and contrasted with civil proceedings – that is, proceedings that are 'non-criminal'. We will also see that even though the ICAO has a very consistent and firm position on matters relating to the prosecution of aircrew of other aviation professionals following an aircraft accident, when it comes to the individual criminal justice systems of member states, the approach taken varies enormously.

There was a time when the ICAO signatories more closely followed the requirements and standards in this area of aviation law, but now it seems that states are interpreting the guidelines quite differently within the context of their own judicial systems. As a

DOI: 10.4324/9781032652146-8

general observation, this seems to be the one area – or at least the most 'high profile' area – of international aviation law where there seems to be a jurisdictional divergence.

It is therefore incumbent upon all ICAO member states – not just those that currently comply with the existing requirements in Annex 13 of the ICAO and who promote the concept of 'just culture' – to take proactive steps towards closing this widening gap. If this area of international aviation law is not more closely harmonized, the aviation industry is at risk, particularly if there were to be a major aviation disaster in which the aforementioned standards and principles were *not* applied.

Varying Approaches to Criminal Liability in Aviation

As we will examine in later chapters, the approach by the ICAO with respect to aircraft accident investigation is such that the investigation of accidents should not be the basis – or even the source – of a prosecution action against aviation personnel. The ICAO advocates that the paramount consideration in an aircraft investigation should be finding the facts and determining the causal factors of the accident, not criminally punishing those who made errors of judgment or mistakes that may have produced tragic consequences.

In contrast to this underlying philosophy and concepts of 'just culture', in some nations there has actually been an increase towards prosecution against those involved in aircraft accidents. Esler (2009) describes the situation:

> It is telling that in some societies, such as Japan, every accident results in a prosecution . . . whereas in the United States, we have never had a commercial pilot prosecuted for criminalization . . . Japan, France, Greece and Italy have all incarcerated controllers. France has pilots in jail, and Italy has put controllers and aviation managers behind bars. There is a crew in Korea that busted minimums on an approach and crashed in Libya, which extradited them back to Korea where they were tried for manslaughter because there were fatalities in the accident. They were convicted and are in jail for life. . . . The tort legal system doesn't exist in most of these countries. Under the US tort system, we can assess all the factors in a case, but these countries don't do that. In Japan, if you kill people, there is no alternative system for publicly assessing culpability, no way to tell the public who was at fault, so they use a criminal trial to fulfil that societal obligation.

As most aviation incidents – and particularly those involving larger aircraft with multi-pilot crews – are the result of human error, the *potential* for legal issues to arise is obviously quite high. In the aviation industry, small human errors can result in large-scale accidents, leading to heavy loss of life which in some jurisdictions is increasingly leading to criminal proceedings against those found to be criminally responsible.

In spite of this huge variance in the approach by nations throughout the world in this area of the law, the primary purpose of this chapter is to provide awareness to aviation practitioners of the varying approaches taken by regulators, governments and the courts on the topic. This is especially the case for those aviation practitioners who may, as part of their employment, be working or based in foreign countries. In the outstanding publication on this area of the law, *Flying in the Face of Criminalization*, Michaelides-Mateou and Mateou (2010: 153) make a very valid observation:

> Even though pilots and air traffic controllers are aware of the possibility that they may face criminal charges after an aviation accident or serious incident, there seems to be a general lack

of awareness among them of the law and of the legal process subsequent to an aviation accident.

In the same publication, the authors go on to explain the extent to which many aviation practitioners are totally oblivious to the legal ramification of their actions or omissions. This situation becomes even more critical when considering the legal systems of countries other than their own:

> Specifically, they [pilots and air traffic controllers] have little knowledge regarding the law of negligence and how this is applied to their professions; nor do they realize that Cockpit Voice Recorders (CVR) transcripts and Flight Data Recorders (FDR) read-outs and statements made by aviation professionals have been admitted in subsequent criminal proceedings. Both pilots and air traffic controllers felt that the fear of prosecution would prevent the voluntary and truthful reporting of incidents and stated that they would be very reluctant to provide relevant information during an investigation for fear of incriminating either themselves or their colleagues. This fear will consequently encourage the hiding of certain errors or mishaps and the opportunity to extract safety lessons may be missed, therefore impeding safety. Pilots and air traffic controllers who are already working under great pressure to maintain a high safety level and achieve high productivity targets due to the economic pressures of the industry, are alarmed that the additional fear of prosecution due to an error will increase their stress and this will have a negative effect on their concentration, decision-making and ultimately on their performance.
>
> This danger was supported by a large majority of aviation professionals who indicated their reluctance and concerns over participating in the investigation subsequent to an aviation accident or serious incident because they feared the legal consequences and punitive measures following the outcome of the investigation.
>
> (Michaelides-Mateou and Mateou 2010: 156)

The fear of criminalization is slowly eroding the safety reporting systems which have been trusted for many years by frontline aviation professionals. Its non-punitive culture allowed the mandatory and voluntary safety reporting programmes to provide valuable information from the reporting of unintentional errors and mishaps.

DEVELOPMENT OF AVIATION CRIMINAL LAW

Classification of Crimes

The basic distinction of what constitutes a crime is similar in both the common law and civil law systems. In a common law system, a crime is generally referred to as an act or omission, which is prohibited under state or federal statutes. In civil law countries, a crime is any act or omission which is punishable under a federal criminal code. It should be noted that the French classification of 'crimes' does not correlate with these definitions, as 'crimes' in French law refer only to serious offences such as murder.

Crimes are generally classified based on the nature and severity of an offence and its outcome. This is pertinent across the majority of both civil and common law systems in countries throughout the world.

Typically, offences in common law countries are classified as either *summary* or *indictable* offences. Summary offences refer to relatively minor offences, such as trespass, and are dealt with summarily in a magistrates' court. This is particularly evident in England

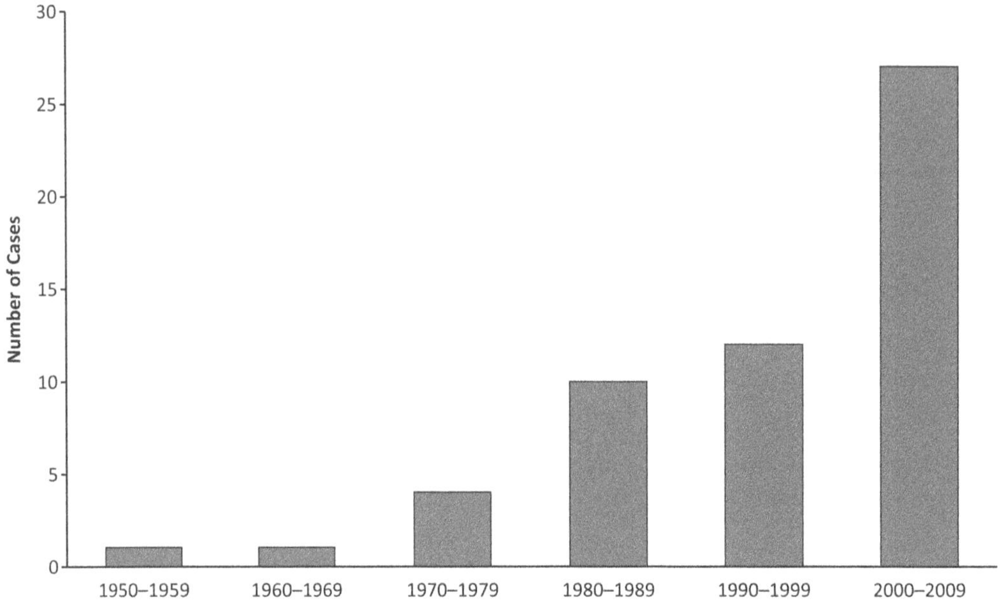

Figure 8.1 The number of worldwide cases of criminalizing human acts in aviation accidents and incidents per decade since 1950

Source: Dekker (2010)

and Australia. Indictable offences, on the other hand, are serious offences such as murder, which are dealt with by a judge and jury. However, some indictable offences such as assault can be dealt with summarily. These are known as *either way* offences in England.

Offences can also be classified as *misdemeanours* and *felonies*, which are usually based on the outcome of the sentencing. Misdemeanours, like summary offences, refer to minor crimes that are punishable by less than one year's imprisonment or a fine. Felonies are the more serious offences and are punishable by one or more year's imprisonment (Speciale 2006). This classification system is primarily used in the USA, but is also evident in the German criminal justice system, which, under its criminal code, classifies offences into either *Vergehen* or *Verbrechen* – misdemeanours or felonies, respectively.

The only distinguishing feature of French criminal law is the tripartite structure of offences. It contains three classifications of offences: *contraventions*, *délits* and *crimes*. *Délits* and *crimes* are similar to misdemeanours and felonies, respectively; however, *contraventions* refer to 'petty offences' which are dealt with by the Police Court and include offences such as speeding. This is also evident in other jurisdictions such as Germany, which has a classification of *ordnungswidrigkeiten*, which are administration offences or infractions which include illegal assembly and disturbing the peace.

PRESUMPTION OF INNOCENCE

The *presumption of innocence* is a principle that underlies most legal systems. It states that an individual is to be considered innocent until he or she is proven otherwise. This principle is often referred to in common law constitutions and is often seen in its Latin form *'Ei incumbit probatio qui dicit, non qui negat'*, meaning 'Proof lies on him who asserts, not on him who denies'.

The principle of the presumption of innocence has also been integrated into many civil law systems, such as the EU, which has included it in Article 48 of the *Charter of Fundamental Rights of the European Union*, which states, 'Everyone who has been charged shall be presumed innocent until proved guilty according to law'. This fundamental right is also highlighted in the *Convention for the Protection of Human Rights and Fundamental Freedoms*, which was written by the Council of Europe and is binding on all EU Member States.

The presumption of innocence is seen as a fundamental human right that should be afforded to all, but this is often not the case in today's media, which is quick to lay blame and portray the accused's guilt.

STANDARD OF PROOF

The principle of the presumption of innocence ensures that an accused is innocent until proven guilty; it is therefore the responsibility of the prosecution to prove guilt. In both the common and civil law systems, the prosecution must prove the accused's guilt in a criminal matter *beyond reasonable doubt*, although some matters of positive defence require the accused to prove but on the lower standard of proof on the *balance of probabilities*, which is generally used as the standard in civil matters (Jackson 2009). This standard may change in cases of strict liability offences, offences where the burden of proof is reversed and when a confiscation order is made.

Regardless of the system of law, the burden of proof in the majority of cases lies on the prosecution, meaning it is their obligation to prove that the accused is guilty of the offence. There are, however, some offences which reverse this onus of proof onto the defendant, such as drug possession offences, as seen in the High Court of Australia case of *He Kaw Teh*.

DOUBLE JEOPARDY

According to the principle of criminal law of *double jeopardy*, no one can be punished for the same crime more than once. If an individual has been acquitted of an offence, they cannot be tried again for the same offence unless there is substantial new evidence (Pengilley and McPhee 1994). For example, if a pilot was charged with involuntary manslaughter after an aviation accident and was acquitted in court, he or she could not be charged with involuntary manslaughter at a later date for the same offence unless significant evidence was later discovered.

SOURCES OF CRIMINAL LAW

The basis for criminal law in countries varies depending on their legal system, which is the main difference in criminal law between countries worldwide. Countries operating with a civil law system, such as France and Germany, have a system of codified laws, which is usually represented in a criminal or penal code. Codified legislation is used primarily as a source of criminal law, although statutes are also used. This is evident in the French *Code penal* and the German *Strafgesetzbuch*.

In common law systems, there are three primary sources of law. These include laws made by the parliament in the form of legislation and statutes, judge-made laws in the form of case law and common law, and finally constitutional laws, which are set out in federal constitutions, such as the Australian Constitution. Common law courts have the authority to make laws where no legislation exists and judges interpret the meaning of statutes and apply them to each case. The *doctrine of precedent* is a unique feature of the common law system and means that a judge at a level in the court system is bound to follow the central legal reasoning (the *ratio decidendi*) of decisions that were made at a higher level in the judiciary hierarchy. Civil law systems, as addressed in Chapter 3, are not bound by this doctrine and in these countries court decisions are not binding on any other court. For this reason, similar cases may come to vastly different conclusions, depending on which court they are heard in and by which judge.

CRIMINAL LIABILITY

Criminal law deals with actions that are seen as harmful as a whole towards the state. It can include acts or omissions where an individual has a legal responsibility to the state to act. For someone to be criminally responsible, he or she must have the capacity to make a voluntary decision to act in a particular way deemed criminal by the state.

Provisions establishing criminal liability are addressed in domestic legislation and vary from state to state.

ELEMENTS OF A CRIME

There are two universal elements of a crime, *mens rea* and *actus reus*, that must be proven to establish criminal responsibility. These elements are addressed throughout the criminal codes and federal statutes around the world and simply represent the 'physical element' and the 'mental element'. The *actus reus* represents the physical act or omission of a legal duty to act that is prohibited under the jurisdictional statutes or criminal code and is commonly referred to as the 'guilty act'. The *mens rea* element of a crime requires the accused to have possessed the necessary intention to commit an offence and is often translated to the 'guilty mind' or 'fault element'. This required state of mind can be shown through intention, knowledge, recklessness and negligence.

Intention

Intention is simply where the outcome of the criminal activity was desired or foreseen as certain and that the accused intended the action to have such consequences. Even if the outcome was not intended but was considered 'highly probable', this would still satisfy the proof of intent.

Knowledge

If the accused had knowledge of the criminal activity in which he or she was involved, the *mens rea* element is satisfied.

Recklessness

The fault element can be shown if the actions of the accused were careless of the possible consequences.

Negligence

An accused can be guilty of the mental element if it can be shown that the accused demonstrated a reckless disregard for the life and safety of others and that if there had not been state intervention, it is likely there would have been adverse outcomes.

Generally, both physical and fault elements need to be proven beyond a reasonable doubt for the prosecution to successfully charge the accused; however, in cases of strict or absolute liability, the *mens rea* or intention does not need to be shown for the accused to be guilty of that offence. This is quite common in aviation offences such as low flying.

AGE OF CRIMINAL RESPONSIBILITY

To be criminally responsible for an offence, it has to be shown that the individual has the capacity to make a voluntary decision to act criminally. As outlined in legislation, children often do not meet this capacity. The age at which a child is able to consciously make a decision is often debated, which is evident in the varying age of criminal responsibility amongst countries. The age of criminal responsibility varies from as young as 7 in Jordan and Pakistan to as old as 18 in Belgium. Generally, it is accepted that by the age of 14, children are able to establish the difference between what is morally right and wrong, which is supported by most countries having an age of criminal responsibility of around 14 years.

STRICT AND ABSOLUTE LIABILITY

Strict and absolute liability offences are generally offences that are recognized as posing a threat to public health and safety which require no proof of any mental state. Many aviation offences are strict liability by nature due to the severe risk to public safety outcomes that they may have. Although the definitions for strict and absolute liability vary considerably between jurisdictions – in fact, some jurisdictions do not differentiate between the terms – the following will provide the aviation practitioner with a sufficient awareness of the concepts.

As addressed in Chapter 5, strict liability offences require no fault element, which means that the defendant can be charged with an offence without it needing to be shown that he or she possessed the required criminal intention, or that the act was done with recklessness, negligence or any knowledge of outcome. Proof beyond reasonable doubt still needs to be shown for the *actus reus* to secure a conviction. There is one defence to strict liability offences, 'honest and reasonable mistake', which notes that an individual will not be found liable for a strict liability offence if he or she can show on the balance of probabilities that at or before the time of the conduct constituting the physical element, he or she was under a mistaken but reasonable belief that certain facts existed and that had those facts existed as the person believed they did, the conduct would not have constituted an offence. Similarly, absolute liability offences refer to offences that are not dependent on the state of mind of the accused; however, there is no defence available to absolute liability offences.

In the aviation industry, offences such as 'low flying' and 'unknowingly overloading aircraft' are classified as strict liability. For example, for a pilot to be charged with low flying as outlined in local regulations, the prosecution does not need to show that the pilot did so intentionally, knowingly, recklessly or even negligently to be charged; it only needs to show that the pilot did actually fly below the minimum height. The only defence in a case like this would be the defence of reasonable mistake of fact. If in this case the pilot had taken into account all of the factors a pilot would normally consider to determine the aircraft's height above the ground, but if the altimeter was displaying an incorrect reading in which the height was being portrayed as above the minimum height and the pilot had no reason to believe the altimeter was not functioning correctly and had no other reason to believe that he or she was flying below the minimum height, then it is likely that he or she could successfully use the defence of reasonable mistake of fact and avoid criminal liability.

Aircrew qualifications are paramount to air safety, and criminal sanctions attach to those who attempt to falsify their experience. In 2019 South African Airways fired a pilot who had been flying undetected with a forged pilot's licence. *USA Today* (5 March 2019) reported

> A South African Airways pilot resigned and now faces criminal charges after the airline discovered he lied about having the correct type of pilot's license to operate international flights. According to the airline, the pilot claimed to have an Airline Transport Pilot License, which all SAA pilots are required to obtain within five years of getting hired. In reality, he possessed a Commercial Pilot License, the airline said, which allows pilots to operate commercial flights, but not long, international flights.

The absolute responsibility cast upon the pilot inevitably carries with it absolute and final authority from take-off to landing. The status of the pilot therefore entails far reaching consequences making an instance of his negligent act open to be interpreted as a dangerous and unlawful act which could justify a charge of manslaughter in the least. Criminality of the act of the pilot lies quite independently of the incontrovertible liability in negligence which would follow from such act.

CORPORATE CRIMINAL LIABILITY

Corporate crime is an area of criminal law which is continuing to expand and is commonly referred to as *white collar crime*. Corporations around the world are under increased scrutiny for behaviour and activities that are seen to be harmful towards individuals and communities. As a result, governments are introducing legislation around the world to criminalize the activities of corporations and to develop corporate criminal liability. Corporate criminal liability has recently been introduced into legislation and exists in many countries, including the USA, England, Australia, France, Germany and Italy (De Maglie 2005; Michaelides-Mateou and Mateou 2010). Changes across European countries and around the world in the legal foundations for corporate criminal liability are reflecting the nature, scope and seriousness of corporate crime (Larsen and Smandych 2008). However, the transnational nature of corporate crimes makes it difficult to monitor and enforce, as there are many global inconsistencies across corporate criminal laws.

Larsen and Smandych (2008) identify the general requirements for corporate criminal liability to be the intent to harm (*mens rea*), a criminal act to cause the harm (*actus reus*) and acting within the scope of the corporate agent's employment. Russell and Gilbert (1999) expand on this and suggest that, for a criminal liability to be established, the act or omission must also be done with the intention to benefit the company.

Some common law countries have enacted corporate manslaughter and corporate homicide statutes, which provide that an organization is guilty of an offence if the way in which its activities are managed or organized causes a person's death, and amounts to a gross breach of a relevant duty of care owed by the organization to the deceased. These statutes apply inter alia to a corporation. The offence is termed 'corporate manslaughter', in so far as it is an offence under the law of England and Wales or Northern Ireland; and 'corporate homicide', in so far as it is an offence under the law of Scotland. An organization that is guilty of corporate manslaughter or corporate homicide is liable on conviction to a fine, and the offence of corporate homicide is indictable only in the High Court of Justiciary.

The possible application of this legislation to air transport is a reality, as exemplified in the Helios trial which opened on 26 February 2009 in Cyprus. The trial pertained to the island's worst air tragedy, when 121 people perished on a charter plane that slammed into a Greek hillside nearly four years previous. According to reports, Helios Airways and four airline officials faced charges of manslaughter and reckless endangerment in one of the most complex and high-profile cases in the eastern Mediterranean island's legal history. Plaintiffs, who were relatives of the dead, called for criminal action against those deemed responsible when the Helios Airways Boeing 737–300 ran out of oxygen and crashed outside Athens in August 2005. It was also reported that, although the authorities did not initially name those to be charged, the accused were known to be officials who held top management positions in the airline at the time of the crash.

Criminal intent is difficult to establish where the defendant is a corporation because, as many argue, corporations do not have a mind and do not have an independent action apart from the decisions that are made by the individuals involved, such as management and directors. Under this view, only natural people can form the necessary criminal intent to constitute a crime. On the other hand, many believe that corporations have the ability to formulate intent through formal decision-making structures and conduct to carry out its operational policies through action by human agents of the corporation.

In Australia – and similar provisions exist in most other countries – changes to their *Interpretation Acts* both federally and throughout the states have led to corporations being classified as legal 'persons', making them capable of holding the mental element of a crime and able to be charged of criminal offences (Bartsch 2024). French law now permits corporations to be charged with criminal offences under a new penal code governing corporate entities. It holds that corporations can be held criminally liable even when the criminal responsibility of a natural person cannot or has not yet been established. However, many corporate crimes, such as criminal negligence, are strict liability, which requires no *mens rea* to be proven.

Corporate Manslaughter

Corporate manslaughter involves the unlawful killing of another person by the act or omission of corporations. In the French Penal Code, 'Causing the death of another person by clumsiness, rashness, inattention, negligence or breach of an obligation of safety or prudence imposed by statute or regulations . . . constitutes manslaughter' (Section 2, Article 221–6). New legislation in the UK, the *Corporate Manslaughter and Corporate Homicide Act 2007*, allows companies to be charged for corporate manslaughter as a result of serious management failures which lead to gross breaches of duty of care, resulting in death.

Case Study: the Air France Concorde Crash 2000

On 25 July 2000, Air France Concorde crashed after a tyre burst on take-off, sending fragments into the fuel tank, fracturing it and causing a fire. All the passengers and crew, and four people on the ground, were killed, with 113 deaths in total. Five officials from Aerospatiale, Air France and Continental Airlines were charged with manslaughter in 2008. All were acquitted in December 2010, except for a Continental engineer who was given a 15-month suspended sentence. A Parisian criminal court ruled that Continental Airlines was criminally responsible for the crash, because a strip of metal that had fallen off one of Continental's airplanes was found to have started the chain of events that led to the accident. The court also fined Continental $266,000 and ordered it to pay the Concorde operator Air France $1.3 million in damages. In 2012 a French appeal court cleared Continental Airlines of criminal responsibility for the crash and also absolved the mechanic of involuntary manslaughter.

In so far as criminalizing corporate activity is concerned, this could set a dangerous trend against efforts by the air transport industries which are calculated to ensure safety. Any extension of these principles of liability to criminal law would cast an undue burden on those involved in providing services that are usually given out by experts such as pilots and surgeons and their employers. They would be forced to concentrate on covering their tracks rather than ensuring the protection of those under their charge.

CRIMINAL PROCEDURES AND TRIALS

Types of Criminal Systems

The process of adjudicating over a criminal trial is either *adversarial* or *inquisitorial* in nature, which prescribes court procedure and the criminal process.

In an adversarial system, each party puts forward its case, usually through legal representatives such as solicitors, barristers or attorneys and the decision is made by an independent and neutral third party (such as a judge, magistrate or tribunal). The decision-maker is to be completely impartial and free from bias and although it does not play an active role in the investigation, it interprets and applies the law. The majority of courts in common law countries follow the adversarial system, except the Coroner's Court, which takes an inquisitorial approach.

Civil law countries on the other hand are more investigative by nature and the notable difference is the judge's active role as investigator. Judges in inquisitorial systems hold significant power and are able to examine and interrogate witnesses and request evidence. Inquisitorial systems also have a strong emphasis on screening and investigative processes, whereas adversarial systems have a stronger focus on the criminal trial (Reichel 2008).

Criminal Process

The criminal process differs between countries, and many are run in either the inquisitorial or adversarial style. However, in recent times, there has been a merging of these styles, with some countries adopting features of both. In this chapter, the procedure has been divided into the following stages: investigation, prosecution, bail, pre-trial proceedings, trial, juries and sentencing.

Investigation In countries that have adopted an adversarial system, the investigation stage is usually performed by the police. The police generally have the power, as prescribed in legislation, to investigate crimes, including rights to search and seize property involved in criminal offences. In the USA, 'probable cause' must be determined for a search warrant to be issued, which is required before any search or seizure occurs.

In countries with an inquisitorial system, the investigation process is the main stage of the criminal process and is predominantly performed by both the police and the prosecutor. In France, the *police judiciarie* or judicial police are given the authority to search and seize under the supervision of district prosecutors (Reichel 2008). The evidence found in this investigation is then passed on to the public prosecutor's office which, depending on the substance of evidence, can bypass the investigation judge and take the matter straight to trial (Jackson 2009).

Prosecution In both legal systems, it is the duty of the police to charge the accused with the offence on behalf of the state, initiating the start of the criminal trial process. The accused is notified of the charge and when he or she is required to attend court.

Bail Bail is the temporary release of an accused person awaiting trial. It often involves a set of conditions imposed on the accused, which could be a monetary value or frequent reporting to police. Bail is commonly granted by police or in court. There is generally a presumption in favour for bail; however, it can be refused if it is believed that the accused poses a severe risk to the community or there is a fear that he or she will not return for the trial proceedings. Bail will usually only be granted for non-violent offenders.

Pre-trial Proceedings There are many mechanisms throughout the world which are put in place before a trial to determine whether there is sufficient evidence, as well as trying to increase the efficiency of the criminal trial. In England, committal proceedings are conducted by magistrates to determine whether there is sufficient evidence for a jury to hold a charge for an indictable offence. Similarly, in the USA, an accused is indicted before a grand jury where the jury determines if there is enough evidence for the case to go to trial.

In civil law systems, this process is known as a 'pre-trial screening' or 'judicial investigation', where it is decided whether the case shall be brought before the court or whether alternate forms of resolution will be taken. In France, this involves the *juge d'instruction* or 'investigation judge', who actively participates in the pre-trial investigation.

Pre-trial proceedings also include plea bargaining. Plea bargaining is commonly referred to as the process where the prosecutor negotiates for a lesser sentence if the accused pleads guilty, ensuring a conviction, and is common in England and the USA. It is not generally used in European countries; however, Germany has adopted the process, and it is usually used for white collar and drug offences. Italy has also adopted a similar procedure, called *trial avoidance mechanisms,* which involves part-agreed sentences that aim to reduce the number of cases going through the court system. The significant difference between these procedures and those in adversarial systems is that in some countries, notably France and Germany, a guilty plea does not eliminate the need for a trial and generally only shortens it.

Trial A trial in an inquisitorial system differs quite substantially from the adversarial system and has an investigative focus, as opposed to two sides competing and arguing their case. In inquisitorial systems, parties must provide all relevant evidence to the court, the judges can also call and actively examine witnesses, and the trial process is essentially an extension of the investigation stage.

On the other hand, adversarial trials have a focus on due process and the judge has notably less power, particularly in relation to deciding which evidence is to be heard and witnesses. Both legal parties – the defence and the prosecution – argue their side, providing evidence and case law to support their argument.

The type of court in which a trial will be heard often varies depending on the severity of the offence; for example, in French law, petty crimes will be heard by the Police Court, whereas felonies will be heard in a higher court known as the Assize Court.

The criminal process in aviation-related cases is usually lengthy, with many cases taking up to a decade to reach the trial stage, such as the Air France Concorde crash in 2000, which did not reach trial until 2010. This has a detrimental effect on aircrew and aviation personnel as it usually results in the suspension of duties, loss of income and irreparable damage to reputation regardless of the outcome of the trial.

Juries Although juries are a unique feature to adversarial systems, merges between common and civil law practices have seen the jury system extend to some inquisitorial systems. Typically, juries comprise 12 randomly selected adults (however, some countries such as Scotland have up to 15 jurors). Jurors are characteristically laypersons who are meant to represent a cross-section of society. A jury must take into account all of the facts presented before it and determine the guilt, or lack thereof, of the accused. Due to the merging of many practices in both the civil and common law systems, some countries such as France have adopted the use of juries in trials involving the most serious offences.

The adoption of juries by inquisitorial systems varies significantly from the jury system, as seen in the common law. Germany, for example, has used 'lay judges' or '*Schöffen*', which are usually two or three citizens who make up a 'mixed bench' with professional judges to adjudicate most criminal cases, with the exception of petty offences and serious political crimes. These lay judges have powers of interrogation, deliberation, voting and sentencing (Reichel 2008).

The voting process of jurors and lay judges varies around the world, with some requiring a unanimous vote and others requiring only a majority vote to determine guilt.

Sentencing The underlying feature of criminal law is to punish those who break laws. Courts try to hand down sentences that are seen as proportionate to the offence committed, taking into account the circumstances and factors surrounding the offence and the offender. Penalties for criminal offences range from minor monetary fines to lengthy imprisonment and, in some countries, the death penalty.

Imprisonment is seen as a last resort, and Reichel (2008) identifies four methods of justification for imprisonment, which include retribution, deterrence, rehabilitation and incapacitation. *Retribution* strongly focuses on vengeance and an 'eye for an eye' approach towards punishment of the offender. *Deterrence* is also a common means of justification and can be divided into *general deterrence*, where other individuals may be deterred or dissuaded from committing a crime, and *specific deterrence*, which suggests that by imprisoning an individual offender, that person is unable to commit any further offences and is very much dissuaded from reoffending after release. *Rehabilitation* is often used to justify incarceration and suggests that imprisonment reforms offenders. Finally, *incapacitation* refers to the restriction of the offender's freedom of movement and is also used to justify home detention.

Around the world, aircrew, aviation professionals, airlines and manufacturers who have been involved in aircraft incidents have been sentenced to significant terms of imprisonment for murder and manslaughter charges, as well as received substantial fines and suffered severe damage to their reputation.

'JUST CULTURE' AND THE INCREASING CRIMINALIZATION OF AVIATION

In the past few decades, there has been a significant shift towards the criminalization of aviation professionals, aircrew, airlines and manufacturers following aviation accidents. As Michaelides-Mateou and Mateou (2010) highlighted, there were 27 cases of aviation accidents that were criminally investigated from 1956 to 1999 (see Figure 8.1). The number of cases between 2000 and 2009 surpassed that figure, with 28 cases being investigated. This significant increase in criminal investigation raises major concerns and issues when trying to determine the appropriate balance between the importance of aircraft investigation and safety with judicial proceedings and achieving 'justice' for those affected.

Annex 13 of the Chicago Convention outlines the operation of accident investigation and judicial proceedings, which raises an important concept of 'just culture'. 'Just culture' is defined by Eurocontrol as 'culture where front line operators or others are not punished for actions, omissions or decisions taken by them that are commensurate with their experience and training, but where gross negligence, willful violations and destructive acts are not tolerated' (Article 2(k) of the Commission Regulation (EU) No 691/2010 of 29 July 2010).

The ICAO argues that it is best only to pursue criminal action if it is deemed to bring safer outcomes for the aviation industry or unless the actions of the people involved show that the incident 'was caused by an act considered, in accordance with the law, to be conduct with intent to cause damage, or conduct with knowledge that damage would probably result, equivalent to reckless conduct, gross negligence or willful misconduct' (Annex 13 of the Chicago Convention).

The inclusion of Annex 13 in the Chicago Convention establishes that there should be recommended procedures in the case of clashes between the accident investigation and judicial trials. However, due to the nature of international treaties, when comparing domestic legislation around the world, there are many inconsistencies, particularly in relation to the treatment of information gained in the process of accident investigation and determining which authority has priority. Annex 13 of the Chicago Convention implies that the main objective of aircraft accident investigation is the prevention of accidents and to increase safety measures as a result – the aim is not to lay blame or determine liability.

In the case of information collected in the accident investigation process, many jurisdictions allow for the information collected to be admissible as evidence in subsequent criminal trials. For example, in New Zealand, there is no absolute guarantee of non-disclosure, whereas US law prohibits disclosure of cockpit voice recordings to the public, except in the event that the courts order the disclosure of information from the investigation process for non-accident investigation purposes. This creates a problem relating to the freedom of information, and a study conducted by Michaelides-Mateou and Mateou (2007) found that a survey of pilots and Air Traffic Control Operators (ATCOs) found that there was a strong fear that the prosecution of aviation offences would prevent the truthful and voluntary reporting of incidents to accident investigation authorities for fear of self-incrimination.

The increased criminalization of aviation accidents has also led to tension between accident investigation authorities and judicial authorities. Although the ICAO states that judicial intervention should not impinge on accident investigations, this is not the case in many countries. In France and Germany, the interest of the judicial authority prevails if there is conflict between the authorities. The French system prioritizes the criminal investigation over accident investigation, whereas in the UK, priority is given to the accident investigation authority to establish the causes and reasons behind an aviation accident to ensure that safety outcomes are prioritized over proportioning guilt and laying blame. A UK publication stresses that '[t]he public interest requires that safety considerations are of paramount importance, the consequence of which may mean that the interests of an [A]AIB investigation have to take precedence over the criminal investigation' (Memorandum of Understanding between the Crown Prosecution Service and the Air Accidents Investigation Branch, Marine Accident Investigation Branch, and Rail Accident Investigation Branch, October 2008).

There is a need to ensure that accident investigation is given priority over judicial proceedings as it is in the best interests of public safety to ensure that the causes of accidents are addressed to avoid the reoccurrence of such accidents. Werfelman (2008) summarizes this point by highlighting the importance of determining the reasons behind an aviation accident:

> The paramount consideration in an aviation accident investigation should be to determine the probable cause of and contributing factors in the accident, not to punish criminally flight crews, maintenance employees, airline or manufacturer executives, regulatory officials or air traffic controllers. By identifying the 'what' and the 'why' of an accident, aviation safety professionals will be better equipped to address accident prevention for the future. Criminal investigations can and do hinder the critical information-gathering portions of an accident investigation, and subsequently interfere with the successful prevention of future aviation industry accidents.

Michaelides-Mateou and Mateou (2007) highlight a significant issue with the increase in criminal prosecution of aviators. A survey of pilots and ATCOs found that the increased fear of criminal prosecution would increase stress and have an adverse effect on their work performance and concentration. This increase in stress could easily cause a human factor-related accident.

Case Study: Falxon 50 EX Jet Crash 2014

On 20 October 2014, the corporate jet of Christophe de Margerie, CEO of Total, a large French oil company, crashed in Moscow, killing all four people on board including de Margerie. The crash was caused by the collision of the jet and a snowplough being driven by a drunk driver on the ground in breach of the relevant rules.

Employees of the Vnukovo air traffic control centre, part of Russia's State Air Traffic Management Corporation, were later charged under Part 3, Article 263 of the Russian Criminal Code for violating the rules of air traffic safety. It was found that the employees neglected their duties by failing to inform the pilots that the snowplough was moving towards and entering the runway. The charges were brought after an investigation by the Interstate Aviation Committee (IAC), and Russian detectives argued that the air traffic controllers (ATCs) could have prevented the collision.

EFFECT OF CRIMINALIZATION ON AVIATION SAFETY

Whilst holding professionals in the aviation industry accountable for criminal offences is vital for the administration of justice, it was found by Michaelides-Mateou and Mateou that the criminalization of pilots and ATCs actually had a negative effect on safety. Many pilots were found to believe that they could not work effectively with the fear of being prosecuted haunting them. ATCOs commonly argued that 'creating a blame culture' was 'counter-productive' for this reason.

In fact, Michaelides-Mateou and Mateou found that a huge majority of aviation professionals expressed reluctance in participating in any post-accident investigation because they were worried about the legal consequences that would come out of any investigative report. This is unfortunate, and undermines the idea in Annex 13 of the

Chicago Convention that technical investigations for accidents are not to be used to apportion blame to any individual. This has been reflected in many jurisdictions. In Australia, for example, section 12AA(3) of the *Transport Safety Investigation Act 2003*, the legislation which establishes Australia's air accident investigation agency, the Australian Transport Safety Bureau (ATSB), makes it expressly clear that the ATSB's role is not to apportion blame or to assist in any court proceedings or to provide the means to determine the liability of any person in respect of a transport safety matter. ATSB reports are not to be used in civil and criminal proceedings as evidence. The same is true in the United States. The National Transport Safety Board (NTSB) has no regulatory or enforcement authority, and any analysis it provides in terms of an aircraft accident and determination of probable cause is inadmissible in a court of law for civil and criminal proceedings. Despite this, however, aviation professionals are still worried to participate.

Michaelides-Mateou and Mateou (2007: 156–60) conclude:

> The fear of criminalization is slowly but surely eroding the safety reporting system which has been trusted for many years by frontline aviation professionals. . . . Holding aviation professionals accountable for their inadvertent acts and omissions has no positive effect on aviation safety and does not minimize or reduce aviation accidents.

LEGISLATION CREATING CRIMINAL OFFENCES IN AVIATION

Aviation Criminal Offences

Generally, aviation criminal offences are activities regarded as disrupting the safety and security of an aircraft, its crew and passengers. As addressed in Chapter 13, there have been significant offences created since the events of 11 September 2001, such as hijacking and terrorism. Some other criminal offences that usually arise from the actions of pilots and aircrew include offences of homicide and endangering human life. This chapter will address the criminal offences likely to affect pilots, aircrew and aviation professionals – mainly homicide and negligence.

Criminal negligence differs between countries; however, the general elements are similar. In cases of criminal negligence, it must be proven that the accused did not comprehend the consequences of his or her behaviour and was unaware of the risk or that he or she was aware of the risk but chose to ignore it (Michaelides-Mateou and Mateou 2010). Criminal negligence can be categorized, and in Canada, for example, criminal negligence is often separated into categories based on the outcome of the offence, such as criminal negligence causing death and bodily harm. Generally, criminal sanctions are imposed for negligent or reckless conduct that results in the death or injury of others (Michaelides-Mateou and Mateou 2010).

There are generally three types of homicide, depending on the state of mind of the accused – these include murder, voluntary manslaughter and involuntary manslaughter.

In cases of manslaughter, it is alleged that the defendant knows 'that the risk of his or her actions may result in death of others, ignores the risk and continues the behaviour anyway' (Michaelides-Mateou and Mateou 2010: 25).

International Law

On 7 December 1944, the world community acknowledged the need to achieve safety in international aviation through uniformity in law by establishing an organization to govern international aviation, conferring upon it quasi-legislative power to prescribe standards governing international aviation safety, and obliging member states to implement these standards through their domestic laws. Such was the importance of the *Convention on International Civil Aviation*, better known as the Chicago Convention, and no fewer than 193 sovereign nations have agreed to comply with the standards prescribed by the ICAO.

With the establishment of the ICAO, the highest possible level of uniformity and consistency across the aviation industry worldwide has been achieved. As observed by Professor Michael Milde (1996: 4): '[c]ivil aviation could not have evolved without worldwide uniformity in regulations, standards and procedures in relation of air navigation'.

Following the Chicago Convention, there have been numerous treaties and conventions made to protect and enhance safety across international aviation. These treaties have also created criminal offences for acts which appear to jeopardize the safety of the aircraft or of persons or property therein. However, the issue with international law lies in its inability to be enforced.

According to accepted principles of law as laid down by international convention, it is incontrovertible that the final responsibility for the safe operation of an aircraft lies with the pilot. The Chicago Convention provides: 'The pilot-in-command shall be responsible for the operation and safety of the aircraft and for the safety of all persons on board, during flight time'. This presumption of responsibility has influenced most states which have signed or ratified the Convention and is reflected clearly in their air navigation laws. These laws have been observed to list requirements which any pilot would naturally comply with. Failure to comply with such regulations renders the pilot liable for prosecution on a criminal charge. In any event, the fundamental postulate which imposes *prima facie* responsibility on the pilot has been accepted as a general principle of liability of the pilot which sets the base for determining his legal status and responsibility.

Domestic Legislation

Criminal legislation is domestic by nature and applies to one particular jurisdiction, albeit a country or state. This causes some significant variations between states and countries as to what is classified as a criminal offence, as well as the criminal proceedings that follow a charge. This can be extremely difficult due to the international nature of aviation.

Although many countries have signed and ratified many international conventions and treaties, which outline offences in relation to particular aviation issues such as security and safety, there are still inconsistencies amongst aviation criminal offences worldwide.

Defences to Aviation Offences

There are many defences available for criminal matters, such as mental illness and duress; however, there are three in particular which are relevant to aviation offences. These include the following.

Necessity The defence of necessity generally states that the accused shall not be found guilty of an offence if he or she was compelled to act criminally due to a sudden or extraordinary emergency. This defence can usually not be used for murder.

Without Fault or Privity The defence of without fault or privity states that an accused is not accountable for committing or omitting an act if he or she did not have knowledge but took all the necessary steps to gain this.

Honest and Reasonable Mistake of Fact As highlighted in the example of low flying, the defence of reasonable mistake of fact finds the accused not guilty of an offence if it can be shown that:

- at the time of the offence, the accused considered whether or not facts existed and was under a mistaken but reasonable belief about those facts; and
- if the state of facts had been as the accused had considered, the act or omission would not have constituted an offence.

It is important that individuals involved in legal proceedings following aviation accidents are aware of legislation from within the jurisdiction and seek legal advice immediately, as well as being aware of their legal rights.

9
Commercial Law and Competition Law

INTRODUCTION

Aviation is big business. The airline sector alone has a global market valuation of USD 996 billion in 2024. The recovery of commercial aviation following the carnage brought about by the coronavirus pandemic has been nothing short of astounding. But during the height of the COVID-19 pandemic, things were tough for the airline industry, both domestically and internationally. Airlines were one of the most affected businesses worldwide. All aviation sectors suffered significant losses in 2020 and 2021 except for air cargo airlines and freight forwarders. Global airline traffic (measured by revenue passenger kilometres) declined by 66 per cent in 2020, and by 58 per cent in 2021, compared to 2019, producing an economic loss of USD 244 billion in 2020 and USD 146 billion in 2021.

In 2024, the world's combined airline fleet is estimated to carry more than 4.96 billion passengers, being a record high and surpassing the pre-pandemic levels. Today, there are over 5,000 airlines issued with International Civil Aviation Organization (ICAO) codes and at any time there are approximately half a billion passengers airborne. In other words, international aviation is a commercial enterprise of global proportions.

As we saw in Chapter 4, such a commercial industry must be regulated to ensure that business operations are conducted efficiently and fairly. Commercial law seeks to fulfil the first of these objectives by allowing businesses to choose from a selection of legal structures the most suitable for their circumstances. Some structures are flexible enough for small businesses, whereas others provide robust protection for the large amounts of capital involved in big business by imposing strict management discipline and limited liability.

Another important aspect of commercial law is that it promotes and enforces fairness through 'competition' or 'antitrust' law. It seeks to preserve the economic freedom of markets by preventing large market players exercising undue control over supply and demand.

Finally, this chapter also considers some special commercial legal rules that apply to aviation and similar transport industries, such as the law of carriage, as well as considering some special features of the law of insurance that apply to aviation and the ways in which airlines acquire their most prominent assets – their aircraft.

BUSINESS STRUCTURES

Businesses exist everywhere around the world and utilize many and varied structures. No two businesses can be considered entirely alike, but there are enough general

DOI: 10.4324/9781032652146-9

similarities between types of businesses that business structures can be separated into only a few categories. The choice of how to structure a business is critical to its success: the wrong structure could mean increased expenditure in terms of legal compliance costs, more stringent financial reporting requirements and, perhaps, less flexibility to take business opportunities as they arise. Selecting the most appropriate legal structure for a business enterprise is thus important to its longevity.

Sole Proprietors

An entrepreneur should feel no impediment in setting up shop and going into business for himself or herself. A *sole proprietor* or *sole trader* is simply a person in business on his or her own account, with no special legal structure surrounding their operations. This is the least legally complex form of business, requiring absolutely no formality to establish, run or dissolve, and allowing the entrepreneur absolute flexibility in operation.

Some jurisdictions provide for registration of a sole proprietor's business name, and such registration is only required when the sole proprietor wishes to trade using a name other than his or her own. In such jurisdictions, registration is typically only to allow for the public to identify the person behind the business name – which is obviously not required when the person trades under his or her own name – and conveys no other legal rights, such as trademark status, which might prevent others from using the name. Registration of a business name is often the only formality required.

The absence of a complicated legal structure surrounding the business both assists the sole proprietor and can greatly reduce establishment costs. It is helpful because of its simplicity: the sole proprietor owns everything in his or her own name and is not required (legally) to share it with anybody. Trading under his or her own name also allows the sole proprietor flexibility to operate the business as he or she sees fit.

However, along with absolute ownership of the business and its profits comes the absolute responsibility and legal liability for its losses. All acts of the business are taken in the name of the sole proprietor personally. This leaves the sole proprietor open, personally, to the legal liability following every action taken during business. Such liability not only extends to contract debts, such as expenses incurred to suppliers, but also to tortious and even criminal liability for injuries it causes: see Chapters 6 and 8.

Sole proprietorship is often considered to be most appropriate to small or very small businesses. In an aviation sense, it could be a useful business structure for a small flying school or air charter operator. However, any budding aeronautical businessperson should check his or her local laws to find out whether an operator of an aircraft is required to be a corporation, as is required in some countries.

Partnerships

Partnerships occur when two or more people enter into business jointly on their own collective account, with a view to making a profit. The presence of more than one person in the partnership introduces some legal complexity to the business structure. A partnership is commonly based on an agreement, usually known as a 'partnership agreement', struck between the partners, which acts as a contract between them. The partnership agreement regulates all aspects of the partnership to the extent not regulated by the law. This agreement covers such things as:

- the amount each partner must contribute to the business;
- how the proceeds of the business are divided between the partners or reinvested in the business;
- any mechanisms to settle disputes that arise between the partners; and
- how to dissolve the partnership.

Partnership law varies between jurisdictions, but may dictate when a partnership exists, what must be included in a partnership agreement, the rules governing the dissolution of a partnership and other default rules that apply in the absence of stipulation in the partnership agreement.

In a partnership, in a similar fashion to a sole proprietorship, the partners share absolute ownership of the property of the business. Legal complexity surrounds where the line is drawn between a partner's own personal property and the 'partnership property' shared by all partners as part of the business. It is here that the partnership, or 'firm', *almost* becomes an entity in itself, and, indeed, for some purposes, it can be considered as such.

Generally speaking, partnership property consists of any plant, equipment and stock used in the business and the money each partner invests in it. It also includes the proceeds of the business. Further, the partners are usually not entitled to any claim on the partnership property during the life of the partnership; their rights exist merely in a share, often defined by the partnership agreement, in the excess of the partnership property over the debts of the partnership business upon winding-up. In the meantime, the partners may decide how and when the revenues or profits of the partnership are paid to the partners.

A partnership, also in a similar fashion to a sole proprietorship, is not a legal entity separate from its owners or managers. It is simply several individuals trading jointly in their own names. As such, the concept of limited liability (which, as will be seen later, applies to corporations) does not apply to partnerships. The partners of any partnership are jointly and severally liable for all the debts of the partnership. The liability is personal in nature, and it is without limit. As such, each partner is personally liable for the full extent of the partnership debts, both in conjunction with the other partners (jointly) and separately to the other partners (severally). Herein lies one of the greatest risks in the partnership business structure: one partner may be held liable for all the partnership debts of the others.

It is here that the law steps in to protect the partners from themselves and each other. Local partnership laws typically provide rules specifying, among other things, that:

- partnership property must be held and applied solely for the benefit of the firm;
- partners acting in the name of the firm must not gain a secret profit;
- all revenues gained and expenses incurred in the name of the firm must be made known to all the other partners;
- the books of the partnership are to be kept at the place of business of the firm and are to be accessible to every partner;
- the firm must indemnify a partner for any actions taken in the course of the firm's business, or actions necessary for the preservation of the firm's business.

In common law countries, these duties are overlaid by what is called a 'fiduciary' duty. The fiduciary duty in this case is essentially a duty placed upon each partner to act in the interests of the firm, rather than in his or her own interests, when conducting firm business.

A partnership automatically dissolves upon the death or retirement of one of the partners. The surviving or remaining partners may constitute a new partnership and carry on the same business, but it is legally a new partnership, not the same old partnership continued. Similarly, in order to add new partners, it is required to dissolve the old partnership (in a legal sense – the partnership business will presumably stay in place physically in most cases) and reconstitute a new partnership with the new partner(s) added.

Professional partnerships – for example, firms of lawyers, accountants or engineers – usually provide in their partnership agreements for automatic reconstitution ('novation') of the partnership upon the death or retirement of a partner.

Limited Partnerships

A limited partnership is a special kind of partnership. In many respects it is similar, if not the same, as an ordinary partnership, but it does have some special features. Like an ordinary partnership, the limited partnership is usually not incorporated, so does not have its own separate legal entity status as a corporation does.

The main difference between the ordinary partnership and the limited partnership is the way in which capital is raised for the business. An ordinary partnership involves the partners investing their own capital and then managing the business. The same can be said of the 'general' partners in a limited partnership. The difference lies in the other class of partners, the 'limited' partners, who invest capital but do not participate in the management of the business. Indeed, the limited partners are generally not permitted to participate – if they do, they 'cross the line' and become general partners.

Limited partners can avail themselves of the advantage of limited liability. The liability of a limited partner is limited to the amount of capital the limited partner invested in the partnership. On the other hand, a general partner's liability is unlimited, and the general partners are jointly and severally liable for the debts of the firm, as they are in an ordinary partnership.

CORPORATIONS

The corporation is a popular form of business in modern society and is especially prevalent in international aviation. The main reason for its popularity in the aviation industry is due to the high capital costs and issues of legal liability arising from aircraft accidents. Companies can and do limit the financial exposure and legal liability of individuals that are part of a corporation, including company directors and senior executives. International airlines often, if not always, conduct their business on a corporate basis. International airports are also usually operated by corporations, and aircraft maintenance and repair organizations are also typically companies. Companies range in size from very small to the largest business entities in existence.

Unfortunately, there is no such thing as 'international corporate law'. Corporations law remains very much a jurisdictionally based law, which is to say that the law pertaining to corporations is very much local rather than international. Some areas of corporate or commercial law, as will be discussed later, are governed by international convention or treaty, but the 'nuts and bolts' of the law relating to companies depends most often upon the law of the country where the company is incorporated. Incorporation is where the company is registered, which is usually the country where it was established. As such, a 'company' is a slightly different thing in each country, and slightly different rules will apply to it.

In the USA, company law is a state matter, so each state has its own corporations' code. This is not the case in some other federations, such as Canada, where corporations law is a matter for the central government, so that one law relating to corporations applies throughout the country.

In Europe, each country also has its own company law, but there is a new entity known as a *Societas Europaea* (SE), which is a type of company incorporated in Europe, rather than in any one country within the EU. With this mix of different company laws internationally, it is surprising that there is such consistency in the basics – the fundamental concepts of corporations and their components – around the world. The following section will discuss these fundamentals briefly.

In general, there are in each jurisdiction a number of different types of companies, each suited for slightly different purposes. A typical division is between 'private' and 'public' companies, which usually refers to who can buy shares: a 'private' company sells shares only to those who it invites to buy them, whereas a 'public' company offers its shares to all on the open market. A number of states in the USA have introduced a form of company known as a 'Limited Liability Company' (LLC). It should be emphasized that this form is *not* a corporation, but is considered an unincorporated business entity, despite being treated as an entity separate from its members, managers and employees.

Separate Legal Entity Essential to the concept of the corporation is the notion that the body formed is a separate legal entity – separate, that is, from its owners and managers. When a company is formed, it is as if a child is born. Upon birth, a child gains legal status as a person and thus gains the right to recognition at law as a being separate from his or her parents. As an individual, the child has the legal ability to participate in society. As the child grows, he or she gains the ability to enter into contracts, to buy and sell property and (from a legal perspective) to sue and be sued. The child is also subject to the law and can be held liable for his or her breaches of the law. Technically, there is no legal barrier to any of this happening from the moment of the child's birth – the only barrier is a physical one, related to the situations in which the child can implicate himself or herself along the path to maturity.

According to Lord Denning in *HL Bolton (Engineering) Co Ltd v TJ Graham & Sons Ltd* [1957] 1 QB 159 at 172:

> A company may in many ways be likened to a human body. It has a brain and nerve centre which controls what it does. It also has hands which hold the tools and act in accordance with directions from the center. Some of the people in the company are mere servants and agents who are nothing more than hands to do the work and cannot be said to represent the mind or will. Others are directors and managers who represent the directing mind and will of the company and control what it does. The state of mind of these managers is the state of mind of the company and is treated by the law as such.

However, the law may (and, in most jurisdictions, does) limit the child's ability to do certain things. It does this through the concept of *legal capacity*. Full legal capacity is the ability to act on one's own behalf in all legal situations, and the law assumes all adults to have this capacity unless they are of unsound mind. Children usually have limited capacity, such as the limited ability to enter into binding contracts only for 'necessities'. A child may still enter into other contracts, but these are said to be 'voidable' at the option of the child – meaning that the child can later choose whether to be bound by the contract or to 'avoid' it.

A company, to complete this rather extended metaphor, becomes a legal person upon incorporation, just as a child becomes a legal person upon his or her birth. The difference is that a company is created *with full legal capacity* at the moment it is incorporated. As such, it is legally separate from the people who constitute it. This concept creates what is known variously as the *veil of incorporation* or the *corporate veil*.

According to Lord Halsbury LC in the old English case of *Salomon v Salomon & Co Ltd* [1897] AC 22:

> It seems to me impossible to dispute that once the company is legally incorporated it must be treated like any other independent person with rights and liabilities appropriate to itself.

The decision in *Salomon v Salomon* was influential across all the common law jurisdictions. The judgment also represents an attempt to 'lift (or pierce) the corporate veil' and hold the members of a company personally responsible for the company's actions. Because of the widespread importance of this decision, a more detailed account of the case follows.

***Salomon v Salomon & Co Ltd* [1897] AC 22, House of Lords**

Aron Salomon was a leather merchant and boot manufacturer trading under the name 'A. Salomon & Co' in Whitechapel High Street towards the end of the nineteenth century. Mr Salomon had traded for approximately 30 years before incorporating a company by the name of 'Aron Salomon & Co Ltd'. At the time, English legislation required a company to be incorporated by seven corporators. Salomon met this requirement by enlisting his wife, daughter and four sons to take shares in the company, as well as taking a share himself. The company was incorporated on 28 July 1892, with a notional share capital comprising 40,000 one pound shares. Upon incorporation, one share was issued to Salomon and to each member of his family (i.e. one share to each of the seven corporators). Salomon's business was then sold to the company for £39,000. The company paid the purchase price by issuing Salomon 20,000 shares as well as 100 debentures (a kind of secured debt instrument), each with a face value of £100 – that is, a secured debt of £10,000. The remaining £9,000 was an unsecured debt to Mr Salomon.

Although his family technically held an interest in the company, Salomon essentially managed it himself in much the same way as he had previously carried on business as a sole proprietor. In the year following incorporation, the company struck hard times. There was a depression and a downturn in the boot trade, leading to strikes. Mr Salomon borrowed £5,000 from Edmund Broderip and immediately invested the money into the company. To secure the loan, the company cancelled Mr Salomon's debentures (at his request) and reissued new debentures to Broderip in the same amount, but paying 8 per cent interest.

The company defaulted on the interest payments to Broderip, who, in September 1893, commenced an action against the company for payment. In order to meet the debt, the company was liquidated, but even after the liquidation there remained a sum of £1,055 owing, which was secured by the debentures. Broderip sued Salomon personally to recover the amount.

At trial, Vaughan Williams J made orders to the effect that the company was merely an agent for Mr Salomon, and that, as such, Mr Salomon was obliged to indemnify the liquidator for the company's unsecured debts, and a lien was placed on all sums payable by the company on the debentures. The Court of Appeal upheld the orders. Lindley LJ said that the six members of Salomon's family were only made members of the company in order to allow Salomon to continue trading as a sole proprietor, but with the benefit of limited liability, and that Parliament had not intended business to be conducted using such a scheme. This was said to amount to a fraud upon creditors. Lopes and Kay LJJ agreed. Lopes LJ, in particular, said:

> The *Joint Stock Companies Act 1856* contemplated the incorporation of seven independent bona fide members, who had a mind and a will of their own, and were not the mere puppets of an individual who, adopting the machinery of the Act, carried on his old business in the same way as before, when he was a sole trader. To legalize such a transaction would be a scandal.

Mr Salomon appealed to the House of Lords. Lord Halsbury LC held that the reasoning of the Court of Appeal was untenable on this point. Essentially, according to his Lordship, the Lords Justices in the Court of Appeal were relying upon a tautology – they had said that the company was incorporated fraudulently, against the intention of Parliament, but also that the company existed and was the agent of Salomon himself. According to this reasoning, the company should not exist because it was not incorporated within the terms of the Act, but it *must* exist in order to be Salomon's agent. His Lordship said quite succinctly: '[e]ither the limited company was a legal entity or it was not'.

Lord Halsbury LC further said that, essentially, the courts cannot speak for Parliament and that to find an intention to prevent such schemes was stretching the meaning of the legislation. Once this point is accepted, it follows that it is also of no consequence that the seven corporators in this case were all members of the same family or that six of them held only a token interest in the company. Lord Macnaghten, agreeing with Lord Halsbury LC, said:

> In order to form a company limited by shares, the Act requires that a memorandum of association should be signed by seven persons, who are each to take one share at least. If those conditions are complied with, what can it matter whether the signatories are relations or strangers? There is nothing in the Act requiring that the subscribers to the memorandum should be independent or unconnected, or that they or any one of them should take a substantial interest in the undertaking, or that they should have a mind or will of their own, as one of the learned Lords Justices seems to think, or that there should be anything like a balance of power in the constitution of the company. In almost every company that is formed the statutory number is eked out by clerks or friends, who sign their names at the request of the promoter or promoters without intending to take any further part or interest in the matter.

In the result, the House of Lords upheld Mr Salomon's appeal and reversed the orders of Vaughan Williams J.

The main principle in *Salomon v Salomon* is that if the statutory conditions for the formation of a company are met, and there is no fraud involved in doing so, the intentions of the company founders are irrelevant to the existence of the company – it exists! Once a company is formed, it becomes an entity separate from its owners and managers. The point was further demonstrated in another English case, which bears some relevance to aviation, in the following Privy Council appeal from a case that originated in the New Zealand courts.

***Lee v Lee's Air Farming Ltd* [1961] AC 12, Privy Council**

Lee's Air Farming Ltd was incorporated in New Zealand by Geoffrey Lee. It operated a business engaged in aerial top dressing. In the company's Articles of Association, Lee was appointed the company's 'governing director' for life and was also employed as its chief pilot. The Articles also gave Lee, as governing director, wide powers to control the company and exercise its powers. Lee also held all the issued share capital in the company, except for one share held by his lawyer. In 1956, Lee was killed when his aircraft crashed whilst he was conducting aerial top-dressing operations in the course of his employment as the company's pilot. Lee's widow sued the company under the company's workers' compensation insurance policy. The relevant statute in New Zealand at the time defined 'worker' as a person who works under a contract of service 'with an employer'. The New Zealand Court of Appeal held that Lee could not be both the governing director, who exercised full control of the company, and also a servant of the company. Mrs Lee appealed to the Privy Council.

Lord Morris of Borth-y-Gest delivered judgment on behalf of the Privy Council. Lord Morris reasoned that Mr Lee was paid wages for his work in the 'arduous and skillful duties of piloting an aeroplane', the airplane belonged to the company, the company kept a wages book, and the work was being done at the request of farmers whose contractual arrangements were with the company (and not with Mr Lee, or anyone else, personally). From these points, his Lordship argued that, whilst piloting the aircraft, Mr Lee could not have been discharging his duties as governing director. Further, Mr Lee operated the air craft pursuant to a contract between himself and the company, which was a separate legal entity. Citing *Salomon*, it was also held that a person can function in dual capacities within a company – in this case, as both governing director and employee. This is not diminished by the fact that Mr Lee was essentially the only person who controlled the company, and that it must be he, and only he, that acted as its agent in all matters, since he and the company were still separate legal entities from each other. The Privy Council upheld Mrs Lee's appeal, overturning the decision of the New Zealand Court of Appeal.

It is perhaps absurd to imagine a negotiating table in this situation, with Mr Lee sitting on both sides, engaging in fierce negotiations with himself as to salary and working conditions. However, the corporate structure permits this wearing of several 'hats': the company is a legal entity separate from all other legal entities, but it should always be remembered that a company can only act through the people who embody it. There is no legal impediment to those people who embody a company also entering into contracts, as separate individuals, with the company.

Limited Liability Separate personality is no comfort to the members of a company if corporate liability to claims of creditors is not limited. If liability were unlimited, the members of a company might be called upon to meet the claims of creditors after the funds of the company are exhausted. Such a notion would strike at the very heart of the concept of corporations, removing one of the main benefits behind the formation of companies in the first place.

Under the doctrine of *limited liability*, the liability of a corporation limited by shares is limited to the amount of its share capital. It is worth pointing out that companies may be formed on the basis of capital other than shares, such as 'by guarantee', but those types of companies are not discussed here. For any shareholder, their liability is limited to the amount left unpaid on the face (or 'par') value of their shares. Generally speaking, once a shareholder has purchased shares, the shareholder is not required to pay any more money into the company because the share price usually represents the full value of the share. In other words, shares are normally taken to be sold at par value, regardless of the actual price paid for them. However, schemes exist whereby the shareholder pays only part of the share price upfront and is then required to pay the rest at a later date, either at specified times, or in response to 'calls'.

It pays to be aware of the existence of the so-called partly paid share. In 2008, a large number of small investors suffered enormous losses after buying partly paid shares in BrisConnections, an Australian company charged with the task of building a toll road between Brisbane Airport and the Brisbane city centre. The company was incorporated in June 2008. Shares were issued at a price of A$3.00, to be paid in instalments of A$1.00 – the first instalment to be paid upon purchase, the next in April 2009 and the third in April 2010. On the first day of trading in the stock, the price fell (from A$1.00) to A$0.41. By mid-September, the price had fallen to A$0.05, and by November 2009, it was A$0.001 – that is, a tenth of a cent, the lowest quotable price on the Australian Stock Exchange.

With the price so low, thousands of small investors bought large amounts of shares. However, very few, if any, had realized that the shares were partly paid, and that buying them meant making a commitment to pay A$1.00 per share in April 2009, and another A$1.00 per share in April 2010. Each share essentially represented A$2.00 in debt. Stories abounded of 'ordinary' people faced with mountainous debts. For example, one man bought 2 million shares at the A$0.001 price for his 82-year-old grandmother. The shares only cost him A$2,000, but this came with an obligation to pay a further A$4 million over the next two years.

The story became even more interesting towards the end of 2008 when Nicholas Bolton, an IT entrepreneur from Melbourne, became involved, buying enough shares to take a stake in the company of almost 20 per cent. For a price of about A$77,800 he purchased 77.8 million shares. Using the voting power he acquired with the shares, Bolton called an extraordinary general meeting in order for shareholders to vote on a resolution to wind up the company. However, on the day before the meeting, Bolton sold his proxy votes (essentially, the right to vote at the meeting) to construction company Thiess John Holland for A$4.5 million. He did not attend the meeting. At the time of print, the saga was still being played out in the Australian courts, with the shareholders bringing a class action (known in Australia as a 'representative action') suit against the company and the company's financial advisors for the share scheme, as well as the scheme's underwriters, in the Federal Court of Australia.

Characteristics of a Corporation

Although a corporation is a legal person in its own right, it is still an 'imaginary' person. It has no body or mind of its own. It cannot see, hear, feel, taste or touch. A corporation is an idea, made out of thin air. As such, it must act through its people. It may be thought, on one level, that a company is properly to be held responsible for the acts of its people, and that might in some circumstances be entirely appropriate.

According to Viscount Haldane LC in *Lennards Carrying Co Ltd v Asiatic Petroleum Co Ltd* [1915] AC 705 at 713:

> My Lords, a corporation is an abstraction. It has no mind of its own any more than it has a body of its own; its active and directing will must consequently be sought in the person of somebody who for some purposes may be called an agent, but who is really the directing mind and will of the corporation, the very ego and centre of the personality of the corporation.

Perhaps the better view, and a view taken in various cases, is that the acts of certain people in the company are the acts of the company itself. On that view, the company is not vicariously liable for the acts of its officers, but those acts are seen as the company acting in its own right, so the company is held directly responsible rather than being responsible through an intermediary such as an employee.

In *Tesco Supermarkets Ltd v Nattrass* [1972] AC 153 at 170, Lord Reid stated:

> A living person has a mind which can have knowledge or intention or be negligent and he has hands to carry out his intentions. A corporation has none of these: it must act through living persons, though not always the same person. Then the person who acts is not speaking or acting for the company. He is acting as the company and his mind which directs his acts is the mind of the company. There is no question of the company being vicariously liable. He is not acting as a servant representative, agent or delegate. He is an embodiment of the company or, one could say, he hears and speaks through the persona of the company, within his appropriate sphere, and his mind is the mind of the company. If it is a guilty mind, then that guilt is the guilt of the company.

As has been stated previously and perhaps slightly repetitiously – but the point is important – a corporation can only act through its people. Those people are typically arranged into various 'organs' of a company, and there is surprising consistency around the world as to the corporate organs provided to exist by the corporate law of various jurisdictions. Generally, a company's organs are its board of directors and its shareholders' meeting.

In some civil law European countries (especially Germany and the Netherlands), a two-tier board of directors is popular, if not required by national legislation (businesspeople in these countries now have the option of incorporating an SE with the option of having a unitary or a two-tier board). The two tiers are quite descriptively named the 'management board' and the 'supervisory board'. Supervisory board members are to supervise the management board to ensure compliance with legal and ethical obligations, including compliance with the company's internal rules. Further, the supervisory board is responsible for appointing and removing members of the management board (Hopt and Leyers 2004). The management board is charged with responsibility for the daily operations of the company and with supervising the company's managers and employees.

Specifics as to the distribution of powers between the board of directors and the shareholders' meeting differ from country to country, so businesspeople would be well advised to check the corporations law of the country in which their company is incorporated (or seek professional legal advice) in order to see who, or which organ, wields the power to make decisions in any given situation. In general, however, it can be said that common law jurisdictions have laws enabling individual corporations to determine for themselves how powers are distributed within their own structures, whereas countries within the civil law tradition place more power in the hands of the shareholders and do this by mandatory statutory provisions (Cools 2004), meaning that the powers are not transferable to the board of directors.

Another concomitant of the artificial nature of a company is that its name could possibly be used in vain by those with sinister intent. Companies could be exposed to improper uses of power in their name and thus could be unfairly exposed to liabilities not of their own making. Without strict controls on who exercises corporate power, the interests of real people – the directors, shareholders, employees and customers of the company – could be adversely affected by charlatans, swindlers and other unsavoury corporate criminals. All this flows from the fact that the company cannot act for itself, so people must act for it. This problem is known in the theory as the 'agency problem' – that is, the company must act through 'agents'.

Avoiding, or at least minimizing, the agency problem involves strict controls on the exercise of corporate power. Controls are provided both by the corporate law in the jurisdiction and by the company's *constitutional documents*. These documents are given various names in different jurisdictions. Some jurisdictions, such as the UK, have only one document known as the 'company constitution', whereas others have multiple documents known variously as the 'corporate charter' and the 'by-laws' (e.g. Delaware in the USA). In the UK and other common law countries, a company's constitutional documents once consisted of its 'certificate of incorporation', which certified that the body named was a company and was brought into existence, and its 'articles of association', which set out the company's internal rules. In jurisdictions where companies only have one constitutional document, this document serves both purposes. Constitutional documents commonly contain such rules as governing the composition of the board, the company's principal objectives, the way in which meetings are conducted, and who may vote and how decisions are reached at meetings.

Directors' Duties

Company directors are the managers of the company. Significant power is placed in the hands of the board of directors and, less directly, in each director personally. Continuing from the discussion of the agency problem, the law imposes various onerous duties upon company directors in relation to their company. In the common law world, the concept of the 'fiduciary duty' of directors is widely known and stringently enforced. The concept is that the company, as a legal person with its own interests, is especially vulnerable to abuse from those who control its actions – particularly its directors. Directors thus come under a legal duty of care towards the company. This is not the same duty as arises in tort. It is in some respects similar, but as a basic concept it is quite different: the director, when given the choice to act in his or her own, in someone else's or in the company's interests, *must* choose to act in the company's interests.

Fiduciary duties are imposed for good reason. In general, the person to whom the duty is owed (in this case, the company) is especially vulnerable to abuse from the person who bears the duty (in this case, the director). The common law position is to impose the duty to act in the interests of the vulnerable in order to discourage behaviour harmful to that person. This was also seen earlier in terms of partnerships, but occurs in other areas of the law, such as agency and trust.

Corporate law in common law jurisdictions takes the fiduciary duty quite seriously, sometimes imposing criminal sanction upon directors who commit egregious breaches of the duty such as using the company to obtain a personal benefit (beyond the remuneration and other benefits they would normally be paid as a director of the company).

There is no doubt that some, if not many, of the readers of this book will at some stage in their professional aviation career be a director of a company or perhaps even a director (possibly a sole director) of their *own* company. Although the precise content and nature of the duties vary in each jurisdiction, the following duties may be considered to be fairly generic and provide some useful practical guidance:

- *Duty to act bona fide in the interests of the company as a whole*: this is essentially the fiduciary duty discussed earlier. In this context, 'the company as a whole' is taken to mean the shareholders as a group. It should, however, be noted that it does not mean any particular shareholder taken individually, but most definitely refers to the preponderance of the interests of the group.
- *Duty to exercise reasonable care and skill*: in conducting the business of the company, the director is required to exercise the care and skill of a reasonably prudent businessperson. The test is an objective test, which is to say that the standard required is not that of what the director thought was 'reasonable care and skill', but that of what the ordinary person equipped with the knowledge of the director in the circumstances would have considered to have been 'reasonable care and skill'.
- *Duty to avoid conflict of interest*: directors must avoid situations where their own interests come into conflict with the interests of the company. To this end, where situations arise within the company business that affect the director's personal interests, the director will, at the very least, have to avoid participating in any board decisions on that subject. In extreme cases, the director may even have to resign his or her position as a director. The situation becomes more complicated when the director is also on the board of another company – the director must also avoid situations where the interests of the two (or many) companies come into conflict. One control on this is to require directors to disclose when they have a material personal interest in a matter, and directors often provide their board colleagues with a standing list of their interests, just in case they come up in board deliberations.
- *Duty to refrain from making a secret profit*: a director must not abuse his or her position as a director in order to obtain personal benefits. Any profits made as a director must be disclosed to the company (the board and the shareholders). The duty includes avoiding taking opportunities presented to the director as a director. Such opportunities are rightfully those of the company. Additionally, information gathered by the company (or by the director on behalf of the company) should only be used in the interests of the company, in the same way that company property is used only in the interests of the company. Profits gained by these means rightfully belong to the company, and any directors making such profits must pay them over to the company.

Overview of the Incoterms 2010

After the foregoing discussion considering the law of carriage, it may be relevant to consider contracts that are peripheral to the carrier's business: contracts for the international sale of goods. These contracts involve the sale of goods from a seller in one country to a buyer in another country. Once the seller and buyer have agreed on the sale of the goods, the goods must be transported to the buyer. In carrying such goods, it is prudent for the carrier to understand which party/parties it may be dealing with at any given point in the transit, and which actions of theirs may be relevant to the contract between buyer and seller – as distinct from the carrier's conception of them as consignor and consignee. Further, carriers as businesses also buy and sell goods internationally, so they may be involved in these contracts as buyer or seller themselves.

In 1936, the International Chamber of Commerce collated a series of standard terms into the system now known as the 'international commercial terms', or *Incoterms*. The Incoterms are standardized forms of contract wording to allocate responsibility for arranging details of the transport of the goods, and for distributing risks and costs as between the seller and buyer of the goods. These terms can be inserted into the contract of sale, which will contain other terms (most notably the price and description of the goods being sold, the identities of the buyer and seller and so on), to address in a standard way the aspects relating specifically to how the goods will be transported. In international commerce, it is important to use such standardized terms where possible in order to avoid or reduce confusion that may arise in dealings over vast distances and in different languages.

The Incoterms have been varied a number of times since 1936, with the current format being released as Incoterms 2010. The most recent version, the ICC Incoterms 2020, came into effect on 1 January 2020. Companies may use earlier versions of the Incoterms as long as it is clear which version is being referenced. This means that the current Incoterms version in 2024 is the Incoterms 2020 version. However, it is also allowed that the Incoterms version in use by a company in 2023 is the Incoterms® 2010 version. Every ten years, the International Chamber of Commerce (ICC) updates the Incoterms.

Incoterms are given three-letter abbreviations and are usually expressed in this shorthand. As such, terms like FOB and CIF have become quite common in the international trade of goods. The structure of the Incoterms is quite simple, selecting a number of events along a journey to be legally significant. The parties simply select which of the terms to incorporate into their contract of sale to select which events will be relevant and for what purpose.

To provide some practical guidance as to how this process may be illustrated, one may consider an ordinary transit in the international shipping of goods to look something like this:

- The goods start at the seller's factory, warehouse or other premises and are taken to the departure point (harbour, port, airport, railway, distribution centre, etc.).
- Customs formalities and clearance for export must be undertaken.
- The carrier loads the goods onto the vehicle (ship, truck, train, aircraft, etc.) for transport.
- The vehicle departs.
- Upon arrival at the destination port, the goods are unloaded from the vehicle.
- Import customs formalities and clearance must be undertaken.
- The goods are collected by the buyer.

In any contract for the international sale of goods, three basic elements must be determined. First, at what point during transit the legal title in the goods passes from the seller to the buyer. This quite clearly enables a determination to be made over who owns the goods at any given time, which may have other legal ramifications flowing from that ownership. The point where title passes is commonly referred to as 'delivery' or the point where the goods are 'delivered'. Second, the contract should stipulate the point during transit at which the risk passes from seller to buyer. Whoever holds the risk at any stage bears the responsibility to repair or replace goods that are damaged or lost. In practical terms, this determines which party pays for and can claim upon any insurance policy covering the goods in transit. Third, which party bears the expense of carriage – that is, which party 'pays the freight'.

The terms are in four groups: E, F, C and D (in the order they are listed in the Incoterms):

- *E-Terms*: these involve the most responsibility for the buyer and almost none for the seller. Title and risk both pass as soon as the goods leave the seller's premises. The buyer must ensure the goods obtain clearance for export.
- *F-Terms*: these begin to share the load. Title and risk pass as the goods are loaded for carriage at the departure point for the main part of the journey, meaning that the goods have passed the export customs frontier, so the seller has obtained clearance for export. The most popular F-Term, FOB ('Free On Board'), involves title and risk passing as the goods pass the ship's rail.
- *C-Terms*: these start to separate the time when title and risk passes. The precise time that risk passes depends upon the C-Term used, but title always passes as the goods are unloaded from the carrier at the destination port. At this point, the goods are still outside the import customs frontier, so the buyer must arrange import clearance.
- *D-Terms*: these involve the most responsibility for the seller. Title and risk both pass as the goods are delivered to the buyer at a nominated point inside the buyer's country (that is, the seller must ensure the goods pass the import customs frontier).

This chapter will not outline all the Incoterms 2020, but a brief overview of those more applicable to air transport are:

- *EXW ('Ex-Works')*: the only E-Term, EXW requires the buyer to arrange all aspects of the journey, taking delivery of the goods at the seller's factory, office or other business premises. This represents the maximum obligation of the buyer, who must arrange for compliance with all export and import formalities and bear all risks of loading at the departure point and unloading at the destination point.
- *FCA ('Free Carrier')*: an F-Term, FCA is similar to the FOB term discussed briefly earlier, but is able to be applied more generally, rather than just to sea or inland water transport. Title and risk both pass when the goods are delivered into the custody of the carrier nominated by the buyer. If the delivery takes place at the seller's premises, 'delivery' is when the goods are loaded onto the carrier's means of transport. If the delivery is to occur at any other place, 'delivery' is when the goods are placed at the disposal of the carrier to take. The buyer is to bear the cost of freight (i.e. the cost of the carriage) and to arrange the contract of carriage. The

seller may arrange the contract of carriage at the request of the buyer or if commercial practice allows it, but it is at the buyer's expense.

- *CPT ('Carriage Paid to . . .')*: CPT requires the seller to arrange the contract of carriage and pay the freight. Delivery occurs, similarly to FCA, when the goods are placed in the custody of the carrier at the departure point. Risk is also similar to the FCA term, passing at the point of delivery. Clearance for export from the seller's country is arranged by the seller, but the buyer must arrange import clearance into the buyer's country.
- *CIP ('Carriage and Insurance Paid to . . .')*: CIP is another C-Term and is identical to CPT, except that the seller must also arrange and pay for insurance for the goods during the carriage. The insurance must be with a reputable insurer, must cover the usual perils in accordance with the Institute Cargo Clauses of the Institute of London Underwriters (which means it does not have to include war, strikes or riots and civil commotion, but must if the buyer requests these additional risks), must cover the whole period until the buyer takes the goods at the destination point and must cover the minimum value of 110 per cent of the sale price under the contract of sale.
- *DAT ('Delivered at Terminal')*: a contract of sale involving a DAT term calls for the seller to arrange export clearance, bear all risks of the transit until delivery, arrange the carrier and pay the freight. Delivery occurs at the destination terminal, whether that is a port, harbour, airport, railway or other international terminal. The buyer is responsible only for obtaining an import clearance and thence any part of the journey within the buyer's country beyond the international frontier.
- *DAP ('Delivered at Place')*: the DAP term goes slightly further than DAT, requiring the seller to deliver the goods at a point within the buyer's country. This means that the seller must arrange for export clearance, bear risks until delivery and arrange and pay for carriers for the entire transit. Delivery takes place at the nominated point within the buyer's country, which might even be the buyer's premises. The buyer must arrange for import clearance and formalities to be complied with, and bears the costs of doing so.
- *DDP ('Delivered Duty Paid')*: DDP is similar to DAT, but the only difference is that the buyer has arranged and paid for import clearance into the buyer's country. Note that this is the maximum level of responsibility for the seller.

STRATEGICAL ALLIANCES AND COMPETITION LAW

Introduction

In the increasingly hostile aviation environment, airlines are increasingly looking to work together to achieve their business goals. Strategic alliances of varying degrees are becoming more prevalent in the global aviation industry, but airlines intending to seek strategic partners need to take care to avoid contravening laws against anti-competitive business practices. Laws such as the 'antitrust' laws in the USA and other competition laws around the world carry serious penalties for breach and also cast a broad net, sometimes reaching across jurisdictions. It is this cross-jurisdictional element that is perhaps the most frightening for international airlines, as British Airways and Qantas discovered in 2006 when they came to the attention of US antitrust regulators, but this will be discussed later. It suffices for now to say that airlines cannot be too careful when it comes to competition law.

What is a Strategic Alliance?

For a long time, airlines have assisted each other through business agreements such as joint marketing campaigns, shared frequent flyer schemes and joint ventures in subsidiary service companies. Since around the beginning of the 1980s, the international industry has undergone significant consolidation through mergers and acquisitions. Airlines have also formed wide-ranging and solid partnerships without actually taking ownership of each other, which has led to the formation, in the late 1990s, of global alliances, the most prominent of which are Star Alliance and Oneworld.

However, not all business deals between airlines can be said truly to be strategic alliances. Most alliances between airlines are strictly commercial and are, perhaps, entered into for more tactical reasons and are more fleeting in nature. Doganis (2001) suggests that a *strategic* alliance is one where the partners co-mingle their assets with a view to achieving a joint set of business objectives. Even this definition, though, still describes strategic alliances within a wide compass.

Strategic alliances fitting this description can range from sharing baggage-handling equipment or airport check-in counters to corporate equity swaps whereby each airline buys a number (sometimes a large number) of shares in the other(s). It is submitted, however, that the definition does not go quite as far as to extend to the merger of two airlines – after such a merger, only one entity remains, and it is difficult for an entity to have a strategic alliance with itself!

Global Alliances

Global alliances emerged in earnest towards the end of the 1990s. Their main characteristic is their sheer size and scope – they typically involve five or more national airlines and significant code-sharing and other forms of coordination involving large parts (if not the whole) of each airline's network. Their broad networks cover the globe, allowing passengers to experience relatively seamless service as they transfer between airlines within an alliance group in different parts of the world.

When joining an alliance, an airline agrees to pool resources with several other carriers to improve the passenger experience. As a result, this allows them to better compete against other carriers. Primarily, alliances operate code-share flights, which allow passengers to book connections across multiple carriers using a singular ticket and booking platform. These alliances give their members many advantages, including increased networks, broader marketing opportunities and broader scope to exploit cost synergies between airlines by code-sharing or contracting technical services such as aircraft maintenance. There are three main global alliances: Star Alliance, Oneworld and SkyTeam.

Star Alliance was the first of the big three alliances to be established. Based in Frankfurt, Germany, the alliance was founded in 1997 with five airlines (Air Canada,

Lufthansa, Scandinavian Airlines, Thai Airways International and United Airlines) and has grown to have 26 member airlines from all parts of the world. Star Alliance member airlines offer a variety of services to each other's passengers including ticketing, check-in services and lounge access. It is the largest global alliance and has the widest network and in 2022 celebrated its 25th anniversary.

The next airline alliance to join the aviation scene was Oneworld. The organization was set up in 1999 and is now headquartered in Fort Worth, home of founder American Airlines, after spending 24 years in New York. The alliance has now expanded to include 14 member airlines and 20 affiliates. Additionally, Fiji Airways is a Oneworld connect partner. Alaska Airlines was a recent addition, only joining in March of 2021. Furthermore, Middle Eastern carrier Oman Air joined the alliance in 2024. Oneworld airlines offer a number of specialized fares, including the world's first multi-airline round-the-world fare.

A most recent newcomer to the global alliance field is SkyTeam, which was founded in 2000 by Aeromexico, Air France, Delta Air Lines and Korean Air. The Netherlands-based alliance now has 20 member airlines with a combined fleet of just over 4,000 aircraft and operates over 15,000 daily departures. The company carries up to 676 million passengers each year to 1,036 destinations. The most recent airline to join the alliance, Virgin Atlantic, entered the association on 1 March 2023 after years of maintaining a close relationship with US legacy carrier Delta Air Lines and European conglomerate Air France-KLM, both SkyTeam members.

Competition Law: General Principles

Competition law seeks to protect the economic integrity of markets. As such, much of the language of competition law – known in the USA as *antitrust law* – is that of economics. What competition law aims to prevent is the loss of 'welfare', which, as an economic concept, is the difference between the current distribution of assets in the market and the distribution that is most economically efficient. To put it perhaps more clearly, competition forces the price of goods (or, in the case of airlines, services) to reach an equilibrium level such that consumers pay the most they are willing to pay for a given quantity of goods or services (and no more), and suppliers simultaneously charge as much as they are willing to receive for the goods or services (and no more).

Economic theory says that this can only occur when there is fair competition in a market. If a monopoly exists in a market or if the suppliers in a market collude to control prices, the price at which goods or services are sold will be artificially high, essentially because the consumer *must* buy the goods or services from the monopolist or the colluding suppliers because there is no alternative.

More specifically, competition law seeks to prevent the abuse of positions of market power. It should be noted that it does not prohibit the mere *gaining* of a position of market power or even the *use* of that position. Such a position may be gained quite legitimately through competitors going out of business in the normal action of the market, and through no fault of the last merchant standing (no fault other than, of course, having a more robust business model or selling a better product, for example). What competition law seeks to avoid in a market is actual *abuse* of a dominant position.

A position of market power is perhaps easier to describe than it is to see. It is a position whereby a supplier can not only influence but can also actually control the price of the goods or services it sells. Certainly, any supplier is legally free to charge whatever it likes for its products, but charging a price so high that consumers avoid buying the product simply does not make economic sense. In a competitive market, suppliers charging too high a price will be undercut by competitors who, theoretically, will then attract more customers. In a market where one or more suppliers exercise market power, those suppliers can restrict the supply of the product without affecting its production costs. The lack of supply causes consumers to be willing to pay more for the product than they otherwise would – a consumer will pay more so that *they* get the product, which is now in limited supply, and not somebody else.

The quintessential example of this behaviour is the oil price crisis of the 1970s. In November 1973, the member nations of the Organization of Petroleum Exporting Countries (OPEC) announced a reduction in its production of crude oil by 25 per cent, with a further 5 per cent reduction in December of that year. At the time, OPEC nations represented 55 per cent of the world's crude oil market (Brankin 2005).

Demand for oil is relatively 'inelastic' in economic parlance, meaning that a change in price has little change in the level of demand amongst consumers. The main reason for this is that many things that use crude oil, such as motor vehicles and aircraft, cannot use something else instead – or, at least, cannot do so easily, especially in 1973. Crude oil, then, is a product without viable substitutes. If there were a viable substitute to crude oil in 1973 (or, indeed, today), consumers would switch to the viable, and presumably cheaper, alternative. In this situation, consumers had no option but to pay the higher price.

OPEC thus manipulated its position of market power. This is not to say that all supply crises such as those that occurred with crude oil in the 1970s are created by the abuse of market power. What was telling in this case was that OPEC had sufficient control of the supply that it could manipulate the price to whatever level it saw fit. In the event, the price of oil increased fourfold and although OPEC nations were selling less oil, they were yielding higher profits due to the greatly inflated price.

Whilst it can easily be seen how a single entity with market power can manipulate the market, such as is the case in a monopoly, where the market consists of just one supplier, the OPEC example shows that market power can also be gained through various suppliers colluding. This is sometimes referred to as a *cartel*. When cartels act to control the price of a product, it is referred to as *price fixing*.

> *Airlines fined over cargo cartel*
>
> In November 2010, a number of airlines were fined by the European Commission (EC) for cartel behavior in breach of the EC competition laws. The airlines were shown to have colluded over the price of international air freight between 1999 and 2006. BBC News reported that the airlines had contacted each other and agreed to charge a fixed price per kilogram for fuel and security surcharges on all shipments of air freight.
>
> Fines were levied on Air France-KLM (€339.6m), British Airways (€104m), Cargolux (€79.9m), Singapore Airlines (€74.8m), SAS (€70.2m), Cathay Pacific (€57.1m), Japan Airlines (€35.7m), Air Canada (€21m), Qantas (€8.9m), and Lan Chile (€8.2m). Lufthansa and Virgin Atlantic were also involved in the cartel, but escaped a fine because it provided information to the EC, thus earning immunity under 'whistleblower' protection provisions.
>
> (BBC News, 9 November 2010)

With reference to the above abstract, all of the companies fined (with the exception of Australian airline Qantas) challenged the decision in the EU's General Court. In December 2015, the General Court annulled the decision concluding there was a procedural error. However, in March 2017, the EC readopted its decision and imposed a fine amounting to €776,465,000. In July 2017, the airlines appealed again.

At the time of writing, proceedings are ongoing. However, British Airways had an appeal in the European Court of Justice dismissed in November 2017.

> The High Court of Australia . . . found that price fixing agreements entered into between Air New Zealand Ltd (Air NZ), PT Garuda Indonesia Ltd (Garuda), and other international airlines, which occurred between 2002 and 2006, breached Australia's competition law.
>
> 'This is a significant win for the Australian Competition and Consumer Commission (ACCC)(Australia's competition watchdog) in the long-running, highly contested air cargo cartel proceedings', ACCC Commissioner Sarah Court said.
>
> The ACCC took action against Air NZ in 2009 and Garuda in 2010 alleging they colluded with other airlines on charges for fuel, security, insurance surcharges, and a customs fee, for the carriage of air freight from origin ports in Hong Kong (both airlines), Singapore (Air NZ) and Indonesia (Garuda) to destination ports in Australia. Under the law as it then stood, the ACCC was required to establish that the conduct occurred in a 'market in Australia'.
>
> The High Court unanimously dismissed the appeals by each airline and held that all aspects of the market, including the presence of customers in Australia, need to be considered in deciding whether a market is 'in Australia'.
>
> (Australian Competition and Consumer Commission, 14 June 2017)

The preceding examples show quite vividly how the same actions can have legal consequences in many jurisdictions, with each country affected wishing to apply its own law to the situation. Airlines should be alive to the possibility that they may be liable in several jurisdictions for the same acts. In many cases, however, the principle of *res judicata*, more simply expressed as 'double jeopardy', would apply to dismiss subsequent cases, but it is within the discretion of local courts within a country to apply the principle in any given case.

The foregoing discussion focuses on behaviours of firms that seek to increase their profits unreasonably at the expense of consumers. Competition law also prohibits behaviours designed to exclude firms from the market. Such behaviours may include those designed to drive competitors out of business (or at least out of the market) as well as those designed to prevent new firms entering the market.

Exclusionary behaviours include such things as *predatory pricing*, *vertical integration*, *exclusive dealing* and *boycotts*. Whilst there are many volumes of complex law behind each of these terms, they can be described simply in the following ways:

- *Predatory pricing* is the sale of a product at below-cost price in order to attract customers away from a competitor, thus driving the competitor out of business. It may also prevent new firms entering into the market who do not have the resources to sell at less than what it costs to make the goods or provide the services. Predatory pricing is characterized by deep price cutting and is also damaging to the predator firm because it also sells products at less than its costs of making them, thus making losses on each sale.
- *Vertical integration* occurs when a firm acquires, merges with or otherwise controls one of its suppliers or one of its customers. For example, consider an airline merger with a travel agent (customer) or with a catering company (supplier), which are both forms of vertical integration. This can reduce competition because it allows a firm greater control over the supply chain, thus making it easier to restrict supply to manipulate costs and prices.

- *Exclusive dealing* and *boycotts* are similar, yet opposite. Exclusive dealing involves a firm agreeing to deal only with a particular firm or group of firms. Boycotts involve a firm or group of firms agreeing to *refuse* to deal with another particular firm or group of firms. Competition is possibly reduced in these situations because firms take control of *demand* for goods and services, directing it either towards or away from specific firms, rather than allowing it to find the level it would naturally have if the market were left to its own devices.

EXTRATERRITORIAL EFFECT

In times not so long past, the USA's Sherman Act, one of the main statutes relating to antitrust law, had an enormous extraterritorial effect – that is, it could be applied to acts taking place outside the USA. Since 2004, the position has been moderated slightly, but the Sherman Act can still have extraterritorial effect. It should be noted, however, that international law allows the laws of a sovereign nation to have effect extraterritorially in certain circumstances, and that the Sherman Act no longer represents an overreaching by the USA, although an argument could be made that it once did. It is used here simply as an example that should be accessible to most readers of this volume.

International aviation law, both in its public and private components, recognizes that sovereign states should not interfere with each other's sovereignty. This principle, which was discussed in some detail in Chapter 1 and is applied by courts around the world, is also known as *comity*. For reasons of comity, a court may refuse to accept jurisdiction to hear a case or it may curtail a ruling or application of law out of respect for the sovereignty of another nation and its courts. As with many aspects of international law, the principle stands on the basis of expected reciprocity – the court of one country acts with comity in the recognition that the courts of the other country also have and will continue to do so. Nevertheless, it is also recognized that a nation's courts can accept jurisdiction and apply and enforce their laws if the interests of the nation are affected.

Early decisions in the US federal courts expressed a certain degree of surprise at the suggestion that the Sherman Act might be applied outside the USA (see, for example, *American Banana Co v United Fruit Co*, 213 US 347 (1909)). In 1945, the Federal Second Circuit rejected the Supreme Court's earlier strict territorial approach, saying that 'any state may impose liabilities, even upon persons not within its allegiance, for conduct outside its borders that has consequences within its borders which the state reprehends' (*United States v Aluminum Co of America (Alcoa)*, 148 F.2d 416 (2nd Cir. 1945)). In the *Alcoa* case, the defendant had a Canadian subsidiary that was engaged in a cartel with various European companies controlling the supply of aluminium to the USA. None of the activity occurred in the USA, but it had significant effects in the USA.

In 1982, Congress enacted the Foreign Trade Antitrust Improvement Act (FTAIA), which clarified the position, imposing certain limitations to the application of the Sherman Act where US commerce was not affected. The legislation, now at 15 USC 6a, provided that the Sherman Act only applies to conduct that has a 'direct, substantial and reasonably foreseeable effect' on trade or commerce that is not with foreign nations or that is import or export trade.

The case of *Hartford Fire v California*, 509 US 764 (1993) seemingly limited the application of the FTAIA by simply not applying it. In this case, the defendants were British reinsurers alleged to be involved in a conspiracy to restrict the terms available under general insurance contracts in the USA. Such restrictions are not illegal under UK law, but are viewed by US law as a breach of antitrust. The Supreme Court of the United States held that the Sherman Act will be applied wherever there is foreign conduct that was 'meant to produce and did in fact produce some substantial effect in the United States', thus reiterating the position set forth in *Alcoa*, putting the focus on the territorial effects of the foreign actions. *Hartford Fire* was later applied by the Federal First Circuit in *United States v Nippon Paper Indus. Co*, 109 F. 3d 1 (1st Cir. 1997) in a criminal case, confirming that the same considerations apply in both civil and criminal matters.

The final position on this matter was elucidated in 2004 in the case of *Hoffman-La Roche Ltd v Empagran SA*, 24 S. Ct 2359 (2004). The Supreme Court applied the FTAIA, holding that the Sherman Act does not apply where the foreign conduct affects consumers both within and outside the USA, *and* the damage suffered by the foreigners is independent of the domestic effects of the foreign conduct. Comity was preserved in this case by the court adopting an interpretation that would not see US law being imposed upon conduct taking place completely outside the USA where the injury to a foreign plaintiff was independent of any local injury within the USA, even if there are indeed local injuries suffered by persons other than the plaintiff. One speculates that the position would have been otherwise had the claim been brought by a US plaintiff – the very same conduct may then have been held in breach of the Sherman Act.

AIRCRAFT LEASING

Introduction

With any business, there is an essential requirement for appropriate and adequate financing of the enterprise. Like the mining, energy and telecommunication sectors, aviation is very capital-intensive, requiring large sums of money in order to initially provide, then maintain and update, the products and services offered. And like many other industries, the product life cycle is shortening. For example, continuous improvements in seating technology require airlines to regularly renew their onboard seating, especially in the premium cabins, in order to keep up with competition.

Since the emergence of the first private aircraft leasing companies in the 1970s, the airline industry has undergone tremendous changes. Supported by several decades of growing demands and rising world economies, the share of leased aircraft across airlines worldwide has grown steadily, exceeding 50 per cent for the first time during the peak of the COVID-19 pandemic.

Aircraft leasing companies are the backbone of modern commercial aviation. Lessors now account for an estimated 60 per cent of new passenger jet deliveries, up from approximately 45 per cent on the eve of the pandemic and just 10 per cent in the mid-1980s. Lessors demonstrated flexibility throughout the COVID-18 pandemic as 86 per cent agreed deferred aircraft lease rentals with their airline customers during the COVID-19 crisis, with a little over half of respondents expecting these deferrals of lease rentals or power by the hour (PBH) to be a short-term measure.

By far the largest asset acquired by any carrier will be its aircraft fleet. The list price for a new Boeing 787–8 Dreamliner is USD 239 million while the purchase price of an Airbus A380 can range from USD 300–400 million depending on the model and specifications. Then you must consider the asset turnover ratio for airlines being typically less than one, that is, more than one dollar of assets is required for every dollar of revenue generated. This is acceptable provided sales margins are large, say 15 per cent. However, the airline industry as a whole struggles to break even on a long-term basis, so the industry has been unable to adequately fund fleet acquisition and expansion for most of its history.

Apart from the financial challenges, there are many risks which are beyond the industry's control: risks such as civil unrest, natural disasters, terrorism and pandemics like SARS and the COVID-19 virus. For government-owned carriers, adequate funding may not be the major issue. However, for publicly listed carriers, there may be difficulties in attracting equity investors, so the only alternative for funds is debt financing.

Surprisingly though, some of the lowest geared airlines (that is, those with low debt) are among the most financially successful airlines, with Southwest Airlines (USA) and Ryanair (Ireland) being two such examples. Because they are so profitable, they can attract equity investors. Southwest, for instance, has stated that around 12 per cent of its cost advantage can be explained by its cheaper financing.

Debt Financing

There are two broad categories of debt financing – borrowing and leasing. If an airline has a high debt to equity ratio (that is, far more borrowing than money provided by shareholders), then this situation can only be sustained in the long term by the airline generating sufficient cash to service that debt. Without sufficient cash, the carrier will have to delay investment in new aircraft and will be unable to renew onboard product offerings. This in turn will have a negative impact on customer perceptions, while increasing expenditure on maintenance and operating costs, for example, a less fuel-efficient fleet versus a younger fleet. Other factors such as on-time performance may also deteriorate, again negatively impacting on customer perceptions, resulting in lower loads and therefore lower revenue. A vicious downward spiral may subsequently develop.

Types of Aircraft Leases To assist the aviation industry with debt financing, a number of specialist financial services companies have been formed to address specific industry needs. Both the major aircraft manufacturers – Boeing and Airbus – have asset-based financing arms. Sixty per cent of all aircraft leases are controlled by just two companies – International Lease Finance Corporation (ILFC) and GE Commercial Aviation Services (GECAS). What gives these leasing companies an edge is that they enjoy weighted average cost of capital of around 7 per cent, while airlines at best have a weighted average cost of capital around 9 per cent or higher.

All these leasing companies specialize in arranging finance and lease structures, managing technical assets, and offering a broad range of financing options and solutions to airlines, which include operating and finance leases, leveraged leasing, sale and leaseback arrangements, and both long-term and short-term financing. Today the percentage of the world's airline's fleet which is leased has grown from around 18 per cent in 1995 to 22 per cent in 2000 and to over 30 per cent in 2011.

Operating leases are generally short term, usually less than ten years in duration, making them attractive when aircraft are needed for a start-up venture or for tentative expansion by an established carrier. The short duration of an operating lease also protects against aircraft obsolescence, an important consideration in many countries due to changing laws on noise and the environment. However, a premium will be paid for the flexibility this type of lease offers. Taxation treatments also need to be considered. In the UK, some operating lease expenses can be capitalized on the company's balance sheet, while in the USA, operating leases are generally reported as operating expenses, similar to fuel, salaries and so on.

A related concept to the operating lease is the *leaseback*. In this situation the airline sells its aircraft for cash to the lessor and then leases the same aircraft back for a specified amount each month.

Finance lease or *capital lease* is the other major category of lease. This is a long-term arrangement where the airline effectively owns the aircraft. It is a more complicated transaction, often involving the creation of a special purpose company which purchases aircraft through a combination of debt and equity financing, and then leases them back to the airline. The airline often has the option to purchase the aircraft at the expiration of the lease, or the aircraft automatically becomes the property of the carrier at the end of the lease. Again, different taxation treatments result from finance leasing, for both the lessor and lessee.

A finance lease can typically contain onerous return conditions, requiring the airline to return the aircraft in 'full life' return condition, thereby incentivizing the airline to exercise its purchase option in the event the leasing is terminated or expires. In these transactions, the lenders' potential claims against the airline may comprise the sum of the return condition claim (for the airline failing to return the aircraft in full life return condition), the termination value claim under the lease (as liquidated damages) and all losses covered by contractual indemnities under the finance lease.

Under common law, the rule of mitigation requires a claimant to take steps to minimize its loss and to avoid taking unreasonable steps that increase its loss, and provides that the injured party cannot recover damages for any loss (whether caused by a breach of contract or breach of duty) which could have been avoided by taking reasonable steps.

Leases can also be very short term in nature, sometimes just one or two sectors. These leases normally cover minor schedule disruptions or for coverage during peaks in maintenance.

Mainly there are three basic types of leases:

- *dry leases*, where only the aircraft, with associated engineering support and insurance, are provided;
- *wet leases*, which cover the aircraft, the associated engineering support and insurance along with all the crew, both technical and cabin; and
- *damp leases*, which cover the aircraft, the associated engineering support and insurance, along with technical crew (pilots).

Obviously, the preceding provides a very superficial account of what is quite a complex area of aviation law. However, because the majority of the worldwide fleet of commercial transport aircraft are subject to financial leasing arrangements, it is necessary to at least provide an overview of this important topic.

AVIATION INSURANCE

Assets used in aviation businesses are large, complex and expensive. They include highly advanced technology such as aircraft, and specialized equipment such as baggage-handling apparatus and ground power units. Aviation businesses also have more ordinary features such as buildings and automobiles, and are exposed to more ordinary risks such as slips and falls and motor accidents. Aviation businesses are also subject to threats that may interrupt their business or otherwise cause a loss of value in their business.

Like other businesses, those in aviation also purchase stock and equipment that may be damaged in transit or later through use. Finally, aviation is just as susceptible (and some would say more susceptible) to accidents (quite apart from aircraft accidents) causing personal injury to staff and customers as any other business. All these risks must be managed, and a part of any risk management plan must be insurance.

Although it is not possible to provide a detailed account of aviation insurance in a text such as this, it is nevertheless important to provide the reader with an overview of the topic and to define the principal terms used in aviation insurance law.

Terminology

Insurance is heavily based on contract law. In an insurance contract, one party (the *insurer*) agrees to pay to the other party (the *insured*) an agreed or calculated amount in the event of any loss incurred by the insured resulting from the occurrence of a specified event or circumstance (the *risk*). The contract is frequently referred to as an *insurance policy* upon which the insured can *claim* if the risk materializes. In return for issuing *cover* (i.e. the promise to pay on valid claims), the insured pays a *premium* to the insurer.

Since the insurer agrees to take on a risk, it is only fair that the insurer be given a full and frank disclosure about the risk, especially its likelihood of occurrence and the damage that may be caused if it does occur. Disclosure allows the insurer to charge a premium appropriate to the risk. In order to ensure fair dealings in this regard, the insured is under a duty of utmost good faith. It is such that in some jurisdictions, a contract of insurance will be voided if it can be shown that the insured either misinformed the insurer or failed to disclose information such that the insurer was misled in a particular matter. It is also on this basis that the insurer accepts the risks described by the insured and only those risks. Due to the complex nature of aviation insurance, prospective insured in the aviation arena would be well advised to use the services of a qualified insurance broker, especially one with experience in aviation insurance.

Lord Mansfield in *Carter v Boehm* (1766) 3 Burr 1905; 97 ER 1162 described the concept: 'Good faith forbids either party . . . concealing what he privately knows, to draw the other into a bargain for his ignorance of that fact'.

If a claimable event occurs, the insurer comes under a duty to restore the insured as best as possible to his or her pre-loss position. The insured should not profit from the claim, and equally the insured should not make a loss – the aim is for the insured to break even, meaning that the claim payout should be equal to the damage suffered. It is said that the insured is thus *indemnified* against loss.

In the UK, an insurance policy cannot exist without the insured having some *insurable interest*. The roots of this concept reach back some centuries, so many jurisdictions with laws based on English law have inherited the concept. However, the insurable interest concept was grounded in firm principle. It stated broadly that an insurance contract is invalid if the insured does not hold an insurable interest in the subject matter of the contract.

A person has an insurable interest if he or she owns the subject matter of the insurance contract or legally bears the risk for its loss or damage. As such, in a sale of goods situation, a person obtains an insurable interest when taking delivery of the goods (in which case the interest lies in the goods themselves) or when the risk passes to that person (in which case the interest lies specifically in the risk). In *Macaura v Northern Assurance Co Ltd* [1925] AC 619, it was held that shareholders do not hold an insurable interest in the property of the company in which they hold shares, and that this principle extends even to majority or controlling shareholders.

The principle behind the insurable interest concept was, first, to ensure that the insured actually had an interest to insure. Otherwise, an insured could profit from the occurrence of an insured event because he or she would stand to lose nothing if it occurs, but, under the policy, would have the right to make a claim. This goes against the principle in insurance law that insurance is merely to indemnify against loss, not to provide a windfall gain for the insured. In this way, the insurable interest prevents gambling or wagering under the guise of an insurance policy.

Second, the insurable interest was said to discourage deliberate destruction of the subject matter. Since the insured's interests were affected if the subject matter were lost or damaged, the insured had nothing to gain except to be restored to his or her pre-loss position, whereas if the insured had no interest, he or she would profit from the loss or damage to the subject matter, which created an incentive to destroy it.

Some jurisdictions, such as Australia (see sections 16 and 17 of the Insurance Contracts Act 1984 (Aust)) and Canada (see *Constitution Insurance Co of Canada v Kosmopoulos* (1987) 34 DLR 208, which overrules *Macaura* in Canadian law), have rejected the concept, instead allowing insurance policies to stand if the insured actually suffered a loss in the event of a claim. Debate continues in the UK as to the abandonment of the insurable interest concept.

WAR IN UKRAINE

The Ukraine conflict has had a seismic impact on the aviation insurance market. Claims under aviation insurance policies have been a key focus as lessors seek to recover losses in respect of aircraft remaining in Russia (which are usually still in the possession and use of Russian airlines). To this end, a flurry of claims has been issued in the English, US and Irish courts.

Aircraft leasing has also been greatly affected since the war commenced. After the Russian invasion of Ukraine, the EU and the UK imposed sanctions prohibiting the leasing of aircraft and aircraft parts to Russian airlines. Notices were issued by the lessors terminating the leases and requesting the aircraft be returned. Aircraft leasing firms are suing dozens of insurers for around $8 billion in a string of lawsuits over the loss of hundreds of aircraft stuck in Russia since Moscow's invasion of Ukraine.

More than 400 leased planes worth around $10 billion are unable to leave Russia after European Union sanctions forced the termination of their leases. Those requests were mostly declined and many of the aircraft are thought to remain under Russian control. Where the lessors have sought to recover their losses from insurers, and those claims for compensation have been denied, there has been a flurry of claims issued in the Commercial Court. Lessors argue the aircraft are covered by policies against war or theft, but insurers point out the planes are undamaged and might yet be returned.

In the future, it would behove insurers and financiers to consider if an analysis of political risks in the country where its clients will be doing business should be factored into their policies, premiums, etc., and to put structures in place for more adequately assessing the risks of insuring and leasing companies doing business with or in countries with volatile political situations.

10
International Carriage by Air

International carriage by air gives rise to a significant amount of international and domestic legal issues, all of which cannot practically be observed in this chapter. And moreover, the issues confronting international air travel are continually changing, as was experienced during the COVID-19 pandemic. Passengers and consignors of freight and cargo became acutely aware of the inadequacies of consumer protection legislation relating to unprecedented disruption of flights brought about by overnight closure of international borders and other network-related chaos.

In this chapter we will initially discuss contracts of carriage by air, a fundamental pillar in international aviation. We will then observe the international legal regime for carriage by air stipulated in the *Convention for the Unification of Certain Rules for International Carriage by Air* (the Montreal Convention), which is the primary air treaty governing international aviation. We will observe the Montreal Convention through its provisions and the case law, and specifically observe recent air tragedies that have given rise to important legal issues. Namely, the Malaysian Airlines disasters in 2014 and the Germanwings tragedy in 2015.

CONTRACTS OF CARRIAGE BY AIR

One of the legal backbones of the aviation business is the contract of carriage. Quite simply, a contract of carriage is a contract between a carrier and another person for the transportation of something from one place to another. That the contract always involves a 'carrier' is quite certain, even if the person entering into the contract on the 'carrier' side is only doing so as the carrier's agent. The other side of the contract is usually one of two kinds of people (or their agents): air passengers or consigners of air freight.

Although this topic was touched upon in Chapter 2 in discussing the Warsaw Convention 1929 and the Montreal Convention 1999, because of the utmost and fundamental importance of this topic to international aviation law, it will be discussed in some detail in the following section.

TERMINOLOGY

To the uninitiated, the terminology involved in contracts of carriage by air – or, for that matter, by sea, road, rail or multimodal transport – can seem daunting, even impenetrable. It pays at the beginning of this discussion to set out some of the terms that will be used.

DOI: 10.4324/9781032652146-10

Perhaps it is best to consider passenger and freight carriage separately. To start with passenger carriage, the traditional position was that a person (the *passenger*) would approach a *travel agent* to buy a *ticket*. The agent would investigate the various options available and would then sell the passenger a suitable ticket. Upon arriving at the airport for the flight, the passenger would approach the airport staff of the airline on whose service the passenger would fly (the *carrier*) and present the ticket. Check-in staff would then issue the passenger a *boarding pass*, which would allow the passenger to be admitted onto the aircraft.

In modern times, the preceding process is still applicable to some passengers, but there is a large and growing movement towards booking fares online. When a passenger books his or her fare online, it is more likely that the passenger is dealing directly with the airline, the effect of which is simply to remove the travel agent from the transaction (however, airlines may still deal through online travel agents or similar intermediaries, and passengers can also choose to buy tickets through travel agents online). Online booking with new online check-in functions also simplifies the boarding process at the airport, but may possibly have legal consequences in relation to contract of carriage and the liability limits under various international conventions. This will be discussed further later.

Turning now to contracts of carriage for air freight, slightly different terminology is used. There is still a *carrier*, which is the airline that carries the freight. Freight is typically sent from one person to another. The person sending the freight is called the *consignor*. A consignor may act through a *freight forwarder*, who then engages the carrier to carry the freight. Consignors usually want the freight to be delivered to another person (i.e. not to themselves, although it is not unknown for a person to send something to himself or herself) at the other end of the journey. The person to whom the freight is being sent is called the *consignee*. When the consignor (or freight forwarder) delivers the freight to the carrier, the carrier will issue the consignor (or freight forwarder) with an *air consignment note* (also known in some places as an *air waybill* and informally as an *airbill*).

Air Consignment Note

The air consignment note serves several functions in that it:

- invokes the limited liability provisions in the Warsaw Convention (discussed later) such that if an air consignment note is not issued, the carrier cannot avail itself of limited liability under the Convention;
- provides evidence of the terms and conditions of the contract of carriage;
- serves as an acknowledgement of receipt of the freight by the carrier; and
- provides evidence of the description and condition of the freight when it was received by the carrier.

It should be noted, however, that the air consignment note is not a document of title. Although it can be seen as the aeronautical equivalent of the bill of lading in shipping, it works slightly differently. A shipping bill of lading is a document of title and is a negotiable instrument – ownership of the cargo may change en route by endorsing the bill of lading and delivering it to the person endorsed on it (usually after selling that person the cargo). The holder of a bill of lading bearing his or her name is entitled to collect the freight from the carrier when it arrives in the destination port. It is possible for a bill of lading to work this way because the consignee is delivered a copy of the bill of lading before (or during the early stages of) the journey.

An air consignment note, on the other hand, is only delivered to the consignee at the same time as the freight is delivered. Thus, title in the freight passes to the consignee at the same time as the air consignment note, allowing no opportunity for the air consignment note to serve such a purpose.

LIABILITY UNDER THE WARSAW SYSTEM

Under the general law, those who cause damage or injury to others are rightfully to be held liable for the consequences. After an aviation incident or accident, what must be determined is whether the carrier is liable and the extent of that liability. For international aviation, the problematic issue is that of which country's law is to apply in any given situation, because applying different laws could lead to different – sometimes vastly different – results.

When the *Convention for the Unification of Certain Rules Relating to International Carriage by Air* – or simply and more commonly called the Warsaw Convention after the city where it was opened for signature – was adopted on 12 October 1929, it represented a framework for a unified system to determine both liability and the assessment of damages. It also introduced limited liability for carriers, but with the proviso that carriers be subject to strict liability.

Without repeating the details of the Warsaw Convention that were provided in Chapter 2 under the section titled 'Public International Aviation Law', the objectives of the Convention can be summarized as follows:

- to protect the infant airline industry by imposing a limitation of liability;
- to benefit passengers with a presumption of liability against the carrier; and
- to achieve the maximum degree of uniformity for the international carriage by air.

A carrier is not liable under the Warsaw Convention if it can prove that it, its servants or agents have taken all necessary measures to avoid the damage, or that it was impossible for such measures to have been taken (Article 20). Further, a carrier may be exonerated wholly or partially from liability where it proves that the damage was caused or contributed to by the negligence of the injured person (Article 21).

Limits upon the liability of carriers for the various heads of damage for which they are liable are set out in Article 22; however, pursuant to Article 25, these limits do not apply if the relevant damage resulted from an act or omission by the carrier, its servants or agents which was done with intent or recklessly and with the knowledge that the damage would probably result, provided the relevant person was acting with the scope of his or her employment. There were, however, a variety of issues with the Warsaw Convention causing its ineffectiveness, subsequently leading to the creation of the Montreal Convention in 1999.

The Warsaw liability system eventually became a hodgepodge of different laws in the form of the Hague Protocol, the Guadalajara Conventions and other international instruments. As a result, it became messy, unclear and confusing. The Hague Protocol

1955 amended Warsaw where, in respect of the carriage, the departure country and destination country are signatories to the Hague Protocol. It raised the limitation of liability pursuant to Article 17 of the Warsaw Convention for the death or injury of passengers to 250,000 *francs Poincare* (or gold francs to be converted into the national currency of the relevant nation) per passenger. It also permitted passengers to recover in excess of the limit where damage was proven to be caused by the carrier's wilful misconduct. Amendments were also made in respect of the relevant time limits for claims concerning damage to baggage or cargo and delay claims and the redefining of certain terms, including 'wilful misconduct'. The Guadalajara Convention responded to commercial aviation arrangements such as leasing, chartering and code-sharing operations, by equating the rights available against the actual carrier to those available against the contracting carrier under the Warsaw Convention. There was also the Montreal Convention No 4 of 1975 which concerned cargo compensation, imposing absolute liability of 17 SDRs (as of 2019 22 SDRs) per kilo unless the consignor provides special notice to the carrier of a particular value of the cargo.

The official French text translated into different things in other languages. For instance, the term 'wilful misconduct' could be interpreted differently in many languages, meaning similar acts of wilful misconduct in different jurisdictions were not being treated uniformly. Consequently, an official English language version of the Montreal Convention was produced to address these language difficulties.

There were also unfortunate implications of the Warsaw scheme for the airline industry. The airline sector was much smaller when Warsaw was created, so liability limits were seen to be too low to reflect the modern industry. An Australian parliamentary report commented that 'it capped air carriers' liability limits at a level appropriate for that era. Those limits are now out of date and unreasonably low'. On the other hand, however, limited liability under Warsaw was also seen to be too lenient for the airline industry in that it would undermine the ability of passengers to achieve adequate compensation. The aim of the Warsaw system, at the end of the day, was to restrict the ability of passengers to make claims for compensation and was inherently protective of the young aviation industry.

The ineffectiveness of these amendments was amplified by other factors. Many countries had not ratified the amendments to the treaty, including the United States. This made it largely difficult to create a uniform system of laws. Not to mention, the compensation system was based on Gold Francs. This was a currency system which became obsolete.

LIABILITY UNDER THE MONTREAL CONVENTION

Readers are advised to consult the section on the Montreal Convention 1999 in Chapter 2 to remind themselves of the limitation on liability imposed by the Convention. Article 1 of the Montreal Convention says that the Convention applies to all international carriage of persons, baggage or cargo performed by aircraft for reward. It applies equally to gratuitous carriage by aircraft performed by an air transport undertaking. Article 17, as contained within Chapter III of the Convention and entitled 'Liability of the Carrier and Extent of Compensation for Damage', significantly provides:

> The carrier is liable for damage sustained in case of death or bodily injury of a passenger upon condition only that the accident which caused the death or injury took place on board the aircraft or in the course of any of the operations of embarking or disembarking.

The liability imposed upon air carriers by the Montreal Convention is not fault based. This gives a passenger or the owner of baggage or cargo very significant advantages in recovering losses incurred from air travel to which the Montreal Convention applies. Passengers are also protected from contractual provisions which purport to relieve or lower an air carrier's liability for losses claimed by a passenger or baggage or cargo owner. While carriers are restricted in their ability to contract out of the Montreal Convention, they are assisted by the certainty and uniformity of the liability system imposed by it.

Liability limits: in terms of ensuring liability limits remain relevant, the International Civil Aviation Organisation every five years updates the Montreal Convention 1999, in respect of the limitation in respect of air carrier liability for loss and damage to cargo during international carriage by air. The maximum liability of air carriers was revised from 19 Special Drawing Rights (SDRs) per kg to 22 SDRs per kg in 2019. This reflects a 13.9 per cent increase over the limits that have been in effect since late 2009 when the last amendment came into force. This has been done to take into account inflationary factors. The increase is based on the 'escalator clause' in Article 24(1) of the Montreal Convention 1999 which requires the ICAO to review the liability limits in the convention every five years.

The revisions were approved by States Parties to the Convention and was effective from 28 December 2019. The increase provides for higher levels of recovery in cases of air cargo claims. However, insurers providing liability insurance cover to international air carriers should also be aware of the revised limits which will naturally also increase their claims exposure due to the increased levels of compensation that shall become due.

The revised limits of liability established under Articles 21 and 22 of the Montreal Convention, in Special Drawing Rights (SDRs), effective as of 28 December 2019 and current as of June 2024, are as set out in the fourth column of the following table:

Montreal Convention of 1999	**Original limit (SDRs)**	**Revised limit (SDRs) as of 30 December 2009**	**Current limit (SDRs) 28 December 2019**
Article 21	100 000	113 100	**128 821**
Article 22, paragraph 1	4 150	4 694	**5 346**
Article 22, paragraph 2	1 000	1 131	**1 288**
Article 22, paragraph 3	17	19	**22**

An 'Accident' for the Purposes of the Montreal Convention

The term 'accident' has been understood to mean slightly different things in many places around the world, but one widely and generally accepted definition arose during the interpretation of the Warsaw Convention in the United States Supreme Court in *Air France v Saks*.

***Air France v Saks* (1985) 470 US 392**

On 16 November 1980, Valerie Saks flew from Paris to Los Angeles on Air France. While descending, Saks felt severe pressure and pain in her left ear. The pain continued after landing. She did not report the pain to Air France staff. Five days after landing, Ms Saks's doctor concluded she had become permanently deaf in her left ear. She filed suit against Air France in California alleging her hearing loss was caused by negligent maintenance and operation of the cabin pressurization system. All evidence submitted to the court found the aircraft's pressurization system worked normally.

At the time of this incident, the Warsaw Convention applied. Article 17 read that

> The carrier is liable for damage sustained in the event of the death or wounding of a passenger or any other bodily injury suffered by a passenger, if the accident which caused the damage so sustained took place on board the aircraft or in the course of any of the operations of embarking or disembarking.

Whilst the wording changed with the Montreal Convention, the case still applies today due to its construction of the term 'accident'.

The court ruled in favour of Air France, as the injury was not caused by an 'accident'. They concluded that liability under Article 17 arose only if a passenger's injury is caused by an 'unexpected or unusual event or happening that is external to the passenger'. If the injury resulted from the passenger's own internal reaction to the normal and expected operation of the aircraft, it will not be found to have been caused by an 'accident'.

Whether or not something is an 'accident' has been the issue in numerous litigations, but it does not always have to be something internal within the aircraft itself as a piece of machinery. The conduct of aircraft staff has been ruled to also constitute an accident, relying on *Saks* for authority. In *Olympic Airways v Husain* (2004) 540 US 644, Dr Hanson and wife Rubina Husain travelled from San Francisco to Athens and Cairo. Hanson, an asthmatic, requested and obtained seats away from the smoking area on the flight to Cairo. For the return flight, Hanson produced a physician's letter explaining his condition, asking the check-in agent to ensure he was not seated in the smoking area. He was seated only three rows in front of the smoking area.

Despite requesting to be moved, no dispensation was made. Exposure to smoke during the flight aggravated Hanson's asthma, and he died from the exposure in-flight despite receiving treatment. There were 11 empty passenger seats on the aircraft, some of which were non-smoking. Hanson's wife, Ms Husain, filed for wrongful death in California, seeking damages under the Warsaw Convention. The issue was whether an airline's unreasonable refusal to assist a passenger who became ill during an international flight, in violation of industry standards and the airline's own policies, constituted an 'accident' within the meaning of Article 17 of the Warsaw Convention. The airline could avoid liability under Article 20 by proving that it took 'all necessary measures to avoid the damage or that it was impossible for [the airline] to take such measures' so the airline had the burden to prove that they took all necessary measures.

The court held that the repeated refusal of petitioner's flight attendant to assign Hanson to another seat was an 'accident' within the meaning of Article 17 of the Warsaw Convention. They applied the definition used in the *Saks* case: 'an unexpected or unusual event or happening that is external to the passenger'. The court reasoned that the flight attendant's conduct was external to the plaintiff's deceased husband and, because it was in 'blatant disregard of industry standards and airline policies', was not expected or usual.

Recovering for Mental Injury

Courts have been generally reluctant to award damages for mental harm under the Montreal Convention, as well as the previous Warsaw Convention. In Article 17 of the Montreal Convention, the term 'wounding' – previously used in Warsaw – was removed. The term 'bodily injury' remains, but mental injury seems to have been excluded. In so refusing to modify the term 'bodily injury', it is considered less likely that a court might find a way to interpret a mental injury as falling within Article 17. Mental injury was an issue in several proceedings under the Warsaw Convention, but they found Warsaw did not cover passengers for mental injury. As such, Montreal probably wouldn't either.

Eastern Airlines Inc v Floyd **(1991) 499 US 530**

In 1983, the defendant's aircraft was flying from Miami to the Bahamas when all three engines failed. The aircraft landed safely after the crew managed to restart one engine; however, some passengers brought claims in respect of mental distress arising from the incident. They had been told their plane would have to land in the ocean due to the engine failures.

The US Supreme Court was required to interpret the original French text of the Warsaw Convention to determine whether the term 'legion corporelle' extended to circumstances in which a claimant under Article 17 had suffered only mental or psychiatric injury. The court held that a carrier cannot be liable where a passenger has not suffered death, physical injury or the physical manifestation of injury. They expressed no view on whether a passenger who suffered both physical and mental injuries could recover under Article 17.

Several months after *Floyd*, the United States District Court for the Eastern District, New York considered a claim concerning pre-death suffering. A passenger suffered a significant amount of conscious pain and suffering, including extreme psychic damage, after his body was torn to shreds when a bomb exploded under the seat of an adjacent passenger. In *In Re Inflight Explosion on Trans World Airlines Inc Aircraft approaching Athens, Greece on April 2, 1986, (Ospina v TWA)* 778 F. Supp 625 (E.D. N.Y. 1991), the Court awarded damages for Mr Ospina because it was found the pain and suffering was a 'direct result' of the physical injury and so was 'damage sustained' under the Warsaw Convention. It was distinguishable from *Floyd* in this way.

Liability of Carriers for Infectious Diseases

As explained earlier most international air carriage is subject to the Montreal Convention which makes airlines prima facie liable for death or bodily injury which is caused by an accident on board an aircraft or during embarkation or disembarkation (see later in this chapter). *Saks case* was precedent for the proposition that an accident is typically defined as an unexpected or unusual event or happening which is external to the passenger. In addition, the internal reaction of a passenger to the usual, normal and expected operation of an aircraft will not constitute an accident and as a result, would not trigger the liability of an airline. However, it is important to note that it is not necessary for the symptoms or conditions to manifest during the flight.

Following the *Povey case* and other DVT claims litigation, the English courts will consider whether one step in a sequence was an unusual or unexpected event and whether this would appear to constitute an accident, triggering the liability of an airline. The key issue is the ability of a passenger to demonstrate that the bodily injury was sustained during the flight or during embarkation or disembarkation and that this constitutes an accident.

If the bodily injury is the transmission of an infectious disease during the flight or during embarkation or disembarkation, it may be difficult for a passenger to isolate an event or events sufficiently clearly during this period which would constitute an accident. This is where a passenger had other opportunities for human contact when the disease could have been transmitted, including using public transport to reach the airport, using airport check-in desks, security screening and immigration facilities, as well as airport retail and food and beverage offerings. Even where a passenger was able to isolate such events to embarkation, disembarkation or during the flight, it would then be necessary to demonstrate that these were unexpected or unusual events. This may also be difficult to achieve where there is widespread media coverage of the disease and its transmission and steps are taken by governments and organizations such as the World Health Organization (WHO) to raise awareness of the disease, the risk of transmission and steps to identify infected individuals and to reduce the risk of transmission. In such circumstances, passengers should be aware of the risk and be taking their own precautions. Whilst this will not absolve airlines of liability, it does make it more difficult for a passenger to claim that transmission was an unexpected or unusual event.

'Embarking' and 'Disembarking'

Article 17 of the Convention reads that the carrier will be liable for damage not only when the accident takes place on board the aircraft, but 'in the course of any of the operations of embarking or disembarking'. The Convention does not define 'embarking' or 'disembarking' and courts have struggled to determine when a passenger begins embarking or completes disembarking. Judges have looked at several factors like the passenger's activity at the time they are injured, restrictions on their movement, the imminence of boarding and the proximity of passengers to the gate. It probably will not be the case that the passenger is embarking if they suffer an injury an hour or two before departure when they are free to roam the airport.

In the US Southern District of New York case *Walsh v KLM N.V.* (SDNY Sept. 12, 2011), it was found that a passenger who tripped and fell on a low-lying metal bar near the departure gate was 'embarking' at the time of his injury. The court reasoned that, 'although he had yet to surrender his boarding pass, he was taking steps toward doing so by approaching the group of people assembled near the gate'. In the case of disembarking, one court explained that descending from the aircraft is the 'commonly understood meaning of disembarkation'. It will seem to be that cases involving issues of embarking and disembarking will tend to be very factually based.

Legal Issues Surrounding the Malaysia Airlines Disasters

In 2014, two major air disasters brought to the forefront of aviation law a significant issue that has persisted to test the ability of the international legal regime to achieve justice. In the following, the author observes the heart-breaking tragedies of MH17 and MH370, two incidents that occurred within a mere four months of one another, and the legal battles that the families of the victims have had to endure.

On 8 March 2014, a Boeing 777 operated by Malaysia Airlines – Flight MH370 – disappeared from the radar on a scheduled flight from Kuala Lumpur to Beijing. All 227 passengers and 12 crew members disappeared. The aircraft reached a cruising level about half an hour after departing, and ten minutes later the captain was instructed to switch radio frequencies. He said 'Goodnight, Malaysia Three Seven Zero'. The aircraft then bizarrely deviated from the scheduled route and flew across Malaysia, Sumatra and then into the Indian Ocean before it disappeared off the radar. At the time of writing, still nobody knows what happened. It is one of the world's strangest modern mysteries. Four months later, Malaysia Airlines Flight 17, a Boeing 777–200ER, was flying from Amsterdam to Kuala Lumpur when it was shot down on 17 July 2014, flying over the warzones of eastern Ukraine. All 298 people on board were killed. The plane crashed near Torez in Donetsk Oblast, in an area controlled by pro-Russian separatist forces fighting in the War in Donbass – part of a broader geopolitical conflict between Ukraine, Russia and a rebellion seeking to separate from Ukraine. A Dutch investigation concluded that the plane was shot down by a Buk surface-to-air missile launched from pro-Russian separatist territory, a system which had been transported from Russia on the day of the crash.

Was Malaysian Airlines negligent in these scenarios? The most obvious problem with MH370 is a lack of evidence, since the aircraft has not been found. Article 21 of the Convention provides, as noted earlier, for two tiers of compensation. Relevantly, the second tier prescribes that liability of the carrier is unlimited and there is *presumed* negligence, with a reversed onus of proof. The onus on the carrier to prove that the damage was not due to its own negligence or that the accident was solely due to a third party's negligence or wrongful act or omission. Article 21 then allows for an exoneration (wholly or partially) for the contributory negligence of the passenger. Since exactly what occurred with the plane is unknown, the facts are near impossible to prove. In tort law, there is the doctrine of *res ipsa loquitur* ('the thing speaks for itself'), which does provide help for some families. This doctrine infers negligence from the very nature of an accident without the need for direct evidence of negligence. Nevertheless, some evidence is still necessary in the case of MH370.

Liability is also an issue with MH17, albeit for very different reasons. The carrier has argued that it is not responsible for its aircraft being shot down. Other airlines were also flying in the area. In fact some airlines, for example British Airways, based upon their internal risk assessments had decided to avoid the area and flight planned accordingly. In its report, however, the Dutch Safety Board noted that Malaysia Airlines did not in fact conduct a risk assessment relating to the route followed (Dutch Safety Board 2015; 214–5; 217–9).

The legal ramifications of these crashes have been vast, with a key issue being liability under the Montreal Convention of airline operators to *non*-passengers who have suffered enormously as a result of the disasters. This has included a range of psychological and financial losses including pure mental harm (nervous shock) and loss of dependency. There is a significant amount of case law for passenger claims dealing with liability for injuries, but essentially none for non-passengers making claims relating to 'death' in Article 17 of the Montreal Convention – and not 'bodily injury'. The leading international authority seems to be the American case of *Zicherman v Korean Airlines*.

***Zicherman v Korean Airlines*, 516 US 217 (1996)**

In 1983, Korean Air Lines Flight 007 was flying en route from New York City to Seoul, South Korea via Anchorage, Alaska. The plane unfortunately strayed into Soviet prohibited airspace and was treated by the Soviet Air Force as a US spy plane. It was shot down over the Sea of Japan with air-to-air missiles after the Air Force had fired several warning shots. All 269 passengers and crew on board were killed.

The Supreme Court of the United States construed the word 'damage in Article 17 of the Warsaw Convention by observing its French counterpart '*dommage*'. Justice Antonin Scalia held that the word should mean '*legally cognizable harm*'. This meant that the Articles in the Convention were essentially a window through to applying domestic law. The court therefore applied section 761 of the *Death on the High Seas Act* 46 USC 761, holding that the petitioners in that case could only recover compensation for pecuniary loss, and not 'loss of society' (i.e. loss of a special relationship such as a husband or a father). *Zicherman* was subsequently applied in further US court decisions.

There are also practical obstacles for plaintiffs in these claims. Malaysia Airlines, at least for MH17, has publicly announced that it would defend claims relying Article 21(2), reversing the onus of proof. Practically, the plaintiffs need to gather the evidence to support their claims. This is clearly problematic. Plaintiffs all around the world cannot simply travel to Ukraine to gather evidence, which is why document access is critical. Flight manuals, logs and records held by the airline would provide valuable information, yet these can be withheld by the airline.

Delay is also a main issue. Litigation over these matters demonstrates that, in reality, the Convention is failing to deliver a mechanism for speedier and a more just dispute resolution procedure for passengers and their loved ones. A recent case heard in Australia illuminates this.

***Pel-Air Aviation Pty Ltd v Casey* [2017] NSWCA 32**

In 2009, Karen Casey was a nurse on board an aeromedical flight conducted by Pel-Air Aviation en route from Sydney to Samoa to Melbourne, and then back to Sydney. In Samoa, a patient and her husband were collected by Ms Casey to be transported back to Melbourne. The weather became aggressive over Norfolk Island, and the captain ditched the aircraft into the ocean. Everybody survived, and was rescued about one and a half hours later. Ms Casey was trapped in her seat for a while prior to eventually freeing herself. She swam to the emergency exit with her life vest and jumped into the ocean, striking her head on the plane's wing. Her life-jacket, furthermore, had only half-inflated. She suffered a range of physical and psychological injuries including but not limited to PTSD, anxiety disorder, hypersensitivity to touch, insomnia and spinal injury. She was from then on unable to complete basic tasks, had problems sleeping and suffered a lack of self-worth, flashbacks and a range of other medical issues. Justice Monika Schmidt in the NSW Supreme Court observed Article 17 of the Montreal Convention, and found that Ms Casey's PTSD was in fact 'bodily injury'.

This was overturned on appeal. Justice Robert Macfarlan in the NSW Supreme Court of Appeal held that 'bodily injury' would be proved if evidence showed there was a 'physical destruction of a part or parts of the brain'.

This case took seven years of legal proceedings, with costs no doubt being enormous. Such delay can cause significant amounts of stress on a plaintiff and their families, which in effect worsens their injuries. In February 2015, about seven years after the crash, the patient for whom the whole flight was made – a woman named Bernie Currall – committed suicide. This only emphasizes the sheer importance of efficiency in modern legal systems, as prolonged litigation can take a huge psychological toll on individuals. Domestic systems around the world are encouraged to review their internal justice systems to ensure proceedings do not endure for nearly a decade.

Liability Flowing From Rogue Pilots: Germanwings Flight 9525

In March 2015, co-pilot Andreas Lubitz intentionally caused a Germanwings Airbus A320–211 en route from Barcelona, Spain to Dusseldorf, Germany to crash over the Alps, killing all 150 people on board (Germanwings, now Eurowings, is a low-cost airline owned by Lufthansa). Lubitz had previously been treated for suicidal tendencies, was depressive and was declared unfit to work. However, he had kept his diagnosis hidden from his employers. When the captain stepped out of the cockpit, Lubitz locked him out and crashed into the mountains. In January 2017, German prosecutors closed their investigation and concluded the co-pilot deliberately crashed the plane. Typically, an airline carrier could disprove negligence in cases of terrorist acts if they can demonstrate that they undertook proper security screening and took all measures to ensure the airline was secure. Andreas Lubitz's acts, however, could probably not be interpreted as terrorist acts. He was an employee, so there are separate legal issues. What issues arise and could the families of the passengers attain compensation?

Prior to any discussion on the provisions of the Montreal Convention, it is likely that courts will apply the law of victims' home country to determine damages. Whilst the Convention imposes strict liability up to 128,828 Special Drawing Rights (SDRs) per passenger, it does not specify amounts for compensation. As such, German compensation law would apply to compensate German families, who constituted the main nationality of passengers on the plane. Unfortunately, German compensation law is not very generous and significantly discourages litigation. This is especially the case when the deceased is single and not earning much income, and is significant because 16 German high school students were killed on the Germanwings incident. So-called bereavement compensation for third parties in Germany is a controversial concept, so lawyers representing families in the Germanwings incident attempted to use the Montreal Convention to steer away from cases being heard in Germany because the Convention allows for numerous forums.

Was the Germanwings crash an 'accident' for the purposes of Article 17? From *Saks*, Article 17 arises only if a passenger's injury is caused by an 'unexpected or unusual event or happening that is external to the passenger'. It would be difficult for Lufthansa's defence team to show that that this was not an accident. The carrier authorized a pilot with suicidal tendencies to fly an airplane, who then intentionally crashed it into the ground. Previous cases have also held that hijackings and terrorist attacks are Article 17 accidents. It was certainly unusual and unexpected and completely external to the passengers. There is therefore strict liability under the Montreal Convention as the carrier 'shall not be able to exclude or limit its liabilities' for claims arising under Article 17 not exceeding 128,828 SDRs. If claims exceed this amount, the carrier will need to prove, under Article 21(2)(a) of the Convention, that the damage was 'not due to the negligence or other wrongful act or omission of the carrier *or its servants* or agents' in order to limit its liability.

This reflects the doctrine of vicarious liability, which was briefly spoken about in Chapter 6. Lufthansa is vicariously liable for the torts committed by its employees, a policy consideration of which is that employers tend to have more assets and income than their employees. It is also believed that somebody carrying on an enterprise ought to bear the risks that arise. Vicarious liability only arises during the course of employment, which is a difficult issue. Employers can tell an employee not to do something, but still be held liable if the employee does it – as long as it is within the course of his or her employment. If, however, an act is so remote that it is unconnected to employment, then the employer might not be liable.

In the Germanwings incident, Lubitz was engaging in an act he was hired to perform, i.e. flying a plane. Just because he was flying in an unauthorized way, it does not technically take that flight outside of his employment.

The Montreal Convention does not, however, govern the laws of vicarious liability. That is left to domestic jurisdiction. Lufthansa's defence may very well make the case that Lubitz was acting outside the scope of his employment, and therefore Lufthansa are not liable. Most recently, cases concerning sexual abuse committed by the employees of schools and religious institutions are dealing with this issue. These cases are particularly concerning because serious criminal acts can be totally contradictory to what employees are employed to do. Lubitz committed a seriously criminal act which, arguably, might bring his acts outside the scope of his employment and Lufthansa could argue their liability should be limited because the damage caused was due to the wrongful act – indeed, the *criminal* act – of its servant.

Some case law has tried to expand the test for vicarious liability. In Australia, for instance, the test in 2016 expanded in a sexual abuse case where a pupil was sexually abused in Prince Alfred College (*A, DC v Prince Alfred College Inc* [2016] HCA 37). His case failed due to lack of evidence and the fact that he had already settled with the college, but the court expanded the test for vicarious liability. The mere fact a person is given an opportunity to commit a tort will not be enough, but where an employer sets an employee up with *occasions* to commit the tort and provides them a position of authority, power, control, trust and intimacy, and then the employee takes advantage of their position with respect to the victims, it may suffice to conclude that their acts were outside the scope of their employment. Lubitz was in a position of control, trust and intimacy as a pilot as all 150 passengers had placed their trust in him as a responsible pilot to navigate them to Dusseldorf in a safe and efficient manner. There could be a case that the entire flight was the 'occasion' to commit the tort, but this is unlikely. The entire flight could conceivably be argued to be the opportunity. The *occasion* may have been when Lubitz locked the pilot outside of the cockpit. This was not provided by Lufthansa, and instead self-inflicted. This might mean that Lubitz was outside the scope of his employment, at least according to the Australian test. However, the occasion to commit the tort may have been provided by the employer by allowing him to fly despite being medically unfit. Vicariously liable, however, is not a settled doctrine.

Many of the passengers are pursuing compensation claims in the United States, where the compensation system tends to be more generous. Passengers have brought claims against a flight school in the US state of Arizona, which had actually trained Lubitz. In March 2017, however, a US judge dismissed a lawsuit saying the better forum is Germany. Under the principle of *forum non conveniens*, judges have the discretion to shift proceedings to a different jurisdiction. Judge Diane Humetewa of a US District Court stated, 'Although Arizona certainly has an interest in this litigation, it is comparatively low when considering the much higher level of public interest in the lawsuit that is likely in Germany given the number of German citizens who lost their lives'. It may be too early to say how this will affect the other families' potential to recover damages.

Indeed, in January 2017, a family of a US mother and daughter killed brought actions against Eurowings (the company under which Germanwings operates), Lufthansa (the parent company of Eurowings) and United Airlines (headquartered in Chicago) in a US District Court in Alexandria, Virginia. United Airlines was added because the family had purchased their tickets for a trip to England and Spain from United and departed on a United flight from Virginia. All airlines are part of a code-sharing alliance allowing each company to book flights on each other's planes, and the family was travelling from Spain to Germany where they planned to transfer to a flight in England. The crash occurred on that flight to Germany. It is argued that Lufthansa and Germanwings were negligent because they did not have a policy requiring at least two flight crew members in the cockpit at all times. In the author's view, there may also be a case that they were negligent in failing to ensure their pilot was medically fit to fly. In March 2017, however, Günter Lubitz, the father of the co-pilot, broke his family's silence and claimed that he had evidence to prove that his son was not depressed. Details have not been released at the time of writing, but it was reported that he had commissioned a journalist with a record of investigating toxic fumes in cabin air on commercial aircraft.

As a closing comment, in our post-pandemic environment, it will be interesting to see whether there will be any litigation arising from claims relating to the transmission of COVID-19 during international carriage by air and whether such claims may give rise to liability under the Montreal Convention 1999. As the Montreal Convention is an international instrument, and as most related litigation centres around an interpretation of the convention, courts irrespective of their jurisdiction, are encouraged to look overseas for guidance on its application and interpretation. And it would come as no surprise to see such litigation initially arise in the US.

11
Airline Operations

INTRODUCTION

The Nature of Airline Operations

Today, there are over 5,000 airlines issued with International Civil Aviation Organization (ICAO) codes and at any time there are approximately half a billion passengers airborne. By any measure the airline industry is big business with a global market valuation of USD 841 billion in 2023. The recovery of commercial aviation following the carnage brought about by the coronavirus pandemic has been nothing short of astounding and demonstrates the resilience of this industry sector.

In 2023 the world's combined airline fleet had carried more than 4.35 billion passengers, being 95 per cent of the pre-pandemic levels. The importance of airlines to the global aviation scene and to international trade and commerce generally cannot be overstated and an understanding of the regulatory framework and associated legal issues is paramount to anyone working in the aviation industry.

This chapter will focus on several major areas within airline operations with a view to highlighting the structure of specific relationships and duties that devolve from the international conventions and state laws that govern aviation. The purpose is not to make the reader an expert in any particular area of airline operations, but rather to raise the main legal and regulatory issues and concepts that arise within the scope of airline activities.

This chapter is presented in such a way as to provide the reader – the aviation practitioner – with an awareness of the scope and broader implications of the aviation legal and regulatory requirements, at both the international and national level, as they apply to airline operations. It would be an impossible and entirely inappropriate challenge to attempt to provide a detailed examination of all the relevant law and rules that apply to airline operations. The international regulations and explanatory material alone in just one area of airline operations would run to hundreds of documents covering many fields of expertise. Also, regulations have the unfortunate, but necessary, characteristic of changing to meet developing needs. Therefore, any attempt to deal in detail with highly specific areas of the regulations would be a futile exercise.

Obviously, there are numerous aspects of airline operations that are regulated by laws and regulations. As we have seen in Chapter 1 nearly all these standards derive from each nation's adoption and ratification of international treaties and in particular the Chicago Convention 1944. We further saw in Chapter 3 how these (and other) international standards became domestic law.

Within this legislative jungle, airlines need to comply with all the relevant aviation law (irrespective of their source), but then as a business they need to expand and, in the case of corporations, provide adequate returns for their shareholders. At the beginning

DOI: 10.4324/9781032652146-11

of the previous decade, the combined profits for airlines globally more than halved each year from USD 16 billion in 2010 to USD 3 billion in 2012. Apart from the three years of devastation caused by the COVID-19 pandemic, the fortunes of the international airline sector over the past three decades have steadily improved but nevertheless now more than ever, airlines need to be able to act like normal businesses.

Apart from the operational and airworthiness requirements prescribed under the various ICAO Annexes, there are also other 'technical' requirements directed at airline operations. Today the environmental impact of aircraft operations is without a doubt one of the most challenging issues facing airlines and the aviation industry in general especially since the introduction of the 2025 Net Zero Emissions targets which have been adopted by both the ICAO and IATA.

In addition to the technical and operational aspects of airline operations – which are the focus of this chapter and Chapter 12 – the commercial structure of the airline industry has also significantly altered, especially over the past few decades. This has occurred mostly as a result of tumultuous change in government policy, including deregulation, ownership restrictions, rapid economic globalization and rationalization, together with infrastructure constraints both on the ground and in the air. The late 1990s saw the introduction of new business arrangements in international aviation with the increase in code-sharing arrangements and other cooperative arrangements and the emergence of global alliances.

This development occurred primarily because of the increasing global nature of international aviation and a general realization of the limitations and inefficiencies inherent to the bilateral framework of international air services agreements. Faced with multiple government restrictions and competition constraints, airlines came together in an attempt to secure revenues and reduce costs. Today, all of the world's major carriers are members of one of the three major global alliances: STAR, Oneworld or SkyTeam.

The most recent arrival on the airline scene is that of low-cost carriers (LCCs). In the post-deregulated domestic aviation sector of many countries and EU's Open Skies policy, the advent and proliferation of LCCs have changed forever the structure of the entire airline industry.

Development of Airline Operations

On 16 November 1909, the world's first airline, DELAG (Deutsche Luftschiffahrts-Aktiengesellschaft or German Airship Company) was established with government assistance and operated airships manufactured by the Zeppelin Corporation. Its headquarters were in Frankfurt. The first fixed wing scheduled airline commenced operations on New Year's Day 1914 from St Petersburg, Florida to Tampa, Florida, a distance of 17 miles. The service was operated by the St Petersburg–Tampa Airboat Line. Although it was a short-lived endeavour of only four months, it paved the way for today's airline industry.

Mr Percival Fansler, a Florida sales representative for a manufacturer of maritime diesel engines, was a major sponsor of the venture. In a brief speech before the flight, as reported by the *Tampa Bay Times* (IATA 2012), Mr Fansler said: 'What was impossible yesterday is an accomplishment today, while tomorrow heralds the unbelievable'. Never were truer words spoken.

Sometimes dubbed the Golden Age of Aviation, the period between the end of World War I (1918) and the beginning of World War II (1939) was characterized by a progressive change from the slow wood-and-fabric biplanes to fast, streamlined metal monoplanes, creating a revolution in commercial aviation. This period also saw the establishment of many airlines, most of which required government support.

With the outbreak of World War II, the development of commercial aviation was rechannelled. Immediately after the end of war in Europe the Chicago Convention provided an opportunity again – after the Paris Convention in 1919 – to test the world reaction to internationalization of civil aviation and at a time when practically the whole world was involved in the most disastrous war in history, during which the airplane, employed as a destructive weapon, had caused the devastation of practically the whole of Europe.

The motivation of states to establish international cooperation in this 'dark time' in human history was evident in delegates having travelled to Chicago at great personal risk during a still-violent period of WWII with many of the countries they represented still occupied. We can gauge how important it was for nations to create uniformity in the set of laws pertaining to civil aviation being recognized at an international level in the following comment made by Chairman of the Conference, Adolf A Berle Jr, at the close of the conference (ICAO 2013):

> As a result of the work of these and many other men, when we leave this Conference we can say to our airmen throughout the world, not that they have a legal and diplomatic wrangle ahead, but that they can go out and fly their craft in peaceful service.

It is highly unlikely that the aviation industry would have achieved such technological progress if not for this unified approach by nations and their governments.

In the following section we will see that to manage an airline, and indeed any operator of an aircraft, helicopter or airship, the operator must satisfy the regulatory authorities that it can do so safely and in conformance with all national and international standards. Airlines are subject to particularly stringent controls. They must, like all other operators, obtain an Air Operator's Certificate (AOC) from the National Aviation Authority (NAA). However, as we shall see in the following sections, to be granted an AOC, they must supply a wide range of manuals and documents for assessment and approval. These typically include the flight manual, the operations manual, the cabin crew maintenance manual and the security manual.

Regulatory Oversight of Airlines

The safety and security of flight is pre-eminent amongst all other considerations of profit and economic viability. There can be no compromise, no shortcuts and no absolution for responsibility. To achieve this, there has evolved a hierarchy of rules and regulations that have their origin in ICAO Standards and Recommended Practices and their application in detailed operating manuals used by airlines, airports, manufacturers, consultants, suppliers and personnel.

In an ideal world, all aviation rules and regulations would be the same in every country. However, it is not an ideal world and because of different national objectives, resources and air transport systems, each country has its own standards. However, as we have observed in earlier chapters, *no* industry has a greater degree of internationally harmonized regulations than the aviation industry. Moreover, the airline sector within the aviation industry – and in particular *international* airlines – has without a doubt greater legislative and regulatory harmonization than any other industry sector in the world.

Essentially, these airline regulatory standards do not deviate very much from each other and where they do, then the ICAO differences are known throughout the system. Without closely supervised and internationally agreed standards uniformly applied across the entire air transport system, we would not enjoy the safety of air travel we have come to expect and often taken for granted.

The key to effective technical regulation of airlines is accountability by all concerned in the management and provision of air transport services. It is also about ensuring that commercial interests do not override or put safety at risk. There is no room for a weak link in the safety chain and in this regard it is essential that all individuals and organizations fulfil their responsibilities. In a practical sense, this means that the 'regulators' must regulate conscientiously and fairly in accordance with international and national legislation, and the 'regulated' must conform to the regulations. Without this partnership, pilots and passengers are put at risk.

In this regard, it may also be noted that although many operators may perceive the regulation of aviation to be an impost which burdens them with additional and unwanted costs, an accident incurs even more severe, and even less wanted, financial and commercial consequences.

The process of supervising the operational areas of airlines is achieved by the state NAAs approving organizations to conduct certain kinds of operations and the master document for sanctioning these operations is the AOC.

Airline Management

Airline management may be regarded as something of a fine art requiring business acumen, sound judgment and knowledge of a vast array of technological assets. The coordination of aircraft, routes, personnel, finance, suppliers, governments, passengers and cargo in competitive markets makes the airline industry one of the most complex industries in the world.

The functions of airline management are essentially little different from any other business enterprise: that is, operating the business safely, profitably and with utmost concern for ensuring compliance with all the applicable legal and regulatory requirements. However, airlines are very complex industrial enterprises, with many different and highly specialized functions.

In the international airline industry, the perennial airline management tug-of-war between the commercial desirability of a course of action and the operational feasibility of achieving it is heavily weighted towards the operational side of the equation. Airline operations, and indeed the entire air transportation system, is a highly regulated activity and, as we have seen in previous chapters, is governed by a complex web of international conventions and national laws. The ultimate purpose of these laws and regulations is to ensure the safety of fare-paying passengers and that of innocent third parties. In its pure form, air safety regulation pays no heed to commercial detail.

The legal obligations of those managing airlines and other aviation businesses within the industry are onerous. Many countries have applied the legal notion of strict liability in the laws governing the airline industry and, as a result, defences for breaches of the various codes have been reduced to an almost insignificant number.

More recently, the airline operational environment has become increasingly complex and the application of high-order technology has accelerated the rate of change within the industry. Airline management are expected to be familiar with these technologies, the benefits that can be gained through their application or adoption and, importantly, the regulatory environment that governs their use.

This is the dynamic environment in which airline management are required to keep abreast of the rapidly changing operational environment and to develop and implement new strategies to provide a competitive edge in an attempt to secure adequate returns for their shareholders.

Responsibilities of Airline Personnel

A careful examination of most state domestic civil aviation law reveals that, when considering the issue of an AOC and for the discharge of many functions prescribed in the statutes, one of the prime areas of regulatory interest is the capability, experience and integrity of the operations management team. Some codes go so far as to prescribe which positions these so-called post holders, senior persons or key personnel must hold. These people must not only meet some stringent experience and qualification requirements but must also be deemed acceptable to the local regulatory authority. Depending upon the system of delegation or authorization by the relevant regulatory authority, an individual may incur personal liability for his or her actions (or omissions) in relation to the performance of their specific delegations or authorizations.

In addition, if one examines the various operational managers' roles in relation to their duty to the company and to the law, it is clear that a significant tension could exist. On the one hand, there is the need to deal with the pressing commercial need in producing revenue, to be a market leader and to run the operation at minimum cost. On the other hand, there are the legal constraints imposed by the state regulations or operational codes. In the middle sits the chief operational officer (COO) – however they may be described.

The operations manager must never think that because the company has an AOC that the individual manager is absolved from personal responsibility either under the regulations and orders or in terms of the civil law duty of care. The system of delegation within an organization makes an individual personally accountable for his or her actions in relation to the applicable operations codes.

The very best way to approach this problem is to be competent and knowledgeable. Be prepared to state your case as to why a particular course of action will conflict with the regulations, but also be prepared to offer advice as to how this problem may be solved.

Also remember that the state regulatory authority is *not* the enemy and that it is usually willing to listen to a well-researched and reasoned case for a variation or concession. Governments often make it one of the duties of the authority to assist the industry. But remember that safety is the authority's primary concern, not profitability. Do not expect an authority to respond instantly or favourably to a poor-quality application requiring immediate action merely because it was submitted by a renowned operator or 'national carrier'. Do expect an authority to be very unimpressed with an application that is just a demand and that demonstrates a clear lack of understanding of the regulations. To make such an approach is to invite delay and to ensure that the authority will develop a very dim view of your organization.

The worst possible scenario for an operator is for it to perform so badly in the regulator's eyes that it is deemed necessary to suspend or otherwise restrict the AOC, intervene in the company's operation, or temporarily or permanently revoke its AOC. An operator that has attracted this level of attention from an authority has a long and difficult road to travel to have its AOC reinstated and to re-establish credibility.

While it is the Chief Executive Officer or CEO (or President in the USA) who normally signs as the person responsible for ensuring all the conditions set out in the AOC are complied with, this task is usually delegated to the two operating departments – flight operations and engineering. Effectively, these departments are the custodians of the AOC. Engineering is primarily concerned with continued airworthiness, but flight operations is often the regulatory contact point for areas such as security and cargo (dangerous goods). In large organizations these can be separate departments.

THE DEVELOPMENT OF AIRLINE OPERATIONS

The First Airlines

The world's first airlines were established in the early 1920s just after the Paris Convention 1919 and not long after the birth of powered flight. The Netherlands' KLM and Australia's Qantas Airways are the two oldest airlines that continue to operate today. Many of these pioneer airlines operated services in aircraft that were only able to carry one passenger over short distances.

Many of the pioneering countries in aviation, such as the USA, Britain, France, the Netherlands and Germany, started scheduled services that primarily appealed to those who wanted to get from point to point more quickly.

By the 1930s, multi-stop long-range services were being operated from Europe to Asia, with travelling times cut in half. For example, Qantas introduced a passenger service in 1935 between Australia and Singapore to link up with Empire Airways services from Britain. The aircraft was a DH86 with six seats. The conditions were cramped and often based on standards found in ships of the time. In the same year, services were introduced between Fukuoka and Taipei, and Penang and Hong Kong.

The early pioneers in aviation followed standards and practices established in the shipping industry and even named the staff after their shipping counterparts, with captains, pilots and stewards becoming a part of aviation. Indeed, for a period in the late 1930s, flying boats were used extensively on scheduled services, strengthening the maritime links. Although there were domestic services from the early days of aviation in many countries, it was the development of international services which had the greatest effect on both commerce and social interaction. There emerged a pattern of separation by regulation and this entity of domestic and international aviation still exists in some countries.

From the earliest days of aviation, international landing rights were traded by nations and it was convenient for the country to nominate its 'flag carrier'. It is usually a government-owned airline as this is sometimes the solely designated international carrier. Many countries, such as the USA, Canada, Australia and a large number of European countries, have more than one international scheduled carrier. Apart from the division between international and domestic, there are other natural groupings in the industry.

The Chicago Convention 1944

The effect that the two World Wars had on the rate of development of aircraft technology and design cannot be overstated. Shortly after the First World War, airline operations throughout the world began to emerge because of the aircraft's increased and proven performance capabilities.

With the outbreak of the Second World War, the development of commercial aviation was rechannelled. Many international commercial airlines were required to operate under wartime priorities for primarily military purposes. Towards the end of 1944, the governments of the allied nations recognized the need to commence post-war planning in international civil aviation. This led to the Chicago Convention of 1944.

The Second World War proved that aircraft could be used as weapons for the exercise of national power and as a possible source of subversion and espionage. It was this environment which prompted the attendance of 54 nation states at the Chicago Convention. While most nations recognized the important commercial and social contributions of airlines, these were considered to be secondary to political and military objectives. This view is consistent with the discussion in Chapter 1 that the overwhelming objective of *all* aviation law globally, dating back to the nineteenth century, was for governments of the world to *control* aviation.

The Chicago Convention provided another opportunity to test the global reaction to the internationalization of civil aviation and at a time when practically the whole world was involved in the most disastrous war in history, during which the plane, employed as a destructive weapon, had caused devastation across practically the whole of Europe.

With this background, the delegates to the Chicago Convention saw subsidized domestic and international airlines as a way of political life. The acceptance of subsidies and the demonstrated willingness of governments to pay them meant that nations could follow bargaining policies at the Conference that were not commercially viable. This explains to a large extent the reason why the Conference failed to reach any general agreement on economic objectives.

TYPES OF AIRLINE OPERATIONS

Scheduled Carriers

Scheduled carriers are characterized by the fact that they operate on a year-round basis independent of whether or not customers appear (but of course may increase or reduce capacity on a demand basis in regulated markets). They are generically grouped into international and domestic operations. The international scheduled services normally

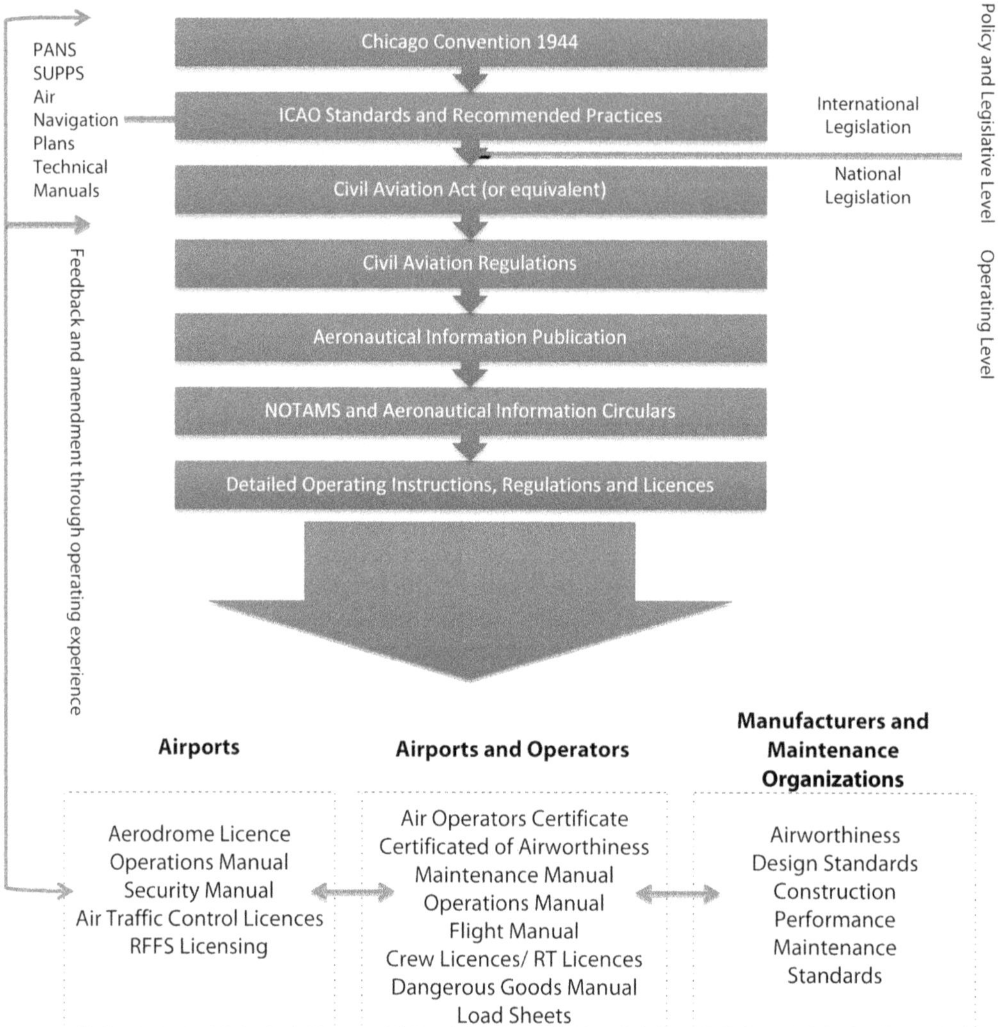

Figure 11.1 Hierarchy of aviation law for airlines

operate within a pattern which has been approved by two governments that have an air service agreement.

Domestically, nations differ, but services range from monopoly carrier systems to deregulated systems where, provided that the carrier proves operational and economic capability, a service can be provided. Scheduled carriers sell air transportation and operate within tariff guidelines imposed by governments, though in practice many markets are deregulated, and the general trend is towards an increasingly liberalized international air transport market, with 'open skies' policies being adopted in more and more regions throughout the world.

Over 240 of the world's scheduled airlines are members of the IATA, which is a body through which they may represent their joint interests. Other regional organizations such as the Asia Pacific Airlines Association (the Orient Airlines Association until 1996) exist and perform similar functions.

Charter Airlines

Charter airlines generally operate flights as seasonal series, ad hoc flights, or they may be chartered by a scheduled carrier. The rules, both domestically and internationally, which govern these types of flights are more liberal and are rarely a feature of bilateral negotiations. The product sold by charter airlines also differs in that it ranges from a total inclusive tour package holiday including accommodation to whole plane charters for a particular purpose, for example, pilgrimage, expeditions, sports, incentive movements and special purposes such as refugee movements and disaster relief.

Regional Airlines

Regional or feeder airlines are known by a number of different terms, which range from commuters and third-level airlines through to supplementary airline operators. These airlines are characterized by the fact that they normally operate aircraft of about 72 seats on lower-density and feeder routes. Their traffic is a mixture of origin/destination traffic and feeders for the major airlines.

Over the last decade, the commuter airlines have undergone a substantial metamorphosis with large expansion and in many cases they have been purchased by larger airlines. They provide, for example, in the USA, air links with smaller communities, but feed on a hub and spoke system of the major carrier. However, some carriers are now disposing of these assets in order to achieve improved balance sheet performance while retaining contractual linkages.

In most countries, there is a thriving aviation airline network which operates short-range services, often of a pioneering nature. This is particularly evident in developing nations.

Low-Cost Carriers (LCCs)

In relative terms, the establishment of LCCs is a relatively modern phenomenon. In the post-deregulated domestic aviation sector, the advent and proliferation of LCCs have changed forever the structure of the airline industry. Traditional airline models – those of the so-called legacy carriers – are being challenged as the proportion of high-yield passengers continues to decline.

The rapid development and proliferation of LCCs provides yet another example of the rate of change of the airline industry and a further reminder of the need for the entire aviation community (including the regulators) to keep pace with the dynamics of the industry to remain relevant and effective.

Cargo and Freight Airlines

Specialist cargo and freight-only airlines have developed around the globe because of the advantages afforded by modern commercial air transportation. Air cargo consists of a wide variety of manufactured goods, agricultural products, animal produce, pharmaceuticals and fashions. High-value livestock is also moved by air. These commodities move around the world by air because it provides a safe, fast and convenient form of transportation. Mail also moves by air, and the growth in small package distribution by air has been the growth phenomenon. Air cargo may also be more economical if the time value of money and the cost of insurance are included in the total cost.

In the early days, air freight was primarily a way of filling up spare capacity on passenger aircraft. Airlines have recently become much more sophisticated in their product definition and now offer a range of distribution options to the customer. Essentially, customers are now offered a range of services at different prices, some of which recognize that the consignee will pay a premium for quick delivery.

Express cargo airlines and the development of substantial hub and spoke networks is another area of significant growth. Basically, the express delivery 'systems' which exist worldwide rely upon dedicated freighters, which range from B747s down to Cessna 208 Caravan aircraft. Although not unique, the Federal Express (FedEx) operation in the USA is the leading company in this field. It is an integrated air/land transport system which is totally controlled by FedEx. It has many thousands of surface vehicles which collect/deliver the packages on the ground and feed them into its major sorting hub at Memphis.

The main features of the express parcels system are overnight delivery, computer tracking of all packages, automatic sorting at the hubs and a strong marketing image. FedEx handles one million packages each night. UPS, TNT and DHL are other companies in this category. They have transformed air distribution in major markets. They also buy capacity from some of the major global airlines to supplement their own in-house uplift.

There is also one significant difference between the product offered by the express freight companies and the airlines. The airlines traditionally only provide carriage from airport to airport, whereas the freight distribution companies, known as 'integrators', provide transport from door to door.

FLIGHT OPERATIONS

Introduction

Flight operations is a generic term which covers a wide range of activities associated with the operation of aircraft. For instance, many aspects of airport and ramp operations such as weight and balance, and load control are usually included as part of flight operations. Indeed, any area of operation for which the chief pilot is held responsible might be considered as flight operations, but in respect of airline operations, the term encompasses far more than this.

An operator would be delighted if only the aircraft and its components were subject to regulatory scrutiny and certification. But, clearly, this would be nonsense as much of the activity in aviation falls within the field of 'operations'. If regulators required that only aircraft and components were subject to close scrutiny and did not apply equal oversight to the operations area, then only half of the necessary supervisory task would be completed. It is the regulator's charter to supervise all areas of activity so as to ensure the safety of the public, third parties and property.

In a similar fashion to that described in Chapter 1, the Chicago Convention obligates the ICAO and contracting states to develop and publish rules for the operation of aircraft. This section will examine the international framework for airline operations and how these are translated from ICAO statements into the various national laws and codes.

Through the national application of the Standards and Recommended Practices contained in Annex 6 of the Chicago Convention, an internationally recognized framework for aircraft operations has been established. When coupled with the Standards of Annex 8, the result is a comprehensive system of rules covering the airworthiness of aircraft and their operation.

Traffic and ground handling (passenger and cargo) are integral parts of operations and are responsible for the processing of passengers and cargo and dispatching aircraft safely and on time.

It is an ICAO standard that states certify operators as competent to conduct operations. Operational approval is granted via the AOC. Without an AOC, commercial operations cannot be undertaken and therefore this certificate ranks with the route licences as the most important approval an operator can obtain. Clearly, it is the operator's responsibility to demonstrate its competence on an initial and continuing basis if the AOC is to be issued and retained.

Annex 6 of the ICAO: Operation of Aircraft

As we will examine in the next section on airline engineering and airworthiness requirements, in the same way that airworthiness finds its roots in the SARPs of an annex to the Chicago Convention, so too does the operation of aircraft. Annex 6 – *Operation of Aircraft* – provides the equivalent guidance for operations as Annex 8 does for the airworthiness of aircraft. While the guidelines are intended to cover international operations, it is usual for the domestic airline requirements to also be substantially in accordance with ICAO policies.

Scope of Airline Operational Activities

In terms of defining the scope of this section, the term 'operations' covers all operational and technical aspects of the airline's flight operations. It may be divided into separate departments for each aircraft type operated by the airline and will have a fleet captain and/or a check and training captain to ensure that crew standards are maintained. The training and checking aspects of flight operations include the certification and operational requirements for flight simulators and other synthetic training devices.

Typical areas of responsibility of airlines' flight operations departments include aircraft flight manual publications, security, fuel, flight and duty time limitations, rostering/crew control performance, extended range operations (EROPs), flight dispatch/planning, minimum equipment lists (MELs), dangerous goods, continued airworthiness, aircraft flight manuals, maintenance manuals, maintenance scheduling, certificate of approval renewals, line maintenance, base maintenance and modifications to MELs.

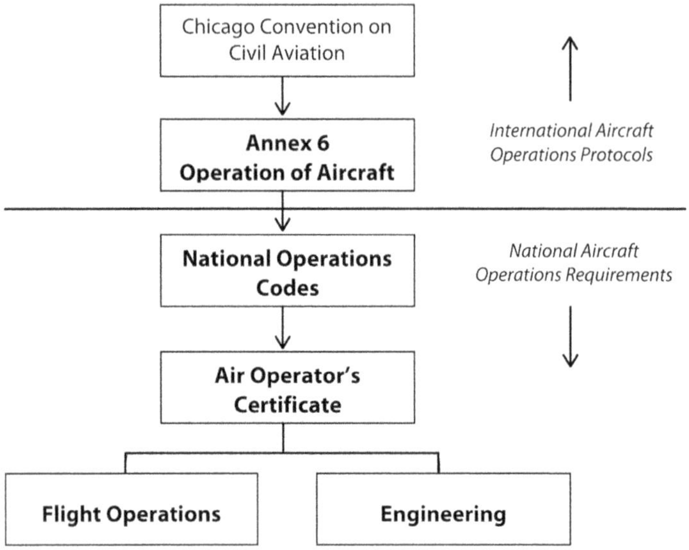

Figure 11.2 The international regulatory framework for airline operations

Annex 6 Requirements

Annex 6 is composed of three parts:

- Part I – SARPs applicable to the operation of planes by operators authorized to conduct *international commercial air transport operations*;
- Part II – SARPs applicable to international general aviation operations;
- Part III – SARPs applicable to international commercial air transport operations or international general aviation operations with helicopters.

However, for the purposes of this section, in illustrating the important relationships and responsibilities, it will only be necessary to deal with Part 1. Annex 6, Part I is divided into 13 chapters, one appendix and seven attachments. These divisions cover the whole gambit of aircraft operations and the main chapters set the SARPs for the following topics:

- flight operations;
- plane performance operating limitations;
- plane instruments, equipment and flight documents;
- plane communications and navigation equipment;
- plane maintenance;
- plane flight crew;
- flight operations officer/flight dispatcher;
- cabin attendants;
- security.

The appendix and attachments of Annex 6, Part 1 go on to address specialized areas such as:

- lights to be displayed on aerodromes;
- flight time and flight duty period limitations;
- first-aid medical supplies;
- plane performance (expanded requirements);
- flight recorders;
- Extended Range Operations (EROP)s;
- AOCs;
- MELs.

As previously stated, there are in excess of 10,000 SARPs covering every conceivable safety, technical and operational aspect of aviation activities.

ICAO Differences

We saw in Chapter 1 that as signatories to the Chicago Convention, all 192 contracting states are expected and indeed obliged to comply with all the SARPs contained in the 19 ICAO Annexes. The option exists, however, to declare a *difference* based on an inability of a state to comply with a particular standard. Each Annex contains a list of differences declared by particular states and what that difference entails.

Many nations have registered differences with the standards contained in Annex 6, but, in general, the intention to have a relatively uniform operations code has been achieved.

ICAO Annexes do not supersede domestic or state laws and therefore each contracting state has to enact domestic legislation – through the legal process of *ratification* – to bring the SARPs into national effect. In this respect, an Annex will normally address the responsibilities of the state; however, Annex 6 is unusual in this respect. While the Annex does set out each state's responsibilities, it also allocates certain responsibilities directly to the operator. In Part I, Chapter 3 – *General*, the international basis of the Annex is brought to light where, for example, it states some operator obligations:

3.1. An operator shall ensure that all employees when abroad know that they must comply with the laws and procedures of those States in which operations are conducted.

3.2. An operator shall ensure that all pilots are familiar with the laws, regulations and procedures, pertinent to the performance of their duties, prescribed for the areas traversed, the aerodromes to be used and the air navigation facilities relating thereto.

In relation to a breach of local regulations or procedures in emergency situations, the Annex goes so far as to allocate to the pilot in command or commander the responsibility for reporting the violation to both the authority in the state of the operator and the local authority. For aircrew, many of these responsibilities will be familiar, but in the form of national legislation or as statements in a company operations manual – Annex 6 is the source document.

Annex 6 also contains the absolute requirement for local authorities to approve operators to conduct commercial air transport operations by way of issuing an AOC.

Domestic Aviation Legislation

It is the responsibility of each contracting state to publish its own rules and regulations for the operation of aircraft or to adopt the code of another state. In many instances, for example, smaller or less developed states have adapted the USA's Federal Aviation Regulations (FARs) as the basis for their domestic civil aviation legislation. In the Pacific, many small island states have adopted the New Zealand Civil Aviation Rules (CARs). In Europe, as we shall see in Chapter 12, the EASA regulations are being progressively adopted by many nations, including by non-EU Member States.

Irrespective of the process, the ICAO requirements are incorporated into each respective state's civil aviation law. How the ICAO standards are incorporated into local legislation is driven by each nation's legal and constitutional framework. The following provides an overview of the varying ways in which states comply with their obligations under the Chicago Convention.

In the USA, a codified approach has been adopted and the FAA publishes its operational requirements as sections of the FARs. On the other hand, for example, in Australia, whose legal system is based on the British common law system, the means of incorporation is via an Act (or statute) of Parliament and the proclamation of subsidiary Regulations and Orders.

Whatever means is used to publish the code, each will contain at least the ICAO minimum requirements. But it should also be remembered that each nation is granted the prerogative to include any other operating rule it deems necessary. As such, one finds a number of fundamental differences between the operating codes.

The various regulations and codes state the requirement but usually give no guidance as to how to achieve compliance. For example, the code will state that operators are required to maintain adequate records of crew flight hours but will not give guidance as to what methods are considered acceptable. Not surprisingly, there is an administrative method in this apparent legal 'madness'.

To provide airline operators with guidance, state authorities normally publish interpretative material that goes into great detail as to how compliance may be achieved. By choosing this approach, it is only necessary to amend the guidance material rather than the code. Any NAA, such as the FAA, will normally have the power to amend guidance material without reference to higher authority, whereas amendment of the code requires government approval.

Interpretative material is normally not considered part of the code (law), but the methods advocated have stood the test of time and are seen by the authorities as satisfying the aims of the regulatory safety system. The authorities would therefore expect that operators adopt these recommended methods and to refuse to do so would cause the regulator to question the operator's suitability to hold an AOC or any other approval it may be seeking. Most authorities, however, retain a flexible approach and are responsive to reasoned arguments for variations or applications of new methods. Indeed, FAA interpretative material usually carries the caveat that the recommended method is one way but not the only way of demonstrating compliance with the law.

THE CAPTAIN AND AIRCREW

The purpose of this section is to provide the reader with an understanding of the operating requirements for the crew of an airliner with an account of the legal liability which flows from the powers and responsibilities of the pilot in command and other crew members involved in commercial transport operations. Although the captain or commander has the superior position in terms of authority and is charged with ultimate responsibility for the safety of the passengers, all operational crew will benefit from an understanding of the captain's legal responsibilities.

Knowledge of the powers and responsibilities of the pilot in command will also benefit other crew members in providing them with a more complete picture of their own legal responsibilities and duties that derive from that authority. Although this section concentrates on the relationship between the pilot in command and other crew in a multicrew environment, many of the comments made, and regulations extracted, apply equally to single pilot and general aviation operations.

Sources of Legal Liability

There are various sources from which the duties of the pilot in command and other aircrew derive. It is important to understand the difference between these sources as the nature of the responsibilities created by each of these sources varies considerably. In Chapter 6, a duty of care arising out of a tortious relationship was distinguished from the duties imposed on the parties to a contract (for which see Chapter 5). This distinction is fundamental and should be fully appreciated.

Another important consideration that flows from the various duties imposed on aircrew is the consequences of a breach of such duties. In some instances, particularly statutory duties, the duty imposed is one of strict liability, the breach of which may attract criminal sanctions.

The main sources from which aircrew duties derive are:

- contractual duties;
- a duty of care arising from the tort of negligence; and
- statutory duties imposed by international standards or domestic aviation law.

Contractual duties are imposed on the pilot in command and other crew members by the terms of their contract of employment. The nature of the duties imposed on employees by a contract of employment is discussed in Chapter 7.

Another source from which contractual duties may arise is the *contract of carriage*: see Chapter 10. In the majority of cases, however, there will be no contractual agreement between any aircrew and either the passengers or the owners of cargo. According to the doctrine of privity of contract, unless someone is a party to a contract, then that party is not liable and it also cannot claim any rights under the terms of that contract. Pilots and other crew members have contracts with the airline and so do passengers and owners of cargo. There is therefore no contract between the passengers or cargo owners and the crew of an aircraft.

The only exception to the preceding is the small number of pilots that may enter formal contracts with their passengers and/or owners of freight. This might occur in general aviation situations where the pilot owns the aircraft or is a freelance pilot offering aircraft charter services. However, the terms of a contract of carriage are largely dictated by statute. Liability of the pilot or carrier to passengers and others will be determined by the classification of operation. For example, is the flight an air transport operation or a private flight? Is it a domestic or international operation? The liabilities and limitations imposed by treaties on operators of international airlines are discussed in more detail in Chapter 10.

A *duty of care* is another source of liability to aircrew. This duty is created by the existence of a certain relationship (the neighbour principle) recognized at law. The pilot in command owes a duty of care to a large number of people, including passengers, fellow crew members and other persons both on the ground and in other aircraft. The scope of this duty at common law is not limited and in Chapter 6 a number of case studies were provided to illustrate the extent to which the courts may hold various airline personnel liable for their tortious acts or omissions.

Statutory duties are those imposed on aircrew by the large amount of aviation-related legislation that specifies the duties required of an individual. The most obvious legislation relating to the duties of aircrew is found in the respective state's civil aviation rules and regulations. Other documentation, such as the airline's operations manual, is equally binding on aircrew. As both the contractual duties and the duty of care of aviation personnel have been discussed elsewhere in this book, it is the statutory duties imposed on aircrew which will now be examined.

Responsibilities of the Aircraft Commander

The prescribed responsibilities imposed by the domestic aviation law of a state will vary, but in general terms the responsibilities are much the same throughout the world because of ICAO standards.

An overview of the scope of the responsibilities typically imposed upon the pilot in command or the commander of an aircraft are:

- start, continuation, diversion and end of a flight by the aircraft;
- operation and safety of the aircraft during flight time;
- the safety of persons and cargo carried on the aircraft;
- the conduct and safety of members of the crew on the aircraft;
- compliance with any information, instructions or directions relating to the start, continuation, diversion or end of a flight that are made available, or issued, under state aviation regulations; and
- the requirements of the operations manual provided by the operator of the aircraft.

In all state regulatory regimes, the pilot in command shall have final authority as to the disposition of the aircraft while he or she is in command and for the maintenance of discipline by all persons on board.

The aircraft commander is also responsible for ensuring that certain duties have been performed before flight. Other individuals may perform these duties; however, the pilot in command has the final responsibility to 'ensure' that the tasks entrusted to them have been complied with.

Typically, the commander will be held responsible to ensure that:

- all required instruments and equipment are functioning properly;
- the gross weight of the aircraft does not exceed the limitation;
- the aircraft is correctly loaded for all stages of flight;
- the fuel supplies are sufficient for a particular flight;
- the required crew members are on board and in a fit state to perform their duties;
- the air traffic control instructions have been complied with;
- the aircraft is safe for flight in all respects; and
- all relevant aeronautical maps, charts and other documentation are carried.

To maintain safe operations, most regulations require the pilot in command to 'ensure' that certain duties are performed, but this does not mean that the pilot in command or captain cannot delegate such duties. The meaning of the word 'ensure' in this context is the subject of some debate. In the New Zealand case of *McNeill v Parmer*, the court considered its meaning in an aviation context.

***McNeill v Parmer*, unreported, Supreme Court of Rotorua, 21 February 1979**

The pilot in command of an aircraft with a certified maximum all-up weight of 8,000 pounds took off 190 pounds overweight. The plaintiff argued that the bulk of this excess was the result of a piece of freight placed on board by a traffic clerk and without the knowledge of the pilot. This additional freight was not recorded on the load sheet. Although the pilot honestly believed the aircraft was correctly loaded, the ruling of the court was that the pilot in command, being responsible for the safety of the aircraft, is under a strict obligation to 'ensure' that all parts of the regulations dealing with weight are complied with. The judgment stated: 'the pilot must, before takeoff, check the cargo which has been loaded, and ensure that all of it appears on the load sheet. This obligation rests on the pilot of a big commercial aircraft such as a Boeing 737 because of an adequate system of supervision and inspection could be established even for an aircraft that size'. Accordingly, the court held that the pilot was guilty of the offence.

Because of the strict wording of the regulation, the pilot was unable to plea the statutory defence of 'without fault or privity'. It is hard to see how, in practical terms, a pilot of a large commercial airliner can 'ensure' that an aircraft is correctly loaded. Pilots rely on approved loading systems and other people certifying that such procedures have been complied with. It seems logical that a pilot's responsibility is limited to taking all reasonable and prudent steps to ensure 'as far as possible' that approved systems have been complied with.

Powers of the Pilot in Command

The varying state regulations bestow upon the captain of an aircraft extremely wide powers over people on board the aircraft. Some of these powers, such as detention without arrest, are unheard of at common law. Other powers come from states' ratification of international conventions, such as the Tokyo Convention 1963. In addition to these statutory powers, there is in common law jurisdictions the power to carry out a 'citizen's arrest' to prevent a breach of the peace.

The most important powers bestowed upon the captain generally include the following:

- to take such action, including the removal of a person from the aircraft or the placing of a person under restraint or in custody, by force, as the pilot considers reasonably necessary to ensure compliance with any rules or regulations in relation to the aircraft; and
- to detain the passengers, crew and cargo for such period as the pilot considers reasonably necessary to ensure compliance with applicable rules or regulations in relation to the aircraft.

This is the most likely offence to be encountered by a crew member and, in particular, by cabin crew in relation to passengers in a state of intoxication. Most airline flight administration manuals give cabin crew the discretion to refuse alcoholic services to disruptive passengers and to prohibit the consumption of alcohol brought on board the aircraft by any passenger. It is important to note that cabin crew should refrain from making reference or accusations as to a passenger's lack of sobriety as this may, in itself, impose liability on the crewmember or airline.

Most state regulations prohibit operating crew members from consuming alcohol in the (usual) eight hours prior to departure. Quite independent of this provision are regulations that state that a crew member is prohibited from so acting if by reason of his or her having consumed, used or absorbed any alcoholic liquor, drug, pharmaceutical or medicinal preparation or other substance, that crew member's capacity to act is 'impaired'. These latter provisions will therefore apply irrespective of any specific time limitation.

Regulators throughout the world have recently begun introducing drug and alcohol testing programmes to further strengthen safety standards in this area.

Flight Attendants

The role of cabin crew in commercial airline operations is essential to the safety and well-being of all passengers. The training required of these professionals is extensive and includes a diverse range of topics, including emergency procedures, first aid and customer service. Irrespective of the specific duties and areas of responsibility of the individual, all cabin crew have a primary responsibility for the safety and comfort of passengers. The flight service director or senior purser is responsible to the captain for the supervision and administration of cabin crew and to ensure that they perform their duties proficiently.

Many of the powers bestowed upon the pilot in command, discussed previously, require delegation to other crewmembers, including cabin crew. It is imperative that each cabin crewmember is aware of his or her company's policy in relation to reporting lines and the chain of command on board the aircraft. If an order or command is given to a flight attendant by a superior crewmember, then under the terms of his or her contract of employment, and in the interests of safety, that person is bound to comply with any such request, provided of course that such a request is lawful and reasonable.

It is also the responsibility of the individual flight attendant to report immediately to a 'superior' crewmember any unusual, emergency or potentially dangerous situations. This might include, for example, any unfamiliar noises, smells, passenger activity or parcels in the cabin during any phase of flight.

THE AIR OPERATORS CERTIFICATE

Introduction

The most important and fundamental legislative requirements in respect of airline operations is the gaining (and retaining) of an Air Operators Certificate, or as more commonly referred, an AOC. This is the basis for regulating all commercial airline operations by safety regulators throughout the world. No air operator activities are permitted unless the operator holds a current AOC which specifies the nature and scope of operations permitted. NAAs may also impose conditions or limitations upon an AOC.

The regulatory requirements pertaining to the issue of an AOC are stated in the individual state's civil aviation acts in regulations. Obviously, these requirements will vary from state to state, but essentially they are all based on ensuring positive safety and security outcomes. In most instances, the AOC regulatory requirements will also require that senior airline managers, post holders and other key personnel in the organization have appropriate experience in air operations to conduct or to carry out the AOC operations safely.

Without a doubt, the AOC ranks with route licences as the most important approval an airline operator can possess. The AOC can be viewed as the over-arching regulatory glue that binds together all of the disparate areas in which an operator is required to display competence and compliance. As we shall see, some of these areas do not necessarily fall neatly into the supervisory envelope of the primary operating departments, namely flight operations and engineering.

Attaining an AOC

Clearly, gaining an AOC by an airline is a major endeavour and maintaining it should be approached with similar enthusiasm. It truly is a management exercise. Setting out to gain an AOC to permit airline operations is a large undertaking – one that will consume considerable time and resources both for the applicant and for the authority. NAAs recognize the difficulties involved in this process and usually provide detailed guidance to applicants through supplementary documents. Additionally, a series of meetings is held at which progress is monitored and verbal and/or written guidance is given.

Some idea of how seriously an authority views the task of issuing an AOC to air transport operators can be gained by looking at the indexes of topics to be assessed contained in each state's regulations relating to air transport operations. All aspects of the operation, engineering included, are subjected to the closest scrutiny to ensure that the safety of the travelling public is guaranteed. Throughout the process, constant dialogue between the authority and applicant should provide the necessary guidance.

Senior Persons These positions within an air operator's organization may be referred to as 'post-holders', 'senior persons' or 'key personnel'. The quality – in terms of experience and qualifications – of the air operator's management team cannot be over stressed. This is not just a focus for the application phase; a quality management team is seen as an ongoing requirement. Accordingly, the operator is often not free to replace senior operations management staff at will. In most jurisdictions, it is necessary to give the authority formal notice of an intention to replace one of these senior people, and that notice must be given well in advance of the event. Most national safety regulators retain the right to either accept or reject the proposal.

Issuing an AOC When the authority is satisfied that the operator is competent, an AOC can be issued. However, here it is worthwhile to point out some differences in approach.

Depending on the legal and constitutional environment in force, some authorities have been granted a form of overall discretion that allows them not to issue an AOC, even though the applicant may superficially appear to have complied with all the requirements – viewed on a segment-by-segment basis. The discretionary provision is normally found in the use of the words of the form 'may issue' instead of 'will issue'. The UK is a country that uses this approach.

The alternative approach can be found in countries such as the USA, Australia and New Zealand. In these countries, the legislation contains direction to the authority that it 'will issue' an AOC if the applicant has met the requirements.

Both systems achieve the same ends. AOCs are only issued to applicants who have demonstrated to the authority's satisfaction that they are completely competent to discharge the responsibilities imposed by the AOC.

AOC Format As required by ICAO Annex 6, the AOC will contain a statement of authority to operate in a particular capacity, with certain aircraft, in a given area or on specified routes, subject to any additional limitations that the authority deems necessary and for a defined period of time. Considering the effort involved in gaining an AOC, it can often appear as a disappointingly small document as it usually runs to only a few pages. It is the operator's responsibility to ensure that all conditions detailed in the AOC are adhered to and made known to company employees.

AOC Renewal An AOC is issued for a specified period, usually a year, and must be renewed. The onus for renewal is placed upon the authority by Annex 6, which requires that states 'establish a system both for the certification and the continued surveillance of the operator to ensure the required standards of operation are maintained' (Annex 6, Attachment F).

The operative word with regard to renewal is surveillance, the implication being that this is a continuous process. Authorities usually appoint officers to supervise individual operators. Periodic inspections are scheduled and snap inspections are also employed as part of a programme aimed at determining continued compliance and satisfactory standards.

Unfortunately, history has shown that inspection programmes can lead to the development of an adversarial relationship, with operators becoming less likely to respond in an open manner. Recently, the inspection method has come to be viewed as an unsatisfactory approach that does not properly facilitate the basic aim – that of increasing safety. Also, under an external inspection-based regime, there is a tendency for operators to rely on the authority to tell them what is wrong, rather than identifying and solving problems themselves.

In an effort to combat those weakness, the authorities in Europe and the USA have recently moved down the 'Quality Management' road and have put in place requirements for an audit-based programme in which the operator is much more involved in self-regulation. This approach has had considerable success as it forces operators to establish, among other things, a Quality System in Flight Operations, something that had previously been confined to the engineering Quality Assurance area.

While the requirement for external inspections still remains, under these new proposals it has been turned into a continuous audit programme. This approach tends to defuse the adversarial atmosphere generated by inspections and has the added benefit of setting an agreed schedule to rectify any problems found. It is a much more collaborative way to tackle the surveillance issue.

Summary The AOC is the airline's approval to conduct business. Without it, the airline's commercial strategies cannot be put into practice. ICAO standards require that operators be certified under the appropriate state regulations to conduct commercial air transport operations. The process of gaining an AOC is complex and relies heavily on the quality, experience and integrity of the operations management team. Once an AOC has been awarded, the operator must protect it at all costs, as to have it revoked or restricted brings not only commercial losses but places the organization in the unenviable and difficult position of having to regain credibility with the supervising authority.

AOC Documentation

There are many documents that are important for the gaining and maintaining of an AOC. Some of these were mentioned earlier where the certification of aircraft was discussed. However, there are two primary documents that are often dismissed by those at the operational coalface but that are the source of information used in company publications.

In this section we will examine the Aircraft (or Airplane) Flight Manual (AFM) and the Master Minimum Equipment List (MMEL).

Aircraft Flight Manual (AFM) The AFM is one of the prime documents associated with the certification of an aircraft. A much-maligned book, for a large transport aircraft, it is truly the province of experts who are able to interpret the generalized way in which it is written. It is the aim of this section to make students and aviation professionals aware of the importance of the AFM and to give a brief description of its construction and administration. The AFM is the pre-eminent document associated with the operation of the aircraft.

In order to certify a new type, the manufacturer must present an AFM for approval. Also, in order to have a Certificate of Airworthiness issued, the aircraft must have an AFM and in order to gain an AOC, an operator must present AFMs for the aircraft intended to be flown. Clearly, this is a very important document.

Given its importance, it is surprising to observe the lack of knowledge that prevails in operations management circles – engineering included – regarding the AFM's status, its use and administration. The understandable tendency is to focus on the company's operations manual and the engineering equivalent, and it is not unusual to find the operations manual referred to as the AFM and vice versa. However, this confusion could lead to a breach of aircraft limitations and non-compliance with mandatory procedures. In the worst-case scenario, breaches of this nature could lead to a revocation of an AOC or, possibly, litigation. The AFM is the primary source of all aircraft operating limitations, procedures and scheduled performance information. As such, the AFM takes precedence over all other operational documents. It needs to be recognized as having this status and should be managed accordingly.

The custodian: traditionally, custodianship of AFMs has rested with the engineering department. The reasoning is that, as the AFM is part of the Certificate of Airworthiness (C of A) documentation, engineering is its right and proper place.

Unfortunately, this view has a number of shortcomings:

- the AFM has nothing to do with the day-to-day business of engineering departments but saves having to have a fully updated version available for the purposes of renewing a C of A;
- all information in the AFM pertains to the aircraft's operation but, for large transport category aircraft, is written in a way to make it usable only by flight operations specialists; and
- if the AFM is retained in the engineering area, there is a strong possibility that flight operations staff will not be made aware of critical changes to procedures, limitations and scheduled performance.

Therefore, it is suggested that the best custodian of the AFM is the flight operations department, subject to the caveat that it is administered by a technically competent group within that organization.

Construction: the AFM is generally composed of five major parts:

1 control pages;
2 limitations;
3 normal procedures;
4 emergency procedures; and
5 scheduled performance.

Additionally, there are often appendices that contain limitations, procedures and performance for different engine types, aircraft configurations and possibly even certain airfields. Appendices can be specific to one operator.

In recent AFMs, performance data have been moved into a digital format and manipulated in computers by performance specialists. Clearly, this brings into question the requirement, contained in some operational codes, to have the AFM available for crews to use on the flight deck.

Configuration Deviation List: it is a requirement that the AFM contains the Configuration Deviation List (CDL) and this is often presented as an appendix to the manual. Operators often choose to also include the CDL in the operations manual as part of the MEL. The CDL lists the authorized deviations from the standard aircraft configuration and contains maintenance and operating instructions on how to operate the aircraft with certain airframe components missing. The CDL is often colloquially referred to as the 'Bits Falling off Aircraft Check List'.

Administration: despite views to the contrary, the AFM is not written in stone. It is a living document that requires constant attention and administration to ensure that a company is fully in compliance with the AFM and is taking advantage of all that can be extracted from the manual to improve commercial performance. Through negotiation with the regulator and the aircraft manufacturer, it is possible to revise the manual and to have data included that enhance commercial capabilities – always subject to the caveat, however, that this needs to conform with the national regulations.

Applicable legislation: when the aircraft certification rules are set, the state of registration will declare the operational rules to which the AFM is to conform. These regulations or rules vary from country to country and manufacturers are set up to produce AFMs written to the various codes. An example of such a difference is the way in which the UK and the USA have accounted for wet runway performance. The UK compiles scheduled take-off data using a wet-runway coefficient of friction – that is, all take-offs are considered to be on a wet runway, even when the runway is dry. The FAA rules assume a dry runway but adjust for wet conditions when required.

Carriage of AFM: there are two reasons why the requirement to carry the AFM on the flight deck remains in most operational codes:

- historically, this has always been so, as when aircraft were much simpler, AFMs were used as pilots' notes. Also, the AFMs for light aircraft are simple documents intended for use by pilots; and
- the AFM is part of the conditions under which the aircraft's C of A is granted and, particularly for international operations, should be on board.

Unfortunately, AFMs for large commercial transport aircraft are highly complex and large documents, extending to several volumes if still in the non-digital format. In addition, the AFM is written in a general manner that allows its application to a wide range of aircraft of that type; in other words, the AFM is not written in the operator-specific mode of an operations manual. As a result, interpreting AFMs has tended to become a specialist task.

Some authorities have recognized this problem and, while retaining the overriding clause in the regulations to cater for smaller types, have granted operators of large transport aircraft dispensation not to carry the AFM.

The operator must accept the responsibility to include all 'relevant' AFM information in the operations manual. Failure to abide by this condition could result in the revocation of the dispensation. For international operations in particular, a copy of the dispensation must be carried on the aircraft. For this dispensation to be issued, the authority must be satisfied that the operator has the management structure and technical competence to administer the necessary support system.

Master Minimum Equipment List (MMEL) The ICAO acknowledges that an operations policy requiring an aircraft to have all systems and equipment serviceable for dispatch would be unrealistic and too restrictive. Indeed, if this policy were applied to modern transport aircraft, it would be in conflict with current design philosophy that uses system redundancy to achieve both increased dispatch reliability and safety.

Furthermore, experience has shown that some systems, or items of equipment, can be unserviceable for certain flight conditions without significantly degrading the safety of the operation. This is not to say that these defects can be carried indefinitely. The ICAO policy makes it abundantly clear that the intention is to facilitate continued safe operation 'within the framework of a controlled programme and sound programme of repairs and parts replacement' (Annex 6, Attachment G of the ICAO).

To help implement this policy, the ICAO requires that the manufacturer, in conjunction with the state of design, prepares a Master Minimum Equipment List (MMEL). The MMEL is approved by the state of design and is the reference on which operators base individual MELs. The MEL is part of the operations manual.

Some authorities may independently publish an MMEL or a supplement to the MMEL if they consider the document issued by the state of design to be inadequate.

Minimum Equipment List (MEL): ICAO policy also requires the state of registration to direct operators to prepare a company MEL for the types in their fleet. The MEL must be based on the MMEL and be approved by the operator's supervising authority.

Though constrained to conform to the MMEL in terms of alleviations, operators have considerable freedom to compile the MEL in the most 'user-friendly' format. There are many variations on this theme, with some MELs incorporating the CDL as well as the maintenance procedures involved in securing the defective system for safe flight. However, the primary requirement is that the MEL clearly states the crew procedures and any performance penalties associated with the degraded system configuration.

State AOC Oversight Programmes

The ICAO has specific standards with respect to the oversight of airlines by the contracting state's aviation regulatory authorities or NAAs. For any regulatory oversight programme to be effective, it is necessary that the system supporting it be dynamic and transparent. This is due to the contemporary characteristics of the industry it is meant to regulate. As developments occur, technologies emerge or new trends evolve, resources should therefore be shifted accordingly. For instance, if surveillance indicates that certain areas or aspects of flight operations or airworthiness are of an ongoing high standard and that these areas are being sufficiently monitored, then it may be appropriate to reallocate resources to other targeted areas.

FAA Oversight of Airlines: in 1998, the USA's FAA began trialling the *Air Transport Oversight System* (ATOS) on ten major airlines. Now fully implemented, this is a systems approach to safety oversight and is designed to use data to identify and correct high-risk areas before they result in incidents or accidents. The ATOS focuses FAA inspectors' efforts on the causes of, and solutions to, the most significant safety deficiencies.

In following the approach of the FAA and other safety regulators throughout the world, these regulators have progressively introduced a *systems approach* to aviation safety oversight. The previous oversight regime by national civil aviation regulators was based on the traditional reactive, product auditing and testing model. As we shall see in Chapter 14, since 2009, the ICAO has mandated that NAAs require the approval of safety management systems for airlines and maintenance organizations.

European Union Oversight of Airlines: the European Union (EU) publishes a list of air carriers that are banned from entering the airspace of any of its Member States, usually for failing to meet EU regulatory oversight standards. The first version of the list was published in 2006, on the legal basis of *Regulation No. 474/2006* of the European Commission, issued on 22 March of that year. The most recent version of the list was published on 30 November 2023 and can be accessed at: https://transport.ec.europa.eu/transport-themes/eu-air-safety-list_en.

The EU *Safety List* (i.e. 'Community list of air carriers which are subject to an operating ban within the Community') actually contains two lists: the first list (Annex A) includes all airlines banned from operating in Europe. The second list (Annex B) includes airlines that are restricted from operating under certain conditions in Europe. Both lists are updated regularly and published in the Official Journal of the European Union. Before taking any action based on the information in these lists, all users should ensure they have the latest version.

OPERATIONAL CONTROL

Overview

In this section we examine the concepts, techniques and tools of operational control. Operational control is both an international ICAO regulatory requirement, founded on the need to manage risk and maintain safety margins, and the means by which an airline retains commercial control over a highly fluid and mobile set of revenue-producing assets – its airborne fleet.

This is the coalface of operations management. It is highly dynamic, yet, by using tools that assist in decision-making, much can be done to ensure that the best outcome is achieved. The system of operational control must be able to access all areas of the organization at all times that the fleet is operational. This crossing of boundaries requires that formal systems of support and communication are established within the organization and that all are aware of the critical nature of this aspect of the business.

However, operational control is not merely an internal function. To a very large extent, operational control is vested in the pilot in command. It is the pilot in command who must make the airborne decisions based on the best information available at the time. Part of the art of operational control is to be able to advise the pilot in command and/or to provide him or her with the information on which a decision can be founded. But there should be no commercial pressure applied, and a regulatory authority would take a very dim view of an operator seeking to bias the pilot in command's decision on the grounds of commercial expediency rather than safety.

Operational Control and Airlines

Management has been variously defined, but most definitions involve the combined action of disciplines such as planning, organizing, leading and controlling in all areas of the business to achieve a set of declared organizational goals. When discussing management, most texts first develop the individual topics separately then weave these into a combined theory, but the focus is usually more at the strategic level.

However, as we have seen throughout this book, aviation is a fast-paced enterprise. While the careful, structured and measured methods referred to in texts are still relevant and applicable, the speed with which this industry operates often forces decisions to be made in timeframes that would be considered unduly hasty in other businesses. Senior management in airlines still deals with the strategic issues and, in terms of day-to-day operations management, these deliberations can seem ponderous. But it should be remembered that it is these strategic visions and directions that determine success or failure in the future.

However, at the operational level, the pace picks up considerably. Consider the daily operational management problems facing a large international airline with a fleet of, say, 500 aircraft. All the longer term issues we have examined in these notes so far, relatively speaking, pale into insignificance when compared with the major tasks of keeping this show on the road. Flight number 123 has diverted to an off-line port with a major engine problem. The weather in Europe has turned very nasty and you have ten aircraft inbound, many of which are likely to divert. What are the legal obligations in a particular situation? What restrictions are therefore created? What then is the optimum solution both legally and commercially? Often it is a matter of making the best out of a bad situation – minimizing damage. But primarily how do we maintain the safety and integrity of the operation?

Other than to describe the elements of operational control, a publication such as this cannot be prescriptive. No two airlines are alike, so how any system is established will depend very much on the individual needs of the airline. The complexity of the system will also depend on the nature, scope and type of operations of that airline.

Operational Control Defined

The term 'operational control' means different things to different people, depending on the regulatory framework in which they operate. On the one hand, the state can assume responsibility and, on the other hand, all responsibility can be thrust upon the aircraft pilot in command. In fact, operational control is a mixture of responsibilities, which change in emphasis according to the phase of flight, the conditions to be encountered and any emergencies that may occur.

ICAO Definition

In Chapter 1 of Annex 6 of the Chicago Convention, operational control is said to relate 'to the exercise of authority over the initiation, continuation, diversion or termination of a flight in the interests of the safety of the aircraft, and the regularity and efficiency of the flight'. If the definition is dissected, three elements can be identified.

Operational control relates to all flight phases, including the initiation or termination of a mission. The primary focus is *safety*. Two secondary objectives are considered – *regularity* and *efficiency*.

Unfortunately, Annex 6 effectively halts the discussion of operational control at this point, save for an assignment of responsibility in Chapter 3. Given the importance of this topic, it is difficult to understand why the ICAO has not seen fit to provide more specific guidance on the matter. Perhaps it is this scarcity of standards or recommended practices that has led to the great variety of operational control solutions and the confusion that exists as to what operational control actually is and who is responsible for its functioning.

We shall return to a broader discussion of this problem after examining the ICAO's recommendation for the assignment of responsibility for operational control.

ICAO Assignment of Responsibility

The next and only other direct reference to operational control in Annex 6 is found in Chapter 3, paragraph 3.3, where it is stated that: 'An operator or a designated

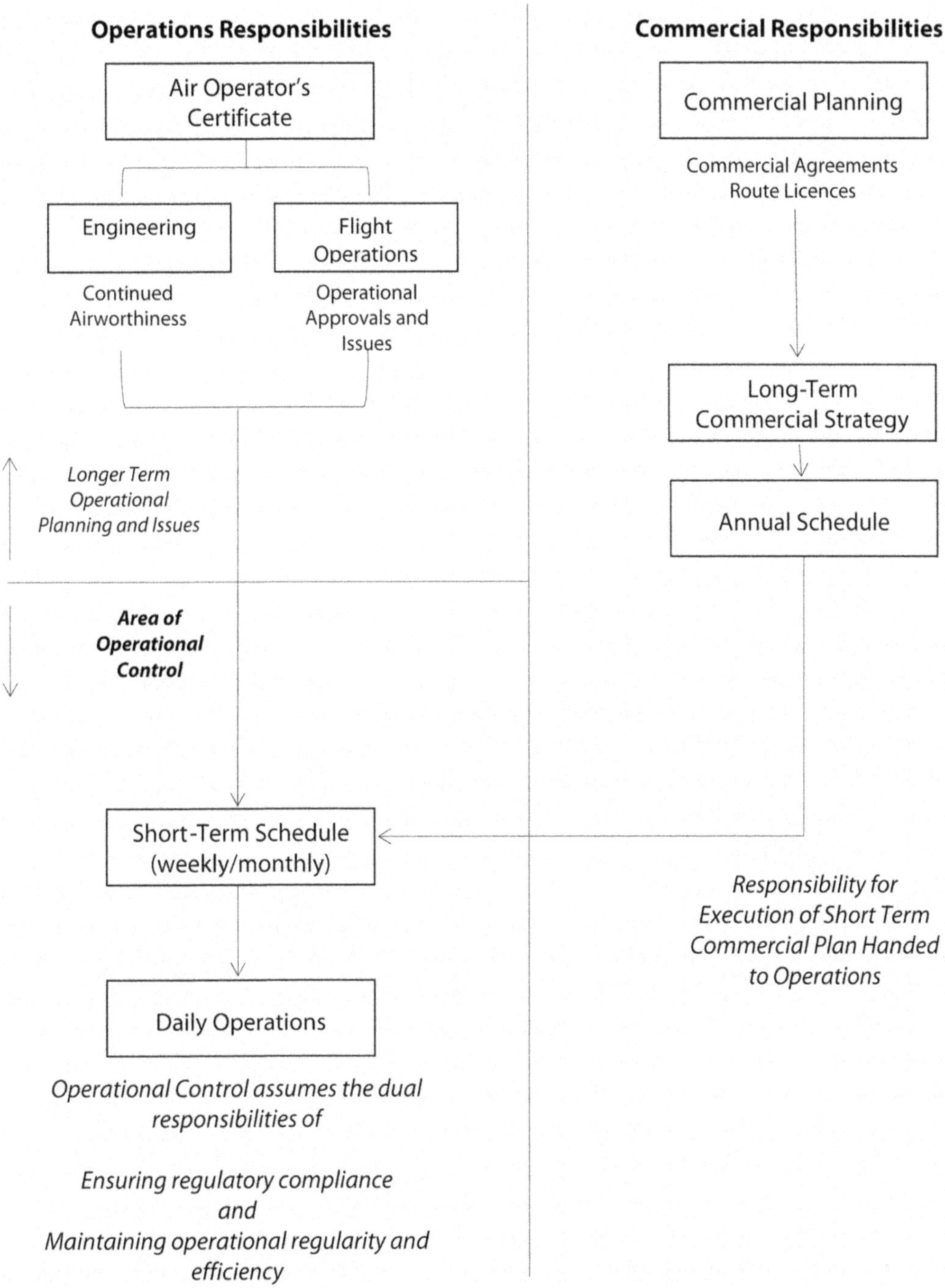

Figure 11.3 Elements of an operational control system

representative shall have responsibility for operational control'. No guidance is given as to what responsibilities an operator or its delegate will assume. At this point in Annex 6, all direct reference to operational control ceases, although one can infer from the subsequent division of responsibilities contained in the Annex that the ICAO considers certain activities to belong to the operator, while others are to remain the exclusive province of the pilot in command of the aircraft.

Possibly, as a result of the lack of SARPs, states have taken widely differing views on this issue. In some countries, operational control is exercised by the state. In other countries, the operator assumes the responsibilities along the lines of the divisions contained in Annex 6, while in some jurisdictions, all responsibility for operational control is thrust upon the aircraft pilot in command.

By way of example, operators in the USA employ licensed dispatchers who retain control over the flight until pushback, whereupon responsibility for operational control, in most respects, shifts to the pilot in command. However, on long-haul operations requiring re-clearance in flight, there have been occasions where the dispatcher has appeared to have the final say as to whether the flight proceeds to the intended destination or diverts. There have been several near-disasters, however, using this approach.

The Flight Plan to 2050

The aviation industry has adopted the goal of reaching net zero carbon emissions by 2050 (icao.int/Newsroom/Pages/States-adopts-netzero-2050-aspirational-goal-for-international-flight-operations.aspx). In October 2022, the UN's International Civil Aviation Organization (ICAO) led two weeks of negotiations involving 184 nations to agree on CO2 emissions reduction measures. These include ramping up innovative aircraft technologies, 'streamlining' flight operations and the increased production and use of sustainable aviation fuels (SAF).

In October 2022 in Montreal, the President of the ICAO Council, Salvatore Sciacchitano stated (ICAO 2022):

> States' adoption of this new long-term goal for decarbonized air transport, following the similar commitments from industry groups, will contribute importantly to the green innovation and implementation momentum which must be accelerated over the coming decades to ultimately achieve emissions-free powered flight.

The airline sectors peak body IATA, on the other hand, says the aviation industry won't be able to completely eliminate emissions at source and will need to mitigate the rest using a variety of offsetting mechanisms. This is the process where emissions are compensated for by the financing of a reduction in emissions elsewhere. Due to the importance of this challenge to the airline sector, these proposed initiatives and other issues relating to the 2050 Zero Emissions Target, are discussed in Chapter 18.

To progress this global challenge, with targets set by international organizations, what is required is a lot more international collaboration to set standards, agreement on a common solution, which may be the catalyst to create the necessary technological solutions and build a new air transport infrastructure, helping developing countries along the way to make the necessary adjustments to a carbon-neutral air transport system.

12
Maintenance Organizations

INTRODUCTION

Airworthiness

Machines have a habit of failing. Fortunately, in the case of flying machines, it does not happen often. Nowadays, rarely does a system or component fail in flight and even if it does, more likely than not there will be a back-up or *redundant* system. In the case of vital components, there may be two redundant systems. In the past century, in terms of airline safety and reliability, aviation has progressed a long way.

In the previous chapter we saw how the airline sector has had to contend with many global challenges. As we have seen, in a most devastating manner, the COVID-19 pandemic brought global air traffic to a sudden halt: airlines between 2020 and 2021 experienced an unprecedented drop in global air traffic of 80 per cent with the closure of state and international borders and grounding of fleets. Such a downturn has had a significant impact on the aerospace industry, including maintenance activities. The demand for maintenance services has been negatively impacted, as service providers have had to adapt to modifications in airline requirements including: a reduction in the number and types of aircraft operated; deprioritization of discretionary maintenance operations; reduction in the average age of fleets after retirement of older aircraft; and recycling of parts from decommissioned aircraft.

In order to cushion the fluctuations in demand for civil aircraft, aircraft maintenance, repair and operations (MROs) and other service providers must analyse options for diversifying their business: expanding into air cargo transport, but also into military air or ground markets. These are some of the challenges currently facing the aviation maintenance sector.

As the reader will recall, the overriding theme of the introductory chapters in this book was that aviation is an extraordinarily complex, worldwide enterprise that functions within an internationally agreed framework of conventions. In this chapter, we continue from the flight operations area of airlines to examine, at a more detailed level, how this cooperative framework extends to the certification and continued airworthiness of aircraft and components.

Aircraft maintenance, engineering and continuing airworthiness keep the aircraft serviceable and may be divided into separate departments for each type of maintenance activity. Often, particularly in smaller airlines and some LCCs, maintenance is contracted out to an approved third-party engineering company, or Maintenance and Repair Organization (MRO). This reduces equipment and staffing costs for the airline and ensures that the aircraft is fully maintained to the appropriate regulatory standard, such as those administered by the Federal Aviation Administration (FAA) in the USA and the European Aviation Safety Agency (EASA) in Europe. A typical structure

DOI: 10.4324/9781032652146-12

involves a separation of line maintenance, heavy maintenance (overhaul) and technical services.

When drafting individual airworthiness codes, states are only constrained to meet the minimum standards contained in Annex 8 of the ICAO and are free to embellish national laws as considered necessary to achieve the basic aim of the safety regulation of their country. Clearly, this approach led to a great variety of rules and caused manufacturers and operators considerable economic hardship where particular rules called for major design changes in order to achieve compliance. Wisely, the major airworthiness authorities have acknowledged this folly and have adopted an active policy of rule harmonization.

Throughout the system of safety regulation, national laws allocate specific responsibilities to both the regulator and the operator. This system of checks and balances has but one aim, the safe operation of aircraft, thereby ensuring the safety of the travelling public. The decision to enter the aviation industry at the operational level means that the operator and manufacturer will be bound by the obligations and duties prescribed in the safety regulation system. There is no escaping these obligations.

Airworthiness Requirements

Beginning with the Chicago Convention, the framework of initial and continued airworthiness is further defined in Annex 8 of the Convention, where both the ICAO airworthiness policy and the minimum agreed international standards for airworthiness are to be found. Contracting states are obligated under the Chicago Convention to either formulate their own airworthiness code or adopt that of another state.

ICAO Policy

The current ICAO policy on airworthiness is found in the Foreword to Annex 8. The last pronouncement on airworthiness policy was made in 1972 and remains in force today.

The policy reads:

a The objective of international airworthiness Standards is to define, for application by the competent national authorities, the minimum level of airworthiness constituting the international basis for the recognition by States under Article 33 of the convention, of certificates of airworthiness for the purposes of the flight of aircraft of other States into or over their territories thereby achieving, among other things, protection of other aircraft, third parties and property.

b The standards developed to meet the objectives stated in a) above are considered by the Council as meeting, in the necessary scope and detail, the obligations of the organization under Article 37 of the convention to adopt International Standards of airworthiness.

c International airworthiness Standards adopted by the Council are recognized as being the complete international code necessary to bring into force and effect the rights and obligations which arise under Article 33 of the convention.

d The technical airworthiness standards of Annex 8 shall be presented as broad specifications stating the objectives rather than the means of realizing these objectives:

ICAO recognizes that national codes of airworthiness containing the full scope and extent of detail considered necessary by individual States are required as the basis for the certification by individual States of airworthiness of each aircraft.

e To assist States in applying the Standards of Annex 8 and in developing their own comprehensive national codes in a uniform manner, detailed guidance shall be developed and published expeditiously in the working languages of the Organization.

It should be noted that to meet the preceding policy objective, the ICAO publishes guidance material entitled the 'Airworthiness Technical Manual'.

In respect of the above ICAO policy, there are a number of important issues:

- The ICAO, while providing guidance to member states, takes no direct part in the initial certification or continuing airworthiness of aircraft. The purpose of the Annex is to establish a minimum standard of airworthiness as the means by which member states may recognize, under the obligations of Article 33 of the Convention, the certificates of airworthiness issued by other member states as being sufficient to ensure safety of other aircraft, third persons and property during international operations where aircraft of one state overfly or operate into another state.
- The standards published in Annex 8 are seen as the complete, but minimum, code necessary for the ICAO to meet the rights and obligations brought into effect by Articles 33 and 37 of the Convention. However, the ICAO has no powers to make national laws and this is explicitly recognized in part d) of the policy statement.
- Article 37 requires that member states publish individual airworthiness codes. National certification codes set the airworthiness standards that particular states apply when considering the initial or continuing issue of a Certificate of Airworthiness for an aircraft or component for which it has design or operational responsibility.
- The ICAO standards merely facilitate international operations and give guidance for minimum standards of airworthiness necessary to meet the member's obligations under the Convention.

ICAO Annex 8: Airworthiness of Aircraft

Background The ICAO Council published the first ICAO standards and recommendations for the airworthiness of aircraft in 1949 as Annex 8 of the Convention. The Annex – entitled *Airworthiness of Aircraft* – contained general airworthiness procedures applicable to all aircraft and the minimum standards for those aircraft intended to be granted a Certificate of Airworthiness under one of the established ICAO aircraft categories.

In 1953, a fundamental review of ICAO policy on international airworthiness was initiated, resulting, in 1956, in the promulgating of a new approach that incorporated two important new principles.

First, the system of ICAO categories for aircraft was abandoned. Instead, Annex 8 was redrafted to include broad standards that defined the minimum basis for the recognition by states of certificates of airworthiness for the purpose of the flight of aircraft of other states. Importantly, these actions were seen as means by which the contracting states could meet their obligations under both Articles 33 and 37 of the Convention. The

Annex thus provides a policy focus for individual airworthiness authorities in that, under the obligations of the Convention, they are expected to concentrate primarily on accident prevention and safety rather than facilitation.

The second leg of the 1956 revision spoke to the status of national regulations. The ICAO declared that the Annex 8 provisions would not replace national airworthiness standards. National codes would contain the full scope and extent of detail considered necessary by individual states for the certification of individual aircraft. Therefore, each state would establish a comprehensive code or select a code from another member state.

Unfortunately, the ICAO made no recommendations as to standardization and, thereafter, a plethora of national airworthiness codes were published, each with differing requirements, but each meeting the intention of the ICAO rulings. It appears that the 1972 ICAO statement of airworthiness policy merely formalized what had been agreed earlier.

Annex 8 Requirements The ICAO Annex opens with a Foreword that contains interesting information, including the ICAO Airworthiness Policy. As a general matter of principle, students and aviation professionals who are not familiar with this area are encouraged to read the Foreword of any Annex or other ICAO publication, as it is here that the policy and procedural aspects that surround this topic will be found. The Foreword contains an outline of the Annex's history; this describes the rationale of both the Annex and of the amendments that have taken place over the years. The applicability of various parts of the Annex is also stated. A further section of the Foreword lays out the required action by contracting states with regard to their obligations under the Convention and in relation to the Annex. Finally, it should be noted that Annex 8 is relatively unique in that it does not contain any recommended practices, only standards.

Annex 8 of the ICAO is divided into four parts:

a Part I – Definitions.
b Part II – Administration – this relates to certificates of airworthiness, proof of compliance with airworthiness codes and continuing airworthiness. It is surprising that an area of such importance is so compact, occupying only four pages of the entire Annex. However, this is consistent with the rationale of broad standards, not precise prescriptions expressed in the ICAO Airworthiness Policy. An Airworthiness Technical Manual (Doc 9051) containing guidance material has been published to provide more detailed guidance on airworthiness matters.
c Part III contains the general standards for areas such as flights, structures, design and construction and so on for airplanes. It is interesting to note that the sequence of chapters used in the Annex is also used in the various national airworthiness codes.
d Part IV relates specifically to the airworthiness of helicopters.

Here it is worth ensuring that the distinction is understood between initial certification and the continuing airworthiness of individual aircraft. The Certificate of Airworthiness referred to in Annex 8 relates to the certificate granted to an individual aircraft by a contracting state under its national airworthiness code. The initial issue of such a certificate can only be accomplished after proving compliance with the appropriate airworthiness requirements, which includes approval of the aircraft design. It is usual that an authority will issue a *Type Design Certificate* in recognition of the fact that the design has met the design requirements; however, individual aircraft are issued a Certificate of Airworthiness which applies only to that aircraft.

Interestingly, Annex 8 recognizes the distinction between those aspects of performance that relate to airworthiness and the operational coverage of performance contained in Annex 6: Operation of Aircraft. The applicability statement contained in the Foreword to Annex 8 explicitly notes that the Annex 6 performance areas are complementary to those of Annex 8, the implication being that both should be read in concert.

The ICAO Council has correctly urged contracting states not to impose on visiting aircraft operational requirements other than those of the state of registry, 'provided that those requirements are not lower than the Standards of Chapter 5 of Annex 6'.

Major Airworthiness (Certification) Codes

The discussion to this point has focused on the international framework for establishing the airworthiness of aircraft. In this section we will turn to the major airworthiness (certification) codes, making a brief examination of two systems, the USA FARs and the European EASA Regulations. The reason for this approach is that, unless an aircraft is intended for use solely within the country of construction, any manufacturer seeking certification for an aircraft will have to comply with one or both of these major codes.

Certification to one of the major codes is a means of establishing that the product has been proven to meet the most accepted and recognized airworthiness standards. However, as allowed under the ICAO protocols, this does not prohibit an importing country from imposing additional requirements where these are considered necessary. Again, the purpose is not to attempt to provide a detailed examination of a code's contents, but rather to look at the structure of each code, seeking commonalities and differences.

Federal Aviation Regulations The US FARs are a well-presented, comprehensive and codified system of legislation, one part of which covers the certification and operation of aircraft. Several sections of the FARs deal with aircraft and component certification, but for the purposes of this section, only two parts need to be considered:

- Part 25 – Airworthiness Standards: Transport Category Aircraft;
- Part 23 – Airworthiness Standards: Normal, Utility, Acrobatic and Commuter Category Aircraft.

The US system of law and administration has forced the Federal Aviation Administration (FAA) to be meticulous in its presentation of regulations and supporting documentation; as such, the FARs are relatively easy to access and interpret.

The first characteristic that strikes the reader is that the regulations are formatted in exactly the same way as Annex 8 of the ICAO. Reference to the index for both the FARs and Annex 8 shows that each follows the same sequence of topics. This is generally true for all airworthiness codes and allows easy use and cross-referencing between documents issued by different countries.

A unique characteristic of the FARs, and one that is forced upon the FAA by the US legal system, is the summary and discussion of each amendment to the regulations.

This documented history stems from the administration's duty under US law to have an open and equitable rule-making process. For major legislation that will have an industry-wide impact, the FAA is obligated to go through a public and transparent rule-making procedure which provides all interested parties with the opportunity to comment and propose changes to any intended regulation.

The process starts with the Notice of Proposed Rulemaking (NPR) and follows a prescribed course, culminating in the summary of amendment action contained in the regulations when the rule is finally incorporated. The great strength of this approach is that the intention and impact of the regulations are made known publicly. On the other hand, some would see the extended time taken in processing changes as possibly detrimental to flight safety and certainly as limiting to the FAA's freedom of action.

Associated with, but not contained in, the FARs is a large body of interpretative material, known as Advisory Circulars, that gives code users guidance as to acceptable means of compliance. These are very detailed documents aimed at specialists in particular areas, for example, design or flight testing. Although the interpretative material gives guidance on acceptable means of compliance, the FAA is not hidebound in its outlook and in each series of regulations or piece of guidance material one can find the statement 'this is one way but not the only way to achieve compliance'. Clearly, this indicates a willingness to consider alternative approaches to certification issues.

Transport versus commuter aircraft (FAR 23 and FAR 25): the airworthiness requirements for a transport category aircraft differ from those of a commuter aircraft, hence the use of two sections of the regulations. The light aircraft code, FAR 23, is less demanding in many ways than the conditions applied to transport category aircraft by FAR 25. While to some this may seem incongruous, the dilemma can be resolved by considering that FAR 23 is a general purpose code aimed at light and utility aircraft which cover a wide range of roles, only some of which involve the carriage of passengers for hire and reward.

The distinction can also be viewed from both technical and economic perspectives. Technically, FAR 25 is much more demanding than FAR 23, requiring for example tight scheduling of take-off performance coupled with stringent flying qualities. These demands can only be met by incorporating, for example, high-powered, expensive engines and high-quality flight control systems, both of which are intended to reduce risk to an acceptable but affordable level. In a large transport category aircraft, the economics of operation allow the high cost of designing and certifying an aircraft to transport category standards to be recovered. This is not the case for a light aircraft. One of the aims of a code such as FAR 23 is to achieve a level of safety commensurate with the nature of the intended operation, thereby making general aviation accessible and affordable. The application of excessively high airworthiness standards to commuter aircraft would make their cost of purchase and operation prohibitive.

The European Aviation Safety Agency With the establishment of the EU came the need to write European law that was applicable to all Member States. Naturally, this has been a slow and convoluted process as it has been necessary to cover a great deal of ground in many fields, just one of which is aviation. Not the least of the difficulties encountered has been reaching an accommodation between a number of states that have a history more focused on fighting than cooperation. This led to the establishment of the Joint Aviation Authority (JAA), which promulgated their Joint Aviation Regulations (JARs) until the establishment of the European Aviation Safety Agency (EASA) in 2003.

Except for the limited rules established by the EU in the field of airworthiness and maintenance prior to the establishment of the EASA, EU Member States were responsible for the regulation of civil aviation safety through their respective NAAs. Although they did their best to harmonize their requirements and practices under the former JAAs, this system led to differing interpretations of harmonized standards, which adversely affected the efficiency of regulation and increased compliance costs for the sector.

Although the EU had been closely associated with the JAA process, the transition to the EASA system and decision-making based on the EU method was decided as a significant improvement in the execution of certification and rule-making tasks. It also reduced fragmentation at the international level by providing the international aviation community with a European interlocutor with enhanced authority and credibility.

The EASA is an agency of the EU with offices in Cologne, Germany, which has been given specific regulatory and executive tasks in the field of civilian aviation safety. It was created on 28 September 2003 and it reached full functionality in 2008, taking over functions of the JAA.

The main responsibilities of the EASA currently include:

- *rule-making*: drafting aviation safety legislation and providing technical advice to the European Commission and to the Member States;
- *inspections,* training and standardization programmes to ensure uniform implementation of European aviation safety legislation in all Member States;
- *safety and environmental type-certification* of aircraft, engines and parts;
- *approval of aircraft design organizations* worldwide and of production and maintenance organizations outside the EU;
- *authorization* of third-country (non-EU) operators;
- *coordination* of the EU Safety Assessment of Foreign Aircraft (SAFA) programme regarding the safety of foreign aircraft using EU airports; and
- *data collection,* analysis and research to improve aviation safety.

In 2023, the EASA welcomed a decision by the European Commission (EC) to bring air traffic management (ATM) into EASA's regulatory framework. The new set of rules lays the groundwork for a more efficient and uniform approach to operations improvement in support of the Single European Sky initiative. For the first time, there will be a single EU regulatory framework covering all aviation domains on the ground and in the sky, driving the transformation of the air transport system.

In respect to airworthiness requirements, the EASA also sets policy for aeronautical repair stations (also referred to as 'Part 145 organizations' in Europe and the USA) and issues repair station certificates for those stations located outside the EU (which permits foreign repair stations to perform work acceptable to the EU on EU aircraft). The EASA has developed regulations for air operations, flight crew licensing and non-EU aircraft used in the EU, and these shall apply after the required European legislation to expand the Agency's remit enters into force (the legislation was first published on 19 March 2008).

Regulations numbering: like the FARs, the EASA rules are formatted to match Annex 8 of the ICAO and are numbered in the same sequence as the FARs. This method of construction has the advantage that the reader only has to use one document when reading the code.

This numbering system has also been adopted in other jurisdictions including in Australia by the Civil Aviation Safety Authority (CASA) with the new Civil Aviation Safety Rules (CASRs). In fact, the new outcome-based style of the Australian CASRs was modelled on the EASA system. The following are examples of some of the EASA parts relating to airworthiness:

- Part 66: Certifying Staff
- Part 145: Maintenance Organization Approval
- Part M: Continuing Airworthiness
- Part 147: Training Organization Requirements
- Part 21: Subpart J Design Organization
- Part 21: Subpart G Production Organization.

It is also worth noting that, as yet, the EASA has not published a Part 23.

Certified on 28 September 2003, the EASA took over responsibility for the airworthiness and environmental certification of all aeronautical products, parts and appliances designed, manufactured, maintained or used by persons under the regulatory oversight of EU Member States.

When an aircraft is certified in an EU country, it will already be certified in the remaining EU Member States. This is in line with Article 11 – Recognition of Certificates – of the EASA Basic Regulation Article 11. In particular, Section 1 of this Article states:

> Member States shall, without further technical requirements or evaluation, recognize certificates issued in accordance with this Regulation. When the original recognition is for a particular purpose or purposes, any subsequent recognition shall cover only the same purpose or purposes.

The certification work also includes all post-certification activities, such as the approval of changes to, and repairs of, aeronautical products and their components, as well as the issuing of airworthiness directives to correct any potentially unsafe situation.

Type-certificates: the EASA has jurisdiction over new type-certificates and other design-related airworthiness approvals for aircraft, engines, propellers and parts. All type-certificates are therefore now issued by the EASA and are valid throughout the EU. It also carries out the same role for foreign organizations involved in the manufacture or maintenance of such products. The EASA relies on NAAs that have historically filled this role and concludes contractual arrangements to this effect.

The EASA works with the NAAs of the EU Member States, but has taken over many of their functions in the interest of aviation standardization across the EU. It is also responsible for assisting the European Commission in negotiating international harmonization agreements with the rest of the world on behalf of the EU Member States and also concludes technical agreements at a working level directly with its counterparts around the world, such as the US FAA.

In summary, the EASA is the centrepiece of the EU's strategy for aviation safety. Its mission is to promote the highest common standards of safety and environmental protection in civil aviation. It develops common safety and environmental rules at the European level. It monitors the implementation of standards through inspections in the Member States and provides the necessary technical expertise, training and research. It works hand in hand with the NAAs, which continue to carry out many operational tasks, such as certification of individual aircraft or licensing of pilots.

Harmonization of Airworthiness Codes As a result of a policy of harmonization, the world's major airworthiness codes – more specifically, those of the FAA and the EASA – are almost indistinguishable and authorities on either side of the Atlantic now generally recognize an airworthiness certification conducted by one authority as being acceptable to the other. Clearly, this has been a major economic benefit to both manufacturers and purchasers alike as it has removed the need for costly and complex dual certification programmes.

For other nations, the harmonization of certification codes has created more of a dilemma. Although national laws and international conventions require the publication of a national airworthiness code, some codes have incorporated some very unique and unusual requirements. While this is allowable under the ICAO provisions, many of these additional requirements are difficult to justify and create significant difficulties for the manufacturer and operator/purchaser. Besides being a potent source of embarrassment, these peculiar requirements are often not seen to materially add to safety, but they most certainly add to the cost of production, certification and, hence, purchase.

The most common means of resolving this dilemma is for states to align their national codes with one or other of the major certification authorities. National operational code differences may still remain, but these are of lesser importance compared to fundamental certification problems. This does not resolve the problem of certification of designs that are not built to a recognizable and accepted code – for example, aircraft and components designed and built in Russia. The resolution of this problem requires careful consideration and extensive negotiation with the regulatory authorities.

AIRWORTHINESS CERTIFICATION

Introduction

The aim of this section is to expand the discussion beyond the major areas of the certification codes. Compliance with the major areas of the codes is only one part of the total certification picture – all components installed in an aircraft must also be certified. Additionally, each country has its own operational requirements that are additional to the certification codes. Clearly, the certification process is complex, convoluted and requires a broad understanding of all the interrelated facets to enable the task to be completed with the minimum of risk, disruption and cost.

This section examines the processes involved in the certification of an aircraft. From the manufacturer's perspective, the first decision in the certification process is whether to be in the game. Not only is the process of building and certifying an aircraft complex, it is also very expensive. The decision to build large transport category aircraft will require the investment of billions of dollars. In some historical cases, the sums required exceed the market value of the manufacturer's company. Clearly, there is a strong motivation to 'get it right'.

While the airworthiness codes are the yardstick by which the airworthiness of a particular type will be measured, these rules provide only the targets for a complex process. A significant part of that process is determining which aspects of the rules will apply to the particular certification. Once the decision has been taken to enter the market, there is a clear need for all concerned to have 'their ducks lined up'. This is particularly relevant to the certification rules that are to be used.

The Corporate Decision

The starting point in this game is the decision to enter. Whether it is a home-built, light twin for a general aviation role or a major manufacturer setting out to build a new passenger aircraft for airline use, the decision has the same scale in terms of the resources that an organization will be required to commit to it.

A book published in the late 1970s, *The Sporty Game*, chronicled the magnitude of decisions taken by companies such as Boeing, Lockheed and McDonnell Douglas, when the company board gives the go-ahead to produce a large transport aircraft. Quite literally, the decision taken bets the company's future against the success of the project. The B777 aircraft cost Boeing in the order of USD 5 billion to develop and bring to the market. The Airbus A380 programme was even more costly and surpassed USD 9 billion. These are colossal amounts of money to place at risk and manufacturers must have compelling cases to place before boards and banks when seeking the funds to finance such a development project.

How does this relate to certification? Having taken the corporate decision to 'bet the company', one can see that the risks in the path ahead had best be fully understood and, where possible, placed in a fixed frame of reference. It is the commercial prerogative of any manufacturer to decide to enter the game and one assumes that this decision would be taken only after comprehensive market research indicated a definite need for the proposed product. However, having taken the decision, it clearly falls upon the company's management to minimize the programme's risk to the greatest extent possible.

Establishing the Ground Rules

One area where this risk minimization process is applied is the series of discussions held with the supervising regulatory authority. These discussions are aimed at establishing the airworthiness/certification rules that will apply.

The applicant will, through a process of meetings and negotiations, come to an agreed position with the regulatory authority as to the full set of rules and conditions that will apply to the construction, testing and certification of the aircraft. Alternatively, if the applicant is an operator seeking to bring a new type onto a country's register of aircraft, it will seek a statement of applicable certification rules together with any 'special conditions' that the local authority wishes to invoke.

While the rules position may appear relatively straightforward on the surface, in practice it is not. Take, for example, a designer who intends to build an experimental light aircraft. This, depending on its intended use, may fall under the rules for experimental aircraft (with all the restrictions this entails) or the designer may choose to build to a light aircraft code such as FAR 23 – optimistically assuming that in the future there will be a wider market for the product. The outcome of this process will be a written statement from the authority outlining the rules and standards that will be used to determine the aircraft's airworthiness and to which the aircraft (or component) must comply. Once stated, the authority and the manufacturer are bound by these conditions.

Simple you say! Not so when you are dealing with large passenger category aircraft that may be a derivative of previous models or with an aircraft built in one country and intended for operations in another.

Taking into consideration the derivative case first, the effort to certify an aircraft classified as a derivative is significantly less than that required for a new type. A product line is an example of the derivative approach – e.g. B747–100, B747–200, B747–300, B747–400. If a manufacturer is successful in its quest to have an aircraft classified as a derivative, it not only avoids the cost of a full certification but may also escape the application of new, and possibly penalizing, certification rules. Generally, new versions of certification rules will be either more penalizing to the product or will add large costs to the development programme, or both.

Despite the passing of 20 years, major changes to the design and massive evolution of the certification standards enabled Boeing to convince the FAA that all B747 models, including the B747–400, should be considered derivatives for certification purposes. Obviously, this result was pleasing from Boeing's point of view as it saved a great deal of time and money by not having to go through a certification programme of the same length and complexity necessary for a new type.

An entirely new type of aircraft will have to meet the latest standard for certification of aircraft in the intended category of operations. This means accepting the costs and effort involved with a full certification programme, a task that can last two or more years compared to a much shorter time for a derivative.

A different set of problems faces an operator that wishes to purchase a foreign-built aircraft for service in its own country. Earlier it was noted that while the authorities were obliged to accept the airworthiness certificates of member states for the purposes of *international operations*, they were *not bound to accept foreign construction and design standards for aircraft intended for use within their own country*.

Indeed, the ICAO makes it very clear that each state has the right to set its own airworthiness standards provided that, at a minimum, these standards meet the ICAO recommended practices. However, this is not an insurmountable problem as an authority will normally provide a comprehensive statement of the basic and additional conditions required for either the type to gain the issue of a Type Certificate or for an individual aircraft to gain a Certificate of Airworthiness.

From an operator's perspective, one can see how vitally important it is to fully define and negotiate these conditions before entering into any purchase agreement. It is catastrophically expensive, possibly to the point of bankruptcy, to discover a major conflict with the airworthiness requirements as the aircraft is presented to the authority for the issue of a Certificate of Airworthiness or a Type Certificate.

The worst situation that can be encountered is to seek to develop a product in an area where no rules exist. Two examples of this situation are those of the supersonic transport Concorde and fly-by-wire flight control systems for civilian airliners. In these cases, authorities and manufacturers had to work together in a highly collaborative manner throughout the certification process to develop an appropriate code. Clearly, this adds to the risk, cost and time taken to complete the programme, but if a company wishes to jump ahead of its competitors, this may be the price it has to pay.

Interestingly, the combined effect of two events has in recent years forced a large degree of harmonization into some areas of the aircraft certification rules. First, the evolution of completely digital aircraft and subsystems has provided manufacturers with the necessary leverage to say to authorities and purchasers alike 'take it as it is with no alterations by way of special conditions (authorities) or differences in specification standard (purchaser)'. The reason for this is that, despite their power and increased capabilities, digital systems are massively expensive to certify and control to airworthiness standards. Manufacturers are unwilling to escalate these costs, which a myriad of variations would do, and thus buyers have that choice removed. Recognizing the economic sense behind the manufacturer's decision, purchasers can also apply pressure on the authorities to accept the standards of one certificating body.

While technology applied the first pressure, European politics gave rise to the second pressure, and this had forced greater harmonization of certification rules. With the coming together of Europe under the banner of the European Parliament, many uniform codes were passed as European law – the EASA Regulations being one example. This code was purposely aligned with the USA's FARs and hence individual European codes have been replaced with a single version.

Most countries have had little choice but to accept this situation, effectively leaving the only scope for individual interpretations to be the operational requirements area.

Development and Testing

Having established the rules, the applicant sets forth to develop and test the new craft with at least the certain knowledge that one set of goalposts has been anchored, but still with all the uncertainties associated with a huge technical task arrayed before him or her.

Again, risk management and minimization are the keynotes. Throughout this phase, an incremental approach is taken to establishing compliance with the certification rules. Life for the manufacturer consists of one round after another of presenting results to the authorities in a step-by-step manner so as to ensure that there are no major conflicts of interpretation. In this way, problems are resolved as they arise and, importantly, at a time when they are most easily rectified at minimum cost.

It is usually the flight test phase of a new type that receives the focus of media attention with VMU tests and maximum braking stops featuring heavily in video releases. But behind the scenes are an army of engineers and other specialists testing all systems and components to establish compliance with the rules. Highly complex rigs are used to test flight control systems, and fuselage and wings are tested to structural failure in large hydraulically powered frames.

In addition to testing the aircraft and its systems, the manufacturer must produce a large volume of documentation. The purpose is twofold:

- first, to substantiate the application for a Type Certificate; and
- second, to provide direction to a purchaser as to how to maintain and operate the aircraft.

The range of documentation produced is substantial; however, in terms of certification, the important ones are:

- birth records for each aircraft;
- the Maintenance Manual (MM);
- the Maintenance Schedule;
- the Aircraft Flight Manual (AFM);
- the Weight and Balance Manual;
- configuration and maintenance procedures (for Extended Twin Operations (ETOPS) capable aircraft);
- the Master Minimum Equipment List (MMEL).

Only when all tests and documentation have been satisfactorily completed and compliance is established can the authority proceed to final certification. Obviously, the onus to demonstrate compliance falls on the manufacturer. The manufacturer will also be facing the considerable commercial pressure of getting the aircraft to the customer at the agreed time. Remember that the authority has no concern with the manufacturer's commercial problems. The only issue for an authority is safety and, in this respect, only compliance with the rules will suffice.

Importation of a Previously Certified Aircraft

The preceding discussion has tended to focus primarily on the certification of a new aircraft type or a derivative. However, most aircraft are either exported new from the country of manufacture or, after service with another organization, imported into another country.

In this case, the operator must make an application to its local authority for a Type Certificate if the type has not appeared on the register before, and in any case, for an individual Certificate of Airworthiness. In reply, the authority is obliged to state the required certification base and any special conditions it wishes to apply for.

The difference between this case and the manufacturer making an application to an original certificating authority is that the responsibility to demonstrate compliance with the regulations falls on the operator. However, the importing authority will open a dialogue with the original certificating body to allow access to airworthiness information. Authorities are usually helpful in these matters, but applicants must be under no illusions as to where the ultimate responsibility lies. An operator is expected to demonstrate a level of knowledge commensurate with its intended role. One can imagine the impression created with a local authority if, for example, a first level airline displayed little or no understanding of the processes and responsibilities involved in acquiring and registering a new aircraft.

To substantiate an application, an operator will be required to submit at least the documentation necessary for an initial Type Certification and in addition will have to provide evidence as to the aircraft's modification status and proof of satisfactory continued airworthiness should the aircraft (or component) already be in service. For an aircraft straight from the factory, this is a relatively easy path to tread; however, if the aircraft has been acquired from a foreign operator, many difficulties can be encountered.

Type Certification

The final step in the certification process is the issue of the Type Certificate. This is the authority's final seal of approval, indicating that the design has met all the required standards and is the manufacturer's signal that it can produce and deliver the aircraft that are now, hopefully, on the order book.

Individual Certificates of Airworthiness

While the Type Certificate certifies the design standard, it is still necessary to give each airframe a Certificate of Airworthiness. The Certificate of Airworthiness indicates that the particular aircraft was, at a point in time, airworthy according to the requirements imposed by the country of registration. If the aircraft is to be delivered to a foreign operator, an Export Certificate of Airworthiness will be issued by the original certificating authority, stating that the aircraft meets the airworthiness standards and is fit for export.

Continued airworthiness will now depend on the operator maintaining the airframe to the standard required by the authority in which the aircraft is registered.

Other Considerations for Achieving Airworthiness Certification

The discussion in the previous sections has focused primarily on the aspects of the airworthiness codes concerned with the airframe/engine combination. These are the sections of the codes most often discussed and, when the certification standard is referred to, it is these major standards that the Type Certificate is thought to hinge on. However, many other components are included in a large transport category or utility category aircraft and these too must be certified under an airworthiness code. Additionally, there are the operational sections of each country's code with which conformity is required if a Certificate of Airworthiness is to be issued.

This section deals briefly with some of these issues. Again, the purpose is not to delve into the intricacies. The objective is to highlight the important points that have to be taken into consideration by an operator who is preparing to purchase an aircraft and who has to reach an understanding with the regulatory authority and, perhaps, the manufacturer as to the standard of the aircraft or component at delivery.

Products and Parts Each authority has a code for controlling the certification of aircraft and for defining the standard of any products and parts that might be fitted to an aircraft. An example of such a code is FAR 21, which deals with the certification procedures for aircraft as a whole and for certain products and parts. The part also details the procedures to be followed in relation to the issue of Type Certificates, amendment or revision of Type Certificates, special category Type Certificates, production certificates and export procedures.

FAR 21 illustrates the point that the process of certification does not stop with the manufacture of the airframe; it extends to the components that go into that machine, the machine as a whole and to the processes which control the issue of the Certificate of Airworthiness, in whatever form these prevail.

The traffic in bogus aircraft components is huge and lucrative. Given the safety implications this represents, the authorities commit considerable time and effort to the detection and prevention of this activity.

Noise Certification As we shall discover in Chapter 16, gone are the days of a manufacturer having complete freedom of action without needing to consider the environmental impact of its efforts. In recent times, noise has become one of the most sensitive environmental issues associated with aircraft and this has led to the development of stringent noise standards or stages. Over time, noise rules have progressively tightened to the extent that now it is almost mandatory for all aircraft to meet the most stringent standard – Stage 3. The environmental effects of aircraft operations – including aircraft noise – are further considered in Chapter 16.

While noise standards are laid down in the ICAO documents, each country has to find a way of incorporating these standards and procedures so as to ensure the consistent measurement of aircraft noise levels. The USA has embodied this procedure in FAR 36, and equivalent measures exist in all national codes.

Operational Certification The final piece in the certification puzzle is the operational requirements imposed by each country on its operators and the aircraft they fly. These requirements are in addition to those imposed by the certification codes and, in general, are peculiar to individual countries. Australia, for example, has its operational requirements, as does the UK and the USA.

When purchasing an aircraft, buyers must establish which of these conditions will apply to their machine. This is done through discussion with the local authority and will, as necessary, have to be conveyed to the manufacturer for inclusion during the aircraft build. Alternatively, some of these requirements can be met by the operator, who will perform minor modifications once it has taken delivery of the aircraft or, alternatively, during refurbishment prior to the issue of a Certificate of Airworthiness.

Operational requirements are not something that can be ignored, as to do so would risk the authority not issuing a Certificate of Airworthiness until compliance was demonstrated. Given today's cost of aircraft financing, any delay in putting the aircraft into revenue service means risking a huge financial loss.

Continuing Airworthiness

The issue of an initial Certificate of Airworthiness merely indicates that at the time the Certificate was issued, the aircraft was airworthy, but in no way does this suggest that the aircraft will remain airworthy indefinitely. Continuing airworthiness is a joint responsibility shared between the state of registration and the operator.

Ensuring the continued airworthiness of the aircraft on its register is one of the major tasks performed by the airworthiness section of any authority.

ICAO Standards for Continuing Airworthiness Once again, we return to Annex 8 to find the ICAO standards for guidance on continued airworthiness.

Part II of the Annex sets out specific standards covering continuing airworthiness. In particular, the Annex covers the following areas:

- Determination of continuing airworthiness: the ICAO is explicit in assigning responsibility for determining continuing airworthiness to the state of registration.
- Publication of requirements for continuing airworthiness: each state must develop or adopt requirements to ensure the continued airworthiness of an aircraft throughout its service life.
- Information related to the continuing airworthiness of aircraft: the Annex stipulates how member states of the Convention are to provide, gather and distribute information relating to the continuing airworthiness of a type for which it either has design responsibility or which it has on its register.

Further areas addressed are the validity of Certificates of Airworthiness and the temporary loss of airworthiness.

National Requirements for Continuing Airworthiness The ICAO makes it clear that it is the responsibility of each state to issue requirements for the continuing airworthiness of aircraft on its register. Having set these requirements, the authority must then enforce them. This is done in two ways:

- First, the authority passes responsibility for day-to-day maintenance to the operator by way of an AOC and other specific approvals to conduct maintenance.
- Second, the authority performs surveillance inspections on aircraft to determine whether the operator is maintaining the aircraft properly, as required under the terms of the AOC and the governing national legislation.

As we have seen in Chapter 8, the failure to properly maintain an aircraft, or a component of an aircraft, can be an offence against the governing law and can be grounds for the temporary or permanent revocation of an AOC. Continuing airworthiness is serious business indeed!

CONCLUSION

The manufacturer's decision to design and build an aircraft, or an operator's to purchase an aircraft, is a commercial one. Clearly, there are likely to be major repercussions for the manufacturer or operator if the applicable airworthiness code is not agreed with the authorities beforehand.

For the manufacturer, the final outcome of the process is the Type Certificate, a document that attests to the airworthiness of the design.

Subsequently, each aircraft will be granted an individual Certificate of Airworthiness, indicating that it has been built to and met, at the time of issue, the airworthiness standards laid out in the Type Certificate and any special conditions that may have been imposed. Continued airworthiness of an individual aircraft is then a matter of the operator maintaining the device in accordance with the agreed maintenance schedule and any other conditions imposed by the authority in the country of registration. The Certificate of Airworthiness is usually renewed annually.

Although the global aviation industry has essentially recovered from the devastation that was COVID-19, and even though the drop in air traffic during the pandemic hit passenger transport hard, the cargo business has shown remarkable resilience and continues to move essential goods. Online sales and the Internet have fuelled this demand and cargo aircraft have become a rare commodity. Governments and companies are competing for aircraft capable of delivering millions of parcels and cargo. Several airlines have adapted their offer with 'ferry' planes, i.e. passenger planes whose holds are entirely filled with cargo. All these shifts in demand need to be supported by effective and efficient maintenance organizations.

As a closing comment, and with an eye to the 2050 Net Zero Emissions target, all sectors of the aviation sector will need to play their part, and this includes maintenance, repair and continuing airworthiness organizations.

13 Aviation Security

INTRODUCTION

The Development of Security Standards

Few people at the time of the first powered flight in 1903 would have perceived that in little over a decade after this marvel, the aircraft would be used as a weapon of destruction against humankind. As we have seen in earlier chapters, even before the scars of the First World War had begun to heal, governments from around the world had gathered in Paris in a feverish attempt to draft universal regulations aimed at controlling this rampaging technology.

As a result of these efforts, 38 nations signed the Paris Convention 1919 to assert the notion of air sovereignty and to prevent a reoccurrence of the tragedy that had left practically all of Europe in a state of devastation. This concept of national sovereignty in certain respects draws parallels with issues related to aviation security – widely considered to be a 'reactive' rather than a 'proactive' aspect of the aviation industry.

Since the first reported aircraft hijacking in the early 1930s, aviation security legislation and regulation has been in a state of constant development because of those who attempted to breach security provisions or engaged in acts of terrorism. There is a broad spectrum in the rationale and philosophy behind these attacks, ranging from political to religious to highly organized crime. However, the escalation of the reported number of hijackings on civil aviation aircraft in the 1960s brought to the fore the importance of developing and implementing an international standard for aviation security.

The Chicago Convention of 1944 led to the creation of the ICAO and with it the creation of international aviation security standards in Annex 17.

Security Conventions

In addition to Annex 17 and its associated security manual (a document to assist states in implementing the SARP associated with Annex 17), there are five principal international legal instruments or conventions that influence the security of civil aviation.

Chicago Convention 1944 for 'Safeguarding International Civil Aviation Against Acts of Unlawful Interference' plays a significant role in the promulgation of aviation security measures on an international scale. As previously stated this Convention has created a regulatory framework through its various Technical Annexes to legally implement its international policies. Annex 17 is the Security Annex.

DOI: 10.4324/9781032652146-13

As is the case with all the standards contained within the ICAO Annexes and indeed the conventions themselves, it is the responsibility of the contracting states to ratify these SARPs within their own nations. However, prior to and in conjunction with the development of Annex 17, there had been a number of aviation security-focused conventions that had begun to address security issues and measures on a global scale.

Tokyo Convention 1963 for 'Offences and Certain Other Acts Committed on Board Aircraft' Specifically, this convention addressed issues regarding offences against penal law and acts which, whether offences or not, 'jeopardized aircraft or of persons and property therein' or 'which jeopardized good order and discipline on board'. This convention also provided guidance on the powers of the aircraft commander (pilot in command), the unlawful seizure of aircraft and the powers and duties of the states themselves.

Subsequent to the events of 11 September 2001 these powers have been significantly increased. In particular Ch III, Art 6, para 2 'Powers of Aircraft Commander' states:

> Any crew member or passenger may also take reasonable protective measures without such authorisation, (meaning that of the Captain) when he has reasonable grounds to believe that such action is immediately necessary to protect the safety of the aircraft or any person or property therein.

This provision allows cabin crews and other specified classes of persons to take restraining action against various forms of behaviour in flight on the behalf of passengers.

Article 10 provides protection against litigation that may ensue:

> For actions taken in accordance with the same convention, neither the aircraft commander, any other member of the crew, any passenger, the owner or operator of the aircraft or the person on behalf the flight was performed, shall be held responsible in any proceedings on account of the treatment undergone by the person against whom the action was taken.

It should be emphasized that if the restraint taken is considered beyond what could be considered 'reasonable force' it is possible that the Article 10 protection would not apply.

Hague Convention 1970 for the 'Suppression of the Unlawful Seizure of Aircraft' In response to the many hijackings that took place throughout the 1960s, this convention addressed the jurisdiction and responsibility of contracting states in dealing with those accused of unlawful seizure and the prosecution and/or extradition of individuals, involving punishment through 'severe penalties'. The various articles of the Convention require contracting states to introduce appropriate measures for the punishment of offenders. It does not prescribe the penalties that should be attached to the various offences but makes it clear that such offences should be regarded as very serious.

Montreal Convention 1971 for the 'Suppression of Unlawful Acts Against the Safety of Aviation' This convention specifically focused on incidents that take place 'in flight' and 'in service', as well as suppressing the possible act of bombing of commercial aircraft and surrounding facilities. Like other conventions, it outlined the jurisdiction of the ruling state to deal with such situations. As a supplement to this convention, the *Montreal Protocol 1988* for the 'Suppression of Unlawful Acts of Violence at Airports Serving International Civil Aviation' was also created to curb the number of terrorist attacks occurring at airports.

In common with the *Hague Convention* an aircraft is considered to be 'in flight' from the moment when the last of its external doors is closed following embarkation until the moment when the first door is opened for disembarkation. In the case of a false landing, the flight is deemed to continue until the competent authorities take responsibility for the aircraft and for the persons and property on board.

An aircraft is generally considered to be 'in service' from the commencement of the pre-flight preparation by ground personnel and/or crew and for a period of 24 hours after landing. The Convention deals with the covert planting of an explosive device and/or the sabotage of aircraft before departure and after arrival (as these stages of flight are not covered in previous conventions).

Montreal Protocol 1988 (Protocol for the Suppression of Unlawful Acts of Violence at Airports Serving International Civil Aviation) Is supplementary to the *Montreal Convention 1971*. The Protocol was introduced to create standards for the suppression of terrorist attacks at airports. Leading up to the introduction of this Protocol, terrorist attacks accounted for the death and injury of a considerable number of people on airports. Although the law of sovereign states covered such incidents, ICAO considered that there should be a global approach to dealing with such matters.

The Beijing Convention 2010 Superseded the Montreal Convention of 1971 as amended by the Montreal Protocol of 1988 when it came into force late in September 2011. Both the original Montreal Convention and Protocol and this Convention are aimed at introducing articles that will protect international civil aviation against unlawful acts that will jeopardize the safety of persons and property, seriously affect the operation of air services and undermine the confidence of the peoples of the world in the safety of civil aviation. At the original time of its introduction in September 1971, there had been numerous instances of bombing and the threatened bombing of commercial flights. The convention deals with acts committed by offenders whilst the aircraft is in flight and when in service.

The Convention urges contracting states to introduce appropriate measures for the punishment of offenders. It does not prescribe the range of punishments that should be introduced to a state's legislation. Punishment is a matter for the state and the drafter of the legislation to complement the Annex.

The listed conventions were considered to be the first and most significant attempts to implement aviation security standards on a worldwide basis. Each of them was ratified by more than 100 sovereign states and for most nations became the 'backbone' for setting domestic aviation security standards, policies and procedures.

Aviation Security and the Industry

'Security', and its allied discipline 'safety', is generally considered as separate issues. In broad terms breaches of security are generally associated with an act of malice on the part of individuals, and breaches of safety are generally associated with acts of carelessness or negligence on the part of individuals.

Although there is a philosophical difference between safety and security both issues relate to events that are caused by the human factor. Proper planning and effective auditing of procedures are an essential part of the protective barriers and defences that form part of risk analysis and risk management programmes.

As previously stated, for a contracting state to comply with international standards it must publish a National Aviation Security Programme. An 'air- port security programme', 'airline security programme' and a 'cargo handling programme' should evolve from the national programme. Security programmes that comply with the provisions of the national programme, may be a:

- programme written and signed off by the carrier, airport, regulated air cargo agent or any other agency required to produce such a document by the contracting state (e.g. the methodology used by Australia and United Kingdom);
- generic programme signed off by the carrier, airport, regulated air cargo agent or other agent, which was published by the contracting state (e.g. the methodology used by the United States Transportation Security Administration); or
- programme written by the carrier, with an addendum meeting specific measures called for by a contracting state, not being the state of registration of the carrier (e.g. the methodology used by the New Zealand Civil Aviation Authority).

Regardless of the basis in which a programme is written, the owner of the programme should understand its content and must implement its provisions strictly. The facilitation of the programme should form part of a security training package.

With Amendment 18 to Annex 17 in November 2022, ICAO amended standards 3.3.1 and 3.3.2 requiring an aircraft operator to establish, implement and maintain an aircraft operator security programme (AOSP) for their host state (standard 3.3.1); and rather than establish, implement and maintain an ASOP for each state that the aircraft operator provides a service, to establish, implement and maintain a Supplementary Station Procedure (SSP) for each location (standard 3.3.2).

This amendment was to reduce the burden on aircraft operators and states to have and maintain ASOP for every state, but rather to hold a SSP which would contain any 'gaps' or 'differences' between the host state AOSP and the overseas state requirements.

Defining 'Aviation Security'

The adoption by so many countries of these crucial security conventions demonstrated to the ICAO the motivation of states to universally harmonize aviation security requirements. It also reinforced the fact that ICAO member states had the power and knowledge to regulate and implement these recommendations in their own countries. In order for this to occur with greater levels of international harmonization, there also needed to be a clear definition as to what aviation security entailed, what was acceptable and what was not.

Annex 17 was thus created and became an additional Annex of the Chicago Convention. It sought to address a range of important issues in the management of aviation security and included guidance on a number of issues in implementing and maintaining security measures and centred on the concept of 'the act of unlawful interference'.

According to the *ICAO Security Document 8973/10* (7th edition), threats to aviation security are considered to be acts of 'unlawful interference' and include actions such as:

- the unlawful seizure of aircraft in flight;
- the unlawful seizure of aircraft on the ground;
- hostage-taking on board aircraft or on aerodromes;
- forcible intrusion on board an aircraft, at an airport or on the premises of an aeronautical facility;
- the introduction on board an aircraft or at an airport of a weapon or hazardous device or material intended for criminal purposes; and
- the communication of false information such as to jeopardize the safety of an aircraft in flight or on the ground of passengers, crew, ground personnel or the general public at an airport or on the premises of a civil aviation facility.

As mentioned previously, any contracting state to the Chicago Convention is required, under international aviation law, to introduce into its domestic law the security standards promulgated by the ICAO and, in this case, Annex 17 of the Convention. Many countries have delegated to separate government bodies or independent agencies the responsibility to administer on behalf of the government aviation security regulations domestically. For instance, in the USA, this responsibility lies with the Transport Security Administration (TSA) and in the EU, this responsibility has most recently been transferred to the European Parliament.

Case Study: the Lockerbie Bombing 1988

Pan Am Flight 103, a Boeing 747, was operating a daily scheduled international flight from London Heathrow to JFK International on 21 December 1988 when a bomb exploded on board, killing all 259 crew and passengers (*Washington Post* 1999). The aircraft crashed in the town of Lockerbie, Scotland, also killing another 11 on the ground. Criminal charges were laid against two Libyan intelligence officers. This tragedy sparked a number of legislative and procedural changes throughout the world, including scrutinizing the process of passenger and baggage screening.

Some of the security changes implemented by the USA in response to the bombing included increased screening of passengers and baggage through both x-ray and physical searches (*Washington Post* 1999). There was also the procedure imposed of ensuring that all baggage could be matched to all passengers boarding any flight. These changes were also reflected through the *Aviation Security Improvement Act 1990,* and similar changes were enforced throughout Europe with the requirements for members to develop a National Aviation Security Programme, which implemented extensive baggage screening procedures.

National Aviation Security Programme

Each signatory to ICAO should have a national aviation security programme that outlines, at the highest level, the roles and responsibilities of government, law enforcement and all aviation industry participants. It will describe minimum operating standards and any differences from ICAO SARPs.

As these documents normally contain security-sensitive information, they are on restricted issue and are therefore not reproduced here. These programmes usually cover the following topics:

- legislation;
- allocation of responsibilities;
- coordination and communication;
- protection of airports, aircraft and air navigation facilities;
- security of persons and items taken aboard aircraft;
- security equipment;
- personnel;
- responses to Acts of Unlawful Interference;
- evaluation and effectiveness (audits);
- contingency plans; and
- incident reporting.

Aviation Security Today

Although aviation security has evolved significantly over the past half-century, the first decade of the twenty-first century has seen its prominence soar. The terrorist attacks on 11 September 2001 were a wake-up call for all within the aviation industry to reassess existing security measures and develop more robust security systems in both the short and long term, and to promulgate them on an international scale. As will be discussed, the USA and the EU have dedicated special departments within existing governing structures to analyse the existing systems in place and to continually monitor and research for more effective methods of counteracting acts of unlawful interference on aircraft.

The extent of the preceding 'call to arms' is reflected in the worldwide budget allocated to aviation security post-9/11. The IATA, which represents over 270 of the world's airlines, estimated that more than $US5 billion was spent by airline members on upgrading security in 2002 alone – and this does not include government expenditure!

The need to increase and improve methods and systems of aviation security to create greater efficiencies is without dispute. The development of more robust security standards through the promulgation of enabling legislation and regulations has provided more effective and robust safeguards against acts of terrorism. Moreover, continual development in security technology, both on the ground and in the air, has been a critical component in the development of a safer and more sustainable aviation industry.

INTERNATIONAL STANDARDS

Annex 17 of the ICAO

Immediately following the Second World War, travel by air became an increasingly popular mode of transport within the commercial sector. For aviation regulators, it was difficult to imagine the many challenges that would be associated with issues relating to security within this rapidly changing and expanding industry. The notion of using aircraft for acts of 'unlawful interference' was still not fully recognized when the various Annexes of the Chicago Convention 1944 were originally drafted. It was only following the increase in violent crimes on civil aviation aircraft that began in deadly earnest in the late 1960s that the ICAO sought to specifically address issues related to acts of unlawful interference on civil aircraft and other similar security breaches.

Annex 17 was introduced by the ICAO Council on 22 March 1974. However, in addition to the creation of Annex 17, subsections of other annexes in the Chicago Convention were also amended to incorporate aspects of aviation security. The other areas of the aviation system that incorporated revised and strengthened aviation security standards included air traffic services, aircraft accident and incident investigation, rules of the air, operation of aircraft, entry and departure of aircraft, aeronautical telecommunications and aerodrome design and operations.

The ICAO provides guidance for member states on the implementation of Annex 17 through the accompanying *Annex 17 Security Manual*, specifying details of the SARPs for member states. It is at the discretion of each member state as to how it chooses to implement the obligations imposed by Annex 17 within its own regulatory regime, but as many of the security standards are quite prescriptive (in terms of their outcomes), there is quite a high level of consistency in the enabling legislation and the resulting security rules and regulations.

Annex 17 is reviewed frequently by the ICAO Aviation Security (AVSEC) panel, which consists of representatives of member states from around the world who are responsible for, *inter alia*, reviewing new intelligence relating to security issues as it comes to hand. Though earlier versions of Annex 17 were focused on issues relating to hijacking, it has since broadened its approach to incorporate acts of sabotage.

AVSEC also provides recommendations on developing security clauses for member states with respect to bilateral Air Services Agreements (ASA). This has allowed aviation security to become a main feature of traffic rights between countries (Milde 2008). The supplementary document to Annex 17, the Security Manual on 'Safeguarding Against Acts of Unlawful Interference' (Doc 8973-Restricted), provides SARPs within five main areas:

1 *National organization and administration*: this outlines the requirement of each state to develop and implement 'regulations, practices and procedures to safeguard against civil aviation acts of unlawful interference' whilst still considering 'safety, regularity and efficiency of flights' (ICAO 2010). This includes the coordination of activities between departments and related agents in addition to cooperating with other ICAO states in the development and exchange of intelligence and information. Also addressed are additional security procedures such as 'the establishment of a national civil aviation security program, management of a quality control program, procedures for handling sensitive information, and the deployment of in-flight security officers and armed personnel'.
2 *Recruitment, selection and training*: this outlines the designation of appropriate authority to develop, implement and maintain security programmes and their coordination. Guidance is provided on national policy and security programmes, including the 'recruitment, selection, training and certification of security staff' in addition to 'the selection and training of non-security staff and training development'.

3 *Airport security, organization, programme and design requirements*: this outlines the requirement to ensure that security programmes are established within airports. Guidance is provided specifically for 'organizational requirements, the airport security programs and airport design'.
4 *Preventive security measures*: this outlines the details of a security programme for airlines which address issues surrounding 'access control, passengers and cabin baggage, potentially disruptive passengers, hold baggage, cargo and mail, aircraft operators, general aviation and aerial work operations'.
5 *Crisis management and response to acts of unlawful interference*: this ensures that personnel and the relevant authorities are trained and able to deal with acts of unlawful interference. This includes 'threat and risk assessment, contingency plans, the collection and transmission of information during an act of unlawful interference, and the subsequent review, analysis and reporting of any act of unlawful interference'.

As mentioned, security issues are also addressed within other parts of the ICAO Annexes. One of these includes Annex 11 for Air Traffic Services which specifies priority assistance and consideration for aircraft deemed to be subject to an act of unlawful interference. More specifically, the Annex addresses the procedure after an aircraft is deemed to be in this 'alert' phase, with regard to informing rescue and coordination centres within the vicinity of the emergency.

Annex 13 on Aircraft Accident and Incident Investigation, addressed in more detail in Chapter 15, also considers acts of unlawful interference, stating that where it is suspected that unlawful interference has taken place during an incident or accident investigation, the aviation security authority for the particular state shall be informed.

Although the creation of Annex 17 provided much guidance on aviation security legislation, it would be a while before union-wide policy would be implemented throughout Europe. However, a number of practices and procedures became almost uniform throughout the EU after a number of security incidents, such as the procedure of matching passengers to checked bags following the Lockerbie bombing in Scotland in 1988 (Poole 2008).

The initial governing body responsible for managing and implementing aviation security measures within the USA was the FAA. As in the case of Europe, in addition to Annex 17, security measures were brought in as a result of the many hijackings that occurred after 1960.

As airlines and airports were responsible for implementing the FAA's regulations themselves, which added to their operational costs, not many pursued the initial pushes for security procedures such as screening at airports (Poole 2008). It was not until after the *Anti-Hijacking Act 1974*, the *Air Transportation Security Act 1974* and the *Aviation Security Improvement Act 1990* that airlines and airports were required to implement these various security strategies (Poole 2008).

The following sections review the main aviation security provisions of the aforementioned statutes.

The Anti-Hijacking Act 1974 Sections of the USA's *Anti-Hijacking Act* included provisions authorizing the President of the United States to suspend air transportation between the USA and nations that 'aided terrorist groups that used the illegal seizure of aircraft as instrumental policy' (Transportation Security Administration 2012). The

Secretary of Transportation was used to imposing sanctions against carriers that did not meet minimum security requirements, maintaining passenger and baggage-screening procedures and refusing flight for passengers who refused to undergo screening or put baggage items through screening.

The Air Transportation Security Act 1974 The provisions of the *Air Transportation Security Act* included the establishment of security programmes throughout the USA. The FAA was responsible for creating regulations for the detection screening of weapons for all passengers and hand baggage. It was also responsible for disclosing or withholding information that was acquired for research purposes on security issues (Transportation Security Administration 2012).

The Aviation Security Improvement Act 1990 As a result of the 1988 Lockerbie bombing, the *Aviation Security Improvement Act* introduced changes to the FAA's security bulletin processes. This most significantly included the creation of Security Directives and Information Circulars and minimized the distribution of security threat information (Transportation Security Administration 2012).

The ratification of Annex 17 by the member states of the ICAO was the first major attempt to 'internationalize' aviation security where no previous legislation or regulation had existed before. The aviation industry was still learning from the challenging times it was experiencing through the number of hijackings and acts of unlawful interference that were occurring. In order to assess the security standards implemented worldwide for its members, the ICAO also developed the *Universal Security Audit Programme* (USAP). Observing the existing security structures in place, this programme aimed to coordinate security measures worldwide.

AVIATION SECURITY POST-9/11

Perhaps the most substantial event to impact aviation security to date was the hijackings of four domestic US flights on 11 September 2001. The events of that day had a disastrous impact upon the development of aviation and were simply beyond the contemplation of most rationally minded people. In an industry where there were many factors to consider in its daily operations, from economics to safety, aviation security was suddenly thrown into the international spotlight for immediate consideration and review. The events of 9/11 would become a catalyst for future changes in aviation security regulation and more generally the development of international aviation law.

Following the terrorist attacks, the ICAO and member state representatives from around the world immediately set about reviewing the security provisions contained in Annex 17. Further amendments to this Annex were introduced on 7 December 2001, with the focus shifting to both the international and domestic aviation sectors. Overall, there were a number of changes made that called for more heavily implemented national security programmes for all the ICAO member states (Spruston 2004).

An important point to note is that prior to 9/11, security implementation in Europe was handled on a relatively separate basis within each country. After the events of 9/11, it was considered essential to implement generic protocols to improve general aviation security for all countries. Uniformity in regulation on civil aviation security in Europe was promulgated by the European Parliament and Council through Regulation No

2320/2002 created in 2002 as a means of better implementing Annex 17 throughout Europe (Poole 2008). This regulation was later revised in 2008 as Regulation No 300/2008.

Regulation No 300/2008

This regulation outlines the practices required for airlines, airports and other services that operate within Europe. The regulations are based on the Annex 17 standards and detail the requirements for screening, training, emergency procedures and other various security controls. In conjunction with the creation and maintenance of security programmes and quality control programmes for each state of the EU, the document also outlines the requirement for each member to present an annual report on the development of Annex 17 and related documents to the European Parliament and Council.

Other areas also addressed within this regulation include:

- common basic standards in accordance with the Annex;
- security costs;
- cooperation with the ICAO;
- security programmes and quality programmes;
- airport, entities, air carrier security programmes; and
- commission inspections and annual reports.

The events of 9/11 and the subsequent review of Regulation No 300/2008 particularly focused on tighter restrictions relating to the screening of passengers, baggage (both checked and hand) and cargo, including the compulsory certification for those who conducted screening. Tighter controls were also implemented on the restricted access areas of airports and aircraft and increased training for employees in aviation security (Kallas 2011). In addition, there were changes made to prevent access to the flight deck of unauthorized personnel and the hardening of flight deck doors to provide protection from explosive devices (Spruston 2004).

For the USA, there were three major pieces of legislation that were either reviewed or developed as a result of the 9/11 attacks. These were the *Transportation Security Act 2001*, the *Maritime Security Act 2002* and the *Homeland Security Act 2002*. Post-9/11, the *Aviation Transportation and Security Act* was updated to incorporate the creation of a new government department entitled the Transportation Security Administration, which took over the duties of the FAA with respect to civil aviation security.

The Transport Security Act 2001

With the passing of the *Homeland Security Act* in 2002, the *Transport Security Act 2001* (the 'TS Act') transferred responsibility for civil aviation security from the Department of Transport to the Department of Homeland Security. The most important provisions of the TS Act include:

- defining the role of the TSA, including the processing of security information and emergency procedures, personnel and services by the under secretary;

- the role of the Transportation Security Oversight Board;
- federal security managers, including the improvement of flight deck integrity and the deployment of federal air marshals;
- the improvement of secure access areas surrounding airports and secure access area control, and the introduction of security programmes at airports;
- crew training for potential threat conditions;
- security screening measures, including the training of those employed in security screening, the introduction of mandatory screening where not already present, explosive detection systems and chemical and biological weapons;
- research and development into security;
- flight school security and the training for specific aircraft;
- increased penalties for interference with security personnel;
- passenger manifests and computer reservation systems;
- aviation security funding and security service fees;
- a reporting culture and flight deck security;
- performance management systems and the allowance of emergency services on board; and
- research and development into aviation security technology.

Similar legislation was implemented through the *Maritime Security Act 2002*, which required more stringent control on maritime technologies and infrastructure. The USA also formed the '9/11 Commission' in 2002 to review the facts and findings resulting from the 9/11 attacks and provide a full report with recommendations, conclusions and corrective measures that could be taken to prevent any future terrorist attacks in the USA (Johnstone 2006).

Further to the establishment of this Commission, in 2004 the USA passed the *Intelligence Reform and Provision Act*, which introduced further changes into the US aviation security system. These additional measures included:

- the TSA being given full access to 'no fly' lists;
- biometrics to confirm the identity of law enforcement and those seeking to gain access to restricted areas in airports and aircraft;
- the screening of those who have access to restricted areas against terrorist watch lists;
- developing advanced airport checkpoint screening services;
- in-flight counter-terrorism training for federal law enforcement;
- anonymity for federal air marshals;
- a programme for training federal air marshals;
- monitoring of checked baggage-screening areas;
- mandating studies on wireless communication for flight crew to communicate on a possible security threat;
- developing standards for security staffing levels at airports;
- further barriers to secure the flight deck; and
- improved tamper-proof pilots' licences.

As demonstrated through the preceding provisions, the events of 9/11 resulted in significant changes in the operation of security systems throughout the world. The events of that day provide an ongoing reminder for the need to consistently review existing security processes and practices throughout the world in an industry that continually demands the minimization of risk.

AVIATION SECURITY IMPLEMENTATION

Airlines and Aviation Security

The restrictions and requirements relating to aviation security on airlines – especially international airlines – became almost universal after 9/11. There are a number of ICAO annexes that, in addition to Annex 17, provide further standards and recommended practices for airlines in handling the events of *unlawful interference*. Changes to rules of the air are contained in Annex 2, Section 3, titled 'Rules of Aircraft and Their Subjectivity to Unlawful Interference'. This Annex provides a directive on airlines informing the appropriate air traffic service of acts of unlawful interference and the procedural steps for the pilot in command or the aircraft's commander in such circumstances. These provisions interface with the procedures outlined in Annex 11 regarding air traffic management services and the priority given to aircraft subjected to unlawful interference.

Entry and Departure of Aircraft Sections of Annex 9 address new requirements with respect to the clearance, arrival and departure of aircraft and the personal identification required for passengers. The Annex 9 SARPs also address the handling and protection of special cargo as well as the selection and loading of cargo and unaccompanied baggage on outbound aircraft at the time of departure. In addition to Annex 9, Annex 10 addresses the reply aircraft transponder codes required to be transmitted ('squawked') in an emergency situation.

Onboard Security Other important changes resulting from the events of 9/11 have been with respect to security requirements on board aircraft. All US airlines and those international airlines that fly into the USA are required to enforce the following procedures and policies. Aircraft must have fortified flight deck doors to protect against firearms and explosives, and all staff must be trained on how to deal with suicidal hijackers, a concept which had not been fully considered prior to 9/11. Domestically within the USA, the number of federal air marshals was also increased and their activities were extended for both international and domestic routes.

Air Cargo Like the increases in passenger screening, security clearances and background checks, additional security procedures were required for all cargo handlers and pre-boarding screening for those who travelled on cargo aircraft and increased restrictions to areas at cargo facilities and airside access.

Prohibited Items There has also been an increase in both the number and range of prohibited items. These proscribed items are either not permitted in handheld baggage – as checked through baggage screening – or for checked baggage, or both. The 2008 ICAO 'List of Prohibited Items' includes the following:

- *guns, firearms and other devices that discharge projectiles*: devices designed to cause serious injury by discharging a projectile, or capable of being mistaken for such devices;

- *stunning devices*: devices designed to stun or immobilize;
- *objects with sharp points or sharp edges*: objects with a sharp point or sharp edge capable of being used to cause serious injury;
- *worker's tools*: tools capable of being used either to cause serious injury or to threaten the safety of aircraft;
- *blunt objects*: objects capable of causing serious injury when used as a weapon;
- *explosives and incendiary substances and devices*: explosive or incendiary substances or devices capable of being used to cause serious injury or threatening the safety of the aircraft – these prohibited items also apply to items placed in the cargo hold of an aircraft;
- *liquids, aerosols and gels (LAGs)*: a limit of one litre on such items (100 millilitres or equivalent for hand baggage).

The last item regarding LAGs was enforced in 2006 after British police uncovered a planned terrorist plot that intended to use explosive liquids on board flights from Britain to the USA and Canada.

***Heinrich v European Commission*, C-345/06 (2009)**

This case challenged the European Parliament Regulation No 2320/2002, which lists the items that passengers were prohibited from bringing on board aircraft. This 'Prohibited Items' list specifically includes any item that could result in acts of unlawful interference, such as 'bludgeons'. The applicant, Mr Heinrich, arrived at Vienna-Schwechat Airport, Austria with tennis racquets that were detected through security screening. It was requested that the applicant remove the items from his hand luggage before boarding the plane as they constituted a prohibited item as prescribed in Annex 17 of the ICAO and Regulation Nos. 2320/2002 and 622/2003, 'Laying down the measures for implementing common basic standards on aviation security'. The applicant had claimed that the actions against him were illegal. The court found that at the time the relevant regulations had not yet been published in the official *Journal of the European Union*, so were not officially proclaimed and the applicant could therefore not be bound by these conditions. The court ruled that document 68/2004 (a later amendment to document 622/2003) had 'no binding force in so far as it seeks to impose obligations on individuals'.

Airports and Aviation Security

Since 9/11, security guidelines for airports are also far more universally harmonized. In addition to the guidelines provided by Annex 17 on aerodrome design and security planning, Annex 14 of the Chicago Convention provides details of the various requirements of aerodrome design and operations. This Annex includes details regarding the parking of aircraft believed to be subject to acts of unlawful interference and describes how they should be isolated from all other operations.

The *Airports Council International* (ACI), which was formed in 1991, became the first worldwide association to represent the common interests of airport operators and foster cooperation with partners throughout the air transport industry. Through the ACI, the airport community has a single voice with respect to airport security issues and other matters of concern for airport operators, and has greatly assisted the move towards a united industry.

The ACI has a close working relationship with the ICAO in respect of the development of international standards relating to airports. The ACI defends the positions of airports and assists with the development of SARPs in the areas of safety, security and environment initiatives. It also advances and protects airport interests in important policy changes on airport charges and regulation, strengthening the hand of airports in dealing with airlines.

One area in which the ACI and other organizations have expended considerable efforts is with respect to the requirements of Annex 17 regarding *emergency response plans* (ERPs). The ICAO requires airport operators to document emergency procedures in the aerodrome's *Emergency Plan* (EP) and to address all aspects of a coordinated response to an airport emergency. Reviews are required both on a full-scale and a partial basis to ensure that the plans can be carried out effectively and to detect any deficiencies.

In the USA, the TSA also provide guidance with regard to the layout, EPs, design, construction and communication of aerodromes for both commercial and general aviation. These procedures are required by the TSA in accordance with the *Aviation Security Improvement Act 1990*, as well as the *Aviation Transport Security Act 2001* and the *Homeland Security Act 2002*. These statutes specify the requirements of aerodromes to secure particular areas of the aircraft, and specific guidelines are detailed in the 'Recommended Security Guidelines for Airport Planning, Design and Construction'.

The requirements for airport security programmes are similarly incorporated throughout Europe. These include the scanning of products and goods, and personal screening. In addition, there are a number of restrictions placed with regard to the carriage of liquids and baggage screening. This also includes a list of 'Prohibited Articles' for the hold and hand luggage and the various screening requirements. As most readers will be aware, on all international flights liquids in containers are not allowed to have a capacity of more than 100 ml. If passengers have a liquid and/or gel (LAGs) container of more than 100 ml they need to be placed in checked baggage, with the exception of certain items such as baby food and medicine. As of 31 January 2014, passengers have been permitted to carry duty free liquids and liquids needed for medical and dietary requirements.

This policy will be monitored by the European Commission to ensure that airports within each Member State are complying with the relevant EU standards and Annex 17 of the ICAO requirements. Document 1486/2003 outlines the requirements for the preparation, procedures and conduct of inspections to ensure that security operations and procedures at airports are standardized. Specifically, this involves a review of the following documentation for each airport according to the original regulation:

- the national civil aviation security programme, including the national civil aviation security training programme;
- the national civil aviation security quality control programme;
- identified airport and air carrier security programmes; and
- the results of the audits referred to in Article 7(1) of Regulation No 2320/2002.

To follow up, a report must be compiled reflecting the findings within six weeks of the conclusion of the audit.

Secure Areas and Airport Access Control The regulations in the USA include the establishment of an *Air Operators' Area,* where only restricted personnel are allowed access and all employees must undergo background checks. These regulations also include, as implemented by the TSA:

- a reduction in airport access points;
- increasing the surveillance of all persons, items and vehicles taken through the airport and secure areas; and
- further and more extensive background checks on airport employees.

Passenger Checkpoint Screening and Checked Baggage These provisions deal with the implementation requirements for standard passenger screening as well as explosive detection for passengers and baggage. In the EU, this has been incorporated through the 'Critical Parts of Security Restrictions at Airports' (Regulation No 1138/2004). This outlines the screening requirements of all staff involved with access to secure areas and already-screened baggage.

Passenger Pre-screening These procedures require the compilation of 'no fly' lists for suspected terrorists – those passengers who are not permitted to board a commercial aircraft or who must go through additional screening. A database of subjects known or suspected to be involved in terrorist activities has been developed that either prohibits air travel or requires additional screening and baggage search in conjunction with the standard security screening requirements.

The 'Shoe Bomb' Incident (2001) On 22 December 2001, American Airlines Flight 63 flying from Charles de Gaulle Airport to Miami International Airport carried passenger Richard Reid. Reid attempted to detonate a bomb planted in the soles of his shoes, but was restrained by cabin crew and passengers. As a result of this incident, screening procedures were introduced and implemented almost universally, which now means that passengers are required to remove footwear for scanning before going through individual screenings at airports.

Security Management Systems

Security, as with all other aspects of aviation operations, is another source of hazards relating to aircraft operations. Accordingly, the risks associated with aviation security hazards are required to be effectively managed to ensure overall safe and efficient operations. While Safety Management Systems (SMS) have been established within airlines for many years, the management of security issues has generally been less formally structured and managed in the aviation sector.

From 1 January 2008 all airlines that are members of International Air Transport Association (IATA) are required to have a Security Management System (SeMS) in place. A SeMS is a more structured and standardized approach to how security processes should be developed and managed to provide better and more uniform standards throughout the aviation industry.

Some aviation organizations and airlines have *integrated* their SMS to include the management of all risks associated with the hazards that may arise within an organization's operating environment. It is not uncommon for aviation security to be included within an organization's integrated SMS. After all, the management of risk is what safety management is all about. Chapter 16 provides a detailed account of SMS in general while the remainder of this section will focus on the effective management of the risks specifically relating to aviation security.

Implementing SeMS as well as an effective and focused threat assessment process should contribute to making security processes proactive. Essentially, a SeMS is an element of corporate management responsibility. A company's security policy to manage security is an integral part of its overall business. Security becomes one of the company's core values by developing a security culture.

As SeMS is based on ICAO Annex 17 standards and the IATA Operational Safety Audit (IOSA) Security Standards most airlines, in compliance with the relevant IOSA standards, already have a quality management system in place in respect to security issues. Each airline must therefore modify its systems to meet the Annex 17 standards and ensure that it satisfies their operating environment. When it comes to aviation security there is never a silver bullet (no pun intended) solution of a 'one size fits all' system.

In order to have an effective SeMS, the system should include the methods and procedures to achieve:

- senior management commitment to security;
- appointment of a head of security;
- creation of a security department organizational structure;
- promotion of a security culture;
- training of security personnel;
- security awareness training for all employees;
- regular evaluation of security personnel;
- effective day-to-day security operations;
- incident and accident investigative reporting;
- continuous correction from the outcome of incident accident investigation report;
- threat assessment;
- risk management;
- emergency response procedures; and
- regular audits and protocols for correction of deficiencies.

It is important that all people involved in prescriptive security arrangements understand, through training and awareness programmes, 'why' security measures are in place and what they will achieve. At times of increased threat people involved in the implementation of additional measures should be made aware of the additional threat and what the additional measures will achieve. This cultural aspect of risk management is imperative to the successful maintenance of both safety and security standards in the industry.

Risk management extends beyond the assessment and management of defined acts of unlawful interference. It is a process that can be applied to any form of unacceptable standard with a view to preventing crime, implementing safety measures or protecting an organization against financial loss. Risk management can only be of value if the true risk is recognized.

Airport Security and Individual Rights

Relevantly, another significant challenge for the international aviation security community is the continual development of technology to constantly improve and counteract security breaches, but also balancing these necessities with the maintenance of individual liberties. Morgan (2001) has suggested that issues that need to be targeted, in addition to the standard passenger screening already implemented, are passenger fingerprinting, retina scans and facial recognition technologies. Ongoing research is also being undertaken with respect to the hardening of aircraft structures to protect from explosives, screening of both passengers and baggage that better coincides with the airport's operations and analysing human factors that assist in more efficient security screening. The following case highlights the importance of such measures particularly in regard to passenger screening.

***United States of America v Abdulmutallab*, United States District Court, E.D. Michigan, Southern Division, 16 September 2011**

On 25 December 2009, Mr Abdulmutallab was convicted of eight charges (including conspiracy to commit an act of terrorism and attempted use of a weapon of mass destruction) for attempting to destroy Northwest Airlines Flight 253 on a flight from Amsterdam to Detroit. As the plane approached Detroit, Abdulmutallab tried, but thankfully failed, to ignite a device (bomb) in his underwear. As a result, he suffered severe burns and was subdued by passengers and crew on the flight. The US Customs and Border Protection was notified of the incident on board and when the plane landed, Customs and Border Protection officers met the plane at the gate. The officers quickly determined that the defendant's burns were far too severe to have been caused by firecrackers. The defendant admitted that he had detonated an explosive device hidden in his underwear while on Flight 253 and that he was acting on behalf of al-Qaeda. A Customs and Border Protection officer had also learned from other federal agents that an explosive device similar to the one used by the defendant had been used previously, although not on a plane. He also knew that the explosive device had no mechanical devices associated with it and was thus problematic because it could defeat airport security and, indeed, had done so in this instance. Mindful of the defendant's self-proclaimed association with al-Qaeda and knowing the group's past history of large, coordinated plots and attacks, the agents feared that there could be additional, imminent aircraft attacks in the USA and elsewhere in the world. The defendant was sentenced to life in prison by a US judge in February 2012.

The preceding case has led to particular implications for security screening at airports around the world. Abdulmutallab's ability to defeat security in Amsterdam contributed to the deployment of full-body scanners at US airports. The TSA was using the scanners in some American cities at the time, but this attack has since accelerated the placement of this technology. The next few paragraphs will discuss the progress and the reasons why there are issues associated with such technology.

Previous technological initiatives regarding security screening have raised issues relating to privacy concerns of the individual. Body scanners were removed from airports within the EU and the USA during 2011 because of such issues. The EU has also continued to support the development of new technology such as higher speed detection that will enable the smoother processing of passenger streams, baggage and cargo at airports. For example, body scanners have been installed across all Australian international airports as part of the Australian government's plan to increase anti-terrorism measures. Legislation allowing for the scanners, designed to locate metal and non-metal items under clothing, has be introduced to support these initiatives.

Individual rights is a critical issue in the discussion of aviation security legislation. Unfortunately, it seems like aviation security legislation keeps getting itself into legal knots by violating such rights.

***Beghal v Director of Public Prosecutions* [2015] UKSC 49**

Ms Beghal was questioned at an airport under UK legislation – the *Terrorism Act 2000* – which requires a person in her position to answer questions asked by police and immigration officers. She refused to answer questions and was convicted of the offence of wilfully failing to do so. She appealed her conviction, arguing that Schedule 7 of the Act (which required her to do those things) was incompatible with certain rights listed in the European Convention for the Protection of Human Rights and Fundamental Freedoms ('the EHCR').

Her appeal was dismissed 4–1, but Lord Kerr delivered a strong dissent criticizing the powers of the police. He argued that there was 'no reasoned justification' for investing officers with a power to stop, search, question and detain anyone passing through a port and charging those who refuse to answer questions. He reasoned that the powers used were interfering with people's right to privacy under Article 8 of the EHCR.

Whilst the legislation in question applied to not just airports, and whilst Ms Beghal's case was dismissed, aviation security conferences – when discussing about the 'speed' of screening and the extra manpower needed to speed up the process, as well as extra police presence – can get carried away and forget about the rights of individuals throughout the process.

AVSEC 2016's agenda made no reference to individual rights, with the agenda being framed on terrorism, the impacts of terrorism, solutions in integrated security risk management – which included creating a 'strong security culture' – followed by workshops on smart security, cyber security and security in airport design. This is not to say that none of these things are important. On the contrary, they are critical. It is merely suggested that throughout all these processes, individual rights should become a topic of discussion. What was positive is that it was mentioned at the conference that airport security should be 'passenger-centric', which could include respecting their rights. Although a difficult task, it is important to balance the interests of individual civil rights and public safety.

Rogue Pilots

One significant, and surprising, issue that has arisen in terms of aviation security is the case of pilots who deliberately crash their own aircraft. Prior to reading on, the reader should remind themselves of the events of the Germanwings incident discussed in Chapter 10. Events such as Germanwings are very tragic because whilst airlines and airports may place large sums of investment into ensuring their procedures are safe, at the end of the day, it is the pilot who is in control. There is only so much airlines and regulators can do to prevent pilots from negligently controlling their own aircraft, let alone deliberately causing a crash.

Shortly after the incident, EASA recommended airlines ensure at least two crew, including at least one pilot, are in the flight crew compartment for the duration of the entire flight. Many airlines changed their policy as a result to reflect this recommendation, now requiring at least two crew members to be present in the cockpit of large jets at all times.

Standard 3.4 of Annex 17 provides for *quality control* and regular background checks on all personnel involved with carrying out security requirements. The Germanwings incident demonstrated that even though the airline had tried to do this, ultimately the pilot did not give them the necessary information. In October 2015, the European Commission developed an Action Plan as a result of recommendations made by EASA on the Germanwings accident. The six EASA recommendations were:

- Maintain the two-persons-in-the-cockpit recommendation, with its benefits being evaluated after one year.
- All airline pilots should undergo psychological evaluation as part of training or before entering service. The airline shall verify that a satisfactory evaluation has been carried out.
- Mandate drugs and alcohol testing as part of a random programme of testing by the operator.
- Establish a robust oversight programme over the performance of aeromedical examiners including the practical application of their knowledge. National authorities should strengthen the psychological and communication aspects of aeromedical examiners' training and practice.
- National regulations must ensure that an appropriate balance is found between patient confidentiality and the protection of public safety. The creation of a European aeromedical data repository is a useful first step to facilitate the sharing of aeromedical information and tackle the issue of pilot non-declaration.
- The implementation of pilot support and reporting systems, linked to the employer Safety Management System within the framework of a non-punitive work environment and without compromising 'Just Culture' principles.

The European Aero-Medical Repository (EAMR) programme is a particularly important recommendation, aiming to 'tackle the issue of pilot non-declaration'. Proposals to amend Part IV Commission Regulation (EU) No 1178/2011 by introducing EAMR provisions are currently being discussed. This was a critical cause of the Germanwings crash, and it should be very interesting to see how this is implemented. Wojciech Rafał Wiewiórowski, the Assistant European Data Protection Supervisor of the European

Commission, wrote that the case for the EAMR was to 'avoid non-declaration of medical issues and forum shopping by pilots by facilitating information sharing between NAAs, aeromedical examiners (AMEs) and aeromedical centres (AMCs) in order to ensure a high level of safety in commercial aviation'. EAMR is said to allow NAAs and AMEs to more easily cross-check self-declarations, as the system automatically informs them if an applicant already has an entry in the system and whether the information is consistent. For example, if a pilot declares never having had a certificate suspended, while EAMR contains information on a past suspension, the system will alert the AME, identifying the record and the relevant authority to be contacted.

In EASA's European Plan for Aviation Safety EPAS 2018–22, EASA launched its action plans to develop a task force with the aims of:

1 carrying out psychological assessments of the flight crew before commencing line flying;
2 enabling, facilitating and ensuring access to a flight crew support programme; and
3 performing systematic drug and alcohol (D&A) testing of flight and cabin crew upon employment.

The author looks forward to EASA's plans being implemented.

Future Challenges

As an ever-expanding and continually changing aspect of aviation activities, security challenges will continue. What many have argued is integral to ensuring protection against acts of unlawful interference and terrorism within the industry is the ongoing need for an internationally integrated and holistic approach to security. The notion that is strongly promoted by the ICAO, the ACI and the IATA is the utmost importance of the security and well-being of air transport passengers and indeed of the general public at large.

Future challenges of aviation security include the continual development and integration of legislation and the regulation of security. Although it is true that aviation security had developed significantly prior to 2001, the challenge now is to ensure its integration into such a large and diverse industry and to incorporate consistent standards worldwide. The aviation systems are only truly as strong and robust as their weakest link.

Case Study: January 2017 Fort Lauderdale Airport Shooting

On 6 January 2017, five people were killed and six were injured in a mass shooting at the baggage claim area in Fort Lauderdale–Hollywood International Airport in Broward County, Florida, USA. The assailant, Esteban Santiago-Ruiz, opened fire on seemingly random people with a 9mm pistol that he had checked in his baggage flying from Anchorage, Alaska, to Fort Lauderdale, Florida. Despite the length that authorities have gone to in order to maximize aviation security, tragic events such as this remind us that the industry needs to be doing more.

International law requires airports to implement security measures in accordance with the relevant national regime. Standard 3.2 of ICAO Annex 17 reads: 'Each Contracting State shall require each airport serving civil aviation to establish, implement and maintain a written airport security programme appropriate to meet the requirements of the national civil aviation security programme' and that states must

> ensure that airport design requirements, including architectural and infrastructure-related requirements necessary for the implementation of the security measures in the national civil aviation security programme, are integrated into the design and construction of new facilities and alterations to existing facilities at airports.

Unfortunately, at the time of the incident in 2017, it was reported that:

> Security at most major airports worldwide is generally focused on protecting aircraft from potential attackers and deadly devices, rather than the airports themselves. As a result, much of the space at terminals is easily accessible to the public, with no formal screening before passengers go through checkpoints to get to their departure gates. . . . It is logistically impractical to try to protect these areas, unfortunately, and the reason is no matter how far you move the boundary out, you will always have some sort of soft target area.
>
> (Ax 2017)

In the United States, Federal Aviation Regulations Part 107 provides for airport security regulations. The federal Transport Security Administration (TSA) permits passengers to carry firearms in their checked luggage – the weapon cannot be loaded, but the rules allow passengers to also carry ammunition (sometimes in the same case). Under Florida's state law, one cannot carry weapons in an airport terminal unless they are still in the case, although, a proposed bill aims to amend the Florida Statutes to allow the open carrying of a handgun in public places. Under Chapter 790, Title XLVI of the Florida Statutes, the Department of Agriculture and Consumer Services is allowed to issue licences to carry concealed firearms. Section 12(a), however, reads that a licence issued does not authorize a person to

> openly carry a handgun or carry a concealed weapon or firearm [into] the inside of the *passenger terminal* and *sterile area* of any airport, provided that *no person shall be prohibited from carrying any legal firearm into the terminal, which firearm is encased for shipment for purposes of checking such firearm as baggage to be lawfully transported* on any aircraft.
>
> (Emphasis added)

Unloaded weapons are not permitted in the terminal, in carry-on or on your person. Passengers may, however, transport unloaded firearms – so long as they are 'legal' firearms – if they are 'encased for shipment', i.e. if they are checked baggage. Whilst Santiago-Ruiz's weapon was unloaded when in checked baggage, he *loaded* it in the airport bathroom after he received his bag. This is obviously a problem.

Since 9/11, most of the safety regulations that were passed were aimed at aircraft, but airport protection was arguably left neglected. Baggage claim, drop-off zones, transportation areas and check-in counters are all open to anyone and they do not have that much of a police presence. If the laws do not change, airports could at least make security in those areas more robust. Simple things could be done such as increasing law enforcement patrols in public places to provide for immediate response. The development of gunshot locators is also a possibility, a system which detects and conveys the location of gunfire using different types of sensors.

The main message of this case is that a balance needs to be achieved between the public's need to freely travel but also to protect them from danger. Logistical impracticability should no longer be an excuse when technology has advanced to the point of producing the innovative types of security measures we are seeing today. Annex 17 makes it perfectly clear that both airline and airport security is critical and an international requirement.

A Concluding Comment

Modern security arrangements, such as enhanced flight deck doors, passenger and CBS, freight screening and the searching of aircraft prior to departure, necessarily impact on carriers, airport operators and the travelling public. They require significant resources and facilities, consume time, incur very significant costs and impinge upon the privacy of passengers and crew. Moreover, the appeal and demand of travel by air to holiday destinations, particularly overseas, is adversely affected by both the inconvenience of these arrangements and the underlying threat that has led to their establishment.

Meeting the demands of security programmes challenges the airlines' ability to achieve on-time performance, and is likely to present continuing difficulties with the recent introduction of new generation aircraft such as the Boeing B787 Dreamliner and the Airbus A350. Throughout the world the cost of these measures is largely met by passengers by the imposition of security-specific ticket levies.

Under the guidance of ICAO, security measures continue to develop. Individual member states to the *Chicago Convention* are obligated to meet the expectations of the global community in this increasingly important area. Many countries have elected to accelerate the introduction of some of ICAO's measures, such as the x-ray screening of 100 per cent of all outbound international checked baggage, and the initiation of screening of some domestic checked baggage.

The overall protection of civil aviation involves an integration of activities by many organizations with the principal objective of securing the various assets of the aviation industry, both tangible and intangible. Ultimately, it is the protection of human life that is paramount.

14
Airport Operations

INTRODUCTION

The 2023 report from the Airports Council International (ACI), based on data from over 2,600 airports across 180 countries, predicts a promising horizon for the global aviation industry. The combined world airports are expected to host over 9.4 billion passengers, surpassing the pre-COVID record of 9.2 billion passengers in 2019. Airports are the critical infrastructure for facilitating the operation and performance of the entire aviation industry.

Airports around the world are operated by various entities including local government authorities, state government instrumentalities, private companies, consortiums and public corporations. As such, they are subject not only to airport-related legislation but also to the statutory requirements that are generally applied to these types of organizations. This chapter will look at the regulatory requirements prescribed in Volume I of Annex 14 and how these requirements are incorporated into different legal systems around the world. For the purposes of this chapter, Volume II (Heliports), and the development of new standards relating to vertiports – for e-VTOL aircraft – will *not* be considered.

The various requirements relating to airports can be broadly categorized as either economic or safety related. The various approaches adopted by American, European and other regulatory agencies will be discussed, with particular attention given to the extent to which Annex 14 requirements have been adopted amongst EASA member states. The commercial aspects of airport operations relating to market power, aeronautical charges and privatization are a growing area of concern for the regulatory authorities. This trend is clearly demonstrated by the industry's efforts to 'bridge the gap' between the extents to which the standardization of economic and safety standards has been implemented.

These challenges, along with environmental sustainability issues that rank highly on the industry's list of priorities, reiterate the volatility which aviation stakeholders, and thus airport operators, are exposed to. In order to ensure the sustainability of airport operations, the international standards and national regulatory requirements imposed on operators need to be developed and implemented within a contemporary mindset which takes into account the issues faced by airport operators today.

The link that the airport operators provide as part of the broader aviation network means that they assume the role of a facilitator for the world's airlines. Moreover, because of the worldwide trend towards privatization of airports, they represent big business. Gone are the days when airports were just a transition between sectors of travel. The modern airport today is a multifaceted enterprise and provides the traveller and other customers with a wide range of products and services.

DOI: 10.4324/9781032652146-14

The universal foundations upon which airport operators base their policies and procedures, as per Annex 14 of the ICAO standards, are now considered.

International Standards

Annex 14 of the ICAO: Aerodromes In 1990, after a series of amendments (39 to be exact), the decision was made by the ICAO to restructure Annex 14 and split it into two volumes: Volume I contains material relating to aerodrome design and operations, whereas Volume II is limited to heliport design. Annex 14 is unique in the sense that it encompasses a broad range of subject areas from planning of airports and engineering, as well as dealing with operational aspects of day-to-day airport operations at the ground level. As mentioned previously in the introduction, this section will deal exclusively with Volume I, since the contents of Volume II (Heliports) are beyond the scope of this chapter.

From the time that Annex 14 was first published, its contents have evolved to keep pace with the dynamically changing industry that airports support. An indication as to how much has changed is demonstrated by the absence of specifications for water aerodromes and aerodromes without runways from the latest version, but which were a significant inclusion back in the mid-1940s at the time when the ICAO was founded. As much as particular components have been phased out, specifications and regulatory guidance for other aspects of modern airport operations have taken their place. For instance, the most recent version of Annex 14, Volume I (for example, runway end safety areas, clearways, stopways and so on) contains today's 'building blocks' upon which the requirements of the core movement area are based – as, for example, with the Annex 14 of the ICAO guidance material.

Classification of Aerodromes

In the late 1990s, the ICAO amended Annex 14 to require contracting states to set up a regime of aerodrome certification for their international airports and recommended that it be extended to any other airport used for public transport. Certification was intended to ensure that facilities, equipment and operational procedures complied with Annex 14 requirements. ICAO Annex 14 sets out the minimum standards to apply to international aerodromes to ensure the safe operation of current aircraft and those planned for introduction. Once ICAO adopts a standard it must be put into effect by each contracting state in its own jurisdiction.

The ICAO enforces the following standards about classifying airports into different categories:

- *certified aerodrome*: an airport served by passenger aircraft with more than 30 seats;
- *registered aerodrome*: aerodromes which do not have to be certified may apply to have their aerodrome registered;
- *other aerodromes*: not to be confused with meaning that *all* other aerodromes include those which do not have to be certified and whose operators choose not to register them. For regulatory purposes, this classification is divided into aerodromes used at least once a week by aircraft with seating for ten to 30 passengers conducting air transport operations. The definition provided by the ICAO also includes aerodromes served by small aircraft of nine or fewer passenger seats.

In most contracting states to the Chicago Convention 1944, the implementation of the ICAO SARPs in respect of airports – and indeed all of the other some 12,000 or so SARPs – is delegated to a particular department or agency. The trend worldwide has been to establish independent statutory authorities separate from the government but usually accountable to a government transport department or ministry. The minimum requirements for certification of the different types of aerodromes are set out in Part 139 (or the state equivalent) of the national civil aviation regulatory regime.

Contracting states are required to notify ICAO of any differences between their national standards and practices and those in Annex 14 and publish them in their Aeronautical Information Publication (AIP). Where there is a difference between an ICAO and MOS standard, the MOS standard prevails. In circumstances where there is no MOS standard equivalent to an ICAO standard and no difference has been notified, the ICAO standard applies.

Aerodrome standards change from time to time to meet identified safety needs, technological changes and changes in international standards and practices. In addition to these international ICAO requirements, national regulatory authorities usually establish a system of registration for airports that do not have to be certified under the ICAO standards and specify (usually by way of delegated legislation or rules) what is required in terms of applicable standards.

In the USA, FAR Part 139, administered by the FAA, has established operating certificate requirements for:

- airports serving scheduled (also known as regular public transport) and unscheduled air carrier operations in aircraft with more than 30 seats;
- airports serving scheduled air carrier operations in aircraft with ten to 30 seats; or
- whether the FAA administrator requires a certificate.

In 2023 there were 5,193 airports in the USA and 520 airports certified under Part 139, with nearly 3,400 existing and proposed airports included under the National Plan of Integrated Airport Systems. This is a plan that provides federal government grants under the Airport Improvement Program (AIP) to airports deemed significant to national air transportation.

European rules for aerodromes require that aerodrome operators put into place and maintain a management system, including a safety management system (SMS) in line with the new ICAO Annex 19. *Regulation (EC) No 139/2014* came into effect on 6 March 2014, establishing requirements and procedures related to aerodromes pursuant to *Regulation (EC) No 216/2008* of the European Parliament. The 2008 regulations require the establishment of Implementing Rules (IRs), in particular concerning the safety regulation of aerodromes. Certificates for aerodromes that were issued prior to 1 December 2014 on the basis of national laws remained valid until they were issued in accordance with the new 2014 regulations. Article 6 prescribes the conversion process of existing aerodrome certificates.

The June 2023 revision to 2014 regulations includes the Easy Access Rules for Aerodromes (EAR for ADR) and incorporates:

- Commission Delegated Regulation (EU) 2022/2074 (https://www.easa.europa.eu/en/document-library/regulations/commission-delegated-regulation-eu-20222074);
- Commission Delegated Regulation (EU) 2022/1645 (https://www.easa.europa.eu/en/document-library/regulations/commission-delegated-regulation-eu-20221645) (applicable from 16 October 2025);

- ED Decision 2022/016/R (Amendment 7) (https://www.easa.europa.eu/en/document-library/agency-decisions/ed-decision-2022016r); and
- ED Decision 2023/003/R (Amendment 8) (https://www.easa.europa.eu/en/document-library/agency-decisions/ed-decision-2023003r).

The 2014 regulations deal with a significant range of subject matters, outlined in Article 1. They set up the conditions for establishing and notifying the certification basis applicable to an aerodrome, including the conditions for issuing, amending, suspending etc. certificates for aerodromes and certificates for organizations responsible for aerodrome operations. Under Article 3, member states are to designate one or more entities as the Competent Authority with the powers and responsibilities for the certification and oversight of aerodromes. States are to ensure that these authorities have the capabilities and resources they needed to fulfil their requirements.

Article 7 allows for deviations from certification specifications, but they must conform to certain conditions as listed in the Article. The concept of the individual aerodrome Certification Basis (CB) includes the possible element of 'special conditions' which provides for the flexibility to the NAA to allow deviations from the European Certification Specifications when:

- the aerodrome has certain 'physical, topographical or similar limitations' related to the location of the aerodrome which results in the certification specifications not being able to be met;
- the aerodrome has novel or unusual design features; or
- experience from the operation of that aerodrome or others with a similar design has shown that safety may be endangered.

As will be explained in more detail later in this chapter, despite the aim of the ICAO being to standardize all aspects of airport operations as much as possible, the implementation and interpretation of the technical material provided in the Annexes will inevitably vary from one nation to the next, due, at least in part, to the disparity in the resources available. Thus, the need for an effective oversight authority exists and with the EASA being assigned the responsibility of more aspects of aviation operations, it is being given the tools to implement change and gradually bridge any gaps in safety standards between one member and another.

For these regulatory authorities, imposing a certification requirement in the short term is considered unrealistic and would lead to inefficient outcomes. Therefore, introducing a certification requirement is considered a long-term objective to enable enough time and resources to be allocated to ensure that the system is fully functional and addresses the safety issues it was designed for. In other instances, basic legal and constitutional provisions were subject to considerable changes, which effectively did not permit relevant legislation processes at all.

SAFETY REQUIREMENTS FOR AIRPORT OPERATORS

Annex 14 of the ICAO sets out the minimum standards that apply to international aerodromes to ensure the safe operation of current aircraft and those planned for introduction. Once the ICAO adopts a standard, it must be 'adopted' or otherwise put into effect by each contracting state in its own jurisdiction. Annex 19 now plays a large role with this, establishing the need for Safety Management Systems (SMSs). Nevertheless, Annex 14 still plays a role in establishing the minimum aerodrome standards necessary to ensure safety of aircraft operations. Much of what Annex 14 provided was copied in the relevant aerodrome sections in Annex 19. For instance, standard 4.1.8 of Annex 19 reads, 'The SMS of an operator of a certified aerodrome, in accordance with Annex 14, shall be made acceptable to the State responsible for the aerodrome's certification'.

As was explained in Chapter 4, contracting states are required to notify the ICAO of any differences between their national standards and practices and those in Annex 14, and then publish any differences in their *Aeronautical Information Publication* (AIP). Where there is a difference between an ICAO and a local standard, the local standard prevails. In circumstances where there is no local standard equivalent to an ICAO standard and no difference has been notified, the ICAO standard continues to apply.

Aerodrome standards change from time to time to meet identified safety needs, technological changes and changes in international standards and practices. In cases where aerodrome operators find it impossible to meet a particular design or operating standard, there are usually provisions in the domestic regulatory regime which permit the operator to apply to its local NAA for an exemption from a particular rule or regulation. The relevant regulatory authority will typically grant such an exemption if it considers there are sufficient alternative safety measures in place so as to achieve 'equivalent safety' standards. The aerodrome operator would normally be required to provide written justification (often in the form of a *safety case*), which may include a risk assessment, to support the application.

Outcome-Based Regulations

Annex 14 of the ICAO and the relevant domestic regulations under Part 139 (or the state equivalent) set out the *minimum* aerodrome standards necessary to ensure the safety of aircraft operations. NAAs require compliance with these minimum, mandatory standards unless an exemption has been granted. Needless to say, the individual nation's regulations cannot and do not attempt to deal with every conceivable safety-related issue that may arise at individual airports. It was mainly due to the increasing complexity and diversity of airport operations that the ICAO decided to mandate the requirement for airport operators to have a NAA-approved SMS. Airport operators were the first sector of the aviation industry in which SMSs were mandated. The traditional, prescriptive, 'one size fits all' style of regulations was simply not effective to cover such diversities of airport operational activities.

The present-day regulatory regime shares the responsibility of aviation safety between industry participants and the regulator. It is no longer sufficient for industry participants to demonstrate compliance with standards and recommended practices relevant to their operation; they must actively identify and manage any risks their activities pose for aviation safety. The management of risk has given rise to the regulator needing to be satisfied that individual airports have a risk-based system in place for identifying and dealing with hazardous or potentially hazardous situations.

This led to the requirement that aerodrome operators must develop and implement a SMS as part of the aerodrome certification process. This had its origins in an amendment to Annex 14 of the ICAO in 2003, with the ICAO standard requiring certification of aerodromes and implementation of SMSs effective from November 2006. Many ICAO member states had mandated for approved SMSs well before the 2006 deadline. The SMS is seen as a means of ensuring that aerodrome operators adopt a proactive approach to safety in addition to compliance with mandatory standards. With the ICAO trend to mandating SMSs for airport operators, airlines and air traffic management (ATM) providers by way of promulgating SARPs it was decided to introduce the new ICAO Annex 19 exclusively for SMS in 2013.

US FAA Requirements

The FAA as the local civil aviation regulator in the USA is entrusted with the responsibility of meeting the USA's obligations to comply with the standards specified by the ICAO. The technical standards that airport operators are expected to meet are contained in FAR Part 139 of the federal regulations, with inspections conducted annually by trained FAA inspectors (35 nationwide, rotated every three years). The FAA can exercise its right to undertake unannounced inspections as part of its surveillance activities.

By way of an overview, the FAA aerodrome inspection and oversight criteria include:

- pre-inspection review;
- briefing of airport management;
- inspection of administrative records and paperwork;
- movement area inspection;
- aircraft fire-fighting and rescue inspection;
- fuelling facilities inspection;
- night inspection; and
- post-inspection briefing with airport management.

In the event that FAA inspectors report non-compliance with regard to any of the standards expected, it has a number of actions in place. Financial penalties are one form of encouraging compliance with the requirements in Part 139, but in the event of severe breaches, the FAA can exercise its right to limit the operational capability of the aerodrome or even go so far as to revoke the operator's certificate.

European EASA Requirements

Since the EASA became operational in 2003, the scope of activities for which it is responsible has gradually broadened. Until recently, safety regulation of aerodromes among EASA member states was a task carried out individually. Although all of these states base their own regulatory reform on the guidance material provided in the ICAO SARPs, individual interpretation and unique characteristics at each airport mean that uniform levels of safety cannot be guaranteed. Close attention will be given later in this section to the extent to which Annex 14 of the ICAO requirements have been adopted by EASA member states to date, but first the process by which the EASA is attempting to unify the region with regard to the safety standards of airport operators will be discussed.

As part of the process of empowering the EASA with the appropriate tools to implement change, the responsibilities of the EASA have been extended to include the areas of Air Traffic Management (ATM), Air Navigation Systems (ANSs) and aerodromes. As a result of this mandate, the EASA rule-making process is under way to develop standardized, comprehensive and mandatory rules with regard to aerodrome design, operations and equipment, underpinned by the contents of SARPs for Annex 14.

The prescriptive style of regulation which for a long time dictated the regulatory regime for the aviation industry is gradually being phased out and replaced with a more outcome-based legislative style which has been shown to deliver more efficient outcomes in complex, modern and diverse industries such as aviation. Moreover, technocentric industries such as aviation are reliant upon the timely uptake of new technologies to provide greater safety and business efficiencies – something that is not always possible under a highly prescriptive regulatory regime.

The rule-making process aims to develop a framework for European airport operators which meets the requirements set out in Annex 14, hence acknowledging that a 'one size fits all' policy will lead to disparities in the level of overall safety between one operator and another, and thus fails to achieve common safety goals. As such, sufficient flexibility must be accounted for to allow for variations in physical limitations and operational specifications (size, type and scope of operations) for airports across the continent.

As previously stated, with the introduction of ICAO Annex – Safety Management in 2013, the responsibility for ensuring compliance with SARPs and other regulations is now placed more on industry stakeholders. Certificate holders now submit 'expositions' for regulatory approval to allow them to more effectively develop procedures that are based on their operating systems. The EASA has adopted a systematic approach to provide greater flexibility for operators, made up of three initial tasks which form the basis of the regulatory development process. These are requirements for:

- aerodrome operator organizations and oversight authorities;
- aerodrome operations; and
- aerodrome design.

Identifying these requirements is an important milestone because it represents the foundations upon which the broader rule-making programme will be based. For the EASA to complete the development and implementation of its rule-making programme for aerodromes by the end of 2013, the individual components which make up each of the aforementioned tasks had to be defined in each of their respective terms of reference (TORs).

The deliverables and the conclusion of this process will include:

- draft Commission regulations prepared by the EASA;
- *Acceptable Means of Compliance* (AMCs), which will provide guidance and technical material to support member states in meeting the specified requirements, as well as providing alternative means by which the same result can be achieved; and
- guidance material or *certification specifications*.

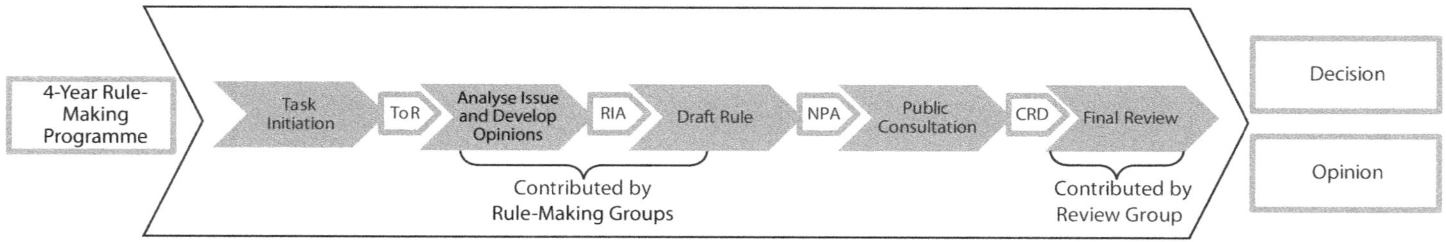

Figure 14.1 The EASA rule-making process

Source: EASA

This range of documentation helps form part of a comprehensive regulatory regime which must be adhered to. Reference to European law and the technical standards in the relevant ICAO Annex should only be made when relevant. The subsections of each step in the process are defined, as well as the method employed and the time allowance given for each phase to be completed. Once the draft is complete, the EASA's consultative bodies, made up of selected experts from NAAs and other industry authorities, review the proposed approach as part of the *rule-making group*.

The benefits that this approach provides are:

- the duplication of rule-making activities is avoided, thus facilitating an efficient allocation of resources;
- the process is completed in a timely manner to ensure that the requirements imposed on operators are in context;
- it provides a holistic view, which takes into consideration the complexities and unique characteristics of a wide range of operators, which consequently facilitates the forming of working relationships between a variety of aviation stakeholders, thereby ensuring coordination and interoperability;
- it enables the sharing of knowledge and experience amongst member states; and
- it considers technological evolution, worldwide best practices and innovations, as well as safety concerns identified by safety analysis and investigations, which otherwise might be difficult to address at an individual state level.

The benefits associated with a uniform approach to safety regulation formed part of the reasoning behind the EASA's decision in 2008 to commission a consultancy to undertake a comprehensive study of its member states. The study determined the extent to which the Annex 14 of the ICAO SARPs had been incorporated into the domestic regulatory framework of all EASA member states. Identifying the variations between the standards set by the ICAO and the application of those same standards amongst all EASA airport operators is the first step towards implementing initiatives to address deficiencies affecting safety.

Although EASA members base their own regulation on the guidance material provided by the ICAO, there are nevertheless significant variations in the individual national approaches. For this reason, there is a need for the EASA to provide effective oversight for the activities of airport operators in the region to ensure that any disparities are identified, addressed and monitored.

It was determined that a consistent application of Annex 14 of the ICAO SARPs can only be achieved provided the following two impediments are effectively overcome:

- The first involves how the various legal implementation processes used across Europe influence the interpretation of the guidance material provided by the ICAO. If the responsibility of implementing the standards set out by the ICAO has been delegated to a NAA, the process of incorporating them into domestic legislation does not necessarily have to be a long, drawn-out process. This sometimes occurs where there has been a 'trade-off' between safety and profitability.
- The second issue that could interrupt the timely and comprehensive implementation of the specifications contained in Annex 14 is the limited capacity of the

authorities whose responsibility it is to implement change. Ensuring that these authorities are sufficiently resourced to carry out their duties is essential for the implementation of regulatory reform staying on schedule and within the timeframe specified during the rule-making process.

MANAGEMENT OF AIRPORTS

Airports are a vital national resource. Traditionally, airports were considered in terms of being an infrastructure provider facilitating the transfer of passengers from one location to another and were normally dependent on finance raised through the public sector. Airports admittedly serve a key role in the transportation of people and goods and in regional, national and international commerce, but this is only part of the story. Today, the airport business has developed into a thriving commercial enterprise, attracting the interest of some of the largest corporations and global consortiums in the world. The diversity and profit-driven nature of the airport business today means that like most other large corporations, the business model must be focused on maximizing the return on investment for its shareholders.

Airports can also be viewed as where the nation's aviation system connects with other modes of transportation and where quite often the national responsibility for managing and regulating air traffic operations intersects with the role of state and local governments or municipalities that frequently own and operate major regional airports. The ownership structure of an airport generally determines whether or not the airport is operated as a commercial enterprise.

There are indications to suggest that non-aeronautical revenue is accounting for a larger proportion of total income amongst many of the world's privatized airports, reaffirming the extent to which the business models of airports have evolved to the point where the movement of aircraft and passengers today represents only a component of the total business. According to the Airports Council International (ACI), airports earn just 18 per cent of their revenue from airlines (*The Economist* 2011).

Privatization

According to Venturini (2009), airport privatization and concession is the infusion of private sector capital to gain partial control over an airport's facilities and services in various degrees and forms. These 'various degrees and forms' represent the source of confusion when categorizing airports as either private or public entities. The ICAO is supportive of private entities operating airports so long as they meet what is considered 'standard' in the provision of airport facilities and management. Standards include:

- non-discrimination in the application of charges;
- no overcharging or other anti-competitive practices or abuse of market power;
- transparency as well as the availability and presentation of all financial data required to determine the basis for charges;
- assessing and encouraging efficiency and efficacy in the operation of providers;
- establishing and reviewing standards, quality and levels of services provided;

- monitoring and encouraging investments in order to meet future demand; and
- ensuring user views are adequately taken into account.

The ICAO also encourages airport operators to develop and implement appropriate performance parameters to facilitate the continuous improvement in the services and facilities supplied. These parameters are described as follows:

- developing and collecting data on performance in the provision of their services (that is, safety standards, on-time performance, flexibility, efficiency, access, environment, cost of services and so on);
- using these parameters to evaluate and improve the quality of the services provided;
- taking these parameters into account to help support their investment decisions;
- undertaking consultation with users to achieve mutual understanding and consensus; and
- developing and maintaining costing systems that allow users and providers to understand the true costs of providing services.

Litigation Involving Airport Ownership Issues

A number of cases involving disputes between the state, the private airport owners and the airlines using the airport facilities have arisen in Germany over the past decade. These cases represent the basis upon which a flawed regulatory regime has been amended to take into consideration contemporary issues facing the airport business. The solution was to form an independent regulatory body to implement UK-style incentive regulation, the need for which has been demonstrated a number of times, such as in the case of Frankfurt following its privatization on 1 June 2001.

The Frankfurt Airport Case On 1 October 2001, Frankfurt Airport sued the airlines using its facilities on the basis of fees it felt it was owed following a proposed fee increase of 12 per cent from 1 January 2000 (prior to privatization). The airport in this instance was unable or unwilling to demonstrate to the airlines that the proposed fee increase was the direct and proportionate result of an increase in costs. The court's decision, handed down in April 2008, found that the airport had not met the 'burden of proof' and that it 'had not demonstrated that the proposed fee was equitable: it was not transparent and there were doubts whether it was properly cost-related' (Littlechild 2011b).

The Dusseldorf Airport Case In an earlier dispute involving a German airport in 1997, Dusseldorf Airport received the advances of the Airport Partners consortium of Hochtief and Aer Rianta, which led to a subsequent partial takeover. The airport was plagued with issues during this period, and with demand warnings and limited slots available, the operator proposed to change the structure of its fees in order to improve its balance sheet. The proposed changes to the structure of fees would mean that a higher proportion of the airport's revenue would be collected from variable fees as opposed to fixed charges paid by the airlines for each movement. After the state regulatory authority negotiated a 7.1 per cent increase in fees (the operator initially proposed a 15 per cent increase) plus charges for noise abatement, Lufthansa, along with a group of 20 smaller airlines, took legal action to oppose the changes.

The airlines were in a predicament. They knew that if they paid the charges before the matter was officially a lawsuit, this would imply acceptance of the charges – at law the principle is known as 'acquiescence' – and hence would make their claims void. On the contrary, if they refused to pay the airport, the operator might well have been within its rights to refuse permission to land. Given that the foundation of the complaint was a civil matter, the airlines decided to pay 50 per cent of the additional fees, knowing that, as a practical matter, it was for the airport to commence legal action if it so desired. Further, if the airport sued, it would consequently be obliged to prove that the fees were set 'according to the principles of equity'. Following the court's initial ruling in June 2001 in favour of the airport, the Court of Appeal in January 2003 'held that the airport had not discharged the burden of proof' and that 'airport charges had to be based on direct costing and contribution margin accounting'. A new agreement was negotiated in December 2004 whereby all parties agreed to a 3.5 per cent increase in charges (down from 7.1 per cent) and agreed to only cover part of the cost of noise abatement (Littlechild 2011b).

Air Traffic Growth

The projected growth in air traffic as a proportion of the increase in capacity around the world (with the number of passengers expected to be 7.8 billion in 2036, double the number of passengers that flew in 2017) has many in aviation concerned that the air transport system will soon be bottlenecked. The benefits associated with inviting private investors to inject much-needed cash into building an adequate airport infrastructure to support the industry is gaining momentum. Despite cases like those explained earlier which may identify particular impediments to a successful change in management structure, privatization still represents the most effective tool available to the airport sector to address the current capacity and equity issues facing the industry. As of 2020, nearly 20 per cent of the world's airports had been privatized. Private equity (PE), usually through dedicated infrastructure funds, are playing an increasing role in privatization, purchasing 102 airports out of a total of 437 that have ever been privatized.

THE ECONOMIC REGULATION OF AIRPORT OPERATIONS

The days where airports were merely considered as the infrastructure necessary to facilitate travel by air are over. Today, airports are seen as businesses in their own right and thus are viewed as attractive sources of investment. The privatization of airports has created a context whereby regulation with regard to the pricing of services supplied is necessary to avoid a situation whereby airport operators are abusing their market power. The ICAO, as with its SARPs with regard to safety, provides guidance material for its members to base their domestic price on as a means to ensure that the prices charged are on par with the services provided, as well as to prevent a price war between airports and their airline clients being passed on to passengers in the form of additional taxes, levies and higher fares.

The ICAO's Policies on Airport Charges

The ICAO's stance with regard to airport charges is that 'users shall ultimately bear their full and fair share of the cost of providing the airport'. The *ICAO Policies on Charges for Airports and Air Navigation Services* (2009) places the onus on the airport operator to ensure that the services which incur charges and the associated costs are readily available and are published regularly as a means of informing the users of airport facilities.

The ICAO also encourages the use of internationally accepted accounting standards for airports as a means of simplifying comparisons between airport operators, as well as ensuring consistency between member states. The charges for which guidance is provided are:

- landing charges;
- parking and hangar charges;
- passenger service charges;
- security charges;
- noise-related charges;
- emissions-related charges; and
- concession and rental charges.

The remainder of this section will focus on how airport operators across the world, operating within different legal jurisdictions, have incorporated the guidance provided by the ICAO regarding the commercial aspects of airport operations into their respective domestic regulatory framework.

North American Regulatory Regimes

In the USA, the FAA is responsible, *inter alia*, for the safety and efficiency of the nation's airport system. These responsibilities were defined in the *Federal Aviation Act 1958* (USA) – inserted into Title 49 of the *United States Code* – following the establishment of the FAA earlier that same year. The FAA utilizes a number of tools through which it carries out its duties with respect to airports, namely direct regulation and contractual obligation, in return for the use of federal grant in-aid funds.

In response to the need for investment into improving airport infrastructure to meet growing demand, the FAA in 1990 introduced what was called a *Passenger Facility Charge* (PFC) programme. Under Title 49 of the *United States Code*, the FAA is able to introduce such an initiative only to address one of three state issues:

1. to preserve/enhance safety, security or capacity;
2. to reduce noise or mitigate impacts; or
3. to enhance competition.

Despite it falling within its scope of responsibilities, the FAA is gradually taking a backseat to negotiations between airport operators and the suppliers of air services over the cost of services supplied. A recent policy statement released by the FAA demonstrates its intention to intervene only when the two parties are unable to reach a common understanding.

The FAA's position with regard to the pricing of airport services can be described as outcome-based, not prescriptive. Its policies specify that all aeronautical users must be given equal access to the airport on fair and reasonable terms by letting airports and users negotiate independently – that is, through commercial negotiation. Only when an agreement is not reached will the FAA step in to mediate the process.

European Regulatory Regimes

As previously indicated, European airports are, for the most part, natural monopolies with significant market power. Given the context in which European airports are operating, the need for economic regulation to be in place which establishes boundaries within which operators must conduct day-to-day operations is essential to ensure that passengers do not bear the brunt of airports abusing their market power. The fact that airports in Europe face limited competition from surrounding airports makes the need for economic regulation to be enforced strictly all the more necessary. Constraining this market power is also desirable, given that it will probably lead to levels of service being on a par with the costs charged, thus achieving efficiency.

In response to the need for rule enforcement with regard to this issue, in 2009 the EU issued a directive on airport charges. The ICAO's policies on airport charges (see the previous section) significantly influenced the EU's policies in relation to this issue and established a framework for the setting of airport charges that takes into consideration the unique characteristics of the European airport sector. The message this directive sends to airport operators is clear: airport charges should be non-disciplinary and transparent. In addition to achieving efficient outcomes, this requirement for transparency facilitates communication between the airport operator and its users.

The introduction of a mandatory consultative process facilitates the bringing together of a variety of stakeholders to the airport business and ensures that the prices set are agreed to it prior to being charged. This process establishes a working relationship between the owner and the users of airport facilities, whilst providing an insight into various aspects of the airport business, both from the operators' and the users' perspectives.

The regulatory landscape in the UK with respect to airport pricing is similar to the rest of the EU, but differs in the sense that UK regulatory authorities utilize (on a very limited basis) a price cap to enforce limitations on the airports they deem to possess market power. If an airport is considered to possess these characteristics, it is said to be 'designated'. For an airport to be designated, it must be determined that:

- the airport is able to acquire substantial market power;
- EU competition law is deemed not to be sufficient to address the risk of persistent pricing above competition levels; and
- the benefits of designation exceed the costs of price regulation.

As of 2011, Heathrow, Gatwick and Stansted are the three airports in the UK which are currently considered to be designated.

THE 'INTERNATIONAL ZONE'

International airport zones are a murky area of international law. ICAO does not really deal with the legal status of these zones, which have a variety of names such as 'transit zones', 'waiting zones' or 'reception centres'. One European case, which will be discussed later, considered evidence of a circular from the Minister of the Interior of France. This circular described the nature of international zones:

> In practice, international zones are to be found mainly at certain ports and airports. At airports, the international zone means the sealed-off area (or one that can be sealed off) used for the arrival of international flights and situated between the passengers' point of arrival and the police checkpoints. Alternatively, a hotel situated in the immediate proximity of the port or airport may be used.

There is no uniform international law to govern these so-called international zones, but despite arguments to the contrary, they are not extraterritorial and are subject to the laws of that country.

***Amuur v France*, 17/1995/523/609, Council of Europe: European Court of Human Rights, 25 June 1996**

In 1992, France established the 'waiting zone' for foreigners who had arrived at an international airport, train station or seaport but were not granted entry by immigration authorities. The space provided for greater policing powers, but lesser rights than provided for under normal French law. The laws of the waiting zone specified that aliens were legally considered to be outside of France and so outside the scope of domestic constitutional protection. It was founded on the legal entry concept, prescribing that mere physical presence on the territory is insufficient to entry and only lawful admission amounts to entry as well as the right to benefit from constitutional protection. France argued therefore that the waiting zone was to be an 'international zone' with extraterritorial application.

Somali aliens were being held at the Hôtel Arcade in Paris (an 'international zone'), but their restriction of movement was to the extent that the Court found that it impinged on their liberties.

At first instance, the Paris *Tribunal de grande* confirmed that the law held no specific rules governing the holding of an asylum-seeker in the international zone for the time strictly necessary for the administrative authorities to consider whether his application is admissible. However, they rejected as 'ill-founded' the defendant's submission that the 'complaint of an interference with personal liberty should be dismissed because the alien was merely prevented from entering France, as he was detained in a place which had to be regarded as an "extension" of the airport's international zone' (see paragraph 22 of the ECHR judgment). The State Counsel's office appealed, and the case eventually went to the ECHR.

The ECHR ruled that despite its name, 'the international zone does not have extraterritorial status' (at paragraph 52). They found that holding defendants in the international zone of Paris-Orly Airport made them 'subject to French law'. Damages were awarded in the sum of FRF 57,000 plus costs.

As we can see, whilst it meant that French legislation had the power to provide for extra policing powers, it did not have the right to circumvent constitutional rights.

FUTURE OF AIRPORT OPERATIONS

According to a recent Global Airport Investment Report it is estimated that global investment in airports will reach USD 2,404 billion by 2040 from USD 200 billion in 2021. Asia Pacific is expected to be the fastest growing and largest market in the 2021–2040 period. The swift economic progression in the Asia Pacific region, spearheaded by powerhouses such as China and India, is driving an increased need for improved and expanded airport facilities. This enhancement is crucial to accommodate the growing demands of both local and international flights. Given its pivotal role in global aviation as a key nexus for flights connecting the Americas, Europe and beyond, the Asia Pacific's commitment to advancing its airport infrastructure is essential for sustaining and elevating its strategic significance in the aviation sector.

The increase in airport investments reflects a multifaceted approach to addressing the growing demands of air travel, economic development, environmental sustainability and digital innovation. The surge in airport investments can be attributed to several key drivers, each reflecting broader trends in global commerce, technology and societal expectations. The following key drivers identified were:

1 The increasing demand for air travel, fuelled by global economic growth and the rising middle class, necessitates the expansion and modernization of airport infrastructure to accommodate higher passenger volumes and enhance operational efficiency. This growth trajectory is prompting stakeholders to invest in enlarging terminals, upgrading facilities and integrating cutting-edge technologies to streamline passenger flow and improve the travel experience.
2 The strategic importance of airports as economic hubs cannot be overstated. Airports play a pivotal role in stimulating local economies, facilitating trade, attracting international business and promoting tourism. By investing in airport development, governments and private entities can spur economic development, create jobs and enhance their regions' connectivity and competitiveness on the global stage.
3 The push towards sustainability and the need to address the environmental impact of aviation, including the ICAO 2050 Net Zero Emissions target, are driving investments in green technologies and sustainable practices. Airports are adopting innovative solutions to reduce carbon footprints, manage waste more efficiently and conserve energy, aligning with broader environmental goals and regulatory requirements.
4 The digital transformation of the aviation industry is a significant factor. Investments in digital technologies, such as biometrics, artificial intelligence and data ana-

lytics, are critical for airports aiming to enhance security, optimize operations and deliver personalized services. These technologies not only improve efficiency and passenger satisfaction but also provide airports with valuable insights to inform strategic decision-making.

Airports are transitioning into global hubs that cater to a broad spectrum of demographics, embracing digital tools to offer personalized, seamless experiences. This approach acknowledges the diversity of passenger needs, leveraging data analytics to tailor services and enhance the overall journey.

CONCLUSION

As we have seen in this chapter, airports are indeed vital national resources. They play a most important role in the transportation of people and goods at the regional, national and international levels. The efficient operation and accessibility of airports is a fundamental requirement for the growth and safety of commercial aviation and therefore its sustainability. Sustainability is becoming a non-negotiable mandate for airports. Initiatives focused on achieving net zero emissions through renewable energy adoption, sustainable construction practices and waste reduction are critical in mitigating the environmental impact of airport operations.

Airports increasingly become multifaceted spaces that blend travel, business and leisure. These 'aerotropolises' are integrated ecosystems offering retail, entertainment and office spaces, transforming airports into destination hubs in their own right. The advent of cognitive computing and the metaverse heralds a new era for airport operations and passenger engagement. Airports are set to become more intelligent, using AI and immersive technologies to streamline processes, from security checks to boarding, and offer virtual experiences that redefine waiting times and spaces.

The uptake of new technologies such as the integration of UAM solutions, drones and e-VTOLs (electric vertical take-off and landing aircraft) is reshaping the concept of urban transportation. This shift not only promises to reduce ground traffic but also to offer faster, more efficient connections between airports and urban centres.

Airports are where the nation's aviation system connects with other modes of transportation and where quite often national responsibility for managing and regulating air traffic operations intersects with the role of state and local governments or municipalities that own and operate most regional airports. In the following chapter, we will examine the remaining component of this intersection in reviewing the system of air traffic management and the underlying legal and regulatory structures that support this system.

15
Air Traffic Management

INTRODUCTION

Air travel has evolved over the years and is now considered one of the safest forms of mass transportation in the world. However, the perception amongst many in the general public indicates that the extent to which the safety of passengers is prioritized is not completely understood or appreciated. The combination of a robust regulatory framework and the rapid development of technology in the field of Air Traffic Management (ATM) has enabled key safety issues, which had previously plagued the industry, to be addressed, improving the overall level of service offered to the travelling public. The ATM system, as complex and technologically advanced as it is, is responsible for ensuring each and every aircraft is provided with the requisite information and support to navigate the airways safely to its intended destination.

In terms of magnitude, the global Air Traffic Management market was valued at USD 8.9 billion in 2021 and is estimated to expand to USD 20 billion by 2027. While this is good news to the ATM sector and the wider aviation industry there are always ongoing challenges. Inflationary pressures, slowing economies and the ongoing impact of Russia-Ukraine War are some of the darker clouds on the radar.

Before embarking upon a detailed discussion of the regulatory and operational structures that support the ATM systems, it is important to articulate the foundation upon which the ATM system is based. The ICAO has defined key terms that it considers important with regard to the provision of ATM services. The following list identifies the key terms used by the ICAO in its guidance material relating to Annex 11:

- *Air Traffic Control (ATC)*: the primary responsibility of the controller is to maintain a safe distance between aircraft and obstacles within a confined airspace and also on the airport surface.
- *Air Space Management (ASM)*: this involves maximizing the utilization of available airspace by applying time sharing and segregation of airspace rules among competing categories of users based on short-term needs.
- *Air Traffic Flow Management (ATFM)*: this ensures an optimum flow of air traffic during times when demand is expected to exceed the available capacity of ATC service.
- *Flight Information Service (FIS)*: this involves collecting, handling and disseminating flight-related information to assist the pilot to conduct his or her flight in a safe and efficient manner.
- *Alerting Service (ALRS)*: this involves initiating an early search and rescue activity for aircraft in distress.

DOI: 10.4324/9781032652146-15

By way of a high-level overview, the interrelationship between these various systems' components can be summarized as follows:

- Air Traffic Service = ATM + FIS + ALRS
- Air Traffic Management = ATC + ASM + ATFM

Today, the travelling public and those working in the industry are fortunate to be living in an era that is underpinned by a robust ATM system. The standards enforced upon *airspace navigation service providers* (ANSP) is one that demands a high degree of conformity to ensure that across the board, a consistently high standard of safety is delivered that ensures seamless transition across sovereign borders.

The foundations of the current framework were established in Annex 11 of the ICAO. This annex is the cornerstone of standardization of this system and for all those involved in the provision of *Air Traffic Services* (ATS), given that its contents includes definitions of key terms, as well as specifying the SARPs applicable in the provision of these services.

Internationally, ICAO has a vision to achieve an integrated, harmonized and interoperable ATM system through what is known as the ICAO Global Operating Concept for Air Traffic Management. A key aspect of realizing the ICAO vision is the wider application and use of satellite surveillance technology (such as ADS-B) and satellite navigation technology (such as the Global Navigation Surveillance System (GNSS)).

The Evolution of Air Traffic Management

As is the case with virtually every aspect of aviation as we know it today, the extent to which the industry has evolved surpasses even the most optimistic predictions made in the days of the Wright brothers at the birth of powered flight. Notwithstanding the humble beginnings of powered flight, the development and implementation of procedures governing the use of airspace and the notion of air sovereignty was already the subject of international debate, despite the very limited number of aircraft that were actually in the air before the First World War: see Chapter 1. However, because of the virtually unlimited amount of airspace and the minimal number of aircraft occupying it, the need for ground-based control of aircraft was insignificant. Moreover, all flights at the time were with visual reference to the ground or water, hence the use of compass and landscape features as cues to self-navigate. Times have changed and the coordination needed to manage thousands of aircraft in the same airspace depends heavily on the reliability of technology to assist the human element in the system.

A rapid increase in the number of mid-air collisions brought about by a combination of uncontrolled airspace and increased traffic – especially during the First World War – reached a point at which a more formal arrangement for the management of airspace was needed to enhance safety and so that the benefits afforded by air travel could be realized. The foundations for the development of what has become today's ATM system can be traced to two milestone events: first, the introduction of 'basic rules of the air' and, second, the founding of the *International Commission for Air Navigation* (ICAN) in 1919. These were the key stepping stones upon which the ATM system as we know it today was founded, and both resulted from the Paris Convention of 1919 (see Chapter 1).

As early as 1920, it became evident that carriage by air was going to revolutionize the logistics and structures of commerce and the military forever. The main impediment to the growth potential being fully realized was the poor state of navigation systems. The speed at which demand for air services grew – particularly as a consequence of wartime priorities – resulted in inadequate research and development in the air safety aspects of flying. Accomplishing a military objective has a totally different set of assumptions and priorities from those required for establishing a commercial system of air travel.

International Air Traffic Standards

The *General Rules for Air Traffic Navigation* as defined by the ICAN were the *only* standards applicable to air navigation at the time, and even then only in those countries that had ratified the Paris Convention 1919. In the late 1920s, a significant rise in aircraft collisions – both with the ground and with other aircraft – prompted a new form of ATC based on visual aids to be introduced. This was a system that saw controllers flag signals to communicate with pilots.

It was not, however, until the Second World War that the potential of radar began to be fully explored, as it was utilized by nations battling in the War for military purposes. In the aftermath of the War, the civil aviation community began to apply the *radio detecting and ranging* or 'radar' technologies developed during wartime for the guidance and surveillance of civil aircraft.

The US Experience

The late 1920s also saw the development and introduction of radio communication devices, including the 'four course radio beacon' and later the 'light beacon'. By 1930, radio-equipped control towers were operating in the USA, which subsequently led to almost all aircraft being equipped with some degree of radiotelephone communication capability. As the benefits of independent navigation capability became evident and the advent of radio transmitters ensured the redundancy of 'flagmen', the potential of ATM to improve safety and efficiency in civil aviation became apparent. It was also clear that ATM would be a function of the resources allocated to the research and development of new and advanced technologies.

The impact of radio transmitters and communication being embraced by the emergent civil aviation industry triggered the establishment of radio-equipped towers. According to Starynin (2005), this in turn facilitated the use of radio communication, not only at towers but also by dispatchers to communicate with flight crews during the en-route phase of flight, as opposed to its initial application only at aerodromes. According to a 2002 report by the US Centennial of Flight Commission, the position of aircraft after departure was determined by controllers using maps and blackboards and little boat-shaped weights that came to be called shrimp boats. Information regarding the status of the flight and conditions on board was transmitted via telephone to airline dispatchers, who relayed this information to flight crews.

The founding of the ICAO came soon after on 6 June 1945, but more specifically the date bears particular significance for ATM and is considered in historical terms as the rebirth of ATC. The ICAO Doc. 7300, which specifies the rules and regulations for air navigation, would from this point on be considered the common set of rules adopted by all member states to the Chicago Convention.

The introduction of radar, which was originally developed by the British for military purposes, represented the second landmark invention of technology following the development of radio communication. This new technology had significant benefits for safety and efficiency, given that it minimized the risk of collision, gave controllers more information upon which they delivered more accurate navigation and importantly reduced the separation minima by half.

In the late 1960s, even greater efficiency was achieved with the introduction of transponders, a device which identified aircraft and thus improved radar performance. These transponders were deemed a requirement for aircraft flying in specific 'positive control' areas. Transponders were used and remain a most important component of today's ATM system, both in the aircraft and as ground-based equipment.

So, by the mid-1940s, the ATM system was becoming more sophisticated and the importance of continued research and development into new technologies was essential, given the increasing demand for air travel and the escalating congestion at major terminal locations. The regulation of air traffic played a central role during the Second World War, and such was its potential that it began to be used as a tool to manipulate the outcome of the conflict. This period in the history of aviation saw many changes which are today considered landmark, and none more so than the advent of jet aircraft in Germany towards the end of the War. It was, however, over a decade, and after the window design faults of the ill-fated Comet aircraft, before the proliferation of the commercial jet airliners with the entry into service of the Boeing B707 and Douglas DC-8 passenger jets.

The ability of jet aircraft to transport greater numbers of passengers led to an unprecedented increase in passenger movements. The US market from 1958 to 1977 registered passenger travel growth of more than 1,000 per cent. By 1958, more people crossed the Atlantic by air than by sea. The use of jet aircraft resulted in more passengers being airborne at any given time and as a result considerable strain was mounting on the air traffic system.

The combination of a disproportional increase in traffic – as compared to the level of infrastructure and resources available – and an experimental era of jet aircraft manufacturing led to spikes in aircraft accidents. One accident involving a mid-air collision between two aircraft over the Grand Canyon, killing 128 people on board both aircraft, in 1956 gave US lawmakers the ammunition to pass the *Federal Aviation Act 1958*. This statute facilitated the establishment of the then Federal Aviation Agency – now called the Federal Aviation Administration (FAA).

The governance and responsibility for civil and military navigation and air traffic control issues were delegated to the FAA, which was instrumental in implementing a series of wholesale changes in the rules governing air traffic management in an effort to reduce the occurrence of avoidable accidents like that which occurred over the Grand Canyon.

The European Experience

In Europe, the accident rate after the introduction of jet aircraft was not sustainable. Due to the improved aircraft performance capabilities of the commercial jet, seating capacity of aircraft increased. Consequently, when aircraft tragedies occurred, they were even more horrific in terms of loss of life. This development, and a series of high-profile jet aircraft accidents, became the catalyst for the establishment of a 'single organization entirely responsible for airspace . . . safety, efficiency and harmony' and provided the necessary powers and the ability to exercise change in each of these areas (Starynin 2005).

The signing of the *International Convention relating to Cooperation for the Safety of Air Navigation* signalled the first step towards establishing EUROCONTROL, which was to become the agency and forum responsible for the future management and regulation of European airspace. The preliminary work required to establish the framework upon which EUROCONTROL was to be based was the setting up of the *Association for the Development of ATC Methods and Equipment*. This body would develop common ATC standards and would then establish the process for adoption and enforcement on all member states – a process which was completed in 1963.

The years thereafter saw the organization segment, with particular areas of specialization assigned to various departments within EUROCONTROL. Technical aspects of equipment and services were assigned to one arm of the organization, whilst training of personnel was another area which received particular focus, especially given the importance of ensuring a standardized level of expertise across all member states. The *Institute of Air Navigation Services* (IANS) was set up to focus exclusively on this aspect of EUROCONTROL's responsibilities.

By the 1970s, second-generation jet aircraft had entered operation and were being acquired by many of the world's international airlines. This coincided with the *era of automation*, which was affecting many aspects of the aviation business, from the operation of aircraft themselves to ticketing, airport operations and ATM. In the USA, for example, by 1975 the FAA had successfully installed a computerized system at all *Air Route Traffic Control Centers* (ARTCCs) across the country, which presented aircraft location, speed and altitude information in real-time in a three-dimensional format. Soon after, this technology was also in use at 61 of the busiest airports across the USA, an upgrade in technology that brought an end to the use of 'shrimp boat markers'.

Given the trend towards bigger aircraft, corresponding with an increased demand for air services and thus a subsequent increase in strain on the ATM system, the FAA established the Central Flow Control Facility. The purpose of this facility, which is still in operation today, was to manage bottlenecks in a manner that caused minimal disruption elsewhere in the network. Being able to isolate any disruptions or spikes in delays to a confined part of the network is indicative of a robust ATM system and a key performance indicator for regulators and ANSPs.

It was during this same period that economic aspects of ATM and the regulations governing the services supplied by ANSPs began to come under scrutiny. The potential for growth if the regulatory noose were loosened was great, given the international nature of aviation. It was important to remember, however, that although this was the primary objective of the airline operators, for the ANSPs and regulators it was a matter of ensuring that excess strain was not placed on the ATM. Although the ATM system had surpassed its humble beginnings, it was still going through an essentially 'trial and error' phase in an attempt to meet the ever-increasing demand for air travel.

Airline Deregulation in the USA

The developments that occurred in the USA from the late 1970s to the early 1990s are a prime example of some of the ramifications of this type of 'trial and error' approach. The *Airline Deregulation Act 1978* had serious short-term ramifications for air transport in the region. The phasing out of economic regulation led to greater competition and lower airfares at a time when there was an increase in operating efficiency – largely as a result of improved aircraft and engine design and manufacture. However, it was not long after this that cracks in the system – which many feared would impede the growth of air transport – began to appear.

This period, appropriately termed the era of 'turbulence in the aviation system', was plagued by a shortage of resources, particularly specialist human resources in the ATM sector. The infrastructure which was underpinning the entire air transport network was insufficient, especially considering that further growth was expected. Industrial action and strikes by overworked and underpaid air traffic controllers were inevitable.

With the advantage of hindsight, this development may have been a blessing in disguise, given the potentially catastrophic ramifications which could have resulted had air transport services continued in the way they were during this period. On 5 August 1981, and after only three days of the national ATC industrial dispute, President Ronald Reagan fired 11,345 striking air traffic controllers when the workers refused to return to work. This subsequently led to the decertification of the *Professional Air Traffic Controller Organization* (PATCO), the union representing the disgruntled air traffic controllers involved in the strike action.

The FAA's failure to resolve the technological deficiencies, which were the cause of computer breakdowns and power outages, continued well into the 1990s. The IATA conducted a study into the cost of these failures to the industry and found that it equated to USD 3.5 billion per year, made up of wasted fuel, poor on-time performance and underutilization of aircraft. In response, the FAA exercised its regulatory powers by developing legislative reform, which it proposed to Congress as an overhaul of the funding options (via trust fund revenues) to finance the acquisition of infrastructure and training of personnel. Despite a number of wholesale changes, including a change in the payment structure of ATM staff which took into consideration the specific duties of each role, as well as the introduction of new technology that brought an end to the use of the systems which were in place from the 1960s, congestion issues continued to trouble the US ATM system.

This was the state of affairs until the opening of Denver International Airport in 1995. This international airport would be used as a blueprint upon which all other international airports in the USA would be modelled. The utilization of parallel runways, which facilitated a significant increase in ATM capacity, was also incorporated into the aerodrome design of the Detroit, Atlanta and Dallas-Fort Worth aerodromes.

The Terrorist Attacks of 2001

For all the research, development and procedural changes that the FAA implemented over the years, nothing could have prepared the US aviation industry for the events which took place on 11 September 2001. A detailed explanation of the aviation security aspects of this event was provided in Chapter 13; here we will consider only the related ATM issues arising from the attacks.

The following list provides a summary of the challenges faced by all those involved in the management of US airspace on that infamous day in aviation history:

- 4,500 planes carrying 350,000 passengers (in US-controlled airspace) were guided to a safe landing;

- within one hour of the order to ground all flights, 75 per cent had landed safely;
- 1,100 of the 4,500 flights airborne at the time had to change course and all were re-routed to a safe destination within 15 minutes of the grounding (this equates to one every second);
- two and half hours after the order to ground all aircraft, all flights (except those involved in the attacks) had made it to a safe destination without incident. This was achieved without minimum separation standards being breached.

The strain placed on the ATM system that day and in the days that followed was substantial to say the least. The strict procedures and mechanisms put into practice played a central role in preventing possible further catastrophes, given the uncertain context that aviation personnel were exposed to on that day. From the perspective of ATM personnel, the grounding of all flights is the most extreme measure which can be taken at any given time, especially when the immediate nature of the order is taken into consideration.

Reflecting on the events that unfolded on 9/11, critical elements that had a bearing on the successful manner in which the situation was handled can be identified, such as the adaptable nature of the ATM network, and the regulatory framework, which provided the foundations and tools to deal with the most serious and uncertain of situations successfully. It is also indicative of a framework capable of successfully adapting to multiple external factors which, when combined, can present a unique, uncertain situation which places a strain on resources.

THE INTERNATIONAL ATM STRUCTURE

Annex 11 of the ICAO: Air Traffic Services

The Chicago Convention 1944 will forever be recognized as a landmark event for aviation. It gave aviation representatives from all over the world an opportunity to establish a common level of understanding on the issues facing aviation and was used as a medium through which a roadmap for the aviation industry was developed.

Due to the minimal amount of air traffic during this period, establishing rules which would govern the control of ATM was not considered a priority. In fact, control of air traffic in 1944 was essentially unknown. The SARPs contained in Annex 11 of the Chicago Convention have expanded in scope over the years to take into consideration all facets of ATM which are applicable in the provision of air traffic services.

The objective of the provision of air traffic services, as defined in Annex 11, is to:

> Prevent collisions between aircraft, whether taxiing on the maneuvering area, taking off, landing, en-route, or in the holding pattern at the destination aerodrome.

The ability to achieve this objective is assisted by the segmentation of airspace into a series of contiguous *flight information regions* (FIRs), which designates the responsible management of portions of airspace to particular ATS providers. Everything from airspace over oceanic regions to mainland areas is assigned to flight information centres and ATC units, which provide the services defined as necessary for that FIR (see, for example, Figure 15.1).

Figure 15.1 Flight information regions over Italy

Source: Wikimedia Commons. Created by pikappa. Licensed under the Creative Commons Attribution-Share Alike 3.0 Unported licence

Classification of Flights

The flight rules applied by aircraft flying through these regions are dependent on whether they are operating under either *instrument flight rules* (IFRs) or *visual flight rules* (VFRs). The IFRs are used when flight outside of visual reference is considered unsafe. Under the IFRs, flight crews rely on the information provided by instruments in the flight deck. The discernible difference between the two sets of rules (apart from the reliance on visual aids as opposed to instruments) is that aircraft flying under VFRs must navigate with primary reference to visual landmarks.

Under the VFRs, it is the responsibility of flight crews to ensure that there is sufficient visibility (or else land, switch to the IFRs or just not fly at all – even *pilots* cannot actually control the weather) and to maintain sufficient clearance from other aircraft, whereas IFR flights are conducted through all but the severest of weather conditions and are thus supplemented with additional ATS, depending on the classification of airspace in which the flight is operating. For example, IFR flights in controlled airspace are provided with ATC services. The same aircraft could be flying through uncontrolled airspace at some point of the flight, at which point flight information services, which include information about the surrounding airspace, are relayed to the pilot, who then accepts responsibility to navigate in a manner which avoids other traffic.

Air Traffic Management Environmental Initiatives

ATM systems are rapidly evolving to meet the increased efficiency, safety, security, environmental and business demands of future aviation. The pursuit of these goals often results in conflict, and the industry is working towards developing a framework within which all these objectives may be pursued without conflicting with each other, all the while operating in a manner which demonstrates that aviation is environmentally conscious. This is not without its challenges.

The degree to which progress has been made can be mainly attributed to the ongoing allocation of financial resources into the development of new technology. Harnessing the knowledge that has been gained over the years and using this as input into the development of technology enables the industry to operate in a manner that facilitates growth without compromising the environment or safety standards. Service providers are today playing a more active role in the research and development of new initiatives, an important hurdle that is slowly being surpassed. Historically, service providers did just that – they provided a service while complying with regulatory requirements. In modern times, however, the scope of a service provider's activities has broadened.

When the process that is undertaken to get an aircraft airborne is broken down into individual phases, it becomes evident that significant efficiency gains remain to be exploited. Reducing taxiing times is practical, and potential technologies to reduce time spent by aircraft during this phase via a more flexible ATM system could reduce wasteful holding on the apron. The same applies to unnecessary airborne holding. Jet engines are much less efficient at lower altitudes, and reducing and eventually eliminating the time spent by aircraft in holding patterns will eliminate a significant issue for aviation and its impact on the environment, not only because of quantitative gains in efficiency but also due to qualitative gains such as reducing the exposure of the community to aircraft noise.

A significant challenge facing aviation at present is the development of a framework that allows for environmental, safety and commercial objectives not to impede each other. Over time, significant improvements have been made that facilitate the pursuit of all these goals. Aviation has entered a crucial phase of its evolution, and the following decades will see significant changes that will make the current systems seem outdated and inefficient.

The ATM system that relies on a network of ground-based navigation points is being phased out. Newer systems see improvements in efficiency and a shift in the way in which aircraft are operated. Traditional, ground-based navigation means passing over fixed points, and 'airways' are drawn between those points. Generally speaking, aircraft flying under the IFRs, which is most airliners, are required to fly along these airways and no other way. The requirement to stick to the airways makes it highly unlikely that the most efficient route is being flown on sectors all over the world. The resulting inefficiency adds approximately 10 per cent to the travel distance on average. However, changes are being made, and these inefficiencies are slowly being identified and addressed. Some ANSPs are even allowing pilots to select optimal routes along which to fly during cruise, rather than forcing them to stick to the airways.

The air transport industry has been making steady progress since the issue of environmental management became topical, and the removal of airspace restrictions forms part of the reason for the success to date. The collaboration of governments, regulators and service providers led to a Europe to China round trip flight being shortened by 15 minutes (as compared to pre-2007 flight times). The sectors affected recorded a reduction in emissions of 84,000 tonnes of carbon dioxide, highlighting the importance of small victories across the global network and reminding the industry and the community that every little bit can count. The decision in Europe to unify the management of air traffic via the formation of the Single European Sky initiative represented a step forward in the direction of removing the outdated notion of ATM within the confines of national boundaries. ATM of the future will be based instead on functional airspace blocks, regardless of whether these blocks cross international boundaries.

Functional airspace blocks may make the airspace itself less complex; however, impediments to achieving efficiency are still present in the form of political obstacles and bureaucracy. The congestion of airspace (because it is still congested) only adds operational complexity to these issues. The situation would be less complex if airspace management was exclusively the responsibility of the ANSPs of individual states. Instead, political considerations must be made and the needs of the military must be considered, and so must national boundaries.

In one sense, larger nations such as the USA, Canada and Australia are fortunate to have such a large portion of airspace falling within one jurisdiction and under the control of a single ANSP. The situation is much more politically complex in Europe, for example, where the Single European Sky initiative requires the cooperation of many jurisdictions within each 'block' of airspace. Essentially, countries are required to partially relinquish control over their sovereign airspace by allowing a foreign or international authority to control the air traffic within it. Advances by countries with large areas of airspace to manage can act as examples for implementation in places like Europe, and may perhaps facilitate agreements between the many and varied jurisdictions involved. However, care must be taken in order to ensure that individual nations retain sovereignty over their territorial airspace in the legal sense as well as in the practical sense. ANSPs must remain sensitive to the wishes of national governments within the airspace they control and must take care to remain politically neutral in the event of conflict between nations. International ANSPs must also tread the fine line of complying with the laws of all the nations whose territorial airspace they control.

Constant Descent Approach (CDA) represents the major proposed change to the operational procedures of aircraft and how they operate in the final phases of flight. To understand exactly what CDA involves and its benefits, the conventional procedures used should be explained. Conventionally, an aircraft is given clearance by ATC from the bottom level of what is called the 'holding stack' (6,000–7,000 feet) to descend to a specific altitude, typically 3,000 feet. The aircraft remains at this altitude until it intersects the 3 degree glide path to the runway. Inefficiencies are identifiable with this approach, since during the level phase of flight, the pilot would need to apply additional engine thrust to maintain speed and altitude.

As the name would suggest, the difference between the conventional approach and CDA is that airspace is managed in such a way that enables aircraft to maintain a more or less constant rate of descent until their destination is reached. Thus, the aircraft remains higher for longer, and this approach eliminates the need for fluctuations in engine power until the time of landing. This has knock-on effects for certain parts of the community exposed to aircraft noise, since the noise impact is mitigated to some extent for those under the flight path. Aircraft emissions are also minimized due simply to the absence of a spike in engine power to maintain level flight. Importantly, a constant, stabilized approach enables flight crew to make a smooth transition to a visual approach once the runway is in sight.

At the moment, the trade-offs between safety, capacity and optimal environmental performance are not well defined. The pursuit of efficiency poses an interesting dilemma for ANSPs – shorter routes negatively impact upon the bottom line and are therefore financially counterproductive (not taking into consideration an increase in capacity). Acknowledging this and working with fellow stakeholders to develop a framework that creates incentives for good environmental performance is the major hurdle standing in the way of ATM reducing its contribution to aviation's carbon footprint.

Safety Management and ATM Systems

With regard to safety management, the enforcement of the SMS requirement by the ICAO for ATM service providers has played a central role in improving safety in aviation as a whole. The implementation of a safety management programme within the context of ATM means that it is essential, given the interlocking nature of aviation service provision, whereby the ATM system is heavily reliant on airport infrastructure and cooperation, hence the need for a common implementation of this standard. Broadly speaking, the ICAO has set minimum requirements which apply to the provision of any service which requires an SMS to be in place. These requirements are:

- identify safety standards;
- ensure that remedial action necessary to maintain an acceptable level of safety is implemented;
- provide for continuous monitoring and regular assessment of the safety level achieved; and
- aim to make continuous improvement to the overall level of safety.

What follows is an excerpt from Annex 11 of the ICAO from the section which identifies this requirement:

> 2.26.1 States shall implement systematic and appropriate ATS safety management programmes to ensure that safety is maintained in the provision of ATS within airspaces and at aerodromes.
>
> 2.26.2 States shall establish the acceptable level of safety and safety objectives applicable to the provision of ATS within their airspace and at their aerodromes.
>
> 2.26.4 States shall identify actual and potential hazards and determine the need for remedial action, ensure that remedial action necessary to maintain an acceptable level of safety

is implemented, and provide for continuous monitoring and regular assessment of the safety level achieved.

2.26.5 Any significant safety-related change to the ATC system, including the implementation of a reduced separation minimum or a new procedure, shall only be effected after a safety assessment has demonstrated that an acceptable level of safety will be met and users have been consulted.

Annex 19 on Safety Management Systems now also relevantly provides:

4.1.7 The SMS of an ATS provider, in accordance with Annex 11, shall be made acceptable to the State responsible for the provider's designation.

Whilst it does not say much about ATS, the creation of Annex 19 meant that the State Safety Oversight System is applicable to the oversight of all product and service providers. Standard 1.1 of Appendix 1 reads:

> The State shall promulgate a comprehensive and effective aviation law, consistent with the size and complexity of the State's aviation activity and with the requirements contained in the Convention on International Civil Aviation, that enables the State to regulate civil aviation and enforce regulations through the relevant authorities or agencies established for that purpose.

These 'relevant authorities' include ATS providers. Standard 1.2 of Appendix 1 also reads that the aviation law 'shall provide personnel performing safety oversight functions access to the aircraft, operations, facilities, personnel and associated records, as applicable, of service providers'. The creation of the SMSs, essentially, was to make the whole process more internationally harmonized and safer.

Applying the SMS requirement with regard to the provision of ATS has contributed to a higher level of safety in international civil aviation. As demand for air services and thus the load placed on the ATM system increases over time, the need for more stringent measures to address safety issues in the provisions of ATS is essential, given the potential for good or bad safety practices to filter through to other aspects of the broader aviation network.

Other components of Annex 11 focus on alerting services for aircraft in distress, infrastructure requirements for air–ground communications, as well as ways to ensure a common level of understanding in terms of contingency measures for identifying air routes in the absence of being able to rely on geographical references.

INTERNATIONAL ATM REGULATORY SYSTEMS

The Chicago Convention established the foundation upon which today's ATM system services the international airline community. The ICAO Doc. 7300 contains the rules and regulations regarding the provision of air navigation services and control. Although the aviation industry prides itself on applying standards on a universal level, it is still worth identifying the various approaches adopted by regulatory agencies across the world to see how they have incorporated the SARPs contained in the ICAO Annexes into the domestic regulatory framework of their respective region. This section focuses on three key aviation markets: Europe (EUROCONTROL), the USA (the FAA) and Australia (the Office of Airspace Regulation).

The European ATM Regulatory System

As was explained earlier in this chapter, the foundation of EUROCONTROL was in direct response to the need for one authority to be designated with the responsibility of incorporating the ICAO SARPs with regard to ATM services across the European region. Much has changed over the years, and many initiatives and policies implemented by EUROCONTROL have contributed to the overall level of safety and efficiency of European aviation, improving the situation to such an extent that it is considered a benchmark for the global aviation community. These standards, adopted from the ICAO guidance material contained in Annex 11, are used as a blueprint upon which EUROCONTROL develops its own regulations, taking into consideration contextual factors in order to establish the best framework upon which it can cater for the European market that it is responsible for serving.

The Structure of EUROCONTROL Given the uniform nature of aviation regulation generally, it is critical for safeguarding measures to be incorporated into any regulatory framework in order to avoid the possibility of the widespread implementation of a standard or practice that is flawed. Given the obligations of all member states to meet the requirements of the regulator, any incorrect information contained in the documentation and guidance material will likely take effect on a grand scale. With this in mind, a *Regulatory Committee* (RC) and a *Regulatory Unit* (RU) were established within EUROCONTROL to act as a mechanism to prevent them from filtering through to the wider aviation community.

The RC allocates a majority of its resources into providing support to the RU, which plays the role of enforcer in the framework and has total control over the implementation of new regulations or amendments to existing ones in member countries. Another of the RU's duties focuses on the *Regulatory Work Programme* (RWP), which was created as a means of monitoring airspace issues amongst members and of identifying if the regulatory documents being delivered to members are achieving the goals set in the broader ATM strategy for that region and the Single European Sky programme (explained in more detail later in this section).

The process by which a regulatory document is constructed and then distributed is systematic. The six steps which make up this process are based on the EUROCONTROL Notice of Proposed Rulemaking (NPR) process, with each phase drawing on the experience and expertise of various stakeholders affected by the proposed regulation. The first major consideration is determining if there is a need for the regulatory change. This is important, given that if the need for action on a matter is proven to be unfounded at a later stage, critical resources and time have been expended, whilst also giving the underlying problem opportunities to affect the normal operating procedures across the region.

Following consultation with recognized experts in the field of interest, a cost-benefit analysis is conducted to determine whether the potential improvement in safety and efficiency justifies the time and resources necessary to enforce the change in all member states. If this is deemed to be the case, a draft version of the regulation is delivered to the *Safety Regulation Commission* (SRC), who has the authority to dismiss the proposal or to accept it. Once receipt of all comments and considerations are acknowledged and the necessary amendments are made, the fifth and sixth phases of the process can be completed. At this stage, the final draft is given to the EUROCONTROL directorate, which represents the final hurdle to the regulation being published.

The rate at which demand for air services is growing is a key consideration for authorities like EUROCONTROL as it tries to establish a framework capable of supporting a rapidly changing industry. Developing initiatives ranging from safety issues influencing the accident rate to addressing capacity issues as well as the long-term impact of the provision of air services on the environment are some of the issues which EUROCONTROL regards as threats to the sustainability of aviation in Europe. Although much has been discussed in this chapter in relation to the harmonized implementation of the ICAO SARPs, the provision of ATC is still very much segmented within the sovereign borders of each member of EUROCONTROL. The *Single European Sky* (SES) aims to primarily address this main impediment to seamless travel and by doing so essentially reforms the architecture of European ATC.

For all the developments in the ATM framework over the years, the underlying foundations have remained unchanged. Such is the scale of the restructuring of the ATM framework to facilitate the adoption of the SES that it will no doubt positively impact on key indicators outside the scope of ATM – that is, economic, environmental, technological and institutional indicators. On 10 March 2004, the European Parliament and the European Council took the first step towards the creation of a SES with the acceptance of the SES's first legislative package being made up of the following:

- the framework for the creation of a SES (No 549/2004);
- the provision of Air Navigation Services (ANS) in a SES (No 550/2004);
- the organization and use of airspace in a SES (No 551/2004); and
- the interoperability of the European Air Traffic Management (EATM) network in a SES (No 552/2004).

It should be noted that as of June 2008, any revisions to SES regulations were adopted under the name SES second package. Within the SES framework, the Single European Sky ATM Research (SESAR) follow-up programme has the goal of creating the future ATM system to be used from 2020 onwards. It is a public–private partnership with EUROCONTROL, the European Commission and many private aviation companies.

Air traffic congestion was a key factor behind these rule changes, given that the strain on resources at the time was resulting in an undersupply of ATS in parts of European airspace. With forecasts indicating a doubling in air traffic levels by 2020, the need for proactive action was necessary. The creation of a common upper European airspace aimed to address this impediment to growth. As a means of ensuring a successful transition to new regulatory obligations, the methodology of the Europeans in relation to the implementation of such large-scale reform has been to facilitate cooperation as a means of ensuring real-time common knowledge of the state of the reform process across the entire industry. Experts and stakeholders affected by the proposed changes are also encouraged to contribute throughout the process to developing the rules.

Based on mandates handed down by the *Single Sky Committee*, EUROCONTROL has a key role to play in the implementation of the SES. The Single Sky Committee, which is made up of two representatives from each member state, provides support to the

European Commission once rules have been drafted. An important aspect of the contribution of the Single Sky Committee is that its advice to the European Commission takes into consideration the interests of all users and thus acts as a point of contact between the industry and the rule-maker.

> The second regulatory package on the Single European Sky (SES II) was approved in 2009 and it changed the SES focus from capacity to general performance. The ultimate goal is to increase the economic, financial and environmental performance of the provisions of European Air Navigation Services. The package created, amongst other things, a comprehensive EU-wide performance scheme (No 691/2010), including the EU-wide performance targets in areas of cost-efficiency, capacity and environment. It also created a notion of 'Functional Airspace Blocks' (FABs), blocks aiming to create enhanced cooperation between the air navigation service providers (ANSPs) and NSAs attain operational efficiency gains. In June 2013, the European Commission proposed an interim update of SES: Single European Sky 2+. This package is aiming for more independence on NSAs, implementing more of a customer focus, diversifying support services and improving FABs to make them more flexible.
>
> (European Commission 2017: 5)

In 2023 the final breakthrough for SES was achieved when the EASA welcomed a decision by the European Commission (EC) to bring air traffic management into EASA's regulatory framework. The new set of rules lays the groundwork for a more efficient and uniform approach to operations improvement in support of the Single European Sky initiative. For the first time, there will be a single EU regulatory framework covering all aviation domains on the ground and in the sky, driving the transformation of the air transport system.

In April 2024 the European Commission adopted a further package of secondary legislation on drones and vertical take-off and landing (VTOL) capable aircraft, which puts the final rules in place for the launch of Urban Air Mobility (UAM), including air taxi services. The legislation introduces a comprehensive set of requirements for piloted electric air taxis, spanning the domains of Air Operations (Air OPS), Flight Crew Licensing (FCL), Standardised European Rules of the Air (SERA) and Air Traffic Management (ATM). It also establishes criteria and processes for the certification and maintenance of drones or RPAS.

The package is the last legislative element required for the launch of air taxi services, complementing other existing legislation. Air taxis will additionally require certification from EASA before such services can become operational in Europe.

The USA's ATM Regulatory System

From initially being a luxury that only a few could consider utilizing, air transportation has evolved into a service readily available to people from virtually all socio-economic backgrounds. As is the case elsewhere in the world, the USA today relies heavily on the safe, reliable and affordable provision of air transportation. Recent years have seen the aviation industry in the USA in survival mode as it struggled to effectively manage multiple stochastic issues, resulting in the sustainability of many airlines being put to the test, a test that many failed to pass. However, for all the obstacles faced, today the demand for air services outweighs any increase in infrastructure and thus has had a detrimental impact on the quality and cost efficiency of air travel and the provision of ATS.

The ATC system in the USA is operated by the FAA. Federal involvement in the provision of ATS can be traced back to the early twentieth century when the need for an established authority to be responsible for the management of such matters first arose. It was as early as 1926 when the passing of the *Air Commerce Act* delegated the enforcement of air traffic rules, the licensing of pilots, the certification of aircraft and the operation of aids for air navigation to the Department of Commerce. Over the next two decades, the federal government's role in the provision of ATS began to increase to the point that by the end of the Second World War, all aspects of ATC were considered federal matters.

It was not until 1958 that all aspects of ATM were consolidated within a single federal agency, a change facilitated by the enactment of the *Federal Aviation Act 1958*. The founding of the FAA brought an end to what was up to that point a scattered approach to ATM issues, whereby multiple agencies were individually managing particular aspects associated with the provision of ATS with minimal (if any) collaboration or coordination.

Jammed airspace has meant that the FAA has had to take a modernized and innovative approach to ATM, which has resulted in the creation of NextGen (Next Generation Air Transportation System) – a system designed to accommodate up to three times the volume of current air traffic in US airspace by more efficient use of airport facilities as well as national airspace. It was originally formed in the early 2000s and began taking form in December 2003 as part of the *Vision 100 – Century of Aviation Reauthorization Act*. It essentially replaces RADAR with 'Automatic Dependent Surveillance-Broadcast' (ADS-B), which is a much more accurate broadcasting systems disseminating information such as speed, location and route to air traffic controllers and other aircraft by using satellite radio signals and ground stations. Interestingly, it provides a new way for pilots and controllers to access information in a digital format – called Data Comm. Information includes things like the transfer of textual clearances, approach procedures and instructions from controllers to pilots and air traffic controllers. As of March 2017, the FAA has said that it has delivered more than USD 2.72 billion in benefits under the NextGen modernization scheme.

In the case of the FAA, projections show that in order for NextGen to be completely operable across the USA over the next 15 years, the FAA would need to allocate USD 1 billion of its budget each year to ensure that a successful, widespread implementation takes place. The magnitude of the task at hand for the FAA is magnified due to the issues it is left to deal with once funding is secured. There exists a need for the fundamental governance principles upon which the organization was founded to be given a contemporary makeover which takes into account the unique contextual changes that have taken place since the founding of the FAA. Displaying an inability to adapt will see the same underlying issues being faced today reappearing in the future. With traffic figures forecast to grow significantly, the situation will worsen when considering that in 20 years' time, nearly twice as many passengers will be occupying the same amount of airspace.

In summary, the three main impediments to sustainable growth facing the FAA are:

- *Inflexible funding*: the emergence of LCCs has had a direct impact on the funding available to the FAA to implement reform. This has resulted in a relative decrease in excise tax collected from certificate holders. This situation has been on the decline since LCCs began to change the face of competition in the airline industry.

For example, 7.5 per cent of fares are collected by the FAA and as competition has increased, airlines have responded by offering cheaper airfares to remain competitive, hence the fall in revenue at the disposal of the FAA.

- *Risks associated with the implementation of new technology*: the FAA's track record in relation to the development and implementation of new technology has not been encouraging. There is not much evidence of a successful implementation of new technology that has delivered the benefits on which the initial proposals were based. Many projects have ended up over budget and have not been completed within the specified timeframe. Industry analysts widely hold the belief that until the reform of ATC is in the hands of an entity outside of the government's control, the risks to which the ATM network in the USA is exposed will never be resolved.
- *Political constraints*: the threat posed by the widespread application of NextGen to the job market within the ATC sector represents a major impediment to receiving full backing from the government, which would assist in fast-tracking its application. The government is reluctant to encourage a fast adoption of this new technology, given that if it does so, it exposes itself to a backlash from the aviation community directly affected. NextGen essentially makes many aviation professionals that today play a key role in the provision of ATS redundant. For example, staff currently employed in en-route control centres and terminal radar approach control facilities face the likely outcome of having their day-to-day tasks completed by automated systems as part of the broader NextGen concept.

Other Regional Issues: The Australian Experience

By way of comparison with Europe and the USA, Australia has a fraction of the volume of air traffic and is also fortunate to be exposed to minimal fluctuations in meteorological patterns; nevertheless, considerable ATM system challenges remain. These include infrastructure renewal, most notably the replacement of ageing radar and navigational aids, and the need for better workforce planning.

Australia remains at the forefront of global air traffic management innovation. OneSKY Australia is a partnership between Airservices Australia – Australia's ANSP – and the Commonwealth Department of Defence that will replace existing civil and military ATM systems with a single system known as the Civil Military Air Traffic Management System (CMATS). Delivery of this new technology will support more efficient service delivery through trajectory-based operations and route optimization.

OneSKY improves safety through shared situational awareness, as it will create one FIR allowing any controller to access the same flight information at any time, which will remove the risk of sharing incorrect information. It will also have the capacity to meet the demands of increasing air traffic growth into the future. OneSKY replaces the Australian Advanced Air Traffic System (TAAATS), which was first commissioned in 2000 and has had over 200 system changes since then.

Since the early 1990s, Australia has led the world in ATM with the introduction of the Australian Advanced Air Traffic System (TAAATS) and the increased use of satellite-based technology – for instance with required navigation performance (RNP) approaches. TAAATS was fully operational by the mid-1990s and is based around two major en route ATC centres at Brisbane and Melbourne. TAAATS offers controllers an integrated air situation display that, amongst other things, has potential to calculate points of conflict dynamically and to display this information on the air situation display. TAAATS has played an integral role in keeping Australian airspace safe for over two decades.

Advances in technology, growth in traffic volumes and the emergence of new industry participants such as UAS and UAV operators, and many other factors, mean the time has come for a new system to lead Australian aviation into the future. However, the industry is rapidly evolving as global demand for air travel increases and technological advancements open up new opportunities. As noted by the then Chair of Airservices (Air Chief Marshal Sir Angus Houston AK, AFC (Ret'd)):

> The factors influencing air space management over the next five years have never been so diverse, complex or exciting. Aviation has always been an industry that thrives on innovation, but the coalescence of technological advancements, globalisation and increased customer expectations is providing an unprecedented context in which we must continue to deliver safety and service excellence.

Australia has continued as a world leader in technological advancement with the transition to the ADS-B system. ADS-B is an advanced surveillance technology that combines a satellite positioning service, aircraft avionics and ground infrastructure to enable more accurate transmission of information between equipped aircraft and ATC. Apart from safety enhancements, this system is potentially a real money saver due to the reduced expenditure for radar equipment on the ground in hostile sites.

The system enables an aircraft fitted with the appropriate avionics to continually and accurately broadcast information, including identification, current position, altitude and velocity. ADS-B uses information from a position service, i.e. the Global Positioning System (GPS), to identify the aircraft's location. This enables more timely and accurate information than that provided by conventional primary or secondary radar.

The pursuit of these objectives is not peculiar to the Australian sector, but like all ANSPs very much depends upon the availability of adequate resources. The short-, medium- and long-term goals for the ATM system in Australia have been identified as such in order to ensure that when the time comes, the regulator and the stakeholders affected are in a position to ensure the complete application of the standards.

The Global Air Traffic Management Operational Concept

Safety regulators and ANSPs throughout the world are cooperating to develop short-, medium- and long-term ATM plans and strategies which are consistent with the international standards contained in the Global Air Traffic Management Operational Concept (GATMOC), which, *inter alia,* outlines the *ICAO Roadmap: Beyond 2025* to develop a harmonized and interoperable ATM system for the global aviation community.

The success but also the greatest challenge for air safety regulators and ANSPs is to consistently implement globally recognized ATM standards. All longer term strategies in relation to ATM must be underpinned by the continued application of the ICAO standards.

Rapid advances in technology have seen the emergence of autonomous aircraft as a new airspace user with many industries such as mining, agriculture and emergency services already embracing the technology. Aerial taxi services, for example, are currently being trialled and it won't be long before their use becomes widespread. This transformation is not without challenges and will require innovative ATM and regulatory solutions to ensure that our skies remain safe for all airspace users and the community.

In general terms, the following list covers the major long-term ATM objectives (2020–25) that will enhance both the levels of safety and operational efficiencies of ATM systems throughout the world. These initiatives include:

- the wider application of satellite technology and monitoring consistency with international timetables, including the provision of required back-up ground-based facilities;
- PBN capability appropriate to the operation to be used by all IFR aircraft; and
- the electronic surveillance of traffic by either aircraft or ANSPs to be ensured for all operations in controlled airspace.

The pursuit for complete harmonization of ATM and navigation systems globally is contingent upon the effective application and safety oversight of SARPs developed by the ICAO. These international standards are designed not only to improve safety and operational efficiency, but also to incorporate mechanisms which ensure that these objectives are *not* achieved at the expense of the environment – a most important topic for the entire aviation and broader community that will be considered in Chapter 17.

How Technology is Revolutionizing the Skies

Air traffic control is a complex, dynamic system that relies on an abundance of technology. It typically involves an interaction between the pilot and a ground station, which monitors and guides aircraft safely through their journeys. In theory, future automation will rely more heavily on AI, which is already making itself known in air traffic control. For instance, Canadian-based company Searidge has developed an AI platform that enhances the decisions of a human traffic controller, with the logic being applied to automated systems of the future.

Of course, it would be unreasonable to assume that all air traffic control will be automated in the future. The level of complexity in some systems means that a human element will always be necessary. This means we must continually look at ways to improve the efficiency and accuracy of manned systems. One such technology is Automatic Dependent Surveillance-Broadcast (ADS-B), a satellite network for air traffic control. Whereas older systems use radar and ground antennas, ADS-B uses satellites to track aircraft and provide accurate real-time information to traffic control.

Using satellites means controllers can plan more efficient routes and help aircraft avoid congested airspace. It also means weather-related decisions can be more accurate, helping aircraft to avoid delays and areas of turbulence. The overall goal is to improve safety and efficiency, which has already been demonstrated in Europe, North America and Australasia.

Back on the ground, augmented reality has the potential to make air traffic controllers' jobs much easier.

NASA is currently developing a system that will overlay flight data on real-world images, and focusing this technology for drone systems and Advanced Air Mobility

(AAM) (nasa.gov/aeronautics/nasas-using-augmented-reality-to-transform-air-traffic-management/). But unsurprisingly, this human-machine interface will be more challenging with unmanned aircraft. There are two possible solutions to this. The first is the growing trend of automation in air traffic control, as this would be ideal for unmanned systems. Automating their interactions with a ground station means the human element can be removed completely, allowing the two systems to communicate seamlessly. But as we have witnessed with tragic mid-air collisions, TCAS interface with ATC requires careful consideration. We need to make automation a better 'team player'.

Advanced air mobility vehicles include electric air taxis, hybrid concepts, autonomous drones and everything in between. First generation of eVTOL aircraft will likely be piloted (airbourne) and rely on traditional systems. To integrate AAM aircraft into the airspace safely, collaboration is required between regulators, OEMs and ANSP. As eVTOL aircraft are still early in the development phase there is time to develop air traffic management systems for the future.

Another emerging area of technological innovation is with the introduction of Digitised Aerodrome Service (DAS) or Digital Towers. Safety regulators and ANSPs throughout the world are cooperating with the first major airport to introduce a digital tower being London City Airport in 2021. There are already digital towers in Sweden, Germany, Argentina, Brazil, Hungary and Norway, with others being installed in Denmark and France.

In Australia, the new AUD 5.3 billion Western Sydney International (WSI) Airport will have digital towers. Sixteen cameras in an array will monitor 360 degrees around the aerodrome and be projected onto screens as a Digitised Aerodrome Service at Eastern Creek 20 kilometres away. In an ABC television interview in March 2024, former head of safety for Qantas Airways and Chair of Avlaw Aviation Consulting, Professor Ronald Bartsch AM, stated (ABC 2024):

> The technology was developed 15 years ago and has been operational for the past decade and has proven to be safe and reliable. It's what they call in the industry a '*safety quinella*' where you have a win-win situation of increased safety and increased efficiency. Australia's adoption of the DAS system at WSI will not see the end of traditionally manned control towers because many are still fit-for-purpose. The introduction of digital towers is no different from how technology has evolved in other areas of aviation. Pilots now use electronic flight bags, rather than carrying maps and charts. Now they're all issued with iPads.

In conclusion it should come as no surprise that technology is changing the way air traffic control works. After all, it's always been a tech-heavy field and an industry that welcomes any way to improve efficiency and safety. We are currently in a period of potentially major industry overhaul, so it will be interesting to see what air traffic control looks like in the next decade or so.

16 Safety Management and Accident Investigation

INTRODUCTION

Throughout this book, reference has been made to the principle of risk management, the aviation safety regulator's primary tool for controlling the risk of aviation activities. While there are formal methods available for the quantification of risk, these are highly specialized techniques that are beyond the scope and requirements of this publication. However, the reader should develop the mindset that the management of risk is the foundation of the aviation safety regulation system and regulators will expect airline executives, operational managers and indeed any aviation professional to approach their duties with the idea of minimizing risk foremost in their minds.

The underlying philosophy of all aviation legislation globally is the promotion of safety in aviation-related activities. Throughout the world, all aviation regulators have safe aviation outcomes as part of their statutory charter. Interestingly, 'safety' is rarely defined or explained in legislation. Indeed, throughout this publication, numerous references have been made to air safety and aviation safety without any definition having yet been provided.

According to a former head of the FAA, 'without a sanctioned definition of safety, there can be no safety yardstick, no safety standard' (Schiavo 1997). Consequently, internationally accepted definitions of safety and safety-related terms will be provided together with an overview of the obligation imposed by the ICAO standards in respect of safety management and accident investigation.

This chapter should provide the reader with a good overview of the framework of aviation safety regulation and the obligations and responsibilities that this system imposes on the regulator, the manufacturer and the operator. The second half of this chapter considers the obligations imposed upon states by the Chicago Convention 1944 with respect to aircraft accidents and serious incidents. These two areas share an underlying rationale: they seek to proactively reduce the level of risk deriving from aviation activities and to promote and enhance the safety of air navigation.

To develop a more comprehensive understanding of any particular aspect of either of these topics, it is necessary to reference the regulations and explanatory material promulgated in the relevant state regulatory authority. Above all, always take the time to discuss your plans in detail with the authority; this will ensure that you and the regulator have agreed on the path ahead and hence costly, time-consuming mistakes will be avoided.

Safety Defined

This chapter begins by explaining the fundamental importance of safety with respect to all aviation activities. In particular, we look at the legislative basis of safety-related

DOI: 10.4324/9781032652146-16

standards and requirements, both those deriving from a state's obligations under the Chicago Convention and also domestic statutory requirements. However, before any meaningful discussion of these topics can be commenced, it is important to clearly articulate the subject matter in question. We must begin by asking: what is safety?

Safety, due to its nebulous nature, is a subjective experience. It has been described as the freedom from those conditions that cause accidents. This assessment would present no difficulties if one could be certain that all the conditions that cause accidents had, in advance, been considered. Unfortunately, history and hindsight have proven to be the only reliable sources of such information.

Other definitions of safety consider something as 'safe' if its risks are judged to be acceptable. This line of reasoning is probably more pragmatic in that it acknowledges both the subjective and relative nature of safety – the need for judgment and a determination of what constitutes an acceptable level of risk. Many state regulators define safety in the following way: 'A state in which the risk of harm (to persons) or damage is limited to an acceptable level'.

Necessarily, whenever judgment is exercised to assess what is 'acceptable', there must be reliance on some predetermined value or objective. Whether we like it or not, any assessment of safety will always be an estimate. The definition of safety used by the CASA in Australia as the basis of its Safety Management System (SMS) implementation programme has been adopted from the ICAO definition. The Australian safety regulator has defined safety as:

> The state in which the probability of harm to persons or of property damage is reduced to, and maintained at, a level which is *As Low as Reasonably Practical* (ALARP) through a continuing process of hazard identification and risk management.
>
> (Emphasis in original)

The elimination of accidents and/or serious incidents and the achievement of similar absolutes of control would certainly be desirable. However, such absolutes of control are unachievable goals in open and dynamic operational contexts. Hazards are inevitable elements of aviation operational contexts. Failures and operational errors will occur in aviation, despite efforts to prevent them. No human activity or human-made system can be guaranteed to be free from hazards and operational errors.

Safety has since around the early 1990s been viewed as the consequence of the management of certain organizational processes, with the final objective being keeping the safety risks of the consequences of hazards in operational contexts under organizational control. The management of these processes is delivered through core business functions and management systems, such as financial management, human resources management, legal management and similar functions.

The Safety Space

The perspective advanced by the ICAO is that, contrary to the 'safety stereotype', safety is not the only priority of aviation organization; rather, safety management must necessarily be balanced against production objectives. The following extract from third edition of the ICAO *Safety Management Manual* (SMM) (2013) presents this balancing process through the concept of 'the safety space':

> The safety space is the zone where an organization balances desired production while maintaining required safety protection through safety risk controls. . . . [D]ecision making should involve an assessment of both the value added to the organization's product or service objectives as well as the safety risks involved. The allocation of excessive resources to protection or risk controls may result in the product or service becoming unprofitable, thus jeopardizing the viability of the organization.

Conversely, the safety space must be sufficient in scope so as to ensure that the risk of accidents occurring is not unacceptable for that organization. As further noted in the SMM, the acceptability of safety performance is often 'influenced by domestic and international norms and culture'. The ICAO considers it necessary for each service provider to define and promulgate a 'safety boundary', which can provide an indication that an unbalanced resource allocation is developing that may produce unacceptable risks. This boundary can and should be subject to review and development in line with changing circumstances.

All aviation organizations, regardless of their nature, have a business component to a greater or lesser degree. Thus, all aviation organizations can be considered business organizations. A simple question is then relevant to shed light on the truthfulness, or lack thereof, of the safety stereotype: what is the fundamental objective of a business organization? The answer to this question is obvious: to deliver the service for which the organization was created in the first place, to achieve production objectives and eventually to deliver dividends to stakeholders.

There is no aviation organization that has been created to deliver only safety. Even organizations that act as guardians of aviation safety are subject to efficiency constraints, internal or external, as dictated by their stakeholders. This includes the ICAO, national and supranational civil aviation authorities, international trade organizations and safety advocate international organizations.

Safety management should therefore be regarded as just another core business function that must be considered at the same level and with the same importance as other core business functions. For aviation organizations to effectively manage this particular business function, safety management should be 'delivered' through an organization's SMS.

THE CONTEMPORARY APPROACH TO SAFETY

From the early 1920s up until the Chicago Convention 1944, commercial aviation lacked comprehensive safety oversight. Technology was unreliable and frail, and the supporting infrastructure was inadequate. Safety oversight by regulatory authorities was inconsistent and mostly reactive, and the hazards underlying aviation operations were not being effectively assessed.

As a consequence, commercial aviation was characterized by a high frequency of accidents. For instance, immediately after the Second World War, airlines in the USA averaged a major passenger accident every 16 days. The fatality rate, measured per 100 million passengers flown, was in excess of 1,300. By the mid- to late 1950s, the rate had fallen to approximately 440. Forty years later in the mid-1990s, the rate had reduced tenfold to 45. From 2003 to 2007, the rate practically stabilized at 2.5 per 100 million passengers flown – a staggering 520-fold reduction in just 60 years.

Safety Methodology

The early safety process by airlines, accident investigation authorities and regulators focused on the need to prevent frequent accidents. Consequently, the investigation of accidents became the principal means of prevention: the 'fly-crash-fix-fly' approach to safety management as summarized here:

> In the past, the improvement of aviation safety was characterized by a fly-crash-fix-fly approach. We would fly airplanes, have the occasional crash, and would investigate the cause(s) to prevent it from happening again. Sometimes the causes would be weather-related or would be caused by a mechanical failure, but more often the cause would be determined as a human error – which usually involved the pilot. Essentially, the prevailing philosophy was once the cause was determined to be the pilot, we simply needed to encourage other pilots not to make the same mistakes.
>
> (Stolzer *et al.* 2008: 13)

The credit for the phenomenal reduction in the rate of accidents since the mid-1940s must be directed to aircraft manufacturers, airline operators and regulatory oversight agencies, and also to a certain extent to safety research by organizations and academics.

ICAO SAFETY REQUIREMENTS

The ICAO Approach to Safety

Since the mid-1990s – around which time the rate of decrease of accidents began to plateau – it became apparent that the effectiveness of safety strategies based on systemic analysis of accident data was nearing its limits. An additional but complementary strategy was required to continue the good work, hence the current worldwide focus by the ICAO on mandating safety management systems and the integration of human factors into these systems.

Back in 1996, the ICAO Air Navigation Bureau (ANB) reconsidered its perspective on a number of issues relating to air safety in relation to the modernization of aviation safety regulatory authorities, and in particular which management practices should be adopted by the ICAO in its pursuit of risk management. In a meeting of aviation experts, the following direction was decided:

> [The] ICAO . . . advocates a proactive approach to safety based upon the *identification* and *cancellation* of *system hazards* and the risks that such hazards involve before they combine with human failures to generate accidents. Within this approach, the process to be pursued is risk management, and the outcome of this process is safety. The management of safety is indeed the management of risk.
>
> (Emphasis added)

Even in the modern context, risk management for safety outcomes requires continued attention and re-evaluation. This is due to the persistent growth of air traffic, the fast pace of technological change, the emergence of new types of hazards and business models, the changing nature of accidents, along with the role of automation in contributing to the increasing complexity of system components.

At the ICAO High-level Safety Conference 2010, a declaration was made for the ICAO to develop a new Annex dedicated to 'safety management responsibilities and processes which would address the safety management responsibilities of States framed under the State Safety Programme (SSP)'. This reflects the ICAO's continuing commitment to safety processes and safety management as a whole.

In response to the 2010 declaration, the ICAO Air Navigation Commission established the Safety Management Panel to provide recommendations for the development of this new Annex. Annex 19 to the Chicago Convention, 'Safety Management', was adopted in February 2013 and became applicable on 14 November 2013.

The new Annex operates alongside the ICAO *Safety Management Manual* (SMM), which was first released in 2006. The third edition (2013) incorporates comprehensive information for the principles and concepts of safety management, as well as detailed guidance on SSP and SMS implementation in accordance with the new Annex 19. The fourth edition of the SMM was published in 2018 (Doc 9859-AN/47, 4th ed, 2018). It contains guidance for mechanisms to facilitate information sharing of best practices from a range of organizations through online media.

The bottom line is that safety risks must be kept under an appropriate level of control notwithstanding the fact that a system as open and dynamic as aviation can still be managed to maintain the appropriate balance between production and protection. However, in its 4th edition in 2018, the Manual (para 2.1.3) changes tack:

> Aviation safety is dynamic. New safety hazards and risks continuously emerge and must be mitigated. As long as safety risks are kept under an appropriate level of control, a system as open and dynamic as aviation can still be kept safe. It is important to note that acceptable safety performance is often defined and influenced by domestic and international norms and culture.

It is noted that there is a difference between the approaches of the 3rd and 4th editions of the Manual, where the focus on 'hazard identification and safety risk management' has been dropped from the former in the latter edition which is satisfied if risks are 'controlled at an acceptable level'.

The elimination of accidents and/or serious incidents and the achievement of similar absolutes of control would certainly be desirable. However, such absolutes of control are unachievable goals in open and dynamic operational contexts. Hazards are integral components of aviation operational contexts. Failures and operational errors will occur in aviation, despite the best and most accomplished efforts to prevent them. No human activity or human-made system can be guaranteed to be absolutely free from hazards and operational errors.

Annex 19: Safety Management

The ICAO stated that Annex 19 would render wide-ranging benefits such as highlighting the importance of proactive safety management at the state level, enhancing safety by consolidating safety management provisions, facilitating the future evolution of safety management provisions, and promoting the further implementation of the SMS and SSP provisions.

Annex 19 contains four tiers of provisions, reflecting the balance to be struck between global consistency and versatility of application in diverse environments. The four tiers are:

1 Standards, whose uniform application is considered obligatory (with mandatory notification procedures in place);

2 Recommended Practices, whose uniform application is considered desirable;
3 Appendices, which form part of both the Standards and Recommended Practices (SARPs); and
4 Attachments, which are material supplementary to the SARPs and are intended largely for guidance on application.

Annex 19 consolidates existing safety management provisions which have been transferred from Annexes 1, 6, 8, 11, 13 and 14. These provisions have been in operation as SARPs dating from 2001 onwards. Moreover, the new Annex incorporates safety-related definitions from across the Chicago Convention into one list of definitions, and has added six new definitions. The approach adopted stresses the importance of a multidimensional, collaborative framework between states and organizations in safety management.

Definitions and Terminology

It is important to have a working definition of a few terms and concepts that are used throughout this publication and are the basis of safety-related legislation throughout the world. It is important that when defining any important terms or processes, there is consistency in the application of such definitions. This is particularly so with respect to aviation because of its global nature and almost universal application of technical standards.

Chapter 1 of Annex 19 defines certain safety-related terms, such as aircraft accidents and incidents, serious incidents and serious injuries. Additionally, the ICAO has notably incorporated a definition of 'safety' in the aviation context:

> *Safety*. The state in which risks associated with aviation activities, related to, or in direct support of the operation of aircraft, are reduced and controlled to an acceptable level.

Beyond this, there are other key terms which need to be clearly and consistently understood by the aviation community when regulating for legislative compliance.

A *hazard* is a source of potential harm or a situation with a potential to cause loss. It is implied that for the consequences of an event to be defined as a hazard, that is, having the potential for causing harm, there is some risk to the human population and therefore absolute safety could not be guaranteed, even if the risk is accepted when judged against some criterion of acceptability.

The ICAO SMM states that a hazard is generically defined as:

> A condition or an object with the potential to cause death, injuries to personnel, damage to equipment or structures, loss of material, or reduction of the ability to perform a prescribed function.

In some respects, this term includes 'condition' or an 'object', which are sometimes classed as incidents, and so these two terms – hazard and incident – are not mutually exclusive. It can be said that all accidents and incidents involve hazards; however, not all hazards result in either an accident or incident.

Risk is defined as the likelihood and consequences of injury or harm occurring. It is the chance of something happening (the event or possibility of an accident) that will have an impact upon objectives and is measured in terms of the product of the likelihood of the event occurring (expressed as either a frequency or probability) and the consequences if the event does occur.

Some commentators see safety as the freedom from risks that are harmful to a person or a group of persons, either local to the hazard, nationally or even worldwide. This implies, however, that safety can be considered in absolute terms – that there can be absolute safety. This simply is not true. As previously stated, safety is a relative concept and is best considered as a state in which an acceptable level of risk exists. And in aviation, as the events of 11 September 2001 have proven, there will always be that element of *unknown* risk.

An acceptable level of safety expresses the safety goals of an oversight authority, an operator or a services provider. From the perspective of the relationship between oversight authorities and operators/services providers, it provides the minimum safety objective(s) acceptable to the oversight authority to be achieved by the operators/services providers while conducting their core business functions. It is a reference against which the oversight authority can measure safety performance, and thereby aligns with the ICAO's concept of the 'safety boundary' outlined in the SMM.

The *as low as reasonably practicable* (ALARP) principle provides a means for assessing the tolerability of risk. A risk is ALARP if the cost of any reduction in that risk is grossly disproportionate to the benefit obtained from the reduction – akin to economic theory and the law of diminishing returns. This comparison may be a quantitative one or may be based on qualitative arguments.

Caution must be exercised when applying the ALARP principle from a public expectation perspective. Fare-paying passengers expect (or even demand) the highest level of safety (and the lowest level of risk). An operator must be able to demonstrate that all other credible risk reduction methods are impractical. There comes a stage, however, when the industry may be unwilling or unable to accept any additional cost to operations from reducing risk in a particular area. The risk appetite or level of risk tolerance will therefore vary with the individual, the organization or the government, which in turn (at least in democratic societies) will reflect what is considered 'acceptable' to the society at large).

A *safety management system* (SMS) can be considered to be a systematic approach to managing safety, including the necessary organizational structures, accountabilities, policies and procedures.

The preceding definitions of safety and safety-related terms show that safety management is all about the effective management of risk. It is not about attempting to achieve absolute safety; rather, it is more about accepting that things will go wrong and about controlling risks to a level that is acceptable, or to a level that is as low as reasonably practical. Safety management involves judgment, assessing priorities and making decisions. It is incumbent upon those responsible for the management of an aviation organization or enterprise to develop a safety culture within that organization that creates and promotes a safe work environment. These are all elements of management in its more general sense. And that is what a CEO does: manage.

The ICAO State Safety Programme

Annex 19: Chapter 3, Appendix 1, as well as Attachment A to the same Annex, include the requirement for member states to establish a State Safety Programme (SSP) aimed at achieving an acceptable level of safety across all aviation activities.

The overall objective of this programme is to harmonize and extend standards and recommended practices relating to safety management to all categories of aviation service providers, including aircraft operators, air navigation service providers, certified aerodrome operators, maintenance organizations, organizations responsible for type design and/or assembly of aircraft and training organizations.

The framework for the implementation and maintenance of a state's safety programme is contained in Chapter 4 of the fourth edition of the ICAO SMM.

Most of Annex 19 consists of provisions which were either duplicated or transferred from other Annexes. Annex 19 Standard 3.1.1 requires each state to establish a State Safety Program (SSP) for the management of safety in the state in order to achieve an 'acceptable level of safety (ALoS) performance in civil aviation'. The SSP must include state safety policy and objectives; state safety risk management; state safety assurance; and state safety promotion. Safety management is a business-like approach to safety which involves four components:

- policy and objectives;
- safety risk management;
- safety assurance;
- safety promotion.

Importantly, these four components of the SSP had previously been 'recommended practices', but Annex 19 has raised them to ICAO 'standard' status and as such, contracting states are now obliged to comply with them.

ICAO Safety Policy and Initiatives

In 1997, the ICAO first began to implement its Global Aviation Safety Plan (GASP), which has functioned as a high-level policy document to promote a 'harmonized, safe and efficient international civil aviation system'. It operates in conjunction with the Global Air Navigation Plan, which serves as an ongoing 15-year strategic methodology with a particular emphasis on long-term foresight and planning.

Global Aviation Safety Plan (GASP) The GASP was introduced with the direct intention of reducing accidents and fatality rates worldwide, 'irrespective of the volume of air traffic'. The ICAO aims to achieve these through enhancing international cooperation networks, so as to improve the ICAO's ability to collect and disseminate safety-related information.

This process of promoting safety awareness through encouraging the sharing and use of aviation safety-related data and information forms one of the fundamental principles of GASP. The ICAO also urges all contracting states to provide the needed support for the various elements of the GASP and to adjust laws to facilitate the voluntary reporting of safety-related events. One of these 'elements' is the review and improvement of existing safety database systems in order to facilitate the publication of safety-related information.

To promote the preceding objective, the ICAO provides safety-related information on the ICAO website. Another related task is the establishment of a comprehensive data analysis and information network. An important process in the GASP is the development of appropriate means to ensure a non-punitive voluntary incident report system.

This is essential to ensure that those with the valuable information are not impeded in divulging this for fear of blame or legal repercussions. Finally, this element also involves participating in the GAIN in order to investigate avenues to reduce impediments to the communication of safety-related information.

The 2017–19 edition of the GASP includes a new global aviation safety roadmap, which was developed to support the ongoing implementation of the GASP in collaboration with various stakeholders.

Global Air Navigation Plan (GANP) The GANP is an overarching policy framework that has a strategic long-term focus for the sustainable growth of global air navigation. It seeks to anticipate future developments and potential challenges and incorporate these considerations into a structured approach, involving states, manufacturers, service providers and operators.

The fifth edition of the GANP, released in 2016, outlines foreseeable challenges in air navigation and provides justification for a consensus-based and transparent framework to proactively address these challenges as they arise.

Safety Collaborative Assistance Networks (SCAN) Arising out of a proposal made at the ICAO High-level Safety Conference in 2010, the SCAN initiative serves as a facilitation channel for the exchange of safety-related information 'regarding financial and technical assistance projects and activities'. It allows donors and assistance providers to communicate regarding current projects and also plan for future assistance endeavours.

Safety Management Systems

Chapter 4 of Annex 19, formerly contained in Annex 6, requires aviation service providers (which includes training organizations, operators, maintenance organizations, design and manufacturing organizations, air traffic services providers and aerodrome operators) to establish a SMS commensurate with its size and the complexity of its aviation products or services. This must include provision for a safety management, accident prevention and flight safety management system.

A framework for its establishment is stipulated in more detail under Appendix 2 to Annex 19. Further detailed guidance for the implementation of a SMS is provided by the ICAO *Safety Management Manual* in Chapter 5.

A safety management system is an integrated set of work practices, beliefs and procedures for monitoring and improving the safety 'health' of all aspects of your operation. It recognizes the potential for errors and establishes robust defences to ensure that errors do not result in incidents or accidents.

As previously stated, a SMS can be defined as a systematic approach to managing safety, including the necessary organizational structures, accountabilities, policies and procedures.

SMSs and associated safety cases can and do make a big difference. Implicit to any effective SMS is the underlying safety culture. The systematic approach means that the hazards of the business are known, understood and demonstrably controlled. There is considerable evidence that those organizations that are most safety-minded are also amongst the most profitable and the amount of money that an effective safety management system can produce is considerable.

Before we consider the ways in which state civil aviation regulatory authorities have set about domestically implementing the ICAO SMS requirements, it is important to appreciate that the international safety system relies upon all nations consistently implementing aviation rules and regulations to ensure that ICAO safety requirements are met. In order for the ICAO to have the confidence that each contracting state to the Chicago Convention is in fact legislating locally the standards contained in the Annexes, it decided to introduce a system of auditing contracting states to ascertain their level of compliance with their obligations under the Convention.

ICAO Safety Oversight

The ICAO Universal Safety Oversight Audit Programme (USOAP) audits commenced, on a voluntary basis, in 1996, and in 1998 became a universal audit programme with all member states of the ICAO being audited on a progressive basis. These multidisciplinary audits promoted a systems-based approach to safety oversight at the national level. It is an approach which fundamentally recognizes the importance of standardization to a safe air transport system.

By the end of 2001, all of the then 185 contracting states to the Chicago Convention had received at least one USOAP audit of legislation, procedures and practices in relation to personnel licensing and the operation and airworthiness of aircraft. In 2004, the ICAO Assembly voted to consider expanding the programme to include audits of all safety-related ICAO Annexes to provide a holistic approach to aviation safety oversight. The programme has progressively been extended to include aerodromes, air traffic services and aircraft accident investigation, and will eventually cover the standards in all safety-related provisions of the Chicago Convention.

From 2007 onwards, the USOAP transitioned into a new framework known as the Continuous Monitoring Approach (CMA), which comprises a more systemic and proactive monitoring process. It employs the 'Online Framework' (OLF) web-based platform, strengthening the flexibility and dynamicity of the USOAP.

In summary, since around the mid-1990s, the ICAO and national aviation authorities worldwide have recognized the industry's need for greater flexibility in an increasingly complex and diverse aviation sector. It has been recognized that there is no silver bullet of regulatory compliance to fit the myriad of varying airline business models.

For this (and other) reasons, the new generation safety regulations are safety outcome-based. Where there is a need for a regulation to specify a particular requirement because of known safety risks, the detail will be mandated. For instance, as we saw in Chapter 11, aircraft certification standards remain highly prescriptive in nature due to the inherent risks known in aircraft manufacture and operation. In most other situations, the operator will take a greater role in developing systems that are acceptable to the regulator. This will provide greater operational flexibility and more efficient operating procedures.

The USOAP CMA will undergo further evolution in the coming years, particularly to ensure better integration with the first amendment to Annex 19, adopted in March 2016. This amendment updated the SSP provisions to more formally align with the State Safety Oversight (SSO) system's '8 Critical Elements'. This integration serves to create a more robust and clearer safety management structure. The first amendment will become applicable in November 2019.

THE OPERATOR'S RESPONSIBILITY FOR SAFETY MANAGEMENT

Overview

History has demonstrated repeatedly that without the complete commitment of the highest management levels within a company, operational safety margins are seriously compromised. This does not suggest that a particular company will have an accident, but it does suggest,

> the management by virtue of being the body responsible for formulating, approving and enforcing policy, must have a profound influence on the operational safety within a company as, through its attitudes and actions, they have a direct bearing in defining the safety culture of an organization.

Managers must advocate the importance of safety and assume responsibility for ensuring that safety accountability remains with those at the top – hence the need for safety management strategies. The term 'safety management' is generally recognized as the management actions required to secure and maintain the necessary levels of safety.

The public and regulatory authorities are increasingly aware of recognizing management's role in air safety by noting changes in investigative reporting procedures requiring executive management involvement, and with the final inquiry report perhaps holding management accountable for a serious incident or accident.

There is now a developing risk that the state may take a hand in prosecuting where a management failure causes death and that failure constitutes conduct falling far short of the standard that can reasonably be expected of an airline operating corporation in the circumstances. Such prosecutions may also satisfy the actual or perceived need of victims of such accidents and their families for revenge or public condemnation of those seen to be responsible for particularly bad accidents.

This 'corporate accountability' is magnified many times over if a company suffers several such incidents or accidents during the course of a few years. In September 2007, a Swiss court convicted three ATC managers on charges of negligent manslaughter and negligent disruption of public transport, and sentenced each to one year in prison.

Role of Senior Management

The majority of AOCs are held by corporations (see Chapter 9); therefore, state safety regulators impose the practical responsibility on the office holders or senior personnel of the company to effectively manage safety within a particular aviation organization. The CEO is at the top of the list. So, although day-to-day responsibility for the diversity of aviation activities may be delegated, should a serious safety issue develop, the local safety regulatory authority's main port of call will be the CEO.

The legal obligations for managing safety have previously been stated and essentially relate to the duty to exercise care and due diligence. The scope of this duty of care is very broad. Every activity covered by the AOC or the Approved Maintenance Organization and everything done in connection with such an activity includes everything within the realm of flight operations, maintenance control and engineering, and as identified in the respective state's aviation rules and regulations. In most countries, these obligations also extend to each director of the company operating an AOC or Approved Maintenance Organization.

In many countries, the person whom the state regulator holds as ultimately responsible for aviation safety within an organization is referred to as the *accountable manager*. This senior manager (often but not always the CEO) within the aviation organization is accountable to the state safety regulator for maintaining safety standards required by regulations and additional standards specified by the AOC holder or applicant.

For instance, in Europe under the EASA, the accountable person for a *Continuing Airworthiness Management Organization* (CAMO) is the same person who is held to be the accountable person for the related AOC. In the case of an approved aircraft *maintenance organization*, the accountable person is again the most senior person within that organization and is generally someone not related to any particular AOC. Obviously, there will be variations as to the names and responsibilities assigned to such persons and other 'responsible managers'.

In the case of corporations, the accountable manager (however described) must have corporate authority for ensuring that all operations and maintenance system activities can be financed and carried out to the standard required. The accountable manager is usually required by legislation to be acceptable to the state regulator.

In the regulation of safety, the accountable manager is a key figure given that his or her influence on the standards of an AOC or maintenance organization is significant. Therefore, the working relationship between the state civil aviation regulator and the accountable manager plays an important part in the regulatory oversight of that aviation organization.

Contracted Aviation Services

In the aviation industry, it is common practice to contract out services for a variety of reasons, but most commonly due to cost benefits and geographical location. Typical service providers include aircraft maintenance, refuelling, catering, ramp operations, flight crew training, flight planning and aircraft performance.

Whether a large corporation or a small business, the contracting authority (that is, the AOC holder or maintenance organization) retains overall responsibility for the safety of services provided by the contractor. By way of example, consider a situation where contracted ground handlers loaded the aircraft in such a configuration that adversely affected the weight and balance and ultimately the performance during take-off, resulting in a runway overrun. The AOC holder would have the ultimate safety accountability. Investigations may reveal that a particular individual was not complying with *standard operating procedures* (SOPs), which may in turn result in the loss of the control and financial ramifications for both the operator and contractor; however, the airline and the AOC holder remain accountable. This situation is consistent with other regulators, such as those covered by workplace safety laws: the operator is presumed to have liability for the actions of its contracted parties.

A SMS must ensure that the level of safety of an organization is not eroded by the inputs, services and supplies provided by external organizations. A good example, in relation to workplace health and safety (WHS) issues, is where an effective SMS may have identified non-compliance-related issues through contractor oversight and/or internal assurance of the contracting service provider.

The operator should ensure that the contracted service provider understands the operator's SMS and its responsibilities relating to it. These factors should be given equal weight with other considerations like price, quality and timely delivery.

Emergency Response Plan (ERP)

As was previously stated in this chapter, the management of safety should be viewed by those responsible and accountable under the legislation as another organizational process that allows aviation organizations to achieve their business objectives through the delivery of their services.

An Emergency Response Plan (ERP) should be established as part of the overall risk management strategies of the organization to provide specific procedures and processes in the occurrence of a major incident or accident or some other 'event' or 'occurrence' that may adversely impact upon the aviation organization's operations. Such an event may relate to the operation of aircraft, but may also include such things as epidemics, major IT or power outages, industrial action or civil unrest and so on. All of these events ought to be identified and considered as part of the organization's overall business resilience strategies.

ICAO Requirements Under Appendix 2 to Annex 19 of the Chicago Convention, the ERP forms an integral part of an airline's SMS. Guidelines relating to ERP content, scope and implementation are provided in Appendix 3 to Chapter 5 of the ICAO SMM. These stipulations operate concurrently with the SMS requirements imposed by a state on aviation service providers.

It may be considered more practical to have the ERP as a stand-alone manual and have cross-references within the SMS manual to the ERP. One of the primary considerations for this is that in a complex or highly complex organization, the ERP may itself be very detailed and required in so many locations that it is better held as a separate document.

An ERP should be established that provides the actions to be taken by the organization or individuals in an emergency. The ERP should be integrated into the SMS and reflect the size, nature and complexity of the activities performed by the organization.

Scope of an ERP An 'occurrence' that is sufficient to activate an ERP may be any one of the following:

- death or serious injury (imminent or on board);
- an aircraft suffering serious damage;
- fire;
- mechanical failure;
- malfunction of an aircraft system;
- flight crew incapacitation;
- low fuel/starvation;
- contamination/dangerous goods;
- rogue passenger;
- food poisoning;
- a bomb or terrorist threat.

Normally, most occurrences which affect the organization are dealt with by individuals as part of their normal duties. However, occurrences such as a major accident or a major security situation will require the coordinated efforts of management and staff and, in certain circumstances, assistance from outside organizations. In these cases, the ERP shall be used as the basis for coordinated action.

Every aviation practitioner within an organization must be fully conversant with their role in emergency situations, and be able to recognize when to activate an ERP. Most civil aviation regulatory authorities require in their respective rules and regulations that an ERP forms part of the airline's SMS.

ACCIDENT INVESTIGATION

Although it is almost universally accepted that travel by air is the safest form of mass transportation, aviation accidents, when they occur, attract significant media and public attention. Consider, for instance, the incredible amount of worldwide publicity that resulted from the Malaysian Airways MH370 and MH17 events – notwithstanding the novelty of both these accidents. However, because of the catastrophic consequences of a single aircraft accident, the level of media attention directed at aviation accidents is nearly always disproportionate to the level of risk this activity poses to society. This view is expressed in the following:

> Aviation safety is an extremely emotive topic. And rightly so. Whenever the safety and wellbeing of humans is concerned there is, and always should be, a high degree of public interest. Aviation is no exception. In fact the scrutiny and monitoring of aviation safety, especially by the media, is to a certain extent out of proportion to the level of risk it poses to the community at large. Whether this level of interest is warranted is a separate issue but the fact remains that aviation safety is prominent in the public eye and always on the mind of even the most seasoned frequent flyer.
>
> (Bartsch 2010: 617)

Air accidents are less tolerable than a simplistic cost-benefit analysis might otherwise suggest. By way of example, Solomon (1993) points out that 100 car accidents, each with a single fatality, are not perceived to be equivalent to a single aviation accident that kills 100 people. Mass media and 'the spectacle' of the event have a lot to do with this perception. However, to put the comparison of the hazards posed by these two modes of transportation into perspective, consider the following: throughout the world, far more people have been killed because of motor vehicle accidents in the past two years than the cumulative total of all those who have died from every fatal aircraft accident since the beginning of aviation in 1783.

With advancements in accident investigation research techniques, legislative initiatives and international cooperation increasing, so too will the travelling public's confidence rise in aviation activities. If all the conditions and factors causally related to aircraft accidents could be identified in advance, then 'zero accidents' may well be an achievable goal. Unfortunately, history and hindsight have repeatedly proven to be the only reliable sources of such information.

The Objectives of Accident Investigation

The prime outcome of an accident or incident investigation is the prevention of future accidents and incidents. In addition, the government and the travelling public expect an open and transparent process regarding the communication and investigation of safety issues. In order to achieve public confidence in the safety of transport, most state accident investigation agencies require that all completed investigations are to be followed by a publicly released final investigation report.

The investigation of aircraft accidents and incidents can have a significant impact upon the development of more effective safety systems. This underlying objective of aircraft accident investigation is fundamental to the ICAO's standards and is well expressed in the following extract from the ICAO *Annual Digest on Aircraft Accidents*:

> Nearly every accident contains evidence which, if correctly identified and assessed, will allow the circumstances and the cause to be ascertained so that corrective action can be undertaken to prevent further accidents.
>
> (ICAO 1974)

This fundamental objective can be contrasted against the retrospective apportionment of liability for an accident or incident that has occurred. It is not the purpose of investigations to assign blame (whether in a strictly legal sense or otherwise), as this may conflict with the prospective focus on the prevention of future accidents and incidents.

The Approach to Aircraft Accident Investigation

From around the early 1990s, there was a change in philosophy in aircraft accident investigations throughout the world. Investigations began to no longer focus on what went on at the 'sharp end', but now also included the latent conditions that developed within the system due to decisions made at the higher levels of management. This systemic approach was based on the Reason Model of organizational conditions, named for Professor James Reason, who conceived it. This model has been adopted by many transport safety investigation agencies throughout the world.

The Reason Model considers that undesirable latent conditions within an organization can go undetected until they contribute to undesirable local conditions (see later) and unsafe acts at the operational level, which can breach the organization's defences. The Model also stated that latent conditions could lead to weaknesses in the organization's defences (Reason 1997).

The main purpose of the investigation of air safety occurrences is the prevention of aircraft accidents through the identification of safety issues. To that end, the primary objective of such an investigation is to establish what happened, how it happened and why it happened. This often requires the examination of the aviation system within which the aircraft was operating.

International Obligations Since the signing of the Chicago Convention on 7 December 1944, the ICAO has since been the basis for agreement and cooperation between contracting states on the standardization of safety and technical aspects of international civil aviation – including accident investigation. Contained within the Convention are a number of articles relating to aviation accident investigation, namely Articles 26 and 37.

Article 26 of the Convention states:

> In the event of an accident to an aircraft of a contracting State occurring in the territory of another contracting State, and involving death or serious injury, or indicating serious technical defect in the aircraft or air navigation facilities, the State in which the accident occurs will

> institute an inquiry into the circumstances of the accident, in accordance, so far as its laws permit, with the procedure which may be recommended by the International Civil Aviation Organization. The State in which the aircraft is registered shall be given the opportunity to appoint observers to be present at the inquiry and the State holding the inquiry shall communicate the report and findings in the matter to that State.

Simply stated, if a foreign aircraft, except for a foreign defence, customs or police aircraft, is involved in an accident in the territory of a contracting state, that state is obliged to investigate the circumstances of the accident and provide a report on the findings of the investigation to the authorities of the country in which the aircraft is registered.

Moreover, Article 37 states:

> Each contracting state undertakes to collaborate in securing the highest practicable degree of uniformity in regulations, standards, procedures, and organization in relation to aircraft, personnel, airways and auxiliary services in all matters in which such uniformity will facilitate and improve air navigation.
>
> To this end the International Civil Aviation Organization shall adopt and amend from time to time, as may be necessary, international standards and recommended practices and procedures dealing with, *inter alia*:
>
> ...
>
> k) Aircraft in distress and investigation of accidents.

As previously stated, Article 38 enables contracting states to notify differences with respect to ICAO standards contained in the 19 Annexes to the Convention.

Annex 13 of the ICAO In accordance with Article 37, the SARPs for aircraft accident investigation were adopted in 1951 by ICAO members and are contained in Annex 13: Aircraft Accident and Incident Investigation. The international procedures for accident investigation are contained in the ICAO *Manual of Aircraft Accident and Incident Investigation*, whose second edition was released in 2015.

It should be noted that, as with all the other ICAO standards, Annex 13 is not the *head of power* or *authority* of the domestic aviation law for aircraft accident investigation, but is the source upon which the domestic law of the contracting state is based.

Annex 13 clearly states that the sole purpose or objective of an investigation shall be: 'The prevention of accidents and incidents and that it is not the purpose of an investigation to apportion blame or liability'.

Importantly, paragraph 5.4.1 of Annex 13 recommends that 'any judicial or administrative proceedings to apportion blame or liability should be separate from any investigation conducted under the provisions of this Annex'. The issue of legal liability generally and criminal liability specifically was discussed in considerable detail in Chapter 8.

Annex 13 was originally intended to apply only to Article 26, that is, accidents involving 'large modern transport aircraft' from another contracting state. More recently, however, the application of Annex 13 has been expanded to include the investigation of serious incidents (in relation to Article 26 aircraft) and to accidents and serious incidents involving domestic aircraft.

The 'Party System' Pursuant to paragraphs 5.18–26 of Annex 13, if an accident or serious incident occurs in a contracting state and involves a foreign-registered aircraft, an accredited representative from the aircraft's country of registration, operator, manufacturer or component designer is entitled to participate in the investigation conducted by the investigation authority. Such representatives and their technical advisers form an integral part of the investigation team and are entitled to participate in all aspects of the investigation, including access to evidence relating to the accident, except where conflicts of interest and confidentiality cannot be managed by the assigned investigator in charge.

Accordingly, such representatives are required to provide unfettered assistance to the investigation process, including full disclosure of all information relevant to the investigation. In addition, those representatives and their advisers must seek permission from the investigation authority to disclose to other parties any information relating to the progress and findings of the investigation. These principles seek to ensure that the investigator in charge is able, without delay, to conduct a comprehensive examination of the circumstances that led to the accident and to communicate critical safety information to relevant parties in a timely fashion.

It should be noted that countries whose citizens suffered fatalities or serious injuries in an accident such as that referred to previously have a right to participate in the investigation as observers. However, the scope of their involvement in the investigation is more limited: see paragraph 5.27 of Annex 13.

To illustrate the application of the preceding provisions, consider the following scenario: Country A's Boeing 777 is involved in an accident within, say, Australian territory.

There are many fatalities, including several citizens and crew from the UK. No unlawful interference is suspected – such events meet the definitional requirements of an accident under Annex 13. The aircraft is registered and operated by Country A but was designed and manufactured in the USA. In such an instance, the Australian Transport Safety Bureau (on behalf of Australia) would be responsible for conducting the accident investigation.

As a minimum, authorized personnel from Country A and the USA would have a right to participate in the investigation as accredited representatives, while authorized persons from the UK would have a right of participation, but with 'observer' status.

International Cooperation Certain obligations exist for contracting states to the Chicago Convention under Annex 13 for the cooperation and participation in the event of aircraft accidents and serious incidents. Upon notification of an accident or serious incident, the state of registry, the state of the operator, the state of design and the state of manufacture shall inform the state of occurrence whether they are going to appoint an accredited representative to participate in the investigation. These requirements are set out in full in paragraph 4.6 of Annex 13. The state conducting the investigation can also request that those states appoint an accredited representative when the accident aircraft is over 2,250 kg.

In accordance with the provisions of paragraph 5.1 of Annex 13, the state of occurrence is required to investigate the circumstances of an aircraft accident and can delegate the whole or any part of the investigation to another state by mutual arrangement.

Quite often, aircraft accident investigation agencies from countries with significant resources and specialist investigators, such as the National Transportation Safety Board of the USA, provide assistance to smaller and developing aviation nations whenever there is a major accident involving a commercial airliner or otherwise requested. Practices like these reflect the collaborative approach to aircraft accident and incident investigations that the ICAO consistently stresses, which is underpinned by the sole objective of preventing future accidents and incidents.

As a final comment it should be remembered that a good safety record is a judgment of past performance but does not guarantee the future, although it is a useful indicator. The following advice was provided by Dr Jonathon Aleck, a former Australian ICAO Council member, at an aviation safety seminar sponsored by the Civil Aviation Safety Authority in Brisbane, Australia, back in October 2003.

> No amount of legally orientated instruction or training can ever fully prepare anyone to respond with absolute certainly to the variety of legal problems and questions each of you face every day – and that you will come to face on a regular basis in connection with the introduction of an SMS. In law, as in any other complex field involving human behaviour, there are far fewer consistently 'correct' answers or solutions than we would like, and a great many things will remain contingent.

Although it is almost universally accepted that travel by air is the safest form of mass transportation, aviation accidents, when they occur, attract significant media and public attention. However, because of the catastrophic consequences of a single aircraft accident, the level of media attention directed at aviation accidents is nearly always disproportional to the level of risk this activity poses to society.

With advancements in accident investigation research techniques, legislative initiatives and international cooperation increasing, so too will the travelling public's confidence rise in aviation activities. If all the conditions and factors causally related to aircraft accidents could be identified in advance then the ultimate goal of 'zero accidents' may well be achievable. Unfortunately, history and hindsight have repeatedly proven to be the only reliable sources of such information.

17 Aviation and the Environment

INTERNATIONAL CONTEXT TO ENVIRONMENTAL ISSUES

Legal and regulatory systems have developed over the past two centuries to manage the effects of human activity on the natural environment. Initially, the object of these systems was to safeguard and improve public health, but the focus has increasingly turned to the preservation of the environment per se. Whilst the law still aims to protect public health, it also aims to protect the health of 'the environment', including flora, fauna and ecosystems. The development of fundamental principles to achieve those aims is slightly outside the scope of this chapter, but the principles themselves will be explained.

It is estimated that civil aviation contributes only 2 per cent of the quantum of greenhouse gases (GHG) emitted globally. However, because much of aviation's GHG as well as water vapour and particulates are injected directly into the upper atmosphere, aviation's contribution to 'greenhouse effect' is estimated to be closer to 3 per cent. It is further estimated that aviation may contribute up to 3–4 per cent of GHG by 2050.

One explanation for this increased share may be that the energy density of current batteries is a fraction of the energy density of fossil fuels. This factor may mean development of sustainably energized aircraft capable of long-distance transportation will be more problematic than developing surface transport modes powered by, for example, lithium-ion batteries and electric motors. Not all greenhouse gases are attributable to burning fossil fuels. Methane is also a greenhouse gas and it is thought the world's bovine population – needed to provide food for the world's human population – also contributes significantly to the problem.

Environmental law is intrinsically an area of law that spans from matters of international concern right down to the minutiae of local issues. As a result, individual nations come under obligations in international law to enact local laws to protect and preserve the local environment and also to protect the broader global environment. These obligations arise in the form of international treaties that many countries have entered into, such as the *United Nations Framework Convention on Climate Change* and its Kyoto Protocol.

The Kyoto Protocol which came into effect in 2005 obliged the 37 industrially developed states who had agreed thereto to work with the International Civil Aviation Organization (ICAO) to achieve the climate change objectives of that treaty. A globally accepted market-based mechanism (MBM) system has been recognized for some time. In 2016, the International Civil Aviation Organization (ICAO) adopted the *Carbon Offsetting and Reduction Scheme for International Aviation* (CORSIA), which was heralded as the first global market-based environmental initiative for any industry sector.

DOI: 10.4324/9781032652146-17

The system applies to international sectors and is based on offsetting, whereby the global aviation sector will offset its emissions through the reduction of emissions elsewhere, and by purchasing credit from a supply and demand-driven 'carbon market' generated by projects that reduce carbon emissions around the world.

The matter of air traffic control being challenged to develop safe traffic flow procedures while minimizing consumption of hydrocarbon fuel was discussed earlier in international design and certification standards for aircraft and engines developed by ICAO and have been enacted domestically in most contracting states to address the issues of both noise and greenhouse gas emission.

For the same reason that aeronautical endeavours were particularly amenable to cooperative regulation at an international level, so too are climate change and other environmental challenges best dealt with through an international cooperative effort. The recent antipathy demonstrated by some world leaders toward the Paris Agreement – which has substantially succeeded the Kyoto Protocol as an international suite of mechanisms to combat catastrophic climate change – threatened to derail those mechanisms.

The Paris Agreement is often referred to as the Paris Accords or the Paris Climate Accords. Adopted in 2015, the agreement covers climate change mitigation, adaptation and finance. The Agreement's central aim is to strengthen the global response to the threat of climate change by keeping a global temperature rise this century well below 2 degrees Celsius above pre-industrial levels and to pursue efforts to limit the temperature increase even further to 1.5 degrees Celsius.

The Paris Agreement opened for signature on 22 April 2016 – Earth Day – at UN Headquarters in New York. It entered into force on 4 November 2016, 30 days after the so-called double threshold (ratification by 55 countries that account for at least 55 per cent of global emissions) had been met. Since then, more countries have ratified and continue to ratify the Agreement, reaching a total in 2024 of 195 Parties out of 198 Parties to the Convention.

Of the various 'greenhouse gases', as referred to in the Paris Agreement, that contribute to the atmospheric insulation, carbon dioxide and nitrous oxide are two significant components that are also by-products of internal combustion engine operations common to nearly all powered flight. Aviation activities are thus clearly identified as part of the problem – and will inevitably have to become part of the solution.

More recently, in Montreal at the 41st ICAO Assembly in 2022, 184 member states adopted the Long Term global Aspirational Goal (LTAG) of net zero carbon emissions from international aviation by 2050 in support of the UNFCCC Paris Agreement's temperature goal to limit global warming to well below 2 degrees Celsius. This was a most important initiative by ICAO in setting the benchmark for the entire international civil aviation industry in respect to climate change.

The LTAG does not attribute specific obligations or commitments in the form of emissions reduction goals to individual states. Each state will contribute to achieving the goal in a socially, economically and environmentally sustainable manner and in accordance with its national circumstances. ICAO recognizes that each state has special circumstances and respective capabilities in the level of development, maturity of aviation markets, sustainable growth of its international aviation, just transition and national priorities of air transport development. Accordingly, member states will inform ICAO of their ability to contribute to the LTAG within their own domestic timeframe.

At the 77th International Air Transport Association (IATA) Annual General Meeting in Boston, USA, on 4 October 2021, a resolution was passed by IATA member airlines committing them to achieving net zero carbon emissions from their operations by 2050. This pledge, consistent with ICAO's goals, brings the entire air transport sector in line with the objectives of the Paris Agreement. ICAO's *Fly Net Zero* commitment is for airlines to achieve net zero carbon emissions by 2050 through a combination of maximum elimination of emissions at the source, offsetting and carbon capture technologies. IATA says the aviation industry won't be able to completely eliminate emissions at the source, and will need to mitigate the rest using a variety of offsetting mechanisms. This is the process where emissions are compensated for by the financing of a reduction in emissions elsewhere.

To provide context to the magnitude of the net zero targets, aircraft emit around 100 times more CO_2 per hour than a shared bus or train ride. The aviation industry contributes an estimated 2.4 per cent of global annual CO_2 emissions, most of it from commercial air services. In quantitative terms, the emissions of global aviation are around 1 billion tonnes of CO_2 per year: more than the emissions of any one of 188 of the 193 contracting states to ICAO. The European Commission predicts that by the middle of the twenty-first century, demand for flying could increase aviation's greenhouse gas emissions by upwards of 300 per cent over 2005 levels if no drastic measures are taken to reduce them.

Amongst the general anthropogenic (human-induced) impacts on the environment to which aviation contributes, aviation has some specific impacts not applicable to other industries. Therefore, as well as adopting the more generally applicable strategies and practices to protect the environment that all industries should adopt, aviation should implement its own techniques to address those issues lying uniquely within its scope to address. In this chapter, more attention will be given to the issues that are specific to aviation.

ENVIRONMENTAL ISSUES IN INTERNATIONAL AVIATION

The Environment

The scope of environmental law is defined entirely by what is meant by 'the environment'. Fisher (2010) notes that 'environment' is actually a term devoid of values, despite its value-laden use in modern discourse. The term implies a location, referring to the things that surround an area or object, and could perhaps be extended to include the relationships between those things. Fisher also notes that 'management' is also a value-free term, so that the term 'management of the environment' is essentially neutral – the 'environment' may be 'managed' in any way we choose.

It is the choice of how to manage the environment that concerns environmental law. However, this does not yet define what is meant by 'the environment'. Bates (2010: 4) outlines several 'environments' that might concern governments attempting to use the law to regulate and manage 'the environment', including 'the natural environment, the built or urban environment, the cultural environment and the economic, social, health and work environments'. Bates also notes the multifaceted and thus complex nature of environmental regulation, suggesting that all these environments overlap and interact.

'Environment', then, could be said to go beyond the mere locational definition that a purely literal reading of the word might entail, and consider broader aspects of the relationship between elements in a complex system, which should be a concept not unfamiliar to those involved in aviation. Vaillancourt summarizes the issue succinctly:

> The environment thus is now considered to be an organized, dynamic and evolving system of natural (i.e. physical, chemical, biological) and human (i.e. economic, political, social and cultural) factors in which living organisms operate or human activities take place, and which has a direct or indirect, immediate or long term effect or influence on these living beings or on human actions at a given time and in a circumscribed area.
>
> (1995: 217)

So, 'the environment' may be considered to include notions of 'location', but also notions of a complex system and the effects that activities may have on that system. It should also be noted that these effects may be either adverse or positive.

Environmental Impacts

Emissions Environmental debate in modern times focuses on the relentless drive to reduce emissions of 'carbon', which is a term often used as shorthand for all the gases listed at Annex A of the Kyoto Protocol but with a particular emphasis on carbon dioxide. The concern with emissions lies in their ability to affect the thermal properties of the atmosphere – specifically its ability both to reflect and to absorb radiation from the sun and also radiation reflected from the surface. Carbon dioxide has long been known to improve the capacity of the atmosphere to absorb radiation, and it has been shown that increasing its concentration in the atmosphere tends to increase the temperature of the atmosphere. Atmospheric science also recognizes that increasing concentrations of other gases, such as those listed at Annex A of the Kyoto Protocol, have a similar effect.

Perhaps the most obvious source of emissions in the aviation industry comes from the aircraft themselves. Aircraft often used for international carriage of passengers and freight have engines that burn kerosene, which is a combustible hydrocarbon. The complete combustion of kerosene releases only carbon dioxide and water vapour into the atmosphere. Aircraft fuels also contain compounds of sulphur, which act as lubricating agents. These compounds when burnt release sulphur dioxide (Daley 2010).

However, complete combustion only occurs in ideal conditions. Such conditions very rarely, if ever, exist in the real world, so combustion of kerosene in aviation is typically incomplete. Incomplete combustion releases the carbon dioxide, water vapour and sulphur dioxide in a similar manner to complete combustion, but also releases (Daley 2010: 21–2):

- nitrogen oxides;
- hydrocarbons;
- carbon monoxide;
- sulphur oxides;
- soot particles.

The sulphur oxides also give rise to sulphate particles, although these are not directly emitted from the engine (Intergovernmental Panel on Climate Change 1999).

What should also be noted is that these emissions are in relatively low quantities. The overwhelming majority of the gas that flows through and is propelled from the back of a jet engine is simply the ambient air – indeed, the main objective of a jet engine is to pull air in through the intake and propel it through its exhaust at a faster speed than which it entered, thus creating a propulsive force. Combustion products such as those discussed earlier are only about 8.5 per cent of the total mass flow that exits the engine. Further, only 0.4 per cent of the volume of the combustion products represents the residual products of incomplete combustion.

Aviation, of course, is not the only industry that releases these gases into the atmosphere. A report in 2007 produced by the UN Intergovernmental Panel on Climate Change (IPCC) said that aviation contributes approximately 2 per cent of all anthropogenic greenhouse gas emissions, but those emissions contribute to approximately 3 per cent of anthropogenic atmospheric *radiative forcing* (Ribeiro *et al.* 2007), an effect more commonly known as the 'greenhouse effect' or 'global warming'. Aviation emissions appear to be more effective at radiative forcing than emissions of other industrial sectors, and this means that aviation should not become complacent that its contribution to greenhouse gas emissions is relatively small.

So, what is the difference? What is it that makes aviation emissions more effective at producing radiative forcing? The primary difference between aviation emissions – that is, emissions from aircraft – is that they are produced at altitude and injected directly into the upper troposphere and the stratosphere, whereas emissions of other industries occur at ground level. There is evidence to suggest that this injection at high levels significantly magnifies the effect that a quantity of greenhouse gas emitted would otherwise have. It is not appropriate here to detail this evidence in any depth, but, for example, it has been noted that the injection of water vapour and particulates directly into the upper levels of the troposphere leads to the formation of condensation trails ('contrails') and increases cirrus cloudiness. Injecting these directly into the stratosphere introduces humidity to a part of the atmosphere that normally has very little. Both these effects tend to increase the capacity of the atmosphere to absorb heat, leading to warming. However, this is offset partially by the additional cirrus clouds formed, increasing the reflection of solar radiation back into space.

There is also cause for concern by EASA on the climate change front. The latest report of the Inter-Governmental Panel on Climate Change (IPCC) released in April 2022 states that anthropogenic emissions are still increasing, but the growth rate of emissions was slower between 2010 and 2019 than between 2000 and 2009. While the price of renewable energy and batteries for passenger electric vehicles has fallen significantly, their adoption continues to rise. However, globally current climate policy responses are not sufficient to reduce greenhouse gas emissions enough to limit global warming to around 1.5 degrees Celsius.

Net anthropogenic GHG emissions have increased since 2010 across all major sectors globally. An increasing share of emissions can be attributed to urban areas. Emissions reductions in CO2 from fossil fuels and industrial processes, due to improvements in energy intensity of GDP and carbon intensity of energy, have been less than emissions increases from rising global activity levels in industry, energy supply, transport, agriculture and buildings.

Noise Amid the intense and increasingly strident public debate about emissions, it would be easy to believe that emissions were the only environmental impact that the aviation industry should concern itself with mitigating. However, environmental regulation in the aviation industry started by focusing on the somewhat more localized impact of noise. Noise is a perennial issue for the aviation industry. What once represented the sound of 'progress' and the coming of a new and exciting era of technology is now an annoyance for those who live and work near airports. Furthermore, excessive exposure to aircraft noise has been shown to have impacts upon the health of those exposed to it.

The ICAO has adapted the 'balanced approach' to aircraft noise management – a concept suggesting that aircraft noise can be reduced through changes made in a number of different areas of aircraft operation, reducing the overall impact of aircraft noise on the community and the surrounding environment. Greater emphasis and responsibility has been placed on the owners and operators of airports to listen to and understand the needs of the community so as to develop and implement procedures that will reduce the impact of aircraft noise. Further changes to the conditions of aircraft noise management will be addressed and implemented through the assistance of ICAO SARPs, especially those within Annex 16. Aircraft noise will continue to remain a growing concern and challenge for all involved and will require substantial community and industry support and collaboration to ensure a sustainable future for aviation.

Airport Operations

To the general public, the responsibility of the aviation industry to manage its detrimental impact on the environment begins and ends with the airlines. For industry and environmental experts, the situation is not quite so simple. The activities of multiple stakeholders, including airport operators, contribute to the industry's total greenhouse gas emissions, and the collaborative efforts of all these stakeholders towards environmental management is the only way that targets will be met.

When compared with other industries, aviation does not rank among the biggest polluters in the world. Air transport services are heavily relied upon, and demand is only showing signs of increasing into the future. Given this reliance by both the corporate world and the travelling public, the cost to the environment is comparatively low. As outlined previously, this equates to approximately 2 per cent of the total anthropogenic carbon dioxide emissions. According to the IPCC, this figure is projected to rise to 4 per cent by 2050 if unmitigated. 'Aviation emissions' is often misconceived to include the contribution of airport emissions, when in fact aviation emissions include only emissions from aircraft, both in flight and on the ground. The importance in distinguishing between the two needs to be recognized in order to avoid inaccurate figures by omission or double counting. The emissions reduction actions of airport operators around the world are gathering momentum; never has the role of the airport operator in minimizing the environmental impact of the aviation industry been greater. The measures being developed and introduced by operators can be categorized into regulatory, technical, operational or economic measures. These are discussed later in relation to the source of the emissions.

Airport Operators Once an understanding is developed as to what constitutes airport emissions, individual sources can be identified in order to facilitate tailor-made solutions being implemented to address different sources of pollution. The World Resources Institute (WRI) has developed a system whereby emissions can be divided into one of three categories based on the ownership and control of airport sources.

Based on this framework, the following initiatives, if implemented appropriately, will assist in the minimization of an airport operator's emissions contribution:

- investing in power, heating and air conditioning systems certified as green technology;
- utilizing energy providers sourcing their services from wind, solar, hydroelectric, geothermal and biomass energy;
- retrofitting of energy-efficient buildings and component technologies, including double-glazing, window tinting, variable shading, natural lighting, etc.;
- updating the airport's fleet vehicles and ground support equipment with newer, greener alternatives;
- reviewing solid waste management procedures.

Another category of activity an airport operator might influence is the 'airport-related activity'. Airport-related activities account for a significant proportion of the total carbon emissions of an airport and yet they are activities with which the airport has no direct relationship – meaning that the airport itself is not the polluter. Transport to and from the airport represents the main source of pollution in this category. So-called kiss-and-fly passengers are those who are dropped off at the airport and picked up again upon arrival. The aggregate result means that for one passenger, up to four car trips might be made for every return flight, highlighting the evident inefficiencies if the travelling public do not have faith in public transport services or there is not sufficient facilitation to use such services. For example, figures released by Manchester Airport attribute 58 per cent of the airport's total carbon emissions to vehicles that carry passengers or staff to and from the airport. Mitigation measures that address pollution as a result of transport, as well as other emissions resulting from airport-related activities, can include the following:

- ensuring a robust public transport network that can comfortably cater to the level of demand;
- launching marketing campaigns in order to educate the public to make environmentally conscious decisions with regard to travel;
- introducing initiatives such as priority queuing, parking discounts and priority parking areas for vehicles using alternative fuel sources, such as hybrid vehicles; and
- investing in infrastructure to facilitate low emission vehicles, for example, providing recharging stations for hybrid or electric vehicles.

Organizations like the ICAO and the IATA have concentrated their efforts with regard to lowering the environmental impact of aviation in areas such as aircraft technology, operational and ATM improvements and the feasibility of alternative fuels. The airport operator is considered an essential medium in this renewed framework. Reviewing the activities of aircraft, in particular those relating to improvements in taxiing and Auxiliary Power Unit (APU) usage, represents the key areas identified where inefficiencies exist. Some mitigation measures include:

- providing, and enforcing the use of, fixed electrical ground power (FEGP) and pre-conditioned air (PCA) supply to aircraft at terminal gates, allowing APUs to be switched off without impeding operational capabilities;
- reducing taxi distances and terminal congestion by evaluating airfield layout;

- the holding of aircraft until a departure slot is available (the holding period should be subject to an APU-off policy that must be enforced); and
- engaging with others who have a presence at the airport, such as ATM and aircraft operators, to identify inefficiencies in relation to arrival and departure procedures.

The common element in all these initiatives is collaboration between the airport operator and other airport users. Establishing a reliable reporting system and effective communication channels is vital. Ultimately, each stakeholder knows something about his or her particular type of operation that others do not, and thus the only way to develop an understanding of the needs of each group is to facilitate the collaboration of all airport users and utilize the expertise at their disposal.

Motivations for Airport Operators to Implement Change

> All facets of the aviation industry must work together to achieve emissions reductions through a comprehensive approach that includes operational advances, technology improvements, alternative fuels, and economic measures.
>
> (Airport Council International 2023)

The central focus for airport operators with respect to environmental management is the reduction of carbon emissions. This is despite the fact that when put into perspective, airport-related activities contribute only 5 per cent of total greenhouse gas emissions from aviation (according to the IPCC). Reporting emissions remains voluntary in many jurisdictions, but some have introduced mandatory reporting schemes. An important development in this regard was the launch of the airport carbon accreditation scheme by the ACI. The scheme, set up in 2009, is based on a four-tier system whereby accreditation is given based on an operator's ability to reduce its carbon footprint. The names given to each tier are: (1) mapping, (2) reduction, (3) optimization and (4) neutrality. Achieving accreditation for 'mapping' simply requires an airport to measure its carbon performance, identify sources of emissions and compile the information in an independently verified report.

Fulfilling the criteria for the 'reduction' award is a matter of proving to inspectors that airport management is putting carbon management procedures into place and that carbon reduction goals have been met. The 'optimization' award recognizes airports that have engaged and reduced emissions from third parties operating out of the site, including airlines, ground-handling groups and catering companies. Finally, airports that have launched environmental projects to offset remaining carbon emissions are awarded the rare 'neutrality' accreditation.

The elimination of 550,000 tonnes of emissions was the result one year on after the launch, and as the roster of accredited airports grows, this number will only rise. Twenty-three airports are currently accredited in some form by the scheme, including major international hubs like London Heathrow, which achieved an optimization award on 11 October 2010. The 23 airports account for around a third of European passenger traffic, and it remains to be seen if this system can be applied on a global scale, whereby emissions are being reduced without the regulatory obligation to do so.

Another motivating factor is the growing movement in the corporate worlds towards corporate social responsibility (CSR). CSR is a form of self-regulation seen in organizations that demonstrate and acknowledge their responsibilities to society, a characteristic of a business that has embedded a strong culture of responsibility in its stakeholders.

With regard to an airport operator, it refers to one that addresses not only the emissions for which it is directly responsible, but also collaborates with airport users who are responsible for the majority of total airport-related emissions. Airports around the world seem to hold a significant status within their local communities as a respectably run operation, and the initiative taken by airport operators to address emission sources for which they are not directly responsible will help build relationships with other stakeholders and the community.

Of course, in some jurisdictions, there are regulatory motivations, if not actual obligations. Indeed, no airport at the time of writing has a regulatory obligation to reduce emissions to certain levels. Having said this, obligations are in place requiring operators to meet other criteria. As climate change regulation evolves, this will likely not be the case going into the future. However, the work of organizations like the ACI has led to airport authorities around the world setting individual emission reduction targets in the absence of legal obligations and repercussions. The introduction of an accreditation programme makes it beneficial for airport authorities to demonstrate to the wider community and other stakeholders operating inside airport facilities that they too have a role to play in the broader aviation community's efforts to minimize its impact on the environment.

In the USA, for example, greenhouse gas reporting is a mandatory requirement applying to businesses that emit more than 25,000 tonnes of carbon dioxide per year. The requirements of those businesses that satisfy this criterion include the submission of annual reports each year, starting in 2011. The EU also requires such reporting in relation to its Emissions Trading Scheme (ETS).

Since the issue of climate change became a contentious political debate, and one that continues to be used as a means by which to influence the public, the regulatory framework within which the aviation stakeholders compete has changed dramatically. The use of legislative reforms to impose obligations on businesses to meet particular standards and targets has demonstrated signs of improving the outlook. On the other hand, room for improvement is vast and much work remains to be done if the industry is to achieve carbon-neutral growth. With regard to airport operators, however, the pursuit of environmentally sustainable solutions has been driven by a series of other initiatives, given the lack of regulatory obligations to reduce emissions. Instead, a series of other drivers for acknowledging the role that the airport plays in the industry's environmental management has arisen. Some of these political and commercial drivers for action include:

- anticipated increases in utility costs (such as water and electricity);
- taking the initiative and making changes that have not been imposed on the operator may give it a commercial advantage by being a pioneer and a benchmark for others to follow;
- the internalization of carbon costs into the price of products and services;
- a commitment to widening corporate responsibility; and
- the threat of carbon limits being imposed on airport operations.

Fundamental Concepts of Environment Law

Whilst it may be that the word 'environment' is, strictly speaking, a value-free term, the law and society have imposed various values upon it. These find their expression, from a legal point of view, in the principles forming the philosophical basis of environmental law. The central principles that will be addressed here are: permanent sovereignty over natural resources; the precautionary principle; the concepts of intragenerational and intergenerational equity; the doctrine of common but differentiated responsibility; and sustainable development.

Permanent Sovereignty Over Natural Resources An enduring principle in international environmental law is the principle of a nation's permanent sovereignty over its natural resources. The principle allows a nation to exercise its will over how natural resources within its jurisdiction (usually its 'territorial' jurisdiction) are accessed and used. The principle emerged in the twentieth century in response to unacceptable colonial practices in earlier times, whereby natural resources of a nation under colonial rule were subject to the will of the colonial rulers and not that of the local government.

In 1974, the UN recognized the principle in General Assembly Resolution 3281 (XXIX), Article 2(1) of which proclaimed that 'every State has and shall freely exercise full permanent sovereignty, including possession, use and disposal, over all its wealth, natural resources and economic activities'. Theoretically, the 'permanent' nature of permanent sovereignty means that a nation's rights in this respect are inalienable (Fisher 2010: 56), but nations may voluntarily restrict their rights or choose not to exercise them. Nations may also become bound, in international law, to limit the exercise of their sovereign rights by submitting to treaties, or through the international acceptance of customary laws.

The right to exercise sovereignty is not unlimited. States have the obligation not to use their natural resources in such a way as to harm the natural resources of another state. This was established in *Trail Smelter Arbitration* (*United States v Canada* (1941) International Environmental Law Reports 231), where the Tribunal said, at 310:

> Under the principles of international law . . . no State has the right to use or permit the use of its territory in such a manner as to cause injury by fumes in or to the territory of another or the properties or the persons therein, when the case is of serious consequence and the injury is established by clear and convincing evidence.

The Precautionary Principle In terms of environmental law, the precautionary principle advocates taking proactive measures to prevent environmental harm rather than waiting for conclusive scientific proof that an action is required or will be successful in obtaining an environmental benefit. Essentially, it makes the default position 'why not' rather than 'why' when considering whether or not to institute a measure to prevent the degradation of the environment in the face of possible serious or irreversible damage and divided scientific opinion. It advocates a cautious approach to any practice that might harm the environment.

The *UN Framework Convention on Climate Change (UNFCCC) 1992* advocates this precautionary approach, exhorting nations to take precautionary measures to protect the environment and also stating that

> where there are threats of serious or irreversible damage, lack of full scientific certainty should not be used as a reason for postponing such measures, taking into account that policies and measures to deal with climate change should be cost-effective so as to ensure global benefits at the lowest possible cost.

Another interpretation suggests that the precautionary principle ensures that policymakers will consider the environmental impact of their actions before implementing them (Cameron and Abouchar 1991).

Similarly, at the 1992 *UN Conference on Environment and Development* (UNCED or 'Earth Summit'), about 200 states adopted the *Rio Declaration on Environment and Development*, Principle 15 of which provided:

> In order to protect the environment, the precautionary approach shall be widely applied by States according to their capabilities. Where there are threats of serious or irreversible damage, lack of full scientific certainty shall not be used as a reason for postponing cost-effective measures to prevent environmental degradation.

Historically, the approach taken before the emergence in the early 1980s of the precautionary principle was the more permissive 'assimilative capacity approach', where the assimilative capacity was the ability of the environment to tolerate anthropogenic disturbances without sustaining unacceptable harm. This approach relied upon two assumptions, the integrity of which could be described as questionable. First, it assumed that science could indeed accurately predict adverse effects on the environment; second, that science could propose and implement effective solutions to identified environmental problems; and, third, that sufficient time to develop and implement these solutions would remain once the adverse effect was identified (McIntyre and Mosedale 1997). Accordingly, the assimilative capacity approach represents an attitude whereby polluters may continue polluting until there is conclusive scientific proof that their actions are causing environmental damage. The precautionary principle reverses this onus of proof, suggesting that where there is cause to question the environmental soundness of any action, the person taking that action should prove that there is no adverse environmental effect before continuing with that action.

An example of judicial consideration of the precautionary principle comes from the courts of Australia. In *Telstra Corporation Ltd v Hornsby Shire Council* (2006) 67 NSWLR 256, Preston CJ in the New South Wales Land and Environment Court provided a detailed summary of the aspects of the precautionary principle and how to apply it. He explained that the principle required two conditions to be fulfilled before it could apply: first, there must be at least a threat of serious or irreversible environmental damage; and, second, there must be a lack of scientific consensus, or a degree of scientific uncertainty, as to the necessity of taking precautionary measures. When these are fulfilled, the effect of the principle is to shift the onus of proof to the person proposing that the threatening action be taken – that is, the decision-maker must assume that the damage will occur if a given project is allowed to proceed, and the person proposing the project must convince the decision-maker that it will not have an adverse effect on the environment. The Chief Judge succinctly summarized the rationale for this reversal of the ordinary onus of proof (at 273):

> The rationale for requiring this shift of the burden of proof is to ensure preventative anticipation; to act before scientific certainty of cause and effect is established. It may be too late, or too difficult and costly, to change a course of action once it is proven to be harmful. The preference is to prevent environmental damage, rather than remediate it. The benefit of the doubt is given to environmental protection when there is scientific uncertainty. To avoid environmental harm, it is better to err on the side of caution.

Intragenerational and Intergenerational Equity The old adage goes that we do not inherit the earth from our ancestors; we borrow it from our children. It is widely attributed to Native American culture and outlines the basic concept behind intergenerational equity. The fundamental idea is to preserve the integrity of the environment available for future generations. This must be done whilst ensuring intragenerational equity, sometimes referred to as 'environmental justice'. To achieve intragenerational equity, the aim is to allow fair and equitable access to natural resources for the present generation. Some authors on the subject of intergenerational equity – for example, Wood (1996: 298–9) – invoke legal philosopher John Rawls, who suggested that rules of fairness should be determined from a conceptual 'original position' by imposing a 'veil of uncertainty'. Under the conceptual 'veil of uncertainty', the decision-maker is entirely unaware of his or her position in society, geography or time (Rawls 1970). Theoretically, then, the decision-maker under the veil will act for the good of all, rather than in self-interest.

In *State of Himachal Pradesh v Ganesh Wood Products*, AIR 1996 SC 149, the Supreme Court of India expressed the concept of intergenerational equity in this way (at 159 [42]):

> Intergenerational equity means the concern for generations to come. The present generation has no right to imperil the safety and well-being of the next generation or the generations to come thereafter.

It may seem that intragenerational and intergenerational equity are polar opposites or, at least, not entirely consistent. However, the better view is that intragenerational equity is very much a part of intergenerational equity – the present generation has an equal right to generations of the past and of the future to access the planet's natural resources (Preston 2005: 175).

Writing extra-judicially, Justice Preston (2005: 176–7) outlines three fundamental principles tying the two concepts together:

- conservation of options: the present generation should aim to preserve or broaden the options available to future generations to use the planet's natural resources;
- conservation of quality: the present generation should sustain or enhance the quality of the environment that is passed on to future generations;
- conservation of access: the present generation should maintain for itself a fair and equitable access to the planet's natural resources in order to improve its own well-being, as long as obligations to future generations are met.

Common but Differentiated Responsibility Debate in the international arena leading up to the signing in 1992 of the UNFCCC surrounded the level of response required by nations (or, more specifically, by different classes of nations) to address climate change. Tension existed between 'developed' and 'developing' nations: the 'developing' nations wanted the opportunity to develop as the 'developed' nations had, regardless of the effect that this might have on the environment. The concept of common but differentiated responsibility recognizes that 'developed' nations have a greater responsibility for having created any anthropogenically induced climate change due to their historical background, and also have a greater capacity to address the problem, so should bear a greater burden to do so.

The 'common' responsibility is the responsibility of all nations to protect the 'common heritage of mankind' (in this case, the environment, but the term has been used in other areas, such as the high seas and outer space). The 'differentiated' responsibility of each nation is determined by its historical trajectory. If it is accepted that development and the emission of carbon dioxide are anthropogenic causes of climate change, then this is based on each nation's respective level of responsibility for causing that change and its capacity to make amends. In a less politically charged setting, it may be described as an efficient allocation of roles in protecting the common environment of all nations to those nations who can protect it best.

A more specific determination of the 'differentiated' responsibility of nations was achieved with the Kyoto Protocol to the UNFCCC in 1997. The Protocol set emissions targets for 37 'developed' nations plus the EU based on the level of emissions that existed in 1990. On average, those nations listed were obliged to meet a target of 95 per cent of their 1990 emissions.

Sustainable Development In a 1999 article in the *Stanford Environmental Journal*, J.B. Ruhl outlined a problem with the then current state of 'environmentalism' and with 'environmentalists' of the time. He argued that environmentalism is a 'worn out label' and said that its permutations are found in a 'sea of bumper sticker slogans and self-righteous, self-anointed "environmentalists"'. In questioning the true character of an environmentalist, he suggested that a brand new label is needed. Rather than being just a superficial title, he suggested a new label corresponding to the visions of a 'unified approach to environment, equality and equity' is needed,

> He suggested that sustainable development was the way of the future. The term 'sustainable development' was coined at the 1987 World Commission on the Environment and Development (also known as the 'Brundtland Commission', after its chairman). The Commission defined the term as being 'development that meets the needs of the present without compromising the ability of future generations to meet their own needs'.
>
> (United Nations World Commission on Environment and Development 1987: 8)

The concept of sustainable development – known sometimes as 'ecologically sustainable development' (ESD) – thus recognizes that the development of human society can and must continue, but it must be done in a way that can be supported by the natural environment. French (2005: 35) described it in this way:

> A political, socio-economic, and potentially moral, objective which may in turn have certain normative consequences, but its origins lie not so much in jurisprudence as in the argument that economic, environmental and social considerations must be integrated if environmental protection and development are to be mutually supportive.

Fisher (2010: 144–5) outlines a definition of ESD by considering the meaning of the individual words. As a compound term, ESD combines the notions of development, ecology and sustainability:

- *Development*: development in this context may be seen as the conversion of resources to be put to valuable use. It is advancement, activity and achievement – an idea of progress.
- *Ecology*: this term is often used interchangeably with 'environment' and its use as such is not inappropriate in this context. As discussed earlier, 'environment' is a neutral term referring to a place. In this context, it is the place from which resources are taken and to which the resources are returned (often as waste) after they are used.

- *Sustainability*: this is the concept of continuing. Here, it is taken to mean that the environment will continue to support future activities of human society.

The fusion of these three concepts is deceptively simple in theory, but incredibly difficult in practice, in which it is difficult to know: (1) how society should develop and how to control that development; and (2) what impact this development will have on the ability of the environment to sustain further development. The concept comes down to an evaluation of the stress that human society places on the environment and whether or not the environment can withstand that stress whilst continuing to support life.

International Agreements

International environmental law has a history extending back to the late nineteenth century in international arbitral tribunals, and later in the International Court of Justice. An in-depth analysis of the development of international environmental law is not appropriate here: instead, this section will address the law as it currently stands.

Treaty or convention law now occupies much of the field of international environmental law, and the conventions in place now make detailed provisions outlining the international obligations of countries in respect of the environment. An early convention was the *Declaration of the United Nations Conference on the Human Environment* (1972), known as the 'Stockholm Declaration'. The Stockholm Declaration outlined the right of humans to 'freedom, equality and adequate conditions of life' (Principle 1) and some general obligations not directed to anyone in particular (and thus directed to everyone), *inter alia*, to preserve and protect natural resources and prevent pollution by toxic substances.

In 1992, as briefly mentioned previously, the 'Earth Summit' was held in Rio de Janeiro. From the Summit, a number of documents and conventions emerged. Relevant here are:

- the *Declaration of the United Nations Conference on Environment and Development* (1992), known as the 'Rio Declaration'; and
- the United Nations Framework Convention on Climate Change (UNFCCC).

The UNFCCC established a 'Conference of the Parties' (COP) as the supreme body of the Convention. At the third session of the Conference of the Parties, held in Kyoto in December 1997, agreement was reached on the Kyoto Protocol 1997 to the *United Nations Framework Convention on Climate Change*. The latest meeting of the COP, its twenty-third, was held in November 2017 in Bonn, Germany.

The Rio Declaration The Rio Declaration outlined 27 principles placing obligations upon nations in relation to the environment and development. The Declaration recognized that development and the environment could no longer be considered separately, and that they must be considered together in order for development to be sustainable (Principle 4).

A number of the principles reiterate the issues discussed previously, such as the permanent sovereignty over natural resources (Principle 2), the precautionary principle

(Principle 15), intergenerational equity (Principle 3) and notions of common but differentiated responsibility (Principles 5–7). Nations also come under the obligation to enact effective environmental legislation (Principle 11), to develop national laws regarding liability and compensation for victims of environmental damage (Principle 13), to provide prior and timely notification and relevant information to other nations potentially affected by activities that may have a significant adverse transboundary effect (Principle 19) and to resolve all environmental disputes peacefully and in accordance with the Charter of the United Nations (Principle 26).

The UN Framework Convention and the Kyoto Protocol

The UNFCCC provides an extensive framework for the protection of the entire 'climate system' (being the atmosphere, hydrosphere, biosphere and geosphere and their interactions: Article 1(3)). The Convention is in four main parts: the objective, several principles, a series of commitments placed upon nations, and the establishment and constitution of the COP.

Article 2 states the objective of the UNFCCC as being to achieve a stabilization of greenhouse gas concentrations in the atmosphere at a level to prevent dangerous anthropogenic interference with the climate system. This is to be done within a timeframe that allows ecosystems to adapt naturally to climate change, without threatening food production or sustainable economic development.

Five principles are outlined in Article 3. The principles have a focus on sustainable development, but also include intergenerational equity (Article 3(1)) and the precautionary principle (Article 3(3)). The notion of common but differentiated responsibility appears in several of the principles (Article 3(1), (2) and (5)), which also direct attention to the specific circumstances of developing countries. Significantly, developed countries should 'take the lead' in combating climate change and its adverse effects.

As for the commitments, all nations are reminded in Article 4 of their common but differentiated responsibility. The provisions of Article 4(1) apply to all parties, both developed and developing, and include obligations to report, share information and technologies, promote the interests of the Convention and participate in international cooperation in addressing climate change.

Article 4(2) contains obligations only binding on developed countries, which are listed in Annex I of the Convention. It should be noted, however, that Article 4(2) applies specifically to those greenhouse gases that are not covered by the *Montreal Protocol on Substances that Deplete the Ozone Layer* (1987). The Montreal Protocol lists a large number of substances in its Annexes A, B, C and E. What is significant about the provisions of the UNFCCC applying to substances *not* controlled by the earlier Montreal Protocol is that emissions of carbon dioxide, perhaps the most destructive greenhouse gas, are now controlled in international law.

The Kyoto Protocol A subsidiary part of the UNFCCC is the Kyoto Protocol, which was created on 11 December 1997 in Kyoto, Japan. It is an international agreement that sets binding targets for nations to reduce greenhouse gas (GHG) emissions. The agreement entered into force on 16 February 2005, 90 days after ratification by the 55th state had occurred. In March 2024, 195 parties (194 states and the EU) had ratified the Kyoto Protocol, which accounts for 63.7 per cent of emissions from Annex I states.

The significance of this protocol was that whereas the UNFCCC *encouraged* states, particularly industrialized nations, to stabilize GHG emissions, the Kyoto Protocol *committed* them to do so. A heavier burden was placed on developed nations through the 'common but differentiated responsibilities' principle, recognizing that they were major contributors to climate change after over 150 years of industrial activity. One of the biggest features of the Kyoto Protocol was the determination of binding targets for Annex I states to reduce GHG emissions by an average of 5 per cent against 1990 levels over the five-year period 2008–12.

Under the Protocol, countries must meet targets primarily through national measures, though it does outline an additional three market-based methods by which targets may be met, namely: emissions trading, the clean development mechanism and joint implementation. These methods are designed to be cost-effective as they encourage green investment by both the public and private sectors.

Annex B of the Kyoto Protocol sets out the emissions targets for each nation listed in Annex I of the UNFCCC. To meet those targets, nations must reduce emissions of the gases listed at Annex A of the Protocol (Article 3(1)). Each party to the Protocol has their own quantified economy-wide emissions targets for 2020. The European Union aims to reduce its emissions by 20–30 per cent (with 1990 as its base year). The US, although it still has not ratified the treaty, aims to reduce its emissions by 17 per cent (with a base level of 2005). Annex A lists the following gases:

- carbon dioxide (CO_2);
- methane (CH_4);
- nitrous oxide (N_2O);
- hydrofluorocarbons (HFCs);
- perfluorocarbons (PFCs);
- sulphur hexafluoride (SF_6).

Carbon dioxide is the main greenhouse gas, so most of the discussion on this topic, especially in the popular media, only speaks of carbon dioxide. Increasingly, the shorthand is becoming even shorter, and people speak of 'carbon' emissions. The reader must be careful to note that all such references really refer to all the gases in Annex A of the Kyoto Protocol.

Under Article 4(1), Annex I nations may collaborate by separate agreement. Any nations entering into such agreements are released from their Annex B targets, but new targets must be set in the agreement, and the targets must add to the same result in terms of emissions as the Annex B targets for the aggregate of the nations in the agreement.

Various mechanisms are endorsed by the Protocol. Article 6 allows for emissions reduction units to be transferred from one nation to another. An emissions reduction unit is created by engaging in a project to reduce emissions in an industry or to enhance the removal of greenhouse gases by sinks. The project must achieve reduced emissions or improved removals over and above what would have been achieved in the ordinary course of things, and must be in addition to national actions undertaken pursuant to obligations under Article 3. Excess units may be sold to other countries under Article 17.

Article 12 defines a 'clean development mechanism' (CDM). The CDM is based on approved projects undertaken by or with the support of Annex I nations in non-Annex I nations. The mechanism allows the Annex I nation to offset its emissions target by the amount of accrued 'certified emissions reductions' from the approved project. At the same time, the non-Annex I nation clearly gains the benefit of emissions reductions while developing in a sustainable way.

Kyoto's Successor?

The Kyoto Protocol was expected to come to an end in 2012. However, the European Union agreed in a conference in Doha, Qatar, to accept a second phase of the Protocol which commenced in 2013, with a mission to achieve emissions targets by 2020. Nations have also sought to establish a successor protocol, forming the basis of discussions at the 15th meeting of the COP to the UNFCCC in Copenhagen in 2009. The result of the Copenhagen meeting was relatively insignificant when compared to Kyoto, as it culminated in a non-legally binding accord between only five states out of the 193 attendees – the USA, China, India, Brazil and South Africa. The accord merely committed individual nations to act independently to address climate change through a 'goal of limiting the global temperature rise to 2 degrees Celsius above pre-industrial levels by 2050'.

Many nations criticized the Copenhagen accord. The criticisms mainly related to the failure of the accord to reach a legally binding agreement and therefore become a successor to the Kyoto Protocol, and a further failure to outline mid-/long-term reduction targets for both industrialized and developing nations.

Although there was a fair degree of international scepticism following the lack of universal support of both the Copenhagen Accord and the Kyoto Protocol there has been a certain renewed sense of optimism with the Paris Agreement taking effect from November 2016. At this stage it is a little too early to determine whether this optimism is well founded or not. No doubt time will tell.

The Paris Agreement

The Paris Climate Conference, held in November and December 2015, was convened in acknowledgement of the need to accelerate anti-global-warming efforts. The Paris Agreement, also known as the Paris Climate Accord, is an agreement within the *United Nations Framework Convention on Climate Change* dealing with greenhouse gas emissions mitigation, adaptation and finance starting in the year 2020.

The primary objective of the conference was to strengthen the worldwide response by all nations into a common cause, combating climate change and adapting to its effects. The Agreement was negotiated by representatives of 196 parties at the 21st Conference of the Parties of the UNFCCC in Paris and adopted by consensus on 12 December 2015. The Agreement came into force on 4 November 2016. As of March 2024, 196 UNFCCC members have signed the agreement and 175 have ratified it. More than 100 developing countries, including China, the world's top carbon emitter, will start taking action by 2024, when hydrofluorocarbons (HFC) consumption levels should peak.

The Agreement aims to respond to the global climate change threat by keeping a global temperature rise this century well below 2.0 degrees Celsius above pre-industrial levels and more ambitiously to pursue efforts to limit the temperature increase even further to 1.5 degrees Celsius. The Agreement obliges each contracting state to determine, plan and regularly report its own contribution it should make in order to mitigate global warming. There is, however, no mechanism to force a country to set a specific target by a specific date, but each target should go beyond previously set targets.

A major setback to the Agreement occurred in June 2017 when President Donald Trump announced his intention for the United States to withdraw from the agreement. As the US is the world's second-worst polluter this created widespread international condemnation. The earliest effective date of withdrawal for the US under the agreement is November 2020, just before the end of President Trump's first term.

The Role of the ICAO

Along with the Annex I nations, the ICAO bears responsibility under the Kyoto Protocol. Article 2(2) of the Protocol reads:

> The Parties included in Annex I shall pursue limitation or reduction of emissions of greenhouse gases not controlled by the Montreal Protocol from aviation and marine bunker fuels, working through the International Civil Aviation Organization and the International Maritime Organization, respectively.

The ICAO thus has the responsibility to coordinate efforts of international civil aviation (technically, the coordination of aviation efforts of those Annex I nations that are also ICAO contracting states) towards reducing emissions from burning aviation fuel. This is a responsibility that the ICAO appears to take seriously. Dr Ruwantissa Abeyratne, the Co-Coordinator of Air Transport Programs and Acting Deputy Director of the Air Transport Bureau of the ICAO, says in his book *Aviation and the Environment* (2009):

> [The] ICAO strives to achieve a balance between the benefit accruing to the world community through civil aviation and the harm caused to the environment in certain areas through the progressive advancement of civil aviation. [The] ICAO is conscious of and will continue to take into account the adverse environmental impacts that may be related to civil aviation activity and its responsibility and that of its Contracting States to achieve maximum compatibility between the safe and orderly development of civil aviation and the quality of the environment.

At the 31st Session of the ICAO Assembly in 1995, it was resolved to adopt at each following ordinary session a consolidated statement of the ICAO's environmental policies. The first such consolidated statement was Resolution A31–11, which collected together various policies then in force. At the latest session, the 39th, held in September–October 2016, Resolution A39–15 stated the continuing ICAO policies in the air transport field.

It should be noted that the ICAO is in an excellent position to orchestrate the global aviation response to environmental issues. The 193 contracting states to the Chicago Convention are in the habit of adhering to directives from the ICAO. It can be argued that, as the ICAO Council Annexes its directives to the Chicago Convention, they become binding upon contracting states in international law. However, even if that is not true, the state of affairs in international aviation is that the contracting states usually consider themselves bound (Kirgis 1995). This gives a resolution of the ICAO Assembly or a directive of the ICAO Council some weight in terms of setting policy.

It is due to this acquiescence of contracting states that the ICAO is in such a position to influence aviation environmental law and policy. In this area, the ICAO Council has established the Committee on Aviation Environmental Protection (CAEP) and the Group on International Aviation and Climate Change (GIACC).

The work of the GIACC has now concluded, with a final report being issued in June 2009, and the Group has now disbanded. Its role was to develop a Programme of Action on International Aviation and Climate Change. It recommended to the Council that it adopt a 'basket of measures' from which contracting states could select their preferred measures to take. These are a set of aspirational goals to reduce emissions. The measures included (ICAO 2009a):

- aircraft-related technology development: new aircraft, retrofitting old aircraft to be more fuel-efficient and the development of alternative fuels;
- improved ATM and infrastructure use: efficient ATM planning, airspace design and usage;
- more efficient operations: minimize weight, maximize load factors, optimize maintenance schedules and use aircraft suitable to the intended role;
- economic/market-based measures: carbon offsetting, emissions trading and emissions charges;
- regulatory/other measures: management of airport movement caps and slots, enhanced weather forecasting and transparent carbon reporting.

The Council fully accepted the GIACC Final Report. A High-Level Meeting on International Aviation and Climate Change (HLM-ENV/09) was held in October 2009 to review the GIACC Final Report. At the Meeting, the following points were agreed upon (ICAO 2009a):

- a global goal of a 2 per cent annual improvement in fuel efficiency until the year 2050 and further exploration of the feasibility of more ambitious medium- and long-term goals, including carbon-neutral growth and emissions reductions;
- the development of a global CO_2 standard for aircraft and the facilitation of further operational changes to reduce aviation emissions;
- the development of a framework for market-based measures in international aviation;
- further elaboration on measures to assist developing states and to facilitate access to financial resources, technology transfer and capacity building; and
- the submission of states' action plans, outlining their policies and actions, and annual reporting of data to the ICAO on their aviation fuel consumption.

The role of the CAEP is technical, developing procedures and conducting research on various areas. These areas presently include aircraft noise, an assessment of the stringency of NO_x emission controls on aircraft engines and a study to quantify the environmental effects of aviation, including climate effects, noise and local air quality (Abeyratne 2009: 95–6).

Carbon Offsetting and Reduction Scheme for International Aviation

A globally accepted market-based mechanism (MBM) system was recognized by ICAO in 2016 in the form of the Carbon Offsetting and Reduction Scheme for International Aviation (CORSIA). The system is based on offsetting, whereby the global aviation sector will offset its emissions through the reduction of emissions elsewhere, and purchasing credit from a supply and demand driven 'carbon market' generated by projects that reduce carbon emissions around the world. Participation in CORSIA is for now voluntary, but as of October 2016, 66 states (accounting for 86.5 per cent of global international aviation activity) announced their voluntary participation. From 2027, however, all states with an individual share of international aviation activities above 0.5 per cent or whose cumulative share reaches 90 per cent of the total must participate in the scheme.

The phases are:

- 2021 to 2023: a 'pilot' voluntary phase of nation-states who elect to be part of the scheme. There will be a review in 2022 to determine if any adjustments need to be made for the continuing effectiveness of the scheme.
- 2024 to 2026: the first voluntary implementation phase.
- 2027 to 2035: the second phase which will include most states except least developed countries (LDCs), small island developing states (SIDS), landlocked developing countries (LLDCs) and countries with a small amount of international air traffic (less than 0.5 per cent of global traffic). Those exempted countries, however, can volunteer. This second phase has triennial technical adjustments to the distribution of obligations between individual airlines, moving towards a more individual approach.

CORSIA is to apply to all aircraft operators on the same routes between states, with the Assembly deciding:

- All international flights on the routes between states, both of which are included in the CORSIA, are covered by CORSIA.
- All international flights on the routes between a state that is included in the CORSIA and another state that is not included in the CORSIA are exempted from the offsetting requirements of the CORSIA.
- All international flights on the routes between states, both of which are not included in the preceding CORSIA, are also exempted.
- New entrants are exempted from CORSIA for three years or until the year in which its annual emissions exceed 0.1 per cent of total emissions in 2020 (whichever occurs earlier). From the subsequent year, the new entrant is included in the scheme and treated in the same way as the other aircraft operators. 'New entrants' are defined by ICAO as 'any aircraft operator that commences an aviation activity falling within the scope of the scheme on or after its entry into force and whose activity is not in whole or in part a continuation of an aviation activity previously performed by another aircraft operator'.
- CORSIA does not apply to low levels of international aviation activity with a view to avoiding administrative burden:
  - aircraft operators emitting less than 10,000 metric tonnes of CO_2 emissions from international aviation per year;
  - aircraft with less than 5,700 kg of Maximum Take Off Mass (MTOM); or
  - humanitarian, medical and firefighting operations.
- The emissions that are not covered by the scheme, as the result of phased implementation and exemptions, are not assigned as offsetting requirements of any aircraft operators included in the scheme.

There are clear flaws with this MBM approach. Its voluntary nature up until 2027 has meant two large aviation markets – those of Russia and India – have decided not to participate. It is therefore difficult to imagine carbon neutral growth being a reality by 2020, which is one of ICAO's environmental objectives. Furthermore, CORSIA lacks clear criteria for what kinds of offsets are favourable or not. Airlines may make their own judgments on what are good offsets for them, rather than for the environment.

The future of CORSIA came into question when in early 2019 the then United States President Donald Trump announced it would withdraw from the Paris Agreement, then on 4 November 2019, the Trump administration gave a formal notice of intention to withdraw, which takes 12 months to take effect. President Trump contended that the agreement would 'undermine' the US economy, and put the US 'at a permanent disadvantage'. Trump's withdrawal from the Paris Agreement impacted other countries by reducing its financial aid to the Green Climate fund. The termination of the USD 3 billion funding ultimately impacted climate change research and decreased society's chance of reaching the Paris Agreement goals, as well as omitted US contributions to the future IPCC reports. The irony is that the US was actually a strong negotiator on behalf of CORSIA in October 2016.

On 20 January 2021, shortly after his inauguration, President Biden signed an executive order to rejoin the Paris Agreement. The United States formally rejoined on 19 February 2021, 107 days after the withdrawal took effect. The Paris Agreement is an unprecedented framework for global action. We know this because all the attending nations designed it to make it a reality. Its purpose is both simple and expansive: to help us all avoid catastrophic global warming and to build resilience around the world to the impacts from climate change we are experiencing on an almost daily basis.

18
Innovation and the 2050 Net Zero Emission Target

INTRODUCTION

It is quite apt that a chapter of this publication be dedicated to the rapidly evolving areas of the aviation industry, and of aviation law, that will be instrumental in attempting to achieve the internationally agreed *Net Zero Emission* target by 2050. Political agreement on targeting net zero for aviation has been complemented by fiscal and regulatory policies throughout the world to promote a variety of initiatives to meet these targets and to provide for a more sustainable aviation sector. Most relevantly, these targets have been agreed to and supported by the International Civil Aviation Organization (ICAO) and the International Air Transport Association (IATA).

To meet these targets, technological innovation is needed across the entire aviation sector including the production of low-emission and sustainable aviation fuels, design improvements in aircraft and engines, and operational fleet optimization. With the escalating increase in aviation traffic in the post-pandemic era, demand restraint scenarios also need to be considered to curb growth in emissions and ultimately reduce them this decade. But to achieve these objectives there needs to be a more collaborative approach, not only between aircraft and engine manufacturers and the airlines and airport operators, but between governments – internationally and domestically – to develop policies and regulations that support and promote these objectives.

NET ZERO EMISSIONS 2050 TARGET

In the previous chapter on environmental law the background to the Net Zero Emissions 2050 target was introduced. While the target is set and the global commitments agreed, it will be critical for progress of the industry, to adopt a united approach by governments and international agencies (especially ICAO), aviation manufacturers, airline and airport operators and industry associations (especially IATA) to meet these timelines based on continued investment in new technologies, innovations and alternative fuel resources. The strategy that will decarbonize aviation the most by 2050 combines more expedient improvements in fuel efficiency with accelerated fleet renewal, maximum use of sustainable aviation fuels (SAF) and hybrid-electric aircraft.

In October 2022, member states of the International Civil Aviation Organization (ICAO) agreed to a long-term aspirational goal (LTAG) of net zero carbon dioxide (CO_2) emissions from aviation by 2050. The agreement signals a turn away from merely offsetting emissions and toward measures to dramatically reduce CO_2 from planes and fuels. It directs the ICAO Council to take the following actions:

DOI: 10.4324/9781032652146-18

- develop and update guidance on the application of control policies and measures for member states, including operational measures, and monitor progress in implementing State Action Plans (SAPs);
- create finance mechanisms to support decarbonization initiatives in developing countries;
- further develop tools to quantify aviation's GHG emissions, including the ICAO Carbon Emissions Calculator; and
- identify the potential impacts of climate change on international aviation and related infrastructure and determine appropriate adaptation measures.

The agreement represents a shift away from previous ICAO climate governance. It favours action to reduce CO_2 from planes and fuels directly, rather than mitigating emissions through the purchase of emissions credit or offsets from other sectors. It envisions deep cuts in aviation CO_2, to near-zero levels by 2050, which ICAO estimates will cost up to USD 4 trillion. And it invites member states to regulate aviation emissions themselves, rather than relying on ICAO to develop minimum global standards covering all countries.

AIRCRAFT AND ENGINE DESIGN AND OPERATIONS

It is quite apparent that while there will likely be technological advances, without major scientific breakthroughs, the aviation industry will need to make significant trade-offs or extend its timeline for reaching net zero emissions, especially if air traffic continues to grow at the forecasted rates. Additionally, the challenge in meeting this goal will also likely impact the cost of aviation. Currently the four main technologies to lower emissions are:

- enhanced aircraft and engine design;
- sustainable aviation fuel (SAF);
- electric-powered aircraft; and
- hydrogen and hybrid propulsion.

Efforts in improving the in-flight energy efficiency through investment in new propulsion, airframes, structures and systems are independent of what type (traditional v SAF) fuel is used for the flight. Airlines are going to have to change the makeup of their fleets and accelerate fleet renewal, aiming to introduce at least two generations of more efficient aircraft into service by 2050.

Historically, new generation aircraft have delivered a 20 per cent reduction in energy use compared to the aircraft they replace. The full transition to the current optimal aircraft technology has not yet been finalized. For example, many Airbus A320s are still being replaced by A320neos, and Boeing 737s by 737-Max. This fleet replacement will already provide an initial reduction in in-flight energy use. Recent technology assessments for evolutionary aircraft predict another 15–20 per cent improvement, compared to the optimal technology available today through the introduction of more efficient engines, lighter materials and improved aerodynamics.

Customers may also need to be a part of the solution. While the costs of upgrading fleet and/or using alternative fuels are more expensive, airlines could give customers the option to choose to fly more fuel efficient or SAF-powered aircraft by offering incentives. Likewise governments around the world may incentivize, possibly by way of subsidies, such initiatives.

Although revolutionary aircraft and propulsion designs are being explored which will still rely on conventional jet fuel or SAF, but which could include technological improvements, they at best are unlikely to provide for improvements in efficiency of more than 10 per cent as compared to current state of the art aircraft types.

IATA's *Fly Net Zero* is the commitment of airlines to achieve net zero carbon by 2050. Achieving net zero by 2050 will require a combination of maximum elimination of emissions at the source, offsetting and carbon capture technologies. IATA has estimated that the relative contribution of each of these initiatives to meet this target are 65 per cent from sustainable aviation fuel; 13 per cent new technology, electric and hydrogen; 3 per cent infrastructure and operational efficiencies; and 19 per cent from offsets and carbon capture.

SUSTAINABLE AVIATION FUELS

According to IATA, the only way to fully decouple the aviation demand growth curve from the emissions curve is to change the source of the CO_2 emissions: the fuel. There are mainly three possible candidates to replace conventional aviation fuel: sustainable aviation fuels (SAF), batteries and hydrogen.

Sustainable aviation fuels are critical to decarbonizing aviation. Currently, demand for aviation fuel is dominated by AVTUR, while SAF currently accounts for less than 0.1 per cent of all aviation fuels consumed; however, high production costs and limited supply has slowed its adoption. Powerplant manufacturers and airlines are increasingly trialling flights that are entirely fuelled by SAF, which can be deployed in current infrastructure, engines and aircraft with minor adjustments to fuel delivery equipment.

According to IATA, sustainable aviation fuels can reduce emissions by 80 per cent and SAF can be made from several sources ranging from agricultural waste to carbon captured from the air. Supporting research and development on advanced biofuel technologies can unlock more abundant and cheaper feedstocks such as agricultural residues, dedicated energy crops and municipal solid waste. SAF also has the advantage that it is fully compatible with existing aircraft and fuelling infrastructure.

Based on current estimates of planned production capacities, SAF will provide just 1–2 per cent of jet fuel demand by 2027. However, IATA estimates that SAF could make up around 65 per cent of the emissions reduction needed by aviation to reach net zero by 2050. But it will require a massive increase in production in order to meet demand. The largest acceleration is expected in the 2030s as policy support becomes global, SAF becomes competitive with fossil kerosene and credible offsets become scarcer. Increasing SAF use in aviation to 10 per cent by 2030 in line with the 2050 net zero emission target will require a significant increase in investment in the capacity to produce SAF, and governments will need to provide supportive policies such as fuel taxes and low-carbon fuels standards.

Governments are increasingly providing fiscal support for SAF production and, in some instances, mandating SAF usage. Production of SAF gained substantial support through the passage in 2022 of the *Inflation Reduction Act* (IRA) in the United States, with USD 3.3 billion in tax credits and a competitive grant programme allocated to SAF.

The IRA provides USD 1.25 per gallon (USD 0.33 per litre) of SAF produced, provided that the lifecycle emissions are no more than 50 per cent of those of fossil jet kerosene. A supplemental 1 cent credit is available for each per cent that the lifecycle emissions reduction exceeds 50 per cent.

In addition to amending the European Union Emissions Trading System to phase out allowances given to the aviation industry by 2026, in Q1 2023 the European Council and Parliament agreed on rules mandating a minimum share of SAF with sub-targets for synthetic fuels. Individual countries such as France and Norway already have SAF blending mandates in place, while Sweden's GHG emissions intensity reduction target will also drive SAF adoption. In 2023, the Swedish Government also announced its aim to invest SEK 15 million (Swedish kronor) annually to support the research and development of electric aircraft. The United Kingdom, following its 2022 Jet Zero pledge, has dedicated GBP 165 million to support SAF projects, with funding allocation running to 2025.

In the Asia–Pacific region, in 2022, Japan proposed legislation mandating that SAF must account for 10 per cent of aviation fuel by 2030. In the same period, the Civil Aviation Administration of China also set ambitions to increase SAF use and lower GHG emissions intensity.

FULL ELECTRIC AIRCRAFT

Full electric battery-powered aircraft have no direct emissions, potentially much lower operational and maintenance costs (dependent on battery durability), high efficiency and far lower noise pollution. However, current battery energy density and weight severely restrict the range of battery electric flights and the size of the aircraft. In September 2022, Eviation performed a test flight of its nine-seat electric aircraft, with an alleged maximum flight range of around 450 km.

The success of deploying electric aircraft technologies will largely depend on the evolution of electric energy storage technologies. The energy density of today's Li-ion batteries is around 200 wh/kg at the pack level, but for short-haul flights over 1,000 km, a battery pack energy density of at least 800 wh/kg would be needed. It is not expected that battery technology will evolve so quickly as to reach those numbers in the next two decades, not even with solid state batteries. Although different companies like CATL in China, or Cuberg and Amprius in the US are announcing advances in lithium-ion technologies that could reach 400–500 wh/kg at the cell level, they usually come with some caveats, the most important of them their cycle life, which attaches a significant cost.

We can anticipate it will take years for those technologies to be fully commercial at competitive levels, and even when that happens their impact will be limited, as at a system level energy densities close to or higher than 500 wh/kg will not be reachable most likely until the end of the next decade. But this does not mean there will not be a case for battery electric aviation before that. There are specific niche applications that are not only a point of entry for battery electric aviation, but a case where the electric aircraft very soon will be clearly superior to conventional aircrafts as the following examples demonstrate.

The first example with a full electric type certificate that hit the market is a small trainer, the Velis Electro. This aircraft has been developed by Pipistrel from Slovenia (acquired by Textron in 2022) and has demonstrated that an application like recreational flight training can be more economically delivered by an electric powerplant. Future additional missions ideally suited for battery electric powerplants are short scenic flights, skydiving and short island hops.

Meanwhile in Australia, Dovetail Electric Aviation is currently developing a conversion of a Cessna Caravan 208 to retrofit, by way of a supplemental type certificate, the conventional single turbine engine with a full electric motor (third party) and a battery pack designed in-house. With a significant number of aircraft in the world in this nine-seat category restricted to operating over short distances, the case for retrofitting these aircraft is compelling with operating costs reduced by 30 per cent or more. New aircraft types are about to enter this market, like the Eviation Alice, which will offer optimized designs to extend range and payload, but presumably with a much higher price tag. That is why a retrofit, as opposed to a new aircraft type, makes more sense in the foreseeable future.

The full potential of all electric aviation will not be realized until superior energy storage solutions can be found. Battery technology will only offer incremental improvements over the next ten years, while other ways to store energy, like hydrogen, can give electric aircraft that extended range if it can be converted into electricity efficiently, as fuel cells are capable of doing.

HYDROGEN-POWERED AIRCRAFT

As was explained in the previous section, current generation full electric aircraft powered by batteries are limited in payload capacity, range and endurance. Tests and prototypes showcase innovations in hydrogen-powered aircraft provide for additional capacities and capabilities. Hydrogen can be used via direct combustion in jet engines, or in fuel cells to generate electricity for electric motors, or a combination of the two. However, using hydrogen in aircraft poses significant challenges, including the need for innovative fuel storage and delivery methods, low-cost and lightweight cryogenic tanks, and redesigned airframes to accommodate them. By 2040, hydrogen aircraft are likely to have a maximum range of under 3,500 km, serving at a maximum about half of all fuel consumption in current commercial aviation operations.

There have been recent test flights in aircraft equipped with fuel cell-powered electric motors. In early 2023, two companies achieved promising results. ZeroAvia flew a 19-seat aircraft equipped with a hydrogen-electric engine on its left wing, and Universal Hydrogen flew a 40-seat regional aircraft at high altitude, with one of its engines powered by a fuel cell. This followed its demonstration of prototype modular capsules that can store hydrogen for up to 100 hours and can be transported by semi-truck.

In terms of larger commercial air transport operations, demonstrations of alternative propulsion systems have been progressing since late 2022. Airbus's ZEROe programme produced a prototype of a cryogenic hydrogen tank that allows hydrogen to be carried in its liquid form at extremely low temperatures. Rolls-Royce and easyJet tested combusting hydrogen to run a regional jet engine with hydrogen produced from wind and tidal power. Avio Aero has launched a demonstration programme for megawatt-level hybrid electric propulsion technologies, coupling a propulsion engine with a fuel cell-powered electric motor. H2FLY has begun the integration of a liquid hydrogen storage system tank in its four-seat aircraft with hydrogen-electric propulsion.

The efforts to introduce hydrogen to power electric powerplants are led by Dovetail Electric Aviation in Australia. Dovetail is adapting the same power-plant used for its battery powered Cessna Caravan to be used in conjunction with a hydrogen fuel cell to extend the range. With agreements with companies like the Korean automotive giant Hyundai to access their fuel cell technology, Dovetail will bring all the required building blocks together to put in the air the first hydrogen powered aircraft in Australia no later than 2025. Following a similar approach to ZeroAvia and Universal Hydrogen, Dovetail will fly a twin engine, in this case a Beechcraft King Air B200, with a hydrogen electric powerplant, but with a more sophisticated and efficient airframe integration.

The adaptation of technologies originating in the automotive industry, compatible mainly due to the similarities in power levels, is an efficient way to progress to the introduction of hydrogen fuel cells into aviation. Regulations relating to smaller air transport category aircraft are a natural platform to test these technologies, as certification of modifications is easier, and also they are the first segment to initially benefit from all the advantages of zero emission powerplants. Although fuel cells and hydrogen storage create an additional level of complexity compared to a battery powered electric aircraft, they still have the potential to significantly reduce operating costs, particularly when the production of hydrogen reaches large industrial scale with reduced production costs.

Regional Air Mobility is the first commercial application that will widely benefit from electrification, particularly when ranges of 300 km and higher are reached, and this is something hydrogen fuel cells can achieve. The so-called thin-haul segment, in other words, short haul routes with insufficient traffic to warrant larger aircrafts (ie, 50 plus seats), may see a renaissance when the hydrogen electric technology can enable flight ranges of between 100 and 300 kilometres.

A 2018 NASA study indicated the number of economically viable Origin-Destination pairs can be multiplied by a factor of 10 if operational costs are reduced for a 19-passenger commuter aircraft flying short distances. Also, consultant firm McKinsey has estimated that the extensive use of regional airports by small aircrafts could bring commercial flight to just within 15 minutes from people's homes to an extra 25 per cent of the total US population. Hydrogen electric commuter aircraft is the technology that can make these changes possible, thanks to its superior economics when fuel cell technology is optimized for aviation. The challenges in terms of added weight and volume to carry hydrogen are way more surmountable for these aircraft flying hundreds of kilometres, compared to 100 plus seater-aircraft flying thousands of kilometres.

Incumbent airlines are also entering the electric aircraft market. In 2022, United Airlines announced a USD 15 million investment in Eve Air Mobility and a conditional purchase agreement for 200 electric vertical take-off and landing (eVTOLs) aircraft plus 200 options. Again, back in Australia, Rex Airlines is leading the charge and investing in this application, due to the nature of its regional network. In January 2024, the Australian Civil Aviation Safety Authority's *Flight Safety* reported that:

> The partnership between Rex and Dovetail was cemented in April 2023 with an 'equity participation agreement' and Rex appointing Prof Ron Bartsch, one of its board members, to the Dovetail board. In June [2023], Dovetail's founder, Mr David Doral, announced that Hyundai Motor Group's business brand, HTWO, will supply a hydrogen fuel cell system to integrate with its EPS for powertrain trials.

Rex Airlines partnered with Dovetail Electric Aviation (owned by Sydney Seaplanes and Dante Aeronautical) to 'pioneer the conversion of turbine powered aircraft to electric, nil-emission propulsion' through the retrofitting of an electric propulsion system (EPS) to an existing (or legacy) aircraft. Rex would provide technical expertise and maintenance support, and some facilities for storage.

Rex and Dovetail's plan, for the time being at least, is to work towards retrofitting the Saab 340 (Rex operate a fleet of over 60 Saab 340 aircraft – the world's largest operator) by first proving the retrofit concept on a Cessna 208 (e-Caravan) and a Beechcraft King Air. The typical hub and spoke regional network may see a transformational change turning into a distributed net- work, provided the technology delivers upon its promise of an efficient hydrogen supply system whether this is based on small electrolysis systems at smaller regional airports generating hydrogen on site with renewable energies, or more centralized mega scale production plants generating clean hydrogen to be transported to those airports by road. The reality is that Australia is very well positioned to efficiently build the required infrastructure that can make hydrogen electric logistically and economically viable and it has a government and safety regulator (CASA) supportive of these initiatives.

When it comes to high-speed long-distance flight, Hypersonix is developing a hydrogen powered scramjet engine called SPARTAN operating up to at least Mach 10, and integrated into their family of hypersonic flyers. Hydrogen is the only fuel capable of powering an airbreathing aircraft at these speeds.

There is no doubt that incremental improvements to engines, materials, aerodynamics and mild hybridization can and should be implemented. Revolutionary designs are needed to achieve efficiency improvements of more than 2 per cent annually in the longer term. However, revolutionary designs are necessary but not sufficient to achieve the 2050 targets. The net zero emissions goal will also require a massive transformation, which will be achieved through a combination of new aircraft technologies, operational measures, alternative fuels, electric or hydrogen-powered aircraft and carbon removals.

REMOTELY PILOTED AIRCRAFT SYSTEMS

Another area of aircraft operations that is having a positive impact upon reducing harmful emissions is the proliferation of drones. This is a rapidly evolving sector of aviation and one that has had – and will continue to have for some considerable time – a significant impact on the development of international aviation law. In society, the term 'drone' is commonly associated with small, 'quadcopter' aircraft. The correct terminology, 'remotely piloted aircraft systems' or RPAS is a more accurate description as it highlights the fact that *any* aircraft flying today has the capacity to be remotely piloted.

The introduction of drones into society has been described as being as significant and revolutionary as the advent of the jet engine. Some commentators go even further. It has been suggested that the drone – or unmanned aircraft as they are more commonly referred to in civilian life – is arguably the greatest aviation innovation since the Wright brothers' Flyer back in 1903. And what is even more amazing about drones is the fact that any aircraft flying today has the ability to be flown without a pilot on board. So are pilotless aircraft to become the horseless carriage of the twenty-first century?

Compared to the challenges that accompany the introduction of any radically new technology, such as the cell phone or the Internet, the integration of unmanned aircraft into society presents even far greater challenges. Managing change in the context of a highly technological and rapidly changing society has, ever since the advent of the traditional piloted aircraft, been the most challenging role of governments and aviation regulators. However, with the rapid emergence of drones into society, unique issues arise that challenge existing assumptions and regulatory models.

Apart from what drones have done and continue to do, for the military, they have already proven themselves as capable of conducting surveillance, boarder patrols, agricultural spraying, searching for missing persons, photography and inspection of emergency situations like bushfires, floods and cyclones. And yes, of course, delivering pizzas. Amazon has estimated that about 85 per cent of what they sell online weighs less than 2 kilogrammes (5 pounds) and with the drones currently available, would be more than capable of delivering your order to your doorstep.

Across all of these applications the issues of safety, privacy and ethics often become topics of debate even before the technology is deployed. While regulators and their regulations may limit the use of drones for commercial and civil purposes from a safety perspective, the major societal issues have been more related to the privacy implications of their usage. Moreover, the unmanned aircraft that seems to be causing most concern in respect to invasion of privacy are those that are being used for recreational purposes with the remote 'pilot' controllers having little or no aviation experience or exposure.

The global economic potential of the civil application of drones is astounding. A recent study estimated the worldwide market for unmanned aircraft systems (UAS) at over USD 150 billion in 2016. Advocates are keen to point out the many and diverse range of ways that they are going to make our lives better. Gretchen West, the Executive Vice President for the US Association for Unmanned Vehicle Systems International (AUVSI), recently stated, 'Really, this technology is an extra tool to help an industry be more effective'. But their potential extends far beyond the domain of traditional piloted aircraft operations.

Many people seem convinced, and with good reason, that unmanned aircraft are about to take over our lives. The reality is a little more complicated. Although drone activity around the world is increasing at an exponential rate in the civilian sector, when it comes to commercial usage, many countries are struggling with how to regulate them. Consequently many states have applied strict limitations and in some instances total bans. But as was so clearly demonstrated with alcohol prohibition in the United States during the 1920s, if there is overwhelming demand for a commodity or service within society, laws and regulations become ineffective and can indeed have the opposite effect to their original purpose. Drones seem to fit squarely into this category.

For governments, corporations and individuals alike it is suggested that a paradigm shift may be required to effectively integrate drones into society. Scary stuff – especially considering the dizzy pace at which drone technology continues to evolve. But it is not only the rapid rate of development of unmanned aircraft systems or UAS technology that requires a recalibration of approach as to how we are to control this new invention. Rather it is the unique characteristics, capabilities and diversity of UAS applications.

If recent drone events are evidence of what the future may behold then we are only at the beginning of the consciousness of human imagination as to what drones may ultimately be capable of. And where the human imagination goes, lawyers will soon follow. Unmanned aircraft give rise to a myriad of legal issues, and all of them, like the technology, in evolution.

Unmanned aircraft technology is evolving faster than our ability to understand how, legally and ethically, to control them. However, if we as a society cannot effectively control drones then apart from the harm, hazards and hindrance they may unleash upon us, any positive contribution or advantages they may afford – and there are many – cannot and will not be fully realized.

For Good and for Bad

The technology for drones appears enticingly cheaper than piloted aircraft and therefore provides a direct cost saving. These savings and benefits also extend to the environment through reduced aircraft emissions. But the integration of drones into society might be more restricted and restrictive than first envisaged. At the most fundamental their potential cannot be fully realized unless and until they are able to share the same domestic airspace with the rest of commercial aviation.

In the past, as with any new and internationally prolific invention, societies and their governments – through their rule-making capacities – have harnessed such technologies for the betterment of society in general. Acknowledging that the sinister, evil, perverted and criminal element will always remain, so long as regulations, and our law enforcement agencies, can keep pace with the technology, the good will always outweigh the bad. Credit card fraud and other cybercrime will persist and so the regulators must remain persistent. The main problem confronting governments in respect to drones is that they 'invaded' well before any effective regulatory regime was established. It's certainly the case of the drone having literally slipped under our radar of consciousness.

Unmanned aircraft nevertheless remain divisively different than previous flying machines and other inventions. Seeing drones in their operating domain is one thing, but the experience of operating this radically new and deeply strange technology is something else. According to some operators the encounter is somewhat surreal.

> A drone isn't just a tool; when you use it you see and act through it – you inhabit it. It expands the reach of your body and senses in much the same way that the Internet expands your mind. The Net extends our virtual presence; drones extend our physical presence.
>
> (Grossman 2013)

Unlike previous technological developments drones are more *agile, accessible, affordable, adaptable* and more capable of *anonymity*. These 'five A' attributes of unmanned aircraft are confronting society and their governments throughout the world. Legislators, public interest groups and certain sectors of society are resistant to the integration of this strange, new technology. They fear, and with good reason, intrusions into their everyday life and privacy violations.

Contrasting drones with traditional manned aircraft becomes even more apparent when one considers their agility. Piloted aircraft are very much constrained by what may be considered their natural limits. Drones have no such constraints, as they have no limitations. Just when we think we have imposed boundaries to harness the invention – technology unleashes the beast. Drones resist all possession. They are capable of a swarming, persistent low-level presence, but above all anonymous. Whereas at times traditional piloted aircraft may be considered to be a necessary inconvenience, many consider drones as an unnecessary evil. Pervasive and uncontrolled or – perhaps even worse – *incapable* of being controlled.

As the rampant pace of drone innovation continues, together with its attributes of agility, accessibility, affordability, adaptability and anonymity, with it comes the potential for widespread abuse by users. The rate of drone developments and the commensurate potential for invasion of privacy together with the threat to national, corporate and personal security has understandably generated considerable public debate.

As in the past the courts have been slow to react when addressing new technologies – credit cards, automatic tellers and the Internet – all of which left society and the general public somewhat vulnerable through abuse and misuse of the new technology. It has been mainly left to governments and regulatory authorities to impose limits and restraints upon the technology and in some instances prohibit their use entirely. The rapid emergence of unmanned aircraft has been no exception. Governments' *modus operandi* in such situations seems to be: 'if we can't control them – ban them'. But alas, the drones have escaped and there's no putting this airborne genie back in the bottle.

The dawn of the age of the drones and the potential they hold, for good and for bad, provides a new challenge, a challenge in which the law needs to catch up. The genie cannot be constrained, but the genie nevertheless needs to be controlled. At present the drone dilemma is very much a case of 'unmanned and uncontrolled'.

Now that we know the nature of the problem that faces society and governments throughout the world, let's look at the phenomenal rate of proliferation of this strange new technology.

The Drones Have Landed and Multiplied

It is now trite to say that drones represent a game-changing development for the aviation industry. While it is estimated that only 2 per cent of current expenditure on UAS in the world encompasses civilian UAS, that percentage is expected to increase exponentially over the next decade. But still there are more unmanned aircraft in the world today than their manned counterpart. In the United States the Association for Unmanned Vehicle Systems International (AUVSI) estimates that upon integration of UAS into the National Airspace System (NAS) and by 2025 more than 100,000 jobs will have been directly created in the US alone and provide an economic impact of USD 82 billion.

Unmanned aircraft systems are poised to become part of everyday air services operations perhaps within the next few years. Needless to say there are significant challenges that need to be addressed in order to seamlessly introduce UAS into civilian airspace. In those countries that have drone regulations most operations are restricted in their operations to segregated airspace – clear of commercial air transportation. At present only about one-third of the 190 countries that are bound under international aviation conventions have enacted drone regulations.

Another challenging aspect of this new type of aircraft is that, since their inception, UAS have become smaller, more sophisticated and increasingly less expensive. Their application is as varied as their design. As was described earlier in this chapter, the rapid pace of UAS technological development can be directly related to what is described as its 'five "A" attributes' of agility, accessibility, affordability, adaptability and anonymity.

In many countries, and in particular in the United States, the most apparent and immediate application of UAS has been in conducting surveillance. This fact is of little surprise considering this was the military application for which drones were originally developed. For example, the Global Hawk drone was initially developed for the US Air

Force towards the end of the 1990s and was first used shortly after the terrorist attacks on the World Trade Center on 11 September 2001. NASA's new Hurricane Hunters are the drones that tracked Bin Laden. Many UAS are fitted with high-resolution cameras and imaging technologies. The research and development arm of the UAS industry is likewise growing exponentially.

Currently, there are hundreds of types and designs of UAS of both fixed wing and rotary variants. Drones range in size from insect-like micro drones to large commercial aircraft. 'Lethal' and 'unobtrusive' micro-drones are currently being developed by the US Air Force to mimic the behaviour of bugs. April 2013 saw the first commercial air transport aircraft to be operated as a Remotely Piloted Aircraft System (RPAS). With two persons on board, the Jetstream 31 type aircraft flew 500 miles in the non-segregated United Kingdom airspace sharing the sky with other commercial airliners. On that day a new chapter in aviation history was written. This revolutionary flight reflects the rapidly expanding use of RPAS for civilian use and simultaneously raises several complex legal issues.

It is this diversity of aircraft design and consequent diversity of application that is raising considerable legal issues. As one commentator (Farber 2014) suggests: 'The defence and aerospace industries are propelling UAS into our lives faster than the courts and lawmakers can prepare for their ubiquitous and powerful presence'.

According to one leading international drone consultancy firm, UAS International, in 2017 in the US alone, over 100 companies manufactured approximately 300 different drones. Worldwide expenditure on drones was in excess of USD 10 billion. In a major report released in May 2016 by PwC, the world's largest professional services firm, the estimated market value of drone-powered solutions is in excess of USD 127 billion.

In the United States it is estimated that by 2020 some 30,000 UAS will be occupying the US national airspace. Further it is predicted that in the same year USD 11.4 billion will be spent per annum on UAS sales with a cumulative total of USD 89 billion over the next decade. The UAS sector is expected to create 70,000 new jobs in the first three years of integration into the NAS and over 100,000 jobs by 2025.

The increased sales of drones have been nothing short of spectacular. In 2014, Australian UAS manufacturer MultiWiiCopter told the Australian Parliament's 'Eyes in the Sky' Inquiry that its local client base included more than 5,000 customers, and consumer UAS vendor Parrot claimed that it has sold 500,000 units globally. Although the market for civil use currently comprises less than 2 per cent of the worldwide market for unmanned aircraft, that could change over the next few years as technology advances and as legislation and regulations allow broader use of unmanned aircraft in unsegregated civilian airspace.

There is absolutely no doubt that there are significant operational and societal benefits that UAS can provide in terms of cost savings, mission diversity and potential reduction in environmental emissions in comparison to piloted aircraft operations. One area in which UAS can provide significant advantages, as compared with manned aircraft, is in the area of reconnaissance and surveillance and this has been the major usage of drones in the US experience. UAS have the ability to be cost-effective while simultaneously improving the efficiency of law enforcement and reducing the risk to law enforcement officials.

The availability of UAS provides domestic law enforcement agencies with the opportunity to operate more efficiently by obtaining otherwise unavailable surveillance information that could potentially lead to greater and more accurate arrests. The use of facial recognition technology is highly effective from a drone vantage point – but equally controversial. In many countries, including the United States and Australia, both the federal and the state police forces have utilized UAS in hostage scenarios with positive outcomes. UAS operations also allow for advanced national security with increased border patrol and coastal surveillance, as well as the opportunity to conduct more sophisticated and effective emergency surveillance and search and rescue missions. Trials of drones for coastal surveillance and border security in the US and many other countries have been undertaken for the past few years.

In a disaster, drones can be quickly deployed to assess affected areas and improve situational awareness, aiding first responders in determining the most effective allocation of resources and delivery of life-saving supplies. Firefighting services are using UAS equipped with thermal imaging software to provide advanced intelligence in respect to the detection and spread of forest and bush fires.

Of the various categories of work potentially open to UAS, other than surveillance applications, an economic study commissioned by the AUVSI suggests that precision agriculture and public safety present the most viable commercial markets, at least in the United States.

What has become a popular and apt descriptor for UAS applications is that they can be used for 'dull, dirty and dangerous' missions where it would be perilous to assign a human pilot for such missions. In his paper, Marshall (2007) describes the history of unmanned or remotely piloted aircraft, the technological challenges facing operators of such systems, and the unique legal and regulatory issues that have arisen because of the rapid evolution of this new, but not-so-new, sector of aviation. In his own words Marshall describes the phrase as follows:

> 'Dull, dirty and dangerous' is a common description of the potential uses and utility of unmanned aircraft, operated as military surveillance and communications platforms, hardened weapons delivery systems, observation and interdiction assets for national security and border protection, and any number of civilian or nonmilitary applications. Scientists use them for intercepting and measuring atmospheric phenomena such as hurricanes, sampling the air quality over disaster areas, and flying through volcanic eruptions where manned aircraft would risk loss of aircraft and human life, a few of the many current and envisioned aviation missions. Any current activity in which airborne assets are deployed in a 'dull' (long endurance, high altitude, fatigue-inducing), 'dirty' (volcanic plumes, chemical spills) or 'dangerous' (high risk, low altitude such as firefighting) environment may potentially be conducted in a safer, less expensive, and more efficient manner with unmanned aircraft.

As a concluding comment to this section, it appears that the potential scope of UAS application is almost limitless. Even the use to date of drones in certain applications far exceeds the capability or efficiencies of traditional piloted aircraft operations. The operational costs of UAS alone are significantly lower than their manned counterparts and some have significantly greater endurance – particularly those that are solar powered or solar assisted. One highly acclaimed UAS commentator (Michaelides-Mateou and Erotokritou 2014) lists a range of civilian applications to include border protection in support of immigration control, law enforcement and homeland security, agricultural use, aerial photography, search and rescue, disaster management (e.g. the Fukushima powerplant explosion in 2011) and leisure activities.

The future use and application of drones seems to be limited only by our imagination. But what effect has this rampaging technology had on society, and how have our established societal controls and values coped? In the following section we will explore the impact of integrating this strange new invention into contemporary society. This presents unprecedented challenges at various levels: into modern society generally; into our legal system; into existing civil aviation regulatory framework; and into unsegregated civilian airspace. Indeed this innovation we call drones essentially represents a fusion of science, society and the law.

RELATIONSHIP BETWEEN THE LAW, TECHNOLOGY AND AVIATION

It was the culmination and convergence of three different technologies that led to the explosion of drone innovation and their proliferation. First there have been dramatic improvements in the efficiencies of drone powerplants, whether it be lightweight electric motors or micro piston-driven or jet engine technology. In respect to electrically powered devices these have been accompanied by commensurate improvements in battery technology.

The second important area of technological development has been in the advancement and availability of Global Positioning Systems or GPS. Their incorporation into everyday life and delivery through our mobile phones and smart devices has been staggering. To be able to determine, with pinpoint accuracy, our position on this planet would have amazed and bewildered our navigational-centric forefathers. Drones avail themselves of this GPS technology and with their three dimensional agility are able to freely locate and perform their mission – whatever that may be.

The final area of scientific advancement has been the remarkable improvements in lightweight cameras with their high-resolution images and versatile operations. Kodak knows only too well – in hindsight – the rate of progress of digital camera technology. Kodak engineer Steven Sasson developed the first digital camera in 1975 with a resolution capability of 0.01 megapixels. Today, many small drones are fitted with 36 megapixel capacity cameras – a staggering 3,600-fold increase in resolution capacity than Kodak's first digital camera.

Apart from these three areas of rapid technological advancement the widespread usage of smart devices, especially mobile phones, provide for seamless and no-cost controlling device platforms through the simple downloading of an app. All these areas of technological development have soared while their costs have been consistently dropping. Attempts in the past to develop useful terrestrial robot-like technology have had limited success. It seems that the clumsy terrestrial robot has finally found its feet – albeit in the sky.

It is the freedom and agility by which aviation operations can readily transcend previously restrictive geographic and political boundaries that truly differentiates flying from all other modes of transport. In respect to drone operations this 'freedom and agility' transcends to an entirely new and unprecedented level. To harness this freedom for the betterment of all, aviation regulation over all forms of aviation – whether of the manned or unmanned variety – provides the requisite authority, responsibility and sanctions. The regulation of aerial activities is as fundamental and rudimentary to the aviation industry as civil order is to modern society. In no other field of human endeavour or branch of law does there exist such a vital yet symbiotic relationship.

It is no revelation that aviation and regulation are intrinsically linked. In fact it is generally recognized that aviation is the most strictly and extensively regulated industry. The preceding view is highlighted in the following extract: 'The aviation industry is what it is today not in spite of, but rather because of, the law that regulates it' (Bartsch 2012b).

But with the UAS generation, as with previous eras of rapid advancement of aircraft design, performance and capability, the law is lagging behind science and technology. The ongoing development and use of unmanned aircraft highlights well the following (Ravich 2009) observation:

> Law lags science; it does not lead it. UAS exemplify the modern information age, an era of computer automation, the Internet, high-definition imagery, and 'smart' technology. More can be done virtually and by remote control today than at any time in history, and the corresponding actual and potential savings of personnel and resources are tangible. In aviation parlance, UAS are the leading edge of contemporary aeronautical science and engineering and a product of a century of manned flight experience. However, UAS operations have outpaced the law in that they are not sufficiently supported by a dedicated and enforceable regime of rules, regulations, and standards respecting their integration into the national airspace.

The capacities of unmanned aircraft systems are increasing while their affordability and thus presence do likewise. The law is undoubtedly having difficulty keeping up, but how long can a regulatory regime based on exceptions and limitations handle the volume of demand for this strange new aircraft type. It is debatable as to whether one regulatory regime can provide both standards-based rules to account for safety concerns and also provide adequate privacy safeguards. Then there are the other areas of the law that involve security, corporate espionage and terrorism that need to be addressed. As mentioned previously, Australia was the first country to introduce regulations relating to unmanned aircraft back in 2002. Not surprisingly, with a mature commercial drone industry having developed in Australia, an Australian company – UAS International – was the first to develop an international UAS standard.

It is important to appreciate that regulations of any kind must be sufficiently flexible to provide beneficial applications of the technology that are not currently contemplated. Drones, like other robots, will continue to challenge lawyers and legal policy makers in the semi-foreseeable future. Legislators have to address the issue of integration, and the solution is unlikely to be addressed purely by regulations – working with industry associations and recognition of industry standards, such as the UAS International Standard, is likely to be an important part of the solution.

Those aspects of integration that are at present creating the greatest challenges derive from the differences between UAS and any previous type or variety of aircraft design and technology. Therefore, from a legal and regulatory perspective, the real integration difficulties stem from the inherent differences and diversities of this new form of aircraft combined with the fact, obviously, that UAS are piloted remotely and in some limited instances, are fully autonomous. And perhaps the most sobering aspect of all is that the rate of advancement of UAS technology is showing absolutely no signs of abating and indeed is continuing to rise at an increasing rate.

Sharing the Sky

As previously stated unmanned aircraft or drones – as they were traditionally referred to – were conceived and developed within a military milieu. Unmanned aerial vehicles

(UAVs) are, as with many previous aviation innovations – including the jet engine – a child of war. It is only a matter of time before we begin to experience their full potential within the civilian and commercial aviation sector. Unlike military drone activities, civilian operations, particularly commercial usage, cannot rely on specially designated and restricted military airspace. Therefore, one of the key issues for operating UAS for civilian purposes will be their integration into non-segregated common airspace.

> Civilian UAVs are intended to operate in a different environment than military UAVs, namely in the common, non-segregated civilian airspace, together with all other air traffic. What is acceptable in military operations and in segregated airspace does not apply to civilian applications. At the moment, UAVs lack formal airworthiness certification by civilian aviation authorities. There are no airworthiness standards and acceptable means of compliance for those technical features of UAV technology, which go beyond traditional manned aircraft. The main obstacle for civilian UAVs to fly in non-segregated airspace is safety.
>
> (Kaiser 2011)

As civilian usage of UAS becomes more and more common and their commercial and operational superiority more demonstrable, the pressure imposed upon governments and regulators for access to unsegregated and ultimately unrestricted civilian airspace will intensify. Of course there will be public outcry from certain sectors of society and individuals, but their cost-benefit superiority will most likely prevail. Such is the nature of democratic societies. Ultimately, UAS will be flying, with the same degree of freedom as manned aircraft, in non-segregated airspace. Therefore a solid legal framework on the international, regional (for example, the European Union and the European Aviation Safety Agency (EASA)) and national level laying down all technical, safety and operational requirements will need to be implemented.

Until now, regulatory authorities have been focusing most of their attention on the issue of developing and imposing limitations on drone usage and made only comparatively few proposals in regard to the creation of an entirely new regulatory framework for their use in common (unsegregated) airspace. Perhaps a better regulatory approach, and one that has been advocated by the International Civil Aviation Organization (ICAO), is to first consider all drones as aircraft and then identify the differences – the 'delta' – in their operations to that of their piloted counterparts. In adopting such an approach the existing, mature and 'safety-proven' regulatory structure can remain and incorporate drones into that regime, as and when the identified 'deltas' are safely addressed.

The diversity of application of UAS usage that differs from that of manned aircraft is what places the adequacy of existing law and regulatory framework under so much pressure. We therefore need to consider the scope of UAS activities and applications (possibly by way of a gap analysis) to ensure that any changes to the regulatory regime will be sufficient to accommodate and harness UAS technology now and well into the future. ABC journalist Mr Mark Corcoran, who is an expert on UAS technology, stated: 'I think that the problem is that the technology is now progressing at such a rate that regulators and legislators risk being buffeted in the slipstream' (O'Sullivan 2014: 45).

The enormity of the task of integrating UAS into unsegregated civil airspace cannot be overstated; however, the legal issues associated with UAS activities are not restricted to safety and technical regulation. While the advantages to society in general of increased usage of UAS is undeniable, because of the uniqueness of this new type of aircraft technology, its increased civilian usage also raises a number of important legal, social and ethical issues.

Most UAS activities, where regulators have permitted operations, are currently constrained to segregated airspace such as low-level airspace (below 400 feet above ground level) test sights, designated danger areas or within temporary restricted areas. On some occasions, UAS operations are permitted in an extremely limited environment outside segregated airspace. To exploit fully the unique operational capabilities of current and future UAS and thus realize the potential commercial benefits of UAS, there is a necessity to be able to access all classes of airspace and operate across national and international borders and airspace boundaries. Such operations must achieve an acceptable (equivalent) level of safety, but regulation should not become so inflexible or burdensome that commercial benefits are either frustrated or denied.

Many regulatory authorities throughout the world have adopted the preceding approach as they transition to a more 'safety systems' and less prescriptive approach to safety regulation. The emphasis is placed more on the operator to demonstrate to the regulator, usually through the development of an exposition, that they have established robust safety systems and procedures that ensure they can carry out their operations safely. The following extract of the Australian Civil Aviation Safety Authority clearly describes the commercial advantages of such an approach:

> Apart from the safety benefits that will be derived from this new regulatory regime clearly articulating the safety outcomes that are required, the new regulations will allow greater operational flexibility for airlines in achieving these safety outcomes. This legislative flexibility will provide significant opportunities for organisations in terms of integrating safety into their business planning processes.

Due to the vast diversity and uniqueness of UAS operations, a highly prescriptive aviation regulatory framework, which is common throughout the world, is simply not practical or feasible to encompass the scope of drone applications. If the legislation is structured in such a way that it prescribes the desired safety outcomes, the operator has the flexibility to structure their procedures so that they are both safe and commercially sustainable.

The viability of the commercial market for UAS, especially in the civil market, is heavily dependent on unfettered access to the same airspace as manned civilian operations to enable sustainable commercial operations. Whilst it is essential that UAS demonstrate an equivalent level of safety compared to manned operations, the current regulatory framework has evolved around the concept of an onboard pilot or pilots. There is a need to develop UAS solutions that assure an equivalent level of safety for UAS operations, which in turn will require adaptation or transition of the current regulatory framework to allow for the concept of the remote pilot without compromising the safety of other airspace users.

One of the major issues facing UAS operations is the demonstration of equivalence (in particular for detect and avoid systems) in the context of an evolving air traffic management (ATM) environment. It is very important to understand that the current ATM environment is not static. Achieving equivalence with manned operations is not a fixed target as there are many significant changes proposed that aim to improve operational efficiency and performance or enhance safety. On the whole, proposed changes to the ATM environment could be seen as advantageous to UAS operations as more and more functions within the environment are automated, thus there is a significant opportunity for the UAS industry to influence the shape of the future ATM environment to support wider UAS operations.

Summing Up

It is impossible to accurately predict the true form of technological advances, or the impact they will have on aviation, society and our legal system. It is equally difficult to envisage their impact or the risks they may impose upon our way of life. Contemporary society has proven to be remarkably adept at integrating and normalizing technological developments, especially once any moral anxiety relating to their introduction subsides. On the other hand, the negative impacts of some technological advancements have only become apparent subsequent to their introduction and integration into society, which makes them much harder to regulate and control.

The challenge for governments throughout the world is to ensure that the risks associated with the introduction of this new technology are managed and balanced in such a manner that permits society to benefit as a whole. The technical standards that UAS will need to meet to be integrated into non-segregated airspace according to the International Civil Aviation Organization are still many years away. It is expected that new technology will resolve many of the issues associated with UAS, including maintaining separation, establishing airworthiness, maintaining contact with air traffic control, loss of link or sight of UAS procedures, and ensuring the security of the link and base station. There epitomizes a touch of irony in that technology created the 'drone' issue but may also prove to be the solution.

As these technical challenges are overcome, authorities will need to be aware of the implications for other stakeholders with aviation responsibilities. For example, it has been suggested that air traffic controllers are best placed to provide separation advice for UAS operators, which arguably effects a de facto transfer of responsibility for separation from the pilot of the UAS to air traffic control. Issues relating to situational awareness and other non-technical aspects of drone operations require special consideration. The human factors element of drone operations is important to consider, both in terms of operations and in terms of developing legislation to integrate drones into unsegregated airspace.

Authorities will also need to ensure that new technologies have demonstrated efficacy, but also that evidentiary requirements are met. For example, the UAS command and control link must be secure and able to detect and monitor when deliberate interference has been attempted. Equally, larger drones may require onboard tamper proof instruments to record the actions of the pilot. In imposing these additional requirements, authorities will have to balance the need for safety against the cost – as per usual cost-benefit analysis.

WHEN IS A DRONE NOT A DRONE: TERMINOLOGY AND DEFINITIONS

In terms of researching and discussing any new technology it is most important to have an accepted definition of the subject matter. Public familiarity with unmanned aircraft, popularly known as drones, comes largely from their use in military operations abroad. Unmanned aircraft or unmanned aerial vehicles (UAVs) are aircraft operated without the possibility of direct human intervention from within or on the aircraft. The simplicity of this definition belies, however, the complexity of classification of unmanned aircraft for regulatory purposes, an issue explored in more detail in the following section.

There is considerable ambivalence about the use of the term 'drone' within this sector of the aviation industry mostly because of its negative military connotations with targeted killing. Lay commentators and media personnel have been corrected, and even been reprimanded by the unmanned aircraft sector for failing to use terms like unmanned aircraft system (UAS), unmanned aerial vehicle (UAVs) or remotely piloted aircraft system (RPAS). As this is a book about aviation law, and all drones are aircraft, therefore it is important that we should discuss the various terms, their origins and how best to describe them in their civilian capacity.

In 2005, the International Civil Aviation Organization (ICAO) decided upon the use of the term 'UAV' and defined it as 'a pilotless aircraft – which is flown without a pilot-in-command on-board and is either remotely and fully controlled from another place . . . or programmed and fully autonomous'. A couple of years later in 2007 the ICAO dispensed with the use of 'UAV' and decided upon 'UAS' as the preferred term and defined it as 'an aircraft and its associated elements which are operated with no pilot on board'.

Another two years later in 2009 the ICAO, in adopting a recommendation of their UAS Study Group, first introduced the term 'remotely piloted aircraft' or RPA. This adaptation was based on the conclusion that only unmanned aircraft that are *remotely* piloted could be integrated alongside manned aircraft into non-segregated airspace (that is airspace used by commercial aviation) and at aerodromes. From that time on the ICAO decided to narrow its focus from *all* unmanned aircraft systems to those that are remotely piloted.

The use of the descriptor 'remote' or 'remotely' as an adjective allows for standard ICAO definitions to continue to be used. Therefore, the definition of a pilot remains unchanged with a *remote* pilot being 'a person charged by the operator with duties essential to the operation of a remotely piloted aircraft and who manipulates the flight controls, as appropriate, during flight time'. Similarly a *remote* pilot-in-command is 'the remote pilot designated by the operator as being in command and charged with the safe conduct of a flight'. A *remote* co-pilot is a 'licensed remote pilot serving in any remote piloting capacity other than as remote pilot-in-command but excluding a remote pilot serving in remote piloting capacity for the sole purpose of receiving flight instruction'. And finally a *remote* flight crewmember is a 'licensed remote crew member charged with duties essential to the operation of a remotely piloted aircraft system during a flight duty period'.

In adopting such taxonomy this provides an efficient way in which the *differences* in operating remotely piloted aircraft can be readily identified. In other words it becomes an exercise in determining the 'delta', that is, that which differs from operating UAS as compared to traditional aircraft operations with the pilot (and other crew members) on board.

The term most commonly used in the United States and by the Federal Aviation Administration (FAA) and increasingly used by the general community and the media, is 'unmanned aircraft system' or UAS. The *FAA Modernization and Reform Act* of 2012 distinguishes between the aircraft and the associated systems by defining an unmanned aircraft as 'an aircraft that is operated without the possibility of direct human intervention from within or on the aircraft'. On the other hand, 'UAS' refers to the airframe as well as the associated communication links and control station and is defined by the FAA as: 'An unmanned aircraft and associated elements (including communication links and the components that control the unmanned aircraft) that is required for the pilot in command to operate safely and efficiently in the national airspace system'.

At the international ICAO RPAS Symposium held in Montreal in September 2017 it was generally agreed that smaller unmanned aircraft (less than 25 kilogrammes) would generally be referred to as UAS or drones. This sector of the unmanned aircraft sector would be unlikely to ever be subject to ICAO international standards and recommended practices (SARPs). Larger and more complex unmanned aircraft, and those not subject to strict domestic restrictions, would be generally referred to as RPAS.

As was stated previously, if the broader benefits that unmanned aircraft operations can provide are to be fully realized, they must be fully integrated into unsegregated airspace both domestically and internationally. Therefore, ultimately UAS terminology must align throughout the world if there is to be international harmonization. For that reason, and with the ICAO having finalized their *Remotely Piloted Aircraft Systems Manual* (RPASM) in 2015, the following definitions from that manual will be used:

- *remotely piloted aircraft (RPA)* – an unmanned aircraft which is piloted from a remote pilot station; and
- *remotely piloted aircraft system (RPAS)* – a remotely piloted aircraft, its associated remote pilot station(s), the required command and control links and any other components as specified in the type design.

The RPASM further defines a 'RPAS operator certificate' as 'a certificate authorising an operator to carry out specified RPAS operations'. Although the term 'UAS' is listed in the manual's glossary of acronyms the term is not defined in the RPASM. As will be discussed in the following section, because the term UAS is broader than RPAS and encompasses all types of unmanned aircraft operating systems, the previous extracted (US Congress) definition of UAS will be adopted throughout this publication.

During its 222nd Session on 1 March 2021, the ICAO Council adopted new and amended Standards and Recommended Practices (SARPs) driving important progress on the international safety and interoperability of remotely piloted aircraft systems (RPAS). The ICAO Remotely Piloted Aircraft Systems Panel (RPASP) has created a draft update of ICAO Document 10019, Manual on Remotely Piloted Aircraft Systems (RPAS).

The new provisions became effective on 12 July 2021, and applicable as of 26 November 2026. The most important pertain to Annex 8 – Airworthiness of Aircraft to the Chicago Convention, and cover certification requirements for remotely piloted airplanes and helicopters, in addition to the remote pilot stations (RPS) they are operated from. The Manual includes a new chapter on 'Integration of RPAS operations into ATM and ATM procedures'.

The practical reality of RPA or UAS operating in the same airspace as manned civil aircraft requires these aircraft to have the ability to act and respond in real-time and comply with instrument flight rules (IFR) and visual flight rules (VFR) as per piloted aircraft. Currently, there is no recognized technology solution that could make these aircraft capable of meeting regulatory requirements to see (detect) and avoid other aircraft, and for the command and control integrity to provide the remotely piloted aircraft with the equivalent level of safety of an aircraft with a pilot on board.

Depending on the situation, unmanned aircraft may be required to 'recognize' aerodrome signs and markings, identify and avoid terrain, identify and avoid severe weather, provide visual separation from other aircraft and avoid collisions. Article 3 of the Chicago Convention also requires civil aircraft to be able to comply with a state's request to land or deviate to a designated airport. One of the greatest challenges of full UAS integration into non-segregated airspace is technology enabling the remote pilot to identify, in real-time, the physical layout of the aerodrome so as to manoeuvre the aircraft safely.

It is these technical aspects of unmanned operations, together with the legal issues associated with determining and apportioning liability, that pose the greatest challenges generally but in particular in respect of fully autonomous operating systems.

FULLY AUTONOMOUS SYSTEMS

A major technical, legal and regulatory challenge of the 'pilotless' element is full automation of flight. The safety of fully autonomous flight necessarily becomes a legal question in terms of the degree of flight control that the related computers are permitted to have and where legal liability might reside. Automation of flight has been progressing at astonishing rates in the past few decades and fully autonomous UAS may still be some way off but will eventually be developed.

One of the most visible effects of automation in the operation of aircraft is the progressive reduction of the number of flight crew in commercial air transport operations. In some instances the reduction has been from six flight crewmembers down to two and potentially, at least technologically, zero. By way of example, post-First World War commercial airline operations typically used to operate with six technical crew members consisting of a pilot-in-command (Captain or Commander), a co-pilot (First Officer), second officer, flight navigator, flight engineer and radio operator. By way of comparison the minimum technical (flight) crew component for the world's largest commercial aircraft – the Airbus A380 – is just two pilots.

Full automation will be the pinnacle of the development of unmanned flight and is strongly spurred by the technical advancement of communication and information technologies and their miniaturization. Remote control and fully automated operations can complement each other in a way that autonomous flight can provide redundancy if a control link fails. Even though partial or fully autonomous flight operations are feasible, both the ICAO and the US Congress consider that there must be human responsibility for, and with authority over, the flight of the unmanned aircraft. Accordingly, mostly based on legal argument, it must be ensured that the responsible remote pilot-in-command can override the autonomous flight mode at any time, when necessary.

In terms of ICAO terminology a RPA or RPAS cannot, by definition, include fully autonomous systems. If this were the case then a consideration of RPAS in not including fully autonomous systems would impose considerable limitations of what is a rapidly developing area of UAS research and technology. For this reason, and to allow consideration of the entire scope of potential unmanned operations, fully autonomous systems will be included in this publication and therefore both terms – RPAS and UAS – will be used as applicable.

The ICAO RPASM defines an 'autonomous aircraft' as 'an unmanned aircraft that does not allow pilot intervention in the management of the flight'. The ICAO RPASM goes on to define an 'autonomous operation' as 'an operation during which a remotely-piloted aircraft is operating without pilot intervention in the management of the flight', which, significantly, does not preclude the existence of a 'remote' pilot.

In summary, the two families of terms differ to the extent that RPA/RPAS excludes fully autonomous flight, whereas UAV/UAS may include or exclude them. As the US Congress requires a pilot-in-command, fully autonomous UAS are excluded from consideration of the FAA – at least at this point in time. The presence and requirement of a remote pilot has led ICAO to define this UAS-type as a remotely piloted aircraft system for the reasons described.

Although the term 'drone' continues to be used as a generic term it is more commonly used to describe the military application of unmanned aircraft operations. With an increasing number of safety regulators throughout the world categorizing small RPAS (less than 2 kg/5 lb) and requiring less stringent regulation, these are increasingly referred to as 'drones' – also by the ICAO. Significantly, however, the word 'drone' does not appear throughout the entire ICAO RPAS Manual. The ICAO, as stated in the RPAS Manual, now considers the term UAV as being 'obsolete' and does not define the term in the Manual.

Elsewhere throughout the world other aviation regulators, for example the European Aviation Safety Agency (EASA) and the Australian Civil Aviation Safety Authority (CASA), in following the ICAO approach, use the terminology 'remotely piloted aircraft' in respect to the civilian usage of unmanned aircraft. The unmanned aircraft or RPA together with the data (command and control) link and ground control units (stations) are, as with the ICAO, collectively and respectively referred to as Unmanned Aircraft Systems (UAS) or Remotely Piloted Aircraft Systems (RPAS).

A CONCLUDING COMMENT

Since its very beginning, aviation was a pioneering and creative industry but, at least in its early years, at the expense of many accidents and the cost of many lives. Today, aviation is based on mature and robust safety systems and cultures. Traditionally it takes years, if not decades, to develop new aircraft types. Innovations are integrated slowly, through the application of strict regulatory controls in accordance with internationally accepted safety and technical standards. The result is a very good safety record.

It is highly attractive to merge the innovative power and competitive pricing of information technologies with aviation. Unmanned aircraft are a product of such a merger. But society continues to struggle to accommodate and integrate unmanned aircraft as governments and their legal systems are overwhelmed by the rate of technological advancement. It is contended that if these aircraft are to be integrated into common, unsegregated civil airspace, then under current laws relating to aircraft certification standards, and in accordance with international conventions, they necessarily must be subject to the same, or at least equivalent, technical and safety standards.

As previously stated any aircraft flying today is capable of being flown by a remotely located pilot. Therefore, if the current level of safety of our air transport system is to be maintained there must be at least an equivalent level of safety for all unmanned operations if they are to share the same airspace.

Public awareness of drones and the political and societal understandings of them are thought to be paramount if there is to be support and acceptance of the technology and its future development. The introduction of UAS into domestic airspace raises never-before-faced safety and integration issues. Of the many challenges facing governments throughout the world and also for UAS manufacturers and operators seeking commercial opportunities in civilian markets, perhaps the most significant is the lack of airspace regulation that covers all existing and contemplated unmanned systems and operations.

Access to the common airspace is the key to everything regarding unleashing the full potential of drones and the benefits they can bestow upon society. To achieve this goal, the focus of new regulations must be to maintain the safety levels the aviation industry has achieved during the past century of piloted operations.

Although the promulgation of ICAO Standards and Recommended Practices (SARPs) for unmanned aircraft is still likely to be at least three years away, the development of industry RPAS standards could be a viable alternative. For instance the Asia-Pacific RPAS Consortium (ARC) in conjunction with UAS International have developed the world's first UAS International Standard (UIS). The UIS was released at the Avalon International Airshow in February 2015 and is rapidly gaining international support as the benchmark standard for UAS operations.

The potential commercial, legal and ethical impact of civilian RPAS operations, perhaps by virtue of their inherent design, seemed to have thus far, slipped under the radar. It is suggested that what is required to address the emerging RPAS issues is a 'whole of government approach' in respect to implementation strategies and due to the unique characteristics of aircraft operations, this needs to be initiated, coordinated and promulgated at the international level.

Perhaps this overview of some of the issues related to the introduction of RPAS into society may provide a wakeup call for governments throughout the world to more aggressively engage in collective and harmonized dialogue to develop effective implementation and integration strategies for civilian RPAS operations. Without exception, this has been the situation with all previous rapid advancements in aircraft design and technology of this magnitude – indeed they have been the basis for international conventions – most notably the Paris Convention 1919 and the Chicago Convention 1944.

It is clear that the regulatory challenge for all countries is the assurance of at least an equivalent level of safety for all drones in common national airspace. There is a crying need for the development of harmonized international rules relating to RPAS operations, but the difficulties and challenges remain. Drone operations are unique and therefore may require unique solutions to the problems and challenges of this strange yet exciting new technology.

Somewhat ironically, this closing chapter of the book about new aircraft types (RPAS, electric and hybrid) and operations (SAF, hydrogen powered) and the challenges presented by the 2050 *Net Zero Emissions* target is the beginning of a new era in aviation. This chapter has attempted to provide an overview of some of these new operations and to create an awareness of the main issues – legal, technical and ethical – and the impact that this transition will have on the travelling public and indeed on society generally.

References and Further Reading

Abeyratne, R. 2009. *Aviation and the Environment*. Baltimore, MD: Publish America.

ACI. 2009. *Policies and Recommended Practices Handbook*. Available at: www.airports.org/aci/aci/file/Publications/2009/ACI_Policies_and_Recommended_Practices_seventh_edition_FINAL.pdf [accessed 13 February 2012].

The Aeroplane. 1944. 'Chicago: A Lost Cause'. *The Aeroplane, 67(1752)*, 685.

Aerostudents. 2011. *Air Traffic Management*. Available at: www.aerostudents.com/files/airTransportation/airTrafficManagement.pdf [accessed 5 September 2012].

Airport Business. 2009. *EASA Preparing Aerodrome Safety Certification Rules*. Available at: www.airport-business.com/2009/12/easa-preparing-aerodrome-safety-certification-rules [accessed 5 September 2012].

Airport Business. 2010. *Airport Safety: The EASA Rulemaking Process Introduced*. Available at: www.airport-business.com/2010/07/airport-safety-the-easa-rulemaking-process-introduced [accessed 5 September 2012].

Airport Council International. 2009. *Position Statement on Climate Change*, 15 June. Available at: http://aci-na.org/static/entransit/ACI-NA_Climate_Change_Position_FINAL.pdf [accessed 5 September 2012].

Airport Council International. 2023. Extract from ACI Media Release. Dated 4 June 2023, Montreal.

Airservices Australia. 2018. *Our Future*. Available at: www.airservicesaustralia.com/about/our-future/ [accessed 20 March 2018].

Allaz, C. 2004. *The History of Air Cargo and Air Mail from the 18th Century*. London: Christopher Foyle Publishing.

Apple, J. and Deyling, R. 1995. *A Primer on the Civil-Law System*. Available at: www.fjc.gov/public/pdf.nsf/lookup/CivilLaw.pdf/../CivilLaw.pdf [accessed 5 September 2012].

Aronowitz, A. *World Factbook of Criminal Justice Systems: Germany*. Available at: www.bjs.gov/content/pub/ascii/WFBCJGER.TXT [accessed 5 September 2012].

ASEAN. 2010. *Joint Ministerial Statement of the 16th ASEAN Transport Ministers' Meeting Bandar Seri Begawan, 11 November 2010*. Available at: www.asean.org/25585.htm [accessed 12 December 2011].

Association of European Airlines. *Open Skies: The US–EU Air Transport Agreement*. Available at: http://files.aea.be/News/News020408.pdf [accessed 5 September 2012].

The Australian. 2003. 'The New Fear of Flying: 100 Years of Flight'. *The Australian, 18*, 11.

Australian Broadcasting Commission. 2024. 'Airport Pioneers Australia's First Digital Air Traffic Control System Off Tarmac'. *B Chandler*. Available at: https://www.abc.net.au/news/brooke-chandler/102272044 [accessed 7 March 2024].

Australian Competition and Consumer Commission. 2017, June 14. Available at: www.accc.gov.au/media-release/high-court-rules-in-acccs-favour-in-air-cargo-cartel-case [accessed 22 March 2018].

Australian National Audit Office. 2016. *Procurement of the International Centre for Complex Project Management to Assist on the OneSKY Australia Program*. Commonwealth of Australia.

Ax, Joseph. 2017. 'Florida Shooting Highlights Limits of U.S. Airport Security'. *Reuters*, 7 January. Available at: www.reuters.com/article/us-florida-shooting-security/florida-shooting-highlights-limits-of-u-s-airport-security-idUSKBN14Q2H7 [accessed 20 February 2017].

Bala, C. 2010. 'Aviation Security: Proactive or Playing Catch-Up?'. *Journal of Aviation Management*, 71–8.

Banner, S. 2008. *Who Owns the Sky?: The Struggle to Control Airspace from the Wright Brothers On*. Cambridge, MA: Harvard University Press.

Bartsch, R.I.C. 1996. *Aviation Law in Australia*, 1st edn. Sydney, Australia: Thomson Reuters.

Bartsch, R.I.C. 2004. *Aviation Law in Australia*, 2nd edn. Sydney, Australia: Thomson Reuters.

Bartsch, R.I.C. 2010. *Aviation Law in Australia*, 3rd edn. Sydney: Thompson Reuters.

Bartsch, R.I.C. 2012a. 'Aviation Expert Discusses Possibility of Qantas Sale'. Television Interview with Host Ticky Fullerton, ABC News 24, The Business, 13 June.

Bartsch, R.I.C. 2012b. *International Aviation Law*. Abingdon: Routledge.

Bartsch, R.I.C. 2024. *Aviation Law in Australia*, 6th edn. Sydney: Thompson Reuters.

Bartsch, Ron. 2021. *The Corona Dilemma: 20–20 Thinking for the Next Normal*. Perth: Vivid Publishing.

Bates, G. 2010. *Environmental Law in Australia*, 7th edn. Sydney: LexisNexis Butterworths.

BBC News. 2010, 9 November. Available at: www.bbc.co.uk/news/business [accessed 6 October 2012].

BBC News. 2011a. *British Airways Cabin Crew Vote for Fresh Strikes*. Available at: www.bbc.co.uk/news/business-12247510 [accessed 5 September 2012].

BBC News. 2011b. *Lufthansa Pilots Win Ageism Case at European Court*. Available at: www.bbc.co.uk/news/world-europe-14899014 [accessed 5 September 2012].

Bofinger, H.C. 2008. *Status of the Liberalisation of Air Transport among ASEAN Countries*. Available at: http://legacy.icao.int/DevelopmentForum/Forum_08/Presentations/Bofinger.pdf [accessed 16 January 2012].

Brankin, S. 2005. 'Introduction' in P. Willis (ed.), *Introduction to EU Competition Law*. London: Informa Professional.

Buckley, C. 2012. 'China Bans Airlines from Joining EU Emissions Scheme'. *Reuters*. Available at: www.reuters.com/article/2012/02/06/us-china-eu-emissions-idUSTRE81500V20120206 [accessed 5 September 2012].

Buyck, Cathy. 2015. 'Has The Single European Sky Project Failed?'. *Aviation Week Network*, 27 February. Available at: http://aviationweek.com/aftermarket-solutions/has-single-european-sky-project-failed [accessed 24 February 2017].

Caldwell, A. 2011. '21 Airlines Fined in Price-Fixing Scheme'. *Associated Press*. Available at: www.msnbc.msn.com/id/41926712/ns/travel-news/t/airlines-fined-price-fixing-scheme/#.TyfurJi-K4UV [accessed 5 September 2012].

Cameron, J. and Abouchar, J. 1991. 'The Precautionary Principle: A Fundamental Principle of Law and Policy for the Protection of the Global Environment'. *Boston College International & Comparative Law Review, 14(1)*, 1.

Campos, N. and Cosmos, A. 2007. *Air Transportation Regulatory Environment: Ownership Liberalization and Open Skies*. Available at: http://web.mit.edu/airlines/industry_outreach/board_meeting_presentation_files/meeting-oct-2007/Cosmas%20-%20Open%20Skies.pdf [accessed 5 September 2012].

CAPA. 2011. *World Airport Rankings*. Available at: www.centreforaviation.com/analysis/world-airport-rankings-2010-big-changes-to-global-top-30-beijing-up-to-2-heathrow-falls-to-4-47882 [accessed 5 September 2012].

Casson, L. 1984. *Ancient Trade and Society*. Detroit, MI: Wayne State University Press.

Cho, George. 2012–13. 'Unmanned Aerial Vehicles: Emerging Policy and Regulatory Issues'. *Journal of Law, Information and Science, 22*, 201.

Chung, C.K. 2004. *The New European Aviation Safety Agency: Is It Europe's Answer to the FAA?* Available at: www.rotor.com/membership/rotor/rotorpdf/p24.pdf [accessed 5 September 2012].

Civil Aviation Authority. *ATS Requirements Overview*. Available at: www.caa.co.uk/default.aspx?catid=2004&pagetype=90 [accessed 5 September 2012].

Clark, Nicola. 2014. 'Air France Pilots End Two-Week Strike'. *New York Times*, 28 September. Available at: www.nytimes.com/2014/09/29/business/international/air-france-pilots-end-two-week-strike.html [accessed 24 February 2018].

Clothier, R. 2008. 'Pilotless Aircraft: The Horseless Carriage of the 21st Century'. *Journal of Risk Research, 11(8)*, 999–1023.

Colegrove, K.W. 1930. *International Control of Aviation*. Boston, MA: World Peace Foundation.

Cools, S. 2004. 'The Real Difference in Corporate Law between the United States and Continental Europe: Distribution of Powers'. Harvard Law School John M. Olin Centre for Law, Economics and Business Discussion Paper Series, Paper 490.

Cooper, J.C. 1968. 'The International Air Navigation Conference Paris 1910'. *Exploration in Aerospace Law*, 105–56.

CRS Report for Congress. *Screening Passengers and Baggage*. Available at: www.law.umaryland.edu/marshall/crsreports/crsdocuments/RL31151_10262001.pdf [accessed 5 September 2012].

Daley, B. 2010. *Air Transport and the Environment*. Aldershot: Ashgate.

Dam, C.V. 2006. *European Tort Law*. Oxford: Oxford University Press.

De Maglie, C. 2005. *Models of Corporate Criminal Liability in Comparative Law*. Available at: http://law.wustl.edu/wugslr/issues/volume4_3/p547deMaglie.pdf [accessed 5 September 2012].

Debost, J. 2007. *France: The New Hiring Contract*. Available at: www.mondaq.com/article.asp?articleid=47750 [accessed 5 September 2012].

Dekker, S. 2010. 'Pilots, Controllers and Mechanics on Trial: Cases, Concerns and Countermeasures'. *International Journal of Applied Aviation Studies, 10(1)*, 31–50.

Dempsey, P.S. 2008. *The Chicago Convention as the Constitution of an International (Civil Aviation) Organization*. Available at: www.mcgill.ca/files/iasl/ASPL633-ICAO.pdf [accessed 5 September 2012].

Dempsey, P.S. 2009. *Airline Regulation: The U.S Example*. Available at: www.mcgill.ca/files/iasl/ASPL614_Airline_Regulation.pdf [accessed 5 September 2012].

Department of Infrastructure and Transport. 2011, July. *Air Traffic Management Future Policy Directions*. Available at: www.infrastructure.gov.au/aviation/atmfuturepolicydirections/files/ATM_Policy_Directions_Paper_Final_July_2011.pdf [accessed 5 September 2012].

Dickson, B. 1994. *Introduction to French Law*. London: Pitman Publishing.

Diederiks-Verschoor, I.H.Ph. 1993. *An Introduction to Air Law*, 2nd edn. The Hague: Kluwer Law International.

Diederiks-Verschoor, I.H.Ph. 2006. *An Introduction to Air Law*, 8th edn. The Hague: Kluwer Law International.

Doganis, R. 2001. *The Airline Business in the Twenty-First Century*. London: Routledge.

Dutch Safety Board. 2015, October. *Crash of Malaysia Airlines flight MH17, Hrabove, Ukraine, 17 July 2014*. The Hague: DSB.

EASA. 2011. *Research Projects – Airports*. Available at: www.easa.eu.int/safety-and-research/research-projects/airports.php#2008-9 [accessed 5 September 2012].

Eastlund, D. 2008. *Open Skies: Opening Up Opportunities*. Available at: www.carlsonwagonlit.com/en/global/tmi/cwt_vision_pdf_en/303_open_skies_en.pdf [accessed 5 September 2012].

The Economist. 2011. *Runways Required*. Available at: www.economist.com/node/18744513 [accessed 5 September 2012].

Esler, D. 2009. *Flight Risk: The Threat of Criminalization*. Available at: www.aviationweek.com/aw/generic/story_generic.jsp?channel=bca&id=news/bca0309p1.xml [accessed 5 September 2012].
Europa. 2008. *EU–US Open Skies: A New Era in Transatlantic Aviation Starts on 30 March*. Available at: http://europa.eu/rapid/pressReleasesAction.do?reference=IP/08/474&format=HTM [accessed 5 September 2012].
European Commission. 2009. *European Air Traffic Management Master Plan*. Available at: http://ec.europa.eu/transport/air/sesar/doc/1-european_atm_master_plan.pdf [accessed 5 September 2012].
European Commission. 2011. *Protecting Civil Aviation Against Terrorism*. Available at: http://ec.europa.eu/transport/air/events/doc/2011-09-27-avsec-conclusions.pdf [accessed 5 September 2012].
European Commission. 2017. *Replies of the Commission to the Special Report of the European Council of Auditors*. Luxembourg: European Union.
European Council of Auditors. 2017. 'Single European Sky: A Changed Culture but Not a Single Sky'. Special Report 18, European Union.
FAA. 2010. *FAA Regulation*. Available at: www.faa.gov/regulations_policies/faa_regulations/ [accessed 5 September 2012].
FAA. 2012. *Part 139 Airport Certification: What Is Part 139?* Available at: www.faa.gov/airports/airport_safety/part139_cert/?p1=what [accessed 5 September 2012].
FAA. 2017. Available at: www.faa.gov/airports/airport_safety/part139_cert/ [accessed 20 March 2018].
Farber, Hillary B. 2014. 'Eyes in the Sky: Constitutional and Regulatory Approaches to Domestic Drone Deployment'. *Syracuse Law Review, 64*(1).
Fauchille, P. 1901. 'Le domaine aérien et le regime juridique des aerostats'. *Revue Générale de Droit International Public, 8*, 414.
Federal Aviation Administration Office of Environment and Energy. *Aviation and Emissions: A Primer*. Available at: http://adg.stanford.edu/aa241/emissions/AEprimer2005.pdf [accessed 5 September 2012].
Fisher, D. 2010. *Australian Environmental Law: Norms, Principles and Rules*, 2nd edn. Sydney: Thomson Reuters.
Flight Global. 2016. *IATA Warns of "Permanent Downward Shift" Following Brexit*, 24 June. Available at: www.flightglobal.com/news/articles/iata-warns-of-permanent-downward-shift-following-b-426690/ [accessed 24 February 2017].
Flight Safety Australia. 2011. *Accidental Justice*. Available at: http://casa.realviewtechnologies.com/default.aspx?iid=51905&startpage=page0000011 [accessed 5 September 2012].
Flight Safety Australia. 2022, Spring. *Culture, Challenge and Catastrophe*. Available at: https://www.flightsafetyaustralia.com/2022/11/culture-challenge-and-catastrophe/ [accessed 8 April 2024].
Flight Safety Australia. 2024. 'Retro but Current'. *Angela Stevenson*. Available at: https://www.flightsafetyaustralia.com/2024/06/retro-but-current/ [accessed 1 July 2024].
Forsyth, P., King, J., Rodolfo, C.L. and Trace, K. 2004. *Preparing ASEAN for Open Sky*. Available at: www.ausaid.gov.au/publications/pdf/asean_open_skies.pdf [accessed 16 January 2012].
French, D. 2005. *International Law and Policy of Sustainable Development*. Manchester: Manchester University Press.
Gallant, K.S. 2009. *The Principle of Legality in International and Comparative Criminal Law*. Cambridge: Cambridge University Press.
Gangopadhyay, P. and Chatterji, M. 2005. *Economics of Globalisation*. Aldershot: Ashgate.
Gilbert, M. and Russell, S. 2002. 'Globalization of Criminal Justice in the Corporate Context'. *Crime, Law and Social Change, 38*(3), 211–38.

Godden, L. 2009. 'Death, Desire, Modernity and Redemption: Climate Change and Public International Environmental Law'. *Melbourne Journal of International Law, 10*(2), 543–78.

Grossman, Lev. 2013. 'Game of Drones'. *Time*, 11 February.

Harvey, Geraint and Turnbull, Peter. 2017. 'Why British Airways Cabin Crew Are Striking'. *The Conversation*, 10 January. Available at: theconversation.com/why-british-airways-cabin-crew-are-striking-70950 [accessed 1 September 2017].

Hasebroek, J. 1965. *Trade and Politics in Ancient Greece*. London: Hafner Publishing.

Hawthorne, M. 2008. 'BrisConnections in an Unguarded Moment'. *The Age*, 27 November. Available at: www.theage.com.au/business/brisconnections-in-an-unguarded-moment-20081126-6iv0.html [accessed 5 September 2012].

Hazeltine, H.D. 1911. *The Laws of the Air*. London, University of London Press.

Heilbronn, G. 2008. *Aviation Regulation and Licensing: The Laws of Australia*. Sydney: Thomson Lawbook Co.

Hopt, J. and Leyers, P. 2004. 'Board Models in Europe: Recent Developments of Internal Corporate Governance Structures in Germany, the United Kingdom, France, and Italy' in L. Timmermann (ed.), *The Verenigde Oostindische Compangnie 1602–2002: 400 Years of Company Law*. The Hague: Kluwer Law International.

House of Representatives Standing Committee on Social Policy and Legal Affairs. 2014. 'Eyes in the Sky: Inquiry into Drones and the Regulation of Air Safety'. The Parliament of the Commonwealth of Australia, Canberra, July.

Hutcheson, S. 2006. *An Introduction to Air Transport*. Sydney: Aviation Training International.

IATA. 2011a. *Early Days*. Available at: www.iata.org/about/pages/history_2.aspx [accessed 5 September 2012].

IATA. 2011b. *Fact Sheet: Industry Statistics, December 2011*. Available at: www.iata.org/pressroom/facts_figures/fact_sheets/Documents/industry-stats-dec2011.pdf [accessed 1 February 2012].

IATA. 2012. *The Story of the World's First Airline 2011*. Available at: https://www.iata.org/en/about/history/flying-100-years/firstairline-story/ [accessed 8 April 2024].

ICAO. *Annex 11 to the Convention on International Civil Aviation: Air Traffic Services*. Available at: http://dcaa.slv.dk:8000/icaodocs/Annex%2011%20-%20Air%20Traffic%20Services/an11_13ed.pdf [accessed 5 September 2012].

ICAO. *Annexes 1 to 18*. Available at: http://legacy.icao.int/eshop/pub/anx_info/annexes_booklet_en.pdf [accessed 5 September 2012].

ICAO. *ICAO Standards and Recommended Practices – SARPs*. Available at: http://atcvantage.com/docs/_ATC_Vantage_ICAO_SMS_Annex_Requirements.pdf [accessed 5 September 2012].

ICAO. *Safety Management SARPs (Extract)*. Available at: www2.icao.int/en/ism/ICAO%20Annexes/Annex%2014.pdf [accessed 5 September 2012].

ICAO. 1974. *Annual Digest on Aircraft Accidents*. Montreal: ICAO.

ICAO. 2008. *Prohibited Items List*. Available at: www.eraa.org/docman/cat_view/86-issues/88-security/335-passenger-security-information- [accessed 5 September 2012].

ICAO. 2009. *ICAO Policies on Charges for Airports and Navigational Services, ICAO Doc. 9082, Eighth Edition*. Montreal.

ICAO. 2009a. *Environment Branch Climate Change*. Available at: http://legacy.icao.int/icao/en/Env2010/ClimateChange.htm [accessed 5 September 2012].

ICAO. 2009b. *Safety Management Manual*. ICAO Doc. 9859. Montreal: ICAO.

ICAO. 2010. *Aviation Security Manual*. ICAO Doc. 8973. Available at: www2.icao.int/en/AVSEC/SFP/Pages/SecurityManual.aspx [accessed 5 September 2012].

ICAO. 2011. *European States Agree on Comprehensive Aviation Security Strategy*. Available at: www.icao.int/Newsroom/Pages/European-States-Agree-on-Comprehensive-Aviation-Security-Strategy.aspx [accessed 5 September 2012].

ICAO. 2013. *1944: The Chicago Conference*. Available at: https://applications.icao.int/postalhistory/1944_the_chicago_convention.htm [accessed 8 April 2024].

ICAO. 2016a. *Annex 19 to the Convention on International Civil Aviation: Safety Management*, 2nd edn. Available at: www.icao.int/SAM/Documents/2017-SSP-GUY/Annex-19-2edEdition_eng.pdf [accessed 2 December 2017].

ICAO. 2016b. *Global Air Navigation Plan*, 5th edn. ICAO Doc. 9750. Available at: www.icao.int/publications/Documents/9750_5ed_en.pdf [accessed 14 December 2017].

ICAO. 2016c. *Global Aviation Safety Plan*, 2nd edn. ICAO Doc. 10004. Available at: www.icao.int/publications/Documents/10004_en.pdf [accessed 13 December 2017].

ICAO. 2018. *Safety Management Manual*, 4th edn. ICAO Doc. 9859. Montreal: ICAO.

ICAO. 2022. *States Adopt Net-Zero 2050 Global Aspirational Goal for International Flight Operations*. Available at: https://www.icao.int/Newsroom/Pages/States-adopts-netzero-2050-aspirational-goal-for-international-flight-operations.aspx [accessed 8 April 2024].

ICAO Pressroom. 2023, June 5. Available at: https://www.iata.org/en/pressroom/2023-speeches/2023-06-05-01/ [accessed 8 April 2024]

Intergovernmental Panel on Climate Change. 1999. *Aviation and the Global Atmosphere*. Cambridge: Cambridge University Press.

Irish Aviation Authority. 2008. 'Disruptive Action by Air Traffic Controllers to Continue'. *BBC Business News*. Available at: www.bbc.co.uk/news/business-12247510 [accessed 5 September 2012].

Jackson, D. 2009. *Adversarial and Inquisitorial Systems*. Available at: www.medicolegal.org.au [accessed 5 September 2012].

Johnstone, R.W. 2006. *9/11 and the Future of Transportation Security*. Westport, CT: Praeger Security International.

Kaiser, Stefan A. 2008. 'Third Party Liability of Unmanned Aerial Vehicles'. *Zeitschrift für Luft- und Weltraumrecht*, *57*, 229.

Kaiser, Stefan A. 2011. 'UAVs and Their Legislation into Non-Segregated Airspace'. *Air and Space Law*, *36*, 162.

Kallas, S. 2011. *10 Years from 9/11: What Has Been Done in Europe to Make Flying Safer from Terrorist Attacks?* Available at: http://ec.europa.eu/commission_2010-2014/kallas/headlines/news/2011/09/10-years-after-9-11_en.htm [accessed 5 September 2012].

Kapnik, Benjamin. 2012. 'Unmanned but Accelerating: Navigating the Regulatory and Privacy Challenges of Introducing Unmanned Aircraft into the National Airspace System'. *Journal of Air Law and Commerce*, *77*, 439–65.

King, J. 2012. 'Introduction to Air Transportation, Course' in *Master of Aviation (Management) Program*. Melbourne: Swinburne University of Technology.

Kirgis, F.L.J. 1995. 'Specialized Law Making Processes' in O. Schachter and C. Joiner (eds.), *United Nations Legal Order*. Cambridge: Cambridge University Press.

Kislov, A. and Krylov, S. 1956. 'State Sovereignty in Airspace'. *International Affairs*, *3*, 35–44.

Kotaite, A. 2000. *Aviation Regulation: New Millennium – New Direction. 56th IATA AGM*. Available at: http://legacy.icao.int/icao/en/pres/pres_sydney.htm [accessed 5 September 2012].

Larsen, N. and Smandych, R. 2008. *Global Criminology and Criminal Justice: Current Issues and Perspectives*. Toronto: University of Toronto Press.

Littlechild, S.C. 2011a. *Australian Airport Regulation: Exploring the Frontier*. Available at: www.accc.gov.au/content/item.phtml?itemId=998759&nodeId=5582b57b97f0a9c6608b41ec07730db [accessed 19 February 2017].

Littlechild, S.C. 2011b. *German Airport Regulation: Framework Agreements, Civil Law and the EU Directive*. Available at: www.accc.gov.au/content/item.phtml?itemId=998755&nodeId=9dde1062c0ce543ad4c4304cc10cd8ed&fn=Paper%20by%20Stephen%20Littlechild%20on%20German%20airport%20regulation.pdf [accessed 5 September 2012].

Markesinis, B.S. 2011. *Tort*. Available at: www.britannica.com/EBchecked/topic/600206/tort [accessed 5 September 2012].

Markesinis, B.S. and Deakin, S. 2003. *Markesinis and Deakin's Tort Law*. Oxford: Clarendon Press.

Markesinis, B.S. and Unberath, H. 2002. *The German Law of Torts*. Oxford: Hart Publishing.

Marsh, P.D.V. 1994. *Comparative Contract Law*. Aldershot: Gower Publishing.

Marshall, Douglas M. 2007. 'Dull, Dirty, and Dangerous: The FAA's Regulatory Authority over Unmanned Aircraft Operations'. *Issues in Aviation Law and Policy*, 10085–109.

Mason, M. 1941. 'The Utility of Consideration: A Comparative View'. *Columbia Law Review*, *41*, 825–48.

Matte, N. 1981. *Treatise on Air-Aeronautical Law*. Montreal: Institute and Centre of Air and Space Law.

Mazur, Michal and Wisniewski, Adam. 2016. 'Clarity from Above'. PwC Global Report on the Commercial Applications of Drone Technology, PwC Poland, May, p. 4.

McIntyre, O. and Mosedale, T. 1997. 'The Precautionary Principle as a Norm of Customary International Law'. *Journal of Environmental Law*, *9*(2), 221–41.

Meiners, R.E., Ringleb, A.H. and Edwards, F.L. 2009. *The Legal Environment of Business*, 10th edn. Independence, KY: South-Western Cengage Learning.

Michaelides-Mateou, S. and Erotokritou, Chrystel. 2014. 'Flying into the Future with UAVs: The Jetstream 31 Flight'. *Air and Space Law*, *39*, 111.

Michaelides-Mateou, S. and Mateou, A. 2007. 'The Effect of the Relationship on Aviation Safety and the Criminalization of Pilots and ATCs'. DProf thesis, Middlesex University.

Michaelides-Mateou, S. and Mateou, A. 2010. *Flying in the Face of Criminalization*. Aldershot: Ashgate.

Milde, M. 1996. 'Enforcement of Aviation Safety Standards – Problems of Safety Oversight'. *German Journal of Air and Space Law*, *45*.

Milde, M. 2008. *International Air Law and ICAO. Essential Air and Space Law Series*, *18*. The Hague: Eleven International Publishing.

Mo, J. 2003. *International Commercial Law*, 3rd edn. Sydney: LexisNexis Butterworths.

Morgan, D. 2001. 'Aviation Security Technologies and Procedures: Screening Passengers for Baggage'. CRS Report for Congress, 26 October.

National Air Traffic Controllers Association. *A History of Air Traffic Control*. Available at: www.natcareloaded.org/library/document-library/20090813115836.ATC%20History%202.pdf [accessed 5 September 2012].

Nijeholt, J.F. 1910. *Air Sovereignty*. The Netherlands, Springer Nature B.V.

North Texas Commission. 2011. *Airport Rankings*. Available at: www.ntc-dfw.org/northtexas/dfwairportrankings.html [accessed 5 September 2012].

Official Journal of the European Commission. 2004. 'Establishing a Common Definition of Critical Parts of Security Restricted Areas at Airports'. Commission Regulation (EC) No 1138/2004, European Commission, 21 June.

O'Sullivan, Emma. 2014. 'Eyes in the Sky: New Technologies Present New Challenges for Law Makers'. *About the House*, August, p. 44.

Paylor, Anne. 2016. 'Sky Fall: Airlines Are Scathing on Single European Sky Progress, but No Clear Solutions in Sight'. *Air Transport World*, 3 March. Available at: atwonline.com/government-affairs/sky-fall [accessed: 1 March 2017].

Pejovic, C. 2001. 'Civil Law and Common Law: Two Different Paths Leading to the Same Goal'. *Victoria University of Wellington Law Review*, *32*(3), 817–42.

Pengilley, W. and McPhee, J. 1994. *Law for Aviators*. Sydney: Legal Books.
Poole, R.W. 2008. 'Towards Risk-Based Aviation Security Policy'. *Organization for Economic and Corporate Development/International Transport Forum, 23*, 1–26. Available at: www.internationaltransportforum.org/jtrc/discussionpapers/DP200823.pdf [accessed 5 September 2012].
Poole, R.W. and Edwards, C. 2010. *Airports and Air Traffic Control*. Available at: www.downsizinggovernment.org/transportation/airports-atc [accessed 5 September 2012].
Preston, B.J. 2005. 'The Role of the Judiciary in Promoting Sustainable Development: The Experience of Asia and the Pacific'. *Asia Pacific Journal of Environmental Law, 9*(2–3), 109.
Productivity Commission. *Economic Regulation of Airports: An International Comparison*. Available at: www.pc.gov.au/__data/assets/pdf_file/0003/111576/19-airport-regulation-draft-appendixc.pdf [accessed 13 February 2012].
Publications Office. 2004. *Regulation (EC) No 549/2004 of the European Parliament and of the Council of 20 March 2004 Laying Down the Framework for the Creation of the Single European Sky (The Framework Regulation) (Text with EEA Relevance) – Statement by the Member States on Military Issues Related to the Single European Sky*. Available at: http://eur-lex.europa.eu/LexUriServ/LexUriServ.do?uri=CELEX:32004R0549:EN:NOT [accessed 5 September 2012].
Quinn, K.P. 2007. 'Battling Accident Criminalization'. *AeroSafety World, 2*(1), 11–4.
Ramaswamy, V., Boucher, O., Haigh, J., Hauglustaine, D., Haywood, J., Myhre, G., Nakajima, T., Shi, G. and Solomon, S. 2001. 'Radiative Forcing of Climate Change' in *Climate Change 2001: The Scientific Basis, Contribution of Working Group I to the Third Assessment Report of the Intergovernmental Panel on Climate Change*. Cambridge: Cambridge University Press.
Ravich, Timothy M. 2009. 'The Integration of Unmanned Aerial Vehicles into the National Airspace'. *North Dakota Law Review, 85*, 597–622.
Rawls, J. 1970. *A Theory of Justice*. Cambridge, MA: Harvard University Press.
Reason, J. 1997. *Managing the Risks of Organizational Accidents*. Aldershot: Ashgate.
Reichel, P.L. 2008. *Comparative Criminal Justice Systems: A Topical Approach*, 5th edn. Upper Saddle River, NJ: Prentice Hall.
Ribeiro, K.S., Kobayashi, S., Beuthe, M., Gasca, J., Greene, D., Lee, D.S., Muromachi, Y., Newton, P.J., Plotkin, S., Sperling, D., Wit, R. and Zhou, P.J. 2007. *Transport and Its Infrastructure in Climate Change 2007: Mitigation*. Cambridge: Cambridge University Press.
Rodrigue, J.P. 2012. *The Geography of Transport Systems*. Available at: http://people.hofstra.edu/geotrans/eng/ch3en/conc3en/airfreedom.html [accessed 5 September 2012].
Rogers, W.V.H. 2010. *Winfield and Jolowicz on Tort*. London: Thomson Reuters (Legal) Ltd.
Rogers Commission. 1987. *Report of the Presidential Commission on the Space Shuttle Challenger Accident*, Volume 1, Chapter 2. U.S. Government Printing Office, Washington, D.C., June 6, 1987.
Ruhl, J.B. 1999. 'Sustainable Development: A Five-Dimensional Algorithm for Environmental Law'. *Stanford Environmental Journal, 18*, 31–65.
Russell, S. and Gilbert, M. 1999. 'Truman's Revenge: Social Control and Corporate Crime'. *Crime, Law and Social Change, 32*(1), 59–82.
Sand, P.H. *et al.* 1960. 'An Historical Survey of International Air Law Before the Second World War'. *McGill Law Journal, 1*(7), 30. Available at: http://lawjournal.mcgill.ca/documents/7/1/sand.pdf [accessed 5 September 2012].
Sanson, M., Anthony, T. and Worswick, D. 2010. *Connecting with Law*, 2nd edn. Oxford: Oxford University Press.
Schiavo, M. 1997. *Flying Blind, Flying Safe*. New York: Avon Books.
Schlesinger, R.B., Mattei, U., Ruskola, T. and Gidi, A. 2009. *Schlesinger's Comparative Law: Cases, Text, Materials*. London: Foundation Press.
Shawcross, C.N., Beaumont, K.M. and Martin, P. 1977. *Air Law*. London: Butterworths.

Shrager, D.S., Frost-Knappman, E. and Riley, S. 1998. *The Quotable Lawyer*. New York: Checkmark Books.

SMH. 2011. *The Case for People Power*. Available at: www.smh.com.au/travel/travel-news/the-case-for-people-power-20110615-1g2p1.html [accessed 5 September 2012].

Solomon, K. 1993. 'Swimming Pool Risks: How Do They Compare to Other Accidental Risks?' *Rand Report*, P-7841.

Somasundaram, N. 2011. *Qantas Grounds Global Fleet over Labor Dispute*. Available at: www.foxbusiness.com/industries/2011/10/29/qantas-grounds-global-fleet-over-labor-dispute [accessed 5 September 2012].

Sosa, A. 2007a. *ASEAN Single Aviation Market*. Available at: http://pdf.usaid.gov/pdf_docs/PNADJ694.pdf [accessed 5 September 2012].

Sosa, A. 2007b. *Philippine Civil Aviation Policy Paper: ASEAN Single Aviation Market*. Available at: http://pdf.usaid.gov/pdf_docs/PNADJ694.pdf [accessed 5 September 2012].

Speciale, R.C. 2006. *Fundamentals of Aviation Law*. New York: McGraw-Hill.

Spruston, D. 2004. *Sharing Responsibility for Security: Changes to Annex 17*. International Business Aviation Council. Available at: www.ibac.org/Files/Security/sharingresponsibility_march04_spruston.pdf [accessed 7 January 2012].

Starynin, D. 2005. *Air Traffic Control in Europe: Regulatory Framework and Implications*. Available at: www.cidd.org/pdf/starynin.pdf [accessed 5 September 2012].

Stolzer, A. *et al*. 2008. *Safety Management Systems in Aviation*. Aldershot: Ashgate.

Stone, H.F. 1915. *Law and Its Administration*. New York: Columbia University Press.

Tan, A.K.J. 2009. *The Proposed Southeast Asian Single Aviation Market*. Available at: www.mcgill.ca/files/iasl/Session_6_Jin_Tan.pdf [accessed 5 September 2012].

Terry, A. and Giugni, D. 2009. *Business and the Law*. Sydney: Cengage Learning Australia.

Transportation Security Administration. 2012. *Statute and Regulation History*. Available at: www.tsa.gov/what_we_do/ssi/history.shtm [accessed 5 September 2012].

Trögeler, M. 2011. *Criminalisation of Air Accidents and the Creation of a Just Culture*. Available at: www.eala.aero/library/Mildred%20Trgeler%20EALA%20prize.pdf [accessed 5 September 2012].

United Nations. 1972. *Declaration of the United Nations Conference on the Human Environment*. 11 ILM 1416.

United Nations. 1987. *Montreal Protocol on Substances that Deplete the Ozone Layer*. 26 ILM 1550.

United Nations. 1992. *Declaration of the United Nations Conference on Environment and Development*. 31 ILM 874.

United Nations World Commission on Environment and Development. 1987. *Our Common Future*. Rio de Janeiro: UNCED.

Unnikrishnan, M. 2007. 'Bush Signs Pilot Retirement Age Act'. *Aviation Week*. Available at: www.aviationweek.com/aw/generic/story_generic.jsp?channel=aviationdaily&id=news/BUSH12177.xml [accessed 8 January 2012].

US Centennial of Flight. *Air Traffic Control*. Available at: www.centennialofflight.gov/essay/Government_Role/Air_traffic_control/POL15.htm [accessed 5 September 2012].

US Centennial of Flight. *International Civil Aviation*. Available at: www.centennialofflight.gov/essay/Government_Role/Intl_Civil/POL19.htm [accessed 5 September 2012].

Vaillancourt, J.G. 1995. 'Environment' in R. Paehlke (ed.), *Conservation and Environmentalism: An Encyclopaedia*. New York: Garland Publishing.

Venturini, A. 2009. *The Role of Privatization in the Future of Airports in the LAC Region*. Available at: www.airports.org/aci/ACI%20LAC/File/Events/Salvador/Presentation%20of%20the%20Speakers/November,%2017th/ALCESTE%20VENTURINI.pdf [accessed 13 February 2012].

Visscher, Charles De. 1957. *Theory and Reality in Public International Law*. London: Oxford University Press.

Vranken, M. 1997. *Fundamentals of European Civil Law*. Sydney: Federation Press.

Washington Post. 1999. *The Bombing of Pan Am Flight 103*. Available at: www.washingtonpost.com/wp-srv/inatl/longterm/panam103/timeline.htm [accessed 5 September 2012].

Weill, A. and Terré, F. 1986. *Droit civil: Les obligations*, 4th edn. Paris: Dalloz.

Werfelman, L. 2008. 'Deterring Criminalization'. *Aerosafety World*, *3*(3), 12–7.

Wood, J.C. 1996. 'Intergenerational Equity and Climate Change'. *Georgetown International Environmental Law Review*, *293*, 298–9.

World Health Organization. 2009. *Night Noise Guidelines for Europe*. Available at: www.euro.who.int/__data/assets/pdf_file/0017/43316/E92845.pdf [accessed 5 September 2012].

List of Cases

Alidair Ltd v Taylor [1978] ICR 445
Baron Bernstein of Leigh v Skyviews and General Ltd [1978] 1 QB 479
Baulderstone Hornibrook Pty Ltd v Qantas Airways Ltd [2003] FCA 174
Berkebile v Brantly Helicopter Corporation, 281 A.2d 707 (Pa. Super 1971)
Bernstein of Leigh (Baron) v Skyviews & General Ltd [1978] 1 QB 479
Bolton v Stone [1951] AC 850
Bruce v Martin-Marietta Corp. and Ozark Airlines, 14 Avi 472 (1976)
Burke v Pan World Airways, Inc., 484 F. Supp. 850 (S.D.N.Y. 1980)
Carlill v Carbolic Smoke Ball Co [1893] 1 QB 256
Carter v Boehm (1766) 3 Burr 1905; 97 ER 1162
Case of Montagnier, Cass civ, 27 October 1885
Cie. Air France v Sté ERVE et al. [1968] RFDA 327
Constitution Insurance Co of Canada v Kosmopoulos (1987) 34 DLR 208
Donoghue v Stevenson [1932] AC 562
Ecuador v Colombia (Aerial Herbicide Spraying Case) International Court of Justice
Edwards v Skyways Ltd [1964] 1 WLR 349
Epoux Saint-Arroman v Réunion des musées nationaux et autres Civ. Ler. (the Poussin case) 13 December 1983, Bull. Cil. No. 293
Fuerschbach v Southwest Airlines, 439 F. 3d 1197 (2006)
Grosse v Purvis [2003] QDC 151
Guille v Swan, 19 Johns 381 (NY Sup Ct, 1822)
HL Bolton (Engineering) Co Ltd v TJ Graham & Sons Ltd [1957] 1 QB 159
Hallock v Trans World Airlines Inc, 364 SW 2d 636 (1963)
Hartford Fire v California, 509 US 764 (1993)
Heinrich v European Commission, C-345/06 (2009)
Hoffman-La Roche Ltd v Empagran SA, 24 S. Ct 2359 (2004)
Lee v Lee's Air Farming Ltd [1961] AC 12
Lenk v Spezia, California Court, 22 December 1949
Lennards Carrying Co Ltd v Asiatic Petroleum Co Ltd [1915] AC 705
Leonard v Pepsico Inc, 210 F 3d 88 (2nd Cir 2000)
Maynard v Stinson Aircraft Corp. [1940] US AvR 71
McNeill v Parmer, unreported, Supreme Court of Rotorua, 21 February 1979
Nichols v Simmonds, Royal Aero Club of Western Australia and Commonwealth [1975] WAR 1
Peter Smythe v Vincent Thomas [2007] NSWSC 844, Supreme Court of New South Wales
Pharmaceutical Society of Great Britain v Boots Cash Chemists Ltd [1953] 1 QB 401
Public Trustee v Commonwealth [1996] NSWSC 110
Qantas Airways Ltd v Christie (1998) 193 CLR 280
Reichsgericht (First Civil State) 14 January 1928
Reichsgericht (Sixth Civil Senate) 11 January 1912 RGZ 78, 171
Roscorla v Thomas (1842) 3 QB 234; 114 ER 496, Court of Queen's Bench
Salomon v Salomon & Co Ltd [1897] AC 22

Scandinavian Airlines System, Inc. v County of Los Angeles, 56 Cal. 2d 11 (1961)
Société des Eaux de Vittel v Dehen & Société Supermag Rennes GP [1962] I 135
State of Himachal Pradesh v Ganesh Wood Products, AIR 1996 SC 149
Tesco Supermarkets Ltd v Nattrass [1972] AC 153
United States v Aluminum Co of America (Alcoa), 148 F.2d 416 (2nd Cir 1945)
United States v Causby, 328 U.S. 256 (1946)
United States v Nippon Paper Indus. Co., 109 F.3d 1 (1st Cir 1997)

Glossary of Legal Terms

Absolute liability The legal responsibility for a breach of law, not dependent on any particular state of mind, and for which no defence is available except an act of God.

Absolute liability offence An offence that does not require proof of any *mens rea* provided the act of the accused is voluntary.

Acceptance The act of agreeing to an offer so as to create a contract.

Actus reus The physical element of a crime; the act itself.

Adversarial A legal approach where two advocates represent their respective parties' positions before an impartial person or group of people – usually a jury or judge, or both.

Agent A person with an authority or capacity to create or affect legal relations between a principal and third parties.

Agreement A negotiated and usually legally enforceable understanding between two or more legally competent parties.

Air law The body of rules governing the use of airspace and its benefit for aviation, the general public and the nations of the world.

Air service agreement An agreement between two countries allowing air services to operate between the two countries and setting out the terms upon which these services are to operate.

Arrest To deprive a person of his or her liberty by force of law.

Assault An act that intentionally or recklessly causes another to apprehend immediate and unlawful personal violence.

Attorney In US law, a lawyer who has been admitted to the Bar and is authorized to practise law.

Aviation law The branch of law that comprises rules and practices which have been created, modified or developed that apply to aviation activities.

Bail The release of a prisoner from lawful custody, usually on conditions including undertakings that may be given.

Bailee A person in possession of goods belonging to another and holding those goods under a *bailment*.

Bailment A contract for the care or safekeeping of property.

Balance of probabilities The weighing up and comparison of the likelihood of the existence of competing facts or conclusions. A fact is proved to be true on the balance of probabilities if its existence is more probable than not, or if it is established by a preponderance of probability.

Barrister In English law and related legal systems, a lawyer, who has been admitted to the Bar, whose main function is to act as an advocate in court.

Barter The exchange of goods or commodities for other goods or commodities without using money.

Battery The reckless or intentional application of force to another person without consent.

Beyond reasonable doubt In criminal proceedings, a standard of proof that stipulates that a change is not proved if the court is not satisfied beyond reasonable doubt that the accused committed the offence charged.

Bilateral contract A contract formed by the exchange of mutual or reciprocal promises.

Binding precedent A precedent made by a court higher in the same hierarchy as the court where a case is heard. The court must follow or apply the precedent if the facts of the case at hand cannot be distinguished from the facts of the precedent case.

Bonus pater familias A man who is the head of a household or the father of a family (French: 'good family father').

Breach of duty of care The negligent or careless conduct, or failure to act, of a person who owes a duty of care to another and who fails to maintain the standard of care necessary to fulfil that duty.

Bush lawyer A layperson who pretends or acts as if they are in fact a lawyer.

'But for' test In tort law, a test applied to establishing causation. It is asked whether the outcome that occurred and resulted in injury to the plaintiff would have occurred without the defendant's actions.

Case A civil or criminal proceeding in a court of law.

Causa A comprehensive term for any proceeding in a court of law whereby an individual seeks a legal remedy.

Causation (*criminal law*) A requirement of the definition of the *actus reus* of a crime.

Causation (*tort law*) The question of whether a plaintiff's loss is the result of the defendant's actions in breach of duty of care.

Chattel Any property other than freehold land.

Civil law (1) The law applying in jurisdictions under a civil law system as opposed to common law.

Civil law (2) A synonym of *private law*, the law relating to the legal relationships between individuals as opposed to *criminal law*.

Civil law system The Western European system of codified laws in contradistinction to the evolutionary body of precedents associated with common law systems.

Claim The assertion of a right or demand to a right to property or to a remedy; a cause of action.

Code A name sometimes given to a statute or law created by a legislature. Used particularly to describe the comprehensive statutes embodying the laws in a civil law system.

Code Civil A code enacted in France embodying the law of rights of persons and of property.

Codification The creation of codes, which are compilations of written statutes, rules and regulations, which inform the public of acceptable and unacceptable behaviour. In common law systems, codification also means the process whereby laws formerly governed by precedent are written into legislative form.

Commercial relations A business relationship.

Commercial transaction A business arrangement or agreement usually involving the alteration of legal rights.

Common law (1) The system of laws existing in a jurisdiction under a *common law system* as opposed to *civil law*.

Common law (2) Laws governed by the development of precedents on a case-by-case basis as opposed to *legislation* or statute law.

Common law system The law system with unwritten law derived from the traditional law of England as developed by judicial precedence, interpretation, expansion and modification.

Compensation The act or process of making amends for injury or loss. Compensation may be in the form of money.

Condition A contractual term, especially an important contractual term. Breach of a condition entitles the other party to terminate the contract immediately.

Conditio sine qua non A causal connection exists between a particular act and an injury when the injury would not have arisen but for the act; necessary condition.

Conflict of laws The area of law dealing with international disputes between private persons or corporations. Determinations in this area include the acceptance of jurisdiction over a dispute and the choice of law to apply in the dispute. Nations may also become involved in this field in relation to their dealings with private persons or corporations, or in other 'business' dealings in which they may engage.

Consensus ad idem A meeting of minds in order to create a contract.

Consent Affirmative acceptance, not merely a standing by and absence of objection.

Consideration The 'price' one party provides in return for the promise of the other. Something of legal value that is given as the value of a contractual promise.

Contract A legally binding promise or agreement.

Contract for services A contractual arrangement by which one person (the contractor) agrees to provide workplace services to another (the principal).

Contract of carriage A contract for transportation of goods (freight or cargo) or passengers.

Contract of employment A contract under which a person (the employee) agrees to work for another person (the employer) in return for some benefit or remuneration from the employer.

Contract of service *see* Contract of employment.

Contributory negligence (*tort law*) The negligence of a defendant that contributed to the defendant's loss or injury. Where a defendant can show that a plaintiff is negligent, the plaintiff's liability for damages is reduced to the extent of the defendant's own contributory negligence.

Control test A test used by the courts to determine whether a person contracted to perform work for another is an employee of the other or an independent contractor. The test asks whether the person for whom the work is being done has lawful authority to direct or command the worker in the performance of the work.

Corpus Iuris Civilis The body of codified legal material commissioned by the Roman Emperor Justinian comprising the *Institutes*.

Crime An act which the state regards as offensive and which may be prosecuted before the courts.

Criminal sanctions A penalty imposed for violating accepted social norms that is of a criminal nature.

Cujus est solum ejus est usque ad coelum (property law) A maxim of Roman law suggesting that the owner of land also owns all the ground beneath it to the centre of the Earth and all the airspace above it to infinity. Translates to 'who owns the soil/land also owns the sky over that property'.

Damage The loss or harm suffered.

Damages A monetary remedy ordered to compensate a party who has suffered loss or harm.

Debt A legal obligation to pay a sum of money to another.

Deed A written document which is intended to act as evidence of an agreement. In the common law, a deed is a formal contract, or a 'contract under seal' and does not require consideration.

Defamation The tort of publishing to persons, other than the person defamed, imputations the effect of which is to lower the reputation of the person in the eyes of the public at large.

Defendant Any legal person against whom relief is sought in a matter or who is required to attend proceedings in a matter, or who is required to attend proceedings in a matter as a party to the proceedings.

Delict A wrong defined in civil law systems.

Deterrence The theory that one of the purposes of punishment is to discourage people from committing crime.

Directive A legislative act that requires member states to achieve a particular result.

Discharged contract A contract in which all parties have fully performed all their obligations. *See also* Executed contract.

Doctrine of precedent The doctrine under which a court is bound to follow previous decisions, unless they are inconsistent with a higher court's decision or wrong in law.

Donee The person who receives a gift.

Donor The person who gives a gift.

Double jeopardy Placing an accused person in peril of being convicted of the same crime in respect of the same conduct on more than one occasion.

Duress Such constraint or coercion as will render void a contract or other legal act entered or performed under its influence.

Duty of care The duty owed to others, a breach of which gives rise to liability for negligence.

Employee A person who performs work under the control of another in exchange for payment for the services that he or she provides.

Employment relationship A contract whereby one party (the employee) agrees to perform certain services for the other party (the employer) in return for remuneration – usually in the form of wages and conditions.

Entry into force When a treaty becomes binding on states that have ratified, it is said to have *entered into force*.

Estoppel When a first person, in doing something, relies on the conduct of a second person to his or her detriment and the second person, well knowing of such reliance, permits the first person to continue to act to his or her detriment, the second person is estopped from denying that he or she consented to the action of the first person.

Evidence Material used to support or prove a fact at issue.

Ex gratia A payment made as a favour.

Executed contract A contract in which all parties have fully performed all their obligations. *See also* Discharged contract.

Executive or executive government In the doctrine of separation of powers, the arm of government responsible for applying and administering the law.

Executory contracts A contract yet to be performed or carried out by one or other party. A contract where any aspect of any party's performance is still outstanding.

Expectation damages A monetary award, usually for breach of contract, of an amount equivalent to the benefit that a party to a contract would have gained had the party in breach performed the contract as agreed.

Express term A term that is expressly stated in a contract by reason of what the parties have written or said.

False imprisonment Unlawfully restraining the liberty of another person without that person's authority.

Felony In common law systems, defined as an indictable offence punishable by penal servitude (imprisonment together with hard labour).

Formal contract A document which is sealed and delivered and intended to take effect as a deed in compliance with legislative provisions.

Fraud An intentional deceit.

Freedoms of the air Freedoms to airlines to cross the territory of another country and conduct commercial services to other countries. The freedoms outlined under the *Air*

Services Transit Agreement (the 'two freedoms agreement') or the *Air Services Transport Agreement* (the 'five freedoms agreement') where all states involved in an air journey adhere to those agreements.

Frustration (*contract law*) Where an event occurs to change the circumstances of the contract so fundamentally as to render the contract impossible to perform.

General deterrence This type of deterrence uses the person sentenced for a crime as an example to induce the public to refrain from criminal conduct.

Good faith Propriety or honesty.

Good Samaritan Someone who renders aid in an emergency to an injured person on a voluntary basis.

Guarantee A contract where one party agrees to promise to pay the debts of another.

Guilty Legally responsible for a criminal offence.

Hearing A trial before an appropriate tribunal.

Hijacking The unlawful seizure of a mode of transport.

Homicide The killing of one person by another.

Honest and reasonable mistake of fact A term that is defined as a defence to an offence where the defendant acts from an honest and reasonable mistake as to existence of facts which, if true, would have made the acts innocent.

Illegal An act which the law forbids; unlawful.

Immovable property In civil law, land and other tangible property not capable of being relocated physically. There is substantial overlap between this and the common law concept of *real property*.

Implied term A term that the parties have not set out, but which is deemed to have been agreed to.

Independent contractor A person who contracts to perform work for another person.

Indictable offences An offence that can be prosecuted on indictment. What comprises an indictable offence differs between the various jurisdictions.

Infringement The encroachment, breach or violation of a right, law, regulation or contract.

Injunction An order made by a court for a person to refrain from engaging in a specified act or from undertaking a specified act. The latter is distinguished from the former by the term *mandatory injunction*.

Inquisitorial system A legal system where the court or a part of the court is actively involved in investigating the facts of the case.

Intention The formation of a purpose or design in mind.

Inter alia A Latin term meaning 'among other things'.

Invitation to treat A request to negotiate or make an offer with a contract in mind.

Judge A judicial officer who presides over an intermediate or superior court.

Judgment The court's decision; may also refer to the reasoning of the judge.

Judiciary In the doctrine of separation of powers, the arm of government responsible for interpreting and enforcing the law.

Jura novit curia A Latin term that means 'a court knows the law'. It is an international law maxim presuming that a court or tribunal knows the law applicable to a given case.

Jurisdiction The scope of a court's power to examine and determine facts, interpret and apply the law, make orders and declare judgment.

Jury A body of people selected to give a verdict on a matter before a court.

Laissez-faire French for 'let it be'. A free enterprise economic system devoid of governmental intervention, which allows market forces (such as demand, supply, prices and competition) to determine the operation of business and trading.

Law Sum total of all those rules of conduct for which there is a state sanction; the subject matter of the discipline of jurisprudence (legal system).

Lawyer A person professionally qualified to practise law.

Legal capacity The power, ability or competence of a person or body.

Legal liability A person's present or prospective legal responsibility, duty or obligation.

Legally enforceable The contract is legally binding.

Legislation Laws enacted by a *legislature*, such as Parliament or Congress.

Legislature In the doctrine of separation of powers, the arm of government responsible for writing and promulgating the law in the form of *legislation*.

Liability Subject to a legal obligation.

Litigation Taking a dispute before a court.

Master An employer (a term that is now seldom used).

Mens rea The mental element of a crime.

Mental injury/illness A condition which seriously impairs, either temporarily or permanently, the mental functioning of a person and is characterized by the presence of at least one of the following symptoms: delusions; hallucinations; serious disorder of the stream of thought; or serious disorder of thought form.

Minor A person under the age of 18.

Misdemeanour An offence less serious than a felony.

Misrepresentation A statement or conduct that is false or misleading.

Mortgage The transfer of an estate or interest in land or other property in order to secure the payment of a debt or other obligation.

Movable property Property capable of being moved physically, such as goods. A civil law concept, with substantial overlap with the common law concept of *personal property*.

Mutual consent An agreement between two parties on terms and conditions of a contract.

Necessity Generally, that which is necessary or indispensable. In *criminal law* it is a defence involving a plea by a person that he or she was compelled by a threat or danger to commit the crime charged.

Negligence An action in tort law under the common law system, the elements of which are: the existence of a duty of care; breach of that duty; and material damage as a consequence of the breach of duty.

No-fault liability This liability is also known as absolute liability. *See* Absolute liability.

Nominal damages Those damages awarded to acknowledge a wrong done against the aggrieved party, but of a merely nominal amount not designed to compensate the party fully.

Nuisance An unlawful interference with another's use of, enjoyment of or right over land.

Objective test/standard Assessing the conduct, mental state or behaviour of a person or the quality of a thing by reference to a standard external to the person who or the thing that is being assessed.

Objet A French term translated to mean 'purpose'. In relation to *contract law* it means the purpose of entering into a contract.

Obligation The binding force of promissory or quasi-promissory comments.

Offer The expression of willingness to contract on terms stated.

Offer to treat A party making an offer to treat is asking for parties to approach him or her so that he or she can select a party with whom to deal.

Offeree The person to whom an offer is made.

Offeror The person who makes the offer.

Party (1) A person immediately concerned with some legal proceeding.

Party (2) In relation to a contract, one of the legal persons who has an obligation under the contract, who may enforce and against whom the contract may be enforced.

Passing off An action to prevent financial loss arising from the defendant's representation that his or her own goods or services are those of the plaintiff.

Past consideration A promise to do something which creates no new obligations.

Performance The completion of an act; an act which, when performed in accordance with the conditions of a contract, discharges that contract.

Personal property In common property law, all forms of property other than *real property*. Includes leases in land, which are referred to as 'chattels real'. There is substantial overlap with the civil law concept of *movable property*.

Persuasive precedent A precedent that is not binding and is made by a court outside the hierarchy of the court where a case is heard. Applying or following the precedent is optional for the court.

Plaintiff A person who seeks relief against any other person by any form of proceedings in a court.

Pleading A court document in which a party sets out its contention of the facts to which the law will be applied. It is a statement of facts only, not an argument as to how the law should apply to the facts or how the case should be decided.

Precedent A judgment or decision cited as justifying a similar result in a later, similar case.

Presumption of innocence A principle that requires the government to prove the guilt of a criminal defendant and relieves the defendant of any burden to prove his or her innocence.

Prima facie At first appearance.

Principal A person who empowers another to act as that person's representative, for example, as an agent or broker.

Private international aviation law This relates to legal *jurisdictional* issues – that is, the scope of the legal authority of a state or body – when conflicts or ambiguities arise between the laws of different states in respect to aviation activities.

Private law The body of laws administering relationships between private individuals.

Privity The doctrine of law that says that only the parties to a contract can enforce the obligations under the contract. This specifically excludes third parties, even those who stand to benefit from the performance of the contract, from enforcing a contract against the parties to it.

Privity of contract A tenet of contract law that only parties to a contract are legally bound by and entitled to enforce it.

Procedural law A body of rules prescribing the manner, form and order in which matters may be dealt with and enforced in a judicial forum.

Product liability A responsibility imposed on a manufacturer, distributor or supplier to warn consumers appropriately about possible detrimental or harmful effects of a product and to foresee how it may be misused.

Proof Evidence which helps establish the existence or non-existence of a fact.

Public international aviation law The agreements relating to aviation between nations, often in the form of international conventions or treaties.

Public law The body of law dealing with the powers, rights and obligations of the government and the governed.

Punitive damages Also known as exemplary damages, damages awarded in addition to general, where the court wishes not only to compensate the victim of a tort but also to punish the defendant.

Pure economic loss Pecuniary loss (loss requiring payment of money) not consequent upon personal injury or physical damage to the plaintiff's property, often arising in the context of negligent misstatements.

Quid pro quo arrangement An arrangement in exchange for another; a fair equivalent. Translates from Latin as 'something for something'.

Ratify or ratification In public international law, the process by which a nation accepts that it is bound by the terms of an international treaty, convention or other international agreement. In some countries, this happens automatically upon the executive government *signing* the agreement.

Real property In common property law, land and interests in land, except for a lease. There is considerable overlap with the civil law concept of *immovable property*.

Reasonably foreseeable Whether a circumstance, event or result is ordinarily, properly or fairly able to be anticipated.

Reasonable person A person who possesses the faculty of reason and engages in conduct in accordance with community standards.

Recklessness Heedless or careless conduct where the person can foresee some probable or possible harmful consequence but nevertheless decides to continue with those actions with an indifference to, or disregard of, the consequences.

Rehabilitation The theory of punishment that the sanctions of the criminal law should re-educate and rehabilitate offenders so that they will be unlikely to reoffend.

Remedy This means available at law or in equity by which a right is enforced or the infringement of a right is prevented, redressed or compensated.

Reparation Making amends for injury or wrong done, often by the payment of compensation.

Res judicata A Latin term which translates to mean a judicially decided matter; the rule that if a dispute is judged by a court of competent jurisdiction, the judgment of the court is final and conclusive as to the rights and duties of the parties involved, and the matter may not be retried, even in another court.

Retribution The theory that the imposition of punishment under the criminal law is justified because a person who inflicts harm should receive harm.

Rule of law The principle that every person and organization, including the government, is subject to the same laws.

Sanctions or penalties A penalty or punishment imposed for a breach of the law, such as imprisonment.

Separation of powers A legal doctrine involving the separation of government power among three organs of government: the *judiciary*, the *legislature* and the *executive*. Power is separated to ensure it does not become concentrated in one place, and a series of checks and balances is instituted to ensure that power cannot be abused by any arm of government. For more information, see definitions of Judiciary, Legislature and Executive.

Signature In international law, a nation's signature on an international treaty, convention or other agreement is taken to be a statement of intention to be bound once the nation has *ratified* the agreement and the agreement has *entered into force*. At this stage, a nation undertakes not to take any steps to frustrate the intention of the treaty, convention or agreement.

Simple contract In common law, a contract that is not special; consideration is an essential element of this type of contract.

Special Drawing Rights An international type of monetary reserve currency created by the International Monetary Fund (IMF).

Specific deterrence This type of deterrence punishes an offender to dissuade that offender from committing crimes in the future.

Spray drift A drift of spray from pesticide applications to any site other than that intended for application.

Stare decisis This is a legal phrase referring to the obligation of courts to honour past precedents; *see also* Doctrine of precedent.

Strict liability Liability which is accountability without the need to prove fault.

Substantive law The branch of the law which creates, defines and regulates people's rights, duties, powers and liabilities.

Sue To bring a civil proceeding against another.

Summary offence An offence not punishable on indictment or for which no procedure is specified.

Theft A general term covering the dishonest appropriation of another's property.

Tort A civil action for wrongs. *See also* Delict.

Trespass A tort involving the direct and unlawful interference with a person or their possession of land or goods.

Trial A civil or criminal proceeding at first instance.

Trier of fact The judicial officer(s) (either judge(s) or a jury) that determines any questions of fact in a legal proceeding.

Trier of law The judicial officer (usually the judge(s)) that determines any questions of law in a legal proceeding.

Trust An equitable obligation which imposes duties on one person (the trustee) for the benefit of another (the beneficiary).

Ultra vires Latin for 'beyond power'. An act beyond the legal power or authority of a person, institution or legislation, and therefore invalid.

Uncodified A system of law that is not codified (creation of codes).

Undue influence In equity, the improper use of influence compelling a person to act without exercising his or her free will.

Unenforceable contract A contract treated as valid in every respect except that one party (or sometimes both parties) cannot be sued in court for breaking the contract.

Unilateral contract Contracts under which only one party is under any obligation following formation of the contract, the other party having performed all its obligations prior to formation.

Verdict The finding of a jury or coroner.

Vicarious liability The liability imposed on one person for the wrongful act of another on the basis of the legal relationship between them, such as that of employer and employee.

Void Without legal effect.

Void ab initio 'Without effect from the beginning'. To be treated as invalid from the outset.

Volenti non fit injuria Means the voluntary assumption of risk. A defence whereby damages cannot be claimed by a party that voluntarily assumes the risk.

Warrant A written authority to do some act.

Warranty A less important contractual term.

White collar crime A broad category of crimes committed by persons from a middle- or upper-class socio-economic background in the course of their occupations.

Wilful misconduct Misconduct which would be regarded seriously by the wider community, irrespective of the state of mind of the actor.

Witness A person who gives evidence at a hearing; to attest by signature.

Work councils A council composed of both employer and employees convened to discuss matters of common interest.

Writ A written order issued in connection with a judicial proceeding.

Glossary of Technical Terms

Air consignment note A note that is issued to the consignor by the carrier to indicate receipt of the goods to be carried under a contract of carriage.

Australian Advanced Air Traffic System The hardware and software system used by Airservices Australia for air traffic control services. It is a computer-based system, which serves as an aid to air traffic controllers.

Boycott A firm or group of firms agreeing to *refuse* to deal with another particular firm or group of firms.

Cabotage The right to transfer passengers or cargo between two points in a foreign country.

Cartel A group of firms colluding in order to manipulate a market using their pooled market power.

Consignee In relation to a contract of carriage, the person to whom the freight or cargo is being sent.

Consignor In relation to a contract of carriage, the person sending the freight or cargo.

Damp lease In terms of an aircraft lease, a lease which covers the aircraft, the associated engineering support and insurance, along with technical crew (pilots).

Digital aerodrome services Also known as Digital Towers, use cameras and sensors to replace traditional physical air traffic control tower.

Dry lease In terms of an aircraft lease, a lease where only the aircraft is leased, with associated engineering support and insurance being provided.

Exclusive dealing An agreement whereby a firm or group of firms agrees to deal only with a particular firm or group of firms.

Finance lease/Capital lease A long-term arrangement where the airline effectively owns the aircraft.

Flight information region The entire area of airspace under the jurisdiction of any single contracting state.

Freight forwarder A person who engages the carrier to carry freight on behalf of the consignor.

Heavier-than-air aircraft An aircraft that becomes airborne through an aerodynamic reaction with the air. *Contrast with* Lighter than air aircraft.

Insurable interest A person has an insurable interest if he or she owns the subject matter of the insurance contract or legally bears the risk for its loss or damage.

Just culture A way of safety thinking that promotes a questioning attitude, is resistant to complacency, is committed to excellence and fosters both personal accountability and corporate self-regulation in safety matters.

Leaseback An agreement whereby an aircraft owner sells their aircraft and then leases the aircraft from the buyer.

Lighter-than-air aircraft An aircraft that becomes airborne by floating on the air by manipulating the air density within an envelope to be less than the ambient air density. This is often done by heating the air or by using a gas that is already lighter than air.

Low-cost carrier An airline that offers generally low fares in exchange for eliminating many traditional passenger services or charging additional fees for those services.

Operating leases A lease contract that allows the use of an asset, but does not convey rights similar to ownership of the asset.

Partnership Two or more people who enter into business jointly on their own collective account, with a view to making a profit.

Predatory pricing The sale of a product at below-cost price in order to attract customers away from a competitor, thus driving the competitor out of business.

Price-fixing Firms in a market agreeing to charge the same price for a product.

Radio detecting and ranging A measuring instrument in which the echo of a pulse of microwave radiation is used to detect and locate distant objects. Abbreviated as 'radar'.

Risk The likelihood and consequences of injury or harm occurring.

Safety management system A systematic approach to managing safety, including the necessary organizational structures, accountabilities, policies and procedures.

Safety quinella A procedure or process whereby both safety and profit are enhanced and, in fact, reinforce each other.

Safety Regulation Commission A commission responsible for the development and uniform implementation of harmonized safety regulatory objectives and requirements for the European Air Traffic Management (ATM) and ensuring their effectiveness through the measurement of safety performance.

Single European Sky A European Commission initiative by which the design, management and regulation of airspace is coordinated throughout the EU.

Sole trader A person who controls and owns a business and is the only key person in the business.

Sovereignty A supreme power or authority; the authority of a state to govern itself or another state.

Vertical integration Where a firm acquires, merges or otherwise controls one of its suppliers or one of its customers.

Wet leases In relation to an aircraft lease, a lease which covers the aircraft, the associated engineering support and insurance along with all the crew, both technical and cabin.

List of Abbreviations

ACI	Airports Council International
ADS-B	Automatic Dependent Surveillance-Broadcast
AEA	Association of European Airlines
AFM	Aircraft Flight Manual
ALARP	As Low As Reasonably Possible
AMC	Acceptable Means of Compliance
ANB	ICAO Air Navigation Bureau
ANSP	Airspace Navigation Service Providers
AOC	Air Operator's Certificate
APU	Auxiliary Power Unit
ARTCC	Air Route Traffic Control Centres
ASA	Air Services Agreement
ASEAN	Association of Southeast Asian Nations
ASM	Air Space Management
ATC	Air Traffic Control
ATCO	Air Traffic Control Officer
ATOS	Air Transport Oversight System
ATS	Air Traffic Services
ATSB	Australian Transport Safety Bureau
BA	British Airways
BASA	Bilateral Air Service Agreements
BGB	*Bürgerliches Gesetzbuch*
BGH	*Bundesgerichtshof*
CAEE	Committee on Aircraft Engine Emissions
CAEP	Committee on Aviation Environment Protection
CAMO	Continuing Airworthiness Management Organization
CAN	Committee on Aircraft Noise
CARs	Civil Aviation Rules
CASA	Civil Aviation Safety Authority
Cass civ/Cass com	*Cour de cassation*
CDA	Constant Descent Approach
CDL	Configuration Deviation List
CDM	Clean Development Mechanism
CEO	Chief Executive Officer
CIP	Carriage and Insurance Paid To
CITEJA	*Comité International Technique d'Experts Juridiques Aériens*
CO_2	Carbon dioxide
C of A	Certificate of Airworthiness
COO	Chief Operational Officer
CPT	Carriage Paid To
CRS	Computer Reservation System

CSR	Corporate Social Responsibility
CVR	Cockpit Voice Recorder
DAP	Deliverable At Place
DAS	Digital Aerodrome Services
DAT	Deliverable At Terminal
DDP	Delivered Duty Paid
DfT	UK Department for Transport
DGCA	Directors General of Civil Aviation
EASA	European Aviation Safety Agency
EC	European Commission
ECJ	European Court of Justice
EEA	European Environmental Agency
EP	Emergency Plan
EROPs	Extended Range Operations
ERP	Emergency Response Plan
ESD	Ecologically Sustainable Development
ETOPS	Extended Twin Operations
ETS	Emissions Trading Scheme
EU	European Union
eVTOL	Electric Vertical Take-Off and Landing
EXW	Ex-Works
FAA	Federal Aviation Administration
FARs	Federal Aviation Regulations
FCA	Free Carrier
FCR	Federal Court Reports
FDR	Flight Data Recorder
FEGP	Fixed Electrical Ground Power
FIR	Flight Information Region
FOB	Free On Board
FRMS	Fatigue Risk Management System
FTAIA	Foreign Trade Antitrust Improvement Act
GAIN	Global Aviation Information Network
GASP	Global Aviation Safety Plan
GATMOC	Global Air Traffic Management Operational Concept
GATS	General Agreement on Trade in Services
GDS	Global Distribution System
GECAS	GE Commercial Aviation Services
GIACC	Group on International Aviation and Climate Change
GNSS	Global Navigation Surveillance System
GPS	Global Positioning System
HFCs	Hydrofluorocarbons
IACA	International Air Charter Association
IANS	Institute of Air Navigation Services
IATA	International Air Transport Association
ICAN	International Commission for Air Navigation
ICAO	International Civil Aviation Organization
IFRs	Instrument Flight Rules
ILFC	International Lease Finance Corporation

ILO	International Labour Organization
Incoterms	International Commercial Terms
IPCC	Intergovernmental Panel on Climate Change
IT	Information Technology
JAA	Joint Aviation Authority
JAR	Joint Aviation Regulations
LAGs	Liquids, Aerosols and Gels
LCC	Low-Cost Carrier
LLC	Limited Liability Company
MALIAT	Multilateral Agreement on Liberalization of International Air Services
MEL	Minimum Equipment List
MM	Maintenance Manual
MMEL	Master Minimum Equipment List
MO	Maintenance Organization
MRO	Maintenance and Repair Organization
MTOW	Maximum Takeoff Weight
NAA	National Aviation Authority
NBW	*Nieuw Burgerlijk Wetboek*
NOx	Nitrogen Oxides
NPR	Notice of Proposed Rulemaking
OPEC	Organization of Oil Producing and Exporting Countries
PASO	Pacific Aviation Safety Office
PATCO	Professional Air Traffic Controller Organization
PBN	Performance Based Navigation
PCA	Pre-Conditioned Air
PFC	Passenger Facility Charge
PFCs	Perfluorocarbons
Qantas	Queensland and Northern Territory Aerial Services
RC	Regulatory Committee
RNP	Required Navigation Performance
RPAS	Remotely Piloted Aircraft Systems
RU	Regulatory Unit
RWP	Regulatory Work Programme
SAF	Sustainable Aviation Fuels
SAFA	Safety Assessment of Foreign Aircraft
SAM	Single Aviation Market
SARPs	Standards and Recommended Practices
SARS	Severe Acute Respiratory Syndrome
SDRs	Special Drawing Rights
SE	*Societas Europaea*
SES	Single European Sky
SMM	Safety Management Manual
SMS	Safety Management System
SOP	Standard Operating Procedures
SRB	Solid Rocket Booster
SRC	Safety Regulation Commission
STOL	Short Take-Off and Landing

TAAATS	The Australian Advanced Air Traffic System
TCAA	Transatlantic Common Aviation Area
TCAS	Traffic Collision Avoidance System
TOR	Terms of Reference
TSA	Transport Security Administration
UK	United Kingdom
UN	United Nations
UNCED	United Nations Conference on Environment and Development
UNFCCC	United Nations Framework Convention on Climate Change
USA	United States of America
USAP	Universal Security Audit Programme
USD	United States Dollar
USOAP	ICAO Universal Safety Oversight Audit Programme
USSR	Union of Soviet Socialist Republics
VFRs	Visual Flight Rules
WRI	World Resources Institute
WTO	World Trade Organization

Index

For Product Safety Concerns and Information please contact our EU
representative GPSR@taylorandfrancis.com
Taylor & Francis Verlag GmbH, Kaufingerstraße 24, 80331 München, Germany

www.ingramcontent.com/pod-product-compliance
Ingram Content Group UK Ltd.
Pitfield, Milton Keynes, MK11 3LW, UK
UKHW052224190926
475702UK00007B/1190
* 9 7 8 1 0 3 2 6 5 2 0 6 1 *